Pebble® Plus

EXtreme Animals

The Fastest Animals

by Catherine Ipcizade

Consulting Editor: Gail Saunders-Smith, PhD

Consultant: Tanya Dewey, PhD
University of Michigan Museum of Zoology

CAPSTONE PRESS

a capstone imprint

Pebble Plus is published by Capstone Press,
151 Good Counsel Drive, P.O. Box 669, Mankato, Minnesota 56002.
www.capstonepub.com

 Books published by Capstone Press are manufactured with paper
containing at least 10 percent post-consumer waste.

Library of Congress Cataloging-in-Publication Data
Ipcizade, Catherine.
  The fastest animals / by Catherine Ipcizade.
    p. cm. — (Pebble plus. Extreme animals)
  Includes bibliographical references and index.
  Summary: "Simple text and photographs present the world's fastest animals"—Provided by publisher.
  ISBN 978-1-4296-5311-4 (library binding)
  ISBN 978-1-4296-6208-6 (paperback)
  1. Animal locomotion—Juvenile literature. 2. Speed—Juvenile literature. I. Title.
QP301.I67 2011
591.47'9—dc22   2010028753

Editorial Credits
Katy Kudela, editor; Heidi Thompson, designer; Marcie Spence, media researcher; Laura Manthe, production specialist

Photo Credits
Alamy: Photoshot Holdings Ltd., cover; Ardea: Tom & Pat Leeson, 15; iStockphoto: BirdofPrey, 13, twphotos, 5;
Nature Picture Library: Doug Perrine, 17; Peter Arnold: Biosphoto/Dragescon-Joffe Alain, 9, Martin Harvey, 7;
Shutterstock: Hedsver van Brug, 11, Mark Beckwith, 1, 19, Sue Robinson, 21

Note to Parents and Teachers

The Extreme Animals series supports national science standards related to life science.
This book describes and illustrates fast animals. The images support early readers in
understanding the text. The repetition of words and phrases helps early readers learn new
words. This book also introduces early readers to subject-specific vocabulary words, which are
defined in the Glossary section. Early readers may need assistance to read some words and to
use the Table of Contents, Glossary, Read More, Internet Sites, and Index sections of the book.

Printed in the United States of America in North Mankato, Minnesota.
092010   005933CGS11

Table of Contents

Fast

They race! They splash! They dive!

These animals aren't just fast.

Their blazing speed is EXTREME.

A killer whale grows as long as a bus.

Size doesn't slow it down.

The killer whale is the fastest

mammal in the sea.

30 miles per hour

(48 kilometers per hour)

5

Some animals save their speed.

A lion rests most of the day.

But watch out!

A chasing lion moves fast.

35 mph

(56 kph)

The ostrich doesn't fly,

but it's the fastest bird on land.

An ostrich can outrun

predators. And it only has

two toes on each foot!

43 mph

(69 kph)

Faster

A greyhound has a long, thin body made for racing. This dog runs almost twice as fast as the quickest human runner.

45 mph
(72 kph)

An American Quarter horse

races to the finish line.

Of all the horse breeds,

it is the fastest

short distance runner.

47 mph

(76 kph)

Pronghorn antelope

live in grasslands.

There are no trees to hide them.

They move as fast as a

roller coaster to outrun predators.

61 mph

(98 kph)

Fastest

No fish swims faster than
the sailfish. With its strong
body and fins, a sailfish
speeds after prey. Its long bill
stuns fish and squid.

68 mph
(109 kph)

The cheetah is the fastest
land animal. Long legs
help this cat run fast.
A cheetah speeds along like
a car on a freeway.

70 mph
(113 kph)

The peregrine falcon is
the fastest animal.
It dives at almost 200 miles
(322 kilometers) per hour. That's
as fast as a small airplane flies.

200 mph
(322 kph)

21

Glossary

bill—the long, pointed snout of a sailfish

breed—a particular type of animal

extreme—very great

fin—a body part that fish use to swim and steer in water

freeway—a wide highway that you can travel on without paying tolls

mammal—a warm-blooded animal with a backbone

predator—an animal that hunts other animals for food

prey—an animal that is hunted by another animal for food

roller coaster—an amusement park ride with a train of cars that travel fast over a track

stun—knock out

Read More

Dahl, Michael. *Fast, Faster, Fastest: Animals that Move at Great Speeds.* Animal Extremes. Minneapolis: Picture Window Books, 2006.

Stout, Frankie. *Nature's Fastest Animals.* Extreme Animals. New York: PowerKids Press, 2008.

Internet Sites

FactHound offers a safe, fun way to find Internet sites related to this book. All of the sites on FactHound have been researched by our staff.

Here's all you do:

Visit *www.facthound.com*

Type in this code: 9781429653114

Super-cool stuff! Check out projects, games and lots more at **www.capstonekids.com**

Index

Word Count: 225

Grade: 1

Early-Intervention Level: 17

Learning to Use

WINDOWS APPLICATIONS

Microsoft

EXCEL 5 FOR WINDOWS

Learning to Use

WINDOWS APPLICATIONS

Microsoft

EXCEL 5 FOR WINDOWS

Gary B. Shelly
Thomas J. Cashman
James S. Quasney

Contributing Author
Steven G. Forsythe

boyd & fraser
publishing company

Special thanks go to the following reviewers of the Shelly Cashman Series Windows Applications textbooks:

Susan Conners, Purdue University Calumet; **William Dorin**, Indiana University Northwest; **Robert Erickson**, University of Vermont; **Roger Franklin**, The College of William and Mary; **Roy O. Foreman**, Purdue University Calumet; **Patricia Harris**, Mesa Community College; **Cynthia Kachik**, Santa Fe Community College; **Suzanne Lambert**, Broward Community College; **Anne McCoy**, Miami-Dade Community College/Kendall Campus; **Karen Meyer**, Wright State University; **Mike Michaelson**, Palomar College; **Michael Mick**, Purdue University Calumet; **Cathy Paprocki**, Harper College; **Jeffrey Quasney**, Educational Consultant; **Denise Rall**, Purdue University; **Sorel Reisman**, California State University, Fullerton; **John Ross**, Fox Valley Technical College; **Lorie Szalapski**, St. Paul Technical College; **Susan Sebok**, South Suburban College; **Betty Svendsen**, Oakton Community College; **Jeanie Thibault**, Educational Dynamics Institute; **Margaret Thomas**, Ohio University; **Carole Turner**, University of Wisconsin; **Diane Vaught**, National Business College; **Dwight Watt**, Swainsboro Technical Institute; **Melinda White**, Santa Fe Community College; **Eileen Zisk**, Community College of Rhode Island; and **Sue Zulauf**, Sinclair Community College.

© **1995 boyd & fraser publishing company**
One Corporate Place • Ferncroft Village
Danvers, Massachusetts 01923

International Thomson Publishing
boyd & fraser publishing company is an ITP company.
The ITP trademark is used under license.

Manufactured in the United States of America

ISBN 0-87709-600-7

7 8 9 10   BC   9 8 7 6

CONTENTS

SPREADSHEETS USING MICROSOFT EXCEL 5 FOR WINDOWS — E1

Arial   10   **B** *I* U

PREFACE

▶ THE WINDOWS ENVIRONMENT

Since the introduction of Microsoft Windows version 3.1, the personal computing industry has moved rapidly toward establishing Windows as the de facto user interface. The majority of software development funds in software vendor companies are devoted to Windows applications. Virtually all PCs purchased today, at any price, come preloaded with Windows and, often, with one or more Windows applications packages. With an enormous installed base, it is clear that Windows is the operating environment for both now and the future.

The Windows environment places the novice as well as the experienced user in the world of the mouse and a common graphical user interface between all applications. An up-to-date educational institution that teaches applications software to students for their immediate use and as a skill to be used within industry must teach Windows-based applications software.

▶ OBJECTIVES OF THIS TEXTBOOK

Learning to Use Windows Applications: Microsoft Excel 5 for Windows was specifically developed for an introductory spreadsheet course. No previous experience with a computer is assumed, and no mathematics beyond the high school freshman level is required. The objectives of this book are as follows:

- ▶ To teach the fundamentals of Windows and Microsoft Excel 5 for Windows
- ▶ To acquaint the student with the proper way to solve spreadsheet problems
- ▶ To use practical problems to illustrate spreadsheet applications
- ▶ To take advantage of the many new capabilities of spreadsheets in a Windows environment (see Figure P-1)

The textbook covers all essential aspects of Excel for Windows. When students complete a course using this book, they will have a firm knowledge of Windows and will be able to solve a variety of spreadsheet problems. Further, because they will be learning Windows, students will find the migration to other Windows applications software to be relatively simple and straightforward.

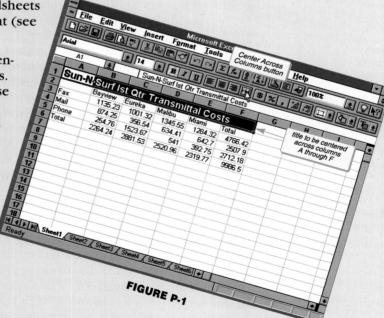

FIGURE P-1

▶ THE SHELLY CASHMAN APPROACH

The Shelly Cashman Series Windows Applications books present word processing, spreadsheet, database, programming, presentation graphics, and Windows itself by showing the actual screens displayed by Windows and the applications software. Because the student interacts with pictorial displays when using Windows, written words in a textbook does not suffice. For this reason, the Shelly Cashman Series emphasizes screen displays as the primary means of teaching Windows applications software. Every screen shown in the Shelly Cashman Series Windows Applications books appears in color, because the student views color on the screen. In addition, the screens display exactly as the student will see them. The screens in this book were captured while using the software. Nothing has been altered or changed except to highlight portions of the screen when appropriate (see the screens in Figure P-2).

The Shelly Cashman Series Windows Applications books present the material using a unique pedagogy designed specifically for the graphical environment of Windows. The textbooks are primarily designed for a lecture/lab method of presentation, although they are equally suited for a tutorial/hands-on approach wherein the student learns by actually completing each project following the step-by-step instructions. Features of this pedagogy include the following:

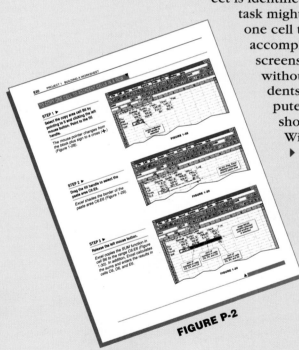

FIGURE P-2

▶ **Project Orientation:** Each project in the book solves a complete problem, meaning that the student is introduced to a problem to be solved and is then given the step-by-step process to solve the problem.

▶ **Step-by-Step Instructions:** Each of the tasks required to complete a project is identified throughout the development of the project. For example, a task might be to save a document on disk, print a document, or copy one cell to adjacent cells in a row using Excel. Then, each step to accomplish the task is specified. The steps are accompanied by screens (see Figure P-2). The student is not told to perform a step without seeing the result of the step on a color screen. Hence, students learn from this book the same as if they were using the computer. This attention to detail in accomplishing a task and showing the resulting screen makes the Shelly Cashman Series Windows Applications textbooks unique.

▶ **Multiple Ways to Use the Book:** Because each step to accomplish a task is illustrated with a screen, the book can be used in a number of ways, including: (a) Lecture and textbook approach — The instructor lectures on the material in the book. The student reads and studies the material and then applies the knowledge to an application on a computer; (b) Tutorial approach — The student performs each specified step on a computer. At the end of the project, the student has solved the problem and is ready to solve comparable student assignments; (c) Reference — Each task in a project is clearly identified. Therefore, the material serves as a complete reference because the student can refer to any task to determine how to accomplish it.

▶ **Windows/Graphical User Interface Approach:** Windows provides a graphical user interface. All of the examples in the book use this interface. Thus, the mouse is used for the majority of control functions and is the preferred user communication tool. When specifying a command to be executed, the sequence is as follows: (a) If a button invokes the command, use the button; (b) If a button is not available, use the command from a menu; (c) If a button or a menu cannot be used, only then is the keyboard used to implement a Windows command.

▶ **Emphasis on Windows Techniques:** The most general techniques to implement commands, enter information, and generally interface with Windows are presented. This approach allows the student to move from one application software package to another under Windows with a minimum amount of relearning with respect to interfacing with the software. An application-specific method is taught only when no other option is available.

▶ **Reference for All Techniques:** Even though general Windows techniques are used in all examples, a Quick Reference chart (see Figure P-3) at the end of each project details not only the mouse and menu methods for implementing a command, but also contains the keyboard shortcuts for the commands presented in the project. Therefore, students are exposed to all means for implementing a command.

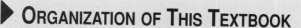

FIGURE P-3

▶ Organization of This Textbook

Learning to Use Windows Applications: Microsoft Excel 5 for Windows consists of an introduction to computers, two projects on Microsoft Windows 3.1, and seven projects on Microsoft Excel 5 for Windows.

An Introduction to Computers

Many students taking a course in the use of Excel will have little previous experience using computers. For this reason, the textbook begins with a section titled *Introduction to Computers* that covers computer hardware and software concepts important to first-time computer users.

Using Microsoft Windows 3.1

To effectively use Microsoft Excel 5 for Windows, students need a practical knowledge of the Microsoft Windows graphical user interface. Thus, two Microsoft Windows projects are included prior to the Excel projects.

Project 1 – An Introduction to Windows   The first project introduces the students to Windows concepts, Windows terminology, and how to communicate with Windows using the mouse and keyboard. Topics include starting and exiting Windows; opening group windows; maximizing windows; scrolling; selecting menus; choosing a command from a menu; starting and exiting Windows applications; obtaining online Help; and responding to dialog boxes.

Project 2 – Disk and File Management   The second project introduces the students to File Manager. Topics include formatting a diskette; copying a group of files; renaming and deleting files; searching for help topics; activating, resizing, and closing a group window; switching between applications; and minimizing an application window to an application icon.

Spreadsheets Using Microsoft Excel 5 for Windows

After presenting the basic computer and Windows concepts, this textbook provides detailed instruction on how to use Microsoft Excel 5 for Windows. The material is divided into seven projects as follows:

Project 1 – Building a Worksheet   In Project 1, students are introduced to Excel terminology, the Excel window, and the basic characteristics of a worksheet and workbook. Topics include starting and exiting Excel; entering text and numbers; selecting a range; using the AutoSum button; copying using the fill handle; changing font size; bolding; centering across columns; using the AutoFormat command; charting using the ChartWizard button; saving and opening a worksheet; editing a worksheet; and obtaining online Help.

FIGURE P-4

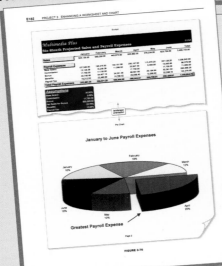

Project 2 – Formulas, Formatting, and Creating Charts   In Project 2, students use formulas and functions to build a worksheet and learn more about formatting and printing a worksheet. Topics include entering formulas; using the AVERAGE, MAX, and MIN functions; formatting text; formatting numbers; drawing borders and adding colors; changing the widths of columns and heights of rows; spell checking; creating a 3-D column chart on a separate sheet; previewing a worksheet; printing a section of the worksheet; and displaying and printing the formulas in a worksheet.

Project 3 – Enhancing a Worksheet and Chart   In Project 3, students learn how to work with larger worksheets, how to create a worksheet based on assumptions, how to use the IF function and absolute references, how to create and format a 3-D pie chart, and how to perform what-if analysis. Topics include using the fill handle to create a series; deleting, inserting, copying, and moving data on a worksheet; displaying and docking toolbars; freezing titles; changing the magnification of worksheets; displaying different parts of the worksheet using panes; changing the type, size, and color of fonts; in-depth charting of data; previewing a printout; printing in landscape; printing to fit; and simple what-if analysis and goal seeking.

Project 4 – Working with Templates and Multiple Worksheets   In Project 4, students learn to create a template and consolidate data into one worksheet. Topics include building and copying a template; multiple worksheets; 3-D references; adding notes; changing page setup characteristics; and finding and replacing data.

Project 5 – Data Tables, Macros Using Visual Basic, and Scenario Manager   In Project 5, students learn more about analyzing data in a worksheet and how to use macros. Topics include applying the PMT function to determine a monthly payment; analyzing data by (1) goal seeking, (2) creating a data table, and (3) creating a Scenario Summary Report worksheet; writing macros in VBA to automate worksheet activities; creating a button and assigning a macro to it; and protecting a worksheet.

Project 6 – Sorting and Filtering a Worksheet Database   In Project 6, students learn how to create, sort, and filter a database. Topics include using a data form to create and maintain a database; creating subtotals; finding, extracting, and deleting records that pass a test; applying database functions; and creating a pivot table.

Project 7 – Object Linking and Embedding (OLE)   In Project 7, students learn to embed and link objects from one application to another. Topics include running multiple applications and switching from one to another; copying an object from one application to another using the three methods: (1) copy and paste, (2) copy and embed, and (3) copy and link; tiling multiple applications; and dragging and dropping between tiled applications.

▶ END-OF-PROJECT STUDENT ACTIVITIES

ach project ends with a wealth of student activities including these notable features:

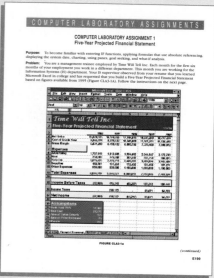

FIGURE P-5

- ▸ A list of key terms for review
- ▸ A Quick Reference that lists the ways to carry out a task using the mouse, menu, or keyboard shortcuts
- ▸ Six Student Assignments for homework and classroom discussion
- ▸ Three Computer Laboratory Exercises that usually require the student to load and manipulate an Excel worksheet from the Student Diskette that accompanies this book
- ▸ Four Computer Laboratory Assignments (see Figure P-5) that require the student to develop a complete project assignment; the assignments increase in difficulty from a relatively easy assignment to a case study

▶ ANCILLARY MATERIALS FOR TEACHING FROM THE SHELLY CASHMAN SERIES WINDOWS APPLICATIONS TEXTBOOKS

 comprehensive instructor's support package accompanies all textbooks in the Shelly Cashman Series.

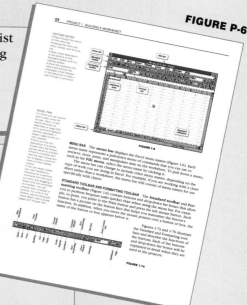

FIGURE P-6

Annotated Instructor's Edition (AIE)   The AIE is designed to assist you with your lectures by suggesting illustrations to use, summarizing key points, proposing pertinent questions, offering important tips, alerting you to pitfalls, and by incorporating the answers to the Student Assignments. There are several hundred annotations throughout the textbook (see Figure P-6).

Computer-Based LCD Lecture Success System   The Shelly Cashman Series proudly presents the finest LCD learning material available in textbook publishing. The Lecture Success System diskette, together with a personal computer and LCD technology, are used in lieu of transparencies. The system enables you to explain and illustrate the step-by-step, screen-by-screen development of a project in the textbook without entering large amounts of data, thereby improving your students' grasp of the material. The Lecture Success System leads to a smooth, easy, error-free lecture.

The Lecture Success System diskette comes with files that correspond to key figures in the book. You load the files that pertain to a project and display them as needed. If the students want to see a series of steps a second time, simply reopen the file you want to start with and redo the steps. This presentation system is available to adopters without charge.

FIGURE P-7

Instructor's Materials This instructor's ancillary (Figure P-7) contains the following:

▸ Detailed lesson plans including project objectives, project overview, and a three-column outline of each project that includes page references and illustration references
▸ Answers to all student assignments at the end of the projects
▸ A test bank of more than 600 True/False, Multiple Choice, and Fill-In questions
▸ Illustrations for every screen, diagram, and table in the textbook on CD-ROM — for selection and display in a lecture or to print and make transparencies.
▸ An Instructor's Diskette that includes the projects and solutions to the Computer Laboratory Assignments at the end of each project
▸ A Lesson Plans and Test Bank Diskette that includes the detailed lesson plans and test bank for customizing to individual instructor's needs

MicroExam IV MicroExam IV, a computerized test-generating system, is available free to adopters of any Shelly Cashman Series textbooks. It includes all of the questions from the test bank just described. MicroExam IV is an easy-to-use, menu-driven software package that provides instructors with testing flexibility and allows customizing of testing documents.

NetTest IV NetTest IV allows instructors to take a MicroExam IV file made up of True/False and Multiple Choice questions and proctor a paperless examination in a network environment. The same questions display in a different order on each PC. Students have the option of instantaneous feedback. Tests are electronically graded, and an item analysis is produced.

▸ ACKNOWLEDGMENTS

The Shelly Cashman Series would not be the success it is without the contributions of outstanding publishing professionals. First, and foremost, among them is Becky Herrington, director of production and designer. She is the heart and soul of the Shelly Cashman Series, and it is only through her leadership, dedication, and untiring efforts that superior products are produced.

Under Becky's direction, the following individuals made significant contributions to these books: Peter Schiller, production manager, Ginny Harvey, series administrator and manuscript editor; Ken Russo, senior illustrator and cover art; Anne Craig, Mike Bodnar, Greg Herrington, Dave Bonnewitz, and Dave Wyer, illustrators; Jeanne Black, Betty Hopkins, and Rebecca Evans, typographers; Tracy Murphy, series coordinator; Sue Sebok and Melissa Dowling LaRoe, copy editors; Marilyn Martin and Nancy Lamm, proofreaders; Henry Blackham, cover and opener photography; and Dennis Woelky, glass etchings.

Special recognition for a job well done must go to James Quasney, who, together with writing, assumed the responsibilities as series editor. Particular thanks go to Thomas Walker, president and CEO of boyd & fraser publishing company, who recognized the need, and provided the support, to produce the full-color Shelly Cashman Series Windows Applications textbooks.

We hope you will find using the book an enriching and rewarding experience.

Gary B. Shelly
Thomas J. Cashman

▶ Shelly Cashman Series – Traditionally Bound Textbooks

The Shelly Cashman Series presents both Windows- and DOS-based personal computer applications in a variety of traditionally bound textbooks, as shown in the table below. For more information, see your boyd & fraser representative or call 1-800-225-3782.

COMPUTER CONCEPTS	
Computer Concepts	Complete Computer Concepts
	Essential Computer Concepts, Second Edition
Computer Concepts Workbook and Study Guide	Workbook and Study Guide with Computer Lab Software Projects to accompany Complete Computer Concepts
Computer Concepts and Windows Applications	Complete Computer Concepts and Microsoft Works 3.0 for Windows (also available in spiral bound)
	Complete Computer Concepts and Microsoft Works 2.0 for Windows (also available in spiral bound)
	Complete Computer Concepts and Microsoft Word 2.0 for Windows, Microsoft Excel 4 for Windows, and Paradox 1.0 for Windows (also available in spiral bound)
Computer Concepts and DOS Applications	Complete Computer Concepts and WordPerfect 5.1, Lotus 1-2-3 Release 2.2, and dBASE IV Version 1.1 (also available in spiral bound)
	Complete Computer Concepts and WordPerfect 5.1, Lotus 1-2-3 Release 2.2, and dBASE III PLUS (also available in spiral bound)
Computer Concepts and Programming	Complete Computer Concepts and Programming in QuickBASIC
	Complete Computer Concepts and Programming in Microsoft BASIC

WINDOWS APPLICATIONS	
Integrated Packages	Microsoft Works 3.0 for Windows (also available in spiral bound)
	Microsoft Works 2.0 for Windows (also available in spiral bound)
Graphical User Interface	Microsoft Windows 3.1 Introductory Concepts and Techniques
	Microsoft Windows 3.1 Complete Concepts and Techniques
Windows Applications	Microsoft Word 2.0 for Windows, Microsoft Excel 4 for Windows, and Paradox 1.0 for Windows (also available in spiral bound)
Word Processing	Microsoft Word 6 for Windows*
	Microsoft Word 2.0 for Windows
	WordPerfect 6 for Windows*
	WordPerfect 5.2 for Windows
Spreadsheets	Microsoft Excel 5 for Windows*
	Microsoft Excel 4 for Windows
	Lotus 1-2-3 Release 4 for Windows*
	Quattro Pro 5 for Windows
Database Management	Paradox 4.5 for Windows
	Paradox 1.0 for Windows
	Microsoft Access 2 for Windows*
Presentation Graphics	Microsoft PowerPoint 4 for Windows

DOS APPLICATIONS	
Operating Systems	DOS 6 Introductory Concepts and Techniques
	DOS 6 and Microsoft Windows 3.1 Introductory Concepts and Techniques
Integrated Package	Microsoft Works 3.0 (also available in spiral bound)
DOS Applications	WordPerfect 5.1, Lotus 1-2-3 Release 2.2, and dBASE IV Version 1.1 (also available in spiral bound)
	WordPerfect 5.1, Lotus 1-2-3 Release 2.2, and dBASE III PLUS (also available in spiral bound)
Word Processing	WordPerfect 6.0
	WordPerfect 5.1
	WordPerfect 5.1, Function Key Edition
	WordPerfect 4.2 (with Educational Software)
	Microsoft Word 5.0
	WordStar 6.0 (with Educational Software)
Spreadsheets	Lotus 1-2-3 Release 2.4
	Lotus 1-2-3 Release 2.3
	Lotus 1-2-3 Release 2.2
	Lotus 1-2-3 Release 2.01
	Quattro Pro 3.0
	Quattro with 1-2-3 Menus (with Educational Software)
Database Management	dBASE IV Version 1.1
	dBASE III PLUS (with Educational Software)
	Paradox 4.5
	Paradox 3.5 (with Educational Software)

PROGRAMMING	
Programming	Microsoft BASIC
	QuickBASIC
	Microsoft Visual Basic 3.0 for Windows*

* Also available as a mini-book in the Double Diamond Edition

▶ SHELLY CASHMAN SERIES – **Custom Edition**™ PROGRAM

I f you do not find a Shelly Cashman Series traditionally bound textbook to fit your needs, boyd & fraser's unique **Custom Edition** program allows you to choose from a number of options and create a textbook perfectly suited to your course. The customized materials are available in a variety of binding styles, including boyd & fraser's patented **Custom Edition** kit, spiral bound, and notebook bound. Features of the **Custom Edition** program are:

▶ Textbooks that match the content of your course
▶ Windows- and DOS-based materials for the latest versions of personal computer applications software
▶ Shelly Cashman Series quality, with the same full-color materials and Shelly Cashman Series pedagogy found in the traditionally bound books
▶ Affordable pricing so your students receive the **Custom Edition** at a cost similar to that of traditionally bound books

The table on the right summarizes the available materials. For more information, see your boyd & fraser representative or call 1-800-225-3782.

COMPUTER CONCEPTS	
Computer Concepts	Complete Computer Concepts
	Essential Computer Concepts, Second Edition
	Introduction to Computers
OPERATING SYSTEMS	
Graphical User Interface	Microsoft Windows 3.1 Introductory Concepts and Techniques
	Microsoft Windows 3.1 Complete Concepts and Techniques
	DOS 6 and Microsoft Windows 3.1 Introductory Concepts and Techniques
Operating Systems	Introduction to DOS 6 (using DOS prompt)
	Introduction to DOS 5.0 (using DOS shell)
	Introduction to DOS 5.0 or earlier (using DOS prompt)
WINDOWS APPLICATIONS	
Integrated Package	Microsoft Works 3.0 for Windows
	Microsoft Works 2.0 for Windows
Word Processing	Microsoft Word 6 for Windows*
	Microsoft Word 2.0 for Windows
	WordPerfect 6 for Windows*
	WordPerfect 5.2 for Windows
Spreadsheets	Microsoft Excel 5 for Windows*
	Microsoft Excel 4 for Windows
	Lotus 1-2-3 Release 4 for Windows*
	Quattro Pro 5 for Windows
Database Management	Paradox 4.5 for Windows
	Paradox 1.0 for Windows
	Microsoft Access 2 for Windows*
Presentation Graphics	Microsoft PowerPoint 4 for Windows
DOS APPLICATIONS	
Integrated Package	Microsoft Works 3.0
Word Processing	WordPerfect 6.0
	WordPerfect 5.1
	WordPerfect 5.1, Function Key Edition
	WordPerfect 4.2
	Microsoft Word 5.0
	WordStar 6.0
Spreadsheets	Lotus 1-2-3 Release 2.4
	Lotus 1-2-3 Release 2.3
	Lotus 1-2-3 Release 2.2
	Lotus 1-2-3 Release 2.01
	Quattro Pro 3.0
	Quattro with 1-2-3 Menus
Database Management	dBASE IV Version 1.1
	dBASE III PLUS
	Paradox 4.5
	Paradox 3.5
PROGRAMMING	
Programming	Microsoft BASIC
	QuickBASIC
	Microsoft Visual Basic 3.0 for Windows*
* Also available as a mini-module	

Introduction to Computers

Objectives

After completing this chapter, you will be able to:

- ▶ Define the term computer and discuss the four basic computer operations: input, processing, output, and storage
- ▶ Define data and information
- ▶ Explain the principal components of the computer and their use
- ▶ Describe the use and handling of diskettes and hard disks
- ▶ Discuss computer software and explain the difference between system software and application software
- ▶ Describe several types of personal computer applications software
- ▶ Discuss computer communications channels and equipment and LAN and WAN computer networks
- ▶ Explain how to purchase, install, and maintain a personal computer system

Every day, computers impact how individuals work and how they live. The use of small computers, called personal computers or microcomputers , continues to increase and has made computing available to almost anyone. In addition, advances in communication technology allow people to use personal computer systems to easily and quickly access and send information to other computers and computer users. At home, at work, and in the field, computers are helping people to do their work faster, more accurately, and in some cases, in ways that previously would not have been possible.

Why Study Computers and Application Software?

T oday, many people believe that knowing how to use a computer, especially a personal computer, is a basic skill necessary to succeed in business or to function effectively in society. As you can see in Figure 1, the use of computer technology is widespread in the world. It is important to understand that while computers are used in many different ways, there are certain types of common applications computer users need to know. It is this type of software that you will learn as you use this book. Given the widespread use and availability of computer systems, knowing how to use common application software on a computer system is an essential skill for practically everyone.

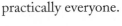

FIGURE 1
Computers in use in a wide variety of applications and professions. New applications are being developed every day.

Before you learn about application software, however, it will help if you understand what a computer is, the components of a computer, and the types of software used on computers. These topics are explained in this introduction. Also included is information that describes computer networks and a list of guidelines for purchasing, installing, and maintaining a personal computer.

What Is a Computer?

The most obvious question related to understanding computers is, "What is a computer?" A computer is an electronic device, operating under the control of instructions stored in its own memory unit, that can accept data (input), process data arithmetically and logically, produce output from the processing, and store the results for future use. Generally the term is used to describe a collection of devices that function together as a system. An example of the devices that make up a personal computer, or microcomputer, is shown in Figure 2.

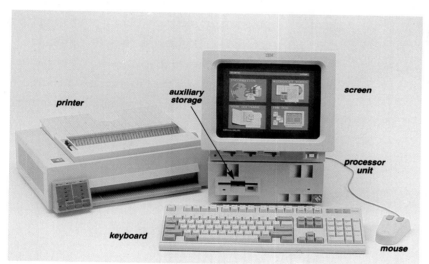

FIGURE 2
Devices that comprise a personal computer.

What Does a Computer Do?

Whether small or large, computers can perform four general operations. These operations comprise the information processing cycle and are: input, process, output, and storage. Collectively, these operations describe the procedures a computer performs to process data into information and store it for future use.

All computer processing requires data. Data refers to the raw facts, including numbers, words, images, and sounds, given to a computer during the input operation. In the processing phase, the computer manipulates the data to create information. Information refers to data processed into a form that has meaning and is useful. During the output operation, the information that has been created is put into some form, such as a printed report, that people can use. The information can also be placed in computer storage for future use.

These operations occur through the use of electronic circuits contained on small silicon chips inside the computer (Figure 3). Because these electronic circuits rarely fail and the data flows along these circuits at close to the speed of light, processing can be accomplished in billionths of a second. Thus, the computer is a powerful tool because it can perform these four operations reliably and quickly.

The people who either use the computer directly or use the information it provides are called computer users, end users, or sometimes, just users.

FIGURE 3
Inside a computer are chips and other electronic components that process data in billionths of a second.

How Does a Computer Know What to Do?

For a computer to perform the operations in the information processing cycle, it must be given a detailed set of instructions that tell it exactly what to do. These instructions are called a computer program, or software. Before processing for a specific job begins, the computer program corresponding to that job is stored in the computer. Once the program is stored, the computer can begin to operate by executing the program's first instruction. The computer executes one program instruction after another until the job is complete.

What Are the Components of a Computer?

To understand how computers process data into information, you need to examine the primary components of the computer. The four primary components of a computer are: input devices, the processor unit, output devices, and auxiliary storage units (Figure 4).

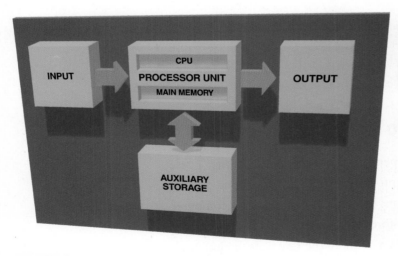

FIGURE 4
A computer is composed of input devices through which data is entered into the computer; the processor that processes data stored in main memory; output devices on which the results of the processing are made available; and auxiliary storage units that store data for future processing.

Input Devices

Input devices enter data into main memory. Many input devices exist. The two most commonly used are the keyboard and the mouse.

The Keyboard   The most commonly used input device is the keyboard, on which data is entered by manually keying in or typing. The keyboard on most computers is laid out in much the same manner as the one shown in Figure 5. The alphabetic keys are arranged like those on a typewriter.

A **numeric keypad** is located on the right side of most keyboards. This arrangement of keys allows you to enter numeric data rapidly. To activate the numeric keypad you press and engage the NUMLOCK key located above the numeric keypad. The NUMLOCK key activates the numeric keypad so when the keys are pressed, numeric characters are entered into the computer memory and appear on the screen. A light turns on at the top right of the keyboard to indicate that the numeric keys are in use.

The **cursor** is a symbol, such as an underline character, which indicates where you are working on the screen. The **cursor control keys**, or **arrow keys**, allow you to move the cursor around the screen. Pressing the UP ARROW (↑) key causes the cursor to move upward on the screen. The DOWN ARROW (↓) key causes the cursor to move down; the LEFT ARROW (←) and RIGHT ARROW (→) keys cause the cursor to move left and right on the screen. On the keyboard in Figure 5, there are two sets of cursor control keys. One set is included as part of the numeric keypad. The second set of cursor control keys is located between the typewriter keys and the numeric keypad. To use the numeric keypad for cursor control, the NUMLOCK key must be disengaged. If the NUMLOCK key is engaged (indicated by the fact that as you press any numeric keypad key, a number appears on the screen), you can return to the cursor mode by pressing the NUMLOCK key. On most keyboards, a NUMLOCK light will indicate when the numeric keypad is in the numeric mode or the cursor mode.

FIGURE 5
This keyboard represents most desktop personal computer keyboards.

The other keys on the keypad—PAGE UP, PAGE DOWN, HOME, and END—have various functions depending on the software you use. Some programs make no use of these keys; others use the PAGE UP and PAGE DOWN keys, for example, to display previous or following pages of data on the screen. Some software uses the HOME key to move the cursor to the upper left corner of the screen. Likewise, the END key may be used to move the cursor to the end of a line of text or to the bottom of the screen, depending on the software.

Function keys on many keyboards can be programmed to accomplish specific tasks. For example, a function key might be used as a help key. Whenever that key is pressed, messages display that give instructions to help the user. The keyboard in Figure 5 has twelve function keys located across the top of the keyboard.

Other keys have special uses in some applications. The SHIFT keys have several functions. They work as they do on a typewriter, allowing you to type capital letters. The SHIFT key is always used to type the symbol on the upper portion of any key on the keyboard. Also, to temporarily use the cursor control keys on the numeric keypad as numeric entry keys, you can press the SHIFT key to switch into numeric mode. If you have instead pressed the NUMLOCK key to use the numeric keys, you can press the SHIFT key to shift temporarily back to the cursor mode.

The keyboard has a BACKSPACE key, a TAB key, an INSERT key and a DELETE key that perform the functions their names indicate.

The ESCAPE (ESC) key is generally used by computer software to cancel an instruction or exit from a situation. The use of the ESC key varies between software packages.

As with the ESC key, many keys are assigned special meaning by the computer software. Certain keys may be used more frequently than others by one piece of software but rarely used by another. It is this flexibility that allows you to use the computer in so many different applications.

The Mouse   A mouse (Figure 6) is a pointing device you can use instead of the cursor control keys. You lay the palm of your hand over the mouse and move it across the surface of a pad that provides traction for a rolling ball on the bottom of the mouse. The mouse detects the direction of the ball movement and sends this information to the screen to move the cursor. You push buttons on top of the mouse to indicate your choices of actions from lists or icons displayed on the screen.

FIGURE 6
The mouse input device is used to move the cursor and choose selections on the computer screen.

The Processor Unit

The **processor unit** is composed of the central processing unit and main memory. The **central processing unit (CPU)** contains the electronic circuits that cause processing to occur. The CPU interprets instructions to the computer, performs the logical and arithmetic processing operations, and causes the input and output operations to occur. On personal computers, the CPU is designed into a chip called a **microprocessor** (Figure 7).

    Main memory, also called **random access memory**, or **RAM**, consists of electronic components that store data including numbers, letters of the alphabet, graphics, and sound. Any data to be processed must be stored in main memory. The amount of main memory in computers is typically measured in kilobytes or megabytes. One **kilobyte (K or KB)** equals 1,024 memory locations and one **megabyte (M or MB)** equals approximately 1 million memory locations. A memory location, or **byte**, usually stores one character. Therefore, a computer with 4MB can store approximately 4 million characters. One megabyte of memory can hold approximately 500 pages of text information.

FIGURE 7
A Pentium microprocessor from Intel Corporation. The microprocessor circuits are located in the center. Small gold wires lead from the circuits to the pins that fit in the microprocessor socket on the main circuit board of the computer. The pins provide an electronic connection to different parts of the computer.

Output Devices

Output devices make the information resulting from processing available for use. The output from computers can be presented in many forms, such as a printed report or color graphics. When a computer is used for processing tasks, such as word processing, spreadsheets, or database management, the two output devices most commonly used are the printer and the television-like display device called a screen, monitor, or CRT (cathode ray tube).

Printers   Printers used with computers can be either impact printers or nonimpact printers. An **impact printer** prints by striking an inked ribbon against the paper. One type of impact printer often used with personal computers is the dot matrix printer (Figure 8).

FIGURE 8
Dot matrix are the least expensive of the personal computer printers. Some can be purchased for less than $200. Advantages of dot matrix printers include the capability to handle wide paper and to print multipart forms.

FIGURE 9

On a dot matrix printer with a nine-pin print head, the letter E is formed with seven vertical and five horizontal dots. As the nine-pin print head moves from left to right, it fires one or more pins into the ribbon, making a dot on the paper. At the first print position, it fires pins 1 through 7. At print positions 2 through 4, it fires pins 1,4, and 7. At print position 5, it fires pins 1 and 7. Pins 8 and 9 are used for lowercase characters such as g, j, p, q, and y that extend below the line.

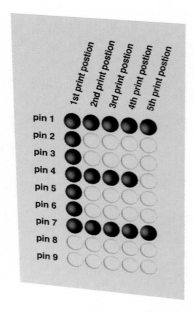

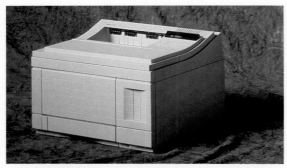

FIGURE 10 ▲

Two types of nonimpact printers are the laser printer (top) and the ink jet printer. Nonimpact printers are excellent for printing work that includes graphics.

FIGURE 11 ▶

Nonimpact printers do an excellent job of printing text in different typefaces, usually referred to as fonts. Technically, a font is a typeface in a particular size. It is common, however, to refer to the different typefaces as fonts. Dot matrix printers can print some fonts but usually at a slower rate and quality than nonimpact printers. The names of four different typefaces (fonts) are shown.

To print a character, a **dot matrix printer** generates a dot pattern representing a particular character. The printer then activates wires in a print head contained on the printer, so selected wires press against the ribbon and paper, creating a character. As you see in Figure 9, the character consists of a series of dots produced by the print head wires. In the actual size created by the printer, the characters are clear and easy to read.

Dot matrix printers vary in the speed with which they can print characters. These speeds range from 50 to more than 300 characters per second. Generally, the higher the speed, the higher the cost of the printer. Compared to other printers, dot matrix offer the lowest initial cost and the lowest per-page operating costs. Other advantages of dot matrix printers are that they can print on multipart forms and they can be purchased with wide carriages that can handle paper larger than 8 1/2 by 11 inches.

Nonimpact printers, such as ink jet printers and laser printers, form characters by means other than striking a ribbon against paper (Figure 10). Advantages of using a nonimpact printer are that it can print graphics and it can print in varying type sizes and styles called **fonts** (Figure 11). An **ink jet printer** forms a character by using a nozzle that sprays drops of ink onto the page. Ink jet printers produce relatively high-quality images and print between 30 and 150 characters per second in text mode and one to two pages per minute in graphics mode.

Laser printers work similar to a copying machine by converting data from the computer into a beam of light that is focused on a photoconductor drum, forming the images to be printed. The photoconductor attracts particles of toner that are fused by heat and pressure onto paper to produce an image. Laser printers produce high-quality output and are used for applications that combine text and graphics such as **desktop publishing** (Figure 12). Laser printers for personal computers can cost from $500 to more than $10,000. They can print four to sixteen pages of text and graphics per minute.

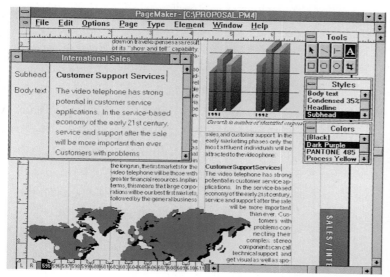

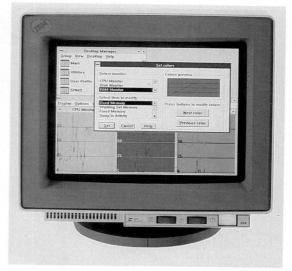

FIGURE 12
High-quality printed documents can be produced with laser printers and desktop publishing software.

Computer Screens   Most full-size personal computers use a TV-like display device called a **screen, monitor,** or **CRT** (cathode ray tube) (Figure 13). Portable computers use a flat panel display that uses **liquid crystal display (LCD)** technology similar to a digital watch. The surface of the screen is made up of individual picture elements called **pixels.** Each pixel can be illuminated to form characters and graphic shapes (Figure 14). Color screens have three colored dots (red, green, and blue) for each pixel. These dots can be turned on to display different colors. Most color monitors today use super VGA (video graphics array) technology that can display 800 × 600 (width × height) pixels.

FIGURE 13
Many personal computer systems now come with color screens. Color can be used to enhance the information displayed so the user can understand it more quickly.

FIGURE 14
Pixel is an abreviation of the words picture element, one of thousands of spots on a computer screen that can be turned on and off to form text and graphics.

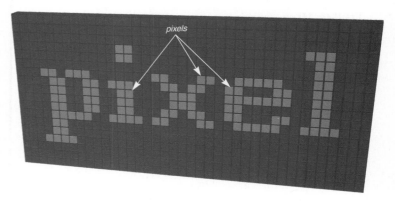

Auxiliary Storage

Auxiliary storage devices are used to store instructions and data when they are not being used in main memory. Two types of auxiliary storage most often used on personal computers are diskettes and hard disks. CD-ROM disk drives are also becoming common.

Diskettes   A **diskette** is a circular piece of oxide-coated plastic that stores data as magnetic spots. Diskettes are available in various sizes and storage capacities. Personal computers most commonly use diskettes that are 5 1/4 inches or 3 1/2 inches in diameter (Figure 15).

FIGURE 15
The most commonly used diskettes for personal computers are the 5 1/4-inch size on the left and the 3 1/2-inch size on the right. Although they are smaller in size, the 3 1/2-inch diskettes can store more data.

To read data stored on a diskette or to store data on a diskette, you insert the diskette in a disk drive (Figure 16). You can tell that the computer is reading data on the diskette or writing data on it because a light on the disk drive will come on while read/write operations are taking place. Do not try to insert or remove a diskette when the light is on as you could cause permanent damage to the data stored on it.

The storage capacities of disk drives and the related diskettes can vary widely (Figure 17). The number of characters that can be stored on a diskette by a disk drive depends on two factors: (1) the recording density of the bits on a track; and (2) the number of tracks on the diskette.

FIGURE 16
A user inserts a 3 1/2-inch diskette into the disk drive of a personal computer.

DIAMETER (INCHES)	DESCRIPTION	CAPACITY (BYTES)
5.25	Double-sided, double-density	360KB
5.25	Double-sided high-density	1.25MB
3.5	Double-sided double-density	720KB
3.5	Double-sided high-density	1.44MB

FIGURE 17
Storage capacities of different size and type diskettes.

Disk drives found on many personal computers are 5 1/4-inch, double-sided disk drives that can store from 360,000 bytes to 1.25 million bytes on the diskette. Another popular type is the 3 1/2-inch diskette, which, although physically smaller, stores from 720,000 bytes to 1.44 million bytes. An added benefit of the 3 1/2-inch diskette is its rigid plastic housing that protects the magnetic surface of the diskette.

The recording density is stated in bits per inch (bpi)—the number of magnetic spots that can be recorded on a diskette in a one-inch circumference of the innermost track on the diskette. Diskettes and disk drives used today are identified as being double-density or high-density. You need to be aware of the density of diskettes used by your system because data stored on high-density diskettes, for example, cannot be processed by a computer that has only double-density disk drives.

The second factor that influences the number of characters that can be stored on a diskette is the number of tracks on the diskette. A **track** is a very narrow recording band forming a full circle around the diskette (Figure 18).

FIGURE 18
Each track on a diskette is a narrow, circular band. On a diskette containing 80 tracks, the outside track is called track 0 and the inside track is called track 79. The disk surface is divided into sectors.

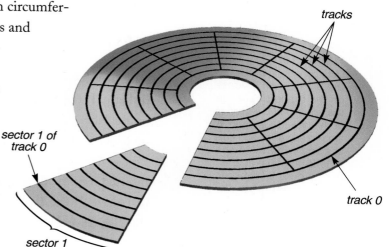

tracks

sector 1 of track 0

sector 1

track 0

The tracks are separated from each other by a very narrow blank gap. Each track on a diskette is divided into sectors. The term sector is used to refer to a pie-shaped section of the disk. It is also used to refer to a section of track. Sectors are the basic units for diskette storage. When data is read from a diskette, it reads a minimum of one full sector from a track. When data is stored on a diskette, it writes one full sector on a track at a time. The tracks and sectors on the diskette and the number of characters that can be stored in each sector are defined by a special formatting program that is used with the computer.

Data stored in sectors on a diskette must be retrieved and placed into main memory to be processed. The time required to access and retrieve data, called the **access time,** can be important in some applications. The access time for diskettes varies from about 175 milliseconds (one millisecond equals 1/1000 of a second) to approximately 300 milliseconds. On average, data stored in a single sector on a diskette can be retrieved in approximately 1/15 to 1/3 of a second.

Diskette care is important to preserve stored data. Properly handled, diskettes can store data indefinitely. However, the surface of the diskette can be damaged and the data stored can be lost if the diskette is handled improperly.

A diskette will give you very good service if you follow a few simple procedures:

1. Keep diskettes in their original box or in a special diskette storage box to protect them from dirt and dust and prevent them from being accidentally bent. Store 5 1/4-inch diskettes in their protective envelopes. Store the container away from heat and direct sunlight. Magnetic and electrical equipment, including telephones, radios, and televisions, can erase the data on a diskette, so do not place diskettes near such devices. Do not place heavy objects on a diskette, because the weight can pinch the covering, causing damage when the disk drive attempts to rotate.

2. To affix one of the self-adhesive labels supplied with most diskettes, it is best to write or type the information on the label before you place the label on the diskette. If the label is already on the diskette, use only a felt-tip pen to write on the label, and press lightly. Do not use ball point pens, pencils, or erasers on lables that are already on diskettes.

3. To use the diskette, grasp the diskette on the side away from the side to be inserted into the disk drive. Slide the diskette carefully into the slot on the disk drive. If the disk drive has a latch or door, close it. If it is difficult to close the disk drive door, do not force it—the diskette may not be inserted fully, and forcing the door closed may damage the diskette. Reinsert the diskette if necessary, and try again to close the door.

The diskette write-protect feature (Figure 19) prevents the accidental erasure of the data stored on a diskette by preventing the disk drive from writing new data or erasing existing data. On a 5 1/4-inch diskette, a write-protect notch is located on the side of the diskette. A special write-protect label is placed over this notch whenever you want to protect the data. On the 3 1/2-inch diskette, a small switch can slide to cover and uncover the write-protection window. On a 3 1/2-inch diskette, when the window is uncovered the data is protected.

FIGURE 19
Data cannot be written on the 3 1/2-inch diskette on the top left because the window in the corner of the diskette is open. A small piece of plastic covers the window of the 3 1/2-inch diskette on the top right, so data can be written on this diskette. The reverse situation is true for the 5 1/4-inch diskettes. The write-protect notch of the 5 1/4-inch diskette on the bottom left is covered and, therefore, data cannot be written to the diskette. The notch of the 5 1/4-inch diskette on the bottom right, however, is open. Data can be written to this diskette.

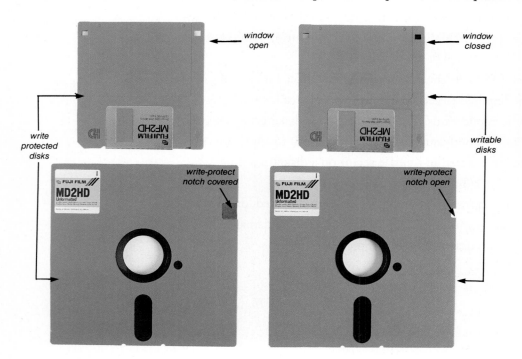

window open

window closed

write protected disks

writable disks

write-protect notch covered

write-protect notch open

Hard Disk   Another form of auxiliary storage is a hard disk. A hard disk consists of one or more rigid metal platters coated with a metal oxide material that allows data to be magnetically recorded on the surface of the platters (Figure 20). Although hard disks are available in removable cartridge form, most disks cannot be removed from the computer. As with diskettes, the data is recorded on hard disks on a series of tracks. The tracks are divided into sectors when the disk is formatted

The hard disk platters spin at a high rate of speed, typically 3,600 revolutions per minute. When reading data from the disk, the read head senses the magnetic spots that are recorded on the disk along the various tracks and transfers that data to main memory. When writing, the data is transferred from main memory and is stored as magnetic spots on the tracks on the recording surface of one or more of the disk platters. Unlike diskette drives, the read/write heads on a hard disk drive do not actually touch the surface of the disk.

The number of platters permanently mounted on the spindle of a hard disk varies. On most drives, each surface of the platter can be used to store data. Thus, if a hard disk drive uses one platter, two surfaces are available for data. If the drive uses two platters, four sets of read/write heads read and record data from the four surfaces. Storage capacities of internally mounted fixed disks for personal computers range from 80 million characters to more than 500 million characters. Larger capacity, stand-alone hard disk units are also available that can store more than one billion bytes of information. One billion bytes is called a gigabyte.

The amount of effective storage on both hard disks and diskettes can be increased by the use of compression programs. Compression programs use sophisticated formulas to replace spaces and repeated text and graphics patterns with codes that can later be used to recreate the compressed data. Text files can be compressed the most; as much as an eighth of their original volume. Graphics files can be compressed the least. Overall, a 2-to-1 compression ratio is average.

CD-ROM   Compact disk read-only memory (CD-ROM) disks are increasingly used to store large amounts of prerecorded information (Figure 21). Each CD-ROM disk can store more than 600 million bytes of data—the equivalent of 300,000 pages of text. Because of their large storage capacity, CD-ROM is often used for multimedia material. Multimedia combines text, graphics, video (pictures), and audio (sound) (Figure 22 on the next page).

spindle
disk surface
read/write head
access arm

FIGURE 20
The protective cover of this hard disk drive has been removed. A read/write head is at the end of the access arm that extends over the recording surface, called a platter.

FIGURE 21
CD-ROM disk drives allow the user to access tremendous amounts of prerecorded information — more than 600MB of data can be stored on one CD-ROM disk.

Computer Software

C omputer software is the key to productive use of computers. With the correct software, a computer can become a valuable tool. Software can be categorized into two types: system software and application software.

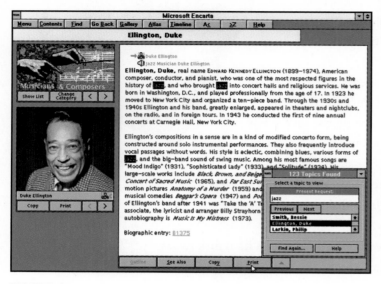

FIGURE 22

Microsoft Encarta is a multimedia encyclopedia available on a CD-ROM disk. Text, graphics, sound, and animation are all available. The camera-shaped icon at the top of the text indicates that a photograph is available for viewing. The speaker-shaped icon just below the camera indicates that a sound item is available. In this topic, if the user chooses the speaker icon with the mouse, a portion of Duke Ellington's music is played.

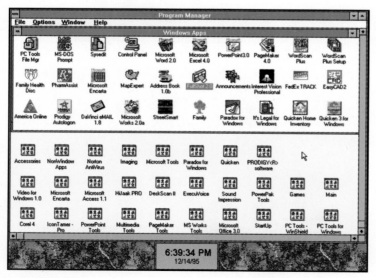

FIGURE 23

Microsoft Windows is a graphical user interface that works with the DOS operating system to make the computer easier to use. The small pictures or symbols on the main part of the screen are called icons. The icons represent different processing options, such as word processing or electronic spreadsheet applications, the user can choose.

System Software

System software consists of programs to control the operations of computer equipment. An important part of system software is a set of programs called the **operating system**. Instructions in the operating system tell the computer how to perform the functions of loading, storing, and executing an application and how to transfer data. For a computer to operate, an operating system must be stored in the computer's main memory. When a computer is started, the operating system is loaded into the computer and stored in main memory. This process is called **booting**. The most commonly used operating system on personal computers is **DOS (Disk Operating System)**.

Many computers use an **operating environment** that works with the operating system to make the computer system easier to use. Operating environments have a **graphical user interface (GUI)** displaying visual clues such as icon symbols to help the user. Each **icon** represents an application software package, such as word processing or a file or document where data is stored. **Microsoft Windows** (Figure 23) is a graphical user interface that works with DOS. Apple Macintosh computers also have a built in graphical user interface in the operating system.

Application Software

Application software consists of programs that tell a computer how to produce information. The different ways people use computers in their careers or in their personal lives, are examples of types of application software. Business, scientific, and educational programs are all examples of application software.

Personal Computer Application Software Packages

P ersonal computer users often use application software packages. Some of the most commonly used packages are: word processing, electronic spreadsheet, presentation graphics, database, communications, and electronic mail software.

Word processing software (Figure 24) is used to create and print documents. A key advantage of word processing software is its capability to make changes easily in documents, such as correcting spelling, changing margins, and adding, deleting, or relocating entire paragraphs. These changes would be difficult and time consuming to make using manual methods such as a typewriter. With a word processor, documents can be printed quickly and accurately and easily stored on a disk for future use. Word processing software is oriented toward working with text, but most word processing packages can also include numeric and graphic information.

Electronic spreadsheet software (Figure 25) allows the user to add, subtract, and perform user-defined calculations on rows and columns of numbers. These numbers can be changed and the spreadsheet quickly recalculates the new results. Electronic spreadsheet software eliminates the tedious recalculations required with manual methods. Spreadsheet information is frequently converted into a graphic form. Graphics capabilities are now included in most spreadsheet packages.

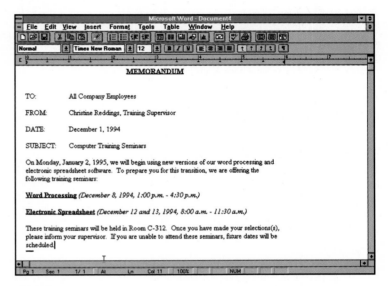

FIGURE 24
Word processing software is used to write letters, memos, and other documents. As the user types words and letters, they display on the screen. The user can easily add, delete, and change any text entered until the document looks exactly as desired. The user can then save the document on auxiliary storage and can also print it on a printer.

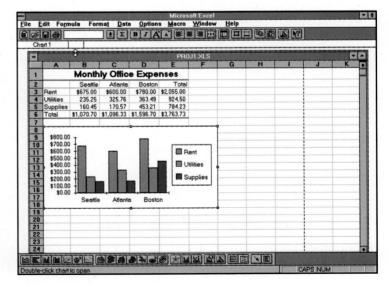

FIGURE 25
Electronic spreadsheet software is frequently used by people who work with numbers. The user enters the data and the formulas to be used on the data and calculates the results. Most spreadsheet programs have the capability to use numeric data to generate charts, such as the bar chart.

Database software (Figure 26) allows the user to enter, retrieve, and update data in an organized and efficient manner. These software packages have flexible inquiry and reporting capabilities that allow users to access the data in different ways and create custom reports that include some or all of the information in the database.

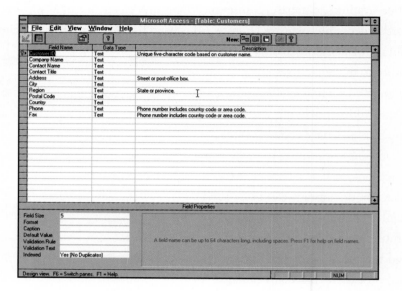

FIGURE 26
Database software allows the user to enter, retrieve, and update data in an organized and efficient manner. This database table illustrates how a business organized customer information. Once the table is defined, the user can add, delete, change, display, print, or reorganize the database records.

Presentation graphics software (Figure 27) allows the user to create documents called slides to be used in making presentations. Using special projection devices, the slides are projected directly from the computer. In addition, the slides can be printed and used as handouts, or converted into transparencies and displayed on overhead projectors. Presentation graphics software includes many special effects, color, and art that enhance information presented on a slide. Because slides frequently include numeric data, presentation graphics software includes the capability to convert the numeric data into many forms of charts.

FIGURE 27
Presentation graphics software allows the user to create documents called slides for use in presentations. Using special projection devices, the slides display as they appear on the computer screen. The slides can also be printed and used as handouts or converted into transparencies to be used with overhead projectors.

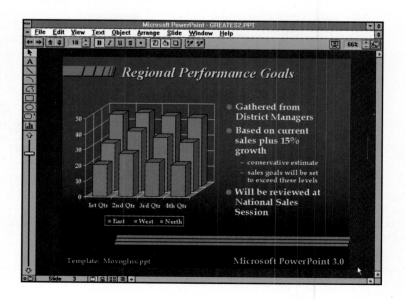

Communications software (Figure 28) is used to transmit data and information from one computer to another. For the transfer to take place, each computer must have communications software. Organizations use communications software to transfer information from one location to another. Many individuals use communications software to access on-line databases that provide information on current events, airline schedules, finances, weather, and hundreds of other subjects.

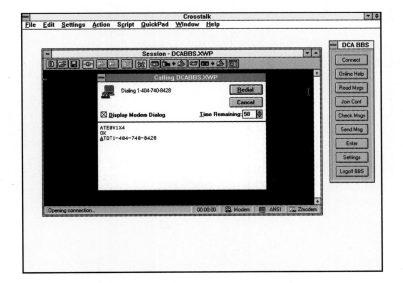

FIGURE 28
Communications software allows users to transmit data from one computer to another. This software enables the user to choose a previously entered phone number of another computer. Once the number is chosen, the communications software dials the number and establishes a communication link. The user can then transfer data or run programs on the remote computer.

Electronic mail software, also called **e-mail** (Figure 29), allows users to send messages to and receive messages from other computer users. The other users may be on the same computer network or on a separate computer system reached through the use of communications equipment and software.

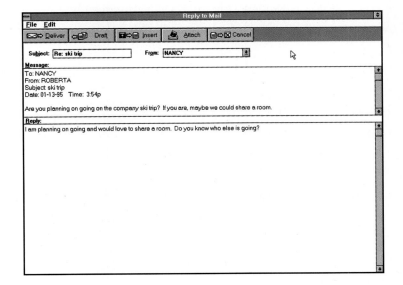

FIGURE 29
Electronic mail software allows users to send and receive messages with other computer users. Each user has an electronic mail box to which messages are sent. This software enables a user to add a reply to a received message and then send the reply back to the person who sent the original message.

What Is Communications?

Communications refers to the transmission of data and information over a communications channel, such as a standard telephone line, between one computer and another computer. Figure 30 shows the basic model for a communications system. This model consists of the following equipment:

1. A computer.
2. Communications equipment that sends (and can usually receive) data.
3. The communications channel over which the data is sent.
4. Communications equipment that receives (and can usually send) data.
5. Another computer.

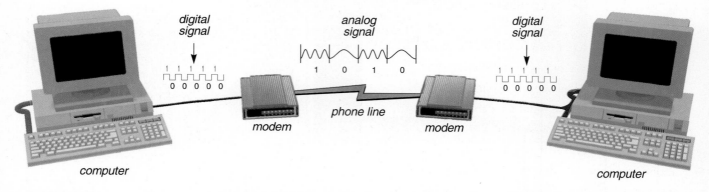

digital signal   analog signal   digital signal

1 0 1 0

phone line

computer   modem   modem   computer

FIGURE 30
The basic model of a communications system. Individual electrical pulses of the digital signal from the computer are converted into analog (electrical wave) signals for transmission over voice telephone lines. At the main computer receiving end, another modem converts the analog signals back into digital signals that can be processed by the computer.

The basic model also includes communications software. When two computers are communicating with each other, compatible communications software is required on each system.

Communications is important to understand because of on-line services and the trend to network computers. With communications equipment and software, access is available to an increasing amount and variety of information and services. **On-line information services** such as Prodigy (Figure 31) and America On-Line offer the latest news, weather, sports, and financial information along with shopping, entertainment, and electronic mail.

International networks such as the Internet allow users to access information at thousands of Internet member organizations around the world. Electronic bulletin boards can be found in most cities with hundreds available in large metropolitan areas. An electronic **bulletin board system (BBS)** is a computer and at least one phone line that allows users to *chat* with the computer operator, called the **system operator (sys op)** or, if more than one phone line is available, with other BBS users. BBS users can also leave messages for other users. BBSs are often devoted to a specific subject area such as games, hobbies, or a specific type of computer or software. Many computer hardware and software companies operate BBSs so users of their products can share information.

Communications Channels

A **communications channel** is the path the data follows as it is transmitted from the
sending equipment to the receiving equipment in a communications system. These
channels are made up of one or more **transmission media**, including twisted pair wire,
coaxial cable, fiber optics, microwave transmission, satellite transmission, and wireless
transmission.

Communications Equipment

If a personal computer is within approximately
1,000 feet of another computer, the two
devices can usually be directly connected by a
cable. If the devices are more than 1,000 feet,
however, the electrical signal weakens to the
point that some type of special communications equipment is required to increase or
change the signal to transmit it farther. A
variety of communications equipment exists
to perform this task, but the equipment most
often used is a modem.

FIGURE 31

Prodigy is one of several on-line service providers offering information on a
number of general-interest subjects. The topic areas display on the right.
Users access Prodigy and other on-line services by using a modem and
special communications software.

Computer equipment is designed to pro-
cess data as **digital signals**, individual electrical
pulses grouped together to represent characters.
Telephone equipment was originally designed
to carry only voice transmission, which is com-
prised of a continuous electrical wave called an **analog signal** (see Figure 30). Thus, a
special piece of equipment called a modem converts between the digital signals and
analog signals so telephone lines can carry data. A **modem** converts the digital signals
of a computer to analog signals that are transmitted over a communications channel. A
modem also converts analog signals it receives into digital signals used by a computer.
The word modem comes from a combination of the words *mo*dulate, which means to
change into a sound or analog signal, and *dem*odulate, which means to convert an analog
signal into a digital signal. A modem is needed at both the sending and receiving ends
of a communications channel. A modem may be an external stand-alone device that is
connected to the computer and phone line or an internal circuit board that is installed
inside the computer.

Modems can transmit data at rates from 300 to 38,400 bits per second (bps).
Most personal computers use a 2,400 bps or higher modem. Business or heavier volume users would use faster and more expensive modems.

Communication Networks

A communication **network** is a collection of computers and other equipment using communications channels to share hardware, software, data, and information. Networks are classified as either local area networks or wide area networks.

Local Area Networks (LANs)

A **local area network**, or LAN, is a privately owned communications network and covers a limited geographic area, such as a school computer laboratory, an office, a building, or a group of buildings.

The LAN consists of a communications channel connecting a group of personal computers to one another. Very sophisticated LANs are capable of connecting a variety of office devices, such as word processing equipment, computer terminals, video equipment, and personal computers.

Three common applications of local area networks are hardware, software, and information resource sharing. **Hardware resource sharing** allows each personal computer in the network to access and use devices that would be too expensive to provide for each user or would not be justified for each user because of only occasional use. For example, when a number of personal computers are used on the network, each may need to use a laser printer. Using a LAN, the purchase of one laser printer serves the entire network. Whenever a personal computer user on the network needs the laser printer, it is accessed over the network. Figure 32 depicts a simple local area network consisting of four personal computers linked together by a cable. Three of the personal computers (computer 1 in the sales and marketing department, computer 2 in the accounting department, and computer 3 in the personnel department) are available for use at all times. Computer 4 is used as a **server**, which is dedicated to handling the communications needs of the other computers in the network. The users of this LAN have connected the laser printer to the server. Using the LAN, all computers and the server can use the printer.

FIGURE 32
A local area network (LAN) consists of multiple personal computers connected to one another. The LAN allows users to share softwre, hardware, and information.

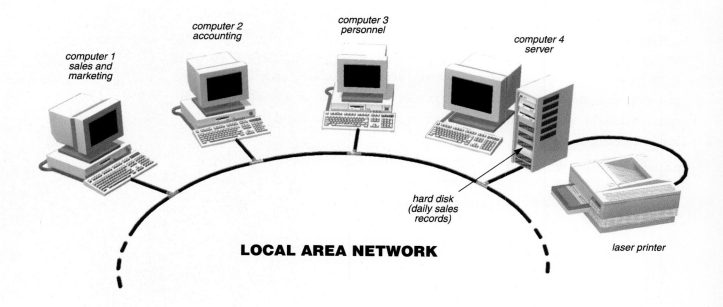

computer 1
sales and
marketing

computer 2
accounting

computer 3
personnel

computer 4
server

hard disk
(daily sales
records)

LOCAL AREA NETWORK

laser printer

Frequently used software is another type of resource sharing that often occurs on a local area network. For example, if all users need access to word processing software, the software can be stored on the hard disk of the server and accessed by all users as needed. This is more convenient and faster than having the software stored on a diskette and available at each computer.

Information resource sharing allows anyone using a personal computer on the local area network to access data stored on any other computer in the network. In actual practice, hardware resource sharing and information resource sharing are often combined. The capability to access and store data on common auxiliary storage is an important feature of many local area networks.

Information resource sharing is usually provided by using either the file-server or client-server method. Using the **file-server** method, the server sends an entire file at a time. The requesting computer then performs the processing. With the **client-server** method, processing tasks are divided between the server computer

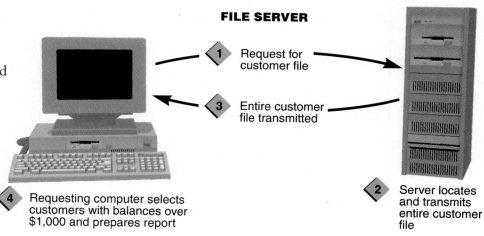

FILE SERVER

1 Request for customer file

3 Entire customer file transmitted

2 Server locates and transmits entire customer file

4 Requesting computer selects customers with balances over $1,000 and prepares report

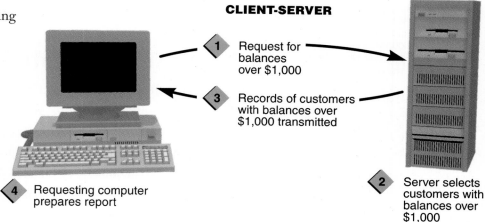

CLIENT-SERVER

1 Request for balances over $1,000

3 Records of customers with balances over $1,000 transmitted

2 Server selects customers with balances over $1,000

4 Requesting computer prepares report

and the *client* computer requesting the information. Figure 33 illustrates how the two methods would process a request for information stored on the server system for customers with balances over $1,000. With the file-server method, all customer records would be transferred to the requesting computer. The requesting computer would then process the records to identify the customers with balances over $1,000. With the client-server method, the server system would review the customers' records and only transfer records of customers meeting the criteria. The client-server method greatly reduces the amount of data sent over a network but requires a more powerful server system.

FIGURE 33
A request for information about customers with balances over $1,000 would be processed differently by the file-server and client-server networks.

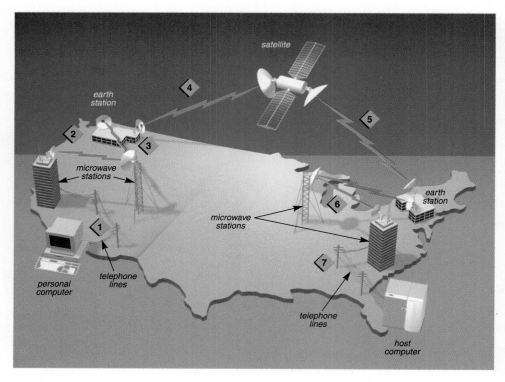

FIGURE 34
A wide area network (WAN) may use a number of different communications channels such as telephone lines, microwaves, and satellites.

Wide Area Networks (WANs)

A wide area network, or WAN, is geographic in scope (as opposed to local) and uses telephone lines, microwaves, satellites, or a combination of communications channels (Figure 34). Public wide area network companies include common carriers such as the telephone companies. Telephone company deregulation has encouraged a number of companies to build their own wide area networks. Communications companies, such as MCI, have built WANs to compete with other communications companies.

How to Purchase a Computer System

The desktop personal computer (PC) is the most widely purchased type of system. The following guidelines assume you are purchasing a desktop IBM-compatible PC, to be used for home or light business use. That is not meant to imply that Macintosh or other non DOS or Windows operating system computers are not worth considering. Software requirements and the need to be compatible with other systems you may work with should determine the type of system you purchase. A portable computer would be an appropriate choice if your situation requires that you have a computer with you when you travel.

1. Determine what applications you will use on your computer. This decision will guide you as to the type and size of computer.

2. Choose your software first. Some packages only run on Macintosh computers, others only on a PC. Some packages only run under the Windows operating system. In addition, some software requires more memory and disk space than other packages.

3. Be aware of hidden costs. Realize that there will be some additional costs associated with buying a computer. Such costs might include; an additional phone line or outlet to use the modem, computer furniture, consumable supplies such as diskettes and paper, diskette holders, reference manuals on specific software

packages, and special training classes you may want to take. Depending on where you buy your computer, the seller may be willing to include some or all of these in the system purchase price.

4. **Buy equipment that meets the** *Energy Star* **power consumption guidelines.** These guidelines require that computer systems, monitors, and printers, reduce electrical consumption if they have not been used for some period of time, usually several minutes. Equipment meeting the guidelines can display the *Energy Star* logo.

5. **Use a spreadsheet like the one shown in Figure 35 to compare purchase alternatives.** Use a separate sheet of paper to take notes on each vendor's system and then summarize the information on the spreadsheet.

6. **Consider buying from local computer dealers and direct mail companies.** Each has certain advantages. The local dealer can more easily provide hands-on support, if necessary. With a mail order company, you are usually limited to speaking to someone over the phone. Mail order companies usually, but not always, offer the lowest prices. The important thing to do when shopping for a system is to make sure you are comparing identical or similar configurations.

System Cost Comparison Worksheet						
		Desired	#1	#2	#3	#4
Base System	Mfr	—	Delway			
	Model		4500X			
	Processor	486DX	486DX			
	Speed	50MHz	50			
	Pwr Supply	200watts	220			
	Exp Slots	5	5			
	Price		$995			
Memory	8MB Ram		incl			
Disk	Mfr		Conner			
	Size	>300MB	340			
	Price		incl			
Diskette	3 1/2					
	5 1/4					
	Combination		$50			
Monitor	Mfr		NEC			
	Model		5FG			
	Size	15in	15			
	Price		$300			
Sound	Mfr		Media Labs			
	Model		Pro			
	Price		$75			
CDROM	Mfr		NEC			
	Speed		450/200			
	Price		$100			
Mouse	Mfr		Logitech			
	Price		incl			
Modem	Mfr		Boca			
	Mod/fax Speeds	14.4/14.4	14.4/14.4			
	Price		$125			
Printer	Mfr		HP			
	Model		4Z			
	Type		laser			
	Speed	6ppm	8ppm			
	Price		$675			
Surge Protector	Mfr		Brooks			
	Price		$35			
Options	Tape Backup					
	UPS					
Other	Sales Tax		0			
	Shipping		$30			
	1 YR Warranty		incl			
	1 YR On-Site Svc		incl			
	3 YR On-Site Svc		$150			
Software	List free software		Windows			
			MS Works			
			diagnostics			
	TOTAL		**$2,535**			

FIGURE 35
A spreadsheet is an effective way to summarize and compare the prices and equipment offered by different system vendors.

7. **Consider more than just price.** Don't necessarily buy the lowest cost system. Consider intangibles such as how long the vendor has been in business, its reputation for quality, and reputation for support.

8. **Look for free software.** Many system vendors now include free software with their systems. Some even let you choose which software you want. Such software only has value, however, if you would have purchased it if it had not come with the computer.

9. **Buy a system compatible with the one you use elsewhere.** If you use a personal computer at work or at some other organization, make sure the computer you buy is compatible. That way, if you need or want to, you can work on projects at home.

10. **Consider purchasing an on-site service agreement.** If you use your system for business or otherwise can't afford to be without your computer, consider purchasing an on-site service agreement. Many of the mail order vendors offer such support through third-party companies. Such agreements usually state that a technician will be on-site within 24 hours. Some systems include on-site service for only the first year. It is usually less expensive to extend the service for two or three years when you buy the computer rather than waiting to buy the service agreement later.

11. **Use a credit card to purchase your system.** Many credit cards now have purchase protection benefits that cover you in case of loss or damage to purchased goods. Some also extend the warranty of any products purchased with the card. Paying by credit card also gives you time to install and use the system before you have to pay for it. Finally, if you're dissatisfied with the system and can't reach an agreement with the seller, paying by credit card gives you certain rights regarding withholding payment until the dispute is resolved. Check your credit card agreement for specific details.

12. **Buy a system that will last you for at least three years.** Studies show that many users become dissatisfied because they didn't buy a powerful enough system. Consider the following system configuration guidelines. Each of the components will be discussed separately:

Base System Components:	Optional Equipment:
486SX or 486DX processor, 33 megahertz	5 1/4" diskette drive
150 watt power supply	14.4K fax modem
160 to 300MB hard disk	laser printer
4 to 8MB RAM	sound card and speakers
3 to 5 expansion slots	CD-ROM drive
3 1/2" diskette drive	tape backup
14" or 15" color monitor	uninterruptable power supply (UPS)
mouse or other pointing device	
enhanced keyboard	
ink jet or bubble jet printer	
surge protector	

Processor: A 486SX or 486DX processor with a speed rating of at least 33 mega-hertz is needed for today's more sophisticated software, even word processing soft-ware. Buy a system that can be upgraded to the Pentium processor.

Power Supply: 150 watts. If the power supply is too small, it won't be able to support additional expansion cards that you might want to add in the future.

Hard Disk: 160 to 300 megabytes (MB). Each new release of software requires more hard disk space. Even with disk compression programs, disk space is used up fast. Start with more disk than you ever think you'll need.

Memory (RAM): 4 to 8 megabytes (MB). Like disk space, the new applications are demanding more memory. It's easier and less expensive to obtain the memory when you buy the system than if you wait until later.

Expansion Slots: 3 to 5 open slots on the base system. Expansion slots are needed for scanners, tape drives, video boards, and other equipment you may want to add in the future as your needs change and the price of this equipment becomes lower.

Diskette Drives: Most software is now distributed on 3 1/2-inch disks. Consider adding a 5 1/4-inch diskette to read data and programs that may have been stored on that format. The best way to achieve this is to buy a combination diskette drive which is only slightly more expensive than a single 3 1/2-inch diskette drive. The combination device has both 3 1/2- and 5 1/4-inch diskette drives in a single unit.

Color Monitor: 14 to 15 inch. This is one device where it pays to spend a little more money. A 15-inch super VGA monitor will display graphics better than a 14-inch model. For health reasons, make sure you pick a low radiation model.

Pointing Device: Most systems include a mouse as part of the base package.

Enhanced Keyboard: The keyboard is usually included with the system. Check to make sure the keyboard is the *enhanced* and not the older *standard* model. The enhanced keyboard is sometimes called the *101* keyboard because it has 101 keys.

Printer: The price of nonimpact printers has come within several hundred dollars of the lowest cost dot matrix printers. Unless you need the wide carriage or multi-part form capabilities of a dot matrix, purchase a nonimpact printer.

Surge Protector: A voltage spike can literally destroy your system. It is low-cost insurance to protect yourself with a surge protector. Don't merely buy a fused multi-plug outlet from the local hardware store. Buy a surge protector designed for com-puters with a separate protected jack for your phone (modem) line.

Fax Modem: Volumes of information are available via on-line databases. In addition, many software vendors provide assistance and free software upgrades via bulletin boards. For the speed they provide, 14.4K modems are worth the extra money. Facsimile (fax) capability only costs a few dollars more and gives you more communication options.

Sound Card and Speakers: More and more software and support materials are incorporating sound.

CD-ROM Drive: Multimedia is the wave of the future and it requires a CD-ROM drive. Get a double- or triple-speed model.

Tape Backup: Larger hard disks make backing up data on diskettes impractical. Internal or external tape backup systems are the most common solution. Some portable units, great if you have more than one system, are designed to connect to your printer port. The small cassette tapes can store the equivalent of hundreds of diskettes.

Uninterruptable Power Supply (UPS): A UPS uses batteries to start or keep your system running if the main electrical power is turned off. The length of time they provide depends on the size of the batteries and the electrical requirements of your system but is usually at least 10 minutes. The idea of a UPS is to give you enough time to save your work. Get a UPS that is rated for your size system.

Remember that the types of applications you want to use on your system will guide you as to the type and size of computer that is right for you. The ideal computer system you choose may differ from the general recommendation that is presented here. Determine your needs and buy the best system your budget will allow.

How to Install a Computer System

1. **Allow for adequate workspace around the computer.** A workspace of at least two feet by four feet is recommended.
2. **Install bookshelves.** Bookshelves above and/or to the side of the computer area are useful for keeping manuals and other reference materials handy.
3. **Install your computer in a well-designed work area.** The height of your chair, keyboard, monitor, and work surface is important and can affect your health. See Figure 36 for specific guidelines.
4. **Use a document holder.** To minimize neck and eye strain, obtain a document holder that holds documents at the same height and distance as your computer screen.

5. **Provide adequate lighting.**

6. **While working at your computer, be aware of health issues.** See Figure 37 for a list of computer user health guidelines.

7. **Install or move a phone near the computer.** Having a phone near the computer really helps if you need to call a vendor about a hardware or software problem. Oftentimes the vendor support person can talk you through the correction while you're on the phone. To avoid data loss, however, don't place diskettes on the phone or any other electrical or electronic equipment.

8. **Obtain a computer tool set.** Computer tool sets are available from computer dealers, office supply stores, and mail order companies. These sets will have the right-sized screwdrivers and other tools to work on your system. Get one that comes in a zippered carrying case to keep all the tools together.

9. **Save all the paperwork that comes with your system.** Keep it in an accessible place with the paperwork from your other computer-related purchases. To keep different-sized documents together, consider putting them in a plastic zip-lock bag.

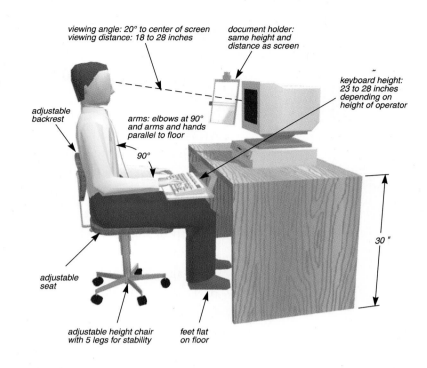

FIGURE 36
More than anything else, a well-designed work area should be flexible to allow adjustment to the height and build of different individuals. Good lighting and air quality should also be considered.

COMPUTER USER HEALTH GUIDELINES
1. Work in a well-designed work area. Figure 36 illustrates the guidelines.
2. Alternate work activities to prevent physical and mental fatigue. If possible, change the order of your work to provide some variety.
3. Take frequent breaks. At least once per hour, get out of your chair and move around. Every two hours, take at least a 15 minute break.
4. Incorporate hand, arm, and body stretching exercises into your breaks. At lunch, try to get outside and walk.
5. Make sure your computer monitor is designed to minimize electromagnetic radiation
6. Try to eliminate or minimize surrounding noise. Noisy environments contribute to stress and tension.
7. If you frequently have to use the phone and the computer at the same time, consider using a telephone headset. Cradling the phone between your head and shoulder can cause muscle strain.
8. Be aware of symptoms of repetitive strain injuries; soreness, pain, numbness, or weakness in neck, shoulders, arms, wrists, and hands. Don't ignore early signs; seek medical advice.

FIGURE 37
All computer users should follow the Computer User Health Guidelines to maintain their health.

10. **Record the serial numbers of all your equipment and software.** Write the serial numbers on the outside of the manuals that came with the equipment as well as in a single list that contains the serial numbers of all your equipment and software.

11. **Keep the shipping containers and packing materials for all your equipment.** This material will come in handy if you have to return your equipment for servicing or have to move it to another location.

12. **Look at the inside of your computer.** Before you connect power to your system, remove the computer case cover and visually inspect the internal components. The user manual usually identifies what each component does. Look for any disconnected wires, loose screws or washers, or any other obvious signs of trouble. Be careful not to touch anything inside the case unless you are grounded. Static electricity can permanently damage the microprocessor chips on the circuit boards. Before you replace the cover, take several photographs of the computer showing the location of the circuit boards. These photos may save you from taking the cover off in the future if you or a vendor has a question about what equipment controller card is installed in what expansion slot.

13. **Identify device connectors.** At the back of your system there are a number of connectors for the printer, the monitor, the mouse, a phone line, etc. If they aren't already identified by the manufacturer, use a marking pen to write the purpose of each connector on the back of the computer case.

14. **Complete and send in your equipment and software registration cards right away.** If you're already entered in the vendors user database, it can save you time when you call in with a support question. Being a registered user also makes you eligible for special pricing on software upgrades.

15. **Install your system in an area where the temperature and humidity can be maintained.** Try to maintain a constant temperature between 60 and 80 degrees farenheight when the computer is operating. High temperatures and humidity can damage electronic components. Be careful when using space heaters; their hot, dry air has been known to cause disk problems.

16. **Keep your computer area clean.** Avoid eating and drinking around the computer. Smoking should be avoided also. Cigarette smoke can quickly cause damage to the diskette drives and diskette surfaces.

17. **Check your insurance.** Some policies have limits on the amount of computer equipment they cover. Other policies don't cover computer equipment at all if it is used for a business (a separate policy is required).

How to Maintain Your Computer System

1. **Learn to use system diagnostic programs.** If a set didn't come with your system, obtain one. These programs help you identify and possibly solve problems before you call for technical assistance. Some system manufacturers now include diagnostic programs with their systems and ask that you run the programs before you call for help.

2. **Start a notebook that includes information on your system.** This notebook should be a single source of information about your entire system, both hardware and software. Each time you make a change to your system, adding or removing hardware or software, or when you change system parameters, you should record the change in the notebook. Items to include in the notebook are the following:

✓ Serial numbers of all equipment and software.

✓ Vendor support phone numbers. These numbers are often buried in user manuals. Look up these numbers once and record all of them on a single sheet of paper at the front of your notebook.

✓ Date and vendor for each equipment and software purchase.

✓ File listings for key system files (e.g., autoexec.bat and config.sys).

✓ Notes on discussions with vendor support personnel.

✓ A chronological history of any equipment or software problems. This history can be helpful if the problem persists and you have to call several times.

3. **Periodically review disk directories and delete unneeded files.** Files have a way of building up and can quickly use up your disk space. If you think you may need a file in the future, back it up to a diskette.

4. **Any time you work inside your computer turn the power off and disconnect the equipment from the power source.** In addition, before you touch anything inside the computer, touch an unpainted metal surface such as the power supply. This will discharge any static electricity that could damage internal components.

5. **Reduce the need to clean the inside of your system by keeping the surrounding area dirt and dust free.** Diskette cleaners are available but should be used sparingly (some owners never use them unless they experience diskette problems). If dust builds up inside the computer it should be carefully removed with compressed air and a small vacuum. Don't touch the components with the vacuum.

FIGURE 38
How a virus program can be transmitted from one computer to another.

6. **Back up key files and data.** At a minimum, you should have a diskette with your **command.com, autoexec.bat,** and **config.sys** files. If your system crashes, these files will help you get going again. In addition, backup any files with a file extension of **.sys.** For Windows systems, all files with a file extension of **.ini** and **.grp** should be backed up.

7. **Protect your system from computer viruses.** Computer viruses are programs designed to *infect* computer systems by copying themselves into other computer files (Figure 38). The virus program spreads when the infected files are used by or copied to another system.

A COMPUTER VIRUS: WHAT IT IS AND HOW IT SPREADS

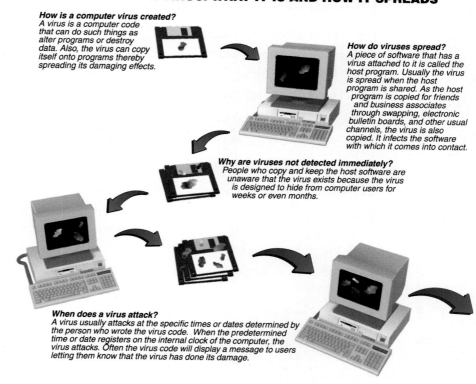

How is a computer virus created?
A virus is a computer code that can do such things as alter programs or destroy data. Also, the virus can copy itself onto programs thereby spreading its damaging effects.

How do viruses spread?
A piece of software that has a virus attached to it is called the host program. Usually the virus is spread when the host program is shared. As the host program is copied for friends and business associates through swapping, electronic bulletin boards, and other usual channels, the virus is also copied. It infects the software with which it comes into contact.

Why are viruses not detected immediately?
People who copy and keep the host software are unaware that the virus exists because the virus is designed to hide from computer users for weeks or even months.

When does a virus attack?
A virus usually attacks at the specific times or dates determined by the person who wrote the virus code. When the predetermined time or date registers on the internal clock of the computer, the virus attacks. Often the virus code will display a message to users letting them know that the virus has done its damage.

Virus programs are dangerous because they are often designed to damage the files of the infected system. Protect yourself from viruses by installing an anti-virus program on your computer.

Summary of Introduction to Computers

As you learn to use the software taught in this book, you will also become familiar with the components and operation of your computer system. When you need help understanding how the components of your system function, refer to this introduction. You can also refer to this section for information on computer communications and for guidelines when you decide to purchase a computer system of your own.

Student Assignments

Student Assignment 1: True/False

Instructions: Circle T if the statement is true or F if the statement is false.

T   F   1. A computer is an electronic device, operating under the control of instructions stored in its own memory unit, that can accept data (input), process data arithmetically and logically, produce output from the processing, and store the results for future use.

T   F   2. Information refers to data processed into a form that has meaning and is useful.

T   F   3. A computer program is a detailed set of instructions that tells a computer exactly what to do.

T   F   4. A mouse is a communications device used to convert between digital and analog signals so telephone lines can carry data.

T   F   5. The central processing unit contains the processor unit and main memory.

T   F   6. A laser printer is an impact printer that provides high-quality output.

T   F   7. Auxiliary storage is used to store instructions and data when they are not being used in main memory.

T   F   8. A diskette is considered to be a form of main memory.

T   F   9. CD-ROM is often used for multimedia material that combines text, graphics, video, and sound.

T   F   10. The operating system tells the computer how to perform functions such as how to load, store, and execute an application program and how to transfer data between the input/output devices and main memory.

T   F   11. Programs such as database management, spreadsheet, and word processing software are called system software.

T   F   12. For data to be transferred from one computer to another over communications lines, communications software is required only on the sending computer.

T   F   13. A communications network is a collection of computers and other equipment that use communications channels to share hardware, software, data, and information.

T F 14. Determining what applications you will use on your computer will help you to purchase a computer that is the type and size that meets your needs.

T F 15. The path the data follows as it is transmitted from the sending equipment to the receiving equipment in a communications system is called a modem.

T F 16. Computer equipment that meets the power consumption guidelines can display the *Energy Star* logo.

T F 17. An on-site maintenance agreement is important if you cannot be without the use of your computer.

T F 18. An anit-virus program is used to protect your computer equipment and software.

T F 19. When purchasing a computer, consider only the price because one computer is no different from another.

T F 20. A LAN allows you to share software but not hardware.

Student Assignment 2: Multiple Choice

Instructions: Circle the correct response.

1. The four operations performed by a computer include _____ .
   a. input, control, output, and storage
   b. interface, processing, output, and memory
   c. input, output, processing, and storage
   d. input, logical/rational, arithmetic, and output

2. A hand-held input device that controls the cursor location is _____ .
   a. the cursor control keyboard
   b. a mouse
   c. a modem
   d. the CRT

3. A printer that forms images without striking the paper is _____ .
   a. an impact printer   b. a nonimpact printer   c. an ink jet printer   d. both b and c

4. The amount of storage provided by a diskette is a function of _____ .
   a. the thickness of the disk
   b. the recording density of bits on the track
   c. the number of recording tracks on the diskette
   d. both b and c

5. Portable computers use a flat panel screen called a _____ .
   a. a multichrome monitor
   b. a cathode ray tube
   c. a liquid crystal display
   d. a monochrome monitor

6. When not in use, diskettes should be _____ .
   a. stored away from magnetic fields
   b. stored away from heat and direct sunlight
   c. stored in a diskette box or cabinet
   d. all of the above

7. CD-ROM is a type of _____ .
   a. main memory
   b. auxiliary storage
   c. communications equipment
   d. system software

8. An operating system is considered part of _____ .
   a. word processing software
   b. database software
   c. system software
   d. spreadsheet software

9. The type of application software most commonly used to create and print documents is _____ .
   a. word processing   b. electronic spreadsheet   c. database   d. none of the above

10. The type of application software most commonly used to send messages to and receive messages from other computer users is _____ .
   a. electronic mail   b. database   c. presentation graphics   d. none of the above

Student Assignment 3: Comparing Personal Computer Advertisements

Instructions: Obtain a copy of a recent computer magazine and review the advertisements for desktop personal computer systems. Compare ads for the least and most expensive desktop systems you can find. Discuss the differences.

Student Assignment 4: Evaluating On-Line Information Services

Instructions: Prodigy and America On-Line both offer consumer oriented on-line information services. Contact each company and request each to send you information on the specific services it offers. Try to talk to someone who actually uses one or both of the services. Discuss how each service is priced and the differences between the two on-line services.

Student Assignment 5: Visiting Local Computer Retail Stores

Instructions: Visit local computer retail stores and compare the various types of computers and support equipment available. Ask about warranties, repair services, hardware setup, training, and related issues. Report on the knowledge of the sales staff assisting you and their willingness to answer your questions. Does the store have standard hardware packages, or are they willing to configure a system to your specific needs? Would you feel confident buying a computer from this store?

Index

Photo Credits

Figure 1, (1) Compaq Computer Corp. All rights reserved.; (2) International Business Machines Corp.; (3) UNISYS Corp.; (4) Compaq Computer Corp. All rights reserved.; (5) International Business Machines Corp.; (6) Zenith Data Systems; (7) International Business Machines Corp.; (8) International Business Machines Corp.; (9) Hewlett-Packard Co.; Figure 2, International Business Machines Corp.; Figure 3, Compaq Computer Corp. All rights reserved.; Figure 5, International Business Machines Corp.; Figure 6, Logitech, Inc.; Figure 7, Intel Corp.; Figure 8, Epson America, Inc.; Figure 10 (top), Hewlett-Packard Co.; Figure 10 (bottom), Epson America, Inc.; Figure 12, Aldus Corp.; Figure 13, International Business Machines Corp.; Figure 15, Jerry Spagnoli; Figure 16, Greg Hadel; Figure 19, Jerry Spagnoli; Figure 20, Microscience International Corp.; Figure 21, 3M Corp.; Illustrations, Dave Wyer.

WINDOWS

USING *M*ICROSOFT *W*INDOWS 3.1

MICROSOFT WINDOWS 3.1

PROJECT ONE

▼

AN INTRODUCTION TO WINDOWS

OBJECTIVES You will have mastered the material in this project when you can:

▶ Describe a user interface
▶ Describe Microsoft Windows
▶ Identify the elements of a window
▶ Perform the four basic mouse operations of pointing, clicking, double-clicking, and dragging
▶ Correct errors made while performing mouse operations
▶ Understand the keyboard shortcut notation
▶ Select a menu
▶ Choose a command from a menu

▶ Respond to dialog boxes
▶ Start and exit an application
▶ Name a file
▶ Understand directories and subdirectories
▶ Understand directory structures and directory paths
▶ Create, save, open, and print a document
▶ Open, enlarge, and scroll a window
▶ Obtain online Help while using an application

▶ INTRODUCTION

The most popular and widely used graphical user interface available today is **Microsoft Windows**, or **Windows**. Microsoft Windows allows you to easily communicate with and control your computer. In addition, Microsoft Windows makes it easy to learn the application software installed on your computer, transfer data between the applications, and manage the data created while using an application.

In this project, you learn about user interfaces, the computer hardware and computer software that comprise a user interface, and Microsoft Windows. You use Microsoft Windows to perform the operations of opening a group window, starting and exiting an application, enlarging an application window, entering and editing data within an application, printing a document on the printer, saving a document on disk, opening a document, and obtaining online Help while using an application.

What Is a User Interface?

A **user interface** is the combination of hardware and software that allows the computer user to communicate with and control the computer. Through the user interface, you are able to control the computer, request information from the computer, and respond to messages displayed by the computer. Thus, a user interface provides the means for dialogue between you and the computer.

Hardware and software together form the user interface. Among the hardware associated with a user interface are the CRT screen, keyboard, and mouse (Figure 1-1). The CRT screen displays messages and provides information. You respond by entering data in the form of a command or other response using the keyboard or mouse. Among the responses available to you are responses that specify what application software to run, when to print, and where to store the data for future use.

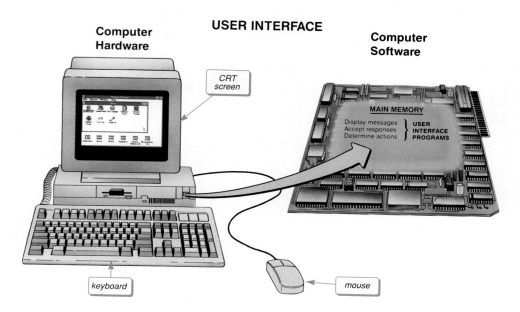

USER INTERFACE   FIGURE 1-1

Computer Hardware

CRT screen

keyboard

mouse

Computer Software

MAIN MEMORY

Display messages
Accept responses
Determine actions } USER INTERFACE PROGRAMS

The computer software associated with the user interface are the programs that engage you in dialogue (Figure 1-1). The computer software determines the messages you receive, the manner in which you should respond, and the actions that occur based on your responses. The goal of an effective user interface is to be **user friendly**, meaning the software can be easily used by individuals with limited training. Research studies have indicated that the use of graphics can play an important role in aiding users to effectively interact with a computer. A **graphical user interface**, or **GUI**, is a user interface that displays graphics in addition to text when it communicates with the user.

▶ MICROSOFT WINDOWS

Microsoft Windows, or Windows, the most popular graphical user interface, makes it easy to learn and work with **application software**, which is software that performs an application-related function, such as word processing. Numerous application software packages are available for purchase from retail computer stores, and several applications are included with the Windows interface software. In Windows terminology, these application software packages are referred to as **applications**.

Starting Microsoft Windows

When you turn on the computer, an introductory screen consisting of the Windows logo, Windows name, version number (3.1), and copyright notices displays momentarily (Figure 1-2). Next, a blank screen containing an hourglass icon (⧗) displays (Figure 1-3). The **hourglass icon** indicates that Windows requires a brief interval of time to change the display on the screen, and you should wait until the hourglass icon disappears.

FIGURE 1-2

FIGURE 1-3

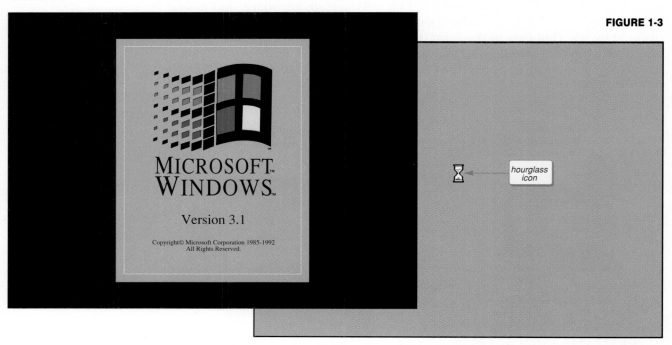

FIGURE 1-4

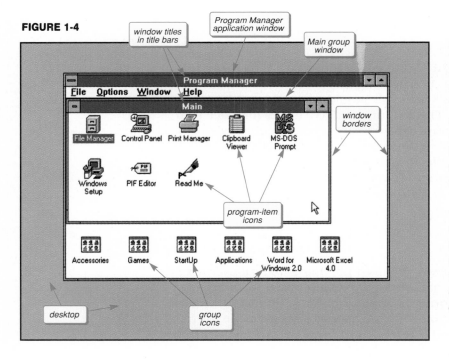

Finally, two rectangular areas, or **windows**, display (Figure 1-4). The double-line, or **window border**, surrounding each window determines their shape and size. The horizontal bar at the top of each window, called the **title bar**, contains a **window title** that identifies each window. In Figure 1-4, the Program Manager and Main titles identify each window.

The screen background on which the windows display is called the **desktop**. If your desktop does not look similar to the desktop in Figure 1-4, your instructor will inform you of the modifications necessary to change your desktop.

The Program Manager window represents the **Program Manager** application. The Program Manager application starts when you start Windows and is central to the operation of Windows. Program Manager organizes related applications into groups and displays the groups in the Program Manager window. A window that represents an application, such as the Program Manager window, is called an **application window**.

Small pictures, or **icons**, represent an individual application or groups of applications. In Figure 1-4 on the previous page, the Main window contains a group of eight icons (File Manager, Control Panel, Print Manager, Clipboard Viewer, MS-DOS Prompt, Windows Setup, PIF Editor, and Read Me). A window that contains a group of icons, such as the Main window, is called a **group window**. The icons in a group window, called **program-item icons**, each represent an individual application. A name below each program-item icon identifies the application. The program-item icons are unique and, therefore, easily distinguished from each other.

The six icons at the bottom of the Program Manager window in Figure 1-4 on the previous page, (Accessories, Games, StartUp, Applications, Word for Windows 2.0, and Microsoft Excel 4.0), called **group icons**, each represent a group of applications. Group icons are similar in appearance and only the name below the icon distinguishes one icon from another icon. Although the program-item icons of the individual applications in these groups are not visible in Figure 1-4, a method to view these icons will be demonstrated later in this project.

▶ COMMUNICATING WITH MICROSOFT WINDOWS

The Windows interface software provides the means for dialogue between you and the computer. Part of this dialogue involves requesting information from the computer and responding to messages displayed by the computer. You can request information and respond to messages using either the mouse or keyboard.

The Mouse and Mouse Pointer

A **mouse** is a pointing device commonly used with Windows that is attached to the computer by a cable and contains one or more buttons. The mouse in Figure 1-5 contains two buttons, the left mouse button and the right mouse button. On the bottom of this mouse is a ball (Figure 1-6).

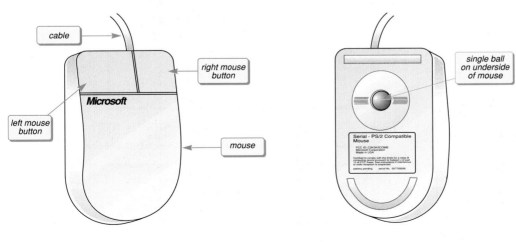

FIGURE 1-5   **FIGURE 1-6**

As you move the mouse across a flat surface (Figure 1-7), the movement of the ball is electronically sensed, and a **mouse pointer** in the shape of a block arrow (↖) moves across the desktop in the same direction.

Mouse moves diagonally across flat surface

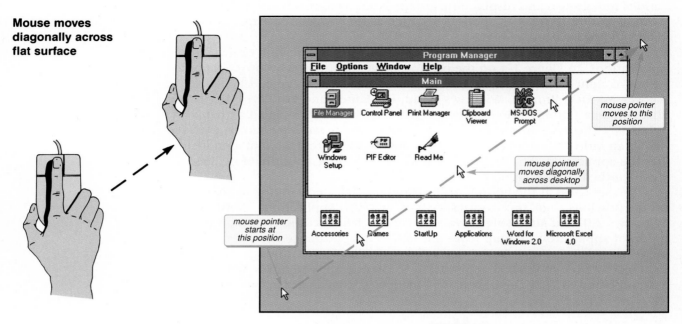

FIGURE 1-7

Mouse Operations

You use the mouse to perform four basic operations: (1) pointing; (2) clicking; (3) double-clicking; and (4) dragging. **Pointing** means moving the mouse across a flat surface until the mouse pointer rests on the item of choice on the desktop. In Figure 1-8, you move the mouse diagonally across a flat surface until the tip of the mouse pointer rests on the Print Manager icon.

Mouse moves diagonally

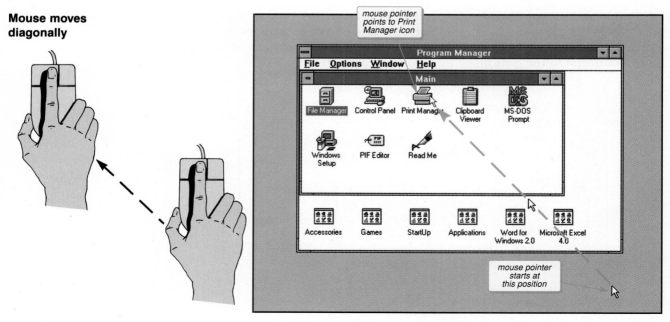

FIGURE 1-8

Clicking means pressing and releasing a mouse button. In most cases, you must point to an item before pressing and releasing a mouse button. In Figure 1-9, you highlight the Print Manager icon by pointing to the Print Manager icon (Step 1) and pressing and releasing the left mouse button (Step 2). These steps are commonly referred to as clicking the Print Manager icon. When you click the Print Manager icon, Windows highlights, or places color behind, the name below the Print Manager icon (Step 3).

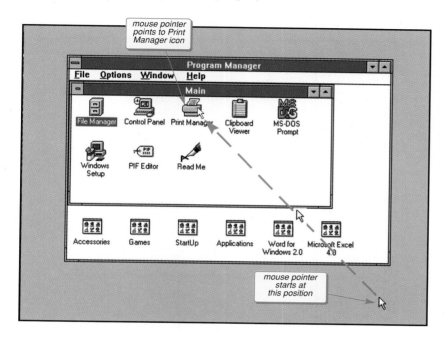

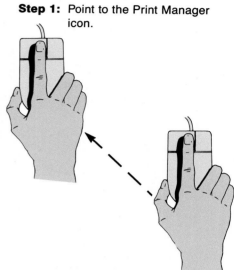

Step 1: Point to the Print Manager icon.

Step 2: Press and release the left mouse button.

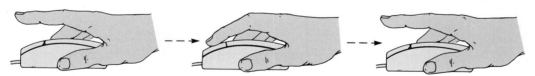

Step 3: Windows highlights the Print Manager name.

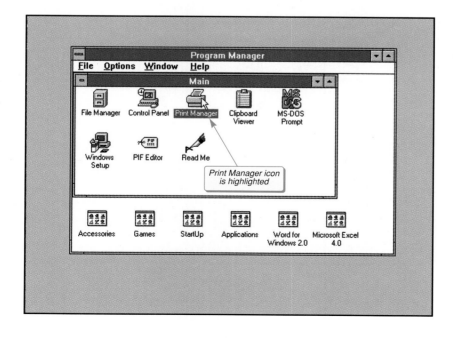

FIGURE 1-9

Double-clicking means quickly pressing and releasing a mouse button twice without moving the mouse. In most cases, you must point to an item before quickly pressing and releasing a mouse button twice. In Figure 1-10, to open the Accessories group window, point to the Accessories icon (Step 1), and quickly press and release the left mouse button twice (Step 2). These steps are commonly referred to as double-clicking the Accessories icon. When you double-click the Accessories icon, Windows opens a group window with the same name (Step 3).

Step 1: Point to the Accessories icon.

Step 2: Quickly press and release the left mouse button twice.

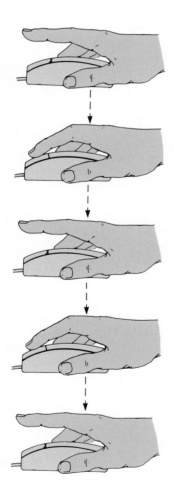

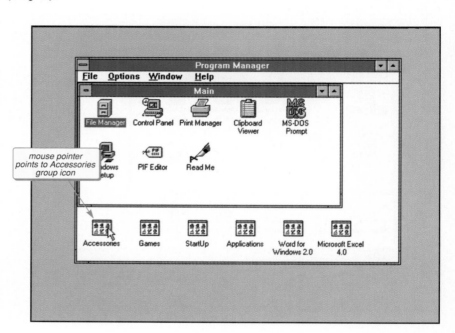

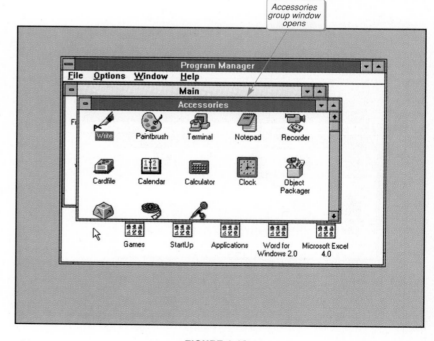

Step 3: Windows opens the Accessories group window.

FIGURE 1-10

Dragging means holding down the left mouse button, moving an item to the desired location, and then releasing the left mouse button. In most cases, you must point to an item before doing this. In Figure 1-11, you move the Control Panel program-item icon by pointing to the Control Panel icon (Step 1), holding down the left mouse button while moving the icon to its new location (Step 2), and releasing the left mouse button (Step 3). These steps are commonly referred to as dragging the Control Panel icon.

In Figure 1-11, the location of the Control Panel program-item icon was moved to rearrange the icons in the Main group window. Dragging has many uses in Windows, as you will see in subsequent examples.

Step 1: Point to the Control Panel icon.

Step 2: Hold down the left mouse button and move the icon to its new location.

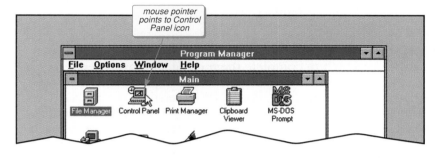

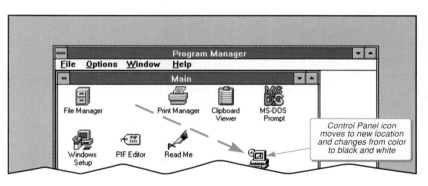

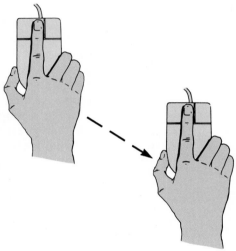

Step 3: Release the left mouse button.

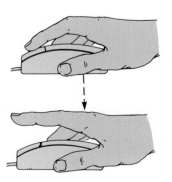

FIGURE 1-11

The Keyboard and Keyboard Shortcuts

The **keyboard** is an input device on which you manually key, or type, data. Figure 1-12 on the next page shows the enhanced IBM PS/2 keyboard. Any task you accomplish with a mouse you can also accomplish with the keyboard. Although the choice of whether you use the mouse or keyboard is a matter of personal preference, the mouse is strongly recommended.

FIGURE 1-12

The Quick Reference at the end of each project provides a list of tasks presented and the manner in which to complete them using a mouse, menu, or keyboard.

To perform tasks using the keyboard, you must understand the notation used to identify which keys to press. This notation is used throughout Windows to identify **keyboard shortcuts** and in the Quick Reference at the end of each project. Keyboard shortcuts can consist of pressing a single key (RIGHT ARROW), pressing two keys simultaneously as shown by two key names separated by a plus sign (CTRL + F6), or pressing three keys simultaneously as shown by three key names separated by plus signs (CTRL + SHIFT + LEFT ARROW).

For example, to move the highlight from one program-item icon to the next you can press the RIGHT ARROW key (RIGHT ARROW). To move the highlight from the Main window to a group icon, hold down the CTRL key and press the F6 key (CTRL + F6). To move to the previous word in certain Windows applications, hold down the CTRL and SHIFT keys and press the LEFT ARROW key (CTRL + SHIFT + LEFT ARROW).

Menus and Commands

A **command** directs the software to perform a specific action, such as printing on the printer or saving data for use at a future time. One method in which you carry out a command is by choosing the command from a list of available commands, called a menu.

Windows organizes related groups of commands into **menus** and assigns a menu name to each menu. The **menu bar**, a horizontal bar below the title bar of an application window, contains a list of the menu names for that application. The menu bar for the Program Manager window in Figure 1-13 contains the following menu names: File, Options, Window, and Help. One letter in each name is underlined.

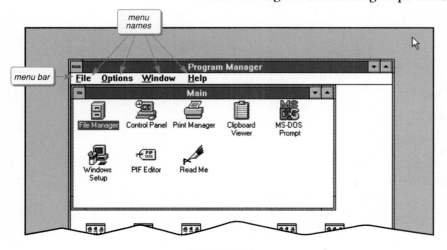

FIGURE 1-13

Selecting a Menu

To display a menu, you select the menu name. **Selecting** means marking an item. In some cases, when you select an item, Windows marks the item with a highlight by placing color behind the item. You select a menu name by pointing to the menu name in the menu bar and pressing the left mouse button (called clicking) or by using the keyboard to press the ALT key and then the keyboard key of the underlined letter in the menu name. Clicking the menu name File in the menu bar or pressing the ALT key and then the F key opens the File menu (Figure 1-14).

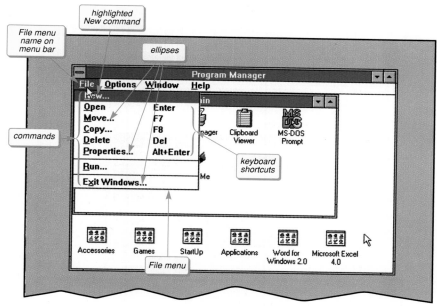

FIGURE 1-14

The File menu in Figure 1-14 contains the following commands: New, Open, Move, Copy, Delete, Properties, Run, and Exit Windows. The first command in the menu (New) is highlighted and a single character in each command is underlined. Some commands (New, Move, Copy, Properties, Run, and Exit Windows) are followed by an ellipsis (...). An **ellipsis** indicates Windows requires more information before executing the command. Commands without an ellipsis, such as the Open command, execute immediately.

Choosing a Command

You **choose** an item to carry out an action. You can choose using a mouse or keyboard. For example, to choose a command using a mouse, either click the command name in the menu or drag the highlight to the command name. To choose a command using the keyboard, either press the keyboard key of the underlined character in the command name or use the Arrow keys to move the highlight to the command name and press the ENTER key.

Some command names are followed by a keyboard shortcut. In Figure 1-14, the Open, Move, Copy, Delete, and Properties command names have keyboard shortcuts. The keyboard shortcut for the Properties command is ALT+ENTER. Holding down the ALT key and then pressing the ENTER key chooses the Properties command without selecting the File menu.

Dialog Boxes

When you choose a command whose command name is followed by an ellipsis (...), Windows opens a dialog box. A **dialog box** is a window that appears when Windows needs to supply information to you or wants you to enter information or select among options.

For example, Windows may inform you that a document is printing on the printer through the use of dialog box; or Windows may ask you whether you want to print all the pages in a printed report or just certain pages in the report.

A dialog box contains a title bar that identifies the name of the dialog box. In Figure 1-15, the name of the dialog box is Print.

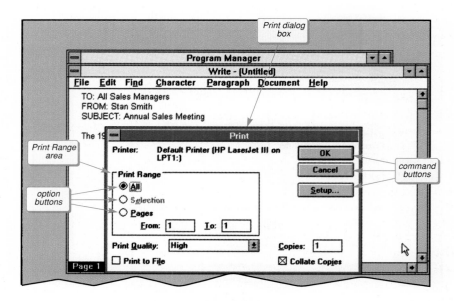

FIGURE 1-15

The types of responses Windows will ask for when working with dialog boxes fall into five categories: (1) Selecting mutually exclusive options; (2) Selecting one or more multiple options; (3) Entering specific information from the keyboard; (4) Selecting one item from a list of items; (5) Choosing a command to be implemented from the dialog box.

Each of these types of responses is discussed in the following paragraphs, together with the method for specifying them.

The Print dialog box in Figure 1-15 opens when you choose the Print command from the File menu of some windows. The Print Range area, defined by the name Print Range and a rectangular box, contains three option buttons.

The **option buttons** give you the choice of printing all pages of a report (All), selected parts of a report (Selection), or certain pages of a report (Pages). The option button containing the black dot (All) is the **selected button**. You can select only one option button at a time. A dimmed option, such as the Selection button, cannot be selected. To select an option button, use the mouse to click the option button or press the TAB key until the area containing the option button is selected and press the Arrow keys to highlight the option button.

The Print dialog box in Figure 1-15 on the previous page also contains the OK, Cancel, and Setup command buttons. **Command buttons** execute an action. The OK button executes the Print command, and the Cancel button cancels the Print command. The Setup button changes the setup of the printer by allowing you to select a printer from a list of printers, select the paper size, etc.

Figure 1-16 illustrates text boxes and check boxes. A **text box** is a rectangular area in which Windows displays text or you enter text. In the Print dialog box in Figure 1-16, the Pages option button is selected, which means only certain pages of a report are to print. You select which pages by entering the first page in the From text box (1) and the last page in the To text box (4). To enter text into a text box, select the text box by clicking it or by pressing the TAB key until the text in the text box is highlighted, and then type the text using the keyboard. The Copies text box in Figure 1-16 contains the number of copies to be printed (3).

FIGURE 1-16

Check boxes represent options you can turn on or off. An X in a check box indicates the option is turned on. To place an X in the box, click the box, or press the TAB key until the Print To File check box is highlighted, and then press SPACEBAR. In Figure 1-16, the Print to File check box, which does not contain an X, indicates the Print to File option is turned off and the pages will print on the printer. The Collate Copies check box, which contains an X, indicates the Collate Copies feature is turned on and the pages will print in collated order.

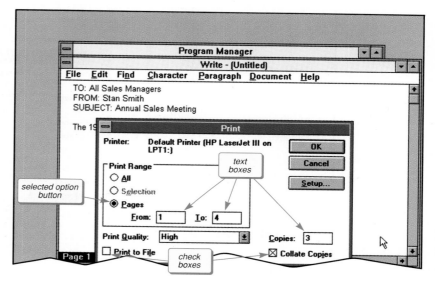

The Print dialog boxes in Figure 1-17 and Figure 1-18 on the next page, illustrate the Print Quality drop-down list box. When first selected, a **drop-down list box** is a rectangular box containing highlighted text and a down arrow box on the right. In Figure 1-17, the highlighted text, or **current selection**, is High.

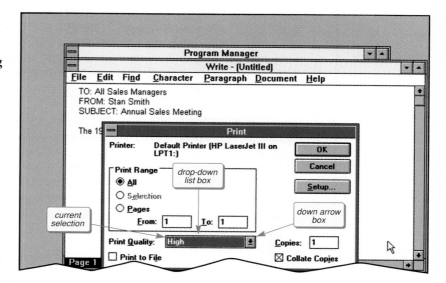

FIGURE 1-17

When you click the down arrow button, the drop-down list in Figure 1-18 appears. The list contains three choices (High, Medium, and Low). The current selection, High, is highlighted. To select from the list, use the mouse to click the selection or press the TAB key until the Print Quality drop-down list box is highlighted, press the DOWN ARROW key to highlight the selection, and then press ALT + UP ARROW or ALT + DOWN ARROW to make the selection.

Windows uses drop-down list boxes when a list of options must be presented but the dialog box is too crowded to contain the entire list. After you make your selection, the list disappears and only the current selection displays.

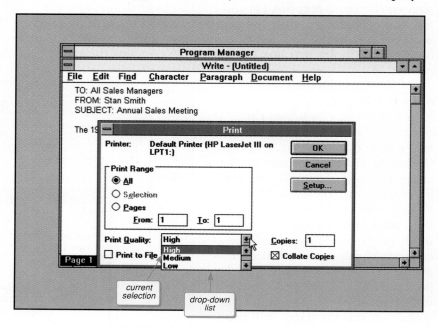

FIGURE 1-18

current selection

drop-down list

▶ USING MICROSOFT WINDOWS

The remainder of this project illustrates how to use Windows to perform the operations of starting and quitting an application, creating a document, saving a document on disk, opening a document, editing a document, printing a document and using the Windows help facility. Understanding how to perform these operations will make completing the remainder of the projects in this book easier. These operations are illustrated by the use of the Notepad and Paintbrush applications.

One of the many applications included with Windows is the Notepad application. **Notepad** allows you to enter, edit, save, and print notes. Items that you create while using an application, such as a note, are called **documents**. In the following section, you will use the Notepad application to learn to (1) open a group window, (2) start an application from a group window, (3) maximize an application window, (4) create a document, (5) select a menu, (6) choose a command from a menu, (7) print a document, and (8) quit an application. In the process, you will enter and print a note.

Opening a Group Window

Each group icon at the bottom of the Program Manager window represents a group window that may contain program-item icons. To open the group window and view the program-item icons in that window use the mouse to point to the group icon and then double-click the left mouse button, as shown in the steps on the next page.

TO OPEN A GROUP WINDOW ▼

STEP 1 ▶

Point to the Accessories group icon at the bottom of the Program Manager window.

The mouse pointer points to the Accessories icon (Figure 1-19).

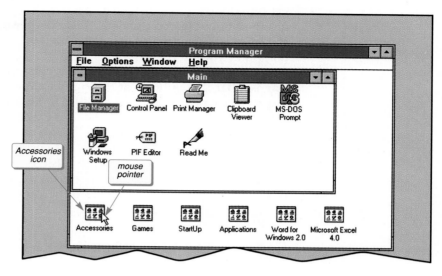

FIGURE 1-19

STEP 2 ▶

Double-click the left mouse button.

Windows removes the Accessories icon from the Program Manager window and opens the Accessories group window on top of the Program Manager and Main windows (Figure 1-20). The Accessories window contains the Notepad icon.

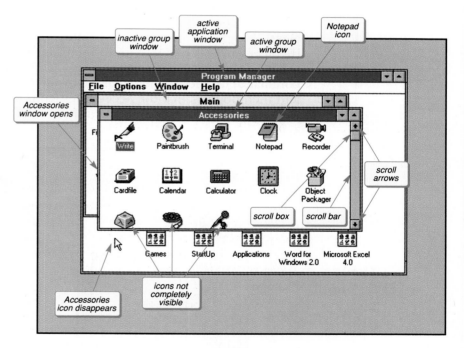

FIGURE 1-20

Opening a group window when one or more group windows are already open in the Program Manager window causes the new group window to display on top of the other group windows. The title bar of the newly opened group window is a different color or intensity than the title bars of the other group windows. This indicates the new group window is the active window. The **active window** is the window currently being used. Only one application window and one group window can be active at the same time. In Figure 1-20 on the previous page, the colors of the title bars indicate that Program Manager is the active application window (green title bar) and the Accessories group window is the active group window (green title bar). The color of the Main window title bar (yellow) indicates the Main window is inactive. The colors may not be the same on the computer you use.

A scroll bar appears on the right edge of the Accessories window. A **scroll bar** is a bar that appears at the right and/or bottom edge of a window whose contents are not completely visible. In Figure 1-20 on the previous page, the third row of program-item icons in the Accessories window is not completely visible. A scroll bar contains two **scroll arrows** and a **scroll box** which enable you to view areas of the window not currently visible. To view areas of the Accessories window not currently visible, you can click the down scroll arrow repeatedly, click the scroll bar between the down scroll arrow and the scroll box, or drag the scroll box toward the down scroll arrow until the area you want to view is visible in the window.

Correcting an Error While Double-Clicking a Group Icon

While double-clicking, it is easy to mistakenly click once instead of double-clicking. When you click a group icon such as the Accessories icon once, the **Control menu** for that icon opens (Figure 1-21). The Control menu contains the following seven commands: Restore, Move, Size, Minimize, Maximize, Close, and Next. You choose one of these commands to carry out an action associated with the Accessories icon. To remove the Control menu and open the Accessories window after clicking the Accessories icon once, you can choose the Restore command; or click any open area outside the menu to remove the Control menu and then double-click the Accessories icon; or simply double-click the Accessories icon as if you had not clicked the icon at all.

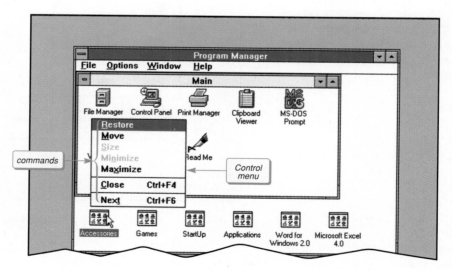

FIGURE 1-21

Starting an Application

Each program-item icon in a group window represents an application. To start an application, double-click the program-item icon. In this project, you want to start the Notepad application. To start the Notepad application, perform the steps on the next page.

TO START AN APPLICATION ▼

STEP 1 ▶

Point to the Notepad icon (Figure 1-22).

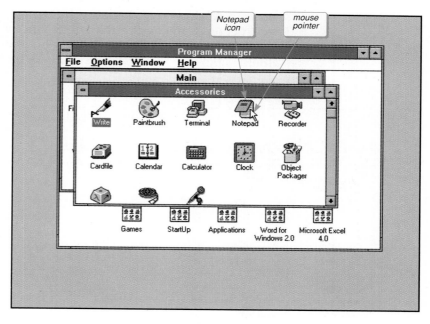

FIGURE 1-22

STEP 2 ▶

Double-click the left mouse button.

*Windows opens the Notepad window on the desktop (Figure 1-23). Program Manager becomes the inactive application (yellow title bar) and Notepad is the active application (green title bar). The word Untitled in the window title (Notepad — [Untitled]) indicates a document has not been created and saved on disk. The menu bar contains the following menus: File, Edit, Search, and Help. The area below the menu bar contains an insertion point, mouse pointer, and two scroll bars. The **insertion point** is a flashing vertical line that indicates the point at which text entered from the keyboard will be displayed. When you point to the interior of the Notepad window, the mouse pointer changes from a block arrow to an I-beam (I).*

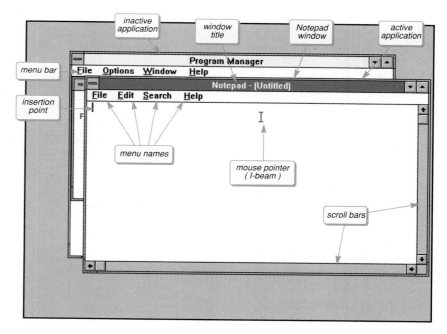

FIGURE 1-23

Correcting an Error While Double-Clicking a Program-Item Icon

While double-clicking a program-item icon you can easily click once instead. When you click a program-item icon such as the Notepad icon once, the icon becomes the **active icon** and Windows highlights the icon name (Figure 1-24). To start the Notepad application after clicking the Notepad icon once, double-click the Notepad icon as if you had not clicked the icon at all.

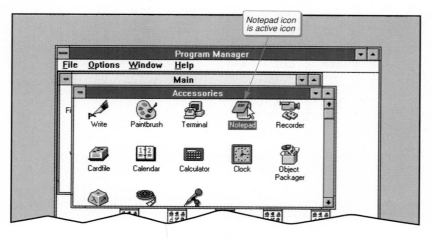

FIGURE 1-24

Maximizing an Application Window

Before you work with an application, maximizing the application window makes it easier to see the contents of the window. You can maximize an application window so the window fills the entire desktop. To maximize an application window to its maximum size, choose the **Maximize button** (▲) by pointing to the Maximize button and clicking the left mouse button. Complete the following steps to maximize the Notepad window.

TO MAXIMIZE AN APPLICATION WINDOW ▼

STEP 1 ▶

Point to the Maximize button in the upper right corner of the Notepad window.

The mouse pointer becomes a block arrow and points to the Maximize button (Figure 1-25).

FIGURE 1-25

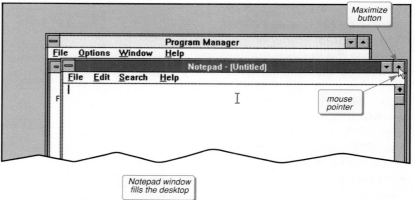

STEP 2 ▶

Click the left mouse button.

The Notepad window fills the desktop (Figure 1-26). The **Restore button** *(▲) replaces the Maximize button at the right side of the title bar. Clicking the Restore button will return the window to its size before maximizing.*

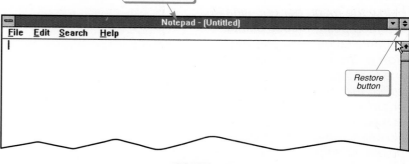

FIGURE 1-26

Creating a Document

To create a document in Notepad, type the text you want to display in the document. After typing a line of text, press the ENTER key to terminate the entry of the line. To create a document, enter the note to the right by performing the steps below.

Things to do today —
1) Take fax\phone to Conway Service Center
2) Pick up payroll checks from ADM
3) Order 3 boxes of copier paper

TO CREATE A NOTEPAD DOCUMENT ▼

STEP 1 ►

Type `Things to do today –` **and press the ENTER key.**

The first line of the note is entered and the insertion point appears at the beginning of the next line (Figure 1-27).

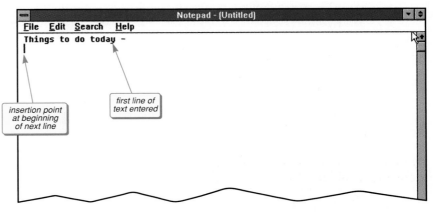

FIGURE 1-27

STEP 2 ►

Type the remaining lines of the note. Press the ENTER key after typing each line.

The remaining lines in the note are entered and the insertion point is located at the beginning of the line following the note (Figure 1-28).

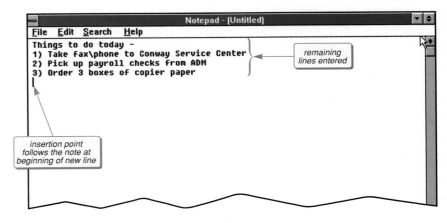

FIGURE 1-28

Printing a Document by Choosing a Command from a Menu

After creating a document, you often print the document on the printer. To print the note, complete the following steps.

TO PRINT A DOCUMENT ▼

STEP 1 ▶

Point to File on the Notepad menu bar (Figure 1-29).

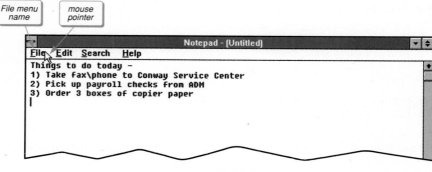

FIGURE 1-29

STEP 2 ▶

Select File by clicking the left mouse button.

Windows opens the File menu in the Notepad window (Figure 1-30). The File menu name is highlighted and the File menu contains the following commands: New, Open, Save, Save As, Print, Page Setup, Print Setup, and Exit. Windows highlights the first command in the menu (New). Notice the commands in the Notepad File menu are different than those in the Program Manager File menu (see Figure 1-14 on page WIN11). The commands in the File menu will vary depending on the application you are using.

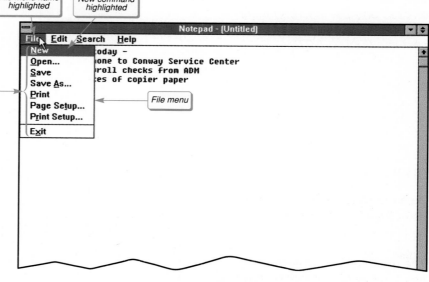

FIGURE 1-30

STEP 3 ▶

Point to the Print command.

The mouse pointer points to the Print command (Figure 1-31).

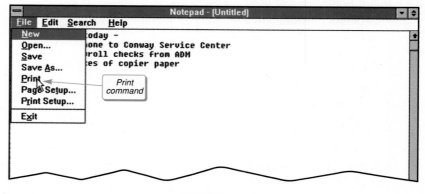

FIGURE 1-31

STEP 4 ▶

Choose the Print command from the File menu by clicking the left mouse button.

Windows momentarily opens the Notepad dialog box (Figure 1-32). The dialog box contains the Now Printing text message and the Cancel command button (Cancel). When the Notepad dialog box closes, Windows prints the document on the printer (Figure 1-33).

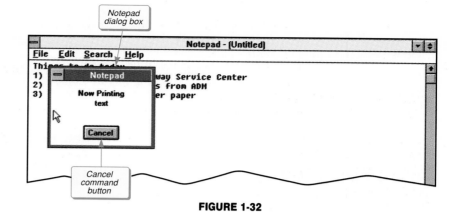

FIGURE 1-32

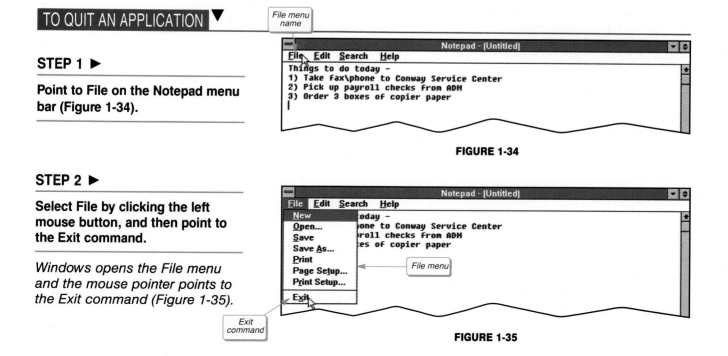

FIGURE 1-33

Quitting an Application

When you have finished creating and printing the document, quit the application by following the steps below and on the next page.

TO QUIT AN APPLICATION ▼

STEP 1 ▶

Point to File on the Notepad menu bar (Figure 1-34).

FIGURE 1-34

STEP 2 ▶

Select File by clicking the left mouse button, and then point to the Exit command.

Windows opens the File menu and the mouse pointer points to the Exit command (Figure 1-35).

FIGURE 1-35

STEP 3 ▶

Choose the Exit command from the File menu by clicking the left mouse button, and then point to the No button.

Windows opens the Notepad dialog box (Figure 1-36). The dialog box contains the following: The message, The text in the [Untitled] file has changed., the question, Do you want to save the changes?, and the Yes, No, and Cancel command buttons. The mouse pointer points to the No button (No). You choose the Yes button (Yes) to save the document on disk and exit Notepad. You choose the No button if you do not want to save the document and want to exit Notepad. You choose the Cancel button to cancel the Exit command.

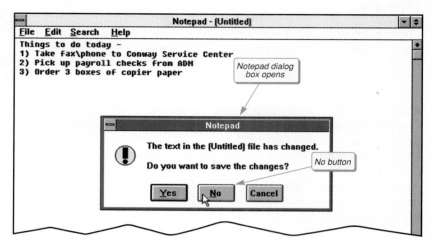

FIGURE 1-36

STEP 4 ▶

Choose the No button by clicking the left mouse button.

Windows closes the Notepad dialog box and Notepad window and exits the Notepad application (Figure 1-37).

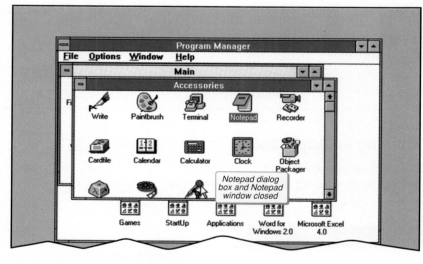

FIGURE 1-37

In the preceding example, you used the Microsoft Windows graphical user interface to accomplish the tasks of opening the Accessories group window, starting the Notepad application from the Accessories group window, maximizing the Notepad application window, creating a document in the Notepad application window, printing the document on the printer, and quitting the Notepad application.

▶ FILE AND DISK CONCEPTS

To protect against the accidental loss of a document and to save a document for use in the future, you should save a document on disk. Before saving a document on disk, however, you must understand the concepts of naming a file, directories, subdirectories, directory structures, and directory paths. The following section explains these concepts.

Naming a File

When you create a document using an application, the document is stored in main memory. If you quit the application without saving the document on disk, the document is lost. To save the document for future use, you must store the document in a **document file** on the hard disk or on a diskette before quitting the application. Before saving a document, you must assign a name to the document file.

All files are identified on disk by a **filename** and an **extension**. For example, the name SALES.TXT consists of a filename (SALES) and an extension (.TXT). A filename can contain from one to eight characters and the extension begins with a period and can contain from one to three characters. Filenames must start with a letter or number. Any uppercase or lowercase character is valid except a period (.), quotation mark (''), slash (/), backslash (\), brackets ([]), colon (:), semicolon (;), vertical bar (|), equal sign (=), comma (,), or blank space. Filenames cannot be CON, AUX, COM1, COM2, COM3, COM4, LPT1, LPT2, LPT3, PRN, and NUL.

To more easily identify document files on disk, it is convenient to assign the same extension to document files you create with a given application. The Notepad application, for instance, automatically uses the .TXT extension for each document file saved on disk. Typical filenames and extensions of document files saved using Notepad are: SHOPPING.TXT, MECHANIC.TXT, and 1994.TXT.

You can use the asterisk character (*) in place of a filename or extension to refer to a group of files. For example, the asterisk in the expression *.TXT tells Windows to reference any file that contains the .TXT extension, regardless of the filename. This group of files might consist of the HOME.TXT, AUTOPART-.TXT, MARKET.TXT, JONES.TXT, and FRANK.TXT files.

The asterisk in MONTHLY.* tells Windows to reference any file that contains the filename MONTHLY, regardless of the extension. Files in this group might consist of the MONTHLY.TXT, MONTHLY.CAL, and MONTHLY.CRD files.

Directory Structures and Directory Paths

After selecting a name and extension for a file, you must decide which auxiliary storage device (hard disk or diskette) to use and in which directory you want to save the file. A **directory** is an area of a disk created to store related groups of files. When you first prepare a disk for use on a computer, a single directory, called the **root directory**, is created on the disk. You can create **subdirectories** in the root directory to store additional groups of related files. The hard disk in Figure 1-38 contains the root directory and the WINDOWS, MSAPPS, and SYSTEM subdirectories. The WINDOWS, MSAPPS, and SYSTEM subdirectories are created when Windows is installed and contain files related to Windows.

HARD DISK

FIGURE 1-38

Directory Structure	Directory Path
🗁 c:\	C:\
🗀 windows	C:\WINDOWS
🗀 msapps	C:\WINDOWS\MSAPPS
🗀 system	C:\WINDOWS\SYSTEM

▶ **TABLE 1-1**

The relationship between the root directory and any subdirectories is called the **directory structure**. Each directory or subdirectory in the directory structure has an associated directory path. The **directory path** is the path Windows follows to find a file in a directory. Table 1-1 contains a graphic representation of the directory structure and the associated paths of drive C.

Each directory and subdirectory on drive C is represented by a file folder icon in the directory structure. The first file folder icon, an unshaded open file folder (🗁), represents the root directory of the current drive (drive C). The c:\ entry to the right of the icon symbolizes the root directory (identified by the \ character) of drive C (c:). The path is C:\. Thus, to find a file in this directory, Windows locates drive C (C:) and the root directory (\) on drive C.

The second icon, a shaded open file folder (🗀), represents the current subdirectory. This icon is indented below the first file folder icon because it is a subdirectory. The name of the subdirectory (windows) appears to the right of the shaded file folder icon. Because the WINDOWS subdirectory was created in the root directory, the path for the WINDOWS subdirectory is C:\WINDOWS. To find a file in this subdirectory, Windows locates drive C, locates the root directory on drive C, and then locates the WINDOWS subdirectory in the root directory.

Because the current path is C:\WINDOWS, the file folder icons for both the root directory and WINDOWS subdirectory are open file folders. An open file folder indicates the directory or subdirectory is in the current path. Unopened file folders represent subdirectories not in the current path.

The third and fourth icons in Table 1-1, unopened file folders (🗀), represent the MSAPPS and SYSTEM subdirectories. The unopened file folders indicate these subdirectories are not part of the current path. These file folder icons are indented below the file folder for the WINDOWS subdirectory which means they were created in the WINDOWS subdirectory. The subdirectory names (msapps and system) appear to the right of the file folder icons.

Since the MSAPPS and SYSTEM subdirectories were created in the WINDOWS subdirectory, the paths for these subdirectories are C:\WINDOWS\MSAPPS and C:\WINDOWS\SYSTEM. The second backslash (\) in these paths separates the two subdirectory names. To find a file in these subdirectories, Windows locates drive C, locates the root directory on drive C, then locates the WINDOWS subdirectory in the root directory, and finally locates the MSAPPS or SYSTEM subdirectory in the WINDOWS subdirectory.

Saving a Document on Disk

After entering data into a document, you will often save it on the hard disk or a diskette to protect against accidental loss and to make the document available for use later. In the previous example using the Notepad application, the note was not saved prior to exiting Notepad. Instead of exiting, assume you want to save the document you created. The screen before you begin to save the document is shown in Figure 1-39. To save the document on a diskette in drive A using the filename, agenda, perform the steps that begin at the top of the next page.

FIGURE 1-39

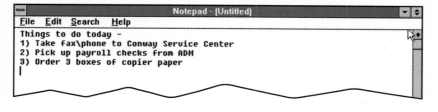

TO SAVE A FILE ▼

STEP 1 ►

Insert a formatted diskette into drive A (Figure 1-40).

The diskette must be properly formatted before being used to save data. To learn the technique for formatting a diskette see Project 2.

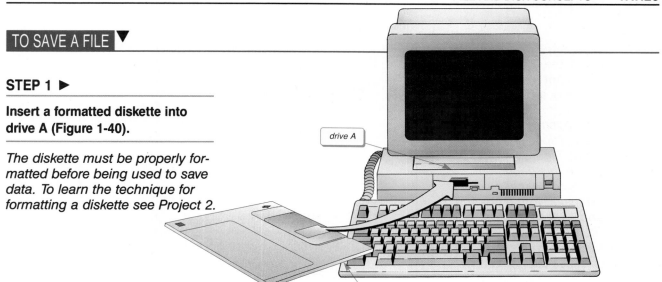

FIGURE 1-40

STEP 2 ►

Select File on the Notepad menu bar, and then point to the Save As command.

Windows opens the File menu in the Notepad window and the mouse pointer points to the Save As command (Figure 1-41). The ellipsis (...) following the Save As command indicates Windows will open a dialog box when you choose this command.

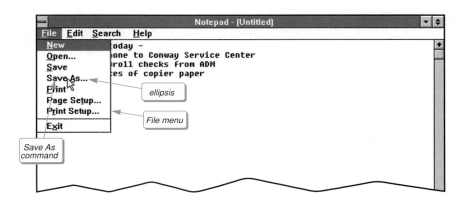

FIGURE 1-41

STEP 3 ►

Choose the Save As command from the File menu by clicking the left mouse button.

The Save As dialog box opens (Figure 1-42). The File Name text box contains the highlighted *.txt entry. Typing a filename from the keyboard will replace the entire *.txt entry with the filename entered from the keyboard. The current path is c:\windows and the Directories list box contains the directory structure of the current subdirectory (windows). The drive selection in the Drives drop-down list box is c:. The dialog box contains the OK (OK) and Cancel (Cancel) command buttons.

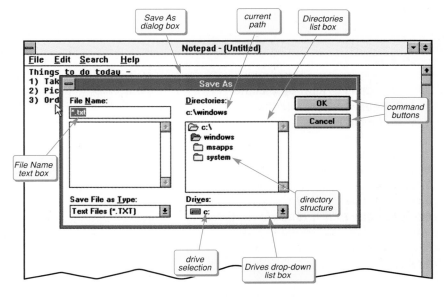

FIGURE 1-42

STEP 4 ▶

Type agenda **in the File Name text box, and then point to the Drives drop-down list box arrow.**

The filename, agenda, and an insertion point display in the File Name text box (Figure 1-43). When you save this document, Notepad will automatically add the .TXT extension to the agenda filename and save the file on disk using the name AGENDA.TXT. The mouse pointer points to the Drives drop-down list box arrow.

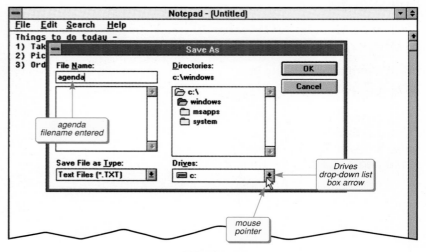

FIGURE 1-43

STEP 5 ▶

Choose the Drives drop-down list box arrow by clicking the left mouse button, and then point to the drive a: icon (▦) in the Drives drop-down list.

Windows displays the Drives drop-down list (Figure 1-44). The drive a: icon and drive c: icon appear in the drop-down list. The mouse pointer points to the drive a: icon.

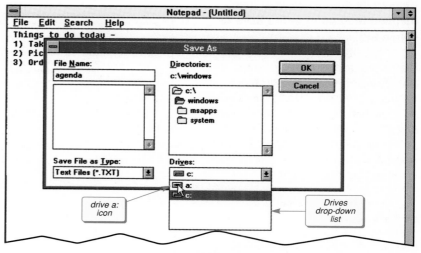

FIGURE 1-44

STEP 6 ▶

Select the drive a: icon by clicking the left mouse button, and then point to the OK button.

The selection is highlighted and the light on drive A turns on while Windows checks for a diskette in drive A (Figure 1-45). The current path changes to a:\ and the Directories list box contains the directory structure of the diskette in drive A.

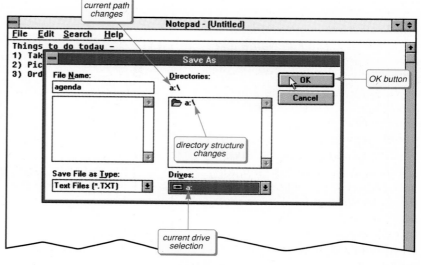

FIGURE 1-45

STEP 7 ►

Choose the OK button in the Save As dialog box by clicking the left mouse button.

Windows closes the Save As dialog box and displays an hourglass icon while saving the AGENDA.TXT document file on the diskette in drive A. After the file is saved, Windows changes the window title of the Notepad window to reflect the name of the AGENDA.TXT file (Figure 1-46).

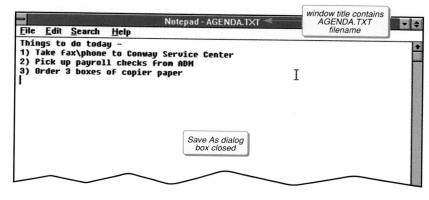

FIGURE 1-46

Correcting Errors Encountered While Saving a Document File

Before you can save a document file on a diskette, you must insert a formatted diskette into the diskette drive. **Formatting** is the process of preparing a diskette for use on a computer by establishing the sectors and cylinders on a disk, analyzing the diskette for defective cylinders, and establishing the root directory. The technique for formatting a diskette is shown in Project 2. If you try to save a file on a diskette and forget to insert a diskette, forget to close the diskette drive door after inserting a diskette, insert an unformatted diskette, or insert a damaged diskette, Windows opens the Save As dialog box in Figure 1-47.

The dialog box contains the messages telling you the condition found and the Retry (Retry) and Cancel buttons. To save a file on the diskette in drive A after receiving this message, insert a formatted diskette into the diskette drive, point to the Retry button, and click the left mouse button.

In addition, you cannot save a document file on a write-protected diskette. A **write-protected diskette** prevents accidentally erasing data stored on the diskette by not letting the disk drive write new data or erase existing data on the diskette. If you try to save a file on a write-protected diskette, Windows opens the Save As dialog box shown in Figure 1-48.

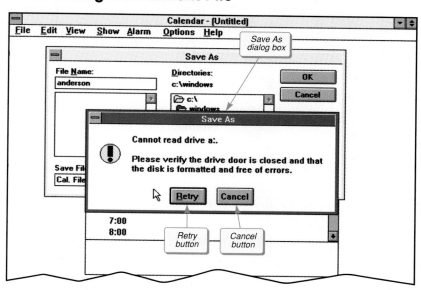

FIGURE 1-47

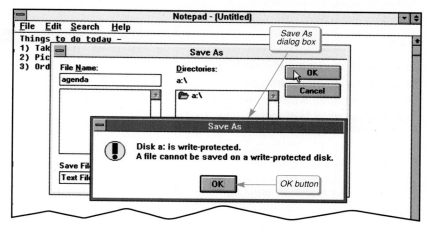

FIGURE 1-48

The Save As dialog box in Figure 1-48 on the previous page contains the messages, Disk a: is write-protected., and, A file cannot be saved on a write-protected disk., and the OK button. To save a file on diskette after inserting a write-protected diskette into drive A, remove the diskette from the diskette drive, remove the write-protection from the diskette, insert the diskette into the diskette drive, point to the OK button, and click the left mouse button.

Quitting an Application

When you have finished saving the AGENDA.TXT file on disk, you can quit the Notepad application as shown in Figure 1-34 through Figure 1-37 on pages WIN21 and WIN22. The steps are summarized below.

TO QUIT AN APPLICATION

Step 1: Point to File on the Notepad menu bar.
Step 2: Select File by clicking the left mouse button, and then point to the Exit command.
Step 3: Choose the Exit command by clicking the left mouse button.

If you have made changes to the document since saving it on the diskette, Notepad will ask if you want to save the changes. If so, choose the Yes button in the dialog box; otherwise, choose the No button.

▶ OPENING A DOCUMENT FILE

C hanges are frequently made to a document saved on disk. To make these changes, you must first open the document file by retrieving the file from disk using the Open command. After modifying the document, you save the modified document file on disk using the Save command. Using the Notepad application, you will learn to (1) open a document file and (2) save an edited document file on diskette. In the process, you will add the following line to the AGENDA.TXT file: 4) Buy copier toner.

Starting the Notepad Application and Maximizing the Notepad Window

To start the Notepad application and maximize the Notepad window, perform the following step.

TO START AN APPLICATION AND MAXIMIZE ITS WINDOW ▼

STEP 1 ▶

Double-click the Notepad icon in the Accessories group window. When the Notepad window opens, click the Maximize button.

Double-clicking the Notepad icon opens the Notepad window. Clicking the Maximize button maximizes the Notepad window (Figure 1-49).

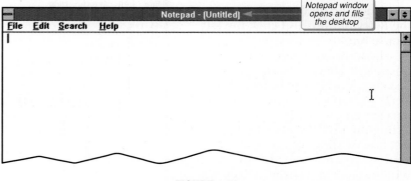

FIGURE 1-49

Opening a Document File

Before you can modify the AGENDA.TXT document, you must open the file from the diskette on which it was stored. To do so, ensure the diskette containing the file is inserted into drive A, then perform the following steps.

TO OPEN A DOCUMENT FILE ▼

STEP 1 ▶

Select File on the menu bar, and then point to the Open command.

Windows opens the File menu and the mouse pointer points to the Open command (Figure 1-50).

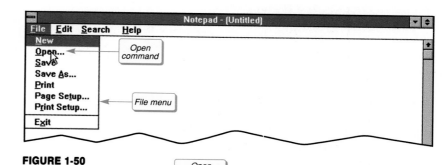

FIGURE 1-50

STEP 2 ▶

Choose the Open command from the File menu by clicking the left mouse button, and then point to the Drives drop-down list box arrow.

The Open dialog box opens (Figure 1-51). The File Name text box contains the *.txt entry and the File Name list box is empty because no files with the .TXT extension appear in the current directory. The current path is c:\windows. The Directories list box contains the directory structure of the current subdirectory (WINDOWS). The selected drive in the Drives drop-down list box is c:. The mouse pointer points to the Drives drop-down list box arrow.

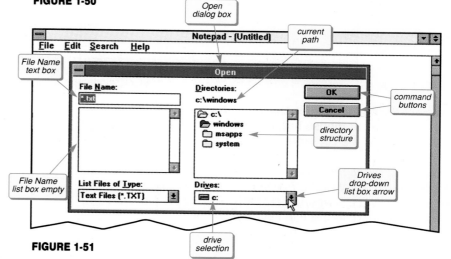

FIGURE 1-51

STEP 3 ▶

Choose the Drives drop-down list box arrow by clicking the left mouse button, and then point to the drive a: icon.

Windows displays the Drives drop-down list (Figure 1-52). The drive a: icon and drive c: icon appear in the drop-down list. The current selection is c:. The mouse pointer points to the drive a: icon.

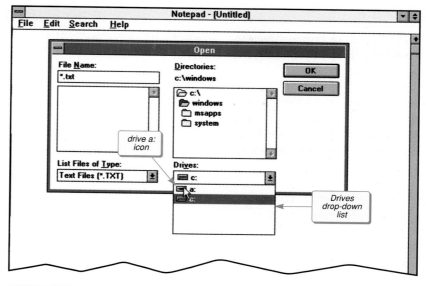

FIGURE 1-52

STEP 4 ▶

Select the drive a: icon by clicking the left mouse button, and then point to the agenda.txt entry in the File Name list box.

The light on drive A turns on, and Windows checks for a diskette in drive A. If there is no diskette in drive A, a dialog box opens to indicate this fact. The current selection in the Drives drop-down list box is highlighted (Figure 1-53). The File Name list box contains the filename agenda.txt, the current path is a:\, and the Directories list box contains the directory structure of drive A. The mouse pointer points to the agenda.txt entry.

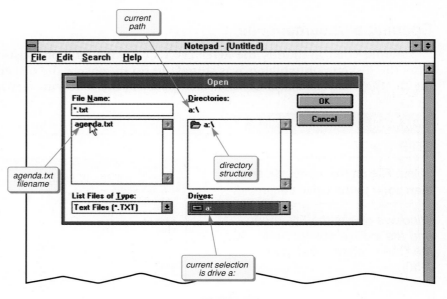

FIGURE 1-53

STEP 5 ▶

Select the agenda.txt file by clicking the left mouse button, and then point to the OK button.

Notepad highlights the agenda.txt entry in the File Name text box, and the agenda.txt filename appears in the File Name text box (Figure 1-54). The mouse pointer points to the OK button.

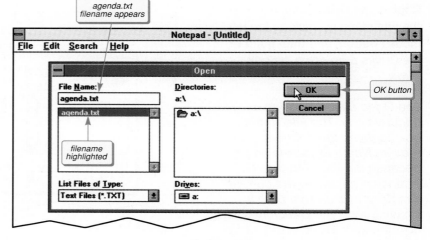

FIGURE 1-54

STEP 6 ▶

Choose the OK button from the Open dialog box by clicking the left mouse button.

Windows retrieves the agenda.txt file from the diskette in drive A and opens the AGENDA.TXT document in the Notepad window (Figure 1-55).

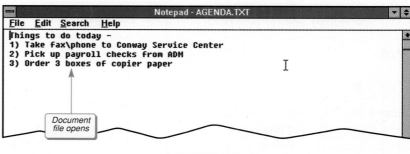

FIGURE 1-55

Editing the Document File

You edit the AGENDA.TXT document file by entering the fourth line of text.

TO EDIT THE DOCUMENT ▼

STEP 1 ▶

Press the DOWN ARROW key four times to position the insertion point, and then type the new line, 4) Buy Copier toner.

The new line appears in the Note-pad document (Figure 1-56).

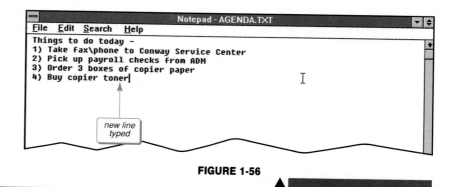

FIGURE 1-56

Saving the Modified Document File

After modifying the AGENDA.TXT document, you should save the modified document on disk using the same AGENDA.TXT filename. To save a modified file on disk, choose the Save command. The Save command differs from the Save As command in that you choose the Save command to save changes to an existing file while you choose the Save As command to name and save a new file or to save an existing file under a new name.

TO SAVE A MODIFIED DOCUMENT FILE ▼

STEP 1 ▶

Select File on the Notepad menu bar, and then point to the Save command.

Windows opens the File menu and the mouse pointer points to the Save command (Figure 1-57).

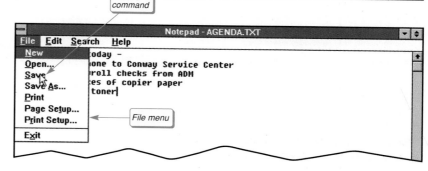

FIGURE 1-57

STEP 2 ▶

Choose the Save command from the File menu by clicking the left mouse button.

Windows closes the File menu, displays the hourglass icon momentarily, and saves the AGENDA.TXT document on the diskette in drive A (Figure 1-58).

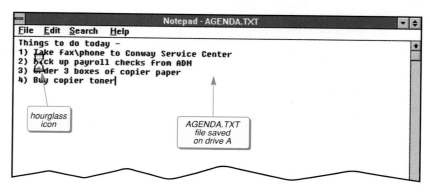

FIGURE 1-58

STEP 3 ▶

Remove the diskette from Drive A (Figure 1-59).

FIGURE 1-59

▲

When you have finished saving the modified AGENDA.TXT file, quit the Notepad application by performing the following steps.

TO QUIT NOTEPAD

Step 1: Select File on the Notepad menu bar.
Step 2: Choose the Exit command.

▶ USING WINDOWS HELP

I f you need help while using an application, you can use Windows online Help. **Online Help** is available for all applications except Clock. To illustrate Windows online Help, you will start the Paintbrush application and obtain help about the commands on the Edit menu. **Paintbrush** is a drawing program that allows you to create, edit, and print full-color illustrations.

TO START AN APPLICATION

STEP 1 ▶

Double-click the Paintbrush icon (🎨) in the Accessories group window in Program Manager, and then click the Maximize button on the Paintbrush — [Untitled] window.

Windows opens and maximizes the Paintbrush window (Figure 1-60).

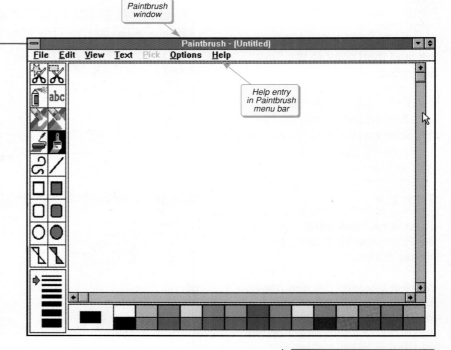

Paintbrush window

Help entry in Paintbrush menu bar

FIGURE 1-60

▲

TO OBTAIN HELP ▼

STEP 1 ►

Select Help on the Paintbrush menu bar, and then point to the Contents command.

Windows opens the Help menu (Figure 1-61). The Help menu contains four commands. The mouse pointer points to the Contents command.

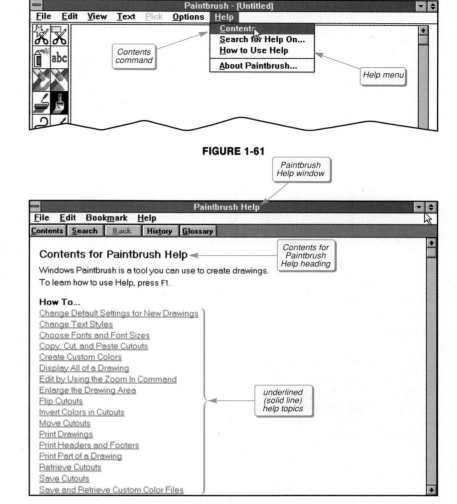

FIGURE 1-61

STEP 2 ►

Choose the Contents command from the Help menu by clicking the left mouse button. Then click the Maximize button on the Paintbrush Help window.

Windows opens the Paintbrush Help window (Figure 1-62), and when you click the Maximize button, it maximizes the window.

FIGURE 1-62

The Contents for Paintbrush Help screen appears in the window. This screen contains information about the Paintbrush application, how to learn to use online Help (press F1), and an alphabetical list of all help topics for the Paintbrush application. Each **help topic** is underlined with a solid line. The solid line indicates additional information relating to the topic is available. Underlined help topics are called jumps. A **jump** provides a link to viewing information about another help topic or more information about the current topic. A jump may be either text or graphics.

Choosing a Help Topic

To choose an underlined help topic, scroll the help topics to make the help topic you want visible, then point to the help topic and click the left mouse button. When you place the mouse pointer on a help topic, the mouse pointer changes to a hand (🖑). To obtain help about the Edit menu, perform the steps on the next page.

TO CHOOSE A HELP TOPIC ▼

STEP 1 ►

Point to the down scroll arrow (Figure 1-63).

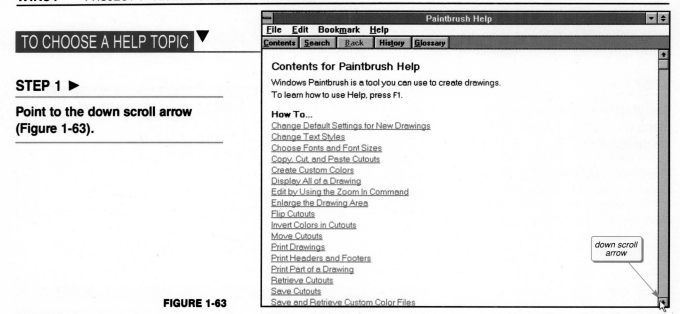

FIGURE 1-63

STEP 2 ►

Hold down the left mouse button (scroll) until the Edit Menu Commands help topic is visible, and then point to the Edit Menu Commands topic.

The Commands heading and the Edit Menu Commands topic are visible (Figure 1-64). The mouse pointer changes to a hand icon and points to the Edit Menu Commands topic.

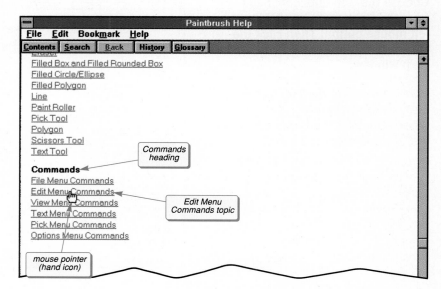

FIGURE 1-64

STEP 3 ►

Choose the Edit Menu Commands topic by clicking the left mouse button.

The Edit Menu Commands screen contains information about each of the commands in the Edit menu (Figure 1-65). Two terms (scroll bar and cutout) are underlined with a dotted line. Terms underlined with a dotted line have an associated glossary definition. To display a term's glossary definition, point to the term and click the left mouse button.

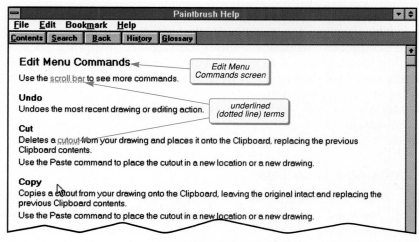

FIGURE 1-65

TO DISPLAY A DEFINITION ▼

STEP 1 ►

Point to the term, scroll bar.

The mouse pointer changes to a hand and points to the term, scroll bar (Figure 1-66).

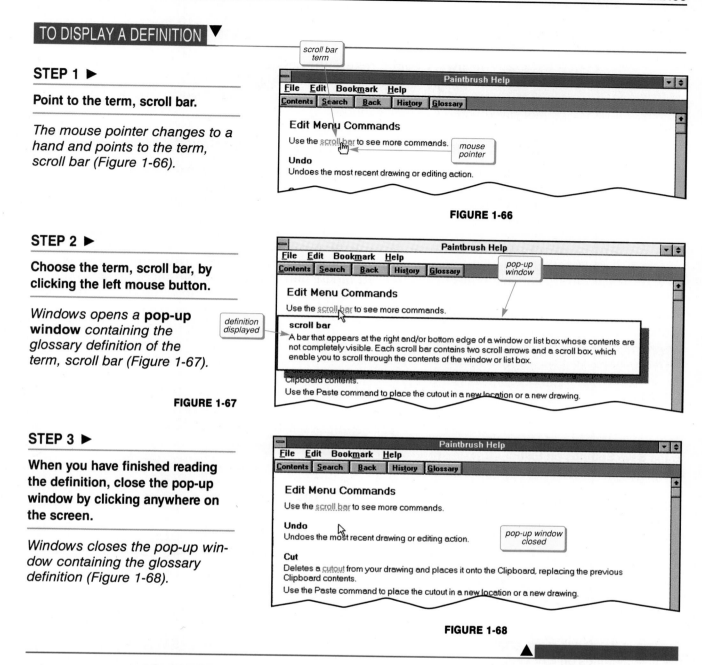

FIGURE 1-66

STEP 2 ►

Choose the term, scroll bar, by clicking the left mouse button.

*Windows opens a **pop-up window** containing the glossary definition of the term, scroll bar (Figure 1-67).*

FIGURE 1-67

STEP 3 ►

When you have finished reading the definition, close the pop-up window by clicking anywhere on the screen.

Windows closes the pop-up window containing the glossary definition (Figure 1-68).

FIGURE 1-68

Exiting the Online Help and Paintbrush Applications

After obtaining help about the Edit Menu commands, quit Help by choosing the Exit command from the Help File menu. Then, quit Paintbrush by choosing the Exit command from the Paintbrush File menu. The steps are summarized below.

TO QUIT PAINTBRUSH HELP

Step 1: Select File on the Paintbrush Help menu bar.
Step 2: Choose the Exit command.

TO QUIT PAINTBRUSH

Step 1: Select File on the Paintbrush menu bar.
Step 2: Choose the Exit command.

▶ QUITTING WINDOWS

Y ou always want to return the desktop to its original state before beginning your next session with Windows. Therefore, before exiting
Windows, you must verify that any changes made to the desktop are
not saved when you quit windows.

Verify Changes to the Desktop Will Not be Saved

Because you want to return the desktop to its state before you started
Windows, no changes should be saved. The Save Settings on Exit command on
the Program Manager Options menu controls whether changes to the desktop
are saved or are not saved when you quit Windows. A check mark (✓) preceding
the Save Settings on Exit command indicates the command is active and all
changes to the layout of the desktop will be saved when you quit Windows. If
the command is preceded by a check mark, choose the Save Settings from Exit
command by clicking the left mouse button to remove the check mark, so the
changes will not be saved. Perform the following steps to verify that changes are
not saved to the desktop.

TO VERIFY CHANGES ARE NOT SAVED TO THE DESKTOP ▼

STEP 1 ▶

**Select Options on the Program
Manager menu bar, and then point
to the Save Settings on Exit
command.**

*The Options menu opens (Figure
1-69). A check mark (✓) precedes the Save Settings on Exit
command.*

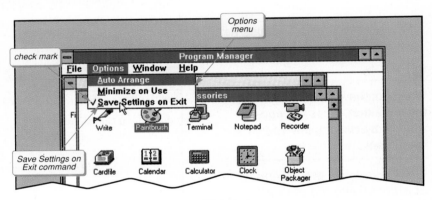

FIGURE 1-69

STEP 2 ▶

**To remove the check mark, choose
the Save Settings on Exit command from the Options menu by
clicking the left mouse button.**

*Windows closes the Options
menu (Figure 1-70). Although not
visible in Figure 1-70, the check
mark preceding the Save Settings
from Exit command has been
removed. This means any
changes made to the desktop will
not be saved when you exit
Windows.*

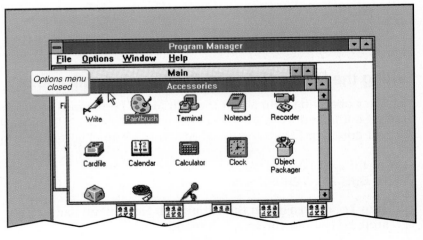

FIGURE 1-70

Quitting Windows Without Saving Changes

After verifying the Save Settings on Exit command is not active, quit Windows by choosing the Exit Windows command from the File menu, as shown below.

TO QUIT WINDOWS ▼

STEP 1 ►

Select File on the Program Manager menu bar, and then point to the Exit Windows command.

Windows opens the File menu and the mouse pointer points to the Exit Windows command (Figure 1-71).

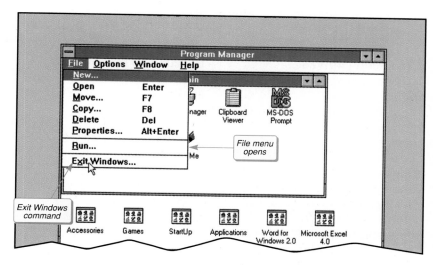

FIGURE 1-71

STEP 2 ►

Choose the Exit Windows command from the File menu by clicking the left mouse button and point to the OK button.

The Exit Windows dialog box opens and contains the message, This will end your Windows session., and the OK and Cancel buttons (Figure 1-72). Choosing the OK button exits Windows. Choosing the Cancel button cancels the exit from Windows and returns you to the Program Manager window. The mouse pointer points to the OK button.

STEP 3 ►

Choose the OK button by clicking the left mouse button.

When you quit Windows, all windows are removed from the desktop and control is returned to the DOS operating system.

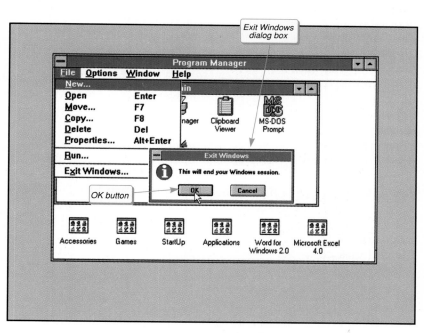

FIGURE 1-72

▶ PROJECT SUMMARY

In this project you learned about user interfaces and the Microsoft Windows graphical user interface. You started and exited Windows and learned the parts of a window. You started Notepad, entered and printed a note, edited the note, opened and saved files, and exited the applications. You opened group windows, maximized application windows, and scrolled the windows. You used the mouse to select a menu, choose a command from a menu, and respond to dialog boxes. You used Windows online Help to obtain help about the Paintbrush application.

▶ KEY TERMS

active icon (*WIN18*)
active window (*WIN15*)
application (*WIN3*)
application software (*WIN3*)
application window (*WIN5*)
check box (*WIN13*)
choosing (*WIN11*)
choosing a command (*WIN11*)
choosing a help topic (*WIN33*)
clicking (*WIN7*)
command (*WIN10*)
command button (*WIN13*)
Control menu (*WIN16*)
creating a document (*WIN19*)
current selection (*WIN13*)
desktop (*WIN4*)
dialog box (*WIN12*)
directory (*WIN23*)
directory path (*WIN24*)
directory structure (*WIN24*)
displaying a definition (*WIN35*)
document (*WIN14*)
document file (*WIN23*)
double-clicking (*WIN8*)
dragging (*WIN9*)
drop-down list box (*WIN13*)
ellipsis (*WIN11*)
edit a document file (*WIN31*)
error correction (*WIN16,*
   WIN18, WIN27)
extension (*WIN23*)
file and disk concepts
   (*WIN22–WIN24*)

filename (*WIN23*)
formatting (*WIN27*)
graphical user interface (GUI)
   (*WIN3*)
group icons (*WIN5*)
group window (*WIN5*)
GUI (*WIN3*)
help topic (*WIN33*)
hourglass icon (*WIN4*)
icons (*WIN5*)
insertion point (*WIN17*)
jump (*WIN33*)
keyboard (*WIN9*)
keyboard shortcuts (*WIN10*)
Maximize button (*WIN18*)
maximizing a window (*WIN18*)
menu (*WIN10*)
menu bar (*WIN10*)
Microsoft Windows (*WIN2*)
mouse (*WIN5*)
mouse operations (*WIN6–WIN9*)
mouse pointer (*WIN6*)
naming a file (*WIN23*)
Notepad (*WIN14*)
online Help (*WIN32*)
opening a document file
   (*WIN28*)
opening a window (*WIN14*)
option button (*WIN12*)
Paintbrush (*WIN32*)
pointing (*WIN6*)
pop-up window (*WIN35*)

printing a document (*WIN20*)
Program Manager (*WIN5*)
program-item icons (*WIN5*)
quitting an application (*WIN21,*
   WIN28)
quitting Windows (*WIN36*)
Restore button (*WIN18*)
root directory (*WIN23*)
saving a document (*WIN24*)
saving a modified document file
   (*WIN31*)
scroll arrows (*WIN16*)
scroll bar (*WIN16*)
scroll box (*WIN16*)
selected button (*WIN12*)
selecting (*WIN11*)
selecting a menu (*WIN11*)
starting an application (*WIN16*)
starting Microsoft Windows
   (*WIN4*)
subdirectory (*WIN23*)
text box (*WIN13*)
title bar (*WIN4*)
user friendly (*WIN3*)
user interface (*WIN3*)
using Windows help (*WIN32*)
window (*WIN4*)
window border (*WIN4*)
window title (*WIN4*)
Windows (*WIN2*)
write-protected diskette
   (*WIN27*)

In Microsoft Windows you can accomplish a task in a number of ways. The following table provides a quick reference to each task presented in this project with it available options. The commands listed in the Menu column can be executed using either the keyboard or mouse.

Task	Mouse	Menu	Keyboard Shortcuts
Choose a Command from a menu	Click command name, or drag highlight to command name and release mouse button		Press underlined character; or press arrow keys to select command, and press ENTER
Choose a Help Topic	Click Help topic		Press TAB, ENTER
Display a Definition	Click definition		Press TAB, ENTER
Enlarge an Application Window	Click Maximize button	From Control menu, choose Maximize	
Obtain Online Help		From Help menu, choose Contents	Press F1
Open a Document		From File menu, choose Open	
Open a Group Window	Double-click group icon	From Window menu, choose group window name	Press CTRL + F6 (or CTRL + TAB) to select group icon, and press ENTER
Print a File		From File menu, choose Print	
Quit an Application	Double-click control menu box, click OK button	From File menu, choose Exit	
Quit Windows	Double-click Control menu box, click OK button	From File menu, choose Exit Windows, choose OK button	
Remove a Definition	Click open space on desktop		Press ENTER
Save a Document on Disk		From File menu, choose Save As	
Save an Edited Document on Disk		From File menu, choose Save	
Save Changes when Quitting Windows		From Options menu, choose Save Settings on Exit if no check mark precedes command	
Save No Changes when Quitting Windows		From Options menu, choose Save Settings on Exit if check mark precedes command	
Scroll a Window	Click up or down arrow, drag scroll box, click scroll bar		Press UP or DOWN ARROW
Select a Menu	Click menu name on menu bar		Press ALT + underlined character (or F10 + underlined character)
Start an Application	Double-click program-item icon	From File menu, choose Open	Press arrow keys to select program-item icon, and press ENTER

STUDENT ASSIGNMENT 1
True/False

Instructions: Circle T if the statement is true or F if the statement is false.

T F 1. A user interface is a combination of computer hardware and computer software.
T F 2. Microsoft Windows is a graphical user interface.
T F 3. The Program Manager window is a group window.
T F 4. The desktop is the screen background on which windows are displayed.
T F 5. A menu is a small picture that can represent an application or a group of applications.
T F 6. Clicking means quickly pressing and releasing a mouse button twice without moving the mouse.
T F 7. CTRL + SHIFT + LEFT ARROW is an example of a keyboard shortcut.
T F 8. You can carry out an action in an application by choosing a command from a menu.
T F 9. Selecting means marking an item.
T F 10. Windows opens a dialog box to supply information, allow you to enter information, or select among several options.
T F 11. A program-item icon represents a group of applications.
T F 12. You open a group window by pointing to its icon and double-clicking the left mouse button.
T F 13. A scroll bar allows you to view areas of a window that are not currently visible.
T F 14. Notepad and Paintbrush are applications.
T F 15. Choosing the Restore button maximizes a window to its maximize size.
T F 16. APPLICATION.TXT is a valid name for a document file.
T F 17. The directory structure is the relationship between the root directory and any subdirectories.
T F 18. You save a new document on disk by choosing the Save As command from the File menu.
T F 19. You open a document by choosing the Retrieve command from the File menu.
T F 20. Help is available while using Windows only in the *User's Guide* that accompanies the Windows software.

STUDENT ASSIGNMENT 2
Multiple Choice

Instructions: Circle the correct response.

1. Through a user interface, the user is able to _____.
   a. control the computer
   b. request information from the computer
   c. respond to messages displayed by the computer
   d. all of the above
2. _____ is quickly pressing and releasing a mouse button twice without moving the mouse.
   a. Double-clicking
   b. Clicking
   c. Dragging
   d. Pointing

3. To view the commands in a menu, you _____ the menu name.
   a. choose
   b. maximize
   c. close
   d. select
4. A _____ is a window that displays to supply information, allow you to enter information, or choose among several options.
   a. group window
   b. dialog box
   c. application window
   d. drop-down list box
5. A _____ is a rectangular area in which Windows displays text or you enter text.
   a. dialog box
   b. text box
   c. drop-down list box
   d. list box
6. The title bar of one group window that is a different color or intensity than the title bars of the other group windows indicates a(n) _____ window.
   a. inactive
   b. application
   c. group
   d. active
7. To view an area of a window that is not currently visible in a window, use the _____.
   a. title bar
   b. scroll bar
   c. menu bar
   d. Restore button
8. The _____ menu in the Notepad application contains the Save, Open, and Print commands.
   a. Window
   b. Options
   c. Help
   d. File
9. Before exiting Windows, you should check the _____ command to verify that no changes to the desktop will be saved.
   a. Open
   b. Exit Windows
   c. Save Settings on Exit
   d. Save Changes
10. Online Help is available for all applications except _____.
    a. Program Manager
    b. Calendar
    c. Clock
    d. File Manager

STUDENT ASSIGNMENT 3
Identifying Items in the Program Manager Window

Instructions: On the desktop in Figure SA1-3, arrows point to several items in the Program Manager window. Identify the items in the space provided.

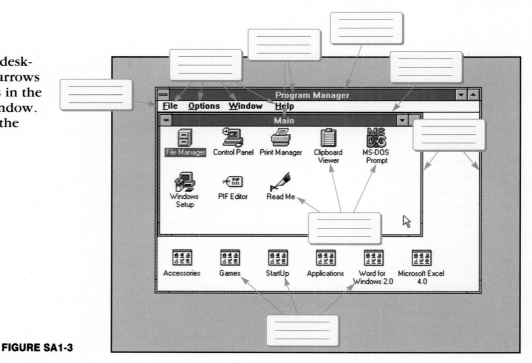

FIGURE SA1-3

STUDENT ASSIGNMENT 4
Starting an Application

Instructions: Using the desktop shown in Figure SA1-4, list the steps in the space provided to open the Accessories window and start the Notepad application.

Step 1: _____

_____

_____

Step 2: _____

_____

_____

Step 3: _____

_____

_____

Step 4: _____

_____

_____

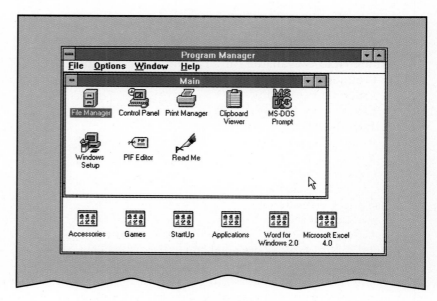

FIGURE SA1-4

COMPUTER LABORATORY EXERCISE 1
Improving Your Mouse Skills

Instructions: Use a computer to perform the following tasks.

1. Start Microsoft Windows.
2. Double-click the Games group icon ( ) to open the Games window if necessary.
3. Double-click the Solitaire program-item icon ( ).
4. Click the Maximize button to maximize the Solitaire window.
5. From the Help menu in the Solitaire window (Figure CLE1-1), choose the Contents command. One-by-one click on the help topics in green. Double-click on the Control-menu box in the title bar of the Solitaire Help window to close it.
6. Play the game of Solitaire.
7. To quit Solitaire choose the Exit command from the Game menu.

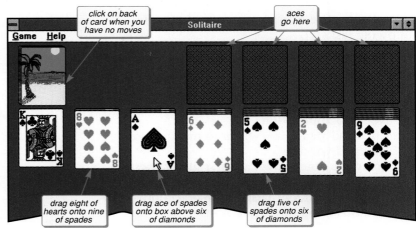

FIGURE CLE1-1

COMPUTER LABORATORY EXERCISE 2
Windows Tutorial

Instructions: Use a computer to perform the following tasks.

1. Start Microsoft Windows.
2. From the Help menu in the Program Manager window, choose the Windows Tutorial command.
3. Type the letter M. Follow the instructions (Figure CLE1-2) to step through the mouse practice lesson. Press the ESC key to exit the tutorial.
4. From the Help menu in the Program Manager window, choose the Windows Tutorial command.

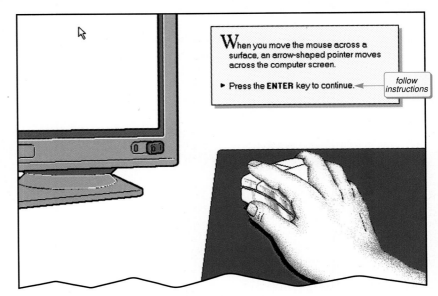

FIGURE CLE1-2

5. Type the letter W. Click the Instructions button (Instructions) and read the information. When you are finished, choose the Return to the Tutorial button (Return to the Tutorial). Next choose the Contents button (Contents) in the lower right corner of the screen.
6. Choose the second item (Starting an Application) from the Contents list. The Windows tutorial will step you through the remaining lessons. Respond as needed to the questions and instructions. Press the ESC key to exit the tutorial.

COMPUTER LABORATORY EXERCISE 3
Creating, Saving, and Printing Documents

Instructions: Use a computer to perform the following tasks.

1. Start Microsoft Windows if necessary.
2. Double-click the Accessories icon to open the Accessories window.
3. Double-click the Notepad icon to start the Notepad application.
4. Click the Maximize button to maximize the Notepad window.
5. Enter the note shown at the right at the insertion point on the screen.
6. Insert the Student Diskette that accompanies this book into drive A.
7. Select the File menu on the Notepad menu bar.
8. Choose the Save As command.
9. Enter grocery in the File Name text box.
10. Change the current selection in the Drives drop-down list box to a:.
11. Click the OK button to save the document on drive A.
12. Select the File menu on the Notepad menu bar.
13. Choose the Print command to print the document on the printer (Figure CLE1-3).
14. Remove the Student Diskette from drive A.
15. Select the File menu on the Notepad menu bar.
16. Choose the Exit command to quit Notepad.

Grocery List —
1/2 Gallon of Low Fat Milk
1 Dozen Medium Size Eggs
1 Loaf of Wheat Bread

```
                        GROCERY.TXT



         Grocery List -
         1/2 Gallon of Low Fat Milk
         1 Dozen Medium Size Eggs
         1 Loaf of Wheat Bread
```

FIGURE CLE1-3

COMPUTER LABORATORY EXERCISE 4
Opening, Editing, and Saving Documents

Instructions: Use a computer to perform the following tasks. If you have questions on how to procede, use the Calendar Help menu.

1. Start Microsoft Windows if necessary.
2. Double-click the Accessories icon to open the Accessories window.
3. Double-click the Calendar icon (⊞) to start the Calendar application.
4. Click the Maximize button to maximize the Calendar window.
5. Insert the Student Diskette that accompanies this book into drive A.
6. Select the File menu on the Calendar menu bar.

7. Choose the Open command.
8. Change the current selection in the Drives drop-down list box to a:.
9. Select the thompson.cal filename in the File Name list box. The THOMPSON.CAL file contains the daily appointments for Mr. Thompson.
10. Click the OK button in the Open dialog box to open the THOMPSON.CAL document. The document on your screen is shown in Figure CLE1-4a.
11. Click the Left or Right Scroll arrow repeatedly to locate the appointments for Thursday, September 29, 1994.
12. Make the changes shown below to the document.

TIME	CHANGE
11:00 AM	Stay at Auto Show one more hour
2:00 PM	Change the Designer's Meeting from 2:00 PM to 3:00 PM
4:00 PM	Remove the Quality Control Meeting

13. Select the File menu on the Calendar menu bar.
14. Choose the Save As command to save the document file on drive A. Use the filename PETER.CAL.
15. Select the File menu on the Calendar menu bar.
16. Choose the Print command.
17. Choose the OK button to print the document on the printer (Figure CLE1-4b).
18. Remove the Student Diskette from drive A.
19. Select the File menu on the Calendar menu bar.
20. Choose the Exit command to quit Calendar.

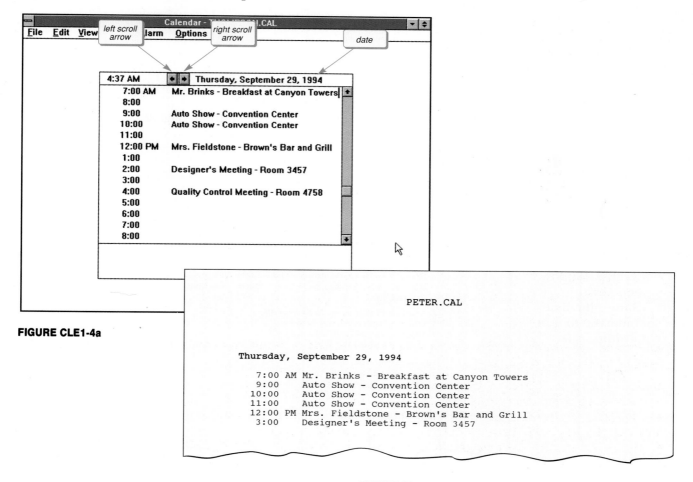

FIGURE CLE1-4a

FIGURE CLE1-4b

COMPUTER LABORATORY EXERCISE 5
Using Online Help

Instructions: Use a computer to perform the following tasks.

1. Start Microsoft Windows if necessary.
2. Double-click the Accessories icon to open the Accessories window.
3. Double-click the Cardfile icon ( ) to start the Cardfile application.
4. Select the Help menu.
5. Choose the Contents command.
6. Click the Maximize button to maximize the Cardfile Help window.
7. Choose the Add More Cards help topic.
8. Select the File menu on the Cardfile Help menu bar.
9. Choose the Print Topic command to print the Adding More Cards help topic on the printer (Figure CLE1-5a).
10. Display the definition of the term, index line.
11. Remove the index line definition from the desktop.
12. Choose the Contents button.
13. Choose the Delete Cards help topic.
14. Choose the Selecting Cards help topic at the bottom of the Deleting Cards screen.

Adding More Cards

Cardfile adds new cards in the correct alphabetic order and scrolls to display the new card at the front.

To add a new card to a file
1 From the Card menu, choose Add.
2 Type the text you want to appear on the underlined index line.
3 Choose the OK button.
4 In the information area, type text.

FIGURE CLE1-5a

15. Select the File menu on the Cardfile Help menu bar.
16. Choose the Print Topic command to print the Selecting Cards help topic (Figure CLE 1-5b).
17. Select the File menu on the Cardfile Help menu bar.
18. Choose the Exit command to quit Cardfile Help.
19. Select the File menu on the Cardfile window menu bar.
20. Choose the Exit command to quit Cardfile.

Selecting Cards

To select a card in Card view
▶ Click the card's index line if it is visible.
   Or click the arrows in the status bar until the index line is visible, and then click it.
   If you are using the keyboard, press and hold down CTRL+SHIFT and type the first letter of the index line.

To select a card by using the Go To command
1 From the Search menu, choose Go To.
2 Type text from the card's index line.
3 Choose the OK button.

To select a card in List view
▶ Click the card's index line.
   Or use the arrow keys to move to the card's index line.

See Also
Moving Through a Card File

FIGURE CLE1-5b

DISK AND FILE MANAGEMENT

OBJECTIVES You will have mastered the material in this project when you can:

▶ Identify the elements of the directory tree window
▶ Understand the concepts of diskette size and capacity
▶ Format and copy a diskette
▶ Select and copy one file or a group of files
▶ Change the current drive
▶ Rename or delete a file

▶ Create a backup diskette
▶ Search for help topics using Windows online Help
▶ Switch between applications
▶ Activate, resize, and close a group window
▶ Arrange the icons in a group window
▶ Minimize an application window to an icon

▶ INTRODUCTION

File Manager is an application included with Windows that allows you to organize and work with your hard disk and diskettes and the files on those disks. In this project, you will use File Manager to (1) format a diskette; (2) copy files between the hard disk and a diskette; (3) copy a diskette; (4) rename a file on diskette; and (5) delete a file from diskette.

Formatting a diskette and copying files to a diskette are common operations illustrated in this project that you should understand how to perform. While performing the Computer Laboratory Exercises and the Computer Laboratory Assignments at the end of each application project, you will save documents on a diskette that accompanies this textbook. To prevent the accidental loss of stored documents on a diskette, it is important to periodically make a copy of the entire diskette. A copy of a diskette is called a **backup diskette**. In this project, you will learn how to create a backup diskette to protect against the accidental loss of documents on a diskette.

You will also use Windows online Help in this project. In Project 1, you obtained help by choosing a topic from a list of help topics. In this project, you will use the Search feature to search for help topics.

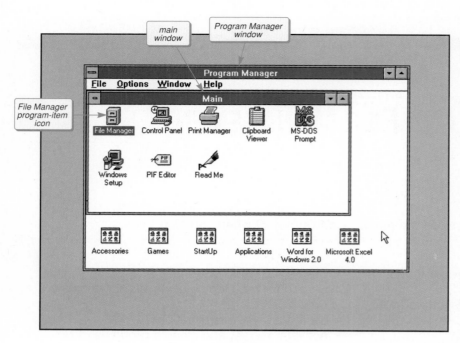

FIGURE 2-1

▶ STARTING WINDOWS

As explained in Project 1, when you turn on the computer, an introductory screen consisting of the Windows logo, Windows name, version number, and copyright notices displays momentarily. Next, a blank screen containing an hourglass icon displays. Finally, the Program Manager and Main windows open on the desktop (Figure 2-1). The File Manager program-item icon displays in the Main window. If your desktop does not look similar to the desktop in Figure 2-1, your instructor will inform you of the modifications necessary to change your desktop.

Starting File Manager and Maximizing the File Manager Window

To start File Manager, double-click the File Manager icon (▤) in the Main window. To maximize the File Manager window, choose the Maximize button on the File Manager window by pointing to the Maximize button and clicking the left mouse button.

TO START AN APPLICATION AND MAXIMIZE ITS WINDOW ▼

STEP 1 ▶

Double-click the File Manager icon in the Main window (see Figure 2-1), then click the Maximize button on the File Manager title bar.

Windows opens and maximizes the File Manager window (Figure 2-2).

FIGURE 2-2

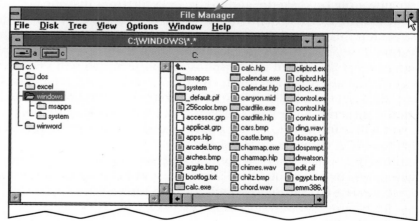

▶ FILE MANAGER

When you start File Manager, Windows opens the File Manager window (Figure 2-3). The menu bar contains the File, Disk, Tree, View, Options, Window, and Help menus. These menus contain the commands to organize and work with the disks and the files on those disks.

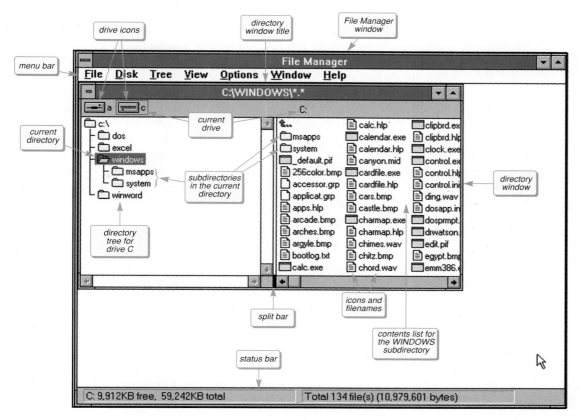

FIGURE 2-3

Below the menu bar is a **directory window** titled C:\WINDOWS*.*. The window title consists of a directory path (C:\WINDOWS), backslash (\), and filename (*.*). The directory path is the path of the current directory on drive C (WINDOWS subdirectory). The backslash separates the path and filename. The filename (*.*) references a group of files whose filename and extension can be any valid filename and extension.

Below the title bar is a horizontal bar that contains two **drive icons**. The drive icons represent the disk drives attached to the computer. The first drive icon (▤ **a:**) represents drive A (diskette drive) and the second drive icon (▤ **c:**) represents drive C (hard drive). Depending upon the number of disk drives attached to your computer, there may be more than two drive icons in the horizontal bar. A rectangular box surrounding the drive C icon indicates drive C is the **current drive**. The entry to the right of the icons (C:) also indicates drive C is the current drive.

The directory window is divided into two equal-sized areas. Each area is separated by a split bar. The **directory tree** in the area on the left contains the directory structure. The **directory tree** in the **directory structure** shows the relationship between the root directory and any subdirectories on the current drive (drive C). You can drag the **split bar** to the left or right to change the size of the two areas.

In the left area, a file folder icon represents each directory or subdirectory in the directory structure (see Figure 2-3). The shaded open file folder (📂) and subdirectory name for the current directory (WINDOWS subdirectory) are highlighted. The unopened file folder icons (📁) for the two subdirectories in the WINDOWS subdirectory (MSAPPS and SYSTEM) are indented below the icon for the WINDOWS subdirectory.

The area on the right contains the contents list. The **contents list** is a list of the files in the current directory (WINDOWS subdirectory). Each entry in the contents list consists of an icon and name. The shaded file folder icons for the two subdirectories in the current directory (MSAPPS and SYSTEM) display at the top of the first column in the list.

The status bar at the bottom of the File Manager window indicates the amount of unused disk space on the current drive (9,912KB free), amount of total disk space on the current drive (59,242KB total), number of files in the current directory (134 files), and the amount of disk space the files occupy (10,979,601 bytes).

▶ FORMATTING A DISKETTE

Before saving a document file on a diskette or copying a file onto a diskette, you must format the diskette. **Formatting** prepares a diskette for use on a computer by establishing the sectors and cylinders on the diskette, analyzing the diskette for defective cylinders, and establishing the root directory. To avoid errors while formatting a diskette, you should understand the concepts of diskette size and capacity that are explained in the following section.

Diskette Size and Capacity

How a diskette is formatted is determined by the size of the diskette, capacity of the diskette as established by the diskette manufacturer, and capabilities of the disk drive you use to format the diskette. **Diskette size** is the physical size of the diskette. Common diskette sizes are 5 1/4-inch and 3 1/2-inch.

Diskette capacity is the amount of space on the disk, measured in kilobytes (K) or megabytes (MB), available to store data. A diskette's capacity is established by the diskette manufacturer. Common diskette capacities are 360K and 1.2MB for a 5 1/4-inch diskette and 720K and 1.44MB for a 3 1/2-inch diskette.

A diskette drive's capability is established by the diskette drive manufacturer. There are 3 1/2-inch diskette drives that are capable of formatting a diskette with a capacity of 720K or 1.44MB and there are 5 1/4-inch diskette drives capable of formatting a diskette with a capacity of 360K or 1.2MB.

Before formatting a diskette, you must consider two things. First, the diskette drive you use to format a diskette must be capable of formatting the size of diskette you want to format. You can use a 3 1/2-inch diskette drive to format a 3 1/2-inch diskette, but you cannot use a 3 1/2-inch diskette drive to format a

5 1/4-inch diskette. Similarly, you can use a 5 1/4-inch diskette drive to format a 5 1/4-inch diskette, but you cannot use a 5 1/4-inch diskette drive to format a 3 1/2-inch diskette.

Second, the diskette drive you use to format a diskette must be capable of formatting the capacity of the diskette you want to format. A 5 1/4-inch diskette drive capable of formatting 1.2MB diskettes can be used to either format a 360K or 1.2MB diskette. However, because of the differences in the diskette manufacturing process, you cannot use a diskette drive capable of formatting 360K diskettes to format a 1.2MB diskette. A 3 1/2-inch diskette drive capable of formatting 1.44MB diskettes can be used to format either a 720K or 1.44MB diskette. Since the 1.44 MB diskette is manufactured with two square holes in the plastic cover and the 720K diskette is manufactured with only one square hole, you cannot use a diskette drive capable of formatting 720K diskette to format a 1.44MB diskette.

The computer you use to complete this project should have a 3 1/2-inch diskette drive capable of formatting a diskette with 1.44MB of disk storage. Trying to format a 3 1/2-inch diskette with any other diskette drive may result in an error. Typical errors encountered because of incorrect diskette capacity and diskette drive capabilities are explained later in this project. For more information about the diskette drive you will use to complete the projects in this textbook, contact your instructor.

Formatting a Diskette

To store a file on a diskette, the diskette must already be formatted. If the diskette is not formatted, you must format the diskette using File Manager. When formatting a diskette, use either an unformatted diskette or a diskette containing files you no longer need. Do not format the Student Diskette that accompanies this book.

To format a diskette using File Manager, you insert the diskette into the diskette drive, and then choose the **Format Disk command** from the Disk menu. Perform the following steps to format a diskette.

TO FORMAT A DISKETTE ▼

STEP 1

Insert an unformatted diskette or a formatted diskette containing files you no longer need into drive A.

STEP 2 ▶

Select the Disk menu, and then point to the Format Disk command.

Windows opens the Disk menu (Figure 2-4). The mouse pointer points to the Format Disk command.

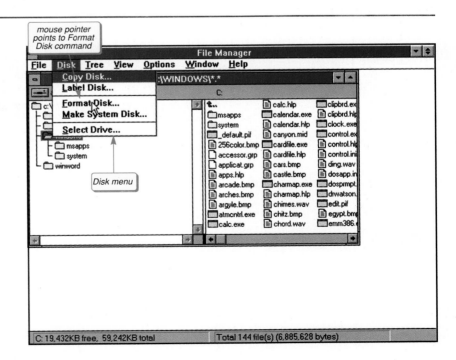

FIGURE 2-4

STEP 3 ▶

Choose the Format Disk command from the Disk menu, and then point to the OK button.

Windows opens the Format Disk dialog box (Figure 2-5). The current selections in the Disk In and Capacity boxes are Drive A: and 1.44 MB, respectively. With these selections, the diskette in drive A will be formatted with a capacity of 1.44MB. The Options list box is not required to format a diskette in this project. The mouse pointer points to the OK button.

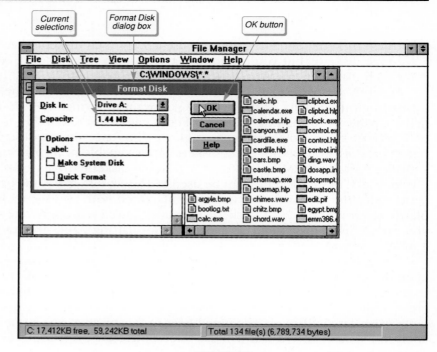

FIGURE 2-5

STEP 4 ▶

Choose the OK button by clicking the left mouse button, and then point to the Yes button.

Windows opens the Confirm Format Disk dialog box (Figure 2-6). This dialog box reminds you that if you continue, Windows will erase all data on the diskette in drive A. The mouse pointer points to the Yes button.

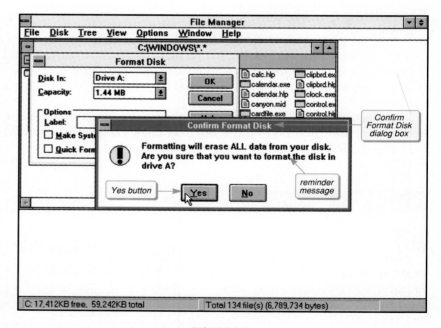

FIGURE 2-6

STEP 5 ▶

Choose the Yes button by clicking the left mouse button.

Windows opens the Formatting Disk dialog box (Figure 2-7). As the formatting process progresses, a value from 1 to 100 indicates what percent of the formatting process is complete. Toward the end of the formatting process, the creating root directory message replaces the 1% completed message to indicate Windows is creating the root directory on the diskette. The formatting process takes approximately two minutes.

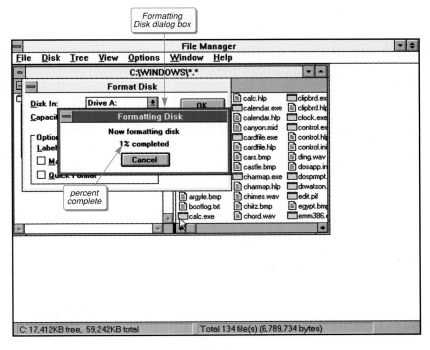

FIGURE 2-7

When the formatting process is complete, Windows opens the Format Complete dialog box (Figure 2-8). The dialog box contains the total disk space (1,457,664 bytes) and available disk space (1,457,664 bytes) of the newly formatted diskette. The values for the total disk space and available disk space in the Format Complete dialog box may be different for your computer.

STEP 6 ▶

Choose the No button by pointing to the No button, and then clicking the left mouse button.

Windows closes the Format Disk and Format Complete dialog boxes.

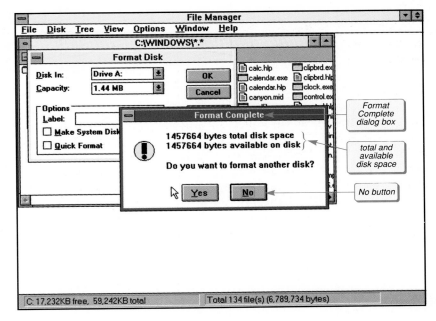

FIGURE 2-8

Correcting Errors Encountered While Formatting a Diskette

When you try to format a diskette but forget to insert a diskette into the diskette drive or the diskette you inserted is write-protected, damaged, or does not have the correct capacity for the diskette drive, Windows opens the Format Disk Error dialog box shown in Figure 2-9. The dialog box contains an error message (Cannot format disk.), a suggested action (Make sure the disk is in the drive and not write-protected, damaged, or of wrong density rating.), and the OK button. To format a diskette after forgetting to insert the diskette into the diskette drive, insert the diskette into the diskette drive, choose the OK button, and format the diskette.

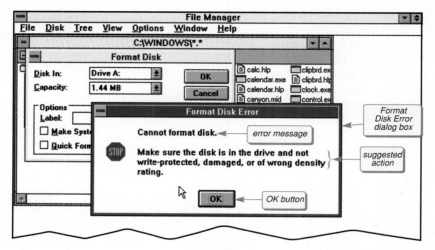

FIGURE 2-9

If the same dialog box opens after inserting a diskette into drive A, remove the diskette and determine if the diskette is write-protected, not the correct capacity for the diskette drive, or damaged. If the diskette is write-protected, remove the write-protection from the diskette, choose the OK button and format the diskette. If the diskette is not write-protected, check the diskette to determine if the diskette is the same capacity as the diskette drive. If it is not, insert a diskette with the correct capacity into the diskette drive, choose the OK button and format the diskette. If the diskette is not write-protected and the correct capacity, throw the damaged diskette away and insert another diskette into drive A, choose the OK button, and format the new diskette.

▶ COPYING FILES TO A DISKETTE

After formatting a diskette, you can save files on the diskette or copy files to the diskette from the hard drive or another diskette. You can easily copy a single file or group of files from one directory to another directory using File Manager. When copying files, the drive and directory containing the files to be copied are called the **source drive** and **source directory**, respectively. The drive and directory to which the files are copied are called the **destination drive** and **destination directory**, respectively.

To copy a file, select the filename in the contents list and drag the high-lighted filename to the destination drive icon or destination directory icon. Groups of files are copied in a similar fashion. You select the filenames in the contents list and drag the highlighted group of filenames to the destination drive or destination directory icon. In this project, you will copy a group of files consisting of the ARCADE.BMP, CARS.BMP, and EGYPT.BMP files from the WINDOWS subdirectory of drive C to the root directory of the diskette that you formatted earlier in this project. Before copying the files, maximize the directory window to make it easier to view the contents of the window.

Maximizing the Directory Window

To enlarge the C:\WINDOWS*.* window, click the Maximize button on the right side of the directory window title bar. When you maximize a directory window, the window fills the File Manager window.

TO MAXIMIZE A DIRECTORY WINDOW ▼

STEP 1 ▶

Click the Maximize button on the right side of the C:\WINDOWS*.* window title bar.

The directory window fills the File Manager window (Figure 2-10). Windows changes the File Manager window title to contain the directory window title (File Manager - [C:\WINDOWS*.]) and removes the title bar of the directory tree window. A Restore button displays at the right side of the File Manager menu bar. Clicking the Restore button returns the directory window to its previous size.*

FIGURE 2-10

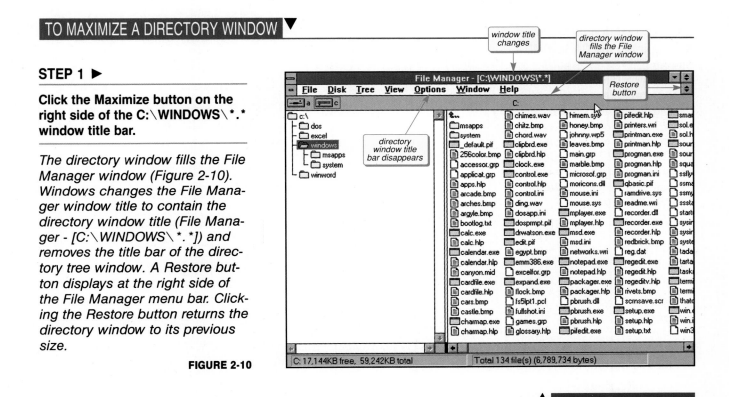

Selecting a Group of Files

Before copying a group of files, you must select (highlight) each file in the contents list. You select the first file in a group of files by pointing to its icon or filename and clicking the left mouse button. You select the remaining files in the group by pointing to each file icon or filename, holding down the CTRL key, clicking the left mouse button, and releasing the CTRL key. The steps on the following pages show how to select the group of files consisting of the ARCADE.BMP, CARS.BMP, and EGYPT.BMP files.

TO SELECT A GROUP OF FILES ▼

STEP 1 ▶

Point to the ARCADE.BMP filename in the contents list (Figure
2-11).

FIGURE 2-11

STEP 2 ▶

Select the ARCADE.BMP file by
clicking the left mouse button, and
then point to the CARS.BMP
filename.

*When you select the first file, the
highlight on the current directory
(WINDOWS) in the directory tree
changes to a rectangular box
(Figure 2-12). The ARCADE.BMP
entry is highlighted, and the
mouse pointer points to the
CARS.BMP filename.*

FIGURE 2-12

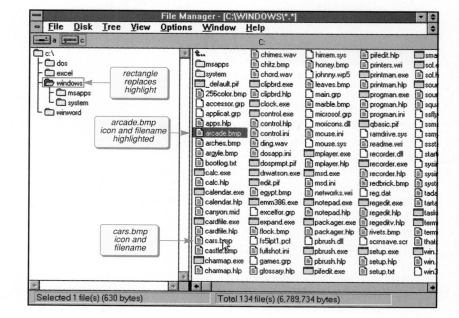

STEP 3 ▶

Hold down the CTRL key, click the
left mouse button, release the CTRL
key, and then point to the
EGYPT.BMP filename.

*Two files, ARCADE.BMP and
CARS.BMP are highlighted
(Figure 2-13). The mouse pointer
points to the EGYPT.BMP
filename.*

FIGURE 2-13

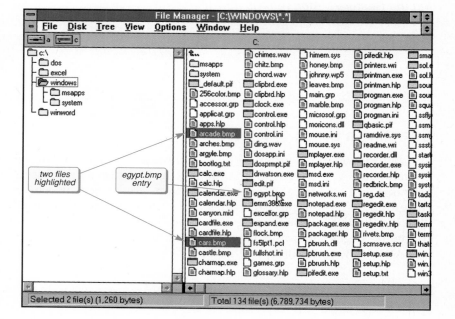

STEP 4 ▶

Hold down the CTRL key, click the left mouse button, and then release the CTRL key.

The group of files consisting of the ARCADE.BMP, CARS.BMP, and EGYPT.BMP files is highlighted (Figure 2-14).

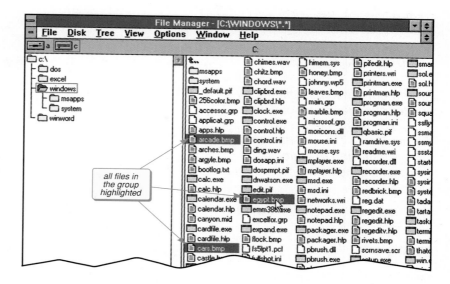

FIGURE 2-14

The ARCADE.BMP, CARS,BMP, and EGYPT.BMP files in Figure 2-14 are not located next to each other (sequentially) in the contents list. To select this group of files you selected the first file by pointing to its filename and clicking the left mouse button. Then, you selected each of the other files by pointing to their filenames, holding down the CTRL key, and clicking the left mouse button. If a group of files is located sequentially in the contents list, you select the group by pointing to the first filename in the list and clicking the left mouse button, and then hold down the SHIFT key, point to the last filename in the group and click the left mouse button.

Copying a Group of Files

After selecting each file in the group, insert the formatted diskette into drive A, and then copy the files to drive A by pointing to any highlighted filename and dragging the filename to the drive A icon.

TO COPY A GROUP OF FILES ▼

STEP 1

Verify that the formatted diskette is in drive A.

STEP 2 ▶

Point to the highlighted ARCADE.BMP entry (Figure 2-15).

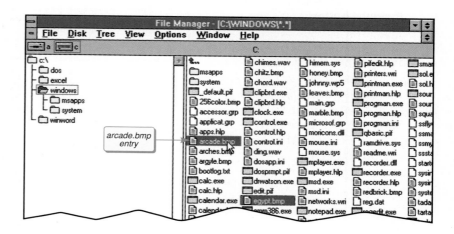

FIGURE 2-15

STEP 3 ▶

Drag the ARCADE.BMP filename over to the drive A icon.

As you drag the entry, the mouse pointer changes to an outline of a group of documents (⊞) (Figure 2-16). The outline contains a plus sign to indicate the group of files is being copied, not moved.

FIGURE 2-16

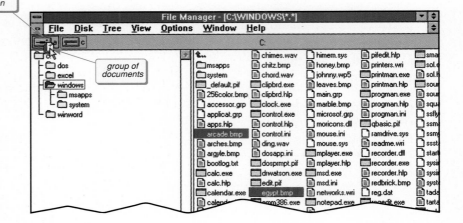

STEP 4 ▶

Release the mouse button, and then point to the Yes button.

Windows opens the Confirm Mouse Operation dialog box (Figure 2-17). The dialog box opens to confirm that you want to copy the files to the root directory of drive A (A:\). The highlight over the CARS.BMP entry is replaced with a dashed rectangular box. The mouse pointer points to the Yes button.

FIGURE 2-17

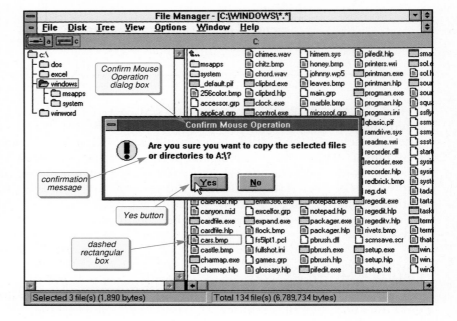

STEP 5 ▶

Choose the Yes button by clicking the left mouse button.

Windows opens the Copying dialog box, and the dialog box remains on the screen while Windows copies each file to the diskette in drive A (Figure 2-18). The dialog box in Figure 2-18 indicates the EGYPT.BMP file is currently being copied.

FIGURE 2-18

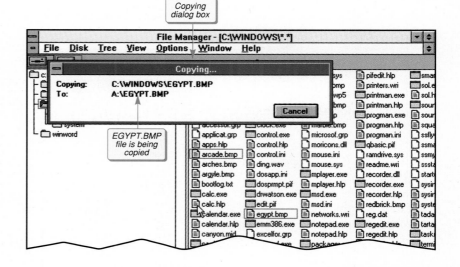

Correcting Errors Encountered While Copying Files

When you try to copy a file to an unformatted diskette, Windows opens the Error Copying File dialog box illustrated in Figure 2-19. The dialog box contains an error message (The disk in drive A is not formatted.), a question (Do you want to format it now?), and the Yes and No buttons. To continue the copy operation, format the diskette by choosing the Yes button. To cancel the copy operation, choose the No button.

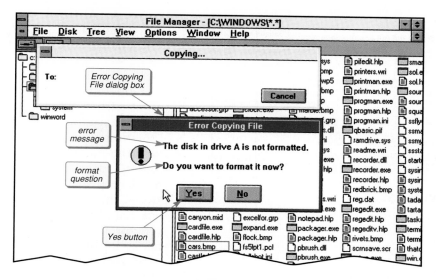

FIGURE 2-19

When you try to copy a file to a diskette but forget to insert a diskette into the diskette drive, Windows opens the Error Copying File dialog box shown in Figure 2-20. The dialog box contains an error message (There is no disk in drive A.), a suggested action (Insert a disk, and then try again.), and the Retry and Cancel buttons. To continue the copy operation, insert a diskette into drive A, and then choose the Retry button.

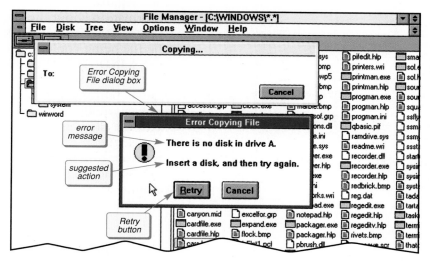

FIGURE 2-20

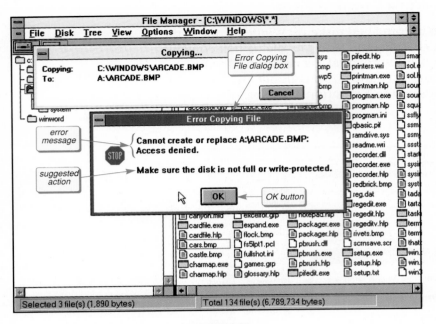

FIGURE 2-21

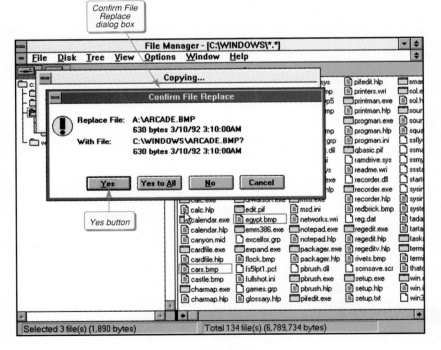

FIGURE 2-22

If you try to copy a file to a diskette that does not have enough room for the file, or you have inserted a write-protected diskette into the diskette drive, Windows opens the Error Copying File dialog box in Figure 2-21. The dialog box contains an error message (Cannot create or replace A:\ARCADE.BMP: Access denied.), a suggested action (Make sure the disk is not full or write-protected.), and the OK button. To continue with the copy operation, first remove the diskette from the diskette drive. Next, determine if the diskette is write-protected. If it is, remove the write-protection from the diskette, insert the diskette into the diskette drive, and then choose the OK button. If you determine the diskette is not write-protected, insert a diskette that is not full into the diskette drive, and then choose the OK button.

Replacing a File on Disk

If you try to copy a file to a diskette that already contains a file with the same filename and extension, Windows opens the Confirm File Replace dialog box (Figure 2-22). The Confirm File Replace dialog box contains information about the file being replaced (A:\ARCADE.BMP), the file being copied (C:\WINDOWS\ARCADE.BMP), and the Yes, Yes to All, No, and Cancel buttons. If you want to replace the file, on the diskette with the file being copied, choose the Yes button. If you do not want to replace the file choose the No button. If you want to cancel the copy operation, choose the Cancel button.

Changing the Current Drive

After copying a group of files, you should verify the files were copied onto the correct drive and into the correct directory. To view the files on drive A, change the current drive to drive A by pointing to the drive A icon and clicking the left mouse button.

TO CHANGE THE CURRENT DRIVE ▼

STEP 1 ▶

Point to the drive A icon.

The mouse pointer points to the drive A icon and the current drive is drive C (Figure 2-23).

FIGURE 2-23

STEP 2 ▶

Choose the drive A icon by clicking the left mouse button.

A rectangular box surrounds the drive A icon and the current drive entry changes to drive A (Figure 2-24). The directory tree of drive A and the contents list consisting of the files in the root directory of drive A display in the directory window. Another rectangular box surrounds the a:\ entry in the directory tree to indicate the current drive is drive A and the current directory is the root directory (\).

FIGURE 2-24

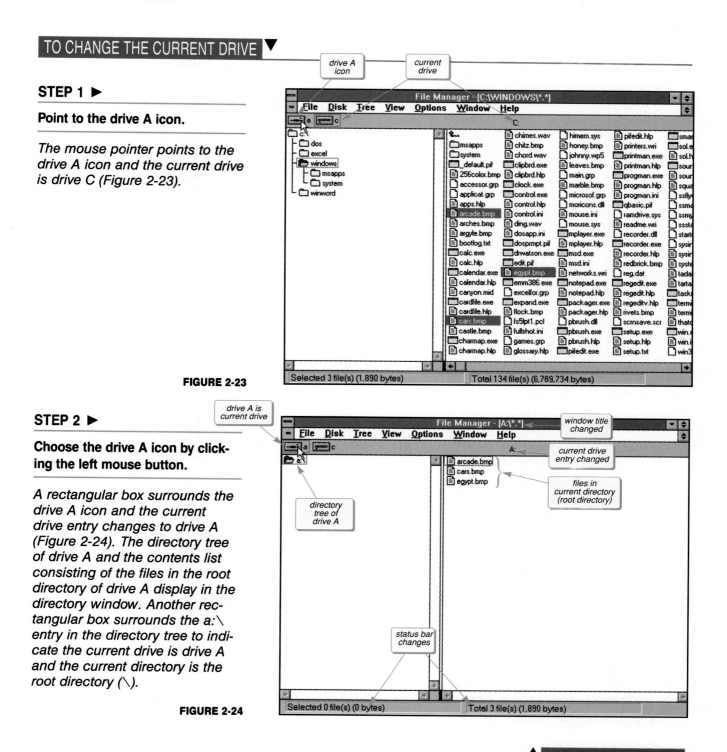

Correcting Errors Encountered While Changing the Current Drive

When you try to change the current drive before inserting a diskette into the diskette drive, Windows opens the Error Selecting Drive dialog box illustrated in Figure 2-25. The dialog box contains an error message (There is no disk in drive A.), a suggested action (Insert a disk, and then try again.), and the Retry and Cancel buttons. To change the current drive after forgetting to insert a diskette into drive A, insert a diskette into drive A, and choose the Retry button.

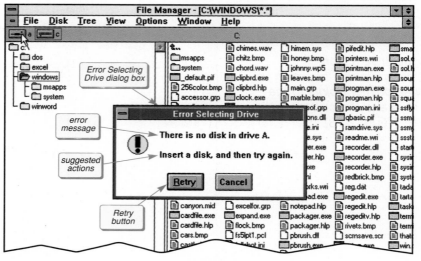

FIGURE 2-25

When you try to change the current drive and there is an unformatted diskette in the diskette drive, Windows opens the Error Selecting Drive dialog box shown in Figure 2-26. The dialog box contains an error message (The disk in drive A is not formatted.), a suggested action (Do you want to format it now?), and the Yes and No buttons. To change the current drive after inserting an unformatted diskette into drive A, choose the Yes button to format the diskette and change the current drive. Choose the No button to cancel the change.

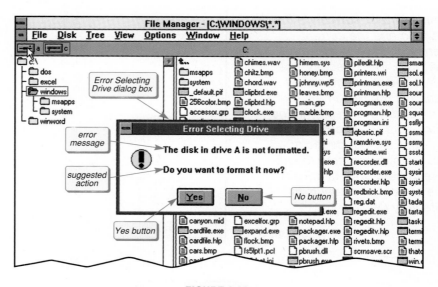

FIGURE 2-26

▶ RENAMING A FILE

Sometimes you may want to rename a file by changing its name or filename extension. You change the name or extension of a file by selecting
the filename in the contents list, choosing the **Rename command**
from the File menu, entering the new filename, and choosing the OK button. In
this project, you will change the name of the CARS.BMP file on the diskette in
drive A to AUTOS.BMP.

TO RENAME A FILE ▼

STEP 1 ▶

Select the CARS.BMP entry by
clicking the CARS.BMP filename in
the contents list.

*The CARS.BMP entry is high-
lighted (Figure 2-27).*

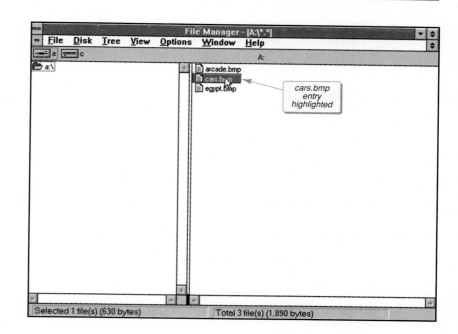

FIGURE 2-27

STEP 2 ▶

Select the File menu, and then
point to the Rename command.

*Windows opens the File menu
(Figure 2-28). The mouse pointer
points to the Rename command.*

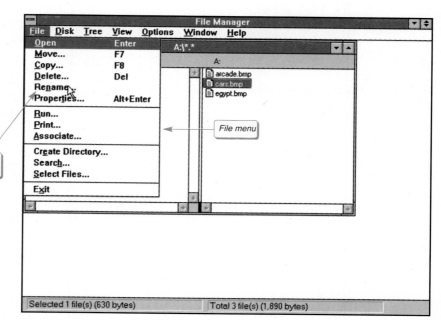

FIGURE 2-28

STEP 3 ▶

Choose the Rename command from the File menu by clicking the left mouse button.

Windows opens the Rename dialog box (Figure 2-29). The dialog box contains the Current Directory : A:\ message, the From and To text boxes, and the OK, Cancel, and Help buttons. The From text box contains the CARS.BMP filename and To text box contains an insertion point.

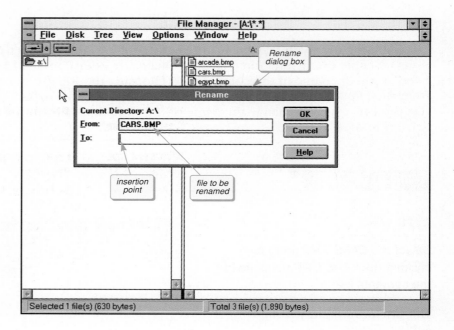

FIGURE 2-29

STEP 4 ▶

Type `autos.bmp` **in the To text box, and then point to the OK button.**

The To text box contains the AUTOS.BMP filename and the mouse points to the OK button (Figure 2-30).

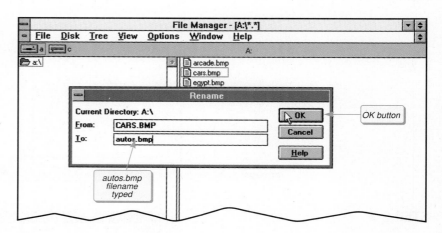

FIGURE 2-30

STEP 5 ▶

Choose the OK button by clicking the left mouse button.

The filename in the cars.bmp entry changes to autos.bmp (Figure 2-31).

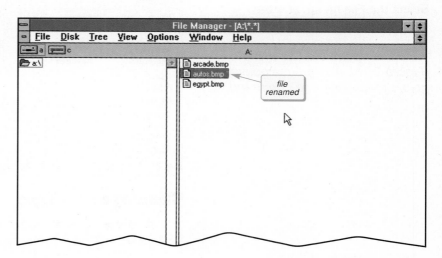

FIGURE 2-31

▶ DELETING A FILE

W hen you no longer need a file, you can delete it by selecting the file-name in the contents list, choosing the **Delete command** from the File menu, choosing the OK button, and then choosing the Yes button. In this project, you will delete the EGYPT.BMP file from the diskette in drive A.

TO DELETE A FILE ▼

STEP 1 ▶

Select the EGYPT.BMP entry.

The EGYPT.BMP entry is high-lighted (Figure 2-32).

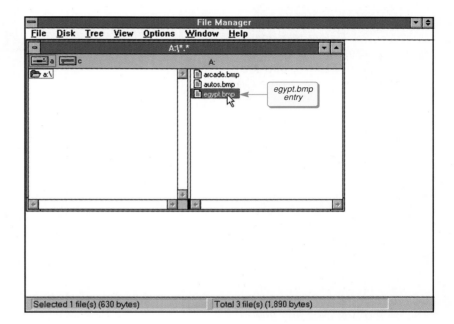

FIGURE 2-32

STEP 2 ▶

Select the File menu from the menu bar, and then point to the Delete command.

Windows opens the File menu (Figure 2-33). The mouse pointer points to the Delete command.

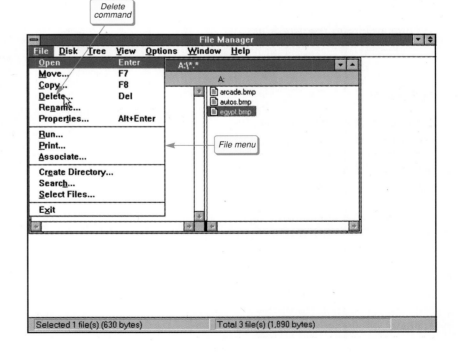

FIGURE 2-33

STEP 3 ▶

Choose the Delete command from the File menu by clicking the left mouse button, and then point to the OK button.

Windows opens the Delete dialog box (Figure 2-34). The dialog box contains the Current Directory: A:\ message, Delete text box, and the OK, Cancel, and Help buttons. The Delete text box contains the name of the file to be deleted (EGYPT.BMP), and the mouse pointer points to the OK button.

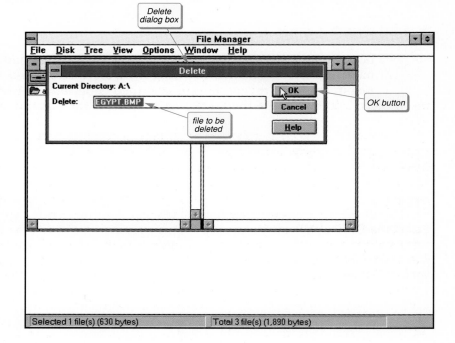

FIGURE 2-34

STEP 4 ▶

Choose the OK button by clicking the left mouse button, and then point to the Yes button.

Windows opens the Confirm File Delete dialog box (Figure 2-35). The dialog box contains the Delete File message and the path and filename of the file to delete (A:\EGYPT.BMP). The mouse pointer points to the Yes button.

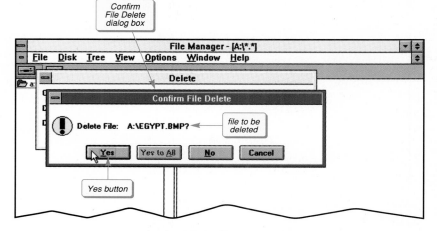

FIGURE 2-35

STEP 5 ▶

Choose the Yes button by clicking the left mouse button.

Windows deletes the EGYPT.BMP file from the diskette on drive A, removes the EGYPT.BMP entry from the contents list, and highlights the AUTOS.BMP file (Figure 2-36).

STEP 6

Remove the diskette from drive A.

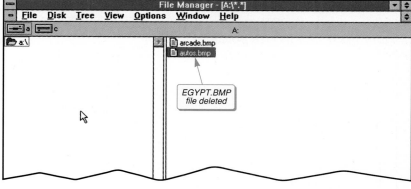

FIGURE 2-36

▶ CREATING A BACKUP DISKETTE

To prevent accidental loss of a file on a diskette, you should make a backup copy of the diskette. A copy of a diskette made to prevent accidental loss of data is called a **backup diskette**. Always be sure to make backup diskettes before installing software stored on diskettes onto the hard drive.

The first step in creating a backup diskette is to protect the diskette to be copied, or **source diskette**, from accidental erasure by write-protecting the diskette. After write-protecting the source diskette, choose the **Copy Disk command** from the Disk menu to copy the contents of the source diskette to another diskette, called the **destination diskette**. After copying the source diskette to the destination diskette, remove the write-protection from the source diskette and identify the destination diskette by writing a name on the paper label supplied with the diskette and affixing the label to the diskette.

In this project, you will use File Manager to create a backup diskette for a diskette labeled Business Documents. The Business Documents diskette contains valuable business documents that should be backed up to prevent accidental loss. The source diskette will be the Business Documents diskette and the destination diskette will be a formatted diskette that will later be labeled Business Documents Backup. To create a backup diskette, both the Business Documents diskette and the formatted diskette must be the same size and capacity.

File Manager copies a diskette by asking you to insert the source diskette into drive A, reading data from the source diskette into main memory, asking you to insert the destination disk, and then copying the data from main memory to the destination disk. Depending on the size of main memory on your computer, you may have to insert and remove the source and destination diskettes several times before the copy process is complete. The copy process takes about three minutes to complete.

TO COPY A DISKETTE ▼

STEP 1 ▶

Write-protect the Business Documents diskette by opening the write-protect window (Figure 2-37).

Business Documents

write-protect window open means diskette is write-protected

FIGURE 2-37

STEP 2 ►

Select the Disk menu from the menu bar, and then point to the Copy Disk command.

Windows opens the Disk menu (Figure 2-38). The mouse pointer points to the Copy Disk command.

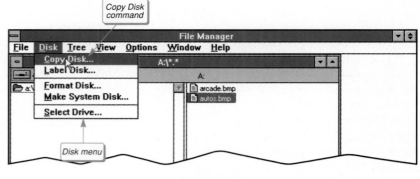

FIGURE 2-38

STEP 3 ►

Choose the Copy Disk command from the Disk menu by clicking the left mouse button, and then point to the Yes button.

Windows opens the Confirm Copy Disk dialog box (Figure 2-39). The dialog box reminds you that the copy process will erase all data on the destination disk. The mouse pointer points to the Yes button.

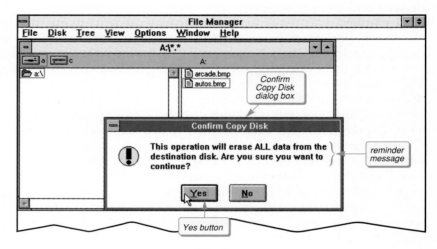

FIGURE 2-39

STEP 4 ►

Choose the Yes button by clicking the left mouse button, and then point to the OK button.

Windows opens the Copy Disk dialog box (Figure 2-40). The dialog box contains the Insert source disk message and the mouse pointer points to the OK button.

STEP 5 ►

Insert the source diskette, the Business Documents diskette, into drive A.

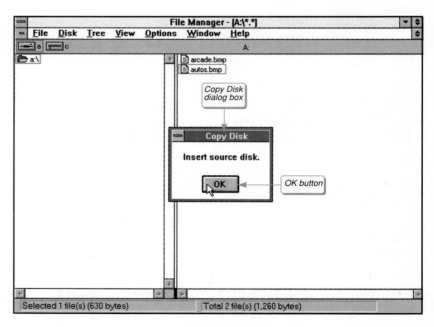

FIGURE 2-40

STEP 6 ►

Choose the OK button in the Copy Disk dialog box by clicking the left mouse button.

Windows opens the Copying Disk dialog box (Figure 2-41). The dialog box contains the messages, Now Copying disk in Drive A:. and 1% completed. As the copy process progresses, a value from 1 to 100 indicates what percent of the copy process is complete.

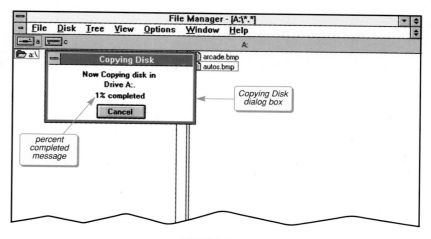

FIGURE 2-41

When as much data from the source diskette as will fit in main memory is copied to main memory, Windows opens the Copy Disk dialog box (Figure 2-42). The dialog box contains the message, Insert destination disk, and the OK button.

STEP 7 ►

Remove the source diskette (Business Documents diskette) from drive A and insert the destination diskette (Business Documents Backup diskette) into drive A.

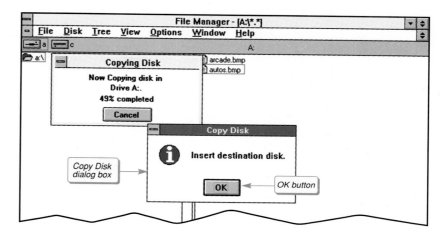

FIGURE 2-42

STEP 8 ►

Choose the OK button from the Copy Disk dialog box.

Windows opens the Copying Disk dialog box (Figure 2-43). A value from 1 to 100 displays as the data in main memory is copied to the destination disk.

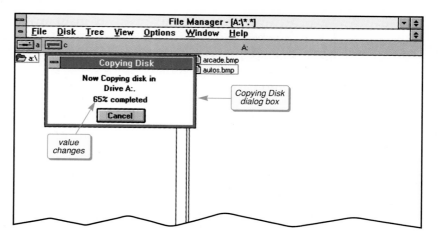

FIGURE 2-43

STEP 9 ▶

Remove the Business Documents Backup diskette from drive A and remove the write-protection from the Business Documents diskette by closing the write-protect window.

The write-protection is removed from the 3 1/2—inch Business Documents diskette (Figure 2-44).

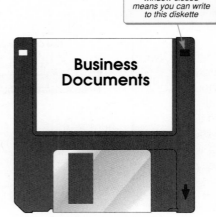

write-protect window closed means you can write to this diskette

Business Documents

FIGURE 2-44

STEP 10 ▶

Identify the Business Documents Backup diskette by writing the words Business Documents Backup on the paper label supplied with the diskette and then affix the label to the diskette (Figure 2-45).

Business Documents Backup

FIGURE 2-45

Depending on the size of main memory on your computer, you may have to insert and remove the source and destination diskettes several times before the copy process is complete. If prompted by Windows to insert the source diskette, remove the destination diskette (Business Documents Backup diskette) from drive A, insert the source diskette (Business Documents diskette) into drive A, and then choose the OK button. If prompted to insert the destination diskette, remove the source diskette (Business Documents diskette) from drive A, insert the destination diskette (Business Documents Backup diskette) into drive A, and then choose the OK button.

In the future if you change the contents of the Business Documents diskette, choose the Copy Disk command to copy the contents of the Business Documents diskette to the Business Documents Backup diskette. If the Business Documents diskette becomes unusable, you can format a diskette, choose the Copy Disk command to copy the contents of the Business Documents Backup diskette (source diskette) to the formatted diskette (destination diskette), label the formatted diskette, Business Documents, and use the new Business Documents diskette in place of the unusable Business Documents diskette.

Correcting Errors Encountered While Copying A Diskette

When you try to copy a disk and forget to insert the source diskette when prompted, insert an unformatted source diskette, forget to insert the destination diskette when prompted, or insert a write-protected destination diskette, Windows opens the Copy Disk Error dialog box illustrated in Figure 2-46. The dialog box contains the Unable to copy disk error message and OK button. To complete the copy process after forgetting to insert a source diskette or inserting an unformatted source diskette, choose the OK button, insert the formatted source diskette into the diskette drive, and choose the **Disk Copy command** to start over the disk copy process. To complete the copy process after forgetting to insert a destination diskette or inserting a write-protected destination diskette, choose the OK button, insert a nonwrite-protected diskette in the diskette drive, and choose the Disk Copy command to start over the disk copy.

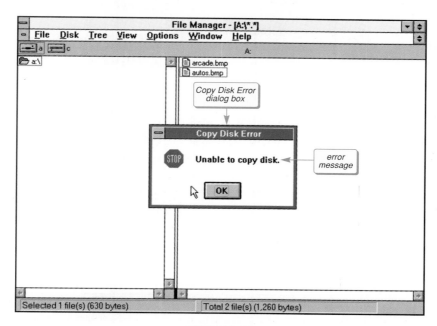

FIGURE 2-46

▶ SEARCHING FOR HELP USING ONLINE HELP

In Project 1, you obtained help about the Paintbrush application by choosing the Contents command from the Help menu of the Paintbrush window (see pages WIN32 through WIN35). You then chose a topic from a list of help topics on the screen. In addition to choosing a topic from a list of available help topics, you can use the Search feature to search for help topics. In this project, you will use the Search feature to obtain help about copying files and selecting groups of files using the keyboard.

Searching for a Help Topic

In this project, you used a mouse to select and copy a group of files. If you want to obtain information about how to select a group of files using the keyboard instead of the mouse, you can use the Search feature. A search can be performed in one of two ways. The first method allows you to select a search topic from a list of search topics. A list of help topics associated with the search topic displays. You then select a help topic from this list. To begin the search, choose the **Search for Help on command** from the Help menu.

TO SEARCH FOR A HELP TOPIC ▼

STEP 1 ►

Select the Help menu from the File Manager window menu bar, and then point to the Search for Help on command.

Windows opens the Help menu (Figure 2-47). The mouse pointer points to the Search for Help on command.

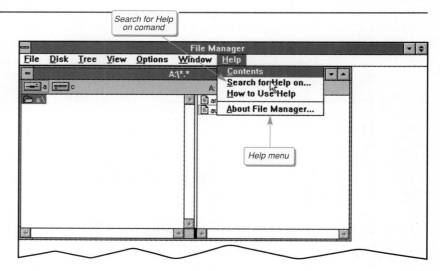

FIGURE 2-47

STEP 2 ►

Choose the Search for Help on command from the Help menu by clicking the left mouse button.

Windows opens the Search dialog box (Figure 2-48). The dialog box consists of two areas separated by a horizontal line. The top area contains the Search For text box, Search For list box, and Cancel and Show Topics buttons. The Search For list box contains an alphabetical list of search topics. A vertical scroll bar indicates there are more search topics than appear in the list box. The Cancel button cancels the Search operation. The Show Topics button is dimmed and cannot be chosen. The bottom area of the dialog box contains the empty Help Topics list box and the dimmed Go To button.

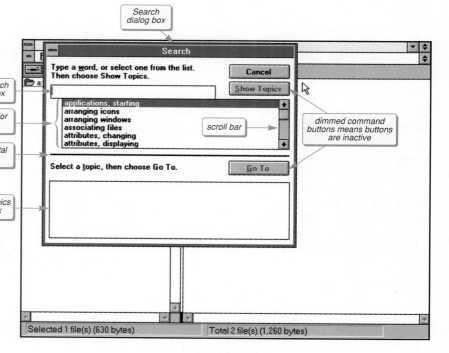

FIGURE 2-48

STEP 3 ►

Point to the down scroll arrow in the Search For list box (Figure 2-49).

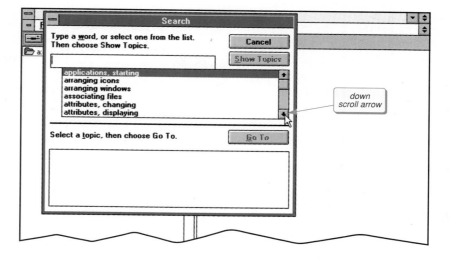

FIGURE 2-49

STEP 4 ►

Hold down the left mouse button until the selecting files search topic is visible, and then point to the selecting files search topic (Figure 2-50).

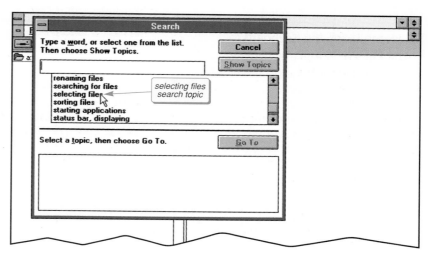

FIGURE 2-50

STEP 5 ►

Select the selecting files search topic by clicking the left mouse button, and then point to the Show Topics button (Show Topics).

The selecting files search topic is highlighted in the Search For list box and displays in the Search For text box (Figure 2-51). The Show Topics button is no longer dimmed and the mouse pointer points to the Show Topics button.

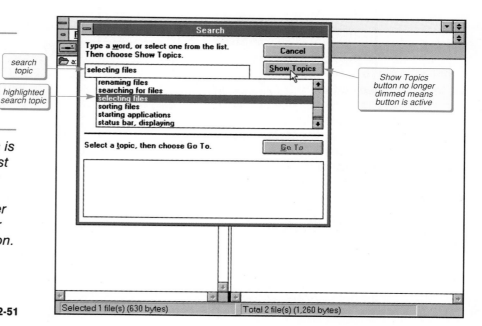

FIGURE 2-51

STEP 6 ▶

Choose the Show Topics button by clicking the left mouse button, and then point to the Using the Keyboard to Select Files help topic.

The Help Topics list box contains four help topics (Figure 2-52). The Go To button (Go To) is no longer dimmed, and the mouse pointer points to the Using the Keyboard to Select Files help topic.

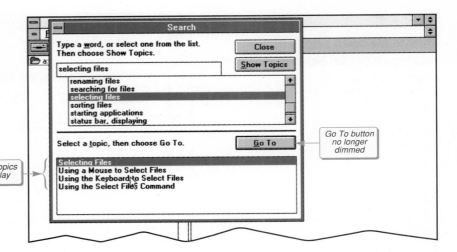

FIGURE 2-52

STEP 7 ▶

Select the Using the Keyboard to Select Files help topic by clicking the left mouse button, and then point to the Go To button.

The Using the Keyboard to Select Files help topic is highlighted in the Help Topics list box and the mouse pointer points to the Go To button (Figure 2-53).

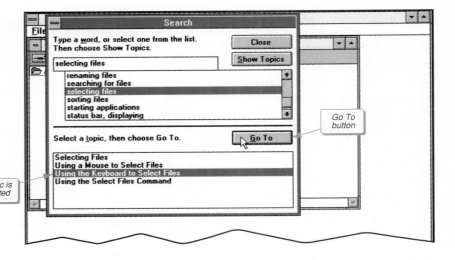

FIGURE 2-53

STEP 8 ▶

Choose the Go To button by clicking the left mouse button.

Windows closes the Search dialog box and opens the File Manager Help window (Figure 2-54). The Using the Keyboard to Select Files screen displays in the window.

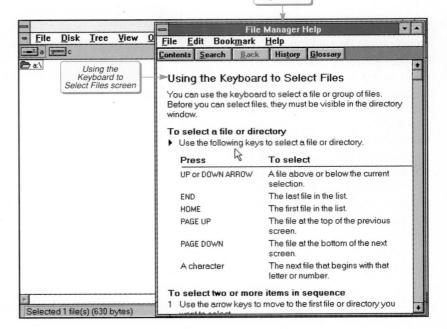

FIGURE 2-54

STEP 9 ▶

Click the Maximize button (⊟) to maximize the File Manager Help window (Figure 2-55).

FIGURE 2-55

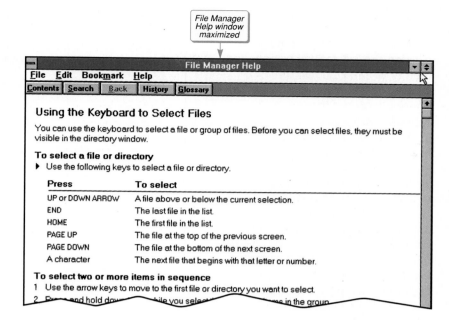

Searching for Help Using a Word or Phrase

The second method you can use to search for help involves entering a word or phrase to assist the Search feature in finding help related to the word or phrase. In this project, you copied a group of files from the hard disk to a diskette. To obtain additional information about copying files, choose the Search button and type `copy` from the keyboard.

TO SEARCH FOR A HELP TOPIC ▼

STEP 1 ▶

Point to the Search button (Search)) (Figure 2-56).

FIGURE 2-56

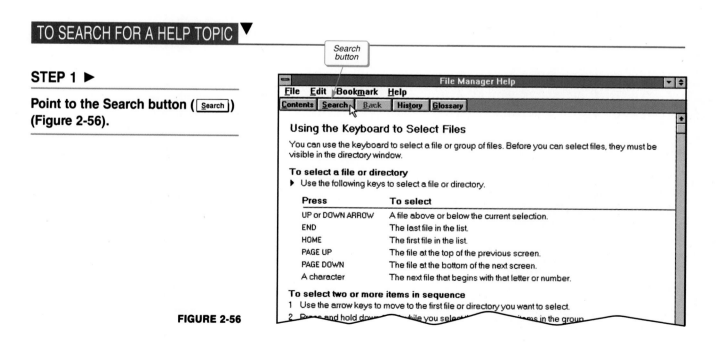

STEP 2 ►

Choose the Search button by clicking the left mouse button, and then type copy.

Windows opens the Search dialog box (Figure 2-57). As you type the word copy, each letter of the word displays in the Search For text box and the Search For Topics in the Search For Topics list box change. When the entry of the word is complete, the word copy displays in the Search For text box and the Search For topics beginning with the four letters c-o-p-y display first in the Search For list box.

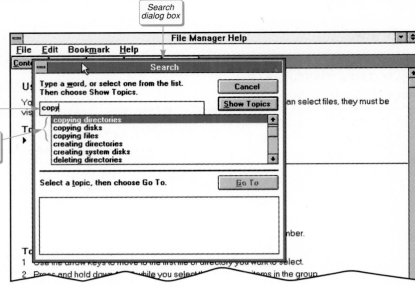

FIGURE 2-57

STEP 3 ►

Select the copying files search topic by pointing to the topic and clicking the left mouse button, and then point to the Show Topics button.

The copying files search topic is highlighted in the Search For list box and displays in the Search For text box (Figure 2-58).

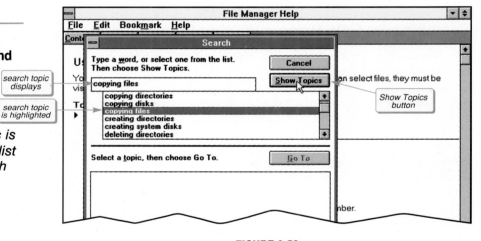

FIGURE 2-58

STEP 4 ►

Choose the Show Topics button by clicking the left mouse button, and then point to the Go To button.

Only the Copying Files and Directories help topic display in the Help Topic list box (Figure 2-59).

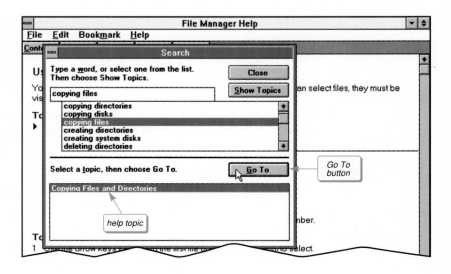

FIGURE 2-59

STEP 5 ▶

Choose the Go To button by clicking the left mouse button.

Windows closes the Search dialog box and displays the Copying Files and Directories help screen (Figure 2-60).

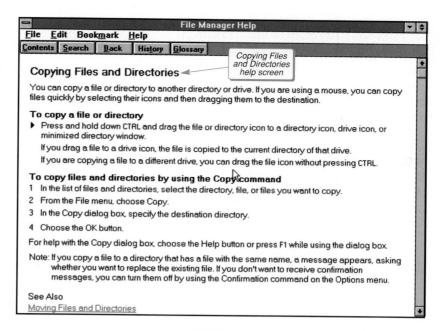

FIGURE 2-60

Quitting File Manager and Online Help

When you finish using File Manager and Windows online Help, you should quit the File Manager Help and File Manager applications. One method of quitting these applications is to first quit the File Manager Help application, and then quit the File Manager application. However, because quitting an application automatically quits the help application associated with that application, you can simply quit the File Manager application to quit both applications. Because the Program Manager and File Manager windows are hidden behind the File Manager Help window (see Figure 2-60), you must move the File Manager window on top of the other windows before quitting File Manager. To do this, you must switch to the File Manager application.

▶ SWITCHING BETWEEN APPLICATIONS

E ach time you start an application and maximize its window, its application window displays on top of the other windows on the desktop. To display a hidden application window, you must switch between applications on the desktop using the ALT and TAB keys. To switch to another application, hold down the ALT key, press the TAB key one or more times, and then release the ALT key. Each time you press the TAB key, a box containing an application icon and application window title opens on the desktop. To display the File Manager window, you will have to press the TAB key only once.

TO SWITCH BETWEEN APPLICATIONS ▼

STEP 1 ▶

Hold down the ALT key, and then press the TAB key.

A box containing the File Manager application icon and window title (File Manager) displays (Figure 2-61).

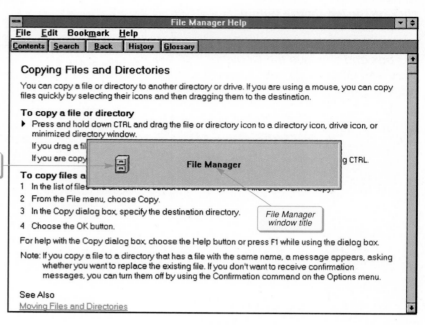

FIGURE 2-61

STEP 2 ▶

Release the ALT key.

The File Manager window moves on top of the other windows on the desktop (Figure 2-62).

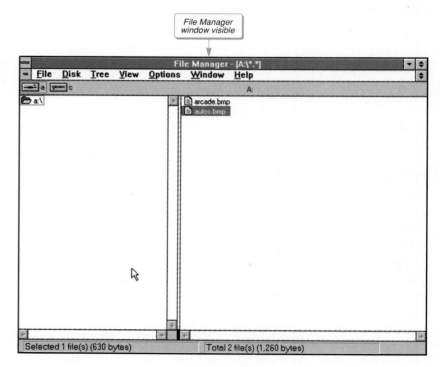

FIGURE 2-62

Verify Changes to the File Manager Window Will Not Be Saved

Because you want to return the File Manager window to its state before you started the application, no changes should be saved. The **Save Settings on Exit command** on the Options menu controls whether changes to the File Manager window are saved or not saved when you quit File Manager. A check mark (✓) preceding the Save Settings on Exit command indicates the command is active and all changes to the layout of the File Manager window will be saved when you quit File Manager. If the command is preceded by a check mark, choose the Save Settings on Exit command by clicking the left mouse button to remove the check mark, so the changes will not be saved. Perform the following steps to verify that changes are not saved to the File Manager window.

TO VERIFY CHANGES WILL NOT BE SAVED ▼

STEP 1 ▶

Select the Options menu from the File Manager menu bar.

The Options menu opens (Figure 2-63). A check mark (✓) precedes the Save Settings on Exit command.

STEP 2 ▶

To remove the check mark, choose the Save Settings on Exit command from the Options menu by pointing to the Save Settings on Exit command and clicking the left mouse button.

Windows closes the Options menu. Although not visible, the check mark preceding the Save Settings on Exit command has been removed. This means any changes made to the desktop will not be saved when you exit File Manager.

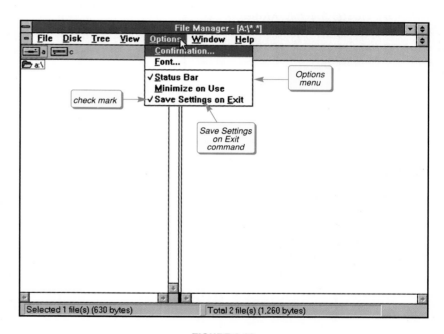

FIGURE 2-63

Quitting File Manager

After verifying no changes to the File Manager window will be saved, the Save Settings on Exit command is not active, so you can quit the File Manager application. In Project 1 you chose the Exit command from the File menu to quit an application. In addition to choosing a command from a menu, you can also quit an application by pointing to the **Control-menu box** in the upper left corner of the application window and double-clicking the left mouse button, as shown in the steps on the next page.

TO QUIT AN APPLICATION ▼

STEP 1 ►

Point to the Control-menu box in the upper left corner of the File Manager window (Figure 2-64).

STEP 2 ►

Double-click the left mouse button to exit the File Manager application.

Windows closes the File Manager and File Manager Help windows, causing the Program Manager window to display.

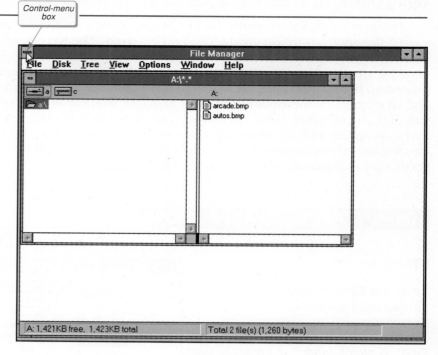

FIGURE 2-64

TO QUIT WINDOWS

Step 1: Select the Options menu from the Program Manager menu bar.
Step 2: If a check mark precedes the Save Settings on Exit command, choose the Save Settings on Exit command.
Step 3: Point to the Control-menu box in the upper left corner of the Program Manager window.
Step 4: Double-click the left mouse button.
Step 5: Choose the OK button to exit Windows.

▶ ADDITIONAL COMMANDS AND CONCEPTS

In addition to the commands and concepts presented in Project 1 and this project, you should understand how to activate a group window, arrange the program-item icons in a group window, and close a group window. These topics are discussed on the following pages. In addition, methods to resize a window and minimize an application window to an application icon are explained.

Activating a Group Window

Frequently, several group windows are open in the Program Manager window at the same time. In Figure 2-65, two group windows (Main and Accessories) are open. The Accessories window is the active group window, and the inactive Main window is partially hidden behind the Accessories window. To view a group window that is partially hidden, activate the hidden window by selecting the Window menu and then choosing the name of the group window you wish to view.

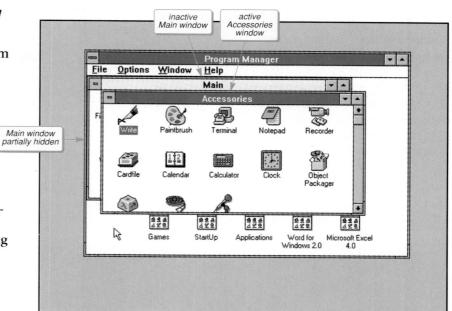

FIGURE 2-65

TO ACTIVATE A GROUP WINDOW ▼

STEP 1 ►

Select the Window menu from the Program Manager menu bar, and then point to the Main group window name.

The Window menu consists of two areas separated by a horizontal line (Figure 2-66). Below the line is a list of the group windows and group icons in the Program Manager window. Each entry in the list is preceded by a value from one to seven. The number of the active window (Accessories) is preceded by a check mark and the mouse pointer points to the Main group window name.

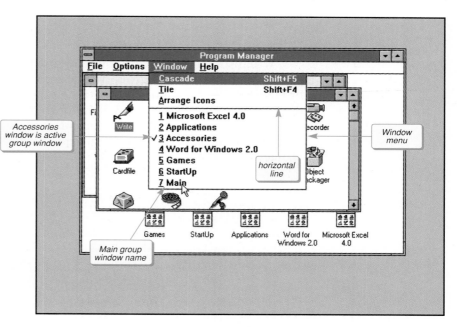

FIGURE 2-66

STEP 2 ▶

Choose the Main group window name by clicking the left mouse button.

The Main window moves on top of the Accessories window (Figure 2-67). The Main window is now the active window.

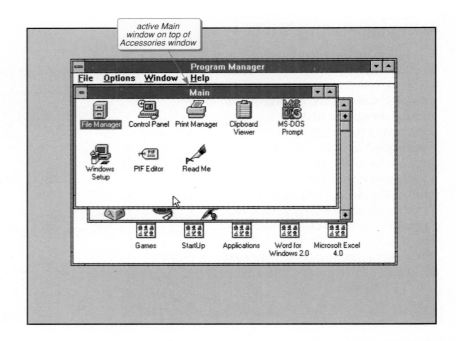

FIGURE 2-67

An alternative method of activating an inactive window is to point to any open area of the window and click the left mouse button. This method cannot be used if the inactive window is completely hidden behind another window.

Closing a Group Window

When several group windows are open in the Program Manager window, you may want to close a group window to reduce the number of open windows. In Figure 2-68, the Main, Accessories, and Games windows are open. To close the Games window, choose the Minimize button on the right side of the Games title bar. Choosing the Minimize button removes the group window from the desktop and displays the Games group icon at the bottom of the Program Manager window.

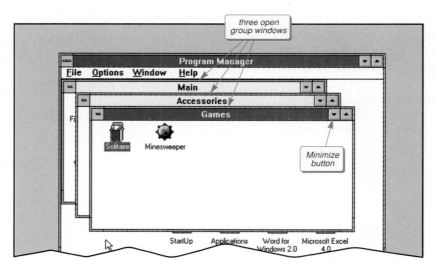

FIGURE 2-68

TO CLOSE A GROUP WINDOW ▼

STEP 1 ►

Choose the Minimize button (▼) on the Games title bar.

The Games window closes and the Games icon displays at the bottom edge of the Program Manager window (Figure 2-69).

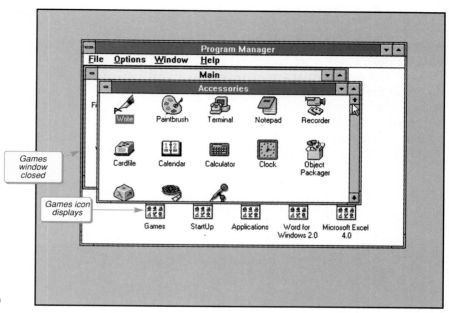

FIGURE 2-69

Resizing a Group Window

When more than six group icons display at the bottom of the Program Manager window, some group icons may not be completely visible. In Figure 2-70, the name of the Microsoft SolutionsSeries icon is partially visible. To make the icon visible, resize the Main window by dragging the bottom window border toward the window title.

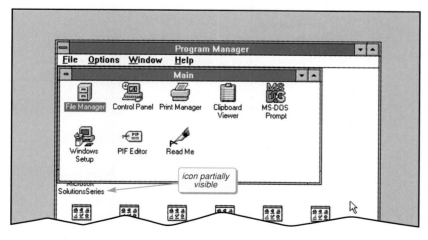

FIGURE 2-70

TO RESIZE A WINDOW ▼

STEP 1 ▶

Point to the bottom border of the Main window.

As the mouse pointer approaches the window border, the mouse pointer changes to a double-headed arrow icon (⇕) (Figure 2-71).

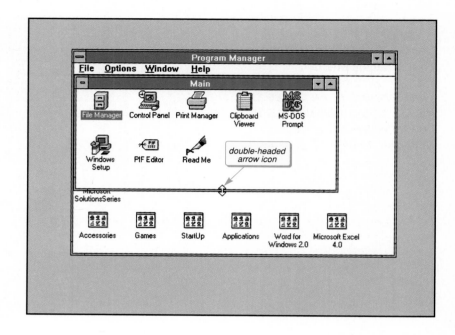

FIGURE 2-71

STEP 2 ▶

Drag the bottom border toward the window title until the Microsoft SolutionsSeries icon is visible.

The Main window changes shape, and the Microsoft SolutionsSeries icon is visible (Figure 2-72).

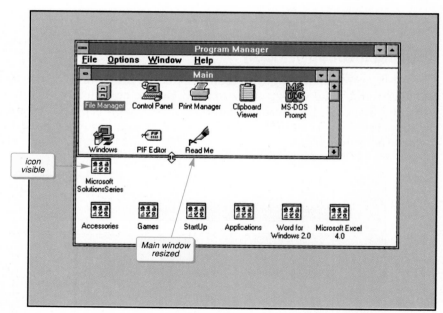

FIGURE 2-72

In addition to dragging a window border to resize a window, you can also drag a window corner to resize the window. By dragging a corner, you can change both the width and length of a window.

Arranging Icons

Occasionally, a program-item icon is either accidentally or intentionally moved within a group window. The result is that the program-item icons are not arranged in an organized fashion in the window. Figure 2-73 shows the eight program-item icons in the Main window. One icon, the File Manager icon, is not aligned with the other icons. As a result, the icons in the Main window appear unorganized. To arrange the icons in the Main window, choose the **Arrange Icons command** from the Window menu.

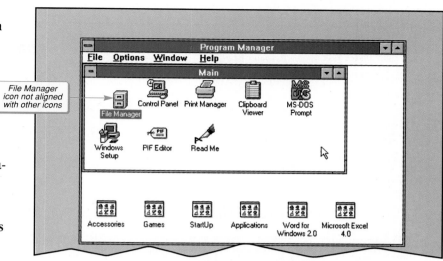

FIGURE 2-73

TO ARRANGE PROGRAM-ITEM ICONS ▼

STEP 1 ▶

Select the Window menu from the Program Manager menu bar, and then point to the Arrange Icons command.

Windows opens the Window menu (Figure 2-74). The mouse pointer points to the Arrange Icons command.

FIGURE 2-74

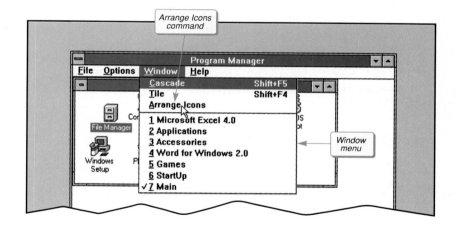

STEP 2 ▶

Choose the Arrange Icons command by clicking the left mouse button.

The icons in the Main window are arranged (Figure 2-75).

FIGURE 2-75

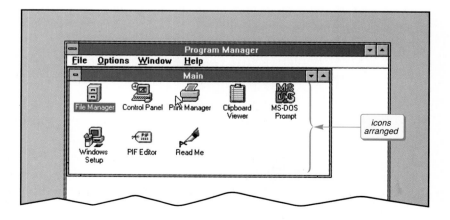

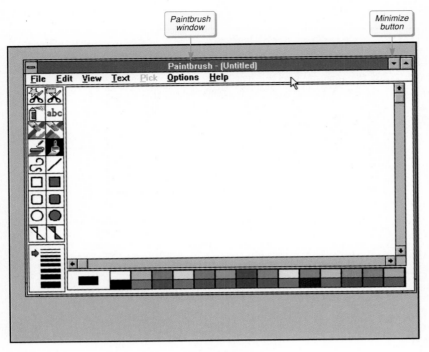

Paintbrush window

Minimize button

FIGURE 2-76

Minimizing an Application Window to an Icon

When you finish work in an application and there is a possibility of using the application again before quitting Windows, you should minimize the application window to an application icon instead of quitting the application. An **application icon** represents an application that was started and then minimized. Minimizing a window to an application icon saves you the time of starting the application and maximizing its window if you decide to use the application again. In addition, you free space on the desktop without quitting the application. The desktop in Figure 2-76 contains the Paintbrush window. To minimize the Paintbrush window to an application icon, click the Minimize button on the right side of the Paintbrush title bar.

TO MINIMIZE AN APPLICATION WINDOW TO AN ICON ▼

STEP 1 ▶

Click the Minimize button on the right side of the Paintbrush title bar.

Windows closes the Paintbrush window and displays the Paintbrush application icon at the bottom of the desktop (Figure 2-77).

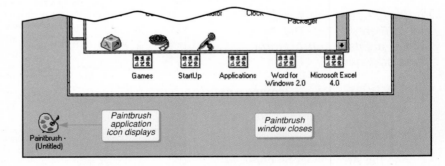

Paintbrush application icon displays

Paintbrush window closes

FIGURE 2-77

After minimizing an application window to an application icon, you can start the application again by double-clicking the application icon.

▶ PROJECT SUMMARY

In this project, you used File Manager to format and copy a diskette, copy a group of files, and rename and delete a file. You searched for help about File Manager using the Search feature of online Help, and you switched between applications on the desktop. In addition, you activated, resized, and closed a group window, arranged the icons in a group window, and minimized an application window to an application icon.

▶ KEY TERMS

application icon (*WIN86*)
Arrange Icons command (*WIN85*)
backup diskette (*WIN47*)
Cascade command (*WIN94*)
contents list (*WIN49*)
Control-menu box (*WIN79*)
Copy Disk command (*WIN67*)
current drive (*WIN48*)
Delete command (*WIN65*)
destination directory (*WIN54*)
destination diskette (*WIN67*)
destination drive (*WIN54*)

directory structure (*WIN49*)
directory tree (*WIN49*)
directory window (*WIN48*)
Disk Copy command (*WIN71*)
Disk menu (*WIN51*)
diskette capacity (*WIN50*)
diskette size (*WIN50*)
drive icon (*WIN48*)
File Manager (*WIN48*)
Format Disk command (*WIN51*)
formatting (*WIN50*)
Help menu (*WIN72*)

Options menu (*WIN79*)
Rename command (*WIN63*)
Save Settings on Exit command (*WIN79*)
Search for Help on command (*WIN72*)
source directory (*WIN54*)
source diskette (*WIN67*)
source drive (*WIN54*)
split bar (*WIN49*)
Tile command (*WIN94*)
Window menu (*WIN81*)

Q U I C K   R E F E R E N C E

In Windows you can accomplish a task in a number of ways. The following table provides a quick reference to each task presented in the project with its available options. The commands listed in the Menu column can be executed using either the keyboard or mouse.

Task	Mouse	Menu	Keyboard Shortcuts
Activate a Group Window	Click group window	From Window menu, choose window title	
Arrange Program-Item Icons in a Group Window		From Window menu, choose Arrange Icons	
Change the Current Drive	Click drive icon		Press TAB to move highlight to drive icon area, press arrow keys to outline drive icon, and press ENTER
Close a Group Window	Click Minimize button or double-click control-menu box	From Control menu, choose Close	Press CTRL + F4
Copy a Diskette		From Disk menu, choose Copy Disk	
Copy a File or Group of Files	Drag highlighted file-name(s) to destination drive or directory icon	From File menu, choose Copy	
Delete a File		From File menu, choose Delete	Press DEL
Format a Diskette		From Disk menu, choose Format Disk	

(continued)

QUICK REFERENCE (continued)

Task	Mouse	Menu	Keyboard Shortcuts
Maximize a Directory Window	Click Maximize button	From Control menu, choose Maximize	
Minimize an Application Window	Click Minimize button	From Control menu, choose Minimize	Press ALT, SPACE BAR, N
Rename a File		From File menu, choose Rename	
Resize a Window	Drag window border or corner	From Control menu, choose Size	
Save Changes when Quitting File Manager		From Options menu, choose Save Settings on Exit if no check mark precedes command	
Save No Changes when Quitting Windows		From Options menu, choose Save Settings on Exit if check mark precedes command	
Search for a Help Topic		From Help menu, choose Search for Help on	
Select a File in the Contents List	Click the filename		Press arrow keys to outline filename, press SHIFT + F8
Select a Group of Files in the Contents List	Select first file, hold down CTRL key and select other files		Press arrow keys to outline first file, press SHIFT + F8, press arrow keys to outline each additional filename, and press SPACEBAR
Switch between Applications	Click application window		Hold down ALT, press TAB (or ESC), release ALT

S T U D E N T   A S S I G N M E N T S

STUDENT ASSIGNMENT 1
True/False

Instructions: Circle T if the statement is true or F if the statement if false.

T F 1. Formatting prepares a diskette for use on a computer.

T F 2. It is not important to create a backup diskette of the Business Documents diskette.

T F 3. Program Manager is an application you can use to organize and work with your hard disk and diskettes and the files on those disks.

T F 4. A directory window title bar usually contains the current directory path.

T F 5. A directory window consists of a directory tree and contents list.

T F 6. The directory tree contains a list of the files in the current directory.

T F 7. The disk capacity of a 3 1/2-inch diskette is typically 360K or 1.2MB.

T F 8. The source drive is the drive from which files are copied.

T F 9. You select a single file in the contents list by pointing to the filename and clicking the left mouse button.

T F 10. You select a group of files in the contents list by pointing to each filename and clicking the left mouse button.

T F 11. Windows opens the Error Copying File dialog box if you try to copy a file to an unformatted diskette.

T F 12. You change the filename or extension of a file using the Change command.

T F 13. Windows opens the Confirm File Delete dialog box when you try to delete a file.

T F 14. When creating a backup diskette, the disk to receive the copy is the source disk.

T F 15. The first step in creating a backup diskette is to choose the Copy Disk command from the Disk menu.

T F 16. On some computers, you may have to insert and remove the source and destination diskettes several times to copy a diskette.

T F 17. Both the Search for Help on command and the Search button initiate a search for help.

T F 18. An application icon represents an application that was started and then minimized.

T F 19. You hold down the TAB key, press the ALT key, and then release the TAB key to switch between applications on the desktop.

T F 20. An application icon displays on the desktop when you minimize an application window.

STUDENT ASSIGNMENT 2
Multiple Choice

Instructions: Circle the correct response.

1. The _____ application allows you to format a diskette.
   a. Program Manager
   b. File Manager
   c. online Help
   d. Paintbrush

2. The _____ contains the directory structure of the current drive.
   a. contents list
   b. status bar
   c. split bar
   d. directory tree

3. The _____ key is used when selecting a group of files.
   a. CTRL
   b. ALT
   c. TAB
   d. ESC

4. After selecting a group of files, you _____ the group of files to copy the files to a new drive or directory.
   a. click
   b. double-click
   c. drag
   d. none of the above

5. The commands to rename and delete a file are located on the _____ menu.
   a. Window
   b. Options
   c. Disk
   d. File

6. The first step in creating a backup diskette is to _____.
   a. write-protect the destination diskette
   b. choose the Copy command from the Disk menu
   c. write-protect the source diskette
   d. label the destination diskette

STUDENT ASSIGNMENT 2 (continued)

7. When searching for help, the _____ button displays a list of Help topics.
   a. Go To
   b. Topics
   c. Show Topics
   d. Search

8. You use the _____ and _____ keys to switch between applications on the desktop.
   a. ALT, TAB
   b. SHIFT, ALT
   c. ALT, CTRL
   d. ESC, CTRL

9. When you choose a window title from the Window menu, Windows _____ the associated group window.
   a. opens
   b. closes
   c. enlarges
   d. activates

10. To resize a group window, you can use the _____.
    a. title bar
    b. window border
    c. resize command on the Window menu
    d. arrange Icons command on the Options menu

STUDENT ASSIGNMENT 3
Identifying the Parts of a Directory Window

Instructions: On the desktop in Figure SA2-3, arrows point to several items in the C:\WINDOWS*.* directory window. Identify the items in the space provided.

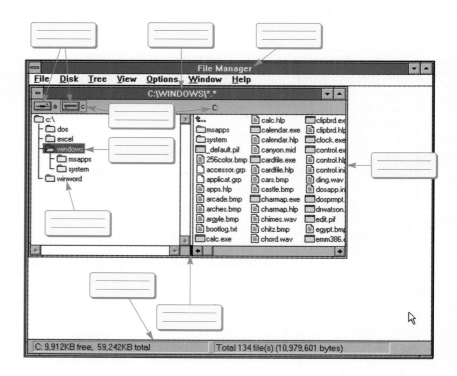

FIGURE SA2-3

STUDENT ASSIGNMENT 4
Selecting a Group of Files

Instructions: Using the desktop in Figure SA2-4, list the steps to select the group of files consisting of the ARCADE.BMP, CARS.BMP, and EGYPT.BMP files in the space provided.

FIGURE SA2-4

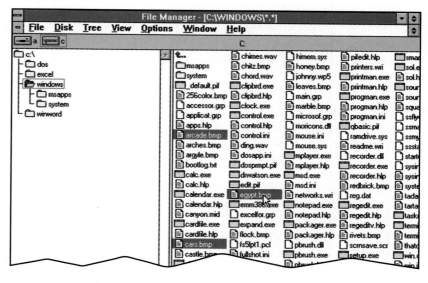

Step 1: _____

Step 2: _____

Step 3: _____

Step 4: _____

STUDENT ASSIGNMENT 5
Copying a Group of Files

Instructions: Using the desktop in Figure SA2-5, list the steps to copy the group of files selected in Student Assignment 4 to the root directory of drive A. Write the steps in the space provided.

FIGURE SA2-5

Step 1: _____

Step 2: _____

Step 3: _____

Step 4: _____

STUDENT ASSIGNMENT 6
Searching for Help

Instructions: Using the desktop in Figure SA2-6, list the steps to complete the search for the Using the Keyboard to Select Files help topic. The mouse pointer points to the down scroll arrow. Write the steps in the space provided.

FIGURE SA2-6

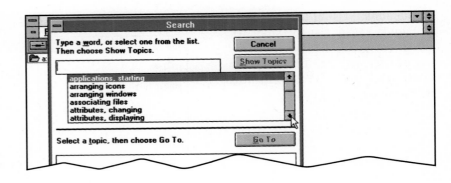

Step 1: _____

Step 2: _____

Step 3: _____

Step 4: _____

Step 5: _____

Step 6: _____

C O M P U T E R   L A B O R A T O R Y   E X E R C I S E S

COMPUTER LABORATORY EXERCISE 1
Selecting and Copying Files

Instructions: Perform the following tasks using a computer.

Part 1:

1. Start Windows.
2. Double-click the File Manager icon to start File Manager.
3. Click the Maximize button on the File Manager window to enlarge the File Manager window.
4. Click the Maximize button on the C:\WINDOWS*.* window to enlarge the C:\WINDOWS*.* window.
5. Select the CHITZ.BMP file.
6. Hold down the CTRL key and click the LEAVES.BMP filename to select the LEAVES.BMP file. The CHITZ.BMP and LEAVES.BMP files should both be highlighted.
7. Insert the Student Diskette into drive A.
8. Drag the group of files to the drive A icon.
9. Choose the Yes button in the Confirm Mouse Operation dialog box.
10. Choose the drive A icon to change the current drive to drive A.
11. Select the CHITZ.BMP file.
12. Choose the Delete command from the File menu.
13. Choose the OK button in the Delete dialog box.
14. Choose the Yes button in the Confirm File Delete dialog box.
15. If the LEAVES.BMP file is not highlighted, select the LEAVES.BMP file.

16. Choose the Rename command from the File menu.
17. Type AUTUMN.BMP in the To text box.
18. Choose the OK button in the Rename dialog box to rename the LEAVES.BMP file.

Part 2:

1. Hold down the ALT key, press the TAB key, and release the ALT key to switch to the Program Manager application.
2. Double-click the Accessories icon to open the Accessories window.
3. Double-click the Paintbrush icon to start Paintbrush.
4. Click the Maximize button on the Paintbrush window to enlarge the Paintbrush window.
5. Choose the Open command from the File menu.
6. Click the Down Arrow button in the Drives drop down list box to display the Drives drop down list.
7. Select the drive A icon.
8. Select the AUTUMN.BMP file in the File Name list box.
9. Choose the OK button to retrieve the AUTUMN.BMP file into Paintbrush.
10. Choose the Print command from the File menu.
11. Click the Draft option button in the Print dialog box.
12. Choose the OK button in the Print dialog box to print the contents of the AUTUMN.BMP file.
13. Remove the Student Diskette from drive A.
14. Choose the Exit command from the File menu to quit Paintbrush.
15. Hold down the ALT key, press the TAB key, and release the ALT key to switch to the File Manager application.
16. Select the Options menu.
17. If a check mark precedes the Save Settings on Exit command, choose the Save Settings on Exit command.
18. Choose the Exit command from the File menu of the File Manager window to quit File Manager.
19. Choose the Exit Windows command from the File menu of the Program Manager window.
20. Click the OK button to quit Windows.

COMPUTER LABORATORY EXERCISE 2
Searching with Online Help

Instructions: Perform the following tasks using a computer.

1. Start Microsoft Windows.
2. Double-click the Accessories icon to open the Accessories window.
3. Double-click the Write icon to start the Write application.
4. Click the Maximize button on the Write window to enlarge the Write window.
5. Choose the Search for Help on command from the Help menu.
6. Scroll the Search For list box to make the cutting text topic visible.
7. Select the cutting text topic.
8. Choose the Show Topics button.
9. Choose the Go To button to display the Copying, Cutting, and Pasting Text topic.
10. Click the Maximize button on the Write Help window to enlarge the window.
11. Choose the Print Topic command from the File menu to print the Copying, Cutting, and Pasting Text topic on the printer.
12. Choose the Search button.
13. Enter the word paste in the Search For list box.
14. Select the Pasting Pictures search topic.
15. Choose the Show Topics button.
16. Choose the Go To button to display the Copying, Cutting, and Pasting Pictures topic.
17. Choose the Print Topic command from the File menu to print the Copying, Cutting, and Pasting Pictures topic on the printer.

COMPUTER LABORATORY EXERCISE 2 (continued)

18. Choose the Exit command from the File menu to quit Write Help.
19. Choose the Exit command from the File menu to quit Write.
20. Select the Options menu.
21. If a check mark precedes the Save Settings on Exit command, choose the Save Settings on Exit command.
22. Choose the Exit Windows command from the File menu.
23. Click the OK button to quit Windows.

COMPUTER LABORATORY EXERCISE 3
Working with Group Windows

Instructions: Perform the following tasks using a computer.

1. Start Windows. The Main window should be open in the Program Manger window.
2. Double-click the Accessories icon to open the Accessories window.
3. Double-click the Games icon to open the Games window.
4. Choose the Accessories window title from the Window menu to activate the Accessories window.
5. Click the Minimize button on the Accessories window to close the Accessories window.
6. Choose the **Tile command** from the Window menu. The Tile command arranges a group of windows so no windows overlap, all windows are visible, and each window occupies an equal portion of the screen.
7. Move and resize the Main and Games windows to resemble the desktop in Figure CLE2-3. To resize a window, drag the window border or corner. To move a group window, drag the window title bar. Choose the Arrange Icons command from the Window menu to arrange the icons in each window.

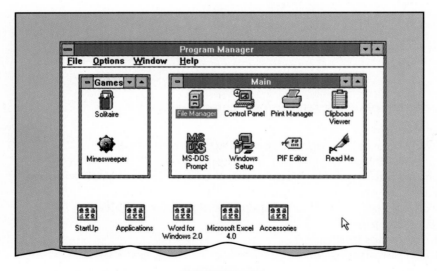

FIGURE CLE2-3

8. Press the PRINTSCREEN key to capture the desktop.
9. Open the Accessories window.
10. Choose the **Cascade command** from the Window menu. The Cascade command arranges a group of windows so the windows overlap and the title bar of each window is visible.
11. Double-click the Paintbrush icon to start Paintbrush.
12. Click the Maximize button on the Paintbrush window to enlarge the Paintbrush window.
13. Choose the Paste command from the Edit menu to place the picture of the desktop in the window.
14. Choose the Print command from the File menu.

15. Click the Draft option button.
16. Choose the OK button in the Print dialog box to print the desktop.
17. Choose the Exit command from the File menu of the Paintbrush window.
18. Choose the No button to not save current changes and quit Paintbrush.
19. Select the Options menu.
20. If a check mark precedes the Save Settings on Exit command, choose the Save Settings on Exit command.
21. Choose the Exit Windows command from the File menu.
22. Click the OK button.

COMPUTER LABORATORY EXERCISE 4
Backing Up Your Student Diskette

Instructions: Perform the following tasks using a computer to back up your Student Diskette.

Part 1:

1. Start Windows.
2. Double-click the File Manager icon to start the File Manager application.
3. Click the Maximize button on the File Manager window to enlarge the File Manager window.
4. Write-protect the Student Diskette.
5. Choose the Copy Disk command from the Disk menu.
6. Choose the Yes button in the Confirm Copy Disk dialog box.
7. Insert the source diskette (Student Diskette) into drive A.
8. Choose the OK button in the Copy Disk dialog box.
9. When prompted, insert the destination diskette (the formatted diskette created in this project) into drive A.
10. Choose the OK button in the Copy Disk dialog box.
11. Insert and remove the source and destination diskette until the copy process is complete.
12. Click the drive A icon to change the current drive to drive A.
13. Press the PRINTSCREEN key to capture the desktop.
14. Select the Options menu on the File Manager menu bar.
15. If a check mark precedes the Save Settings on Exit command, choose the Save Settings on Exit command.
16. Choose the Exit command from the File menu on the File Manager menu bar to quit File Manager.

Part 2:

1. Double-click the Accessories icon to open the Accessories window.
2. Double-click the Paintbrush icon to start Paintbrush.
3. Click the Maximize button to enlarge the Paintbrush window.
4. Choose the Paste command from the Edit menu to place the picture of the desktop in the window.
5. Choose the Print command from the File menu.
6. Click the Draft option button.
7. Choose the OK button in the Print dialog box to print the picture of the desktop on the printer.
8. Choose the Exit command from the File menu.
9. Choose the No button to not save current changes and quit Paintbrush.
10. Select the Options menu.
11. If a check mark precedes the Save Settings on Exit command, choose the Save Settings on Exit command.
12. Choose the Exit Windows command from the File menu of the Program Manager menu bar.
13. Click the OK button to quit Windows.
14. Remove the diskette from drive A.
15. Remove the write-protection from the Student Diskette.

SPREADSHEETS

USING MICROSOFT EXCEL 5 FOR WINDOWS

$\mathcal{M}$ICROSOFT $\mathcal{E}$XCEL 5 FOR $\mathcal{W}$INDOWS

BUILDING A WORKSHEET

OBJECTIVES You will have mastered the material in this project when you can:

- ▸ Start Excel
- ▸ Describe the Excel worksheet and workbook
- ▸ Select a cell or range of cells
- ▸ Enter text and numbers
- ▸ Use the AutoSum button to sum a range of cells
- ▸ Copy a cell to a range of cells using the fill handle
- ▸ Change the size of the font in a cell
- ▸ Bold entries on a worksheet
- ▸ Center cell contents over a series of columns
- ▸ Apply the AutoFormat command to format a range

- ▸ Use the reference area to select a cell
- ▸ Create a column chart using the ChartWizard
- ▸ Save a workbook
- ▸ Print a worksheet
- ▸ Open a workbook
- ▸ Quit Excel
- ▸ Correct errors on a worksheet
- ▸ Use Excel online Help
- ▸ Use Excel online tutorials
- ▸ Use the TipWizard
- ▸ Plan a worksheet

▶ WHAT IS EXCEL?

xcel is a spreadsheet program that allows you to organize data, complete calculations, make decisions, graph data, and develop professional look- ing reports. The three major parts of Excel are:

- ▸ *Worksheets* Worksheets allow you to enter, calculate, manipulate, and analyze data such as numbers and text.
- ▸ *Charts* Charts pictorially represent data. Excel can draw two-dimensional and three-dimensional column charts, pie charts, and other types of charts.
- ▸ *Databases* Databases manage data. For example, once you enter data onto a worksheet, Excel can sort the data, search for specific data, and select data that meets certain criteria.

▶ PROJECT ONE — SUN-N-SURF 1ST QUARTER TRANSMITTAL COSTS

To illustrate the features of Microsoft Excel, this book presents a series of projects that use Excel to solve typical business problems. Project 1 uses Excel to produce the worksheet and column chart shown in Figure 1-1.

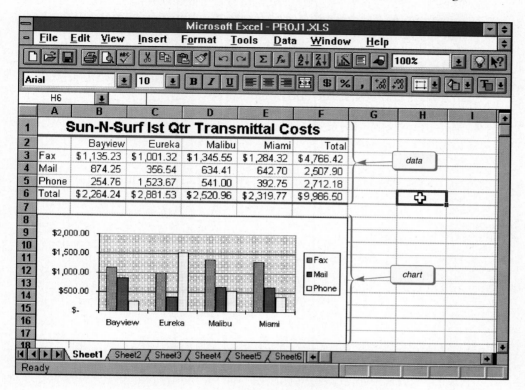

FIGURE 1-1

The worksheet contains the Sun-N-Surf 1st Quarterly Transmittal Costs (Fax, Mail, and Phone) for four locations — Bayview, Eureka, Malibu, and Miami. The worksheet also includes total transmittal costs for each city, each type of transmittal device, and the total transmittal cost for the quarter. Excel calculates the totals by summing the appropriate numbers.

Beneath the worksheet, Excel displays a column chart that it easily creates from the data contained in the worksheet. The column chart compares the three transmittal costs for each of the four cities. For example, you can see from the column chart that for the Eureka office during the first quarter, the greatest transmittal expense was the phone and the smallest transmittal expense was the mail.

Worksheet and Column Chart Preparation Steps

The steps on the next page provide you with an overview of how the worksheet and chart in Figure 1-1 will be built in this project. If you are building the worksheet and chart in this project on a personal computer, read these ten steps without doing them.

1. Start the Excel program.
2. Enter the worksheet title (Sun-N-Surf 1st Qtr Transmittal Costs), the column titles (Bayview, Eureka, Malibu, Miami, and Total), and the row titles (Fax, Mail, Phone, and Total).
3. Enter the first quarter costs (fax, mail, phone) for Bayview, Eureka, Malibu, and Miami.
4. Use the AutoSum button to calculate the first quarter totals for each city, for each type of transmittal, and for the total quarterly transmittal cost for Sun-N-Surf.
5. Format the worksheet title (center it across the five columns, enlarge it, and make it bold).
6. Format the body of the worksheet (add underlines, display the numbers in dollars and cents, and add dollar signs).
7. Direct Excel to create the chart.
8. Save the workbook on disk.
9. Print the worksheet.
10. Quit Excel.

The following pages contain a detailed explanation of each of these steps.

▶ STARTING EXCEL

o start Excel, the Windows Program Manager must display on the screen and the Microsoft Office group window must be open. Perform the following steps to start Excel.

TO START EXCEL ▼

STEP 1 ▶

Use the mouse to point to the Microsoft Excel program-item icon in the Microsoft Office group window (Figure 1-2).

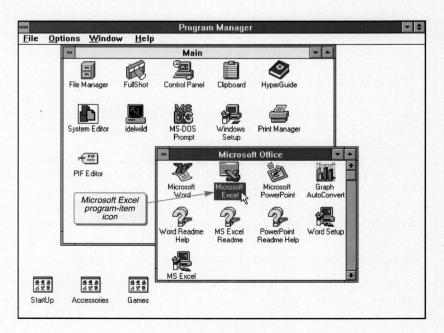

FIGURE 1-2

STEP 2 ▶

Double-click the left mouse button. If necessary, enlarge the window by clicking the Maximize button in the upper right corner of the window.

Excel displays an empty workbook titled Book1 (Figure 1-3).

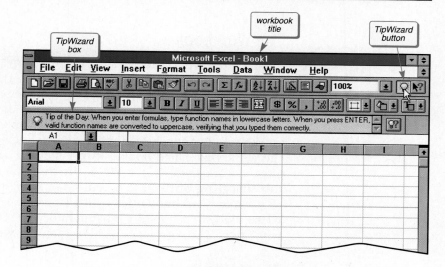

FIGURE 1-3

STEP 3 ▶

If the TipWizard box displays (Figure 1-3), point to the TipWizard button on the Standard toolbar (🔍) and click the left mouse button.

Excel removes the TipWizard box from the window and increases the display of the worksheet (Figure 1-4). The purpose of the TipWizard box will be discussed later in this project.

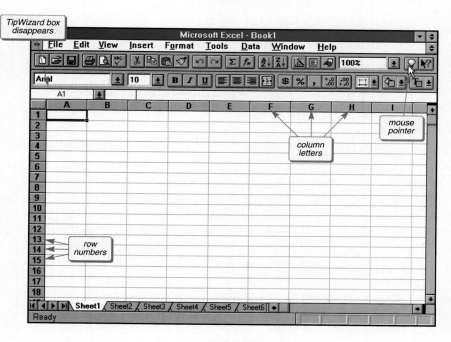

FIGURE 1-4

▶ THE EXCEL WINDOW

The Excel window consists of a variety of features to make your work more efficient. It contains a title bar, menu bar, toolbars, formula bar, the worksheet window, sheet tabs, scroll bars, and the status bar. Each of these Excel window features and its components is described in this section.

The Workbook

When Excel starts, it creates a new empty workbook, called Book1. The **workbook** (Figure 1-5), is like a notebook. Inside the workbook are sheets, called **worksheets**. On each worksheet you can enter any number of sets of data and charts. Usually, however, you enter one set of data and possibly one or more charts per worksheet. Each sheet name appears on a **sheet tab** at the bottom of the workbook. For example, Sheet1 is the name of the active worksheet displayed in the workbook called Book1. If you click the tab labeled Sheet2, Excel displays the Sheet2 worksheet. To the left of the sheet tabs are the tab scrolling buttons. The **tab scrolling buttons** can be used to scroll through the sheet tabs.

A new workbook opens with 16 worksheets. If necessary, you can add additional worksheets up to a maximum of 255. This project will only use the Sheet1 worksheet. Later projects will use multiple worksheets.

The Worksheet

The worksheet is organized into a rectangular grid containing columns (vertical) and rows (horizontal). A column letter above the grid, also called the column heading, identifies each **column**. A row number on the left side of the grid, also called the row heading, identifies each **row**. Nine complete columns (A through I) and eighteen complete rows (1 through 18) of the worksheet display on the screen when the worksheet is maximized and the TipWizard box is closed (Figure 1-5).

Cell, Gridlines, Active Cell, and Mouse Pointer

The intersection of each column and row is a **cell**. A cell is the basic unit of a worksheet into which you enter data. A cell is referred to by its unique address, or **cell reference**, which is composed of the coordinates of the intersection of a column and a row. To identify a cell, specify the column letter first, followed by the row number. For example, cell reference D3 refers to the cell located at the intersection of column D and row 3 (Figure 1-5).

The horizontal and vertical lines on the worksheet itself are called **gridlines**. Gridlines make it easier to see and identify each cell on the worksheet. If desired, you can remove the gridlines from the worksheet, but it is recommended that you leave the gridlines on.

One cell on the worksheet, designated the **active cell**, is the one in which you can enter data. The active cell in Figure 1-5 is A1. Cell A1 is identified in two ways. First, a heavy border surrounds the cell. Second, the **active cell reference** displays immediately above column A in the **reference area** in the formula bar.

The mouse pointer can become one of fourteen different shapes, depending on the task you are performing in Excel and the pointer's location on the screen. The mouse pointer in Figure 1-5 has the shape of a block plus sign (✛). The mouse pointer displays as a block plus sign whenever it is located in a cell on the worksheet.

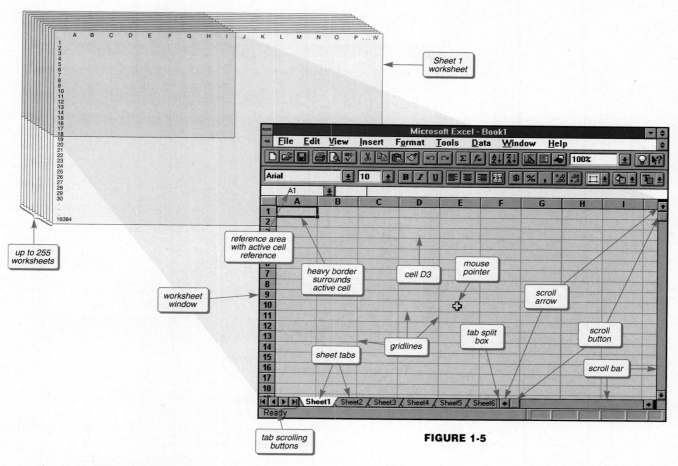

FIGURE 1-5

Another common shape of the mouse pointer is the block arrow (⬚). The mouse pointer turns into the block arrow whenever you move it outside the window or when you drag cell contents between rows or columns.

The other mouse pointer shapes are described when they appear on the screen during this and subsequent projects.

Worksheet Window

Each worksheet in a workbook has 256 columns and 16,384 rows for a total of 4,194,304 cells. The column headings begin with A and end with IV. The row headings begin with 1 and end with 16,384. Only a small fraction of the active worksheet displays on the screen at one time. You view the portion of the worksheet displayed on the screen through a **worksheet window** (Figure 1-5). Below and to the right of the worksheet window are the **scroll bars**, **scroll arrows**, and **scroll boxes,** which you can use to move the window around the active worksheet. To the right of the sheet tabs is the tab split box. You can drag the **tab split box** to increase or decrease the length of the horizontal scroll bar.

Menu Bar, Standard Toolbar, Formatting Toolbar, Formula Bar, and Status Bar

The menu bar, Standard toolbar, Formatting toolbar, and formula bar appear at the top of the screen just below the title bar (Figure 1-6 on the next page). The status bar appears at the bottom of the screen.

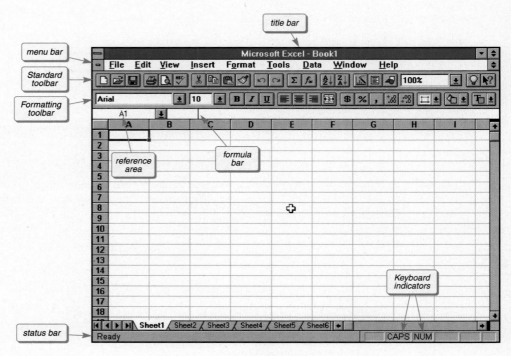

FIGURE 1-6

MENU BAR   The **menu bar** displays the Excel menu names (Figure 1-6). Each menu name represents a pull-down menu of commands that you can use to retrieve, store, print, and manipulate data on the worksheet. To pull down a menu, such as the **File menu**, select the menu name by clicking it.

The menu bar can change to include other menu names, depending on the type of work you are doing in Excel. For example, if you are working with a chart sheet rather than a worksheet, the menu bar will consist of menu names for use specifically with charts.

STANDARD TOOLBAR AND FORMATTING TOOLBAR   The **Standard toolbar** and **Formatting toolbar** (Figure 1-6) contain buttons and drop-down list boxes that allow you to perform frequent tasks quicker than when using the menu bar. For example, to print, you point to the Print button and press the left mouse button. Each button has a picture on the button face that helps you remember the button's function. In addition, when you move the mouse pointer over a button or box, the name of the button or box appears below it.

Figures 1-7a and 1-7b illustrate the Standard and Formatting tool-bars and describe the functions of the buttons. Each of the buttons and drop-down list boxes will be explained in detail when they are used in the projects.

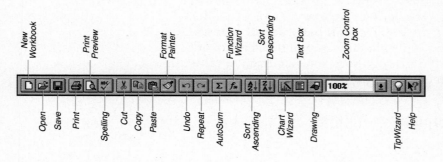

FIGURE 1-7a

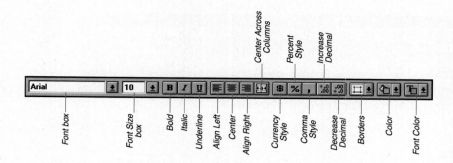

FIGURE 1-7b

Excel has several additional toolbars you can activate through the View menu on the menu bar.

FORMULA BAR   Below the Formatting toolbar is the **formula bar** (Figure 1-6). As you type, the data appears in the formula bar. Excel also displays the active cell reference on the left side of the formula bar in the reference area.

STATUS BAR   The left side of the **status bar** at the bottom of the screen displays a brief description of the command selected (highlighted) in a menu, the function of the button the mouse pointer is on, or the current activity (mode) in progress (Figure 1-6). **Mode indicators**, such as Enter and Ready, specify the current mode of Excel. When the mode is Ready, as shown in Figure 1-6, Excel is ready to accept the next command or data entry. When the mode indicator is Enter, Excel is in the process of accepting data for the active cell.

Keyboard indicators, such as CAPS (Caps Lock), OVR (overtype), and NUM (Num Lock), indicate which keys are engaged and display on the right side of the status bar within the small rectangular boxes (Figure 1-6).

▶ SELECTING A CELL

To enter data into a cell, you must first select it. The easiest way to **select a cell** (make active) is to use the mouse to move the block plus sign to the cell and click the left mouse button.

An alternative method is to use the **arrow keys** that are located just to the right of the typewriter keys on the keyboard. An arrow key selects the cell adjacent to the active cell in the direction of the arrow on the key.

You know a cell is selected (active) when a heavy border surrounds the cell and the active cell reference displays in the reference area in the formula bar.

▶ ENTERING TEXT

In Excel, any set of characters containing a letter is considered **text**. Text is used to place titles on the worksheet, such as the spreadsheet titles, column titles, and row titles. In Project 1 (Figure 1-8 on the next page), the centered worksheet title Sun-N-Surf 1st Qtr Transmittal Costs identifies the worksheet. The column titles are the names of cities (Bayview, Eureka, Malibu, and Miami) and Total. The row titles (Fax, Mail, Phone, and Total) identify the data in each row.

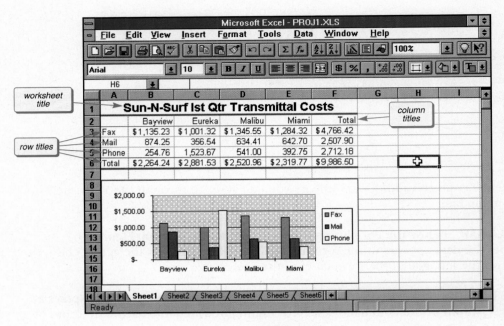

FIGURE 1-8

Entering the Worksheet Title

The following example explains the steps to enter the worksheet title into cell A1. Later in this project, the worksheet title will be centered over the column titles.

TO ENTER THE WORKSHEET TITLE ▼

STEP 1 ►

Select cell A1 by pointing to it and clicking the left mouse button.

Cell A1 becomes the active cell and a heavy border surrounds it (Figure 1-9).

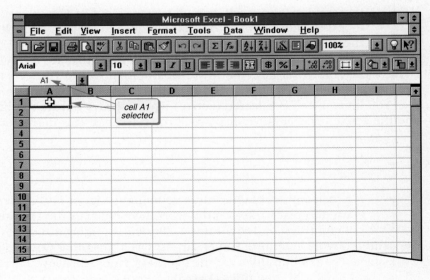

FIGURE 1-9

STEP 2 ▶

Type Sun-N-Surf 1st Qtr Transmittal Costs

*When you type the first character, the mode indicator in the status bar changes from Ready to Enter and Excel displays two boxes: one called the **cancel box** (☒) and the other called the **enter box** (☑) in the formula bar (Figure 1-10). The entire title displays in the formula bar. The text also appears in cell A1 followed immediately by the insertion point. The **insertion point** is a blinking vertical line that indicates where the next character typed will appear.*

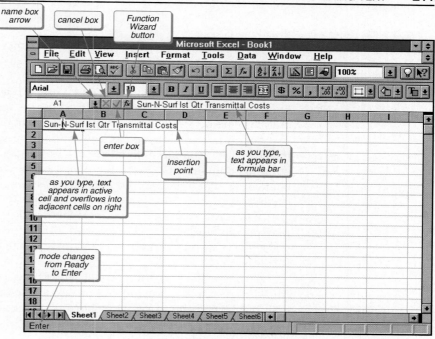

FIGURE 1-10

STEP 3 ▶

After you type the text, point to the enter box (Figure 1-11).

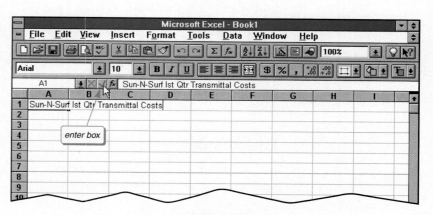

FIGURE 1-11

STEP 4 ▶

Click the left mouse button to complete the entry.

Excel enters the worksheet title in cell A1 (Figure 1-12).

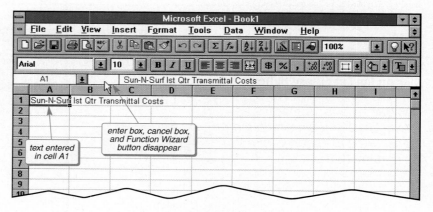

FIGURE 1-12

In the previous example, instead of using the mouse to complete an entry, you can press the **ENTER key** after typing the text. Pressing the ENTER key replaces Step 3 and Step 4.

When you complete a text entry into a cell, a series of events occurs. First, Excel positions the text **left-justified** in the active cell. Therefore, the S in the company name Sun-N-Surf begins in the leftmost position of cell A1.

Second, when the text is longer than the width of a column, Excel displays the overflow characters in adjacent cells to the right as long as these adjacent columns contain no data. In Figure 1-12, the width of cell A1 is approximately nine characters. The text entered consists of 35 characters. Therefore, Excel displays the overflow characters in cells B1, C1, and D1 because all three cells are empty.

If cell B1 contained data, only the first nine characters of cell A1 would display on the worksheet. Excel would hide the overflow characters, but they would still remain stored in cell A1 and display in the formula bar whenever cell A1 was the active cell.

Third, when you complete an entry into a cell by clicking the enter box or pressing the ENTER key, the cell in which the text is entered remains the active cell. If pressing the ENTER key changes the active cell, then select the Move Selection after Enter check box on the Edit tab that displays when you choose the Options command from the Tools menu.

Correcting a Mistake While Typing

If you type the wrong letter and notice the error before clicking the enter box or pressing the ENTER key, use the **BACKSPACE key** to erase all the characters back to and including the one that is wrong. To cancel the entire entry before entering it into the cell, click the cancel box in the formula bar or press the **ESC key**. If you see an error in a cell, select the cell and retype the entry. Later in this project, additional error-correction techniques are covered.

Entering Column Titles

To enter the column titles, select the appropriate cell and then enter the text, as described in the following steps.

TO ENTER THE COLUMN TITLES ▼

STEP 1 ▶

Select cell B2 by pointing to it and clicking the left mouse button.

Cell B2 becomes the active cell. The active cell reference in the reference area changes from A1 to B2 (Figure 1-13).

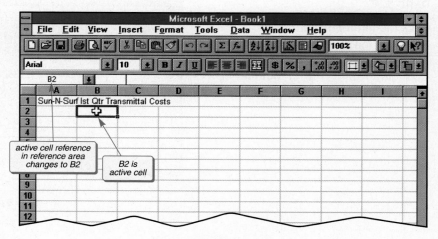

FIGURE 1-13

STEP 2 ▶

Type the column title Bayview

Excel displays Bayview in the formula bar and in cell B2 (Figure 1-14).

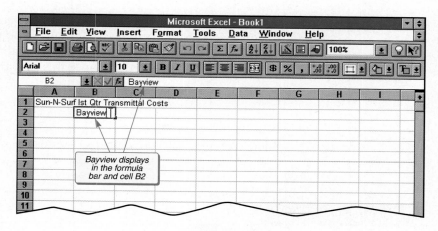

FIGURE 1-14

STEP 3 ▶

Press the RIGHT ARROW key.

Excel enters the column title, Bayview, in cell B2 and makes cell C2 the active cell (Figure 1-15). When you press an arrow key to complete an entry, the adjacent cell in the direction of the arrow (up, down, left, or right) becomes the active cell.

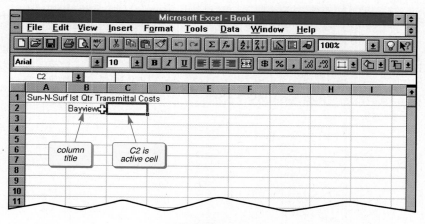

FIGURE 1-15

STEP 4 ▶

Repeat Step 2 and Step 3 for the remaining column titles in row 2. That is, enter Eureka **in cell C2,** Malibu **in cell D2,** Miami **in cell E2, and** Total **in cell F2. Complete the last column title entry in cell F2 by clicking the enter box or by pressing the ENTER key.**

The column titles display left-justified as shown in Figure 1-16.

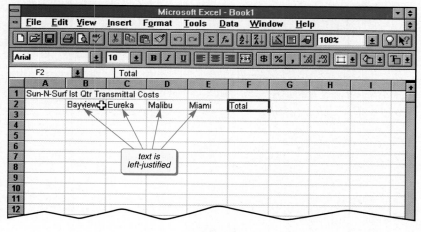

FIGURE 1-16

To complete an entry in a cell, use the arrow keys if the next entry is in an adjacent cell. If the next entry is not in an adjacent cell, click the next cell in which you plan to enter data or click the enter box in the formula bar or press the ENTER key and then use the mouse to select the appropriate cell for the next entry.

Entering Row Titles

The next step in developing the worksheet in Project 1 is to enter the row titles in column A. This process is similar to entering the column titles and is described in the following steps.

TO ENTER ROW TITLES

STEP 1 ▶

Select cell A3 by pointing to it and clicking the left mouse button.

Cell A3 becomes the active cell (Figure 1-17). The cell reference in the reference area changes from F2 to A3.

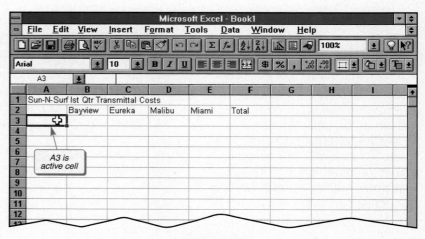

FIGURE 1-17

STEP 2 ▶

Type Fax **and press the DOWN ARROW key.**

Excel enters the row title Fax in cell A3 and cell A4 becomes the active cell (Figure 1-18).

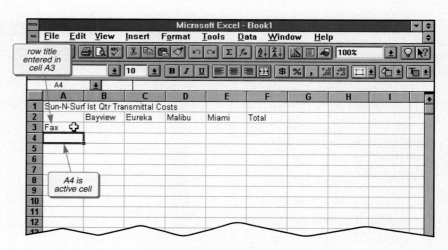

FIGURE 1-18

STEP 3 ▶

Repeat the procedure used in Step 2 for the remaining row titles in column A. Enter Mail in cell A4, Phone in cell A5, and Total in cell A6. Complete the last row title in cell A6 by clicking the enter box or by pressing the ENTER key.

The row titles display as shown in Figure 1-19.

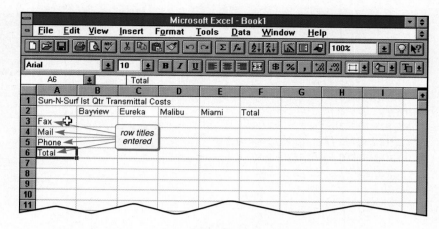

FIGURE 1-19

▶ ENTERING NUMBERS

In Excel, you can enter numbers into cells to represent amounts. **Numbers** can include the digits zero through nine and any one of the following special characters:

+ - ( ) , / . $ % E e

If a cell entry contains any other character (including spaces) from the keyboard, Excel interprets the entry as text and treats it accordingly. Use of the special characters is explained when they are required in a project.

In Project 1, the costs for Fax, Mail, and Phone for each of the four cities (Bayview, Eureka, Malibu, and Miami) are to be entered in rows three, four, and five. The following steps illustrate how to enter these values one row at a time.

TO ENTER NUMERIC DATA ▼

STEP 1 ▶

Select cell B3 by pointing to it and clicking the left mouse button.

Cell B3 becomes the active cell (Figure 1-20).

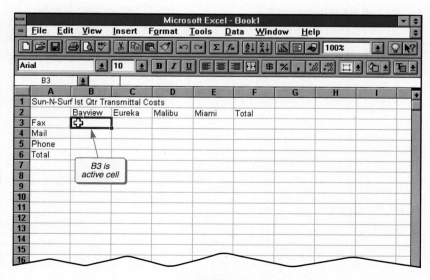

FIGURE 1-20

STEP 2 ▶

Type `1135.23` **and press the** RIGHT
ARROW **key.**

Excel enters the number 1135.23
right-justified *in cell B3 and*
changes the active cell to cell C3
(Figure 1-21). The numbers on the
worksheet are formatted with dol-
lar signs and cents later in this
project.

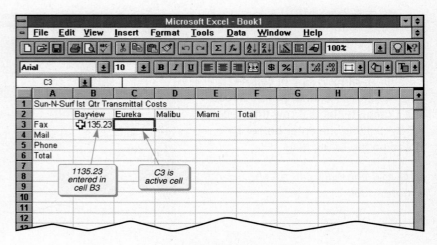

FIGURE 1-21

STEP 3 ▶

Enter `1001.32` **in cell C3,** `1345.55`
in cell D3, and `1284.32` **in cell E3.**

Row 3 now contains the first
quarter fax costs all right-justified
(Figure 1-22).

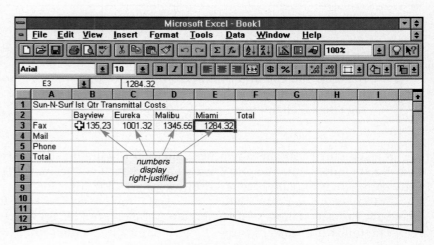

FIGURE 1-22

STEP 4 ▶

Select cell B4 (Figure 1-23).

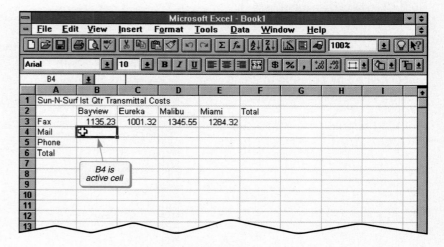

FIGURE 1-23

STEP 5 ▶

Enter the 1st Quarter mail costs for the four cities (874.25 for Bayview, 356.54 for Eureka, 634.41 for Malibu, and 642.7 for Miami) and the first quarter phone costs for the four cities (254.76 for Bayview, 1523.67 for Eureka, 541 for Malibu, and 392.75 for Miami).

The first quarter mail and phone costs for the four cities display in row 4 and row 5 (Figure 1-24).

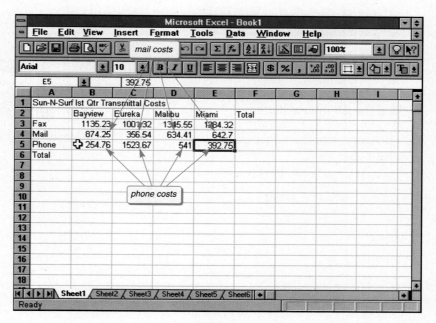

FIGURE 1-24

Step 1 through Step 5 complete the numeric entries. Notice several important points. First, you are not required to type dollar signs and trailing zeros. Later, dollar signs will be added as previously shown in Figure 1-1 on page E3. However, when you enter a number that has cents, you must add the decimal point and the numbers representing the cents when you enter the number.

Second, Excel stores numbers **right-justified** in the cells which means they occupy the rightmost positions in the cells.

Third, Excel will calculate the totals in row 6 and in column F. Indeed, the capability of Excel to perform calculations is one of its major features.

▶ CALCULATING A SUM

The next step in creating the Sun-N-Surf 1st Qtr Transmittal Costs worksheet is to determine the total costs for the Bayview office. To calculate this value in cell B6, Excel must add the numbers in cells B3, B4, and B5. Excel's **SUM function** provides a convenient means to accomplish this task.

To use the SUM function, you must first identify the cell in which the sum will be stored after it is calculated. Then, you can use the **AutoSum button** (Σ) on the Standard toolbar to enter the SUM function.

Although you can enter the SUM function in cell B6 through the keyboard as =SUM(B3:B5), the following steps illustrate how to use the AutoSum button to accomplish the same task.

TO SUM A COLUMN OF NUMBERS ▼

STEP 1 ►

Select cell B6 by pointing to it and clicking the left mouse button.

Cell B6 becomes the active cell (Figure 1-25).

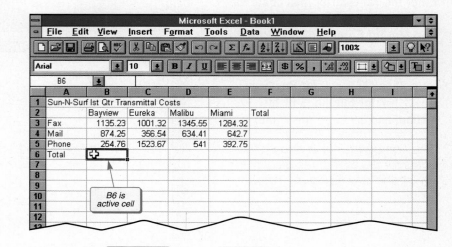

FIGURE 1-25

STEP 2 ►

Point to the AutoSum button on the Standard toolbar and click the left mouse button.

*Excel responds by displaying =SUM(B3:B5) in the formula bar and in the active cell B6 (Figure 1-26). The =SUM entry identifies the SUM function. The B3:B5 within parentheses following the function name SUM is Excel's way of identifying the cells B3, B4, and B5. Excel also surrounds the proposed cells to sum with a moving border, also called the **marquis**.*

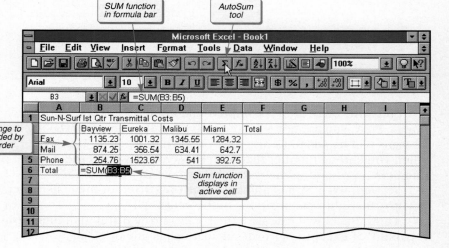

FIGURE 1-26

STEP 3 ►

Click the AutoSum button a second time.

Excel enters the sum of the costs for Bayview (2264.24 = 1135.23 + 874.25 + 254.76) in cell B6 (Figure 1-27). The function assigned to cell B6 displays in the formula bar when cell B6 is the active cell.

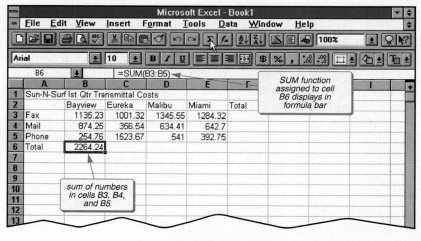

FIGURE 1-27

When you enter the SUM function using the AutoSum button, Excel automatically selects what it considers to be your choice of the group of cells to sum. The group of cells B3, B4, and B5 is called a range. A **range** is a series of two or more adjacent cells in a column or row, or a rectangular group of cells. Many Excel operations, such as summing numbers, take place on cells within a range.

In proposing the range to sum, Excel first looks for a range of cells with numbers above the active cell and then to the left. If Excel proposes the wrong range, you can drag the mouse pointer to select the correct range anytime prior to clicking the AutoSum button a second time. You can also enter the correct range in the formula bar by typing the beginning cell reference, a colon (:), and the ending cell reference.

When using the AutoSum button, you can click it once and then click the enter box or press the ENTER key to complete the entry. However, double-clicking the AutoSum button is the quickest way to enter the SUM function.

▶ USING THE FILL HANDLE TO COPY A CELL TO ADJACENT CELLS

O n the Sun-N-Surf 1st Qtr Transmittal Costs worksheet, Excel must also calculate the totals for Eureka in cell C6, for Malibu in cell D6, and for Miami in cell E6. Table 1-1 illustrates the similarity between the entry in cell B6 and the entries required for the totals in cells C6, D6, and E6.

▸ **TABLE 1-1**

CELL	SUM FUNCTION ENTRIES	REMARK
B6	=SUM(B3:B5)	Sums cells B3, B4, and B5
C6	=SUM(C3:C5)	Sums cells C3, C4, and C5
D6	=SUM(D3:D5)	Sums cells D3, D4, and D5
E6	=SUM(E3:E5)	Sums cells E3, E4, and E5

To place the SUM functions in cells C6, D6, and E6, you can follow the same steps that were shown in Figures 1-25 through 1-27. A second, more efficient method is to copy the SUM function from cell B6 to the range C6:E6. The cell being copied is called the **copy area**. The range of cells receiving the copy is called the **paste area**.

Notice from Table 1-1 that although the SUM function entries are similar, they are not exact copies. Each cell to the right of cell B6 has a range that is one column to the right of the previous column. When you copy cell addresses, Excel adjusts them for each new position, resulting in the SUM entries illustrated in Table 1-1. Each adjusted cell reference is called a **relative reference**.

The easiest way to copy the SUM formula from cell B6 to cells C6 and D6 is to use the fill handle. The **fill handle** is the small rectangular dot located in the lower right corner of the heavy border around the active cell (Figure 1-27). The following steps show how to use the fill handle to copy one cell to adjacent cells.

TO COPY ONE CELL TO ADJACENT CELLS IN A ROW ▼

STEP 1 ►

Select the copy area cell B6 by pointing to it and clicking the left mouse button. Point to the fill handle.

The mouse pointer changes from the block plus sign to a cross (✚) (Figure 1-28).

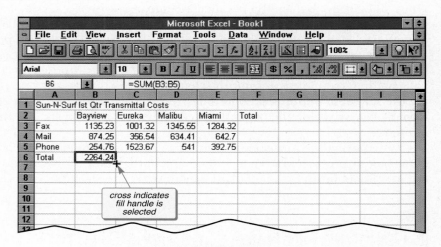

FIGURE 1-28

STEP 2 ►

Drag the fill handle to select the paste area C6:E6.

Excel shades the border of the paste area C6:E6 (Figure 1-29).

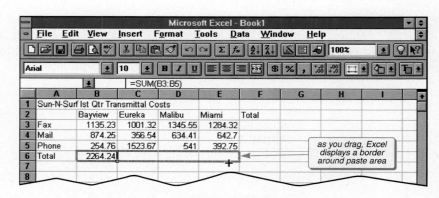

FIGURE 1-29

STEP 3 ►

Release the left mouse button.

Excel copies the SUM function in cell B6 to the range C6:E6 (Figure 1-30). In addition, Excel calculates the sums and enters the results in cells C6, D6, and E6.

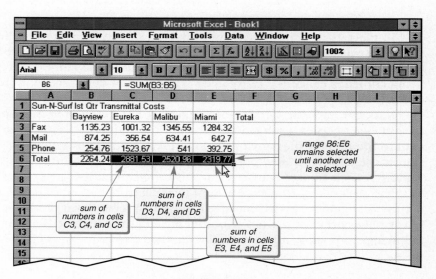

FIGURE 1-30

After the copy is complete, the range remains selected. To remove the range selection, select any cell.

Summing the Row Totals

The next step in building the Sun-N-Surf 1st Qtr Transmittal Costs worksheet is to total the fax, mail, phone, and company total costs and place the sums in column F. The SUM function is used in the same manner as it was when the costs by city were totaled in row 6. However, in this example, all the rows will be totaled at the same time. The following steps illustrate this process.

TO SUM THE ROWS

STEP 1 ►

Select cell F3 by pointing to it and clicking the left mouse button.

Cell F3 becomes the active cell (Figure 1-31).

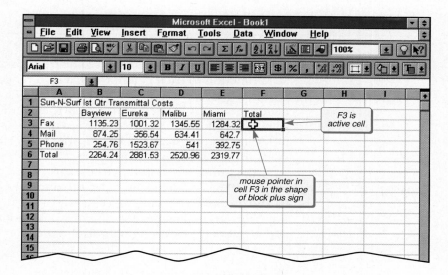

FIGURE 1-31

STEP 2 ►

With the mouse pointer in cell F3 and in the shape of a block plus sign (✚), drag the mouse pointer down to cell F6.

Excel highlights the range F3:F6 (Figure 1-32).

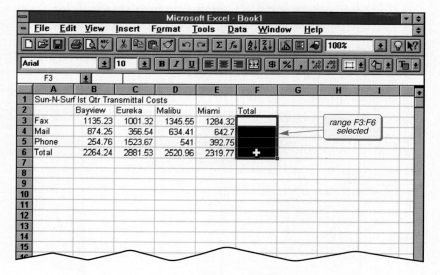

FIGURE 1-32

STEP 3 ▶

Point to the AutoSum button on the Standard toolbar and click.

Excel assigns the functions =SUM(B3:E3) to cell F3, =SUM(B4:E4) to cell F4, =SUM(B5:E5) to cell F5, and =SUM(B6:E6) to cell F6, and then computes and displays the sums in the respective cells (Figure 1-33).

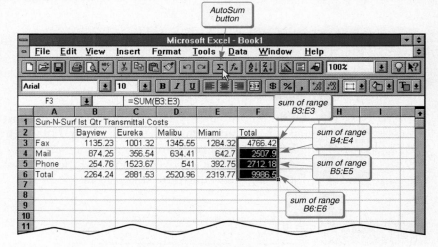

FIGURE 1-33

Because a range was selected next to rows of numbers, Excel assigned the SUM function to each cell in the selected range. Thus, four SUM functions with different ranges were assigned to the selected range, one for each row. This same procedure could have been used earlier to sum the columns. That is, rather than selecting cell B6 and double-clicking the AutoSum button and then copying the SUM function to the range C6:E6, you could have selected the range B6:E6 and clicked the AutoSum button once.

An alternative to finding the totals in row 6 and column F is to select the range B3:F6. This range includes the numbers to sum plus an additional row (row 6) and an additional column (column F). Next, click the AutoSum button. Excel immediately assigns the appropriate SUM functions to the empty cells in the range and displays the desired totals all at once.

▶ FORMATTING THE WORKSHEET

T he text, numeric entries, and functions for the worksheet are now complete. The next step is to format the worksheet. You **format** a worksheet to emphasize certain entries and make the worksheet easier to read and understand.

Figure 1-34a shows the worksheet before formatting it. Figure 1-34b shows the worksheet after formatting it. As you can see from the two figures, a worksheet that is formatted is not only easier to read, but it looks more professional.

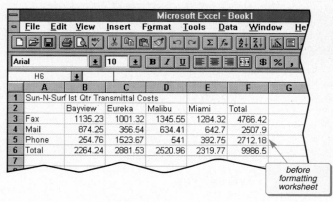

FIGURE 1-34a

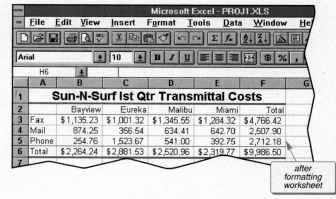

FIGURE 1-34b

To change the unformatted worksheet in Figure 1-34a to the formatted worksheet in Figure 1-34b, begin by bolding the worksheet title, Sun-N-Surf 1st Qtr Transmittal Costs, in cell A1. Next, enlarge the title and center it across columns A through F. Finally, format the body of the worksheet using the AutoFormat command. The body of the worksheet, range A2:F6, includes the column titles, row titles, and numbers. The result is numbers represented in a dollars-and-cents format, dollar signs in the first row of numbers and the total row, and underlines that emphasize portions of the worksheet.

The process required to format the Sun-N-Surf 1st Qtr Transmittal Costs worksheet is explained on the following pages.

Font, Font Size, and Font Style

Characters that appear on the screen are a specific shape and size. The **font type** defines the appearance and shape of the letters, numbers, and special characters. The **font size** specifies the size of the characters on the screen. Character size is gauged by a measurement system called points. A single **point** is about 1/72 of one inch in height. Thus, a character with a **point size** of 10 is about 10/72 of one inch in height.

Font style indicates how the characters appear. They may be normal, bold, underlined, or italicized.

When Excel begins, the default font type for the entire worksheet is Arial with a font size of 10 points, no bold, no underline, and no italic. With Excel you have the capability to change the font characteristics in a single cell, a range of cells, or for the entire worksheet.

To change the worksheet title (Sun-N-Surf 1st Qtr Transmittal Costs) from the Excel default presentation (Figure 1-34a) to the desired formatting (Figure 1-34b), these procedures must be completed: (a) the characters must be changed from normal to bold; (b) the size of the characters must be increased from 10 point to 14 point; and (c) the worksheet title must be centered across columns A through F of the worksheet.

Although the three procedures will be carried out in the order presented, you should be aware that you can make these changes in any order.

TO APPLY THE BOLD FORMAT TO A CELL ▼

STEP 1 ▶

Select cell A1 (Figure 1-35).

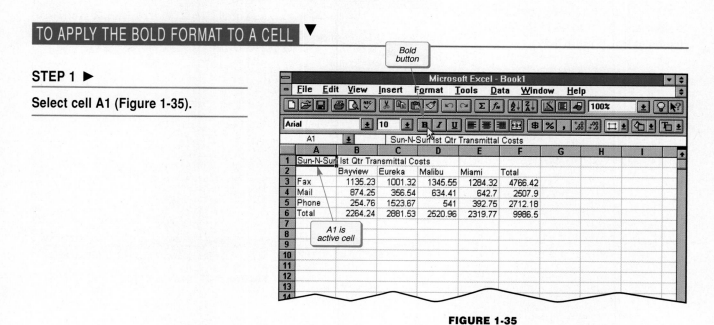

FIGURE 1-35

STEP 2 ▶

Click the Bold button (🅱) on the Formatting toolbar.

Excel applies a bold format to the worksheet title, Sun-N-Surf 1st Qtr Transmittal Costs (Figure 1-36).

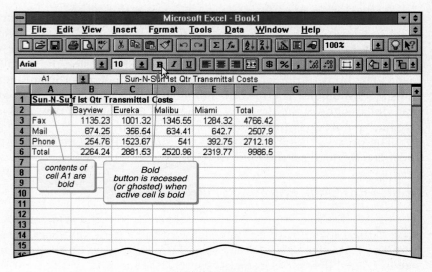

FIGURE 1-36

When the active cell is bold, the Bold button is recessed (or **ghosted**) as shown in Figure 1-36. Clicking the Bold button a second time removes the bold format and the Bold button is no longer be recessed.

Increasing the font size is the next step in formatting the worksheet title.

TO INCREASE THE FONT SIZE ▼

STEP 1 ▶

With cell A1 selected, click the Font Size box arrow on the Formatting toolbar and point to 14 in the drop-down list box (Figure 1-37).

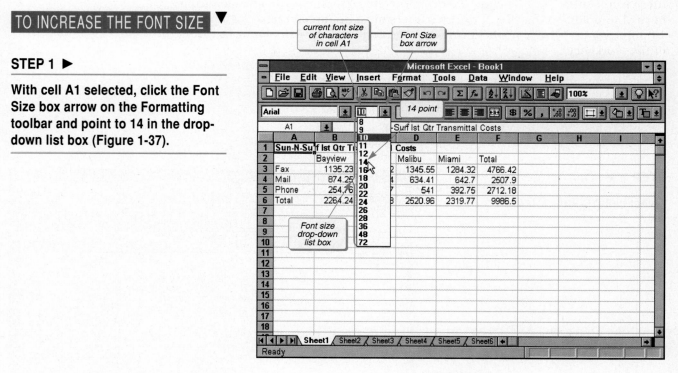

FIGURE 1-37

STEP 2 ▶

Click the left mouse button to choose 14 point.

The characters in the worksheet title in cell A1 increase from 10 point to 14 point (Figure 1-38).

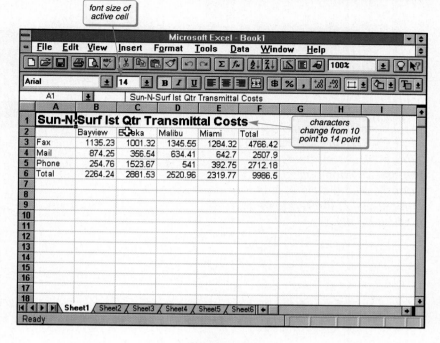

FIGURE 1-38

The final step in formatting the worksheet title is to center it over columns A through F.

TO CENTER A CELL'S CONTENTS ACROSS COLUMNS ▼

STEP 1 ▶

With cell A1 selected, drag the block plus sign to the rightmost cell (F1) in the range over which to center.

When you drag the mouse pointer over the range A1:F1, Excel highlights the cells (Figure 1-39).

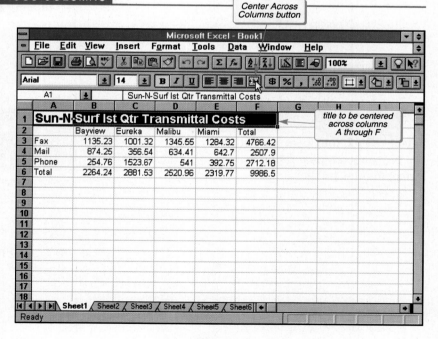

FIGURE 1-39

STEP 2 ▶

Click the Center Across Columns button ( ) on the Formatting toolbar.

Excel centers the contents of cell A1 across columns A through F (Figure 1-40). For the Center Across Columns button to work properly, all the cells except the leftmost cell in the range of cells must be empty.

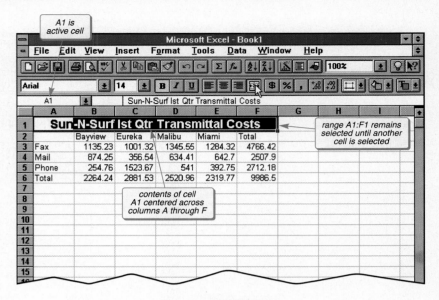

FIGURE 1-40

To remove the selection from range A1:E1, select any cell on the worksheet.

▶ USING AUTOFORMAT TO FORMAT THE WORKSHEET

xcel has several customized format styles called **table formats** that allow you to format the body of the worksheet. The table formats can be used to give a worksheet a professional appearance. Follow these steps to automatically format the range A2:F6 in the Sun-N-Surf 1st Qtr Transmittal Costs worksheet.

TO USE THE AUTOFORMAT COMMAND ▼

STEP 1 ▶

Select cell A2, the upper left corner cell of the rectangular range to format (Figure 1-41).

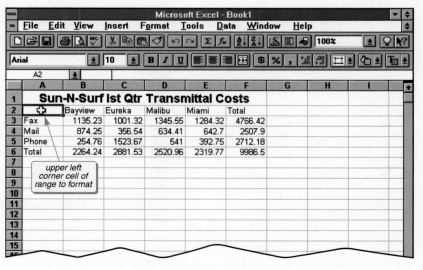

FIGURE 1-41

STEP 2 ▶

Drag the mouse pointer to cell F6, the lower right corner cell of the range to format, and release the left mouse button.

Excel highlights the range to format (Figure 1-42).

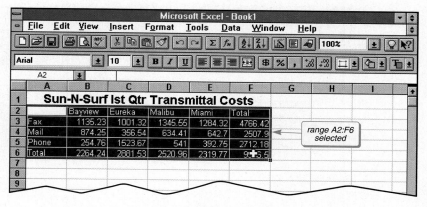

FIGURE 1-42

STEP 3 ▶

Select the Format menu.

The Format menu displays (Figure 1-43).

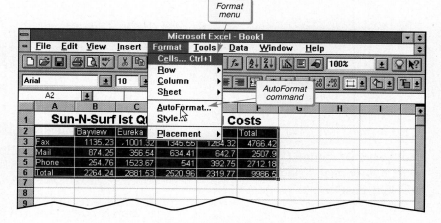

FIGURE 1-43

STEP 4 ▶

Choose the AutoFormat command.

*Excel displays the **AutoFormat dialog box** (Figure 1-44). On the left side of the dialog box is the Table Format list box with the Table Format name Simple highlighted. In the Sample area of the dialog box is a sample of the format that corresponds to the highlighted Table Format name, Simple.*

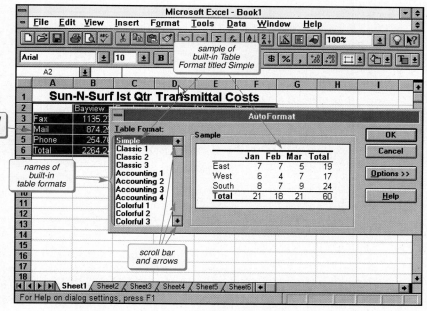

FIGURE 1-44

STEP 5 ▶

Point to Accounting 2 in the Table Format list box and click.

The Sample area in the dialog box now shows the Accounting 2 format selected (Figure 1-45).

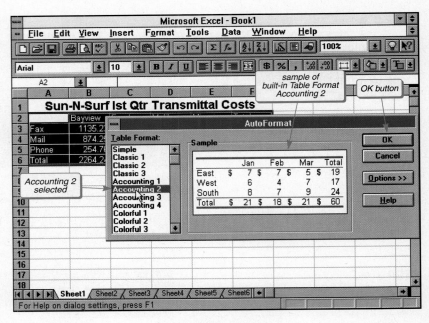

FIGURE 1-45

STEP 6 ▶

Choose the OK button (OK) in the AutoFormat dialog box. Select cell H6 to deselect the range A2:F6.

Excel displays the worksheet with the range A2:F6 using the customized format, Accounting 2 (Figure 1-46).

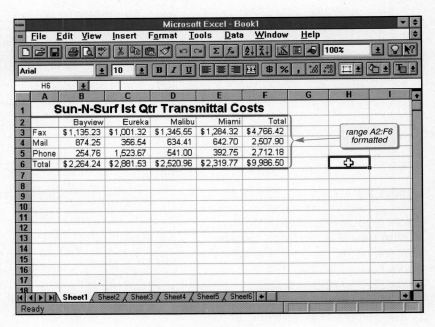

FIGURE 1-46

Excel provides fifteen customized format styles from which to choose. Each format style has different characteristics. The format characteristics associated with the customized format, Accounting 2 (Figure 1-46), include right-justification of column titles, numeric values displayed as dollars and cents, comma placement, numbers aligned on the decimal point, dollar signs in the first row of numbers and in the total row, and top and bottom borders emphasized. The width of column A has also been reduced so the longest row title fits in the column.

The worksheet is now complete. The next step is to chart the Sun-N-Surf 1st Qtr Transmittal Costs for the four offices. To create the chart, the active cell must be cell A2, the cell in the upper left corner of the range to chart. To select cell A2, you can move the mouse pointer to it and click. This is the procedure used in previous examples. You can also use the reference area in the formula bar to select a cell.

Using the Reference Area to Select a Cell

The reference area is located in the left side of the formula bar. To select any cell, click in the reference area and enter the cell reference of the cell you want to select. The following steps show how to select cell A2.

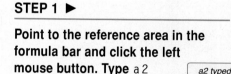
TO USE THE REFERENCE AREA TO SELECT A CELL ▼

STEP 1 ►

Point to the reference area in the formula bar and click the left mouse button. Type a 2

Even though cell H6 is the active cell, the reference area displays the cell reference a2 (Figure 1-47).

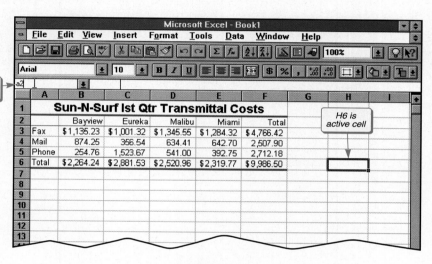

FIGURE 1-47

STEP 2 ►

Press the ENTER key.

Excel changes the active cell from cell H6 to cell A2 (Figure 1-48).

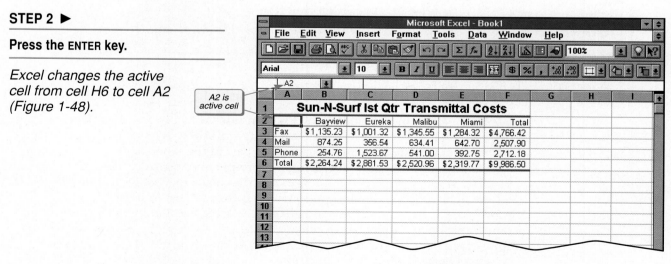

FIGURE 1-48

As you will see in later projects, besides using the reference area to select any cell, you can also click the Name box arrow to the right of the reference area to assign names to a cell or range of cells.

Excel supports several additional ways to select a cell. They are summarized in Table 1-2.

▸ **TABLE 1-2**

KEY, BOX, OR COMMAND	FUNCTION
ARROW	Selects the adjacent cell in the direction of the arrow on the key.
HOME	Selects the cell at the beginning of the row that contains the active cell and moves the window accordingly.
CTRL+HOME	Selects cell A1 or the cell below and to the right of frozen titles and moves the window to the upper left corner of the worksheet.
CTRL+ARROW	Selects the border cell of the worksheet in combination with the arrow keys and moves the window accordingly. For example, to select the rightmost cell in the row that contains the active cell, press CTRL+RIGHT ARROW. You can also press the END key, release it, and then press the arrow key to accomplish the same task.
Go To command on Edit menu	Selects the cell in the worksheet that corresponds to the cell reference you enter in the Go To dialog box and moves the window accordingly. You can press F5 as a shortcut to display the Go To dialog box.
Find command on Edit menu	Finds and selects a cell in the worksheet with specific contents that you enter in the Find dialog box. If necessary, Excel moves the window to display the cell. You can press SHIFT+F5 to display the Find Dialog box.
Reference Area	Selects the cell in the workbook that corresponds to the cell reference you enter in the reference area.
PAGE UP	Selects the cell one window up from the active cell and moves the window accordingly.
ALT+PAGE UP	Selects the cell one window to the left and moves the window accordingly.
PAGE DOWN	Selects the cell one window down from the active cell and moves the window accordingly.
ALT+PAGE DOWN	Selects the cell one window to the right and moves the window accordingly.

▶ ADDING A CHART TO THE WORKSHEET

T he column chart drawn by Excel in this project is based on the data in the Sun-N-Surf 1st Qtr Transmittal Costs worksheet (Figure 1-49). It is called an **embedded chart** because it is part of the worksheet.

For Bayview, the light blue column represents the quarterly cost of faxing ($1,135.23), the purple column represents the quarterly cost of mailing ($874.25), and the light yellow column represents the quarterly cost of using the phone ($254.76). For Eureka, Malibu, and Miami, the same color columns represent the comparable costs. Notice in this chart that the totals from the worksheet are not represented because the totals were not in the range specified for charting.

Excel derived the dollar values along the y-axis (or vertical axis) of the chart on the basis of the values in the worksheet. It also automatically determines the $500.00 increments. The value $2,000.00 is greater than any value in the worksheet, so it is the maximum value Excel included on the chart.

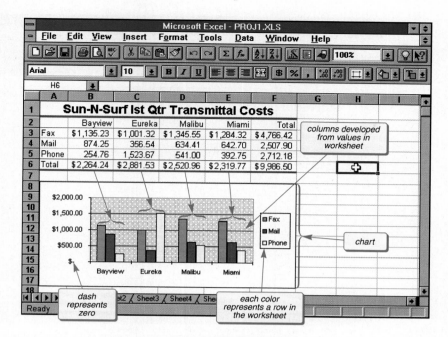

FIGURE 1-49

To draw a chart like the one in Figure 1-49, select the range to chart, click the **ChartWizard button** (⬛) on the Standard toolbar, and select the area on the worksheet where you want the chart drawn. In Figure 1-49, the chart is located immediately below the worksheet. When you determine the location of the chart on the worksheet, you also determine its size by dragging the mouse pointer from the upper left corner of the chart location to the lower right corner of the chart location.

Follow these detailed steps to draw a **column chart** that compares the Sun-N-Surf 1st Qtr Transmittal Costs for the four cities.

TO DRAW AN EMBEDDED COLUMN CHART ▼

STEP 1 ▶

With cell A2 selected, position the block plus sign within the cell's border (Figure 1-50).

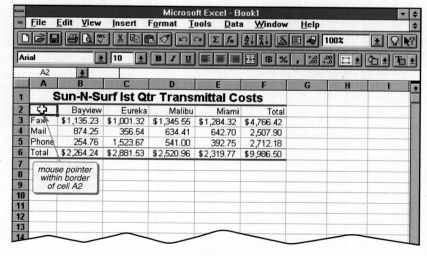

FIGURE 1-50

STEP 2 ▶

Drag the mouse pointer to the lower right corner cell (cell E5) of the range to chart (A2:E5).

Excel highlights the range to chart (Figure 1-51).

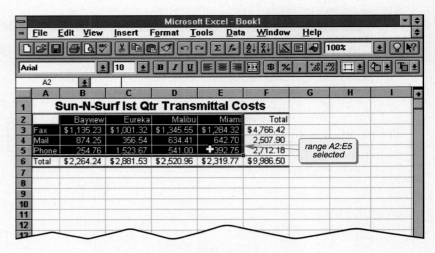

FIGURE 1-51

STEP 3 ▶

Click the ChartWizard button on the Standard toolbar and move the mouse pointer into the window (Figure 1-52).

The mouse pointer changes to a cross hair with a chart symbol (+ᵢₗ) (Figure 1-52).

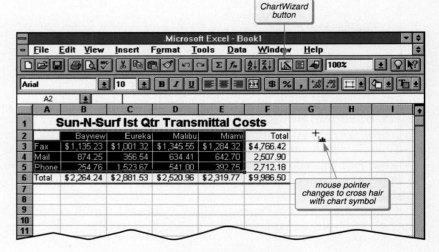

FIGURE 1-52

STEP 4 ▶

Move the mouse pointer to the upper left corner of the desired chart location, immediately below the worksheet (cell A8).

A moving border surrounds the range to chart A2:E5. (Figure 1-53).

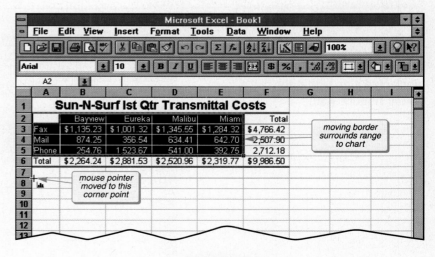

FIGURE 1-53

STEP 5 ▶

Drag the mouse pointer to the lower right corner of the chart location (cell F17).

The mouse pointer is positioned at the lower right corner of cell F17, and the chart location is surrounded by a solid line rectangle (Figure 1-54).

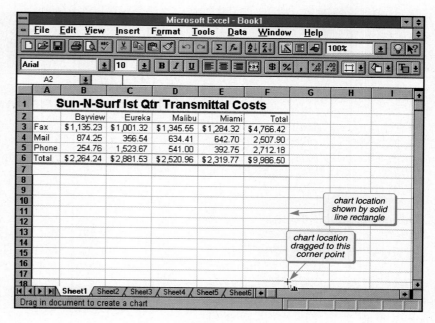

FIGURE 1-54

STEP 6 ▶

Release the left mouse button.

Excel responds by displaying the ChartWizard dialog box (Figure 1-55).

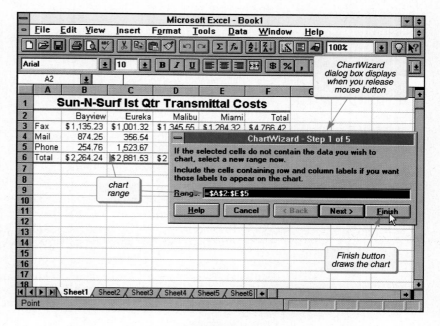

FIGURE 1-55

STEP 7 ▶

In the ChartWizard dialog box, choose the Finish button (Finish).

Excel draws a column chart over the chart location comparing the Sun-N-Surf first quarter transmittal costs for the four cities (Figure 1-56). The small selection squares, or handles, on the border of the chart area indicate the chart is selected. While the chart is selected, you can click on and drag the chart to any location on the worksheet. You can also resize the chart by dragging on the handles.

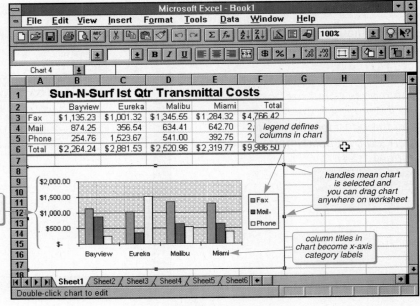

FIGURE 1-56

STEP 8 ▶

Select a cell outside the chart location to remove the chart selection.

The embedded column chart in Figure 1-56 compares the first quarter transmittal costs for each city. It also allows you to compare the costs between the cities. Notice that Excel automatically selects the entries in the row at the top of the range (row 2) as the titles for the x-axis (or horizontal axis) and draws a column for each of the twelve cells containing numbers in the range. The small box to the right of the column chart in Figure 1-56 contains the legend. The **legend** identifies each column in the chart. Excel automatically selects the leftmost column of the range (column A) as titles within the legend. Excel also automatically scales the y-axis on the basis of the magnitude of the numbers in the graph range.

Excel offers 15 different chart types from which you can choose. The **default chart type** is the chart Excel draws when you initially create the chart. When you first load Excel on a computer, the default chart type is the two-dimensional column chart. You can change the chart type by double-clicking the chart and choosing the Chart Type command on the Format menu. The Chart Type command only appears on the Format menu when the chart is active. Subsequent projects will discuss changing charts, sizing charts, and adding text to charts.

▶ SAVING THE WORKBOOK

While you are building a worksheet, the computer stores it in main memory. If the computer is turned off, or if you lose electrical power, the workbook is lost. Hence, it is mandatory to save on disk any workbook that you will use later. The steps below and on the next two pages illustrate how to save a workbook to drive A using the Save button on the Standard toolbar. Be sure you have a formatted disk in drive A.

TO SAVE THE WORKBOOK ▼

STEP 1 ▶

Click the Save button (▣) on the Standard toolbar.

Excel responds by displaying the Save As dialog box (Figure 1-57).

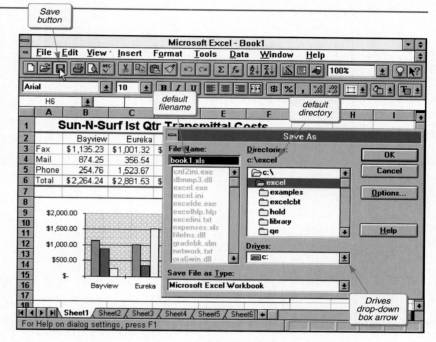

FIGURE 1-57

STEP 2 ▶

Type `proj1` in the File Name text box.

The filename proj1 replaces book1.xls in the File Name text box (Figure 1-58).

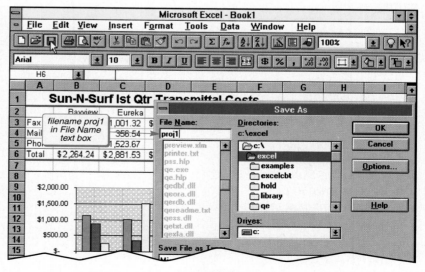

FIGURE 1-58

STEP 3 ▶

Click the Drives drop-down box arrow.

A list of available drives displays (Figure 1-59). If the drive A symbol does not appear in the Drives drop-down list, use the UP ARROW key on the scroll bar.

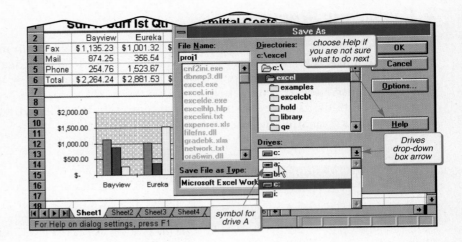

FIGURE 1-59

STEP 4 ▶

Select drive A (▭a:) and point to the OK button.

Drive A becomes the selected drive (Figure 1-60).

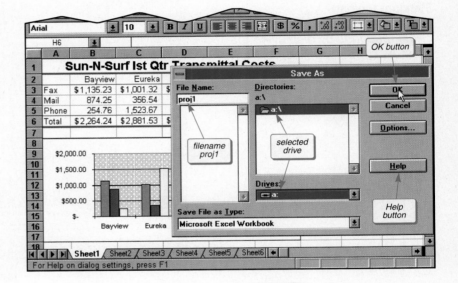

FIGURE 1-60

STEP 5 ▶

Choose the OK button in the Save As dialog box.

Excel displays the Summary Info dialog box with the Title, Subject, Author, Keywords, and Comments boxes empty. If you wish, you may enter information such as a title, subject area, author name and keywords in the Summary Info dialog box as shown in Figure 1-61. If you enter information into the text boxes, be sure to press the TAB key to advance from one text box to the next.

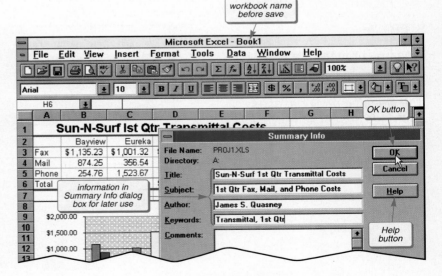

FIGURE 1-61

STEP 6 ▶

Choose the OK button in the
Summary Info dialog box.

*Excel saves the workbook to drive
A using the filename PROJ1. XLS.
Excel automatically appends to
the filename proj1 the extension
.XLS, which stands for Excel worksheet. Although the Sun-N-Surf
1st Qtr Transmittal Costs worksheet is saved on disk, it also
remains in main memory and displays on the screen (Figure
1-62).*

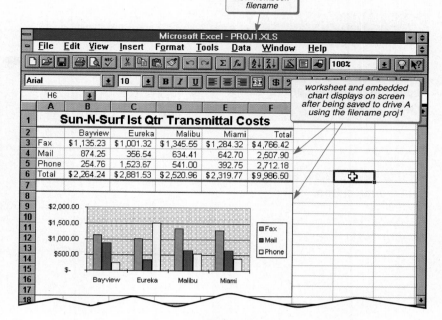

FIGURE 1-62

While Excel is saving the workbook, it momentarily changes the word Ready
in the status bar to Saving PROJ1.XLS. It also displays a horizontal bar next to the
words Saving PROJ1.XLS indicating the amount of the workbook saved. After the
save operation is complete, Excel changes the name of the workbook in the title
bar from Book1 to PROJ1.XLS (Figure 1-62).

▶ PRINTING THE WORKSHEET

nce you have created the worksheet and saved the workbook on disk, you
may want to print the worksheet. A printed version of the worksheet is
called a **hard copy** or **printout**.

There are several reasons why you may want a printout. First, to present the
worksheet to someone who does not have access to your computer, it must be in
printed form. In addition, worksheets and charts are often kept for reference by
persons other than those who prepare them. In many cases, the worksheets are
printed and kept in binders for use by others. This section describes how to print
a worksheet.

By default, Excel prints the gridlines that display on the screen along with the
worksheet. To print without gridlines, you must turn them off by removing the X
in the Gridlines check box on the **Sheet tab** in the Page Setup dialog box. In this
section, you will see that some dialog boxes are made up of tabs, each with its
own name. A **tab** in a dialog box contains selections that are grouped under the
tab name.

A number of ways to remove gridlines from the printout are available using
the Page Setup command. One way is to choose the Page Setup command from
the File menu. Another way is to use the shortcut menu. Excel provides a **shortcut menu** that contains the commands most often used for the current activity. To
activate the shortcut menu that pertains to the entire workbook, point to the
menu bar and click the right mouse button as described in the following steps.

TO PRINT A WORKSHEET ▼

STEP 1 ▶

Ready the printer according to the printer instructions.

STEP 2 ▶

Point to the menu bar and click the right mouse button.

Excel displays the shortcut menu (Figure 1-63).

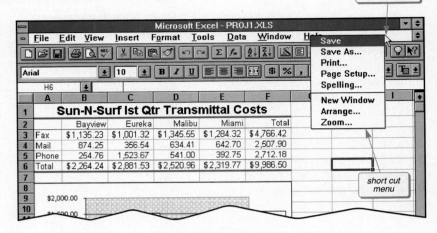

FIGURE 1-63

STEP 3 ▶

Choose the Page Setup command from the shortcut menu.

Excel displays the Page Setup dialog box (Figure 1-64). The Page tab displays.

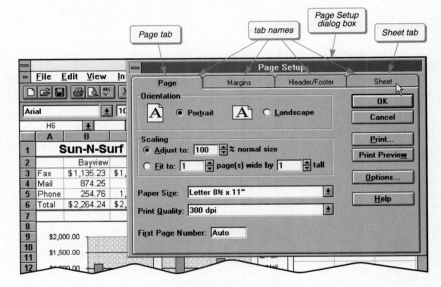

FIGURE 1-64

STEP 4 ▶

Click the Sheet tab in the Page Setup dialog box.

Excel displays the Sheet tab in place of the Page tab (Figure 1-65).

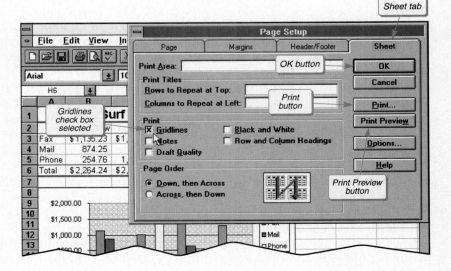

FIGURE 1-65

STEP 5 ▶

If an X appears in the Gridlines check box in the Print area of the Sheet tab, select the check box by clicking it so the X disappears.

The Gridlines check box is empty (Figure 1-66). The gridlines on the screen will not print.

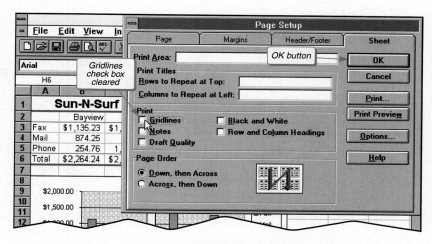

FIGURE 1-66

STEP 6 ▶

Choose the OK button in the Page Setup dialog box.

The Page Setup dialog box disappears and the worksheet and embedded chart display with a dashed line showing the right boundary of the page that Excel will print (Figure 1-67).

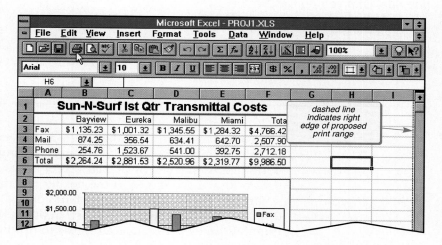

FIGURE 1-67

STEP 7 ▶

Click the Print button (🖨) on the Standard toolbar.

Excel displays the Printing dialog box (Figure 1-68) that allows you to cancel the print job at any time while the system is internally creating the worksheet to send to the printer. When the Printing dialog box disappears, the printing begins.

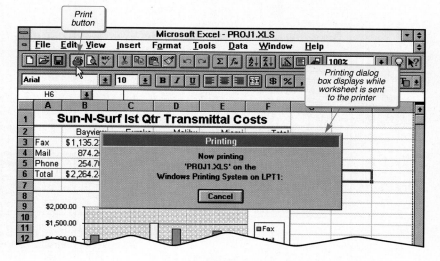

FIGURE 1-68

STEP 8 ▶

When the printer stops, retrieve the printout (Figure 1-69).

STEP 9 ▶

Point to the Save button on the Standard toolbar and click.

Excel saves the workbook with the page setup characteristics shown in Figure 1-66. Saving the workbook after changing the page setup means that you do not have to perform Step 2 through Step 6 the next time you print the worksheet and chart unless you want to make other page setup changes.

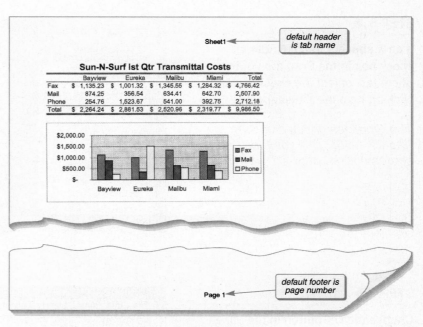

FIGURE 1-69

Notice in Figure 1-69 that Excel adds a header and footer. A **header** is a line of text that prints at the top of each page. A **footer** is a line of text that prints at the bottom of each page. By default, Excel prints the name on the worksheet tab at the bottom of the screen as the header and the page number as the footer.

If you already know the Gridlines check box is clear, then you can skip Step 2 through Step 6 in the previous list. In other words, if the printer is ready, click the Print button on the Standard toolbar to print the worksheet and chart.

▶ EXITING EXCEL

After you build, save, and print the worksheet and chart, Project 1 is complete. To quit Excel and return control to Program Manager, perform the following steps.

TO EXIT EXCEL ▼

STEP 1 ▶

Point to the Control-menu box in the title bar (Figure 1-70).

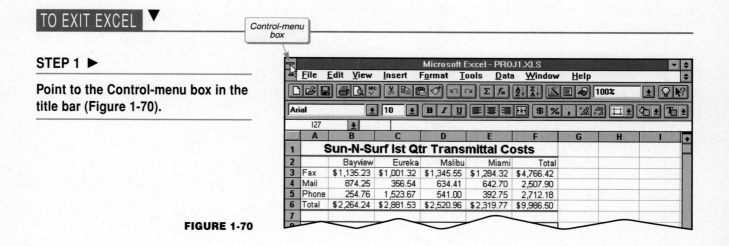

FIGURE 1-70

STEP 2 ▶

Double-click the left mouse button.

If you made changes to the work-book, Excel displays the question, Save changes in 'PROJ1. XLS'? in the Microsoft Excel dialog box (Figure 1-71). Choose the Yes button to save the changes to PROJ1. XLS before quiting Excel. Choose the No button to quit Excel without saving the changes to PROJ1. XLS. Choose the Can-cel button to terminate the Exit command and return to the workbook.

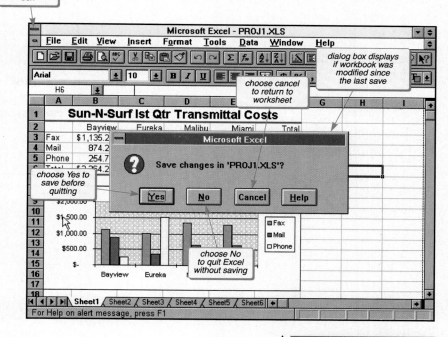

FIGURE 1-71

Rather than double-clicking the Control-menu box in the title bar you can also quit Excel by choosing the Exit command on the File menu.

▶ OPENING A WORKBOOK

Earlier, you saved the workbook built in Project 1 on disk using the file-name PROJ1.XLS. Once you have created and saved a workbook, you will often have reason to retrieve it from disk. For example, you may want to enter revised data, review the calculations on the worksheet, or add more data to the worksheet. After starting Excel (see page E4), you can use the following steps to open PROJ1.XLS using the Open button (⊞).

TO OPEN A WORKBOOK ▼

STEP 1 ▶

Point to the Open button on the Standard toolbar and click.

Excel displays the Open dialog box.

STEP 2 ▶

If drive A is not the selected drive, select drive A in the Drives drop-down list box (refer to Figures 1-59 and 1-60 on page E36 to review this technique). Select the filename proj1.xls by clicking the filename in the File Name list box (Figure 1-72).

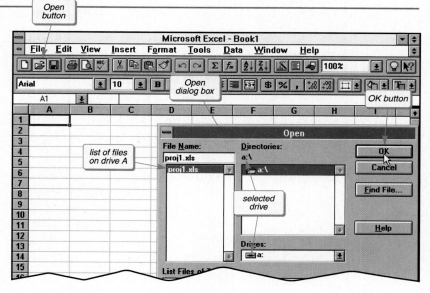

FIGURE 1-72

STEP 3 ▶

Choose the OK button in the Open
dialog box.

*Excel loads the workbook
PROJ1. XLS from drive A into
main memory, and displays it on
the screen (Figure 1-73).*

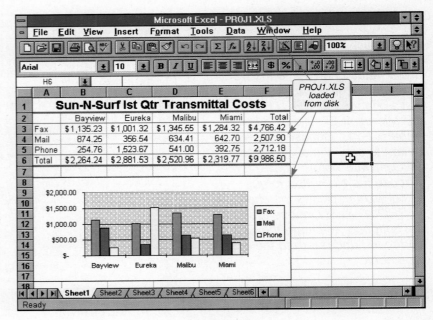

FIGURE 1-73

▶ CORRECTING ERRORS

Several methods are available for correcting errors on a worksheet. The
one you choose will depend on the severity of the error and whether you
notice it while typing the data in the formula bar or after you have
entered the incorrect data into the cell.

Correcting Errors Prior to Entering Data into a Cell

If you notice an error prior to entering data into a cell, use one of the following techniques:

1. Use the BACKSPACE key to erase the portion in error and then type the correct characters; or
2. If the error is too severe, click the cancel box or press the ESC key to
   erase the entire entry in the formula bar and reenter the data from the
   beginning.

In-Cell Editing

If you find an error in the worksheet after entering the data, you can correct
the error in one of two ways:

1. If the entry is short, select the cell, retype the entry correctly, and click the
   enter box or press the ENTER key. The new entry will replace the old entry.
2. If the entry in the cell is long and the errors are minor, the **Edit mode** may
   be a better choice. Use the Edit mode as described at the top of the next
   page.

a. Double-click the cell containing the error. Excel switches to Edit mode, the cell contents appear in the formula bar, and a flashing insertion point appears in the cell (Figure 1-74). This editing procedure is called **in-cell editing** because you can edit the contents directly in the cell. The cell contents also appear in the formula bar. An alternative to double-clicking the cell is to select the cell and press the function key F2.

b. Make your changes, as specified below:

(1) To insert between two characters, place the insertion point between the two characters and begin typing. Excel inserts the new characters at the location of the insertion point.

(2) To delete a character in the cell, move the insertion point to the left of the character you want to delete and press the **DELETE** key, or place the insertion point to the right of the character you want to delete and press the BACKSPACE key. You can also use the mouse to drag over the character or adjacent characters to delete and press the DELETE key or click the Cut button (🔥) on the Standard toolbar.

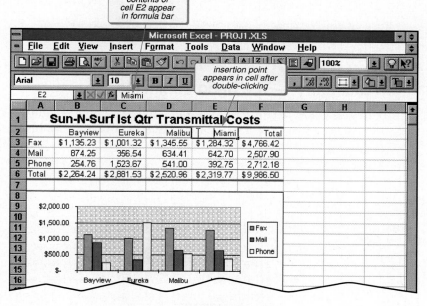

FIGURE 1-74

When you have finished editing an entry, click the enter box or press the ENTER key.

When Excel enters the Edit mode, the keyboard is usually in **Insert mode** (OVR does not display in the status bar). In Insert mode, as you type a character, Excel inserts the character and moves all characters to the right of the typed character one position to the right. You can change to **Overtype mode** (OVR displays in the status bar) by pressing the **INSERT key**. In Overtype mode, Excel overtypes the character to the right of the insertion point. The INSERT key toggles the keyboard between Insert mode and Overtype mode.

While in Edit mode, you may have occasion to move the insertion point to various points in the cell, select portions of the data in the cell, or switch from inserting characters to overtyping characters. Table 1-3 summarizes the most common tasks used during in-cell editing.

▸ **TABLE 1-3**

TASK	MOUSE	KEYBOARD
Move the insertion point to the beginning of data in a cell	Point to the left of the first character and click	Press HOME
Move the insertion point to the end of data in a cell	Point to the right of the last character and click	Press END
Move the insertion point anywhere in a cell	Click the character at the appropriate position	Press RIGHT ARROW or LEFT ARROW
Highlight one or more adjacent characters	Drag the mouse pointer over adjacent characters	Press SHIFT+RIGHT or LEFT ARROW
Select all data in a cell	Double-click the cell with the insertion point in the cell	
Delete selected characters	Click the Cut button on the Standard toolbar	Press DELETE
Toggle between Insert and Overtype modes		Press INSERT

Undoing the Last Entry — The Undo Command

Excel provides an Undo button (⟲) on the Standard toolbar (Figure 1-75) that you can use to erase the most recent cell entry. Thus, if you enter incorrect data in a cell, click the Undo button and Excel changes the cell contents to what they were prior to entering the incorrect data.

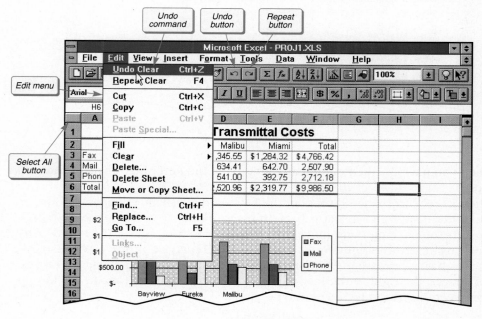

FIGURE 1-75

Using the Undo button you can undo more complicated worksheet activities than a single cell entry. For example, most commands you issue can be undone if you choose the Undo command before making another entry. The general rule is that the Undo command can restore the worksheet data and settings to what they were the last time Excel was in Ready mode. If Excel cannot undo an operation, then the button is inoperative. Next to the Undo button on the Standard toolbar is the Repeat button (⬚). The Repeat button allows you to repeat the last activity.

Finally, you can choose the Undo command from the Edit menu rather than using the Undo button. If Excel cannot undo an operation, then the words, Can't Undo, appear on the Edit menu in place of Undo.

Clearing a Cell or Range of Cells

It is not unusual to enter data into the wrong cell or range of cells. In such a case, to correct the error, you might want to erase or clear the data. **Never press the SPACEBAR to enter a blank character to clear a cell.** A blank character is text and is different than an empty cell, even though the cell may appear empty.

Excel provides three methods to clear the contents of a cell or a range of cells.

TO CLEAR CELL CONTENTS USING THE FILL HANDLE

Step 1: Select the cell or range of cells and point to the fill handle so the mouse pointer changes to a cross.
Step 2: Drag the fill handle back into the selected cell or range until a shadow covers the cell or cells you want to erase.
Step 3: Release the left mouse button.

TO CLEAR CELL CONTENTS USING THE DELETE KEY

Step 1: Select the cell or range of cells to be cleared.
Step 2: Press the DELETE key.

TO CLEAR CELL CONTENTS USING THE CLEAR COMMAND

Step 1: Select the cell or range of cells to be cleared.
Step 2: Choose Clear from the Edit menu.
Step 3: Choose All.

You can also select a range of cells and click the Cut button on the Standard toolbar, or choose the Cut command on the Edit menu. However, in addition to deleting the contents from the range, they also copy the contents of the range to the Clipboard.

Clearing the Entire Worksheet

Sometimes, everything goes wrong. If this happens, you may want to clear the worksheet entirely and start over. To clear the worksheet, follow these steps.

TO CLEAR THE ENTIRE WORKSHEET

Step 1: Select the entire worksheet by clicking the Select All button (⬚)which is just above row heading 1 and immediately to the left of column heading A (Figure 1-75).
Step 2: Press the DELETE key or choose the Clear command from the Edit menu and choose All.

TO DELETE AN EMBEDDED CHART

Step 1: Click the chart.
Step 2: Press the DELETE key or choose the Clear command from the Edit
menu and choose All.

An alternative to using the Select All button and the DELETE key or Clear command from the Edit menu to clear an entire worksheet is to delete the sheet from the workbook by using the Delete Sheet command on the Edit menu or choose the Close command on the File menu to close the workbook. If you choose the Close command to close a workbook, click the New Workbook button on the Standard toolbar or choose the **New command** on the File menu to begin working on an empty workbook.

▶ EXCEL ONLINE HELP

At any time while you are using Excel, you can select the **Help menu** to gain access to the **online Help** (Figure 1-76). The Excel Help menu provides a table of contents, a search command for navigating around the online Help, and an index of Help topics you may use to request help. Pressing function key F1 also allows you to obtain help on various topics.

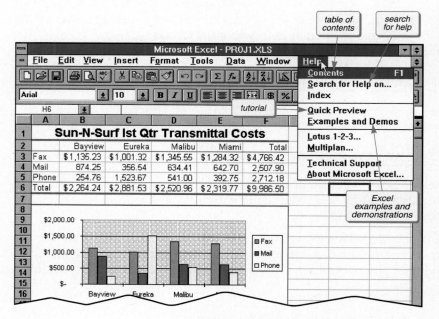

FIGURE 1-76

The **Quick Preview command** on the Help menu steps you through four short **tutorials** (Figure 1-77) that introduce you to the basics of Excel. Below each topic, Excel tells you approximately how long it will take to step through the tutorial (usually 4 to 7 minutes). The lesson titled Getting Started is highly recommended to help you become familiar with Excel. Before you begin the quick preview of Excel, click the Save button to save the workbook with your latest changes.

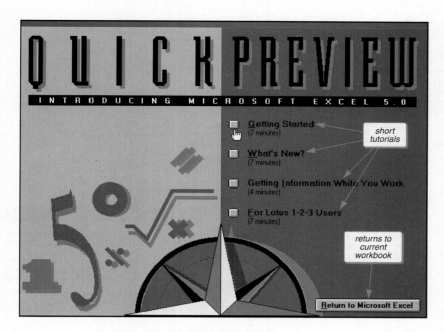

FIGURE 1-77

In many Excel dialog boxes you can click a Help button to obtain help about the current activity on which you are working. If there is no Help button in a dialog box, press function key F1 while the dialog box is on the screen.

Help Button on the Standard Toolbar

To use Excel online Help, you can click the **Help button** ( ) on the Standard toolbar (top screen of Figure 1-78 on the next page). Move the arrow and question mark pointer ( ) to any menu name, button, or cell, and click to get context-sensitive help. The term **context-sensitive help** means that Excel will display immediate information on the topic to which the arrow and question mark pointer is pointing. For example, clicking the Bold button displays the **Help window** shown in the bottom screen of Figure 1-78.

To print the Help information in the Help window, choose the **Print Topic command** from the File menu in the Help window. You close a Help window by choosing Exit from the File menu in the Help window.

Excel online Help has features that make it powerful and easy to use. The best way to familiarize yourself with the online Help is to use it.

Excel Online Examples and Demonstrations

To improve your Excel skills, you can step through the examples and demonstrations that come with Excel. Choose the **Examples and Demos command** on the Help menu (Figure 1-76). Excel responds by displaying the screen shown in Figure 1-79 on the next page. Click any of the twenty buttons to select a category of examples and demonstrations. Excel then displays a list of subtopics from which to choose. The Examples and Demos command provides interactive practice sessions on the features of Excel.

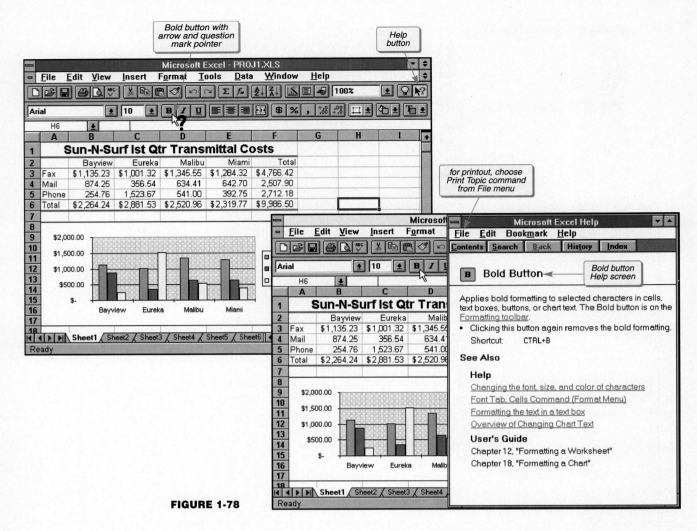

FIGURE 1-78

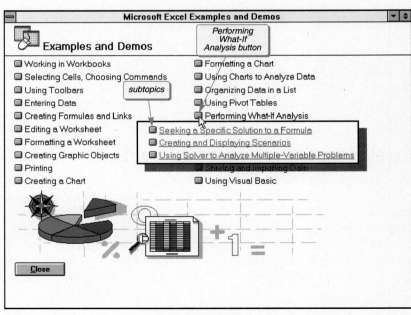

FIGURE 1-79

Information at Your Fingertips — TipWizard

Excel displays tips on how to work more efficiently in the **TipWizard Box**. When toggled on, the TipWizard Box displays at the top of the screen between the Formatting toolbar and formula bar (Figure 1-80). You toggle the TipWizard Box on or off by clicking the **TipWizard button** on the Standard toolbar. If toggled on when you start Excel, the TipWizard Box begins with a tip of the day. As you work through creating and editing a workbook, Excel adds tips to the TipWizard Box. The tips explain how to complete the activities you just performed more efficiently. You can scroll through these tips using the arrows to the right of the Tip-Wizard Box.

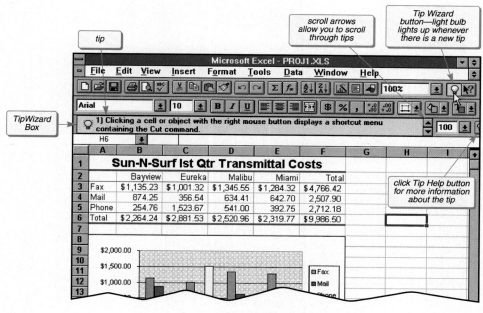

FIGURE 1-80

If the TipWizard Box is toggled off and Excel has a tip to offer you, the bulb on the TipWizard button lights up. To view the tip, click the TipWizard button.

▶ PLANNING A WORKSHEET

At the beginning of this project, the completed Sun-N-Surf 1st Qtr Transmittal Costs worksheet was presented in Figure 1-1 on page E3 and then built step by step. In the business world, you are seldom given the worksheet specifications in this form. Usually, the specifications for a worksheet are given to you verbally or in paragraph form on paper, and it is your responsibility to plan the worksheet from start to finish. Careful planning can significantly reduce your effort and result in a worksheet that is accurate, easy to read, flexible, and useful.

In planning a worksheet, you should follow these steps: (1) define the problem; (2) design the worksheet; (3) enter the worksheet; and, (4) test the worksheet. The following paragraphs describe these four steps in detail and outline how the Sun-N-Surf 1st Qtr Transmittal Costs worksheet in Figure 1-1 was planned.

Define the Problem

In this first step, write down on paper the following information:

1. The purpose of the worksheet.
2. The results or output you want, including such items as totals and charts.
3. Identify the data needed to determine the results.
4. List the required calculations to transform the data to the desired results.

Figure 1-81 shows one way to define the Sun-N-Surf 1st Qtr Transmittal Costs problem.

<u>Purpose of Worksheet</u> Create a worksheet that lists the first quarter transmittal costs and their totals for Sun-N-Surf.

<u>Expected Results</u> Display the first quarter transmittal costs and totals for each office and their totals for each category, and for the company. Draw a column chart that compares the costs within each office.

<u>Required Data</u> Obtain the first quarter Fax, Mail, and Phone transmittal costs for the four offices.

<u>Required Calculations</u> Use the SUM function to calculate the total transmittal costs for each office, each category, and for the company.

FIGURE 1-81

Design the Worksheet

In this second step, outline the worksheet on paper. Include the worksheet title, column titles, row titles, totals, and chart location if required.

Don't worry about the specific formats that will eventually be assigned to the worksheet. Figure 1-82 illustrates the outline for the Sun-N-Surf 1st Qtr Transmittal Costs worksheet. The series of 9s in Figure 1-82 indicates numeric entries.

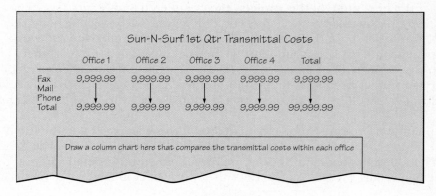

Sun-N-Surf 1st Qtr Transmittal Costs

	Office 1	Office 2	Office 3	Office 4	Total
Fax	9,999.99	9,999.99	9,999.99	9,999.99	9,999.99
Mail	↓	↓	↓	↓	
Phone					
Total	9,999.99	9,999.99	9,999.99	9,999.99	99,999.99

Draw a column chart here that compares the transmittal costs within each office

FIGURE 1-82

3. Which of the following is a valid number you can enter on a worksheet?
   a. 3.25
   b. 3.25%
   c. $3.25
   d. all of the above

4. When you enter text into the active cell, the text is _____ in the cell.
   a. aligned to the right
   b. aligned to the left
   c. centered
   d. decimal-aligned

5. Keyboard indicators display in the _____ bar.
   a. status
   b. menu
   c. title
   d. button

6. Excel uses the _____ between cell references to indicate a range.
   a. period (.)
   b. colon (:)
   c. semicolon (;)
   d. tilde (~)

7. To display a shortcut menu, _____.
   a. click the right mouse button
   b. click the left mouse button
   c. choose the Shortcut command from the File menu
   d. click the Select All button

8. The fill handle is located _____.
   a. on the menu bar
   b. on the toolbar
   c. on the heavy border that surrounds the active cell
   d. in the status bar

9. Which one of the following will quit Excel and return control to Windows?
   a. double-click the Control-menu box
   b. choose the Close command from the File menu
   c. click the New Workbook button on the Standard toolbar
   d. choose the Clear command from the Edit menu

10. To select the entire worksheet, click the _____.
    a. Select All button
    b. ChartWizard button
    c. Open button
    d. Save button

STUDENT ASSIGNMENT 3
Understanding the Excel Worksheet

Instructions: In Figure SA1-3, arrows point to the major components of the Excel window and bars. Identify the various parts of the windows and bars in the space provided.

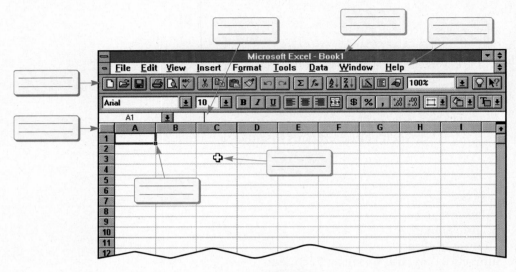

FIGURE SA1-3

STUDENT ASSIGNMENT 4
Understanding Toolbars

Instructions: In the worksheet in Figure SA1-4, arrows point to several of the buttons on the Standard and Formatting toolbars. In the space provided, briefly explain the purpose of each button.

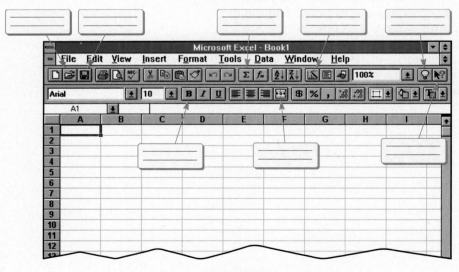

FIGURE SA1-4

STUDENT ASSIGNMENT 5
Understanding the Formula Bar on the Worksheet

Instructions: Answer the following questions concerning the contents of the formula bar area in Figure SA1-5.

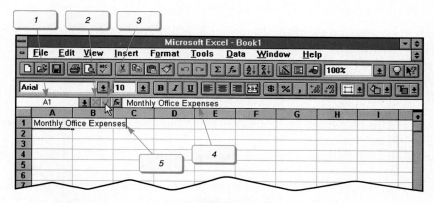

FIGURE SA1-5

1. What does the A1 signify in the reference area on the left side of the formula bar? _____
2. What is the purpose of the box in the formula bar that contains the letter X? _____
3. What is the purpose of the box in the formula bar that contains the check mark? _____
4. How would you complete the entry of the text in the formula bar, Monthly Office Expenses, into cell A1 without using the mouse and maintain cell A1 as the active cell? _____
5. What do you call the vertical line that follows the text in cell A1? _____

STUDENT ASSIGNMENT 6
Understanding the AutoSum Button on the Standard Toolbar

Instructions: Answer the following questions after reviewing the entries on the worksheet in Figure SA1-6.

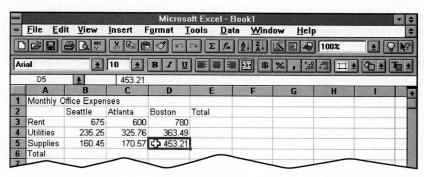

FIGURE SA1-6

1. List the steps to use the AutoSum button to sum the range B3:B5 and assign it to cell B6. Then, copy the SUM function to cells C6 and D6.

   _____

2. List the steps to use the AutoSum button on the Standard toolbar to sum the range B3:D5 and produce both the row totals and column totals in the most efficient manner.

   _____

COMPUTER LABORATORY EXERCISE 1
Using the Help Menu, Help Button, and Excel Tutorial

Part 1 Instructions: Start Excel and perform the following tasks using a computer.

1. Choose the Contents command from the Help menu on the menu bar.
2. Click Reference Information.
3. Click Parts of the Microsoft Excel Screen.
4. Click Sheet Tab.
5. Read the paragraph. Use the scroll arrow in the lower right corner of the Help window to scroll through and read the rest of the topic.
6. Ready the printer and choose Print Topic from the File menu in the Help window to print a hard copy of the Sheet Tab help topic.
7. To return to the original Help screen, click the Contents button in the upper left corner of the Help window.
8. Use the technique described in Steps 3 and 4 to display help on any other topic listed.
9. To close the Help window, double-click the Control-menu box in the Help window title bar.
10. Click the Help button on the Standard toolbar.
11. Point at the AutoSum button and click.
12. Ready the printer and choose Print Topic from the File menu in the Help window.
13. Close the Help window as described in Step 9.

Part 2 Instructions: Start Excel and perform the following tasks using a computer.

1. Choose Quick Preview from the Help menu and select, one at a time, these previews: Getting Started and Getting Information While You Work.
2. Close the Quick Preview by clicking on the Close button (Close) in the lower left corner of the screen and then click the Return to Microsoft Excel button (Return to Microsoft Excel) in the lower right corner of the screen.

Part 3 Instructions: Start Excel and perform the following tasks using a computer.

1. Choose Examples and Demos from the Help menu.
2. Click the Using Toolbars button.
3. Click the Displaying, Hiding, and Moving Toolbars button.
4. Read the information on the screen and then click the Practice (Practice) button in the lower right corner of the screen.
5. Read the information about displaying a toolbar and click the Hint button (Hint) in the lower right corner of the information box.
6. Read the hint and click the Show me button (Show Me) in the lower right corner of the hint box.
7. Read the information in the show me box and observe the floating toolbar that appears on the sample worksheet on the screen.
8. Close the Examples and Demos by clicking the Close button in the lower left corner of the show me box. Next, click the Close button in the lower left corner of the Examples and Demos screen.

COMPUTER LABORATORY EXERCISE 2
Formatting a Worksheet

Instructions: Start Excel. Open the workbook CLE1-2 from the subdirectory Excel5 on the Student Diskette that accompanies this book. The worksheet is shown at the top of Figure CLE1-2. Perform the tasks at the top of the next page to change it so it resembles the worksheet in the lower portion of Figure CLE1-2.

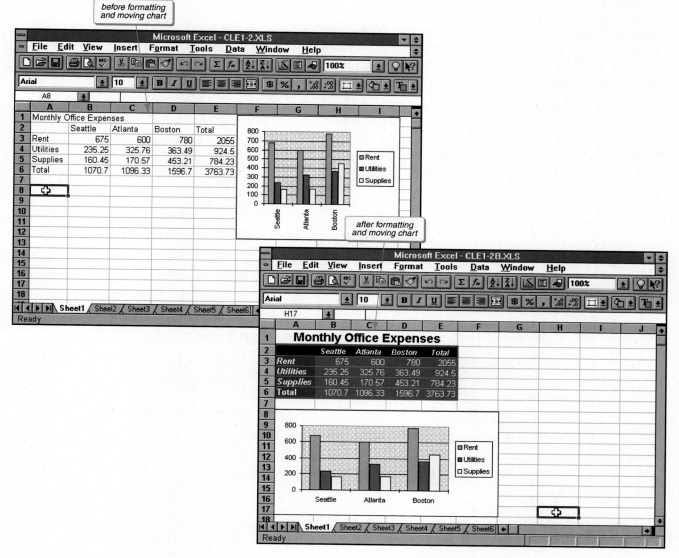

FIGURE CLE1-2

(continued)

COMPUTER LABORATORY EXERCISE 2 (continued)

1. Increase the font size of the worksheet title in cell A1 to 14 point by clicking the Font Size box arrow on the Formatting toolbar and selecting 14 in the Font Size drop-down list box.
2. Bold the worksheet title in cell A1.
3. Center the worksheet title in cell A1 across columns A through E.
4. Select the range A2:E6.
5. Choose the AutoFormat command from the Format menu and review the seventeen formats in the Sample box by selecting each one using the mouse.
6. Select the Colorful 1 format and choose OK from the AutoFormat dialog box.
7. Move the chart from its current location to the range A8:F17 as shown in the lower portion of Figure CLE1-2.
8. Choose the Page Setup command from the shortcut menu or File menu. Select the Sheet tab. Turn Gridlines off. Choose OK from the Page Setup dialog box.
9. Click the Print button on the Standard toolbar to print the worksheet with the new format.
10. Save the workbook using the filename CLE1-2B.
11. Select the column chart and delete it using the DELETE key.
12. Click the Print button to print the worksheet.
13. Choose the Close command from the File menu to close the workbook.

COMPUTER LABORATORY EXERCISE 3
Changing Data in a Worksheet

Instructions: Start Excel. Open the workbook CLE1-3 from the subdirectory Excel5 on the Student Diskette that accompanies this book. As shown in Figure CLE1-3, the worksheet is a semiannual income and expense worksheet. Perform the tasks at the top of the next page.

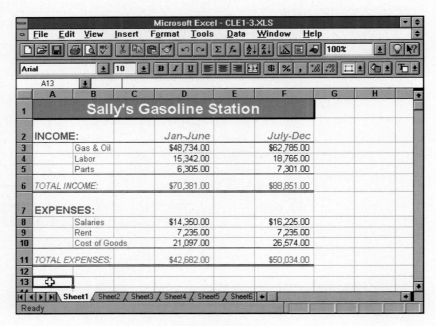

FIGURE CLE1-3

1. Make the changes to the worksheet described in the table below. As you edit the values in the cells containing numeric data, watch the total income (cells D6 and F6) and total expenses (cells D11 and F11). Each of the values in these four cells is based on the SUM function. When you enter a new value, Excel automatically recalculates the SUM functions. After you have successfully made the changes listed in the table, the total incomes in cells D6 and F6 should equal $126,882.00 and $127,811.00, respectively. The total expenses in cells D11 and F11 should equal $50,689.00 and $53,685.00, respectively.
2. Save the workbook using the filename CLE1-3B.
3. Print the revised worksheet without gridlines.

CELL	CURRENT CELL CONTENTS	CHANGE CELL CONTENTS TO
A1	Sally's Gasoline Station	Sal's Gas Station
D3	48734	48535
F3	62785	61523
D5	6305	63005
F5	7301	47523
D8	14350	22357
F8	16225	19876

COMPUTER LABORATORY ASSIGNMENTS

COMPUTER LABORATORY ASSIGNMENT 1
Building and Modifying a College Cost Analysis Worksheet

Purpose: To become familiar with building a worksheet, formatting a worksheet, embedding a column chart, printing a worksheet, and saving a workbook.

Problem: As a student assistant working in the Financial Aid office, you have been asked by the director to project the expenses for attending college for two semesters and a summer session. The estimated costs are shown in the table on the next page.

Instructions: Perform the tasks below and on the next page:

1. Create the worksheet shown in Figure CLA1-1 on the next page using the numbers in the table. Enter the text and numbers into the cells described in the worksheet.
2. Direct Excel to determine the totals for Semester 1, Semester 2, Summer, Tuition, Books, Lab Fees, and a total for the three semesters.

(continued)

COMPUTER LABORATORY ASSIGNMENT 1 (continued)

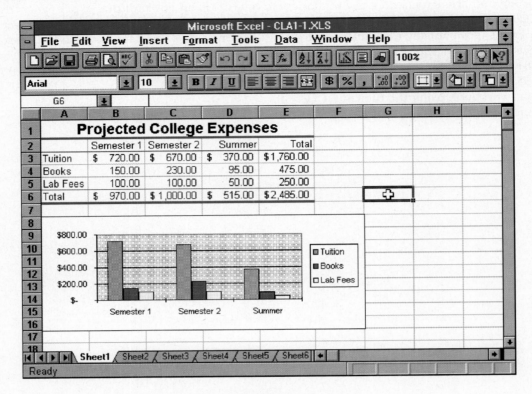

FIGURE CLA1-1

	SEMESTER 1	SEMESTER 2	SUMMER
TUITION	720.00	670.00	370.00
BOOKS	150.00	230.00	95.00
LAB FEES	100.00	100.00	50.00

3. Format the worksheet title, Projected College Expenses, as 14 point, bold, and centered over columns A through E.
4. Format the range A2:E6 using the table format Accounting 2 as shown in the worksheet in Figure CLA1-1.
5. Use the ChartWizard button to draw the column chart shown on the worksheet in Figure CLA1-1. Chart the range A2:D5.
6. Enter your name in cell A19. Enter your course, computer laboratory assignment number (CLA1-1), date, and instructor name below in cells A20 through A23.
7. Save the workbook using the filename CLA1-1.
8. Print the worksheet with cell gridlines off.
9. Increase the tuition by $200.00 for Semester 1 and Semester 2. Increase the cost of books by $25.00 for all three semesters. Increase the Lab fees by $25.00 for Semester 2. The three semester totals should be $1,195.00, $1,250.00, and $540.00, respectively. Print the worksheet containing the new values with cell gridlines off.

COMPUTER LABORATORY ASSIGNMENT 2
Creating a Daily Sales Report Worksheet

Purpose: To become familiar with building a worksheet, formatting a worksheet, embedding a column chart, printing a worksheet, and saving a workbook.

Problem: The Music City company has hired you to work in its Information Systems Department as a part-time consultant. The president of the company has requested that a worksheet be created showing a daily sales summary report for the company's three stores. The request has been turned over to you to handle. The report is to list the daily sales in each store for compact discs (CDs), cassettes, and videos. The daily sales are shown in the table below.

Instructions: Perform the tasks below and on the next page:

1. Create the worksheet shown in Figure CLA1-2 using the numbers in the table below.

	STORE 1	STORE 2	STORE 3
CDs	775.29	600.51	995.17
CASSETTES	550.38	425.43	605.24
VIDEOS	350.65	250.33	400.17

2. Direct Excel to determine the totals for Store 1, Store 2, Store 3, CDs, Cassettes, Videos, and all the stores.

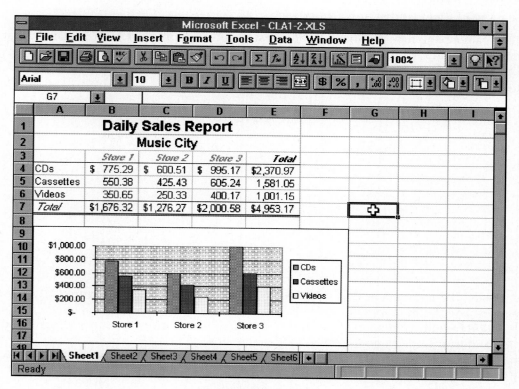

FIGURE CLA1-2

(continued)

COMPUTER LABORATORY ASSIGNMENT 2 (continued)

3. Format the worksheet title, Daily Sales Report, as 14 point, bold, and centered over columns A through E.
4. Format the worksheet subtitle, Music City, as 12 point, bold, and centered over columns A through E.
5. Format the range A3:E7 using the table format Accounting 1 as shown on Figure CLA1-2.
6. Use the ChartWizard button to draw the column chart shown on the worksheet in Figure CLA1-2. Chart the range A3:D6.
7. Enter your name in cell A19. Enter your course, computer laboratory assignment number (CLA1-2), date, and instructor name below the chart in cells A20 through A23.
8. Save the workbook using the filename CLA1-2.
9. Print the worksheet with cell gridlines on.
10. Print the worksheet with cell gridlines off. Save the workbook using the filename CLA1-2.
11. Make the following changes to the daily sales: Store 1, CDs — $546.34, Store 2, Videos — $395.45, and Store 3, Cassettes — $943.67. The new three-store totals should be $1,447.37, $1,421.39, and $2,339.01.
12. Select the chart and increase its width by one column.
13. Print the modified worksheet with cell gridlines off.

COMPUTER LABORATORY ASSIGNMENT 3
Creating a Personal Financial Statement

Purpose: To become familiar with building a worksheet, formatting a worksheet, embedding a column chart, printing a worksheet, and saving a workbook.

Problem: To obtain a bank loan, the bank has requested you to supply a personal financial statement. The statement is to include your average monthly income for the last three years and all major expenses. The data required to prepare your financial statement is shown in the table below.

	1993	1994	1995
INCOME:			
Wages	1200.00	1450.00	1550.00
Tips	300.00	425.00	550.00
EXPENSES:			
Rent	650.00	700.00	850.00
Utilities	125.00	150.00	160.00
Insurance	125.00	140.00	200.00
Other	200.00	250.00	290.00

Instructions: Using the numbers in the table, create the worksheet shown in Figure CLA1-3 including the chart of expenses. Use the AutoSum button to calculate the total income and total expenses for each of the three years. Enter your name in cell A19 and your course, computer laboratory assignment number (CLA1-3), date, and instructor name in cells A20 through A23.

To format the worksheet, use the table format Accounting 1 for the Income table and then again for the Expenses table.

Save the workbook using the filename CLA1-3. Print the worksheet without cell gridlines.

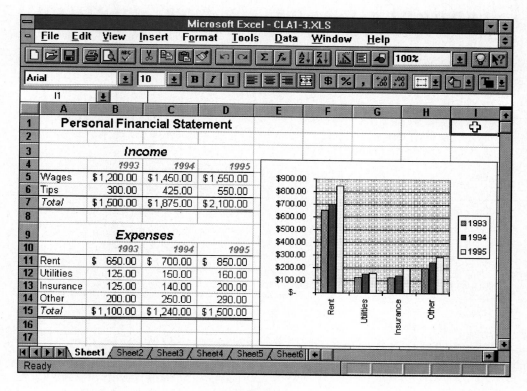

FIGURE CLA1-3

COMPUTER LABORATORY ASSIGNMENT 4
Planning a Weekly Expense Account Report

Purpose: To provide practice in planning and building a worksheet.

Problem: While in college, you are serving an internship in the Office Automation department of the Academic Textbook Company (ATC). ATC is a publishing company that sells textbooks to high schools and colleges throughout the United States. The company has sales representatives that are reimbursed for the following expenses: lodging, meals, and travel.

You have been asked to create for distribution a worksheet that the sales representatives can use as a weekly expense report. Beginning next month, the weekly expense report must be submitted by each sales representative to the regional sales manager of the company by Wednesday of the following week. The sheet should summarize the daily expenses and the total weekly expense. Expenses are only paid for Monday, Tuesday, Wednesday, Thursday, and Friday, the days on which the sales representatives can call upon teachers at the schools.

Instructions: Design and create the Weekly Expense Report. Develop your own test data. Submit the following:

1. A description of the problem. Include the purpose of the worksheet, a statement outlining the results, the required data, and calculations.
2. A handwritten design of the worksheet. This document should be approved by your manager (your instructor) before you build the worksheet.
3. A printed copy of the worksheet without cell gridlines.
4. A one-page, double-spaced typewritten description of the worksheet explaining to the sales representatives its purpose, how to retrieve it, how to enter data into it, save it, and print it.
5. Use the techniques you learned in this project to format the worksheet. Include a column chart that compares the daily costs.
6. Enter your name, course, computer laboratory assignment number (CLA1-4), date, and instructor name below the chart in column A. Save the workbook using the filename CLA1-4.

MICROSOFT EXCEL 5 FOR WINDOWS

P R O J E C T   T W O

▼

FORMULAS, FORMATTING, AND CREATING CHARTS

OBJECTIVES You will have mastered the material in this project when you can:

▸ Enter a formula
▸ Use the Point mode to enter formulas
▸ Identify the arithmetic operators +, −, *, /, %, and ^
▸ Determine a percentage
▸ Apply the AVERAGE, MAX, and MIN functions
▸ Change a cell's font
▸ Change the font of individual characters in a cell
▸ Color the characters and background of a cell
▸ Align text in cells
▸ Add borders to a range of cells
▸ Change a column width or row height to best fit

▸ Change the width of a series of adjacent columns
▸ Change the height of a row
▸ Check the spelling of a worksheet
▸ Create a chart on a separate sheet
▸ Format chart items
▸ Rename sheet tabs
▸ Preview how a printed copy of the worksheet and chart sheet will look
▸ Print an entire workbook
▸ Print a partial or complete worksheet
▸ Display and print the formulas version of a worksheet
▸ Print to fit
▸ Distinguish between portrait and landscape orientation

▶ INTRODUCTION

I n Project 1, you learned about entering data, summing values, making the worksheet easier to read, and drawing a chart. You also learned about online Help and saving, printing, and loading a workbook from disk into main memory. This project continues to emphasize these topics and presents some new ones.

The new topics include entering formulas, changing fonts, coloring characters in a cell and the background of a cell, adding borders, changing the widths of columns and heights of rows, spell checking, using additional charting techniques, and producing alternative types of printouts. One alternative display and printout shows the formulas rather than the values in the worksheet. When you display the formulas in the worksheet, you see exactly what text, data, formulas, and functions you have entered into it.

E66

▶ PROJECT TWO — AWESOME SOUND INTERNATIONAL SALES ANALYSIS

The worksheet in Project 2 (Figure 2-1) contains a sales report for the month of May that shows the gross sales, returns, net sales, and percent returns by division for Awesome Sound International. In addition, for the gross sales, returns, net sales, and percent returns, the worksheet includes totals in row 9, averages in row 10, and highest and lowest values in rows 11 and 12. On a separate sheet, a 3-D column chart compares the sales by division.

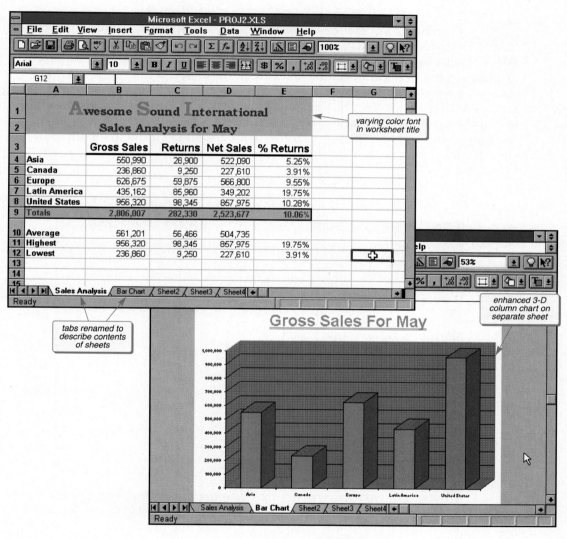

FIGURE 2-1

To improve the appearance of the worksheet and to make it easier to read, the numbers in the worksheet are formatted. The widths of columns A through E and the heights of rows 3 and 10 are increased to add more space between the titles and numbers.

In Figure 2-1, the gross sales in column B and the returns in column C make up the data sent to the accounting department from the division offices throughout the world. You enter the numbers into the worksheet in the same fashion as described in Project 1.

Each division's net sales figure in column D is equal to the gross sales in column B minus the returns in column C and is calculated from a formula. Each division's percent return in column E is the quotient of the returns in column C divided by the gross sales in column B. Row 9 contains the total gross sales, total returns, total net sales, and percent returns for all sales. Finally, rows 10 through 12 contain the average, maximum and minimum gross sales, returns, and net sales.

▶ ENTERING THE TITLES AND NUMBERS INTO THE WORKSHEET

T he worksheet title and subtitle in Figure 2-1 on the previous page are centered over columns A through E in rows 1 and 2. Because the centered text must first be entered into the leftmost column of the area over which it is to be centered, it will be entered into cells A1 and A2. The column headings in row 3 begin in cell B3 and extend through cell E3. The row titles in column A begin in cell A4 and continue down to cell A12. The numbers are entered into the range B4:C8. The total gross sales in cell B9 and the total returns in cell C9 are determined using the SUM function. The steps required to enter the worksheet title, column titles, row titles, numbers, and determine the totals in cells B9 and C9 are outlined in the remainder of this section and are shown in Figure 2-2.

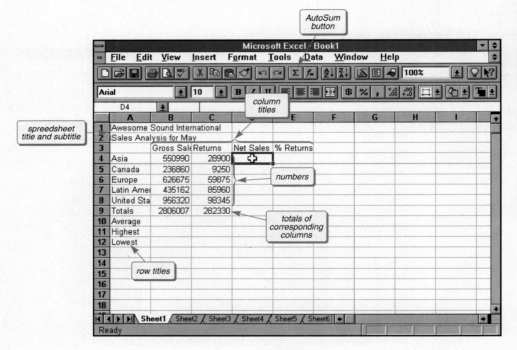

FIGURE 2-2

TO ENTER THE WORKSHEET TITLES

Step 1: Select cell A1. Type Awesome Sound International and click the enter box or press the ENTER key

Step 2: Select cell A2. Type Sales Analysis for May and click the enter box or press the ENTER key.

The worksheet titles display as shown in cells A1 and A2 of Figure 2-2.

TO ENTER THE COLUMN TITLES

Step 1: Select cell B3. Type `Gross Sales` and press the RIGHT ARROW key.

Step 2: Enter the column titles `Returns`, `Net Sales`, and `% Returns` in cells C3, D3, and E3 in the same fashion as described in Step 1.

The column titles display as shown in row 3 of Figure 2-2. Don't be concerned that a portion of the column title Gross Sales is hidden. Later, the column widths will be increased so it will display in its entirety.

TO ENTER THE ROW TITLES

Step 1: Select cell A4. Type `Asia` and press the DOWN ARROW key.

Step 2: Enter the row titles `Canada`, `Europe`, `Latin America`, `United States`, `Totals`, `Average`, `Highest`, and `Lowest` in cells A5 through A12.

The row titles display as shown in column A of Figure 2-2.

TO ENTER THE NUMBERS

Step 1: Enter `550990` in cell B4 and `28900` in cell C4.

Step 2: Enter `236860` in cell B5 and `9250` in cell C5.

Step 3: Enter `626675` in cell B6 and `59875` in cell C6.

Step 4: Enter `435162` in cell B7 and `85960` in cell C7.

Step 5: Enter `956320` in cell B8 and `98345` in cell C8.

The numeric entries display as shown in the range B4:C8 of Figure 2-2.

TO ENTER THE TOTALS

Step 1: Select the range B9:C9.

Step 2: Click the AutoSum button on the Standard toolbar.

Step 3: Select cell D4.

The totals for the gross sales and returns display in cells B9 and C9, respectively (Figure 2-2).

▶ ENTERING FORMULAS

The net sales for each division, which displays in column D, is equal to the corresponding gross sales in column B minus the corresponding returns in column C. Thus, the net sales for the Asia division in row 4 is obtained by subtracting 28900 (cell C4) from 550990 (cell B4).

One of the reasons Excel is such a valuable tool is because you can assign a **formula** to a cell and Excel will calculate the result. In this example, the formula in cell D4 subtracts the value in cell C4 from the value in cell B4 and displays the result in cell D4. The steps to enter the formula using the keyboard are described on the next page.

TO ENTER A FORMULA THROUGH THE KEYBOARD ▼

STEP 1 ►

Select cell D4. Type =b4-c4

The formula displays in the formula bar and in cell D4 (Figure 2-3).

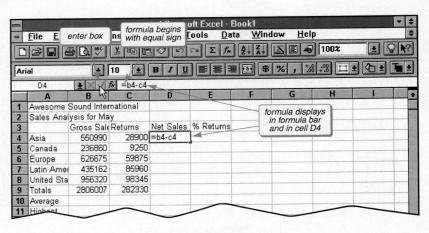

FIGURE 2-3

STEP 2 ►

Click the enter box or press the ENTER key.

Instead of displaying the formula in cell D4, Excel completes the arithmetic indicated by the formula and displays the result, 522090 in cell D4 (Figure 2-4).

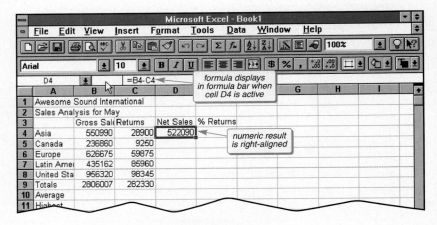

FIGURE 2-4

The equal sign (=) preceding b4-c4 is an important part of the formula. It alerts Excel that you are entering a formula or function and not text, such as words. The minus sign (–) following b4 is the arithmetic operator, which directs Excel to perform the subtraction operation. Other valid Excel arithmetic operators include + (**addition**), * (**multiplication**), / (**division**), % (**percentage**), and ^ (**exponentiation**).

You can enter formulas in uppercase or lowercase, and you can add spaces between the arithmetic operators to make the formulas easier to read. That is, =b4-c4 is the same as =B4-C4, =b4 - c4 or =B4 - C4. Notice in Figure 2-4 that Excel displays the formula in the formula bar in uppercase when cell D4 is the active cell even though it was entered earlier in lowercase.

Except for row references, the formulas required to compute the net sales for the other regions in column D are the same as the formula in cell D4. Hence, you can use the fill handle in the lower right corner of the heavy border that surrounds the active cell (Figure 2-4) to copy cell D4 down through the range D5:D9.

TO COPY A FORMULA IN ONE CELL TO ADJACENT CELLS ▼

STEP 1 ►

Select cell D4, the cell to copy. Point to the fill handle.

The mouse pointer changes to a cross (Figure 2-5).

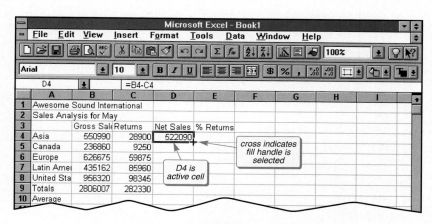

FIGURE 2-5

STEP 2 ►

Drag the fill handle down to select the range D5:D9 and then release the left mouse button.

Excel copies the formula in cell D4 (=B4-C4) to the range D5:D9 and displays the net sales for the remaining divisions (Figure 2-6).

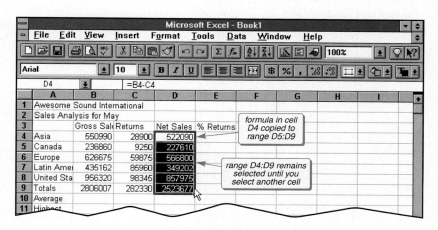

FIGURE 2-6

Select any cell to remove the selection from the range D4:D9.

When Excel copies the formula =B4-C4 in cell D4 to the range D5:D9, the row references in the formula are adjusted as the formula is copied downward. For example, the formula assigned to cell D5 is =B5-C5. Similarly, Excel assigns cell D6 the formula =B6-C6, cell D7 the formula =B7-C7, cell D8 the formula =B8-C8, and cell D9 the formula =B9-C9. When you copy downward, the row reference changes in the formula.

Order of Operations

In the formulas in column D, only one arithmetic operation is involved, subtraction. When more than one operator is involved in a formula, Excel uses the same order of operations that algebra follows. Moving from left to right in a formula, the **order of operations** is as follows: first negation (-), then all percents (%), then all exponentiations (^), then all multiplications (*) and divisions (/), and finally all additions (+) and subtractions (-). You can use **parentheses** to override the order of operations. All operations within parentheses ae performed before the operations outside the parentheses.

For example, following the order of operations, 8 * 5 - 2 is equal to 38. However, 8 * (5 - 2) is equal to 24 because the parentheses instruct Excel to subtract 2 from 5 before multiplying by 8. Table 2-1 illustrates several examples of valid formulas.

▸ **TABLE 2-1**

FORMULA	REMARK
=E3	Assigns the value in cell E3 to the active cell.
=5 + -10^2	Assigns 105 to the active cell.
=7 * F5 or =F5 * 7 or =(7 * F5)	Assigns seven times the contents of cell F5 to the active cell.
=525 * 15%	Assigns the product of 525 times 0.15 to the active cell.
=-G44 * G45	Assigns the negative value of the product of the values contained in cells G44 and G45 to the active cell.
=2 * (J12 - F2)	Assigns the product of two times the difference between the values contained in cells J12 and F2 to the active cell.
=A1 / C6 - A3 * A4 + A5 ^ A6	From left to right: first exponentiation (A5 ^ A6), then division (A1 / C6), then multiplication (A3 * A4), then subtraction (A1 / C6 - A3 * A4), and finally addition (A1 / C6 - A3 * A4 + A5 ^ A6). If cells A1 = 10, A3 = 6, A4 = 2, A5 = 5, A6 = 2, and C6 = 2, then Excel assigns the active cell the value 18 (10 / 2 - 6 * 2 + 5 ^ 2 = 18).

▶ ENTERING FORMULAS USING THE POINT MODE

In the worksheet shown in Figure 2-1 on page E67, the percent returns for each division display in column E. The percent returns for the Asia division in cell E4 is equal to the returns (cell C4) divided by the gross sales (cell B4). Recall that the slash (/) represents the operation of division.

Rather than entering the formula =c4/b4 in cell E4 completely through the keyboard as was done with net sales in cell D4, the following steps show how to use the mouse and the Point mode to enter a formula. **Point mode** allows you to select cells to be used in a formula by using the mouse.

TO ENTER A FORMULA USING POINT MODE ▼

STEP 1 ▶

Select cell E4. Type the equal sign (=) in the formula bar to begin the formula and click cell C4.

Excel responds by highlighting cell C4 with a moving border and by appending cell C4 to the equal sign in the formula bar and in cell E4 (Figure 2-7).

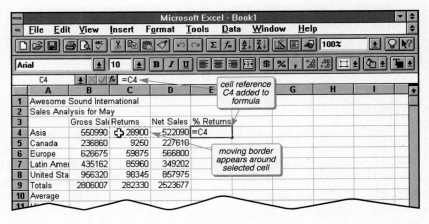

FIGURE 2-7

STEP 2 ▶

Type the slash (/) in the formula bar and click cell B4.

Excel highlights cell B4 with a moving border and appends cell B4 to the slash (/) in the formula bar and in cell E4 (Figure 2-8).

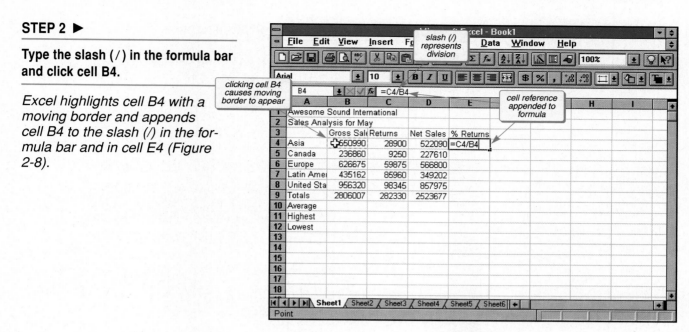

FIGURE 2-8

STEP 3 ▶

Click the enter box or press the ENTER key.

Excel determines the quotient of =C4/B4 and stores the result, 0.052451, in cell E4 (Figure 2-9).

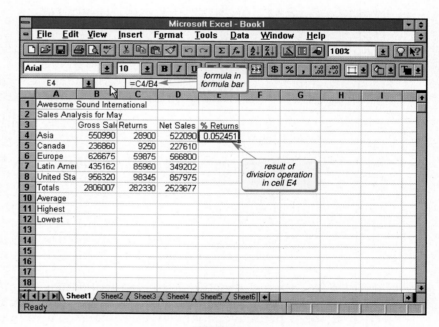

FIGURE 2-9

Later in this project the percent returns, 0.052451, will be formatted to 5.25%.

To complete the percent returns for the remaining divisions and the total line in row 9, use the fill handle to copy cell E4 to the range E5:E9. Perform the following steps to complete the copy.

TO COPY A FORMULA IN ONE CELL TO ADJACENT CELLS

Step 1: Select E4, the cell to copy. Point to the fill handle.
Step 2: Drag the fill handle down to select the range E5:E9 and then release
the left mouse button.

*Excel copies the formula in cell E4 to the range E5:E9 and displays the per-
cent returns in decimal form for those cells (Figure 2-10).*

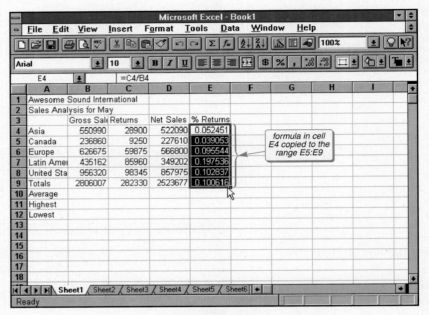

FIGURE 2-10

▶ USING THE AVERAGE, MAX, AND MIN FUNCTIONS

The next step in creating the Sales Analysis report is to compute the
average gross sales, place it in cell B10, and then copy it to the range
C10:D10 to calculate the average returns and average net sales. The
average gross sales can be computed by assigning to cell B10 the formula
=(B4 + B5 + B6 + B7 + B8) / 5, but Excel includes an **AVERAGE function** that
is much easier to use.

A **function** is a prewritten formula that takes a value or values, performs an
operation, and returns a value or values. The values that you give to a function to
perform operations on are called the **arguments**. All functions begin with an
equal sign and include the arguments in parentheses after the function name. For
example, in the function =AVERAGE(B4:B8), the function name is AVERAGE and
the argument is the range B4:B8. Perform the following steps to assign the AVER-
AGE function to cell B10.

TO FIND THE AVERAGE OF A GROUP OF NUMBERS ▼

home.htm

<AHREF= classes.htm>

STEP 1 ▶

Select cell B10. Type =average(

Excel displays the beginning of the AVERAGE function in the formula bar and in cell B10 (Figure 2-11).

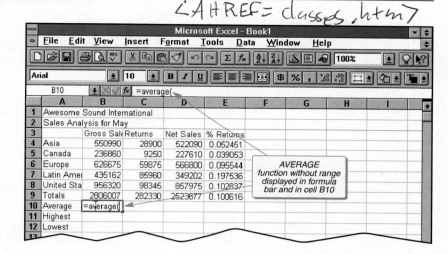

FIGURE 2-11

STEP 2 ▶

Select cell B4, the first end point of the range to average. Drag the mouse pointer down to cell B8, the second end point of the range to average.

A marquis surrounds the range B4:B8. When you select cell B4, Excel appends cell B4 to the left parenthesis in the formula bar and highlights cell B4 with a moving border. When you begin dragging, Excel appends a colon (:) to the function and also the cell reference of the cell where the mouse pointer is located (Figure 2-12).

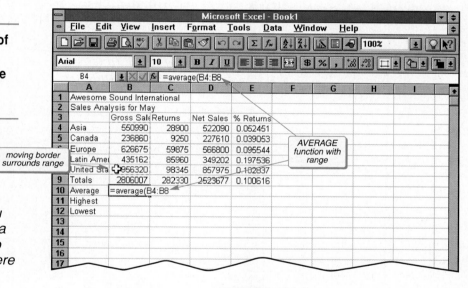

FIGURE 2-12

STEP 4 ▶

Release the left mouse button, and then click the enter box or press the ENTER key.

Excel computes the average, 561201.4, of the five numbers in the range B4:B8 and assigns it to cell B10 (Figure 2-13).

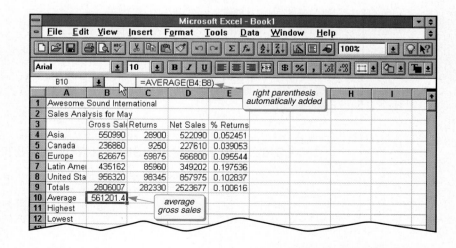

FIGURE 2-13

Notice that Excel automatically appends the right parenthesis to complete the AVERAGE function when you click the enter box or press the ENTER key. The AVERAGE function requires that the range (the argument) be included within parentheses following the function name.

The example just illustrated used the Point mode to select the range following the left parenthesis. Instead of using Point mode, you can type the range. If you decide to type a range, remember that the colon (:) separating the endpoints of the range is required punctuation.

The next two required entries are the average returns in cell C10 and the average net sales in cell D10. Except for the ranges, these two entries are identical to the AVERAGE function in cell B9. Thus, you can use the fill handle to copy cell B10 to the range C10:D10.

Notice this project does not average in cell E10 the percent returns in column E because these values use different denominators. Thus, the average percent returns would make no sense.

TO COPY A FUNCTION IN ONE CELL TO ADJACENT CELLS

Step 1: Select cell B10, the cell to copy. Point to the fill handle.
Step 2: Drag the fill handle across the range C10:D10 and then release the left mouse button.

Excel copies the AVERAGE function in cell B10 to the range C10:D10 and displays 56466 in cell C10 and 504735.4 in cell D10 (Figure 2-14).

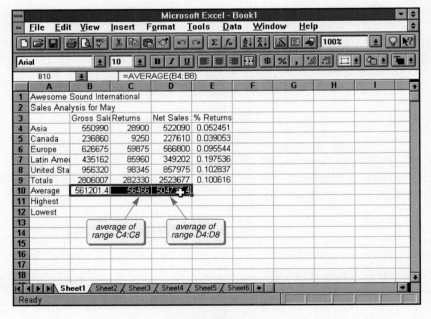

FIGURE 2-14

Calculating the Highest Value in a Range Using the MAX Function

The next step is to select cell B11 and determine the highest value in the range B4:B8. Excel has a function for displaying the highest value in a range called the **MAX function**. Enter the function name and use the Point mode as described in the steps on the opposite page.

TO FIND THE HIGHEST NUMBER IN A RANGE.

Step 1: Select cell B11. Type =max(

Step 2: Select cell B4, the first end point of the desired range. Drag the mouse pointer down to cell B8, the second end point of the desired range.

Step 3: Release the left mouse button and then click the enter box or press the ENTER key.

Excel determines the highest value in the range B4:B8 as 956320 (cell B8) and displays it in cell B11 (Figure 2-15).

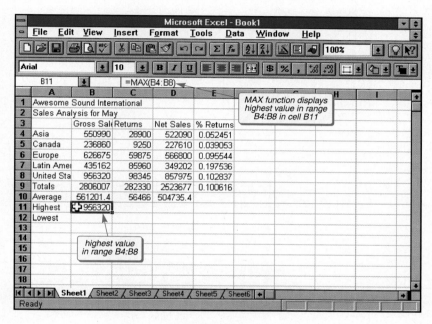

FIGURE 2-15

Certainly it would be as easy as entering the MAX function to scan the range B4:B8 to determine the highest value in the range B4:B8 and enter the number 956320 as a constant in cell B11. The display would be the same as shown in Figure 2-15. However, if the values in the range B4:B8 change, cell B11 would continue to display 956320. By using the MAX function, you are guaranteed that Excel will recalculate the highest value in the range B4:B8 each time a new value is entered into the worksheet.

Calculating the Lowest Value in a Range Using the MIN Function

The next step is to enter the **MIN function** in cell B12 to determine the lowest value in the range B4:B8. Although you could enter the MIN function in the same fashion as the MAX function, the following steps show an alternative using Excel's **Function Wizard button** on the Standard toolbar.

TO ENTER A FUNCTION USING THE FUNCTION WIZARD BUTTON ▼

STEP 1 ▶

Select cell B12 and point to the
Function Wizard button (⨍ₓ) on the
Standard toolbar (Figure 2-16).

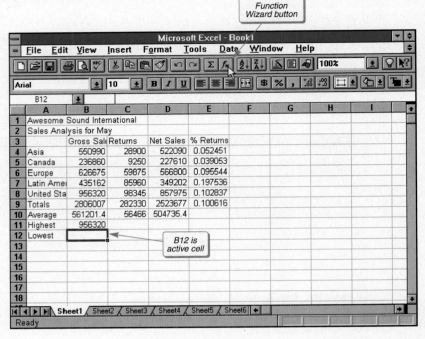

FIGURE 2-16

STEP 2 ▶

Click the Function Wizard button.
Select MIN in the Function Name list
box and point to the Next button
(Next).

*Excel displays the Function
Wizard – Step 1 of 2 dialog box
with Most Recently Used selected
in the Function Category list box,
MIN selected in the Function
Name list box, and the mouse
pointer pointing to the Next button
(Figure 2-17).*

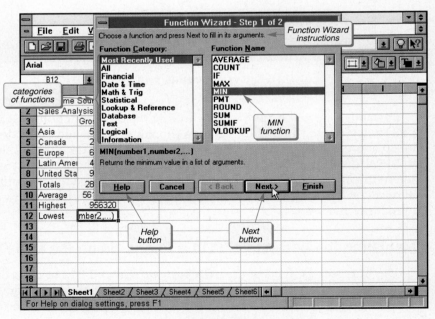

FIGURE 2-17

STEP 3 ▶

Choose the Next button.

Excel displays the Function Wizard – Step 2 of 2 dialog box.

STEP 4 ▶

Use the mouse and Point mode to select the range B4:B8 on the worksheet and then point to the Finish button (Finish).

Excel enters the range in the number 1 box and displays the result of =MIN(B4:B8) in the Value box (236860) of the dialog box (Figure 2-18).

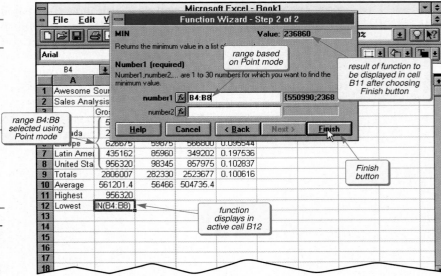

FIGURE 2-18

STEP 5 ▶

Choose the Finish button.

Excel determines the lowest value in the range B4:B8 and displays it in cell B12 (Figure 2-19).

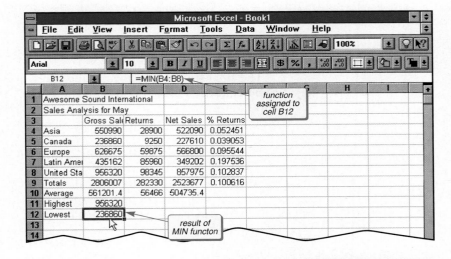

FIGURE 2-19

You can see from the previous example that using the Function Wizard button on the Standard toolbar allows you to easily enter a function into a cell without requiring you to memorize its format. Any time you are to enter a function, simply click the Function Wizard button on the Standard toolbar, select the desired function, and enter the arguments.

An alternative to using the Function Wizard button on the Standard toolbar, is to use the Function Wizard button, which is next to the enter box on the formula bar. This button only displays when the formula bar is active (see Figure 2-12 on page E75) and is primarily used to enter a function in the middle of a formula you are entering into a cell. A third alternative for entering a function into a cell is to choose the Function command on the Insert menu.

Thus far, you have learned to use the SUM, AVERAGE, MAX, and MIN functions. Besides these four functions, Excel has more than 400 additional functions that handle just about every type of calculation you can imagine. These functions are categorized as shown in the Function Category box in Figure 2-17.

To obtain a list and description of the available functions, choose the Contents command from the Help menu. When Excel displays the Microsoft Excel Help screen, choose Reference Information. Then choose Worksheet Functions, and finally choose Alphabetical List of Worksheet Functions or choose Worksheet Functions listed by Category. Use the Print command on the File menu of the Microsoft Help Screen to obtain a hardcopy of any desired topics.

In the Function Wizard dialog box in Figure 2-18 on the previous page, there are five buttons from which to choose. If a button is dimmed (or ghosted), that means you cannot choose it. The functions of the five Function Wizard buttons are described in Table 2-2.

▶ **TABLE 2-2**

BUTTON	FUNCTION
Help	Displays help on the Function Wizard
Cancel	Cancels the Function Wizard and returns you to the worksheet
Back	Displays the previous dialog box
Next	Displays the next dialog box
Finish	Assigns the cell the selections made thus far

Copying the MAX and MIN Functions

The final step before formatting the worksheet is to copy the MAX and MIN functions in the range B11:B12 to the range C11:E12. Using the fill handle you can complete the copy. This example illustrates that the fill handle can be used to copy a range of cells to an adjacent range.

TO COPY A RANGE OF CELLS TO ANOTHER RANGE USING THE FILL HANDLE

Step 1: Select the range B11:B12. Point to the fill handle.
Step 2: Drag the fill handle to the right to select the range C11:E12 and then release the left mouse button.

Excel copies the MAX function across the range C11:E11 and the MIN function across the range C12:E12 (Figure 2-20).

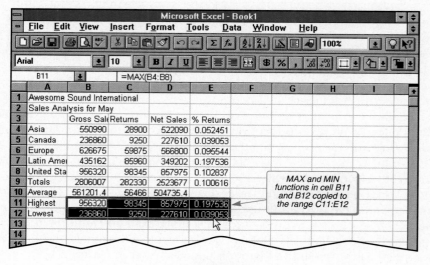

FIGURE 2-20

Here again, you must remember that Excel adjusts the ranges in the copied function so each function refers to the column of numbers above it. Review the numbers in rows 11 and 12 in Figure 2-20. You should see that each MAX function is determining the highest value in the column above it for rows 4 through 8 and each MIN function is determining the lowest value in the column above it for rows 4 through 8.

Select any cell in the worksheet to remove the selection from the range B11:E12. This concludes entering the data and formulas into the worksheet. The next step is to apply formatting to the worksheet so it is easier to read. However, before moving on, it is best to save the workbook.

▶ SAVING AN INTERMEDIATE COPY OF THE WORKBOOK

A good practice is to save intermediate copies of your work. That way, if your computer loses power or you make a serious mistake, you can always retrieve the latest copy from disk. It is recommended that you save an intermediate copy of the worksheet every 50 to 75 keystrokes. Use the Save button on the Standard toolbar often, because you can save keying time later if the unexpected happens. For the following steps, it is assumed you have a formatted disk in drive A.

TO SAVE AN INTERMEDIATE COPY OF THE WORKBOOK ▼

STEP 1 ▶

Click the Save button on the Standard toolbar. When the Save As dialog box displays, type `proj2` in the File Name box. If necessary, use the Drives box to change to drive A.

The Save As dialog box displays as shown in Figure 2-21.

STEP 2 ▶

Choose the OK button from the Save As dialog box, and then choose the OK button in the Summary Info dialog box.

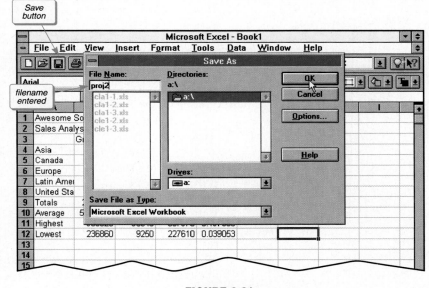

FIGURE 2-21

After Excel completes the save, the worksheet remains on the screen with PROJ2.XLS in the title bar. You can immediately continue with the next activity.

▶ APPLYING FORMATS TO THE WORKSHEET

 lthough the worksheet contains the data, formulas, and functions that make up the Sales Analysis Report, the text and numbers need to be formatted to improve their appearance and readability.

In Project 1, you used the AutoFormat command to apply formatting to the majority of the worksheet. However, you may not always find an acceptable Format Table layout to use. This section describes how to change the unformatted worksheet in Figure 2-22a to the formatted worksheet in Figure 2-22b without using the AutoFormat command.

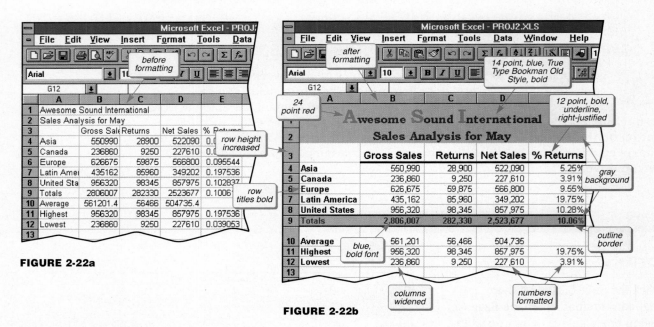

FIGURE 2-22a

FIGURE 2-22b

The type of formatting required in the Project 2 worksheet is outlined as follows:

1. Worksheet titles
   a. font type — TrueType (TT) Bookman Old Style (or TT Courier New if your system does not have TT Bookman Old Style)
   b. font size — 14
   c. font style — bold
   d. font color — blue
   e. font size and font color of first character in each word in main title — 24 red.
   f. alignment — center across columns A through E
   g. background color (range A1:E2) — gray
2. Column titles
   a. font size — 12
   b. font style — bold
   c. alignment — right-justified
   d. border — underline
3. Row titles
   a. font style — bold
4. Total line
   a. font style — bold
   b. font color — blue
   c. background color — gray
   d. border — outline

5. Numbers in range B4:D12
   a. Comma style with no decimal places
6. Numbers in range E4:E12
   a. Percent style with two decimal places
7. Increase the column widths as follows: A to best fit; B to 13.71 characters; C and D to 11.00 characters; and E to 12.14 characters.
8. Increase the heights of rows 3 and 10 to 24.00 points

All of the above formatting can be applied by using the mouse and Formatting toolbar.

Applying Formats to the Worksheet Titles

To emphasize the worksheet title in cells A1 and A2, the font type, size, style, and color are changed as described in the following steps.

TO APPLY FORMATS TO THE CHARACTERS IN THE WORKSHEET TITLE ▼

STEP 1 ▶

Select the range A1:A2.

STEP 2 ▶

Click the Font box arrow on the Formatting toolbar and point to TT Bookman Old Style (or TT Courier New if your system does not have TT Bookman Old Style).

The Font drop-down list box displays (Figure 2-23).

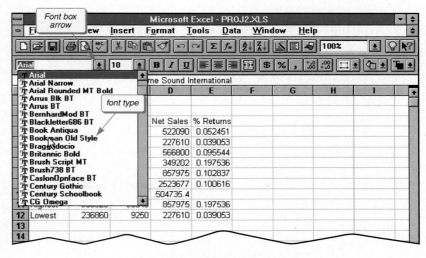

FIGURE 2-23

STEP 3 ▶

Click the left mouse button to choose TT Bookman Old Style (or TT Courier New). Click the Font Size box arrow on the Formatting toolbar and point to 14.

The characters in cells A1 and A2 display using TT Bookman Old Style (or TT Courier New). The mouse pointer points to 14 in the Font Size drop-down list box (Figure 2-24).

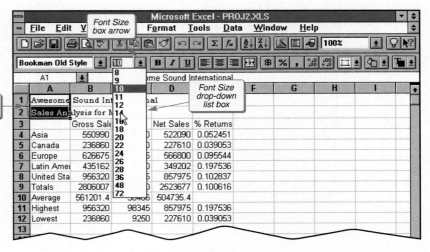

FIGURE 2-24

STEP 4 ▶

Click the left mouse button to change the font size to 14 point and click the Bold button on the Formatting toolbar.

The font in cells A1 and A2 displays in 14 point bold (Figure 2-25). Excel automatically increases the row heights of rows 1 and 2 so the larger characters fit in the cells.

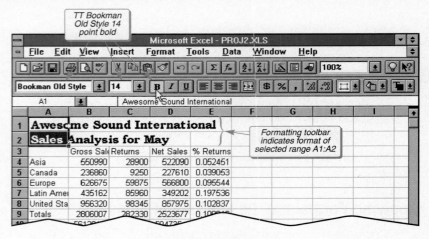

FIGURE 2-25

STEP 5 ▶

Click the Font Color button arrow ( ) on the Formatting toolbar and point to the dark blue color (column 1, row 4) on the Font Color palette.

Excel displays the Font Color palette (Figure 2-26).

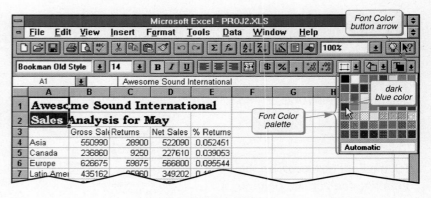

FIGURE 2-26

STEP 6 ▶

Click the left mouse button to choose the dark blue font color.

Excel changes the font color of the characters in cells A1 and A2 from black to dark blue.

STEP 7 ▶

Double-click cell A1 to edit the contents of the cell. Drag across the letter A in Awesome. Click the Font Size box arrow and point to 24.

Excel enters the Edit mode and the letter A in Awesome is selected (Figure 2-27). The Font Size drop-down list box displays.

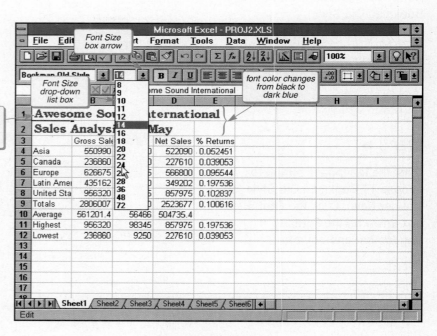

FIGURE 2-27

STEP 8 ▶

Click the left mouse button to choose 24. Click the Font Color button arrow, and then point to the color red (column 3, row 1) on the Font Color palette.

The letter A in Awesome increases to 24 points and the mouse pointer points to the red color on the palette (Figure 2-28).

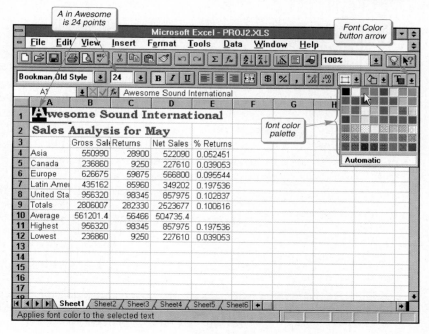

FIGURE 2-28

STEP 9 ▶

Click the left mouse button to choose the red font color for the selected letter A in Awesome.

STEP 10 ▶

Repeat Step 7 through Step 9 for the letter S in Sound and the letter I in International. To choose red using the Font Color button, click the Font Color button, which displays the last color applied.

STEP 11 ▶

Click the check box on the formula bar or press the ENTER key to complete editing the contents of cell A1.

The text making up the worksheet titles displays in the desired format (Figure 2-29).

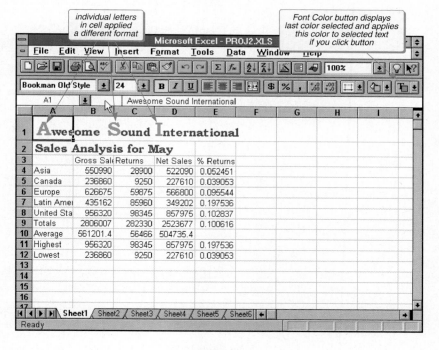

FIGURE 2-29

Excel allows you to change the font of individual characters in a cell or all of the characters in a cell, in a range of cells, or in the entire worksheet. You can also change the font any time while the worksheet is active. For example, some Excel users prefer to change the font before they enter any data. Others change the font while they are building the worksheet or after they have entered all the data. When developing presentation-quality worksheets, several different fonts are often used in the same worksheet.

Recall that the Bold button is like a toggle switch. Click it once and Excel bolds the selected range. Click it again with the same range selected and Excel removes the bold style.

The next step is to center the worksheet titles across columns A through E.

TO CENTER THE WORKSHEET TITLE

Step 1: Select the range A1:E2.
Step 2: Click the Center Across Columns button on the Formatting toolbar.
Step 3: Select cell B3.

Excel centers the worksheet titles in cells A1 and A2 across columns A through E (Figure 2-30).

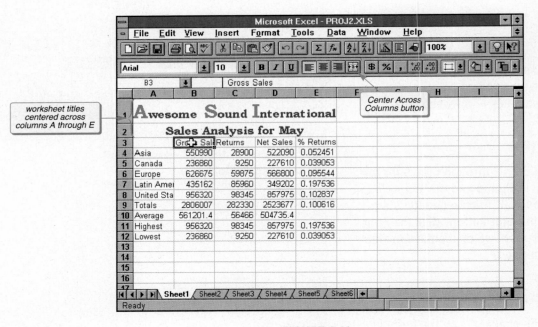

FIGURE 2-30

The final format to be applied to the worksheet title is the gray background color (Figure 2-22b on page E82). This format will be completed later when the background color of the totals in row 9 is applied.

Applying Formats to the Column Titles

According to Figure 2-22b, the text making up the column titles in row 3 are a font size of 12, a font style of bold, aligned right-justified, and underlined. The following steps apply these formats to the column titles.

TO APPLY FORMATS TO THE COLUMN TITLES ▼

STEP 1 ▶

Select the range B3:E3. Click the Font Size box arrow on the Formatting toolbar and point to 12.

The Font Size drop-down list box displays (Figure 2-31).

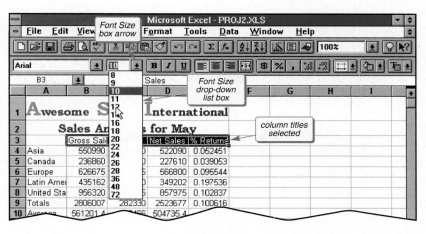

FIGURE 2-31

STEP 2 ▶

Click the left mouse button to choose 12 point. Click the Bold button and then the Align Right button (▤) on the Formatting toolbar, and point to the Borders button arrow (▣▼) on the Formatting toolbar.

Excel applies 12 point bold and right-aligns the text in the column titles (Figure 2-32).

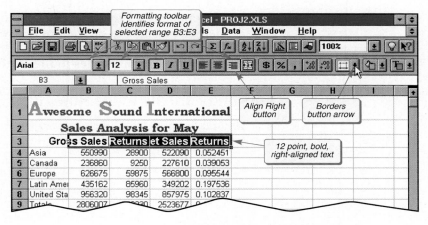

FIGURE 2-32

STEP 3 ▶

Click the Borders button arrow and point to the second border in the second row on the Borders palette.

The Borders palette displays (Figure 2-33). Any border selected will be applied to the selected range.

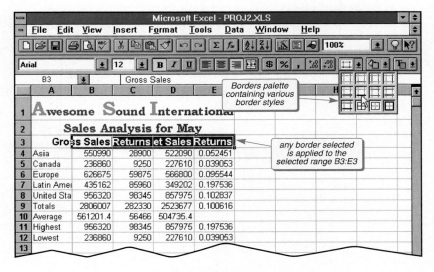

FIGURE 2-33

STEP 4 ▶

Click the left mouse button to choose the underline style, and select any cell on the worksheet.

Excel draws an underline below the column titles in row 3 (Figure 2-34).

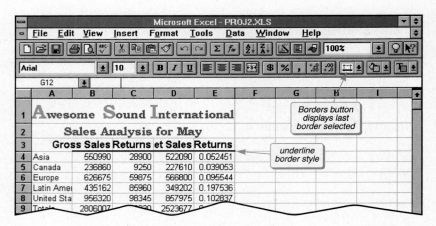

FIGURE 2-34

Notice, thus far, how all the formats have been applied using the mouse and Formatting toolbar. An alternative method to formatting the selected cells is to choose the Cells command on the **Format menu** or the **Format Cells command** on the shortcut menu. In either case, the Format Cells dialog box displays which allows you to apply format styles to the selected cells.

Applying Formats to the Row Titles

The next step is to bold the row titles in column A. Perform the following steps to complete this task.

TO APPLY FORMATS TO THE ROW TITLES

Step 1: Select the range A4:A12.
Step 2: Click the Bold button on the Formatting toolbar.

Excel bolds the text in the range A4:A12 (Figure 2-35).

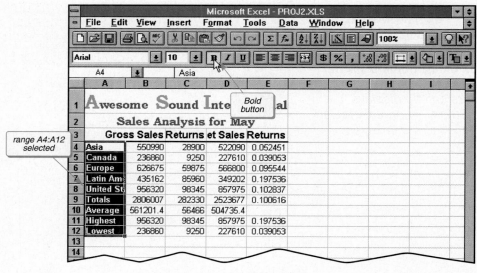

FIGURE 2-35

Applying Formats to the Totals Row and Changing the Background Color of the Worksheet Titles

According to Figure 2-22b on page E82 the totals in row 9 are formatted in a bold style and colored blue. To make the totals stand out, an outline surrounds the totals and the background is colored gray. The **background color** of a cell is the color of the area behind the characters in a cell. The background color of the worksheet titles (A1:E2) is also gray. To illustrate how you can select a **nonadjacent range** using the CTRL key, the background color of the worksheet titles will be changed at the same time the background color of the totals row is changed. Follow these steps to apply the desired format styles.

TO APPLY FORMATS TO THE TOTALS ROW AND CHANGE THE BACKGROUND COLOR ▼

STEP 1 ▶

Select the range A9:E9. Click the Bold button twice. Click the Borders button arrow, and point to the bold outline border on the Borders palette.

The Borders palette displays (Figure 2-36). The Bold button is clicked twice because cell A9 in the range A9:E9 is already bold.

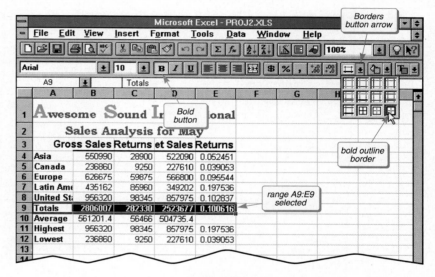

FIGURE 2-36

STEP 2 ▶

Click the left mouse button to choose the bold outline border and then click the Font Color arrow and point to the dark blue color (column 1, row 4) on the Font Color palette.

Excel draws an outline around the totals and the Font Color palette displays (Figure 2-37).

STEP 3 ▶

Click the left mouse button to choose the dark blue color on the Font Color palette.

Excel colors the font blue in the range A9:E9.

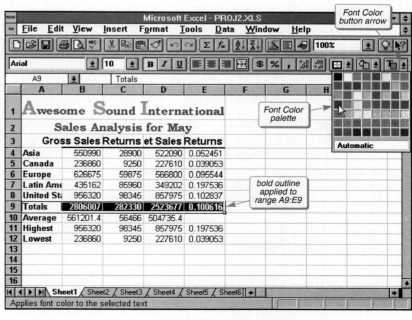

FIGURE 2-37

STEP 4 ▶

With the range A9:E9 selected, hold down the CTRL key and drag across the range A1:E2. Point to the Color button arrow ( ) on the Formatting toolbar.

The nonadjacent ranges A1:E2 and A9:E9 are selected (Figure 2-38).

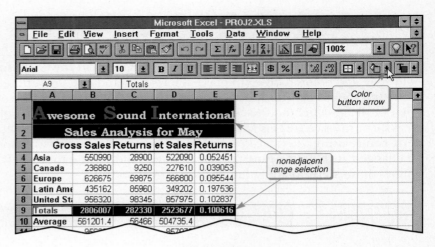

FIGURE 2-38

STEP 5 ▶

Click the left mouse button and point to the light gray color (column 7, row 2) on the Color palette (Figure 2-39).

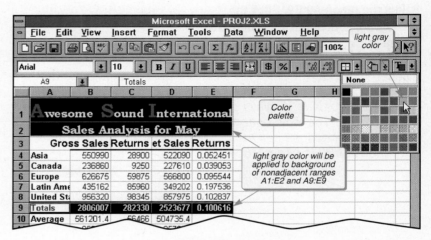

FIGURE 2-39

STEP 6 ▶

Click the left mouse button to choose the light gray color.

Excel colors the background of the nonadjacent ranges A1:E2 and A9:E9 light gray (Figure 2-40).

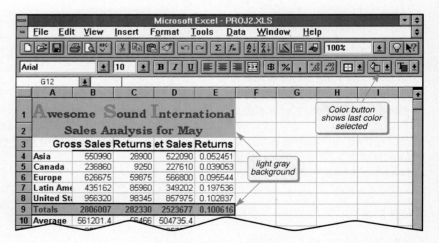

FIGURE 2-40

In the previous steps, you learned how to outline a range of cells, how to select nonadjacent ranges, and how to color the background of a range of cells. These format styles along with the ones previously discussed will allow you to develop professional looking worksheets that will be easy to read and understand.

▶ APPLYING NUMBER FORMATS

hen using Excel, you can apply formats to represent dollar amounts, whole numbers with comma placement, percentages, and decimal numbers through the use of buttons on the Formatting toolbar.

According to Figure 2-22b on page E82, the numbers in columns B through D are formatted to the Comma style with no decimal places. The **Comma style** inserts a comma every three positions to the left of the decimal point. The numbers in the % Returns column are formatted to the Percent style with two decimal places. The **Percent style** inserts a percent sign (%) to the right of the number.

The remainder of this section describes how to use the Comma style, Percent style, Increase Decimal, and Decrease Decimal buttons on the Formatting toolbar to format the numbers in the worksheet. Besides inserting a comma in a number, the **Comma Style button** adds two decimal places to the right of the decimal point. Because this project requires no decimal places in the dollar amounts, the **Decrease Decimal button** on the Formatting toolbar is used to eliminate the decimal places.

The **Percent style button** displays a number in Percent style with no decimal places. Because this project requires two decimal places in the % Returns column, the **Increase Decimal button** is used to add two decimal places. Follow these steps to apply number formatting.

TO APPLY NUMBER FORMATS TO THE WORKSHEET ▼

STEP 1 ▶

Select the range B4:D12. Point to the Comma Style button ( ) on the Formatting toolbar (Figure 2-41).

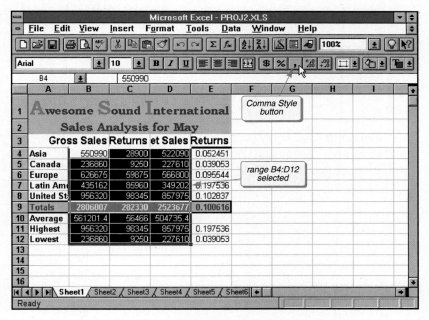

FIGURE 2-41

STEP 2 ▶

Click the left mouse button to apply the Comma style and point to the Decrease Decimal button (⊞) on the Formatting toolbar.

*The majority of numbers in the range B4:D12 display as a sequence of **number signs** (#) indicating they are too large to fit in the width of the cells (Figure 2-42).*

FIGURE 2-42

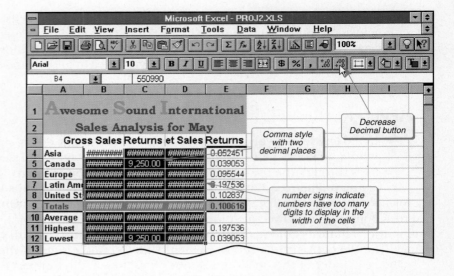

STEP 3 ▶

Click the Decrease Decimal button twice to eliminate the two decimal places in the numbers in the range B4:D12.

The majority of numbers in the range B4:D12 display as whole numbers with comma placement (Figure 2-43). Later the column widths will be increased so the remaining numbers will display properly.

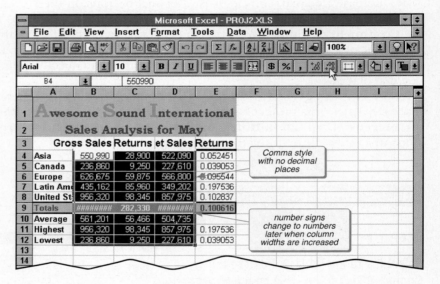

FIGURE 2-43

STEP 4 ▶

Select the range E4:E12 and point to the Percent style button (⊞) on the Formatting toolbar (Figure 2-44).

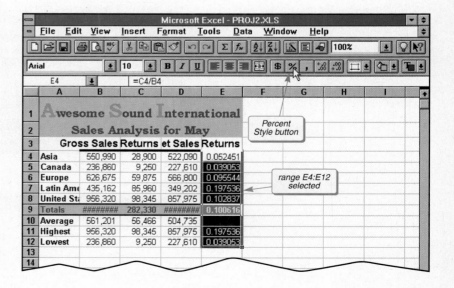

FIGURE 2-44

STEP 5 ▶

Click the left mouse button to apply the Percent style. Then, point to and click the Increase Decimal button ( ) twice.

The decimal numbers in column E display using the Percent style with two decimal places (Figure 2-45).

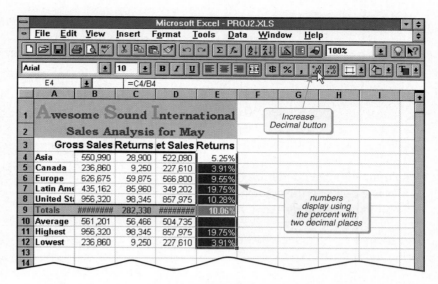

FIGURE 2-45

Excel rounds a number to fit the format selected. For example, in cell E4, Excel rounds the actual value 0.052451 up to 5.25%. In cell E8, Excel rounds the actual value 0.102837 down to 10.28%.

Applying Number Formats Using the Cells Command on the Format Menu or Format Cells Command on the Shortcut Menu

Thus far, you have been introduced to two ways to apply number formats in a worksheet. In Project 1, you formatted the numbers using the AutoFormat command on the Format menu. In the previous section, you were introduced to using the Formatting toolbar as a means of selecting a format style. A third way to format numbers is to use the Cells command on the Format menu or the Format Cells command on the shortcut menu. Using the Cells command allows you to display numbers in any desired format you can imagine.

▶ CHANGING THE WIDTHS OF COLUMNS AND HEIGHTS OF ROWS

When Excel begins and the blank worksheet displays on the screen, all the columns have a default width of 8.43 characters and a height of 12.75 points. At any time, you can change the width of the columns or height of the rows to make the worksheet easier to read or to ensure that entries will display properly in the cells to which they are assigned. The width of columns is measured in characters. A **character** is defined as TT Arial, 10 point, the default font used by Excel.

Changing the Widths of Columns

Excel provides two ways to increase or decrease the width of the columns in a worksheet. First, you can change the width of one column at a time. Second, you can change the width of a series of adjacent columns. This project demonstrates both methods.

When changing the column width, you can manually set the width or you can instruct Excel to size the column to best fit. **Best fit** means that the width of the column will be increased or decreased so the widest entry will fit in the column.

TO CHANGE THE WIDTH OF A COLUMN TO BEST FIT ▼

STEP 1 ▶

Position the mouse pointer on the border line between the column A and column B headings above row 1.

The mouse pointer becomes a split double arrow () (Figure 2-46).

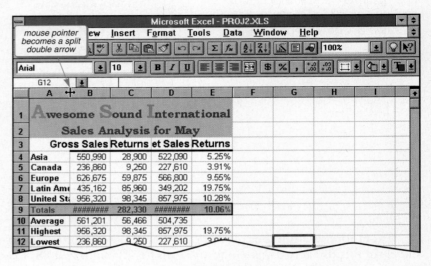

FIGURE 2-46

STEP 2 ▶

Double-click the left mouse button.

The width of column A increases just enough so the widest entry in column A, Latin America, fits in cell A7 (Figure 2-47).

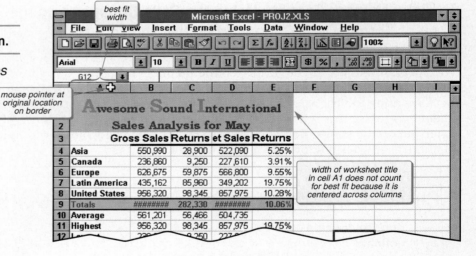

FIGURE 2-47

Compare the entries in column A of Figure 2-47 to Figure 2-46. Notice how Excel has increased the width of column A just enough so all the characters in column A display. To determine the exact character width of column A, you can move the mouse pointer to the border line between the column A and column B headings. When the mouse pointer changes to a split double arrow, hold down the left mouse button. Excel displays the new column width (13 for column A) in place of the cell reference in the reference area in the formula bar.

Recall that the worksheet title, Awesome Sound International, is assigned to cell A1. Because it was centered earlier across columns A through E, Excel does not take the width of the title into consideration when determining the best fit for column A.

If you decide to undo a new column width prior to entering the next command or data item, you can choose the Undo Column Width command from the Edit menu.

The next step is to change the column widths of column B to 13.71, columns C and D to 11.00, and column E to 12.14. In these cases, best fit will not be used because more space is preferred between the columns to improve the appearance of the report.

TO CHANGE THE WIDTH OF COLUMNS ▼

STEP 1 ►

Position the mouse pointer on the border line between the column B and column C headings above row 1 and drag to the right until the number 13.71 displays in the reference area in the formula bar.

A dotted line shows the new right border of column B and the number 13.71 displays in the reference area in the formula bar (Figure 2-48).

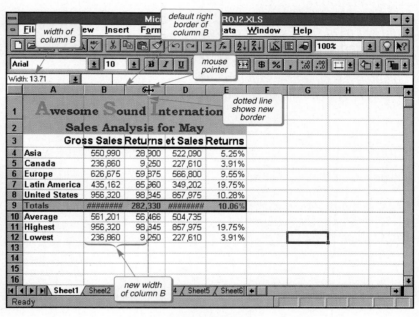

FIGURE 2-48

STEP 2 ►

Release the left mouse button.

Excel sets the width of column B to 13.71 (Figure 2-49).

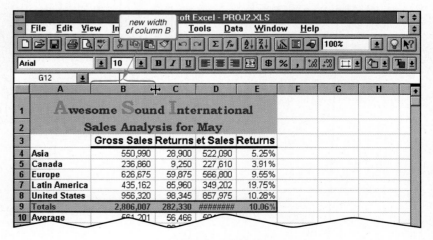

FIGURE 2-49

STEP 3 ▶

Drag the mouse pointer from column heading C through column heading D and then release the left mouse button to select both columns. Move the mouse pointer to the right border of column heading D. When the mouse pointer changes to a split double arrow, drag to the right until a width of 11.00 displays in the reference area in the formula bar.

Columns C and D are selected and the right border of column D is dragged to the right until the width in the Reference area in the formula bar is 11.00. Excel displays a vertical dotted line, that when added to the width of column D, indicates the column width that will be assigned to columns C through D (Figure 2-50).

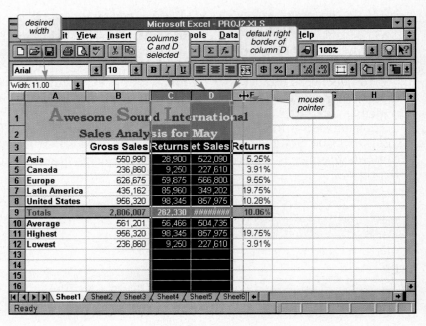

FIGURE 2-50

STEP 4 ▶

Release the left mouse button.

Excel assigns a new width of 11.00 characters to columns C and D (Figure 2-51).

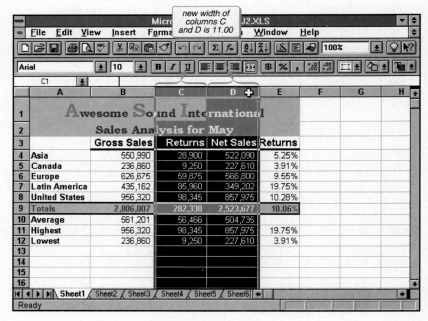

FIGURE 2-51

STEP 5 ▶

Click column heading E to select the column. Click the right mouse button to display the shortcut menu. Point to the Column Width command (Figure 2-52).

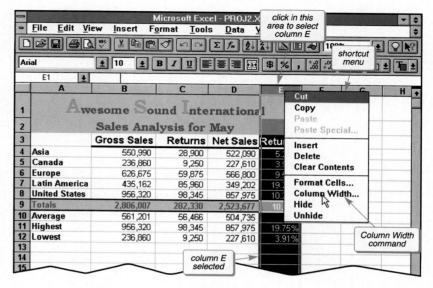

FIGURE 2-52

STEP 6 ▶

Choose the Column Width command. When the Column Width dialog box displays, type the number 12.14 in the Column Width box and point to the OK button.

The Column Width dialog box displays, which allows you to enter a column width between 0 and 255 (Figure 2-53).

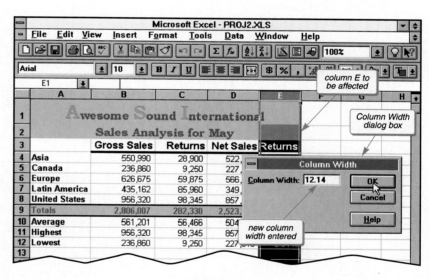

FIGURE 2-53

STEP 7 ▶

Choose the OK button.

The width of column E increases from the default 8.43 to 12.14 characters (Figure 2-54).

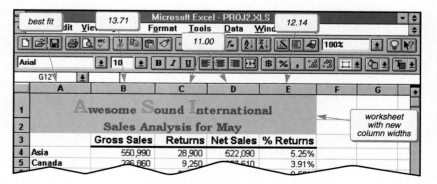

FIGURE 2-54

Step 6 and Step 7 show that you can use the Column Width command instead of dragging the mouse to change the column width. Select any cell in the column or range of columns to be affected, choose the **Column command** from the Format menu or the Column Width command from the shortcut menu, and type in the desired width. The Column Width command only appears on the shortcut menu when one or more entire columns are selected. You select entire columns by dragging through the column headings. Use the Column Width command instead of the mouse when you want to increase or decrease the column width significantly.

The column width can vary between zero and 255 characters. When you decrease the column width to zero, the column is hidden. **Hiding columns** is a technique you can use to hide sensitive data on the screen that you don't want other people to see. When you print a worksheet, hidden columns do not print. To unhide a hidden column, position the mouse pointer to the left of the heading border where the the hidden column is located and drag to the right.

Changing the Heights of Rows

When you change the font size of a cell entry, such as Awesome Sound International in cell A1, Excel automatically adjusts the row height to the best fit. You can also manually adjust the height of a row to add space that improves the appearance of the worksheet. The row height is measured in point size. The default row height is 12.75 points. Recall from Project 1 that a point is equal to 1/72 of an inch. Thus, 12.75 points is equal to about one-sixth of an inch.

The following steps show how to use the mouse to increase the height of rows 3 and 10 from their default height to 24.00 points so there is extra space between the worksheet subtitle in row 2 and the column titles in row 3 and the totals in row 9 and the averages in row 10. In the following example, the CTRL key is used to select the nonadjacent rows 3 and 10 and the bottom border of row 10 is dragged down until the row height in the reference area in the formula bar is 24.00 points.

TO INCREASE THE HEIGHT OF A ROW BY DRAGGING THE MOUSE ▼

STEP 1 ▶

Click row heading 3. Hold down the CTRL key and click row heading 10. Release the CTRL key. Move the mouse pointer to the border line between row headings 10 and 11. Drag the mouse down until a height of 24.00 displays in the reference area in the formula bar.

Excel displays a horizontal dotted line (Figure 2-55). The distance between the dotted line and the top of row 10 indicates the new row height for rows 3 and 10.

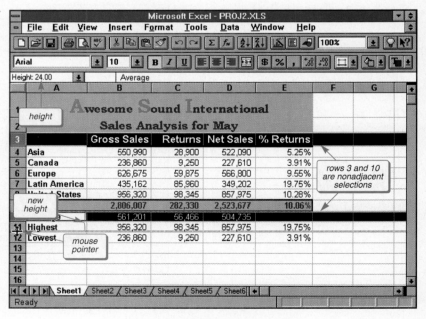

FIGURE 2-55

STEP 2 ▶

Release the left mouse button.

Rows 3 and 10 have a new height of 24.00 points (Figure 2-56).

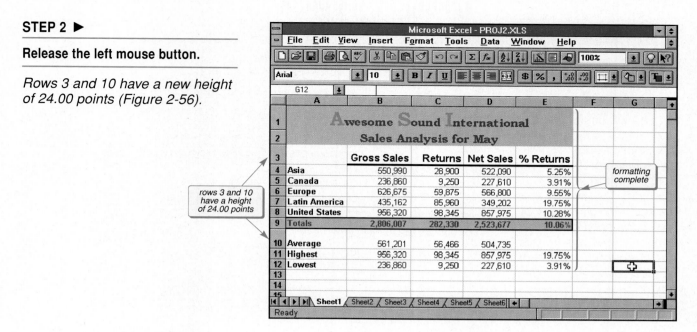

rows 3 and 10 have a height of 24.00 points

formatting complete

FIGURE 2-56

The row height can vary between zero and 409 points. When you decrease the row height to zero, the row is hidden. To show a hidden row, point just below the row heading border where the row is hidden and drag down.

To use a dialog box to change the row height, select any cell in the row or a series of cells down a column, choose the **Row command** from the Format menu or the **Row Height command** from the shortcut menu, and type the desired height in the Row Height dialog box. As with the Column Width command, the Row Height command only shows on the shortcut menu when one or more rows are selected.

If for some reason you want to switch back to the default row height, simply move the mouse pointer to the row border and double-click.

The task of formatting the worksheet is complete. The next step is to check the spelling of the worksheet.

▶ CHECKING SPELLING

E xcel has a spell checker you can use to check the worksheet for spelling errors. The spell checker checks for spelling errors against its standard dictionary. If you have any specialized terms that are not in the standard dictionary, you can add them to a **custom dictionary** through the **Spelling dialog box**.

When the spell checker finds a word that is not in the dictionaries, it displays the word in the Spelling dialog box so you can correct it if it is misspelled.

You invoke the spell checker by clicking the **Spelling button** on the Standard toolbar or by choosing the Spelling command from the Tools menu. To illustrate Excel's reaction to a misspelled word, the word Lowest in cell A12 is purposely misspelled as Liwest, as shown in Figure 2-57 on the next page.

TO CHECK SPELLING IN THE WORKSHEET ▼

STEP 1 ▶

Select cell A1. Click the Spelling button (🔤) on the Standard toolbar.

The spell checker begins checking the spelling of the text in the worksheet with the active cell (cell A1) and continues checking to the right and down row by row. If the spell checker comes across a word that is not in the standard or custom dictionaries, it displays the Spelling dialog box (Figure 2-57).

STEP 2 ▶

When the spell checker displays a word in the Change To box, select one of the six buttons to the right in the Spelling dialog box.

In Figure 2-57, the word Lowest in cell A12 is misspelled as Liwest. The spell checker displays its best guess of the word you wanted (Lowest) in the Change To box. Because Lowest is in fact the correct spelling, choose the Change button (Change).

STEP 3 ▶

Choose the OK button when Excel displays the Microsoft Excel dialog box to indicate the spell check is complete (Figure 2-58).

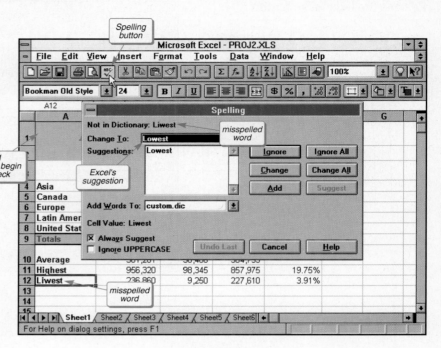

FIGURE 2-57

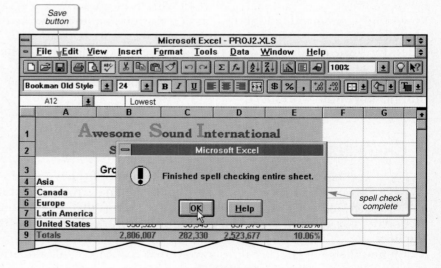

FIGURE 2-58

When the spell checker identifies a word not in the dictionaries, it changes the active cell to the cell containing the word not in the dictionaries. The Spelling dialog box (Figure 2-57) lists the word not in the dictionaries, a suggested correction, and a list of alternative spellings. If you agree with the suggested correction in the Change To box, choose the Change button. To change the word throughout the worksheet, choose the Change All button (Change All).

If one of the words in the Suggestions list box is correct, select the word and choose the Change button or double-click the word. If none of the listed words is correct, type the correct word and choose the Change button. To skip correcting the word, choose the Ignore button (Ignore). To have Excel ignore the word for the remainder of the worksheet, choose the Ignore All button (Ignore All).

Consider these additional points regarding the spell checker:

1. To check the spelling of the text in a single cell, double-click the cell and click the Spelling button on the Standard toolbar.
2. When you select a single cell and the formula bar is not active before invoking the spell checker, Excel checks the entire worksheet, which includes the worksheet, notes, and embedded charts.
3. If you select a range of cells before invoking the spell checker, Excel only checks the spelling of the words in the selected range.
4. To check the spelling of a chart, select the chart before invoking the spell checker.
5. To check the spelling of all the sheets in a workbook, choose the Select All Sheets command from the sheet tab shortcut menu, and then invoke the spell checker. You display the sheet tab shortcut menu by pointing to it and clicking the right mouse button.
6. If you select a cell other than cell A1 before you start the spell checker, a dialog box displays after Excel checks to the end of the worksheet asking if you want to continue checking at the beginning.
7. To add words that are not in the standard dictionary to the custom dictionary, choose the Add button (Add) in the Spelling dialog box (Figure 2-57) when Excel identifies the word.

▶ SAVING THE WORKBOOK A SECOND TIME USING THE SAME FILENAME

E arlier, you saved an intermediate version of the workbook using the filename PROJ2.XLS. To save the workbook a second time using the same filename, click the Save button on the Standard toolbar (Figure 2-58). Excel automatically stores the latest version of the worksheet under the same filename PROJ2.XLS without displaying the Save As dialog box as it did when you saved the workbook the first time.

If you want to save the workbook under a new name, choose the Save As command from the File menu or shortcut menu. For example, some Excel users use the Save button to save the latest version of the workbook to the default drive. They then use the Save As command to save a second copy to another drive.

You can also instruct Excel to automatically create a backup of a workbook on the default drive every time you save it by choosing the Options button (Options...) in the Save As dialog box and selecting the Always Create Backup check box. A **backup** copy is the previous version of the worksheet, renamed with a .BAK extension. Saving a backup copy of the workbook is another form of protection against losing all your work.

▶ CREATING A 3-D COLUMN CHART ON A CHART SHEET

The next step in this project is to draw the 3-D column chart shown in Figure 2-59. A **column chart** is used to show trends and comparisons. Each column emphasizes the magnitude of the value it represents. The column chart in Figure 2-59 compares the gross sales for the month of May for the international divisions. It is easy to see from the column chart that the United States had the greatest gross sales and Canada had the smallest gross sales.

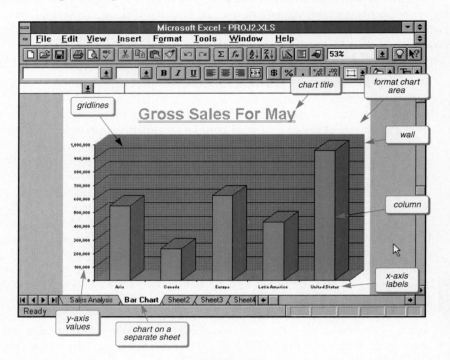

FIGURE 2-59

The column chart in Figure 2-59 differs from the one in Project 1 in that it is not embedded in the worksheet. Instead, it is created on a separate sheet, called a **chart sheet**.

The range of the worksheet to graph is A4:B8 (see Figure 2-60). The division names in the range A4:A8 identify the columns and show at the bottom of the column chart. The entries in column A are called the **category names.** The range B4:B8 contains the data that determines the magnitude of the columns. The entries in column B are called the **data series**. Because there are five category names and five numbers in the data series, the column chart contains five columns.

Drawing the 3-D Column Chart

In Project 1, you used the ChartWizard button on the Standard toolbar to draw an embedded 2-D column chart. Embedded means the chart is on the same sheet with the worksheet. Anytime you want to create an embedded chart, the ChartWizard button is the best choice. However, you will often want to create a chart on a sheet separate from the worksheet, but in the same workbook. To create a chart on a separate sheet, use the **Chart command** on the **Insert menu**. This command takes you into the ChartWizard, but first asks you if you want to create the chart on the same sheet or a separate sheet.

The following steps illustrate how to create a 3-D column chart on a separate sheet.

TO DRAW A 3-D COLUMN CHART ON A CHART SHEET ▼

STEP 1 ►

Select the range A4:B8. Choose the Chart command on the Insert menu. Point to the As New Sheet command on the cascading menu.

*Excel displays a cascading menu that allows you to choose where the chart will be created (Figure 2-60). A **cascading menu** is one that displays to the right of the current menu with a list of commands.*

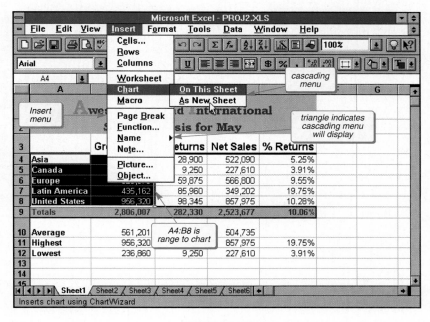

FIGURE 2-60

STEP 2 ►

Choose the As New Sheet command from the cascading menu.

Excel displays the ChartWizard – Step 1 of 5 dialog box which displays the selected range in the worksheet (Figure 2-61). You can type in a new range or use the mouse to change the range in the worksheet if you decide you want to change your original selection.

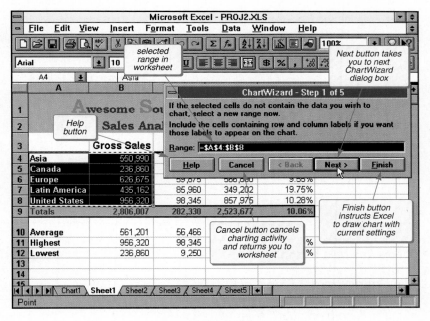

FIGURE 2-61

STEP 3 ►

Choose the Next button. Select the 3-D Column chart in the ChartWizard – Step 2 of 5 dialog box (Figure 2-62).

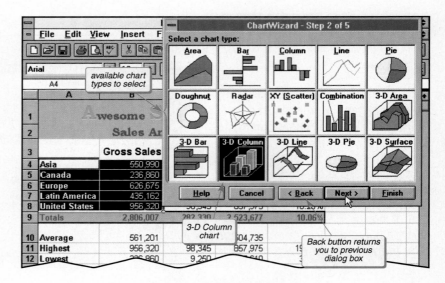

FIGURE 2-62

STEP 4 ►

Choose the Next button. Select format number 4 for the chart (Figure 2-63).

The ChartWizard – Step 3 of 5 dialog box displays with eight different 3-D formats from which to select.

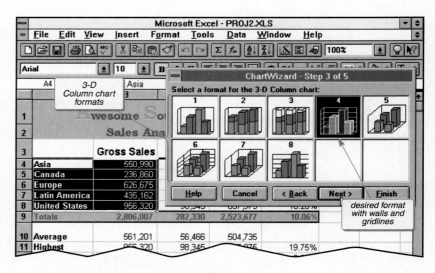

FIGURE 2-63

STEP 5 ►

Choose the Next button.

The ChartWizard – Step 4 of 5 dialog box displays with a sample of the 3-D column chart. (Figure 2-64).

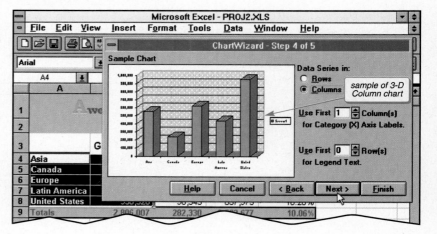

FIGURE 2-64

STEP 6 ▶

Choose the Next button. Select the No option button in the Add a Legend? area. Select the Chart Title box. Type Gross Sales For May **in the Chart Title box (Figure 2-65).**

The ChartWizard – Step 5 of 5 dialog box displays. You have the opportunity in this dialog box to add a chart title, y-axis title, x-axis title, and select whether or not you want legends to display alongside the chart. Excel dynamically changes the sample chart in the dialog box as you enter titles.

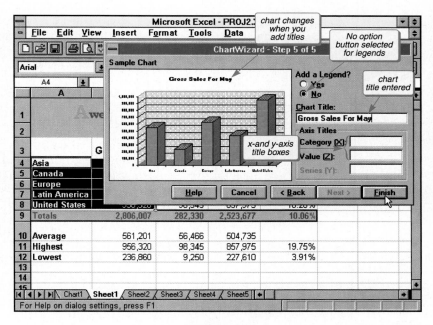

FIGURE 2-65

STEP 7 ▶

Choose the Finish button.

Excel displays the 3-D column chart on a separate sheet (Figure 2-66).

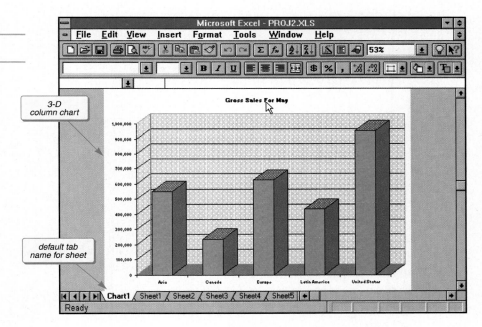

FIGURE 2-66

Each column in the chart in Figure 2-66 represents a division of the company. The names of the divisions display below the corresponding columns on the **x-axis**. The values along the **y-axis** (the vertical line to the left of the columns) are automatically determined by Excel from the highest and lowest gross sales amounts in the range B4:B8 of the worksheet.

Notice in the five ChartWizard dialog boxes (Figures 2-61 through 2-65 on pages E103 through E105) that you can return to the previous ChartWizard dialog box by choosing the Back button. The functions of the buttons for the Chart-Wizard dialog box are the same as those described for the Chart Wizard dialog box in Table 2-2 on page E80.

Enhancing the 3-D Column Chart

Excel allows you to change the appearance of any chart item labeled in Figure 2-59 on page E102. All you have to do is double-click the chart item you want to change and Excel displays a dialog box containing the changeable characteristics. To change the 3-D column chart in Figure 2-66 so it looks like the one in Figure 2-59, the following changes must be made:

1. Chart title — increase the font size, add a double-underline, and change the font color to red.
2. Walls — change the color to a light blue.
3. Columns — change the color to red.

Applying Formats to the Chart Title

Perform the following steps to increase the chart title font size, double-underline the chart title, and change the color of the chart title to red.

TO APPLY FORMATS TO THE CHART TITLE ▼

STEP 1 ▶

Double-click the chart title. Click the Font tab.

The Font tab displays in the Format Chart Title dialog box.

STEP 2 ▶

Select 36 in the Size list box and Double in the Underline drop-down list box. Click the Color box arrow and select the color red (column 3, row 1) on the palette.

The Format Chart Title dialog box should display as shown in Figure 2-67.

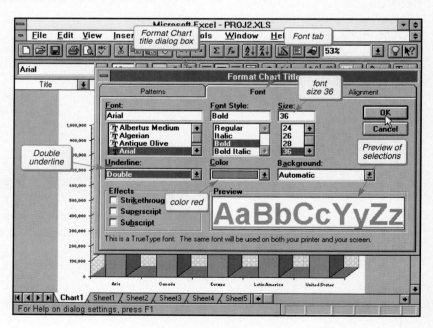

FIGURE 2-67

STEP 3 ▶

Choose the OK button.

Excel displays the column chart with the chart title formatted as required (Figure 2-68).

FIGURE 2-68

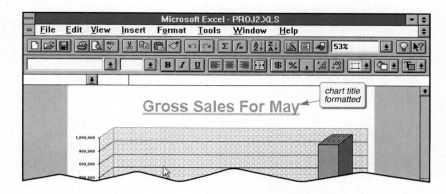

Compare the chart title in Figure 2-68 to the one in Figure 2-66 on page E105. You can see that the chart title stands out after formatting is applied. One of the drawbacks to increasing the font size of the chart title is that Excel decreases the size of the chart itself to make room for the larger font. However, you can select the chart and increase its size if you so desire.

Notice that when you double-click the chart title, Excel immediately opens the Format Chart Title dialog box which includes three tabs — Patterns, Font, and Alignment. Click any tab to display it.

An alternative to formatting the chart title by double-clicking it is to click it to select it and use the buttons on the Formatting toolbar.

Applying Formats to the Walls and the Columns

The next step is to format the walls and the columns. The **walls** are behind and to the left of the columns in the chart. The following steps show how to select a chart item and use the Formatting toolbar to format it.

TO APPLY FORMATS TO THE WALLS AND COLUMNS ▼

STEP 1 ▶

Click any part of the walls except on a gridline.

Black handles surround the walls.

STEP 2 ▶

Click the Color button arrow on the Formatting toolbar and point to the light blue color (column 1, row 5) on the color palette.

The Color palette displays (Figure 2-69).

FIGURE 2-69

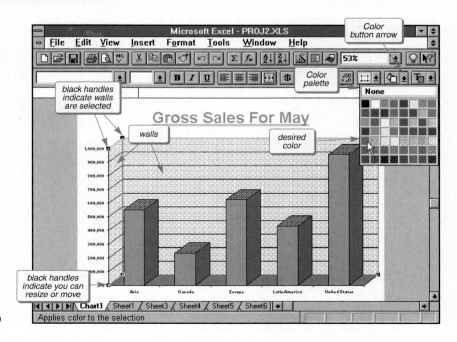

STEP 3 ▶

Click the left mouse button.

Excel changes the color of the walls to a light blue (Figure 2-70).

STEP 4 ▶

Click any one of the five columns.

White handles surround the columns in the chart.

STEP 5 ▶

Click the Color button arrow on the Formatting toolbar and point to red (column 3, row 1) on the color palette.

The Color palette displays (Figure 2-70).

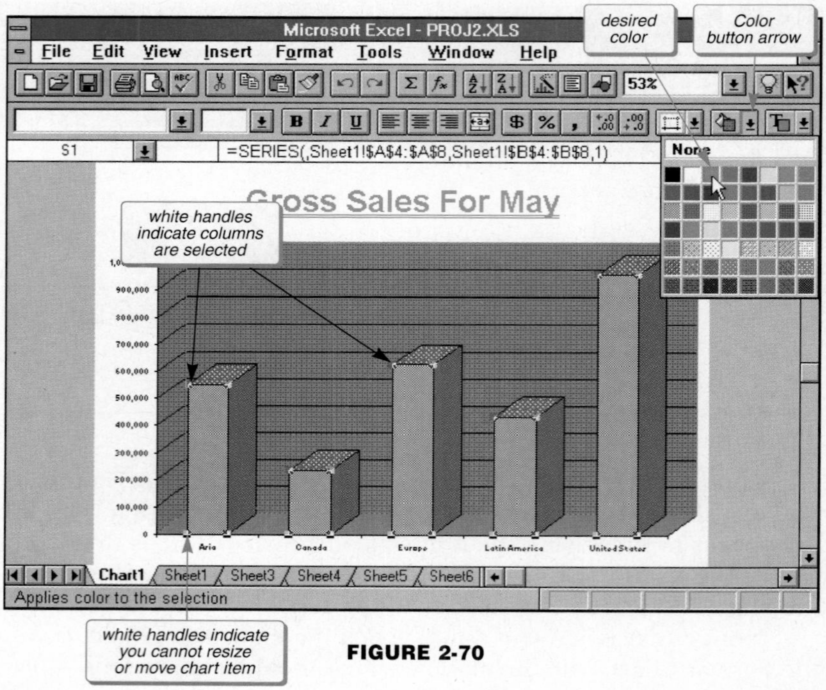

STEP 6 ▶

Click the left mouse button.

The formatted 3-D column chart displays as shown in Figure 2-71.

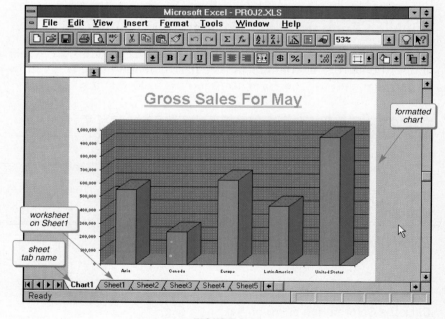

FIGURE 2-70

FIGURE 2-71

You can easily format the chart to a variety of styles. The four ways to apply formats to chart items are:

1. Double-click a chart item and select format styles from a dialog box; the technique applied on the chart title.

2. Click a chart item and use the buttons on the Formatting toolbar; the technique applied on the chart walls and columns in the previous steps.
3. Click a chart item, click the right mouse button to display the shortcut menu, and choose the command that describes the selection, such as Format Walls.
4. Click a chart item, select the Format menu, and choose the command that describes the selection, such as Selected Walls.

One of the commands available on the shortcut menu or the Format menu is the AutoFormat command. The **AutoFormat command** allows you to change the 3-D column chart to any of the other fourteen chart types displayed in Figure 2-62 on page E104.

When you select a chart item, Excel surrounds it with white selection squares or black selection squares, also called **handles**. Chart items marked with **white handles** (such as the columns in Figure 2-70) can be formatted, but cannot be moved or resized. Chart items marked with **black handles** can be formatted, moved, and resized. For example, in Figure 2-69, you can drag the handles on the corners of the wall to resize the chart and change it's perspective.

Changing the Names on the Sheet Tabs and Rearranging the Order of the Sheets

At the bottom of the screen (Figure 2-71) are the tabs that allow you to display any sheet in the workbook. By default, the tab names are Sheet1, Sheet2, and so on. When you draw a chart on a separate sheet, Excel assigns the name Chart1 to the sheet tab. The following steps show you how to rename the sheet tabs and reorder the sheets so the worksheet comes before the chart sheet.

TO RENAME THE SHEET TABS AND REARRANGE THE ORDER OF THE SHEETS ▼

STEP 1 ▶

Double-click the sheet tab named Chart1 at the bottom of the screen.

Excel displays the Rename Sheet dialog box.

STEP 2 ▶

Type Bar Chart **in the Name box.**

The Rename Sheet dialog box displays as shown in Figure 2-72.

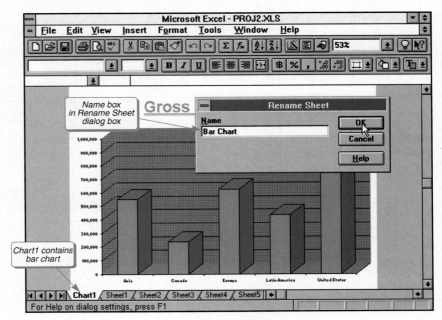

FIGURE 2-72

STEP 3 ▶

Choose the OK button.

Excel renames the Chart1 tab Bar Chart (Figure 2-73).

STEP 4 ▶

Double-click the Sheet1 tab.

Excel displays the Rename Sheet dialog box.

STEP 5 ▶

Type Sales Analysis **in the Name box.**

The Rename Sheet dialog box displays as shown in Figure 2-73.

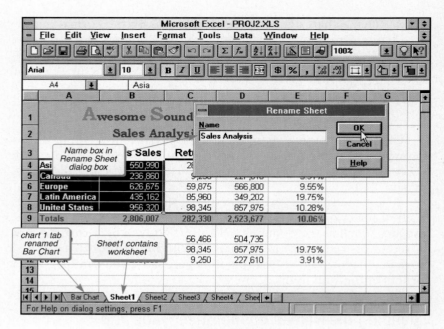

FIGURE 2-73

STEP 6 ▶

Choose the OK button.

Excel renames the Sheet1 tab Sales Analysis (Figure 2-74).

STEP 7 ▶

Point to the Sales Analysis tab and drag it over the Bar Chart tab (Figure 2-74).

The mouse pointer changes to a pointer and a document. A small dark triangle indicates where the Sales Analysis sheet will be moved.

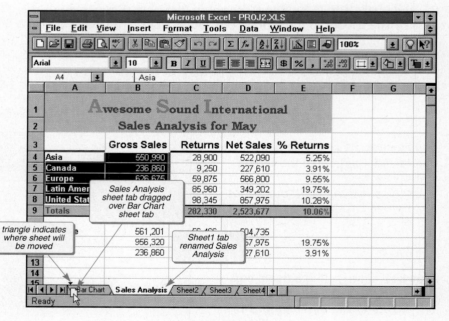

FIGURE 2-74

STEP 8 ▶

Release the left mouse button.

*Excel moves the sheet named Sales Analysis in front of the sheet named Bar Chart. The workbook for Project 2 is complete (Figure 2-75). You can also move a sheet by choosing the **Move or Copy Sheet** command on the Edit menu.*

STEP 9 ▶

Click the Save button on the Standard toolbar to save the workbook to disk using the filename PROJ2.

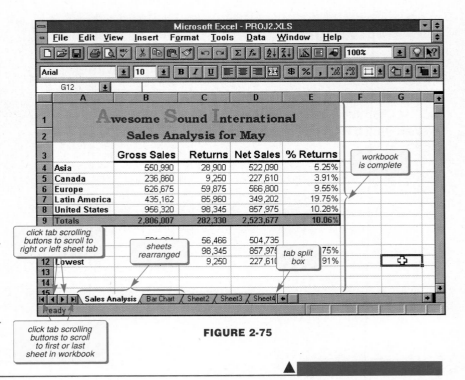

FIGURE 2-75

The previous steps showed you how to rename the sheet tabs at the bottom of the screen and how to resequence them. Sheet names can be up to 31 characters in length. The longer the tab names, the fewer tabs will show. However, you can increase the number of tabs that show by dragging the **tab split box** next to the scroll arrow (Figure 2-75) to the right. This will reduce the size of the scroll bar at the bottom of the screen. Double-click the tab split box to reset it to its normal position.

You can also use the **tab scrolling buttons** to the left of the sheet tabs (Figure 2-75) to scroll between sheet tabs. The leftmost and rightmost tab scrolling buttons scroll to the first or last sheet tab in the workbook. The two middle tab scrolling buttons scroll one sheet tab to the left or right. Tab scrolling buttons do not select sheet tabs. Click a sheet tab to select it.

▶ PREVIEWING AND PRINTING THE WORKBOOK

I n Project 1, you printed the workbook (the worksheet with the embedded chart) without previewing it on the screen. By previewing the workbook, you see exactly how it will look without generating a hard copy. Previewing a workbook can save time, paper, and the frustration of waiting for a printout only to find out it is not what you want.

The **Print Preview command**, as well as the Print command, will only preview selected sheets. You know a sheet is selected when the sheet tab at the bottom of the screen is white. Thus, in Figure 2-75 the Sales Analysis sheet is selected, but the Bar Chart tab is not. To select additional sheets, hold down the SHIFT key and click any sheet tabs you want included in the preview or printout.

TO PREVIEW THE WORKBOOK AND PREPARE IT FOR PRINTING ▼

STEP 1 ►

Hold down the SHIFT key and click the Bar Chart tab. Point to the Print Preview button (🔍) on the Standard toolbar.

Both sheets are selected (Figure 2-76).

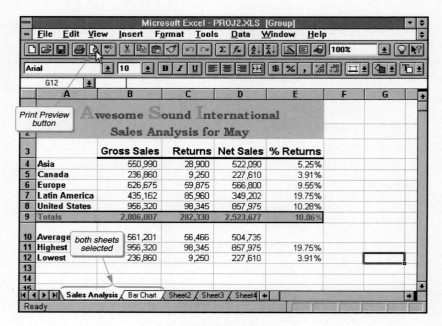

FIGURE 2-76

STEP 2 ►

Click the Print Preview button.

*Excel displays a preview of the worksheet (possibly with cell gridlines) in the **preview window** and the mouse pointer changes to a magnifying glass (🔍) (Figure 2-77).*

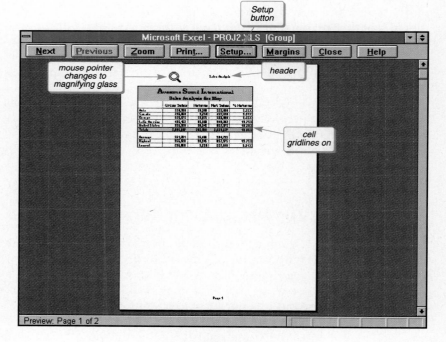

FIGURE 2-77

STEP 3 ▶

If the cell gridlines display in the preview as in Figure 2-77, click the Setup button (Setup...) at the top of the preview window. Click the Sheet tab and clear the Gridlines check box in the Print area so the cell gridlines in the preview do not print.

Excel displays the Page Setup dialog box with the Gridlines check box cleared (Figure 2-78).

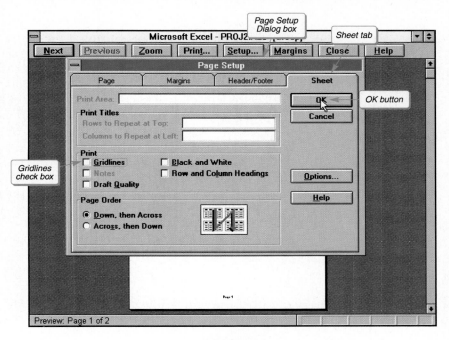

FIGURE 2-78

FIGURE 2-79a

STEP 4 ▶

Choose the OK button in the Page Setup dialog box.

Excel displays the preview of the worksheet without cell gridlines (Figure 2-79a).

STEP 5 ▶

Click the Next button (Next) to display a preview of the chart.

A preview of the column chart displays (Figure 2-79b).

STEP 6 ▶

Click the Close button (Close) in the preview window to return to the workbook.

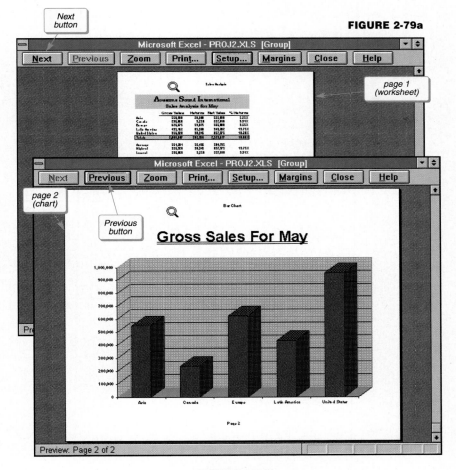

FIGURE 2-79b

Excel displays several buttons at the top of the preview window (Figure 2-79 on the previous page). The first two buttons on the left allow you to page back and forth in a multiple-page worksheet. You use the Zoom button (Zoom) for magnifying or reducing the print preview. Clicking the mouse when the pointer displays as a magnifying glass on the worksheet carries out the same function.

When you click the Print button (Print...), Excel displays a Print dialog box that allows you to print the worksheet. The Setup button displays the same Print Setup dialog box that displays when you choose the Print Setup command from the File menu. The Margins button (Margins) allows you to adjust the top, bottom, left, and right margins, and the column widths. Whatever margin or column width changes you make with the Margins button remain with the worksheet when you close the preview window. The Close button closes the preview window and the workbook redisplays in the Excel workbook window. The Help button (Help) allows you to obtain help on previewing a printout.

Because a change was made in the Print Setup dialog box, Excel draws a dashed line on the worksheet to show the right edge of the page. This is illustrated in Figure 2-80.

After closing the preview window, you can print the worksheet using the Print button on the Standard toolbar.

TO PRINT THE WORKBOOK ▼

STEP 1 ▶

Ready the printer.

STEP 2 ▶

With both sheets selected, point to the Print button on the Standard toolbar (Figure 2-80).

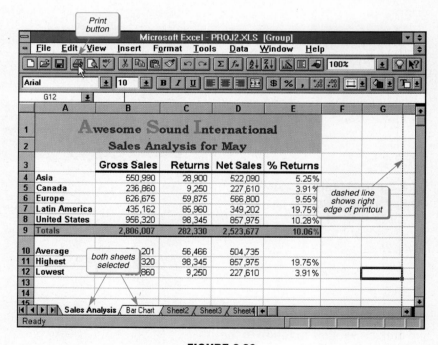

FIGURE 2-80

STEP 3 ►

Click the left mouse button.

Excel prints the worksheet and column chart on the printer (Figure 2-81).

STEP 4 ►

Hold down the SHIFT key and click the Sales Analysis tab at the bottom of the window to deselect the Bar Chart tab.

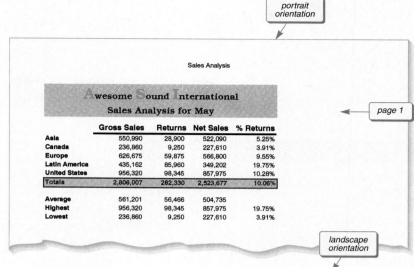

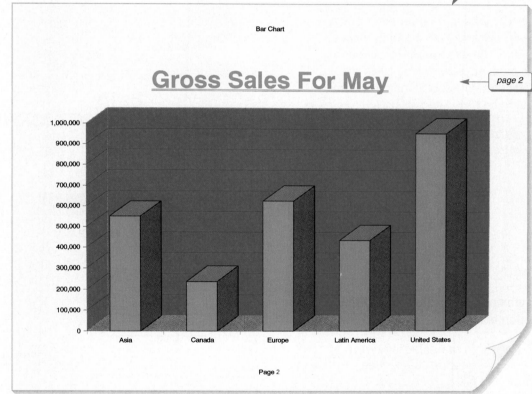

FIGURE 2-81

Notice that the worksheet prints in portrait orientation and the chart prints landscape orientation. **Portrait orientation** means the printout is across the page width of 8.5 inches. **Landscape orientation** means the printout is across the page length of 11 inches. Excel automatically selects landscape orientation for the chart.

▶ PRINTING A SECTION OF THE WORKSHEET

Y ou may not always want to print the entire worksheet. You can print portions of the worksheet by selecting the range of cells to print and then selecting the Selection option button in the Print dialog box. Perform the following steps to print the range A3:C8.

TO PRINT A SECTION OF THE WORKSHEET ▼

STEP 1 ▶

Ready the printer.

STEP 2 ▶

Select the range A3:C8. Point to the menu bar and click the right mouse button. Choose the Print command from the shortcut menu. Click the Selection option button in the Print dialog box.

Excel displays the Print dialog box (Figure 2-82).

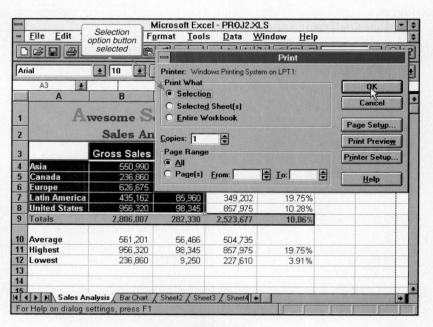

FIGURE 2-82

STEP 3 ▶

Choose the OK button in the Print dialog box.

Excel prints the selected range of the worksheet on the printer (Figure 2-83).

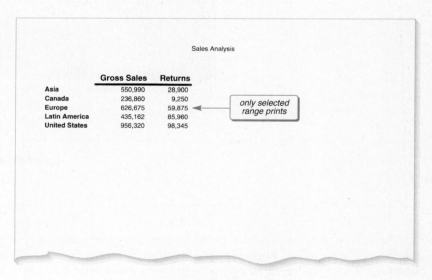

FIGURE 2-83

In the Print What area in the Print dialog box, there are three option buttons (Figure 2-82). The Selection option button instructs Excel to print the selected range. The Selected Sheet(s) option button instructs Excel to print the active sheet (the one displaying on the screen) or the selected sheets. Finally, the Entire Workbook option button instructs Excel to print all the sheets in the workbook. Selecting Entire Workbook is an alternative to selecting tabs by holding down the SHIFT key and clicking tabs to select their sheets. To deselect sheets, click the tab of the one you want to keep active. Next, hold down the SHIFT key and click the active sheet tab again.

▶ DISPLAYING AND PRINTING THE FORMULAS IN THE WORKSHEET

T hus far, the worksheet has been printed exactly as it appears on the screen. This is called the **values version** of the worksheet. Another variation that you can display and print is called the formulas version. The **formulas version** displays and prints what was originally entered into the cells instead of the values in the cells. You can toggle between the values version and formulas version by pressing CTRL+` (single quotation mark next to the 1 key).

The formulas version is useful for debugging a worksheet because the formulas and functions display and print out, instead of the numeric results. **Debugging** is the process of finding and correcting errors in the worksheet.

When you change from values to formulas, Excel increases the width of the columns so the formulas and text do not overflow into adjacent cells on the right. Thus, the worksheet usually becomes significantly wider when the formulas display. To fit the wide printout on one page you can use the **Fit to option** in the Page Setup dialog box and landscape orientation. To change from values to formulas and print the formulas on one page, perform the following steps.

TO DISPLAY THE FORMULAS IN THE WORKSHEET AND FIT THE PRINTOUT ON ONE PAGE ▼

STEP 1 ▶

Press CTRL+` (single quotation mark next to 1 key).

Excel changes the display of the worksheet from values to formulas (Figure 2-84). The formulas in the worksheet display showing unformatted numbers, formulas, and functions that were assigned to the cells. Excel automatically increases the width of the columns.

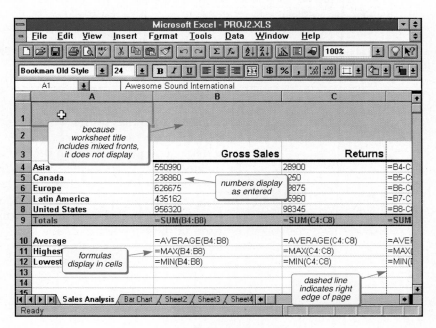

FIGURE 2-84

STEP 2 ▶

Choose the Page Setup command from the shortcut menu or File menu. From the Page Setup dialog box, click the Page tab, select the Landscape option, and Fit to option to fit the wide printout on one page in landscape orientation.

Excel displays the Page Setup dialog box with the Landscape and Fit to options selected (Figure 2-85).

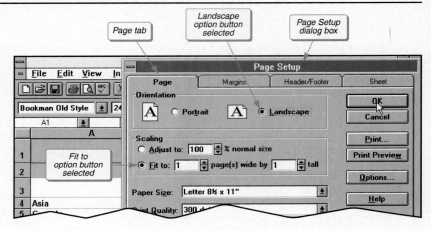

FIGURE 2-85

STEP 3 ▶

Choose the OK button from the Page Setup dialog box. Ready the printer and click the Print tool on the Standard toolbar.

Excel prints the formulas in the worksheet on one page in landscape orientation (Figure 2-86).

STEP 4 ▶

When you're finished with the formulas version, press CTRL+`` ` `` (single quotation mark next to 1 key) to display the values version.

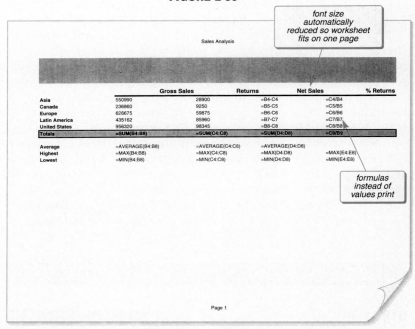

FIGURE 2-86

Although the formulas in the worksheet were printed in the previous example, you can see from Figure 2-84 on page E117 that the display on the screen can also be used for debugging errors in the worksheet.

The formulas in the worksheet were printed using the fit to option so they would fit on one page. Anytime characters extend past the dashed line that represents the rightmost edge of the printed worksheet, the printout will be made up of multiple pages. If you prefer to print the worksheet on one page, select the Fit to option button in the Page Setup dialog box (Figure 2-85) before you print.

An alternative to using CTRL+`` ` `` to toggle between formulas and values is to select the Formulas check box on the View tab. You display the View tab by choosing the Options command on the Tools menu.

Changing the Print Scaling Option Back to 100%

Depending on your printer driver, you may have to change the Print Scaling option back to 100% after using the Fit to option. Follow the steps below to reset the Scaling option so future worksheets print at 100%, instead of being squeezed on one page.

TO CHANGE THE PRINT SCALING OPTION BACK TO 100%

Step 1: Choose the Page Setup command from the shortcut menu or File menu.
Step 2: Select the Adjust to option button in the Scaling area.
Step 3: If necessary, type 100 in the Adjust to box.
Step 4: Choose the OK button in the Page Setup dialog box.

Through the Adjust to box you can specify the percentage of reduction or enlargement in the printout of a worksheet. The default percentage is 100%. The 100% automatically changes to the appropriate percent whenever you select the Fit to option.

▶ PROJECT SUMMARY

In Project 2, you learned how to enter formulas, calculate an average, find the highest and lowest numbers in a range, change fonts, draw borders, apply number formats, and change column widths and row heights. The techniques and steps presented showed you how to chart on a separate sheet, rename sheet tabs, preview a worksheet, print a workbook, print a section of a worksheet, and display and print the formulas in the worksheet using the Fit to option.

▶ KEY TERMS AND INDEX

addition operator *(E70)*
arguments *(E74)*
Align Left button *(E121)*
Align Right button *(E87)*
As New Sheet command *(E102)*
AutoFormat command *(E109)*
AVERAGE function *(E74)*
background color *(E89)*
backup *(E101)*
best fit *(E94)*
cascading menu *(E102)*
category names *(E102)*
character *(E93)*
Cells command *(E93)*
Chart command *(E102)*
chart sheet *(E102)*
Chart title box *(E105)*
Color button *(E107)*
Color palette *(E107)*
column chart *(E102)*
Column command *(E98)*
column width *(E93)*
Column Width command *(E97)*
Column Width dialog box *(E97)*
Comma style *(E91)*
Comma Style button *(E91)*
custom dictionary *(E99)*
data series *(E102)*
debugging *(E117)*

Decrease Decimal button *(E91)*
division operator *(E70)*
exponentiation operator *(E70)*
Fit to option *(E117)*
Font box *(E83)*
Font Color button *(E84)*
Font Color palette *(E89)*
font color *(E84)*
font size *(E84)*
Font Size box *(E83)*
font styles *(E83)*
Format Cells command *(E88)*
Format menu *(E88)*
formatting numbers *(E91)*
formula *(E69)*
formulas version *(E117)*
function *(E74)*
Function Wizard button *(E77)*
handles *(E109)*
hiding columns *(E98)*
Increase Decimal button *(E91)*
Insert menu *(E102)*
landscape orientation *(E115)*
MAX function *(E76)*
MIN function *(E77)*
Move or Copy sheet command *(E111)*
multiplication operator *(E70)*
negation operator *(E71)*

nonadjacent range *(E89)*
number sign *(E92)*
order of operations *(E71)*
parentheses in formulas *(E71)*
Percent style *(E91)*
Percent Style button *(E91)*
percentage operator *(E70)*
Point mode *(E72)*
portrait orientation *(E115)*
preview window *(E112)*
previewing a worksheet *(E112)*
Print Preview button *(E112)*
Print Preview command *(E111)*
Rename Sheet dialog box *(E109)*
Row command *(E99)*
row height *(E98)*
Row Height command *(E99)*
select sheets *(E117)*
shortcut menu *(E116)*
Spelling button *(E99)*
Spelling dialog box *(E99)*
subtraction operator *(E70)*
tab scrolling buttons *(E111)*
tab split box *(E111)*
values version *(E117)*
walls of chart *(E107)*
white handles *(E109)*
x axis of chart *(E105)*
y axis of chart *(E105)*

In Microsoft Excel, you can accomplish a task in a number of ways. The following table provides a quick reference to each task presented in this project with its available options. The commands listed in the Menu column can be executed using either the keyboard or mouse. Many of the commands in the Menu column are also available on the shortcut menu.

Task	Mouse	Menu	Keyboard Shortcuts
Add a Border	Click Borders button arrow on Formatting toolbar	From Format menu, choose Cells, then select Border tab	Press CTRL+1 Press CTRL+SHIFT+<- (remove border)
Apply Comma Style	Click Comma Style button on Formatting toolbar	From Format menu, choose Cells, then select Number tab	Press CTRL+SHIFT+I
Apply Percent Style	Click Percent Style button on Formatting toolbar	From Format menu, choose Cells, then select Number tab	Press CTRL+SHIFT+%
Change a Column Width	Drag column heading border; double-click column heading right border for best fit	From Format menu, choose Column	Press CTRL+0 (Hide) Press CTRL+SHIFT+) (Unhide)
Change Font Color	Click Font Color arrow on Formatting toolbar	From Format menu choose Cells, then select Font tab	Press CTRL+1
Change Font Size	Click Font Size arrow on Formatting toolbar	From Format menu choose Cells, then select Font tab	Press CTRL+1
Change Font Type	Click Font Type arrow on Formatting toolbar	From Format menu choose Cells, then select Font tab	Press CTRL+1
Change a Row Height	Drag row heading border, double-click row heading bottom border for best fit	From Format menu, choose Row	Press CTRL+9 (Hide) Press CTRL+SHIFT+((Unhide)
Check Spelling	Click Spelling button on Standard toolbar	From Tools menu, choose Spelling	Press F7
Decrease Decimal Places	Click Decrease Decimal button on Formatting toolbar	From Format menu, choose Cells, then select Number tab	Press CTRL+1
Display a Shortcut Menu	Click right mouse button		
Fit to Print Across Page		From File menu, choose Page Setup, then select Page tab	Press CTRL+P and choose Page Setup button
Increase Decimal Places	Click Increase Decimal button on Formatting toolbar	From Format menu, choose Cells, then select Number tab	Press CTRL+1
Left Align Text	Click Align Left button on Formatting toolbar	From Format menu, choose Cells, then select Alignment tab	Press CTRL+1
Move a Sheet	Drag sheet tab to new location	From Edit menu, choose Move or Copy Sheet	

Task	Mouse	Menu	Keyboard Shortcuts
Print Preview	Click Print Preview button on Standard toolbar	From File menu, choose Print Preview	Press CTRL+P and choose Print Preview button
Print an Entire Workbook		From File menu, choose Print	Press CTRL+P
Print a Selected Range		From File menu, choose Print	Press CTRL+P
Rename a Sheet Tab	Double-click tab	From shortcut menu, choose Rename	
Right-Align Text	Click Align Right button on Formatting toolbar	From Format menu choose Cells, then select Alignment tab	Press CTRL+1
Select Sheets	Hold down SHIFT key and click desired sheet tab		
Shade Cells or a Range of Cells	Click Color button on Formatting toolbar	From Format menu, choose Cells, then select Patterns tab	Press CTRL+1
View the Formulas Version or the Values Version		From Tools menu, choose Options, then select View tab	Press CTRL+'

S T U D E N T   A S S I G N M E N T S

STUDENT ASSIGNMENT 1
True/False

Instructions: Circle T if the statement is true or F if the statement is false.

T F   1. Click the right mouse button to display the shortcut menu.

T F   2. Use the Currency Style button on the Formatting toolbar to change the entry in a cell to different international monetary value.

T F   3. The minimum column width is zero.

T F   4. If you assign a cell the formula =8 / 4, the number 2 displays in the cell.

T F   5. To remove decimal places in an entry, click the Increase Decimal button.

T F   6. In the formula =8 + 6 / 2, the addition operation (+) is completed before the division operation (/).

T F   7. The formulas =a2 - a3, =A2 - A3, and =A2-A3 result in the same value being assigned to the active cell.

T F   8. The Function Wizard button on the Standard toolbar must be used to enter functions.

T F   9. If you use the Point mode to enter a formula or select a range, you must click the enter box to complete the entry.

T F   10. Use the AVERAGE function to assign a cell the average of the entries in a range of cells.

T F   11. To save an intermediate copy of the workbook to disk, you must choose the Save As command from the File menu.

T F   12. If you save a workbook a second time using the Save button, Excel will save it under the same filename that was used the first time it was saved.

STUDENT ASSIGNMENT 1 (continued)

T   F   13. If the function =SUM(B4:B8) assigns a value of 10 to cell B9, and B9 is copied to C9, cell C9 may or may not equal 10.

T   F   14. To select a second sheet, hold down the SHIFT key and click its tab.

T   F   15. When a number is too large to fit in a cell, Excel displays asterisks (*) in place of the number in the cell.

T   F   16. It is not possible to apply different format styles to individual characters in a cell.

T   F   17. Use the Font box to change the font in a cell or range of cells.

T   F   18. To increase or decrease the width of a column, use the mouse to point to the column heading name and drag it to the left or right.

T   F   19. To select an entire row, click the row heading.

T   F   20. When the formulas in the worksheet display, Excel displays numeric and text entries without the format applied to them.

STUDENT ASSIGNMENT 2
Multiple Choice

Instructions: Circle the correct response.

1. Which one of the following arithmetic operations is completed first if they are all found in a formula with no parentheses?
    a. +   b. -   c. ^   d. *

2. The Comma Style button on the Formatting toolbar causes 5000 to display as:
    a. $5,000   b. 5000   c. 5,000   d. 5,000. 00

3. Which one of the following formulas is valid?
    a. =C3 + b3   b. =c3 + b3   c. =C3 + B3   d. all of these

4. When you use the Print Preview button on the Standard toolbar, the mouse pointer becomes a _____ when it is pointed at the worksheet.
    a. cross   b. magnifying glass   c. split double arrow   d. block plus sign

5. The maximum height of a row is approximately _____ points.
    a. 100   b. 200   c. 300   d. 400

6. A listing on the printer of the worksheet in which formulas display instead of numbers is called the _____ version of the worksheet.
    a. formulas   b. displayed   c. formatted   d. content

7. If 0. 052451 is assigned to a cell that is formatted by clicking the Percent Style button and clicking the Increase Decimal button twice on the Formatting toolbar, then the cell contents display as _____.
    a. 5. 25%   b. 5. 24%   c. 0. 05%   d. 5. 00%

8. Which one of the following describes a column width where the user has requested that Excel determine the width to use?
    a. custom fit   b. usual fit   c. close fit   d. best fit

9. The function =AVERAGE(B3:B7) is equal to _____.
    a. =b3 + b4 + b5 + b6 + b7 / 5   c. both a and b
    b. =(b3 + b4 + b5 + b6 + b7) / 5   d. none of these

10. To print two sheets in the workbook at one time, first select the two sheets by holding down the _____ key and clicking the sheet that is not selected, and then clicking the Print button on the Standard toolbar.
    a. SHIFT   b. CTRL   c. ALT   d. ESC

STUDENT ASSIGNMENT 3
Entering Formulas

Instructions: Using the values in the worksheet in Figure SA2-3, write the formula that accomplishes the task for each of the following items and manually compute the value assigned to the specified cell.

FIGURE SA2-3

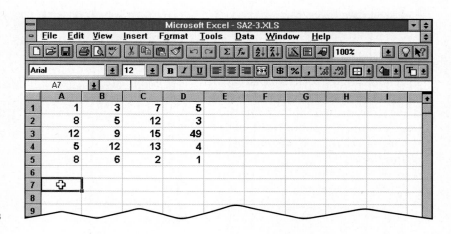

1. Assign cell A7 the product of cells A2 and D2.

   Formula: _____   Result: _____

2. Assign cell F4 the product of cells B1, C1, and D5.

   Formula: _____   Result: _____

3. Assign cell D6 the sum of the range B1:C2, less cell A5.

   Formula: _____   Result: _____

4. Assign cell G2 five times the quotient of cell B2 divided by cell B1.

   Formula: _____   Result: _____

5. Assign cell E1 the sum of the range of cells D2:D5 minus the product of cells C1 and C3.

   Formula: _____   Result: _____

6. Assign cell G6 the result of cell A5 less cell A4 raised to cell B1.

   Formula: _____   Result: _____

7. Assign cell A6 the expression $(X \char94 2 - 4 * Y * Z) / (2 * Y)$ where the value of X is in cell C2, the value of Y is in cell D2, and the value of Z is in cell D4.

   Formula: _____   Result: _____

STUDENT ASSIGNMENT 4
Understanding Formulas

Instructions: Figure SA2-4 displays the formula version of a worksheet. In the space provided, indicate in the fill-ins, the numeric value assigned to the cells if the numbers display instead of the formulas.

1. D1 _____

2. D2 _____

3. D3 _____

4. A4 _____

5. B4 _____

6. C4 _____

7. D4 _____

Microsoft Excel - SA2-4.XLS

	A	B	C	D	E
1	3	2	5	=A1 + B1 + C1	
2	7	7	6	=A3 * B2 - C3	
3	5	3	9	=2 * (B3 + C1)	
4	=A2 ^ B1	=20 / (A3 + C1)	=A1	=A2 ^ B3 - C3 * B2	
5					
6					
7					
8					
9					

FIGURE SA2-4

STUDENT ASSIGNMENT 5
Understanding Functions

Instructions: Figure SA2-5 displays the formula version of a worksheet. In the space provided, indicate the numeric value assigned to the cells if the numbers display instead of the functions.

1. D1 _____
2. D2 _____
3. D3 _____
4. A4 _____
5. B4 _____
6. C4 _____
7. D4 _____

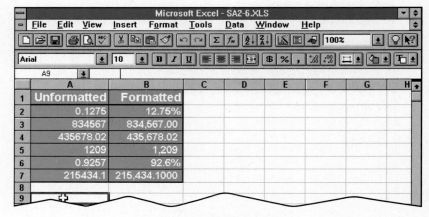

FIGURE SA2-5

STUDENT ASSIGNMENT 6
Applying Number Formats

Instructions: Indicate the buttons you would use on the Formatting toolbar to apply formats to the numbers in column A of Figure SA2-6 so they appear the same as the corresponding number in column B of Figure SA2-6.

Cell	Button(s)
B2	_____
B3	_____
B4	_____
B5	_____
B6	_____
B7	_____

FIGURE SA2-6

C O M P U T E R   L A B O R A T O R Y   E X E R C I S E S

COMPUTER LABORATORY EXERCISE 1
Using the Search for Help on Command on the Help Menu

Instructions: Start Excel and perform the following tasks using a computer.

1. Choose the Search for Help on command from the Help menu.
2. Type column width in the Search dialog box and choose the Show Topics button. With the topic, Adjusting column width, highlighted in the lower list, choose the Go To button. Read the information

displayed on the topic. Ready the printer. Click the Print button in the How To window. Click the Close button in the How To window. Double-click the Control-menu box in the Help window to close.

3. Choose the Search for Help on command from the Help menu. Type `borders` and click the Show Topics button. Select the topic Tips for Formatting Data in the lower list and choose the Go To button. Read the information and print the information by choosing Print Topic from the File menu in the Help window. Close the Help window.

4. Choose the Search for Help on command from the Help menu. Type `function wizard` and choose the Show Topics button. Select New Function Wizard and Help for Worksheet Functions from the lower list. Read and print the information in the Help window. Close the Help window.

COMPUTER LABORATORY EXERCISE 2
Applying Formats and Copying Formulas and Functions

Instructions: Start Excel. Open the workbook CLE2-2 from the subdirectory Excel5 on the Student Diskette that accompanies this book. The worksheet resembles the Awesome Sound International Sales Analysis worksheet created in Project 2. Perform the tasks below and on the next page so the worksheet CLE2-2 appears the same as the one shown in Figure CLE2-2.

FIGURE CLE2-2

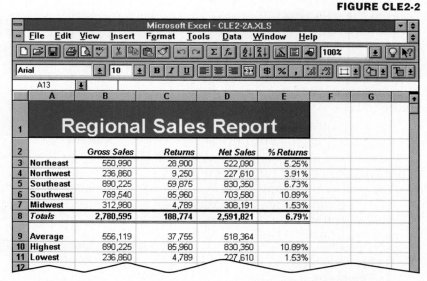

1. Copy the formula in cell E3 to the range E4:E8.
2. Use the appropriate function in cell B10 to calculate the maximum value in the range B3:B7. Copy cell B10 to the range C10:E10.
3. Use the appropriate function in cell B11 to calculate the minimum value in the range B3:B7. Copy cell B11 to the range C11:E11.
4. Enter your name, course, computer laboratory exercise number (CLE2-2), date, and instructor name in cells A13 through A17.
5. Save an intermediate copy of the workbook. Use the filename CLE2-2A.
6. Apply the following formats to the worksheet title in cell A1: (a) bold; (b) font size 24; (c) text color white (column 2, row 1 on the Color palette); (d) center across columns A through E; (e) background color of range A1:E1 green (column 2, row 2 on the Color palette); and (f) bold outline around the range A1:E1.
7. Change the column width as follows: (a) column A to best fit; (b) columns B through D to 13.00; and (c) column E to 11.00.
8. Bold, italicize, and right-align the column titles in the range B2 through E2. Draw a bold bottom border below row 2 in the range B2:E2 and below row 7 in the range A7:E7.
9. Bold the row titles in the range A3:A11, italicize the row title in cell A8, and bold the totals in the range B8:E8.
10. Draw a double underline border below row 8 in the range A8:E8.
11. Apply the Comma style with no decimal places to the range B3:D11.
12. Apply the Percent style with two decimal places to the range E3:E11.
13. Change the row height for row 1 to 45 points and the row height for rows 2 and 9 to 24 points.

(continued)

COMPUTER LABORATORY EXERCISE 2 (continued)

14. Save the workbook a second time using the same filename.
15. Preview the worksheet. Print the worksheet without gridlines.
16. Save the workbook again.
17. Print the range A2:C9.
18. Press CTRL+` (next to 1 key) to change the display from values to formulas. Print the formulas in the worksheet. After printing the formulas, change the display back to values by pressing CTRL+`.
19. Hide columns B and C by changing their column widths to zero. Print the worksheet.

COMPUTER LABORATORY EXERCISE 3
Changing Values in a Worksheet and Changing Appearance of a Chart

Instructions Part 1: Start Excel and perform the following tasks to change values in a worksheet. Open the worksheet CLE2-3 from the sub-directory Excel5 on the Student Diskette that accompanies this book. The worksheet CLE2-3 is shown in Figure CLE2-3a.

FIGURE CLE2-3a

1. Increase the Quantity On Hand amounts in column F as listed in the table to the right. Notice as you change the values in column F that the values in column G change accordingly. You should end up with the following totals: cell G11 is $20,189.18; cell G12 is $812.50; cell G13 is $5,756.70; and cell G14 is $2,523.65.
2. With gridlines off, print a copy of the worksheet with the new values.
3. Close the workbook without saving the changes.

Instructions Part 2: Perform the following tasks to change the appearance of the bar chart that accompanies worksheet CLE2-3 to make it look like Figure CLE2-3b.

1. Open the worksheet CLE2-3.
2. Click the Bar Chart tab at the bottom of the screen to display the worksheet's accompanying bar chart. Steps 3, 4, and 5 will change the chart you see on your screen to look like the one in Figure CLE2-3b.

	OLD QUANTITY ON HAND	NEW QUANTITY ON HAND
Roadhandler	25	40
Whitewalls	140	155
Tripod	10	25
Maxidrill	6	21
Normal Saw	1	16
Router	8	23
Radial Saw	3	18
Oxford Style	28	43

3. Move the columns in the chart so they are in the sequence shown in Figure CLE2-3b by (a) selecting any column on the chart; (b) clicking the right mouse button; (c) selecting Format 3-D Column Group; (d) displaying the Series Order tab; (e) one by one selecting the name in the Series Order box that corresponds to each column; (f) clicking the Move Up button or the Move Down button until the columns are in the same sequence as shown in Figure CLE2-3b; and (g) choosing the OK button.

4. Change the color of the chart walls to blue (column 8, row 1 on the Color palette). You must first click the chart wall (not a gridline) to change the color.

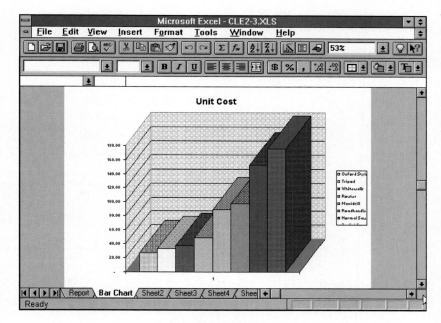

FIGURE CLE2-3b

5. Change the perspective of the chart to agree with the perspective shown in Figure CLE2-3b by (a) clicking on the chart; (b) moving the mouse pointer to the black handle located at the upper left corner of the chart; (c) clicking the handle (the mouse pointer will change to a cross shape); dragging the chart to a new location; and (d) releasing the left mouse button.

6. Click the Report tab at the bottom of the screen to return to the worksheet and enter your name, course, computer laboratory exercise number (CLE2-3B), date, and instructor name in cells A16 through A20.

7. Save the modified workbook. Use the filename CLE2-3B.

8. Print both the worksheet and the column chart.

COMPUTER LABORATORY ASSIGNMENTS

COMPUTER LABORATORY ASSIGNMENT 1
Building a Monthly Sales Analysis Worksheet and 3-D Column Chart

Purpose: To become familiar with building a worksheet that includes formulas, formatting a worksheet, using the recalculation features of Excel, printing different versions of the worksheet and building a 3-D column chart based on values in the worksheet.

Problem: The computer consulting firm you and a friend started recently on a part-time basis has received its first contract. The client has specified in the contract that you are to build a monthly sales analysis worksheet that determines the sales quota and percentage of quota met for the following salespeople:

NAME	SALES AMOUNT	SALES RETURNS	SALES QUOTA
Sandy Lane	$15,789.00	$245.00	$12,000.00
George Ade	8,500.00	500.00	10,000.00
Mary Markam	17,895.00	1,376.00	12,000.00
Tom Rich	12,843.00	843.00	11,000.00

(continued)

COMPUTER LABORATORY ASSIGNMENT 1 (continued)

Part 1 Instructions: Perform the following tasks to build the worksheet shown in Figure CLA2-1a.

FIGURE CLA2-1a

1. Use the Select All button and the Bold button to bold the entire worksheet.
2. Increase the widths of columns A through F to 13.00 characters.
3. Enter the worksheet title, Monthly Sales Report, in cell A1, column titles in row 2, and the row titles in column A as shown in Figure CLA2-1a.
4. Enter the sales data described in the previous table in columns A, B, C, and E as shown in Figure CLA2-1a. Do not enter the numbers with dollar signs or commas.
5. Obtain the net sales in column D of the worksheet by subtracting the sales returns in column C from the sales amount in column B. Enter the formula in cell D3 and copy it to the range D4:D6.
6. Obtain the above quota amounts in column F by subtracting the sales quota in column E from the net sales in column D. Enter the formula in cell F3 and copy it to the range F4:F6.
7. Obtain the totals in row 7 by adding the column values for each salesperson. The averages in row 8 contain the column averages.
8. In cell A9, enter the % of Quota Sold title with equal signs and the greater than sign to create the arrow shown in Figure CLA2-1a. Obtain the percent of quota sold in cell C9 by dividing the total net sales amount in cell D7 by the total sales quota amount in cell E7.
9. Change the worksheet title font in cell A1 to CG Times and increase its size to 22 point. Center the title across columns A through F.
10. Italicize the column titles in row 2. Right-align the titles in columns B through F. Draw a bold bottom border in the range A2:F2.
11. Select the ranges A1:F1 and A7:F7. Change the background color to purple (column 1, row 2 of the Color palette). Change the text color of the worksheet title to white (column 2, row 1 of the Color palette). Outline both of these ranges with a bold border as shown in Figure CLA2-1.
12. Increase the height of row 1 to 42.00 points and increase the heights of rows 2, 8, and 9 to 24.00 points.
13. Use the buttons on the Formatting toolbar to apply number formats in the range B3:F8 to the Comma style with two decimal places. Format cell C9 to the Percent style with two decimal places.
14 Change the color of cell C9 to yellow (column 4, row 5 of the Color palette) and place an outline around it.

15. Enter your name, course, computer laboratory assignment number (CLA2-1), date, and instructor name below the entries in column A in separate cells.
16. Save the workbook using the filename CLA2-1A.
17. Print the worksheet without gridlines.
18. Save the workbook again.
19. Display the formulas by pressing CTRL+`. Print the formulas in the worksheet using the Fit to option button in the Scaling area on the Page tab in the Page Setup dialog box. After printing the worksheet, reset Scaling by selecting the Adjust to option button on the Page tab in the Page Setup dialog box and changing the percent value to 100%. Change the display from formulas back to values by pressing CTRL+`.
20. Print only the range A2:B8.

Part 2 Instructions: Increment each of the four values in the sales quota column by $1,000.00 until the percent of quota sold in cell C9 is below, yet as close as possible to, 100%. All four values in column E must be incremented the same number of times. The percent of quota sold in cell C9 should equal 98.23%. Save the workbook as CLA2-1B. Print the worksheet without cell gridlines.

Part 3 Instructions: With the percent of quota sold in cell C9 equal to 98.23% from Part 2, decrement each of the four values in the sales return column by $100.00 until the percent of quota sold in cell C9 is below, yet as close as possible to, 100%. Decrement all four values in column C the same number of times. Your worksheet is correct when the percent of quota sold in cell C9 is equal to 99.74%. Save the workbook as CLA2-1C. Print the worksheet without cell gridlines.

Part 4 Instructions: Select the range A3:B6. Use the Chart command on the Insert menu to create a chart on a new sheet. Draw a 3-D Column Chart with a number 4 format like the one shown in Figure CLA2-1b. Notice the following about the chart: (a) the data series for this chart is in columns; (b) there is no legend on the chart; and (c) the chart does have a title of Monthly Sales by Salesperson. Next, change the color of the chart background to yellow (column 4, row 5 on the Color palette) and change the color of the columns to purple (column 1, row 2 on the Color palette). Change the font size of the chart title to 24 point and the color of the text to the same color as the columns. Rename the Sheet tabs at the bottom of the screen to read Sales for the sheet tab corresponding to the worksheet and Bar Chart for the sheet tab corresponding to the chart. Rearrange the order of the sheet tabs so the worksheet appears first with the chart following it. Save the workbook as CLA2-1D. Print the entire workbook without cell gridlines.

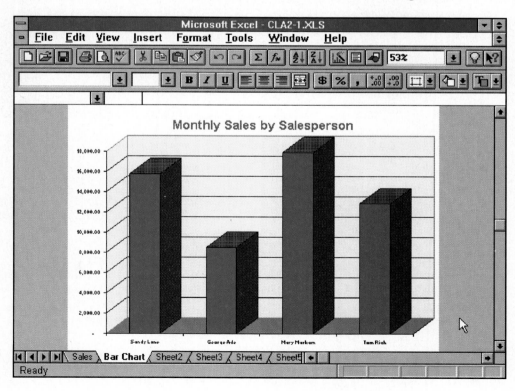

FIGURE CLA2-1b

COMPUTER LABORATORY ASSIGNMENT 2
Building a Biweekly Payroll Worksheet

Purpose: To become familiar with entering complex formulas.

Problem: You are employed by the Payroll department of a construction firm. You have been asked to prepare a biweekly payroll report for the following six employees:

EMPLOYEE	RATE PER HOUR	HOURS	DEPENDENTS
Col, Lisa	12.50	81.00	2
Fel, Jeff	18.00	64.00	4
Di, Marci	13.00	96.25	0
Sno, Niki	4.50	122.50	1
Hi, Mandi	3.35	16.50	1
Bri, Jodi	10.40	80.00	3

Instructions: Perform the following tasks to create a worksheet similar to the one in Figure CLA2-2.

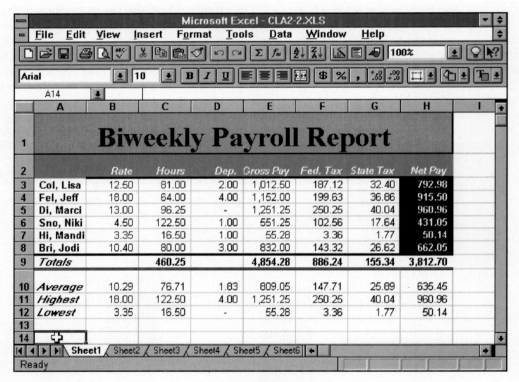

FIGURE CLA2-2

1. Enter the worksheet title, Biweekly Payroll Report, in cell A1. Enter the column titles in row 2, the row titles in column A, and the data in columns B through D from the above table as shown in Figure CLA2-2.

2. Use the following formulas to determine the gross pay, federal tax, state tax, and net pay:
   a. Gross Pay = Rate * Hours (Hint: Assign the first employee in cell E3 the formula =B3 * C3, and copy the formula in E3 to the range E4:E8 for the remaining employees.)
   b. Federal Tax = 20% * (Gross Pay - Dependents * 38. 46)
   c. State Tax = 3. 2% * Gross Pay
   d. Net Pay = Gross Pay - (Federal Tax + State Tax)
3. Show totals for the hours, gross pay, federal tax, state tax, and net pay in row 9.
4. Determine the average, highest, and lowest values of each column in rows 10 through 12 by using the appropriate functions.
5. Do the following to apply formatting to the worksheet title in cell A1: (a) bold; (b) change the font style to TrueType Times New Roman; (c) increase the font size to 18 point; (d) individually change the first character in each word to 28 point; (e) center the title across columns A through H; (f) change the background color of the range to red (column 3, row 1 on the Color palette); and (g) draw a bold outline around the range A1 through H1.
6. Use the buttons on the Formatting toolbar. Apply the Comma style with two decimal places to the range B3:H12. Notice that Excel displays a dash in any cell that has a value of zero and has been formatted to the Comma style.
7. Bold, italicize, and right-align the column titles and draw a bold border under them in the range B2:H2. Change the background color for the range A2:H2 to gray (column 8, row 2 on the Color palette) and change the column title text to white (column 2, row 1 on the Color palette).
8. Select the range H3:H8 and change the background color to black (column 1, row 1 on the Color palette) and change the text color to white (column 2, row 1 on the Color palette). Draw an outline around this range.
9. Bold the names and row titles in column A. Italicize the row titles and change the Font style to MS Sans Serif in the range A9:A12.
10. Change the heights of rows 2 and 10 to 24.00 points and the width of columns A through H to 9.00 points. Draw the borders above and below the totals in row 9 as shown in Figure CLA2-2.
11. Enter your name, course, computer laboratory assignment number (CLA2-2), date, and instructor name below the entries in column A in separate but adjacent cells.
12. Save the workbook using the filename CLA2-2.
13. Preview the worksheet. Print the worksheet with gridlines off.
14. Save the workbook a second time.
15. Press CTRL+` to change the display from values to formulas. Print the formulas to fit on one page in the worksheet. After the printer is finished, reset the worksheet to display the numbers by pressing CTRL+`. Reset Scaling to 100% by selecting the Adjust to option button on the Page tab in the Page Setup dialog box and setting the percent value to 100%.
16. Increase the number of hours worked for each employee by 7. 5. Total net pay (cell H9) should be 4,168.38. Print the worksheet with the new values. Do not save the worksheet with the new values.

COMPUTER LABORATORY ASSIGNMENT 3
Determining the Monthly Accounts Receivable Balance

Purpose: To become familiar with entering and copying formulas, applying formatting to a worksheet, creating a bar chart, and printing different versions of the worksheet.

Problem: You are enrolled in a sophomore Office Information Systems course in which the students are given projects in the local business community. You have been assigned to LakeView Hardware. LakeView Hardware wants you to generate a much-needed report that summarizes their monthly accounts receivable balance. The monthly information contained in the table on the next page is available for test purposes.

(continued)

COMPUTER LABORATORY ASSIGNMENT 3 (continued)

ACCOUNT NUMBER	CUSTOMER NAME	BEGINNING BALANCE	PURCHASES	PAYMENTS	RETURNS
A203	Kelly	1,782.32	324.12	400.00	6.25
C609	Bates	235.68	23.00	25.00	23.15
F812	Webb	435.92	10.00	50.00	212.25
F933	Silver	1,678.54	212.78	25.00	15.00
H234	Abram	3,098.75	89.43	10.00	45.00

Part 1 Instructions: Construct a worksheet similar to the one shown in Figure CLA2-3a. Include all six fields in the report plus the service charge and new balance. (Assume no negative unpaid monthly balances.) Use the following formulas to determine the service charge and the new balance at the end of month for each account:

a. Service Charge = 2.25% * (Beginning Balance - Payments - Returns)
b. New Balance = Beginning Balance + Purchases - Payments - Returns + Service Charge

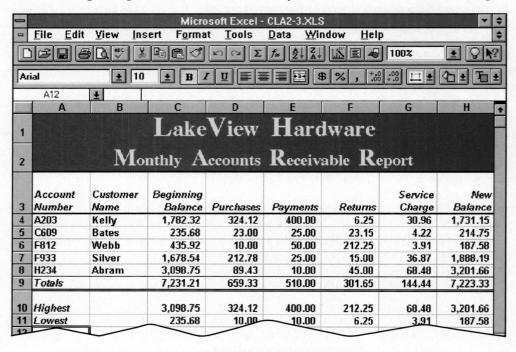

FIGURE CLA2-3a

Perform the following tasks:

1. Use the Select All button and Bold button on the Formatting toolbar to bold the entire worksheet.
2. Assign the worksheet title, LakeView Hardware, to cell A1. Assign the worksheet subtitle, Monthly Accounts Receivable Report, to cell A2.
3. Enter the column titles in the range A3:H3 as shown in Figure CLA2-3a. In the column titles that contain two words (such as Account Number in cell A3), press ALT+ENTER after the first word and ENTER after the second word.
4. Enter the account numbers and row titles in column A
5. Cell C10 should contain the appropriate function to calculate the maximum value in the range C4:C8. Copy cell C10 to the range D10:H10.
6. Cell C11 should contain the appropriate function to calculate the minimum value in the range C4:C8. Copy cell C11 to the range D11:H11.

7. Change the worksheet title font in cell A1, to CG Times 22 point. Change the font size of the first letter of each word in the worksheet title to 28 point. Format the worksheet subtitle font in cell A2 to CG Times 16 point and the first letter of each word in the subtitle to 24 point.

8. Select the range A1:H2 and change the background color to blue (column 5, row 1 of the Color palette). Change the text color in the range A1:H2 to yellow (column 3, row 4 of the Color palette). Center both the worksheet title and subtitle across the range A1:H2. Change the heights of rows 1 and 2 to 30.00 points.

9. Change the widths of columns A through H to 10.00 points. Italicize the column titles and place a bold border below them. Right-align the column titles in the range C3:H3. Change the row height of row 3 to 42.00 points.

10. Italicize the titles in rows 9, 10, and 11. Change the height of row 10 to 24.00 points. Select row 9 and place a single upper border and double underline border in the range A9:H9.

11. Using the buttons on the Formatting toolbar, apply the Comma style with two decimal places to the ranges C4:H11.

12. Enter your name, course, computer laboratory assignment number (CLA2-3), date, and instructor name below the entries in column A in separate but adjacent cells.

13. Save the workbook using the filename CLA2-3.

14. Print the worksheet in landscape orientation without gridlines.

15. Save the workbook again.

16. Print the range A3:C9 in portrait orientation.

17. Press CTRL+` to change the display from values to formulas. Print to fit on one page in landscape orientation, the formulas in the worksheet. After the printer is finished, reset the worksheet to display values by pressing CTRL+`. Reset Scaling to 100% by selecting the Adjust to option button on the Page tab in the Page Setup dialog box and setting the percent value to 100%.

Part 2 Instructions: Select the range B4:C8. Use the Chart command on the Insert menu, to create a chart as a new sheet. Draw a 3-D Bar Chart with a number 1 format like the one shown in Figure CLA2-3b. Notice the following about the chart: (a) the data series for this chart is in columns; (b) there is no legend on the chart; and (c) the chart does have a title of Monthly Accounts Receivable. Once the chart is drawn, change the color of the chart walls to medium blue (column 1, row 3 on the Color palette) and change the color of the bars to yellow (column 3, row 4 on the Color palette). Change the font size and color of the title to 18 point with a color of dark blue (column 1, row 4 on the Color palette). Rename the sheet tabs at the bottom of the screen to read Report for the sheet tab corresponding to the worksheet and Bar Chart for the sheet tab corresponding to the chart. Rearrange the order of the sheet tabs so the worksheet appears first with the chart following it. Save the workbook using the filename CLA2-3A. Print the chart.

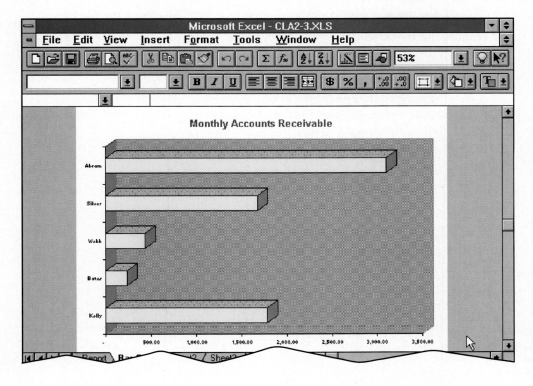

FIGURE CLA2-3b

COMPUTER LABORATORY ASSIGNMENT 4
Inflation Gauge

Purpose: To become familiar with planning a worksheet.

Problem: You are employed as a summer intern by the State Budget department. One of the department's responsibilities is to report to the state legislature the expected inflation rate of food for the next year. They obtain their data by selecting a few often-used grocery items and keeping track of the prices over a period of time. They then determine and report the individual inflation rates and the expected prices in one year. As a summer intern with a knowledge of Excel, they have asked you to create an Inflation Gauge worksheet.

Instructions: Perform the following tasks to determine the price change, inflation rate, and expected price using the pricing information data below.

ITEM	CURRENT PRICE	BEGINNING PRICE	NUMBER OF WEEKS
1 doz. eggs	$0.93	$0.92	13
1 lb. butter	2.59	2.50	15
1 gal. milk	1.92	1.85	18
1 loaf bread	1.10	1.07	6

Assign these three formulas to the first item — 1 doz. eggs in row 4 — and copy them to the rest of the items.
   a. Price Change = 52 * (Current Price - Beginning Price) / Weeks
   b. Inflation Rate = Price Change / Beginning Price
   c. Price in One Year = Current Price + Inflation Rate * Current Price

Use the techniques you learned in this project to apply formatting to the worksheet and to illustrate totals. Enter your name, course, computer laboratory assignment number (CLA2-4), date, and instructor name below the entries in column A in separate but adjacent cells. Save the worksheet using the filename CLA2-4. Submit the following:

1. A description of the problem. Include the purpose of the worksheet, a statement outlining the results, the required data, and calculations.
2. A handwritten design of the worksheet.
3. A printed copy of the worksheet without cell gridlines.
4. A printed copy of the formulas in the worksheet.
5. A short description explaining how to use the worksheet.
6. Draw a chart that compares the inflation rate of the four items in the worksheet. Apply appropriate formatting to the chart.

MICROSOFT EXCEL 5 FOR WINDOWS

▼

ENHANCING A WORKSHEET AND CHART

OBJECTIVES You will have mastered the material in this project when you can:

- ▶ Use the fill handle to create a series of month names
- ▶ Copy a cell's format to another cell using the Format Painter button
- ▶ Copy a range of cells to a nonadjacent paste area
- ▶ Freeze the column and row titles
- ▶ Insert and delete cells
- ▶ Format numbers by entering them with a format symbol
- ▶ Display the system date using the NOW function and format it
- ▶ Use the IF function to enter one value or another in a cell on the basis of a logical test
- ▶ Copy absolute cell references

- ▶ Italicize text
- ▶ Add a drop shadow to a range of cells
- ▶ Display and dock toolbars
- ▶ Create a 3-D pie chart
- ▶ Explode a 3-D pie chart
- ▶ Rotate a chart
- ▶ Add an arrow and text to a chart
- ▶ Use the Zoom Control box to change the appearance of the worksheet
- ▶ View different parts of the worksheet through window panes
- ▶ Use Excel to answer what-if questions
- ▶ Analyze worksheet data by using the Goal Seek command

▶ INTRODUCTION

This project introduces you to techniques to enhance your ability to create worksheets and draw charts. You will learn about alternative methods for entering values in cells and formatting them. You will also learn how to use absolute cell references and how to use the IF function to assign one value or another to a cell based on a logical test.

In the previous projects, you learned how to use the Standard toolbar and Formatting toolbar. Excel has several other toolbars that can make your work easier. One such toolbar is the **Drawing toolbar**, which allows you to draw shapes, arrows, and drop shadows around cells you want to emphasize in the worksheet.

Worksheets are normally much larger than those presented in the previous projects. Worksheets that extend beyond the size of the window present a viewing problem because you cannot see the entire worksheet at one time. For this reason, Excel provides several commands that allow you to rearrange the view on the screen to display critical parts of a large worksheet. These commands allow you to maintain the row and column titles on the screen at all times by freezing the titles and to view different parts of a worksheet through window panes.

From your work in Projects 1 and 2, you are aware of the ease in creating charts. This project goes a step further and introduces you to methods for improving a chart's appearance. With only a little effort, you can use Excel to create, display, and print professional looking charts and convey your message in a dramatic pictorial fashion.

When you set up a worksheet, you should use as many cell references in formulas as possible, rather than constant values. The cell references in a formula are often called assumptions. **Assumptions** are cells whose values you can change to determine new values for formulas. This project emphasizes the use of assumptions and introduces you to answering what-if questions such as: What if you decrease the base salary assumption (cell B15 in Figure 3-1a) by 1% — how would the decrease affect the total projected payroll expenses (cell H12 in Figure 3-1a)? This capability of quickly analyzing the effect of changing values in a worksheet is important in making business decisions.

FIGURE 3-1a

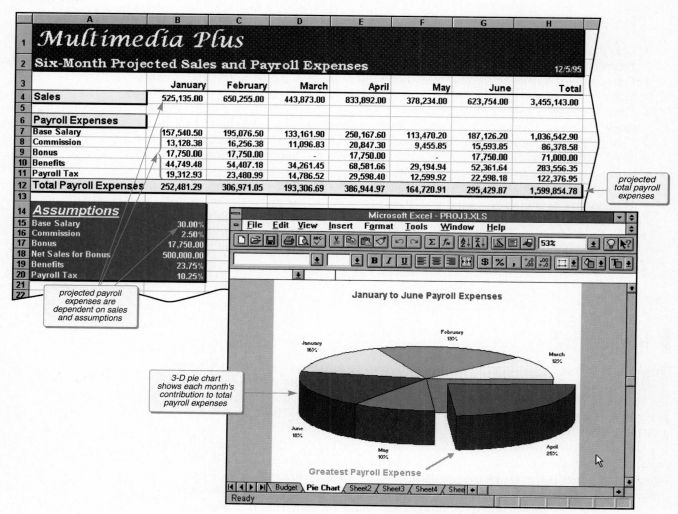

FIGURE 3-1b

▶ PROJECT THREE — MULTIMEDIA PLUS SIX-MONTH PROJECTED SALES AND PAYROLL EXPENSES

T he worksheet in Figure 3-1a contains a company's projected sales and payroll expenses for a six-month period. The date in cell H2 (12/5/95) indicates that the January to June projections are being made a month before the six-month period begins. The sales in row 4 are estimates based on previous years' sales. In addition, the worksheet includes the projected six-month total sales in cell H4.

Each of the monthly projected payroll expenses in the range B7:G11 — base salary, commission, bonus, benefits, and payroll tax — is determined by taking a percentage of the corresponding monthly sales in row 4. The percent values (assumptions) located in the range B15:B20 are as follows:

1. The monthly base salary is 30% of the projected sales.
2. The monthly commission is 2.5% of the projected sales.
3. The monthly bonus is $17,750 if the monthly projected sales exceed the net sales for bonus in cell B18 ($500,000).
4. The monthly benefits is 23.75% of the projected sales.
5. The monthly payroll tax is 10.25% of the projected sales.

The total projected payroll expenses for each month in row 12 of Figure 3-1a are the sum of the corresponding monthly projected expenses in rows 7 through 11. Finally, the six-month totals in column H are determined by summing the monthly values in each row.

Because the monthly expenses in rows 7 through 11 are dependent on the percent expenses and bonus (assumptions), you can use Excel's what-if capability to determine the impact of changing these percent expenses on the total payroll expenses in row 12.

The 3-D pie chart (Figure 3-1b) shows the contribution of each month to the total projected payroll expenses for the six-month period. The slice representing April has been slightly removed from the main portion of the pie to emphasize the fact that it is expected to contribute more to payroll expenses than any other. The text, Greatest Payroll Expense, at the bottom of the chart sheet and an arrow pointing to the April slice are also used to highlight the April slice.

Worksheet and Chart Preparation Steps

The following list is an overview of how the worksheet in Figure 3-1a and chart in Figure 3-1b will be built in this project. If you are building the worksheet and chart in this project on a personal computer, read these 15 steps without doing them.

1. Start the Excel program.
2. Assign the bold style to all the cells in the worksheet.
3. Enter the worksheet titles, column titles, and row titles. Increase the column widths.
4. Save the workbook.
5. Enter the assumptions in the range B15:B20.
6. Enter the projected sales in row 4.
7. Display the system date in cell H2.
8. Enter the formulas that determine the payroll expenses (B7:G12) and the totals in column H.
9. Format the worksheet so it appears as shown in Figure 3-1a.
10. Create the 3-D pie chart using the nonadjacent range selections B3:G3 and B12:G12.
11. Format the pie chart.

12. Check spelling, preview, print the worksheet and chart, and save the workbook.
13. Use the Zoom Control box on the Standard toolbar to change the appearance of the worksheet.
14. Divide the window into panes.
15. Analyze the data in the worksheet by changing the assumptions (B15:B20) and by goal seeking.

The following sections contain a detailed explanation of each of these steps.

Starting Excel

To start Excel, follow the steps you used at the beginning of Project 1. These steps are summarized below.

TO START EXCEL

Step 1: From Program Manager, open the Microsoft Office group window.
Step 2: Double-click the Excel program-item icon.
Step 3: If necessary, enlarge the window by clicking the maximize button in the upper right corner of the screen.

Changing the Font of the Entire Worksheet to Bold

The first step in this project is to change the font of the entire worksheet to bold, so all entries are emphasized.

TO CHANGE THE FONT OF THE ENTIRE WORKSHEET TO BOLD

Step 1: Click the Select All button immediately above row heading 1.
Step 2: Click the Bold button on the Standard toolbar.

There is no immediate change on the screen. However, as you enter text and numbers into the worksheet, Excel will display them in bold.

Entering the Worksheet Titles

There are two worksheet titles, one in cell A1 and one in cell A2. In the previous projects, the titles were centered over the worksheet. With large worksheets that extend beyond the width of a window, it is best to display them in the upper left corner as shown in Figure 3-1a on page E136.

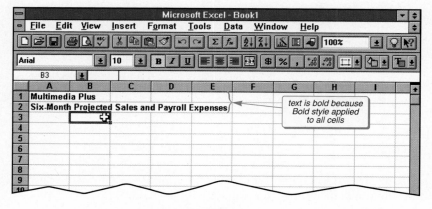

FIGURE 3-2

TO ENTER THE WORKSHEET TITLES

Step 1: Select cell A1 and type
Multimedia Plus
Step 2: Select cell A2 and type
Six-Month Projected
Sales and Payroll
Expenses
Step 3: Select cell B3.

The worksheet titles in cells A1 and A2 display in bold (Figure 3-2).

▶ USING THE FILL HANDLE TO CREATE A SERIES

In Projects 1 and 2, you used the fill handle to copy a cell or a range of cells to adjacent cells. You can also use the fill handle to automatically create a series of numbers, dates, or month names. Perform the following steps to enter the month name January in cell B3, format cell B3, and then create the remaining five month names, February, March, April, May, and June, in the range C3:G3 (see Figure 3-5).

TO USE THE FILL HANDLE TO CREATE A SERIES OF MONTH NAMES ▼

STEP 1 ▶

With cell B3 selected, enter January**. On the Formatting toolbar, choose 11 point in the Font Size box, click the Align Right button, and choose a heavy bottom border from the Borders palette. Point to the fill handle.**

The text, January, in cell B3 displays using the applied formats (Figure 3-3). The mouse pointer changes to a cross.

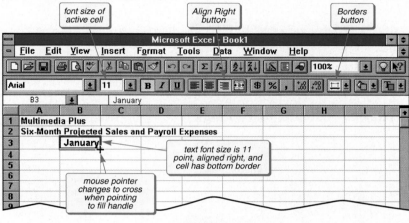

FIGURE 3-3

STEP 2 ▶

Drag the fill handle to the right to select the range C3:G3.

Excel displays a light border that surrounds the range selected (Figure 3-4).

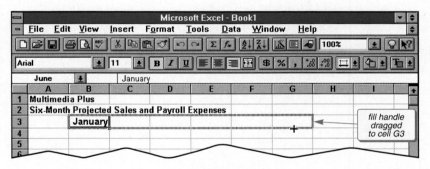

FIGURE 3-4

STEP 3 ▶

Release the left mouse button.

Using January in cell B3 as the basis, Excel creates the month name series, February through June, in the range C3:G3 (Figure 3-5). The formats applied to cell B3 are copied (propagated) to the range C3:G3.

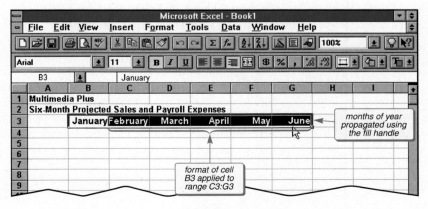

FIGURE 3-5

Besides creating a series of values, the fill handle also copies the format of cell B3 (11 point, right-aligned, and heavy bottom border) to the range C3:G3. If you drag the fill handle past cell G3 (after June) in Step 2, Excel continues to increment the months and will logically repeat January, February, and so on.

You can create different types of series using the fill handle. Table 3-1 illustrates several examples. Notice in Examples 4 through 7 in Table 3-1 that if you use the fill handle to create a series of numbers or nonsequential months, you are required to enter the first number in the series in one cell and the second number in the series in an adjacent cell. You then select both cells and drag the fill handle across the paste area.

If you want to use the fill handle to copy the same text, such as January, to each cell in the paste area without creating a series, hold down the CTRL key while you drag.

▶ **TABLE 3-1**

EXAMPLE	CONTENTS OF CELL(S) COPIED USING FILL HANDLE	NEXT THREE VALUES OF EXTENDED SERIES
1	6:00	7:00, 8:00, 9:00
2	Qtr3	Qtr4, Qtr1, Qtr2
3	Quarter 1	Quarter 2, Quarter 3, Quarter 4
4	Jul-93, Oct-93	Jan-94, Apr-94, Jul-94
5	1999, 2000	2001, 2002, 2003
6	1, 2	3, 4, 5
7	200, 195	190, 185, 180
8	Sun	Mon, Tue, Wed
9	Tuesday	Wednesday, Thursday, Friday
10	1st Part	2nd Part, 3rd Part, 4th Part
11	-1, -3	-5, -7, -9

Customizing the Series

You can instruct Excel on what type of series you want to create by using the **AutoFill shortcut menu** or **Fill command** on the Edit menu. To display the AutoFill shortcut menu, point to the fill handle. When it changes to a cross, hold down the right mouse button. The mouse pointer changes from the cross to a block arrow ( ). Drag the fill handle over the desired range. Then, release the right mouse button and the AutoFill shortcut menu displays. You can then select the type of series you want to create.

▶ COPYING A CELL'S FORMAT USING THE FORMAT PAINTER BUTTON

Because it is not part of the series, the last column title, Total, in cell H3 must be entered separately. Furthermore, to ensure that it appears the same as the other column titles, the same formats applied to the months must be applied to cell H3. Excel has a button on the Standard toolbar, called the **Format Painter** ( ), which allows you to copy a cell's format to another cell. The following steps enter the column title, Total, in cell H3 and format the cell using the Format Painter button.

TO COPY A CELL'S FORMAT ▼

STEP 1 ▶

Select cell H3 and enter Total

STEP 2 ▶

Select cell G3 and click the Format Painter button on the Standard toolbar. Move the mouse pointer over cell H3.

The mouse pointer changes to a block plus sign and paint brush (🔲🖌) (Figure 3-6).

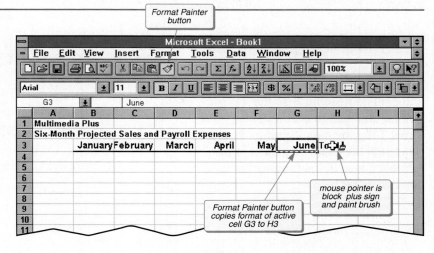

FIGURE 3-6

STEP 3 ▶

Click the left mouse button to assign the format of cell G3 to H3. Select cell A4.

The format of cell G3 (11 point, right-aligned, and a heavy bottom border) is applied to cell H3 (Figure 3-7).

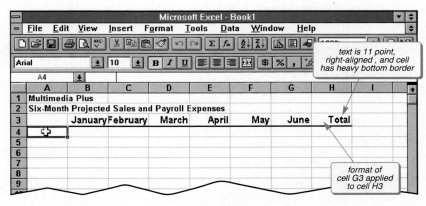

FIGURE 3-7

The Format Painter button can be used to copy the formats of a cell to a range or to copy a range to another range. To copy formats to a range of cells, select the cell or range to copy from, click the Format Painter button, and then drag through the range you want to paste the formats to.

If you want to copy formats to more than one range (nonadjacent ranges), double-click the Format Painter button and then, one by one, drag through the ranges. Finally, click the Format Painter button to deactivate it.

▶ INCREASING THE COLUMN WIDTHS AND ENTERING ROW TITLES

In Project 2, you increased the column widths after entering the values into the worksheet. Sometimes, you may want to increase the column widths before you enter the values and then, if necessary, adjust them later. The following steps increase the column widths and add the row titles in column A down to Assumptions in cell A14. The last step saves the workbook using the filename PROJ3.XLS.

TO INCREASE COLUMN WIDTHS AND ENTER ROW TITLES ▼

STEP 1 ▶

Move the mouse pointer to the border between column heading A and column heading B so the pointer changes to a split double arrow. Drag the mouse pointer to the right until the width displayed in the reference area in the formula bar is equal to 25.00.

The distance between the left edge of column A and the vertical dotted line below the mouse pointer shows the proposed column width and 25.00 displays in the reference area (Figure 3-8).

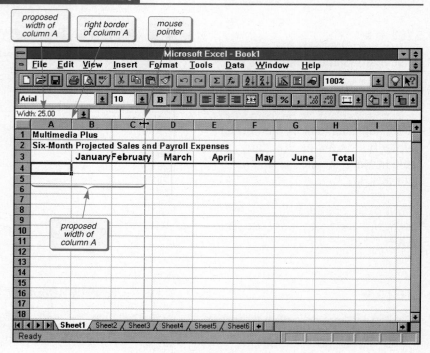

FIGURE 3-8

STEP 2 ▶

Release the left mouse button. Select columns B through G by pointing to column heading B and dragging though column heading G. Move the mouse pointer to the borderline between column headings G and H and drag the mouse to the right until the width displayed in the reference area is 13.00.

The distance between the left edge of column G and the vertical line below the mouse pointer shows the proposed column width and 13.00 displays in the reference area (Figure 3-9).

STEP 3 ▶

Release the left mouse button. Use the technique in Step 1 to increase the width of column H to 15.00.

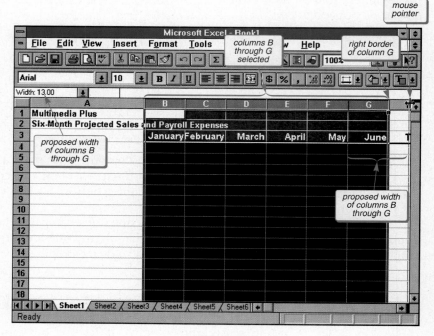

FIGURE 3-9

STEP 4 ▶

Enter Sales **in cell A4,** Payroll Expenses **in cell A6,** Base Salary **in cell A7, and** Commission **in cell A8. Enter** Bonus **in cell A9,** Benefits **in cell A10,** Payroll Tax **in cell A11,** Total Payroll Expenses **in cell A12, and** Assumptions **in cell A14 as shown in Figure 3-10. Click the Save button on the Standard toolbar. Type the filename** PROJ3 **in the File Name box. If necessary, select drive A in the Directories box. Choose the OK button. If a Summary Info dialog box displays, choose the OK button.**

The workbook name in the title bar changes from Book1 to PROJ3.XLS (Figure 3-10). Only columns A through E display in the window.

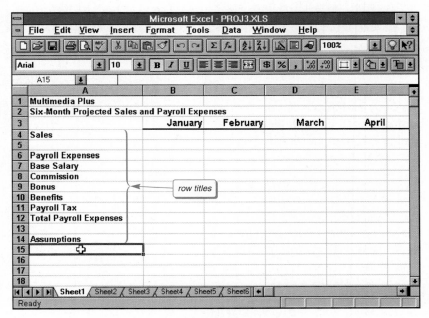

FIGURE 3-10

▶ COPYING A RANGE OF CELLS TO A NONADJACENT PASTE AREA

According to Figure 3-1a on page E136, the row titles in the Assumptions table in the range A15:B20 are the same as the row titles in the range A7:A11, except for the additional entry in cell A18. Hence, the range A7:A11 can be copied to the range A15:A19 and the additional entry in cell A18 can be inserted. Notice that the range to copy (A7:A11) is not adjacent to the paste area (A15:A19). In the first two projects, the fill handle worked well for copying a range of cells to an adjacent paste area, but you cannot use the fill handle to copy a range of cells to a nonadjacent paste area.

A more versatile method of copying a cell or range of cells is to use the Copy button and Paste button on the Standard toolbar. You can use these two buttons to copy a range of cells to an adjacent or nonadjacent paste area.

When you click the **Copy button** (🖹), it copies the contents and format of the selected range and places the entries on the Clipboard, replacing the Clipboard's contents. The **Copy command** on the Edit menu or shortcut menu works the same as the Copy button.

The **Paste button** (🖹) copies the contents of the Clipboard to the paste area. The **Paste command** on the Edit menu or shortcut menu works in the same way as the Paste button. You can also complete the paste operation by pressing the ENTER key.

TO COPY A RANGE OF CELLS TO A NONADJACENT PASTE AREA ▼

STEP 1 ▶

Select the range A7:A11 and click the Copy button on the Standard toolbar. Scroll down until row 20 is visible and then select cell A15, the top cell of the paste area.

Excel surrounds the range A7:A11 with a marquis when the Copy button is clicked (Figure 3-11). Excel also copies the values and formats of the range A7:A11 onto the Clipboard.

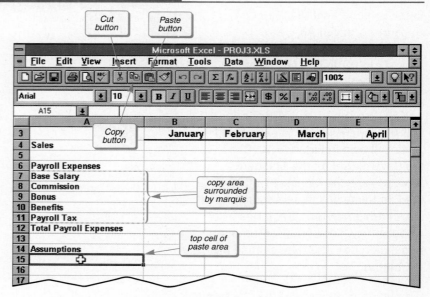

FIGURE 3-11

STEP 2 ▶

Press the ENTER key to complete the copy.

Excel copies the contents of the Clipboard (range A7:A11) to the paste area A15:A19 (Figure 3-12).

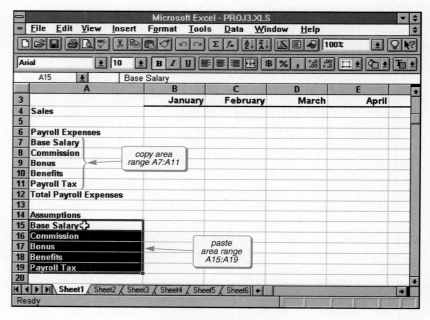

FIGURE 3-12

Notice in Figure 3-11 that you are not required to highlight the entire paste area (A15:A19) before pressing the ENTER key to complete the copy. Because the paste area is exactly the same size as the range you are copying, you need to select only the top left cell of the paste area. In the case of a single column range such as A15:A19, the top cell of the paste area (cell A15) is the upper left cell of the paste area.

When you complete a copy, the values and formats in the paste area are replaced with the values and formats on the Clipboard. Any data contained in the paste area prior to the copy and paste is lost. If you accidentally delete valuable data, immediately click the Undo button on the Standard toolbar or use the **Undo Paste command** from the Edit menu to undo the paste.

Whenever you want to copy a range only once, it is more efficient to use the ENTER key to complete the copy than it is to use the Paste button.

When you use the ENTER key to paste, the contents on the Clipboard are erased after the copy is complete. When you paste using the Paste button or Paste command on the Edit menu or shortcut menu, the contents of the Clipboard remain available for additional copying. Thus, if you plan to copy the cells to more than one paste area, click the Paste button or choose the Paste command from the Edit menu or shortcut menu instead of pressing the ENTER key. Then, select the next paste area and invoke the Paste command again. If you paste using the Paste button or the Paste command from the Edit menu or shortcut menu, the marquis around the range to copy remains to remind you that the copied range is still on the Clipboard. To erase the marquis, press the ESC key.

Using Drag and Drop to Move or Copy Cells

You can use the mouse to move or copy cells. Select the copy area and point to the border of the range. You know you are pointing to the border of a range when the mouse pointer changes to a block arrow. To move the selected cells, drag the selection to its new location. To copy a range, hold down the CTRL key while dragging. Then release the left mouse button before you release the CTRL key. Using the mouse to move or copy cells is called **drag and drop**.

Another way to move cells is to select them, click the Cut button on the Standard toolbar, select the new area, and then click the Paste button on the Standard toolbar or press the ENTER key. You can also use the **Cut command** on the Edit menu or shortcut menu to copy the selected cells to the Clipboard and delete them from their current location.

Moving Cells Versus Copying Cells

In Excel, moving cells is not the same as copying cells. When you copy cells, the copy area remains intact. When you move cells, the original location is blanked and the format is reset to the default. Copy cells to duplicate them on the worksheet. Move cells to rearrange a worksheet.

▶ INSERTING AND DELETING CELLS IN A WORKSHEET

t any time while the worksheet is on the screen, you can add cells to insert new data or delete cells to remove unwanted data. You can insert or delete individual cells, a range of cells, entire rows, or entire columns.

Inserting Rows

The **Rows command** on the Insert menu or the **Insert command** on the shortcut menu allows you to insert rows between rows that already contain values. In the Assumptions table at the bottom of the worksheet, room must be made between rows 17 and 18 to add a row for the Net Sales for Bonus (see Figure 3-1a on page E136). The following steps show how to accomplish the task of inserting a new row into the worksheet.

TO INSERT ROWS ▼

STEP 1 ▶

Click row heading 18 to select the entire row.

STEP 2 ▶

Position the mouse pointer within the selected row and click the right mouse button.

The shortcut menu displays as shown in Figure 3-13.

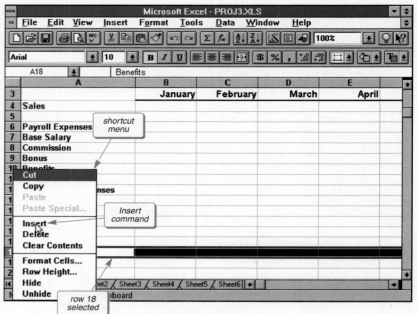

FIGURE 3-13

STEP 3 ▶

Choose the Insert command.

Excel inserts a new row by pushing down all rows below and including row 18, the one originally selected (Figure 3-14).

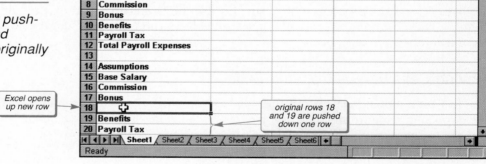

FIGURE 3-14

If the rows pushed down include any formulas, Excel adjusts the cell references to the new locations. Thus, if a formula in the worksheet references a cell in row 18 before the insert, then after the insert, the cell reference in the formula is adjusted to row 19.

The primary difference between the Insert command on the shortcut menu and the Rows command on the Insert menu is that you must select entire rows to insert rows when you use the Insert command on the shortcut menu. The Rows command on the Insert menu only requires that you select a cell in the row to push down or a range of cells to indicate the number of rows to insert. Inserted rows duplicate the format (including colors) of the row above them.

Inserting Columns

Inserting columns into a worksheet is achieved in the same way as inserting rows. To insert columns, begin your column selection immediately to the right of where you want Excel to insert the new blank columns. Select the number of columns you want to insert. Next, choose the Columns command from the Insert menu or the Insert command from the shortcut menu. Here again, if you use the **Columns command**, you need to select only the cells in the columns to push to the right; whereas, you must select entire columns to use the Insert command on the shortcut menu. Inserted columns duplicate the format of the column to their left.

Inserting Individual Cells or a Range of Cells

The Insert command on the shortcut menu or the Cells command on the Insert menu allows you to insert a single cell or a range of cells. However, be aware that if you shift a single cell or a range of cells, they may no longer be lined up with their associated cells. To ensure that the values in the worksheet do not get out of order, it is recommended that you insert only entire rows or entire columns.

Deleting Columns and Rows

The **Delete command** on the Edit menu or shortcut menu removes cells (including the data and format) from the worksheet. Deleting cells is not the same as clearing cells. The Clear command described earlier in Project 1, clears the data out of the cells, but the cells remain in the worksheet. The Delete command removes the cells from the worksheet and moves rows up when you delete rows or moves columns to the left when you delete columns.

Excel does not adjust cell references to the deleted row or column in formulas in the worksheet. Excel displays the error message **#REF!** (meaning cell reference error) in those cells containing formulas that reference cells in the deleted area. For example, if cell A7 contains the formula =A4 + A5 and you delete row 5, then Excel assigns the formula =A4 + #REF! to cell A6 (originally cell A7) and displays the error message #REF! in cell A6, which was originally cell A7.

Deleting Individual Cells or a Range of Cells

Although Excel allows you to delete an individual cell or range of cells, be aware if you shift a cell or range of cells on the worksheet, they may no longer be lined up with their associated cells. For this reason, it is recommended that you delete only entire rows or entire columns.

▶ ENTERING NUMBERS WITH A FORMAT SYMBOL

The next step is to enter the row title, Net Sales for Bonus, in cell A18 and enter the assumption values in the range B15:B20. These numbers can be entered as decimal numbers as was done in Projects 1 and 2 and formatted later, or you can enter them with format symbols. When you enter a number with a **format symbol**, Excel immediately applies number formatting to the cell. Valid format symbols include the percent sign (%), comma (,), and dollar sign ($). If the number entered is a whole number, then it displays without any decimal places.

▶ **TABLE 3-2**

FORMAT SYMBOL	ENTERED IN FORMULA BAR	DISPLAYS IN CELL	COMPARABLE FORMAT
$	$112	$112	Currency (0)
	$3798.12	$3,798.12	Currency (2)
	$44,123.3	$44,123.30	Currency (2)
,	7,876	7,876	Comma (0)
	4,913.6	4,913.60	Comma (2)
%	4%	4%	Percent (0)
	6.1%	6.10%	Percent (2)
	7.25%	7.25%	Percent (2)

If the number has one or more decimal places, then Excel displays the number with two decimal places. Table 3-2 illustrates several examples of numbers entered with format symbols. The number in parentheses in column 4 indicates the number of decimal places.

The following steps describe how to complete the entries in the Assumptions table.

TO ENTER A NUMBER WITH A FORMAT SYMBOL ▼

STEP 1 ▶

Select cell A18 and enter the text Net Sales for Bonus

STEP 2 ▶

Enter 30.00% **in cell B15,** 2.50% **in cell B16,** 17,750.00 **in cell B17,** 500,000.00 **in cell B18,** 23.75% **in cell B19, and** 10.25% **in cell B20.**

The entries display in a format based on the format symbols entered with the numbers (Figure 3-15).

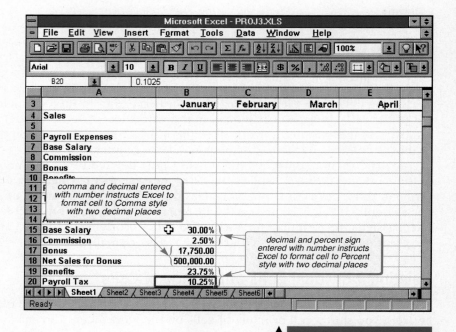

FIGURE 3-15

▶ FREEZING WORKSHEET TITLES

F reezing worksheet titles is a useful technique for viewing large work sheets that extend beyond the window. For example, when you scroll down or to the right, the column titles in row 3 and the row titles in column A that define the numbers disappear off the screen. This makes it difficult to remember what the numbers represent. To alleviate this problem, Excel allows you to freeze the titles so they remain on the screen no matter how far down, or to the right, you scroll.

Follow these steps to freeze the worksheet titles and column titles in rows 1 through 3, and the row titles in column A using the **Freeze Panes command** on the Window menu.

TO FREEZE COLUMN AND ROW TITLES ▼

STEP 1 ►

Select cell B4, the cell below the column headings you want to freeze and to the right of the row titles you want to freeze. Select the Window menu (Figure 3-16).

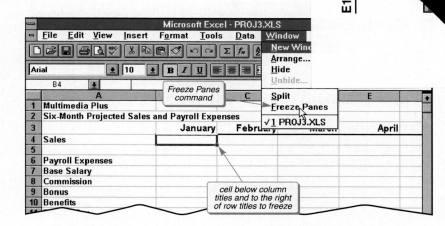

FIGURE 3-16

STEP 2 ►

Choose the Freeze Panes command.

Excel splits the window into two parts. The right border along column A changes to a thin black line indicating the split between the frozen row titles in column A and the rest of the worksheet. The bottom border in row 3 changes to a thin black line indicating the split between the frozen column titles in rows 1 through 3 and the rest of the worksheet (Figure 3-17).

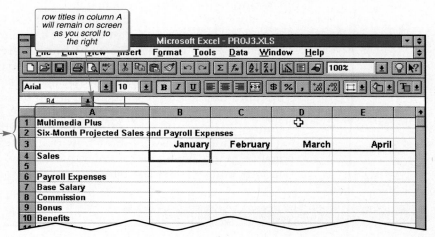

FIGURE 3-17

The row titles in column A remain on the screen even when you use the right scroll arrow to move the window to the right to display column G.

The titles are frozen until you unfreeze them. Later steps in this project show you how to use the Unfreeze Panes command.

Entering the Projected Sales

The next step is to enter the projected sales and their total in row 4.

TO ENTER THE PROJECTED SALES

Step 1: Select cell B4. Enter 525135 in cell B4, 650255 in cell C4, 443873 in cell D4, 833892 in cell E4, 378234 in cell F4, 623754 in cell G4.

Step 2: Select cell H4, click the AutoSum button twice.

The projected sales for the last three months and the total projected sales display as shown on the next page in Figure 3-18. Notice that columns B, C, and D have scrolled off the screen, but column A remains because it was frozen earlier.

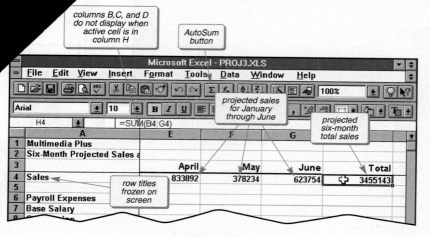

FIGURE 3-18

▶ DISPLAYING THE SYSTEM DATE

The worksheet in Project 3 (Figure 3-1a on page E136) includes a date stamp in cell H2. A **date stamp** is the system date of which your computer keeps track. If the computer's system date is set to the current date, which it normally is, then the date stamp is equivalent to the current date. In information processing, a report such as a printout of the worksheet is often meaningless without a date stamp. For example, the date stamp in Project 3 is useful for showing when the six-month projections were made.

To enter the system date in a cell in the worksheet use the **NOW function**. The NOW function is one of fourteen date and time functions available in Excel. When assigned to a cell, the NOW function returns a decimal number in the range 1 to 65,380, corresponding to the dates January 1, 1900 through December 31, 2078 and the time of day. Excel automatically formats the number representing the system's date and time to the date and time format m/d/yy h:mm where the first m is the month, d is the day of the month, yy is the last two digits of the year, h is the hour of the day, and mm is the minutes past the hour.

The following steps show how to enter the NOW function and change the format from m/d/yy h:mm to m/d/yy where m is the month number, d is day of the month, and yy is the last two digits of the year.

TO ENTER AND FORMAT THE SYSTEM DATE ▼

STEP 1 ▶

Select cell H2 and click the Function Wizard button on the Standard toolbar.

The Function Wizard – Step 1 of 2 dialog box displays.

STEP 2 ▶

Select Date & Time in the Function Category box and select NOW in the Function Name box.

The Function Wizard – Step 1 of 2 dialog box displays as shown in Figure 3-19.

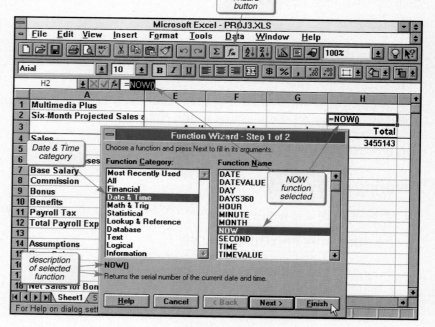

FIGURE 3-19

STEP 3 ▶

Choose the Finish button.

Excel displays the system date and system time in cell H2 using the default date and time format m/d/yy h:mm (Figure 3-20).

FIGURE 3-20

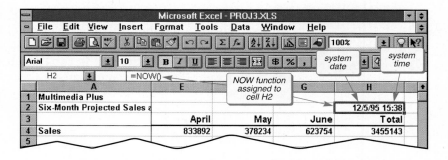

STEP 4 ▶

With cell H2 selected and the mouse pointer within the cell, click the right mouse button.

Excel displays the shortcut menu (Figure 3-21).

FIGURE 3-21

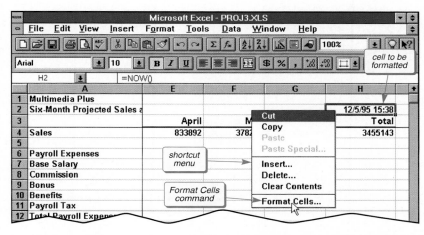

STEP 5 ▶

Choose the Format Cells command. If necessary, click the Number tab, select Date in the Category box, and select m/d/yy in the Format Codes box.

Excel displays the Format Cells dialog box with Date and m/d/yy selected (Figure 3-22).

FIGURE 3-22

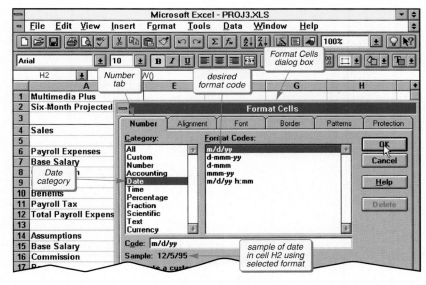

STEP 6 ▶

Choose the OK button in the Format Cells dialog box.

Excel displays the date in the form m/d/yy (Figure 3-23).

FIGURE 3-23

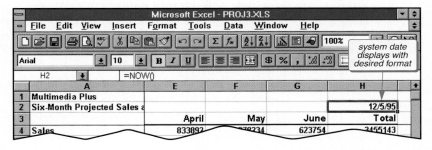

Notice in Figure 3-23 the date displays in the cell right-aligned because Excel treats a date as a number. If you format the date by applying the **General format** (Excel's default for numbers), the date displays as a number. To format a cell to General, select the All category in the Format Cells dialog box and then select General. For example, if the system time and date is 12:00 noon on December 5, 1995 and the cell containing the NOW function is assigned the General format, then Excel displays the following number in the cell:

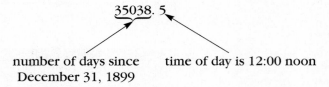

35038. 5

number of days since   time of day is 12:00 noon
December 31, 1899

The whole number portion of the number (35038) represents the number of days since December 31, 1899. The decimal portion (.5) represents the time of day (12:00 noon).

▶ ABSOLUTE VERSUS RELATIVE ADDRESSING

The next step is to enter the formulas that determine the projected payroll expenses in the range B7:G11 (Figure 3-1a on page E136). The projected payroll expenses are based on the projected sales in row 4 and the assumptions in the range B15:B20. The formulas for each column are the same, except for the sales in row 4. Thus, the formulas can be entered for January in column B and copied to columns C through G. The formulas for determining the January projected payroll expenses are shown in Table 3-3.

▸ **TABLE 3-3**

CELL	PAYROLL EXPENSE	FORMULA	COMMENT
B7	Base Salary	=B15 * B4	Base Salary % times January Sales
B8	Commission	=B16 * B4	Commission % times January Sales
B9	Bonus	=IF(B4 >= B18, B17, 0)	Bonus equals value in cell B17 or zero
B10	Benefits	=B19 * (B7 + B8 + B9)	Benefits % times sum of Base Salary, Commission, and Bonus
B11	Payroll Tax	=B20 * (B7 + B8 + B9)	Payroll Tax % times sum of Base Salary, Commission, and Bonus

The problem is, if you enter these formulas in column B and then copy them to columns C through G, Excel automatically adjusts the cell references for each column. Thus, after the copy, the February base salary in cell C7 would be =C15 * C4. The cell reference C4 (February sales) is correct. However, cell C15 is empty. What is needed here is a way to keep a cell reference in a formula the same when it is copied. The formula for cell C7 should read =B15 * C4 instead of =C15 * C4.

Excel has the ability to keep a cell reference constant when it copies a formula or function by using a technique called **absolute referencing**. To specify an absolute reference in a formula, add a dollar sign ($) to the beginning of the column name, row name, or both in formulas you plan to copy. For example, $B$15 is an absolute reference and B15 is a relative reference. Both reference the same cell. The difference shows when they are copied. A formula using $B$15 instructs Excel to use the same cell (B15) as it copies the formula to a new location. A formula using B15 instructs Excel to adjust the cell reference as it copies. Table 3-4 gives some additional examples of absolute references. A cell reference with one dollar sign before either the column or the row is called a **mixed cell reference**.

Entering the January Base Salary and Commission Formulas

The following steps show how to enter the base salary formula (=$B$15 * B4) in cell B7 and the commission formula (=$B$16 * B4) in cell B8 for the month of January using the Point mode. When you enter an absolute reference, you can type the $ or you can press F4 with the insertion point in, or to the right of, the cell reference you want to change to absolute.

▶ **TABLE 3-4**

CELL REFERENCE	MEANING
$B$15	Both column and row references remain the same when you copy this cell reference because they are absolute.
B$15	The column reference changes when you copy this cell reference to another column because it is relative. The row reference does not change because it is absolute.
$B15	The row reference changes when you copy this cell reference to another row because it is relative. The column reference does not change because it is absolute.
B15	Both column and row references are relative. When copied to another row and column, both the row and column in the cell reference are adjusted to reflect the new location.

TO ENTER THE JANUARY BASE SALARY AND COMMISSION FORMULAS ▼

STEP 1 ▶

Select cell B7. Type the equal sign (=) and click cell B15. Press F4 to change B15 to an absolute reference in the formula. Type the asterisk (*) and click cell B4.

The formula displays in cell B7 and in the formula bar (Figure 3-24).

STEP 2 ▶

Click the enter box in the formula bar or press the ENTER key.

Excel displays the result (157540.5) in cell B7 (Figure 3-25).

STEP 3 ▶

Select cell B8. Type the equal sign (=) and click cell B16. Press F4 to change cell B16 to an absolute reference in the formula. Type the asterisk (*) and click cell B4. Click the enter box or press the ENTER key.

Excel displays the result of the formula (13128.375) in cell B8 (Figure 3-25).

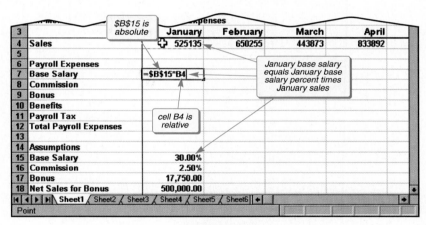

FIGURE 3-24

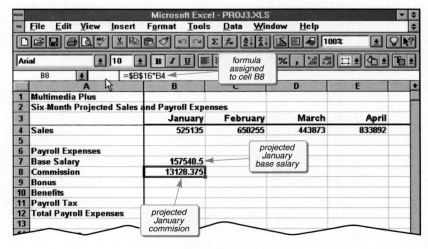

FIGURE 3-25

When you enter a formula that contains an absolute reference, you can use the F4 key to cycle the cell reference on which the insertion point is positioned, or immediately to the right of, from relative to absolute to mixed.

▶ MAKING DECISIONS — THE IF FUNCTION

If the January sales in cell B4 are greater than or equal to the net sales for bonus in cell B18, then the January bonus in cell B9 is equal to the amount in cell B17 (17,550.00); otherwise, cell B9 is equal to zero. One way to assign the bonus in row 9 is to manually compare the sales for each month in row 4 to the net sales for bonus in cell B17 and enter 17750 when the corresponding month sales equals or exceeds the amount in cell B17. However, because the data in the worksheet changes each time you prepare the report, you will find it preferable to automatically assign the monthly bonus to the entries in the appropriate cells. What you need in cell B8 is an entry that displays 17750 or zero, depending on whether the projected January sales in cell B4 is greater than or equal to or less than the number in cell B18.

Excel has the **IF function** that is useful when the value you want to assign to a cell is dependent on a logical test. A **logical test** is made up of two expressions and a comparison operator. Each expression can be a cell reference, a number, text, a function, or a formula. A **comparison operator** is one of the following: > (greater than), < (less than), = (equal to), >= (greater than or equal to), <= (less than or equal to), <> (not equal to). For example, assume you assign cell B9 the IF function:

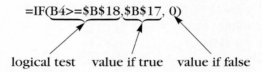

If the January projected sales in cell B4 are greater than or equal to the value in cell B18, then 17,750 displays in cell B9. If the January projected sales in cell B4 are less than the value in cell B18, then cell B9 displays a zero.

The general form of the IF function is:

=IF(logical-test, value-if-true, value-if-false)

The argument, value-if-true, is the value you want displayed in the cell when the logical-test is true. The argument, value-if-false, is the value you want displayed in the cell when the logical-test is false.

Table 3-5 lists the valid comparison operators and examples of their use in IF functions.

▶ **TABLE 3-5**

COMPARISON OPERATOR	MEANING	EXAMPLE
=	Equal to	=IF(A5 = B7, A22 - A3, G5 + E3)
<	Less than	=IF(E12 / D5 < 6, A15, B13 - 5)
>	Greater than	=IF(=SUM(A1:A5) > 100, 1, 0)
>=	Greater than or equal to	=IF(A12 >= $E$2, A4 * D5, 1)
<=	Less than or equal to	=IF(A1 + D5 <= 10, H15, 7 * A3)
<>	Not equal to	=IF(C5 <> B5, "Valid", "Invalid")

The following steps assign the IF function =IF(B4>= $B$18,$B$17,0) to cell B9. This function will determine whether the worksheet projects a bonus or not for January.

TO ENTER AN IF FUNCTION ▼

STEP 1 ▶

Select cell B9 and type
`=if(b4>=$b$18,$b$17,0`

The IF function displays in cell B9 and in the formula bar (Figure 3-26).

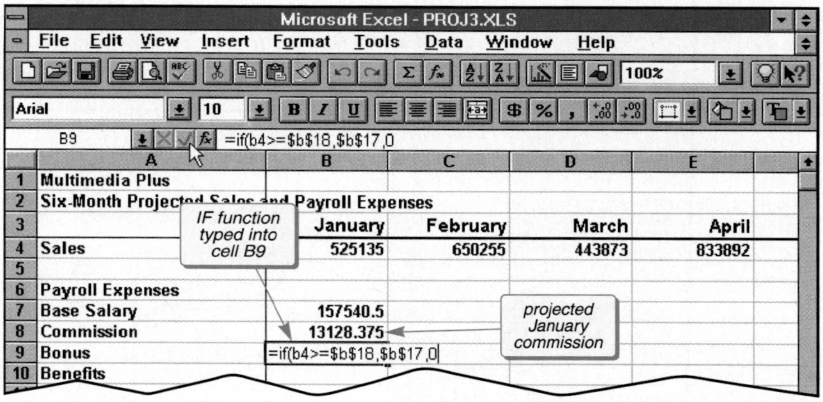

FIGURE 3-26

	A	B	C	D	E
1	Multimedia Plus				
2	Six-Month Projected Sales and Payroll Expenses				
3		January	February	March	April
4	Sales	525135	650255	443873	833892
5					
6	Payroll Expenses				
7	Base Salary	157540.5			
8	Commission	13128.375			
9	Bonus	=if(b4>=b18,b17,0			
10	Benefits				

IF function typed into cell B9

projected January commission

STEP 2 ▶

Click the enter box in the formula bar or press the ENTER key.

Excel displays 17750 in cell B9 because the value in cell B4 is greater than or equal to the value in cell B18 (Figure 3-27). Recall that it is not necessary to type the closing parenthesis when you enter a function.

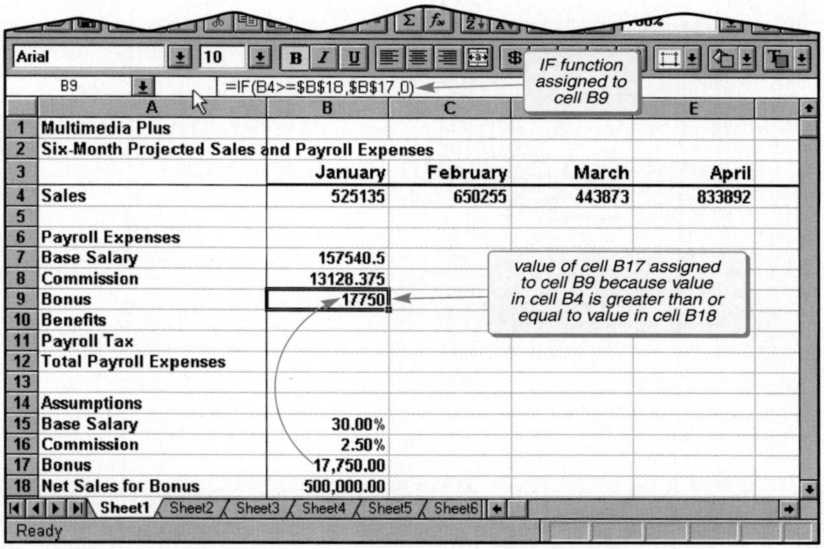

FIGURE 3-27

B9   =IF(B4>=$B$18,$B$17,0)

IF function assigned to cell B9

	A	B	C		E
1	Multimedia Plus				
2	Six-Month Projected Sales and Payroll Expenses				
3		January	February	March	April
4	Sales	525135	650255	443873	833892
5					
6	Payroll Expenses				
7	Base Salary	157540.5			
8	Commission	13128.375			
9	Bonus	17750			
10	Benefits				
11	Payroll Tax				
12	Total Payroll Expenses				
13					
14	Assumptions				
15	Base Salary	30.00%			
16	Commission	2.50%			
17	Bonus	17,750.00			
18	Net Sales for Bonus	500,000.00			

value of cell B17 assigned to cell B9 because value in cell B4 is greater than or equal to value in cell B18

Ready

The value that Excel displays in cell B9 depends on the values assigned to cells B4, B17, and B18. For example, if the projected sales in cell B4 are reduced below 500,000, then the IF function in cell B9 will change the display from 17750 to zero. Changing the net sales for bonus in cell B18 to a greater amount has the same effect.

Entering the January Benefits, Payroll Tax Formulas, and Total Payroll Expenses

The January projected benefits in cell B10 are equal to the benefits percent in cell B19 times the sum of the January projected base salary, commission, and bonus in cells B7, B8, and B9. In the same manner, the January projected payroll tax in cell B11 is equal to the payroll tax percent in cell B20 times the sum of the January projected base salary, commission, and bonus in cells B7, B8, and B9. The total January projected payroll expenses in cell B12 are equal to the sum of the January projected payroll expenses in the range B7:B11. The steps on the next page enter the three formulas into the worksheet.

TO ENTER THE JANUARY BENEFITS AND PAYROLL TAX FORMULAS AND TOTAL PAYROLL EXPENSES

Step 1: Select cell B10. Enter =b19*(b7+b8+b9)
Step 2: Select cell B11. Enter =b20*(b7+b8+b9)
Step 3: Select cell B12. Click the AutoSum button on the Standard toolbar twice.

The January projected benefits, payroll tax, and total payroll expenses display in cells B10, B11, and B12 (the left screen in Figure 3-28).

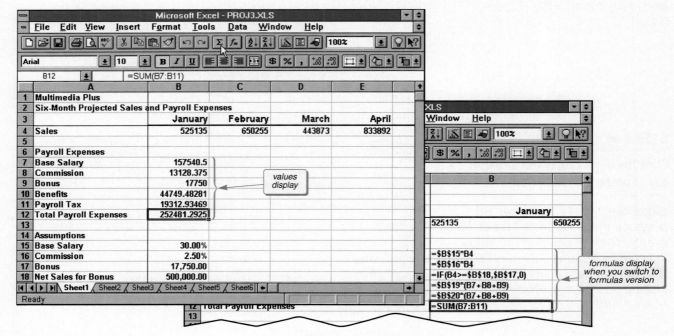

FIGURE 3-28

You can view the formulas in the worksheet by pressing CTRL+` (left apostrophe key — next to the number 1 key on the keyboard). The display changes from the left screen in Figure 3-28 to the right screen in Figure 3-28. Press CTRL+` to display the values again.

TO COPY THE JANUARY PROJECTED PAYROLL EXPENSES AND TOTALS USING THE FILL HANDLE ▼

STEP 1 ▶

Select the range B7:B12. Point to the fill handle near the lower right corner of cell B12.

The range B7:B12 is selected, and the mouse pointer changes to a cross (Figure 3-29).

FIGURE 3-29

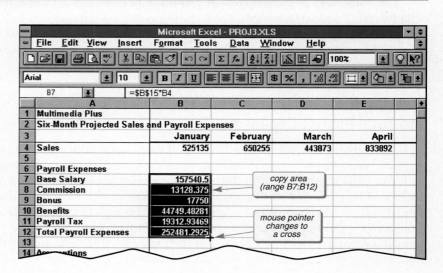

STEP 2 ▶

Drag the fill handle to select the
paste area, range C7:G12, and then
release the left mouse button.

*Excel copies the formulas in the
range B7:B12 to the paste area
C7:G12. The last three columns of
the paste area display as shown in
Figure 3-30.*

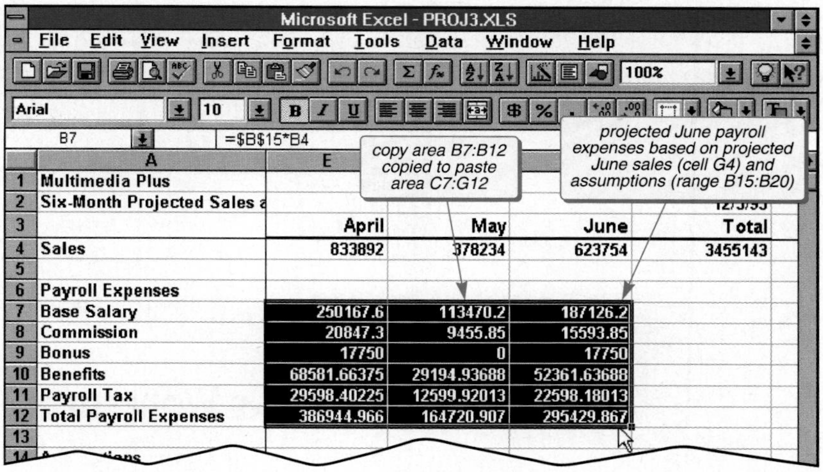

FIGURE 3-30

Determining the Projected Total Payroll Expenses

Follow these steps to determine the total projected payroll expenses in the
range H7:H12.

**TO DETERMINE THE PROJECTED
TOTAL PAYROLL EXPENSES**

Step 1: Select the range H7:H12.
Step 2: Click the AutoSum button on the Standard
toolbar.

*The projected total payroll
expenses display in the range
H7:H12 (Figure 3-31).*

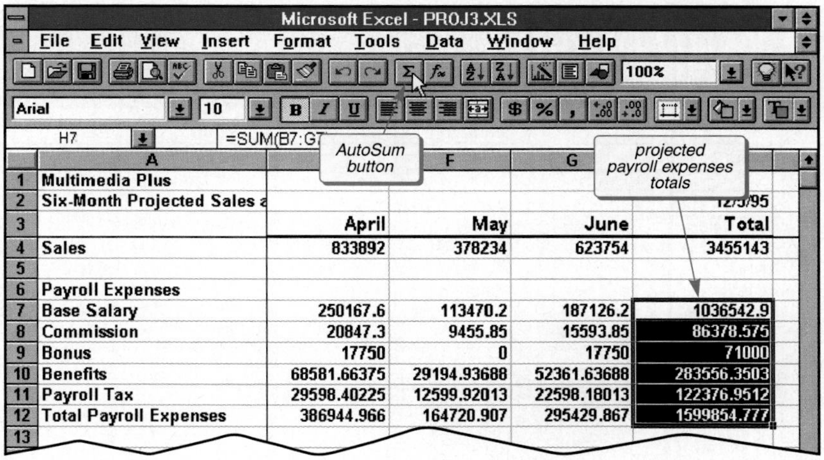

Unfreezing Worksheet Titles
and Saving the Workbook

FIGURE 3-31

All the text, data, and formulas have been entered into the worksheet. The
next step is to improve the appearance of the worksheet. Before modifying the
appearance, the following steps unfreeze the titles and save the workbook under
its current filename PROJ3.XLS.

TO UNFREEZE THE WORKSHEET TITLES AND SAVE THE WORKBOOK

Step 1: Select cell B4 to clear the range selection from the previous steps.
Step 2: Select the Window menu and point to the **Unfreeze Panes
command** (Figure 3-32 on the next page).
Step 3: Choose the Unfreeze Panes command.
Step 4: Click the Save button on the Standard toolbar.

*Excel unfreezes the titles so column A scrolls off the screen when you scroll
to the right and the first three rows scroll off the screen when you scroll
down. The workbook is saved using the filename PROJ3.XLS.*

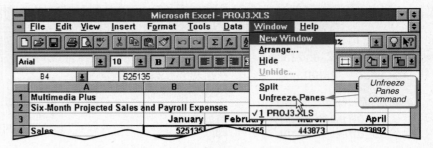

FIGURE 3-32

▶ FORMATTING THE WORKSHEET

T he worksheet in Figure 3-32 determines the projected payroll expenses. However, its appearance is uninteresting, even though some minimal formatting was done earlier. This section will complete the formatting of the worksheet so the numbers are easier to read and to emphasize the titles, assumptions, categories, and totals (Figure 3-33).

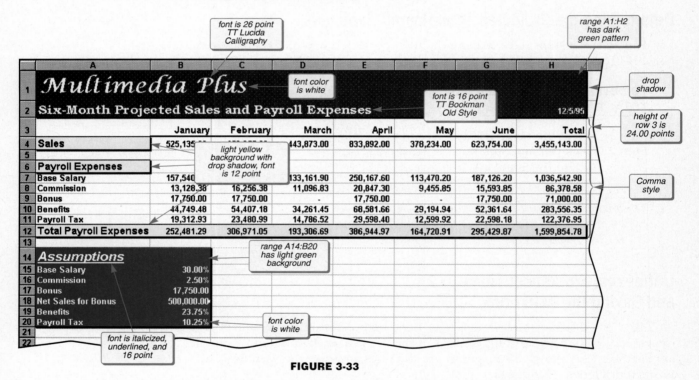

FIGURE 3-33

Formatting the Projected Sales and Payroll Expenses

Apply the Comma style to the projected sales and payroll expenses as described in the following steps.

TO FORMAT THE PROJECTED SALES AND PAYROLL EXPENSES

Step 1: Select the range B4:G12.
Step 2: Click the Comma Style button on the Formatting toolbar.

Excel formats the range B4:H12 to the Comma style (Figure 3-34).

Not all the cells in the range formatted have numbers. Some of the cells are empty (range B5:H6). Applying the Comma style to the empty cells has no impact on the worksheet because the format remains hidden unless numbers are entered into these cells.

An alternative way to apply the Comma style to the range B4:G12 is to use the Format Painter button on the Standard toolbar. For example, you could select cell B17, which was formatted earlier to the Comma style, click the Format Painter button, and drag over the range B4:G12.

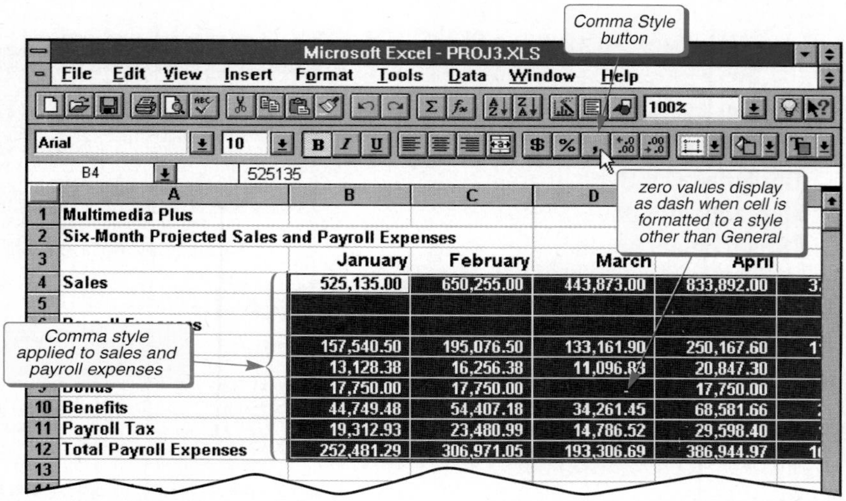

Compare cell D9 in Figure 3-34 to Figure 3-31. Notice that Excel changes a zero value to a dash (-) when the cell is assigned the Comma style. The dash (-) means the cell contains a numeric value of zero.

FIGURE 3-34

Formatting the Titles

To emphasize the worksheet titles in cells A1 and A2, the font type, size, and color are changed as described in the following steps.

TO FORMAT THE TITLES ▼

STEP 1 ►

Select cell A1. Click the Font arrow on the Formatting toolbar. Scroll down until TT Lucida Calligraphy displays. If your system does not have TT Lucida Calligraphy, select another font.

The Font drop-down list box displays (Figure 3-35).

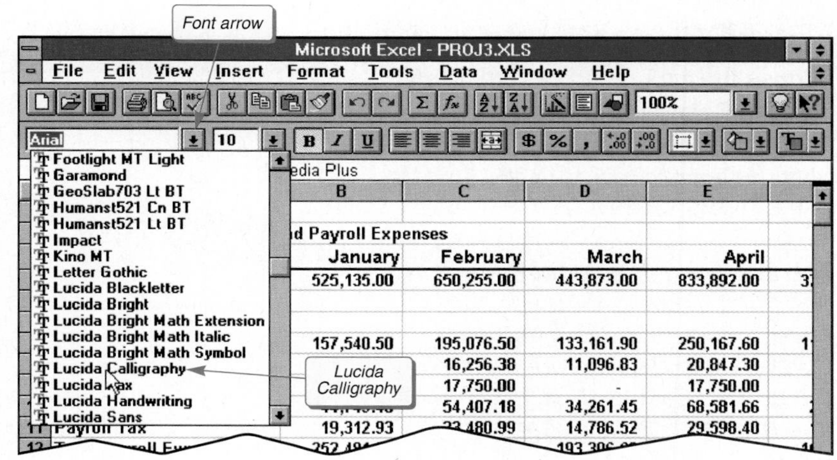

FIGURE 3-35

STEP 2 ►

Choose TT Lucida Calligraphy. Click the Font Size arrow and choose 26.

The title in A1 displays as shown in Figure 3-36.

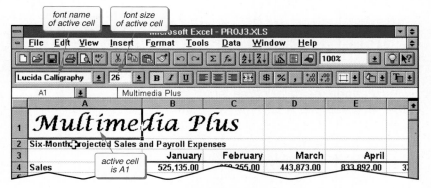

FIGURE 3-36

STEP 3 ▶

Select cell A2. Click the Font arrow on the Formatting toolbar. Choose TT Bookman Old Style. If your system does not have TT Bookman Old Style, select another font. Click the Font Size arrow and choose 16.

The subtitle in cell A2 displays as shown in Figure 3-37.

FIGURE 3-37

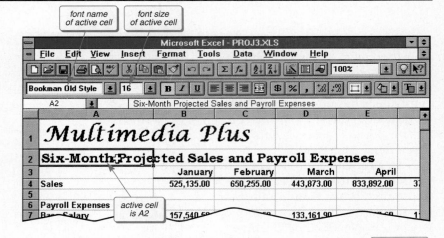

STEP 4 ▶

Select the range A1:H2. Click the Color button arrow on the Formatting toolbar and point to the dark green pattern (column 3, row 7) on the Color palette.

The Color palette displays as shown in Figure 3-38.

FIGURE 3-38

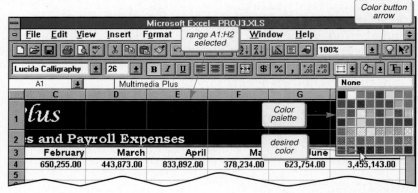

STEP 5 ▶

Choose the dark green pattern. Click the Font Color button arrow on the Formatting toolbar and point to white (column 2, row 1) on the Font Color palette.

The background color of the range A1:H2 changes to the dark green pattern (Figure 3-39). The Font Color palette displays. Because the range remains selected, the true background color does not show.

STEP 6 ▶

Choose white for the font in the titles.

Excel changes the color of the font in the titles from black to white (see Figure 3-33 on page E158).

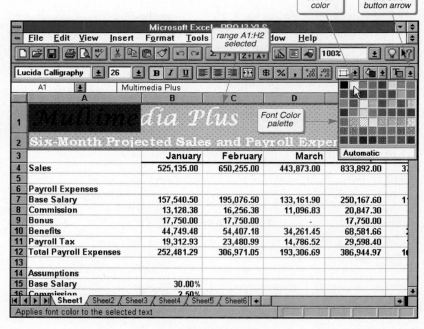

FIGURE 3-39

With the range A1:H2 selected, the next step is to add a drop shadow. To add a drop shadow, the Drawing toolbar must display on the screen. The following section describes how to display and dock an inactive (hidden) toolbar.

Displaying the Drawing Toolbar

Excel toolbars can display more than 200 buttons. Most of the buttons display on thirteen built-in toolbars. You can also create customized toolbars containing the buttons that you often use. Two of the thirteen built-in toolbars are the Standard toolbar and Formatting toolbar that usually display at the top of the screen. Another built-in toolbar is the Drawing toolbar. The **Drawing toolbar** provides tools that can simplify adding lines, boxes, and other figures to a worksheet. You can display the Drawing toolbar using one of the following techniques:

1. Point to a toolbar and click the right mouse button to display a shortcut menu of toolbars. Choose the Drawing toolbar from the list of toolbars.
2. Choose the Toolbars command from the View menu. Select the Drawing toolbar from the list in the Toolbars dialog box.
3. Click the Drawing button on the Standard toolbar.

Perform the following steps to display and then dock the Drawing toolbar at the bottom of the screen.

TO DISPLAY THE DRAWING TOOLBAR ▼

STEP 1 ►

Point to the Drawing button (▨) on the Standard toolbar.

STEP 2 ►

Click the left mouse button.

The Drawing toolbar displays (Figure 3-40). Excel locates the Drawing toolbar on the screen wherever it displayed and in whatever shape it displayed the last time it was used.

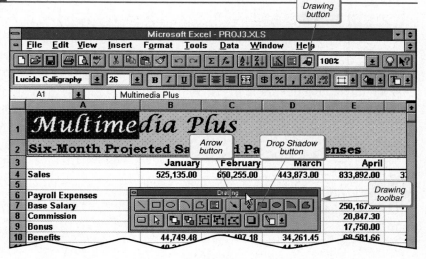

FIGURE 3-40

This project uses the Drop Shadow and Arrow buttons (Figure 3-40). To obtain information on any button, perform the following steps.

TO LIST THE FUNCTIONS OF BUTTONS ON A TOOLBAR

Step 1: From the Help menu, choose the Search for Help on command.
Step 2: When the Search dialog box displays, type `buttons` in the top box and choose the Show Topics button (Show Topics).
Step 3: Select Using Toolbar Buttons in the lower box and choose the Go To button (Go To) scroll down and choose the topic Button Category Summary .
Step 4: Choose the Drawing Buttons Category (or any other category of buttons). When you're finished with one category, click the Back button (Back) to select another category of buttons.
Step 5: When you are finished, double-click the Control-menu box in the Help window.

Moving and Shaping a Toolbar

The Drawing toolbar in Figure 3-40 is called a **floating toolbar** because you can move it anywhere in the window. You move the toolbar by positioning the mouse pointer in a blank area within the toolbar (not on a button) and dragging it to its new location. A floating toolbar always displays in its own window with a title bar and Control-menu box. As with any window, you can drag the toolbar window borders to resize it and you can click the Control-menu box in the title bar to hide a floating toolbar.

Sometimes, a floating toolbar gets in the way no matter where you move it. Hiding the toolbar is one solution. However, there are times when you want to keep it active because you plan to use it. For this reason, Excel allows you to locate toolbars on the edge of its window. If you drag the toolbar close to the edge of the window, Excel positions the toolbar in a **toolbar dock**.

Excel provides four toolbar docks, one on each of the four sides of the window. You can add as many toolbars to a dock as you want. However, each time you dock a toolbar, the window decreases slightly in size to compensate for the room taken up by the toolbar. The following steps show how to dock the Drawing toolbar at the bottom of the screen below the scroll bar.

TO DOCK A TOOLBAR AT THE BOTTOM OF THE SCREEN ▼

STEP 1 ▶

Position the mouse pointer in a blank area in the Drawing toolbar.

STEP 2 ▶

Drag the Drawing toolbar below the scroll bar at the bottom of the screen and release the left mouse button.

Excel docks the Drawing toolbar at the bottom of the screen (Figure 3-41).

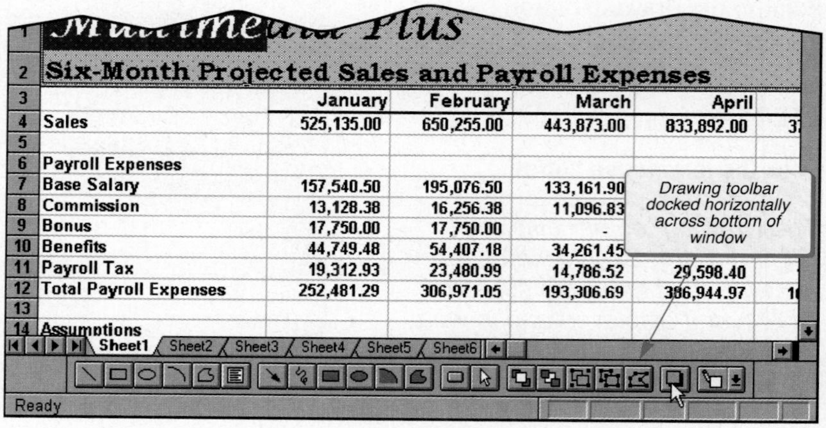

FIGURE 3-41

Compare Figure 3-41 to Figure 3-40 on the previous page. Notice how Excel automatically resizes the Drawing toolbar to fit across the window and between the scroll bar and status bar. Also, the heavy window border that surrounded the floating toolbar has changed to a thin border. To move a toolbar to any of the other three docks, drag the toolbar to the desired edge before releasing the left mouse button. A toolbar that has a drop-down list box, such as the Pattern button (▣) on the right side of the Drawing toolbar cannot be docked on the left or right edge of the window. To change a docked toolbar to a floating toolbar, double-click a blank area in the toolbar.

Adding a Drop Shadow to the Title Area

With the Drawing toolbar at the bottom of the screen, the next step is to add the drop shadow to the selected title area in the range A1:H2.

TO ADD A DROP SHADOW ▼

STEP 1 ▶

With the range A1:H2 selected, point to the Drop Shadow button (▣) on the Drawing toolbar.

STEP 2 ▶

Click the left mouse button. Select any cell in the worksheet to deselect the drop shadow assigned to the the range A1:H2.

Excel adds a drop shadow to the title area in the range A1:H2 (Figure 3-42).

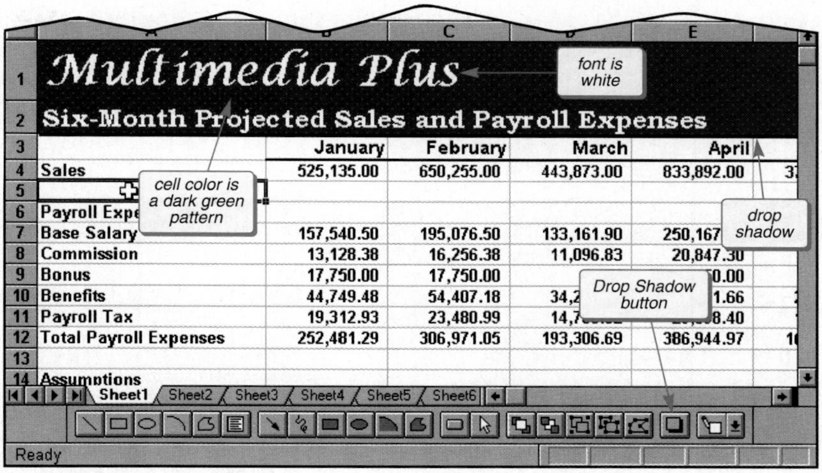

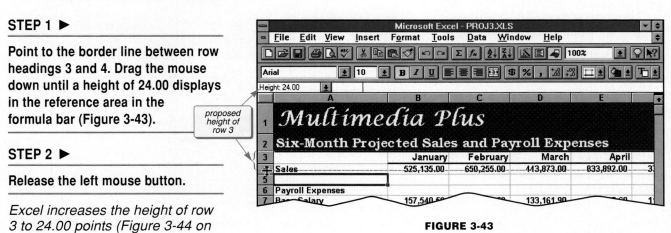

FIGURE 3-42

When you add a drop shadow to a range, Excel selects the drop shadow and surrounds it with black handles. To deselect the drop shadow, select any cell.

To remove an unwanted drop shadow, point to it and click the left mouse button. Next, press the DELETE key. You should also notice that the handles surrounding the drop shadow are black, meaning you can move and resize it.

Increasing the Height of the Row Containing the Column Headings

Row 3 contains the column headings. The next step is to increase the white space between the worksheet title and the column titles by increasing the height of row 3 to 24.00 points.

TO INCREASE THE HEIGHT OF A ROW ▼

STEP 1 ▶

Point to the border line between row headings 3 and 4. Drag the mouse down until a height of 24.00 displays in the reference area in the formula bar (Figure 3-43).

STEP 2 ▶

Release the left mouse button.

Excel increases the height of row 3 to 24.00 points (Figure 3-44 on the next page).

FIGURE 3-43

Changing Font Size, Adding Color, and Adding Drop Shadows to the Category Row Titles and Total Payroll Expenses Row

This project requires a font size of 12 point in cells A4, A6, and A12. Also, cells A4, A6, and the range A12:H12 all require the same background color and drop shadows (see Figure 3-33 on page E158). The following steps change the font size in cells A4, A6, and A12 and then add the background color and drop shadows.

TO CHANGE FONT SIZE , ADD COLOR, AND A DROP SHADOW TO NONADJACENT SELECTIONS ▼

STEP 1 ►

Select cell A4. Hold down the CTRL key and select cells A6 and A12. Click the Font Size arrow on the Formatting toolbar and choose 12 from the drop-down list.

The font size in cells A4, A6, and A12 changes to 12 point.

STEP 2 ►

Select cell A4. Hold down the CTRL key and select cell A6. Hold down the CTRL key and select the range A12:H12. Click the Color button arrow on the Formatting toolbar.

The nonadjacent ranges are selected and the Color palette displays (Figure 3-44).

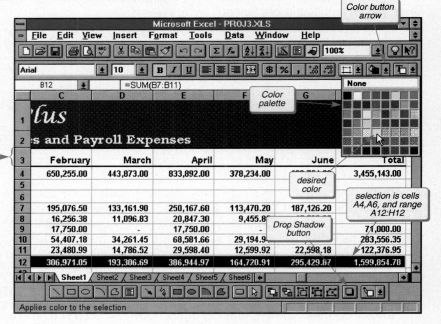

FIGURE 3-44

STEP 3 ►

Choose light yellow (column 4, row 5) on the Color palette. Click the Drop Shadow button on the Drawing toolbar.

Excel colors the nonadjacent selection and adds a drop shadow to cells A4, A6, and the range A12:H12. The drop shadow on the range A12:H12 remains selected (Figure 3-45).

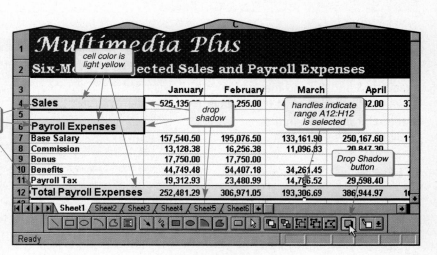

FIGURE 3-45

An alternative to formatting all three areas at once is to select each one separately and apply the formats. Although formatting cell A4 first, and then using the Format Painter button on the Standard toolbar may sound like a good idea, the drop shadow is considered a shape and not a format. Thus, Excel would not paint the drop shadow on cell A6 and the range A12:H12. However, it would paint the background color and change the font size.

Formatting the Assumptions Table

The last step to improving the appearance of the worksheet is to format the Assumptions table in the range A14:B20. Project 3 in Figure 3-33 on page E158 requires a 16 point underlined italics font for the title in cell A14. The background of the range A14:B20 is colored light green, and a drop shadow surrounds it.

TO FORMAT THE ASSUMPTIONS TABLE ▼

STEP 1 ▶

Select cell A14. Click the Font Size arrow on the Formatting toolbar and choose 16 point. Click the Italic button (*I*) and Underline button (U) on the Formatting toolbar.

The table heading, Assumptions, displays as shown in Figure 3-46.

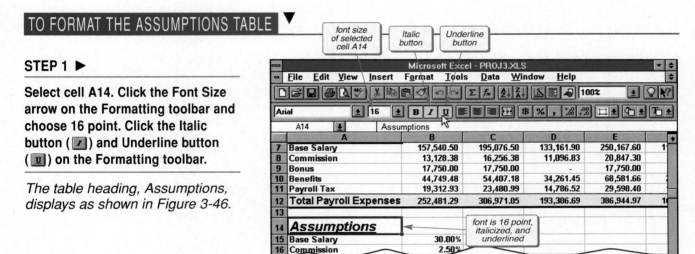

FIGURE 3-46

STEP 2 ▶

Select the range A14:B20. Click the Color button arrow on the Formatting toolbar. Point to the color green (column 2, row 2) of the Color palette.

The Color palette displays as shown in Figure 3-47.

STEP 3 ▶

Click the left mouse button to choose the color green. Click the Font Color button on the Formatting toolbar.

The background of the Assumptions table is colored green and the font is colored white.

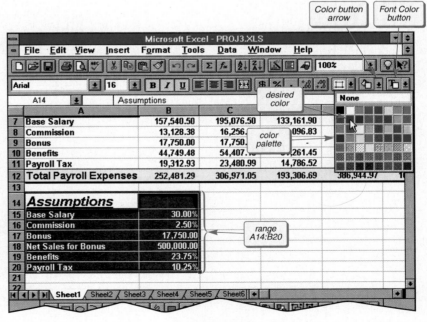

FIGURE 3-47

STEP 4 ▶

Click the Drop Shadow button on the Drawing toolbar. Select cell D20.

The Assumption table displays as shown in Figure 3-48.

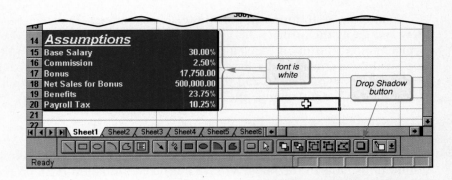

FIGURE 3-48

Because the last font color applied to the worksheet titles was white and Excel applies the last color used, you can click the Font Color button instead of the arrow to choose the color white.

Notice when you apply the **italic** font style to a cell, Excel slants the characters slightly to the right as shown in cell A14 in Figure 3-48. Applying underlining to a font is different from assigning a bottom border to a cell. When you **underline**, only the characters in the cell are underlined. When you assign a bottom border to a cell, the border displays whether or not characters are in the cell.

▶ HIDING A TOOLBAR

With the formatting of the worksheet complete, the next step is to hide the Drawing toolbar docked at the bottom of the screen. As shown in the following steps, you can hide the Drawing toolbar by clicking on the Drawing button on the Standard toolbar.

TO HIDE THE DRAWING TOOLBAR ▼

STEP 1 ▶

Point to the Drawing button on the Standard toolbar.

STEP 2 ▶

Click the left mouse button.

The Drawing toolbar is removed from the screen (Figure 3-49).

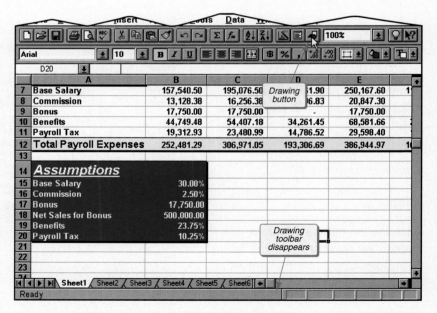

FIGURE 3-49

If you want to hide other toolbars displaying on the screen, use one of the following techniques:

1. Drag the toolbar onto the screen and double-click its Control-menu box.
2. Choose the Toolbars command from the View menu and remove the X from the selected toolbar to hide and then choose the OK button.
3. Point to the toolbar you want to hide, click the right mouse button to display the shortcut menu, and click its name in the shortcut menu to hide it.

The worksheet is complete. Before moving on to create the pie chart, save the workbook by clicking the Save button on the Standard toolbar.

▶ ADDING A PIE CHART TO THE WORKBOOK

FIGURE 3-50

T he next step in this project is to draw the 3-D pie chart on a separate sheet as shown in Figure 3-50. A **pie chart** is used to show how 100% of an amount is divided. Each slice (or wedge) of the pie represents a contribution to the whole. The pie chart in Figure 3-50 shows the contribution of each month to the total projected payroll expenses.

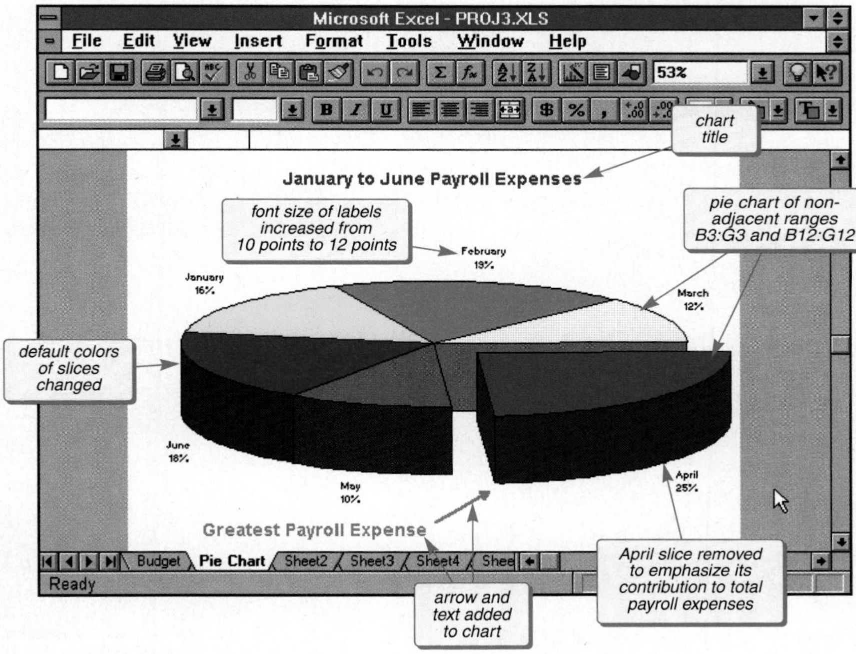

The cells in the worksheet to graph are the nonadjacent ranges B3:G3 and B12:G12 (see Figure 3-51). The month names in the range B3:G3 will identify the slices. The cells in row 3 are the category names. The range B12:G12 contains the data that determines the size of the slices. The cells in row 12 make up the data series. Because there are six months, the pie chart has six slices.

This project also calls for emphasizing the month with the greatest projected payroll expenses (April) by offsetting its slice from the main portion and adding an arrow and the text, Greatest Payroll Expense. A pie chart with one or more slices offset is called an **exploded pie chart**.

Drawing the Pie Chart

To draw the pie chart on a separate sheet, select the nonadjacent ranges B3:G3 and B12:G12 and choose the Chart command from the Insert menu. Once the chart is created, it will be formatted as shown in Figure 3-50 in the following fashion:

1. Increase the font size and color the font in the chart title.
2. Increase the font size of the labels that identify the slices.
3. Explode the April slice.
4. Rotate the pie chart so the April slice will display more prominently.
5. Change the color of the slices of the pie chart.
6. Add the words, Greatest Payroll Expense, below the pie chart.
7. Add and format an arrow pointing from the text box to the April slice.

TO DRAW A PIE CHART ▼

STEP 1 ►

Select the range B3:G3. Hold down the CTRL key and select the range B12:G12. Choose the Chart command from the Insert menu

The Chart cascading menu displays (Figure 3-51).

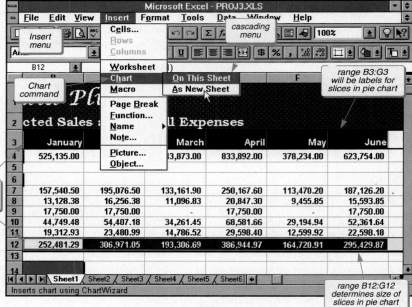

FIGURE 3-51

STEP 2 ►

Choose the As New Sheet command from the Chart cascading menu.

Excel displays the ChartWizard Step – 1 of 5 dialog box, which shows the selected range to chart (Figure 3-52).

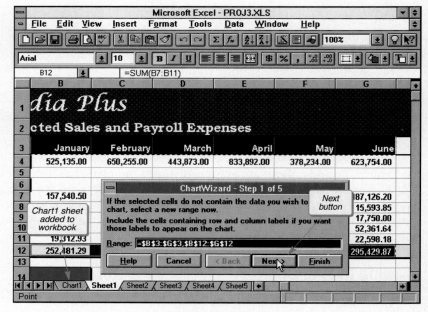

FIGURE 3-52

STEP 3 ▶

Choose the Next button in the ChartWizard – Step 1 of 5 dialog box.

The ChartWizard – Step 2 of 5 dialog box displays with fifteen charts from which to choose (Figure 3-53). The first nine charts in the dialog box are two-dimensional. The last six charts are three-dimensional.

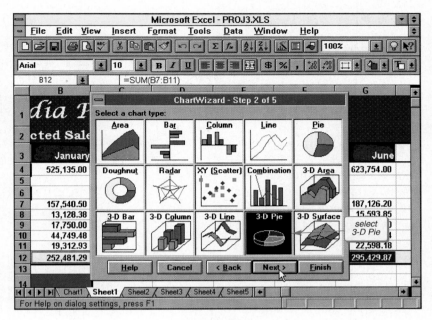

FIGURE 3-53

STEP 4 ▶

Select 3-D Pie (column 4, row 3).

Excel highlights the 3-D pie chart.

STEP 5 ▶

Choose the Next button in the ChartWizard – Step 2 of 5 dialog box.

The ChartWizard – Step 3 of 5 dialog box displays with seven different built-in pie chart formats from which to choose (Figure 3-54).

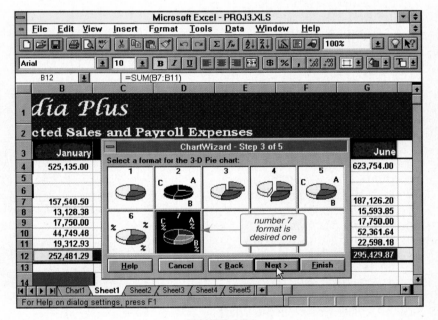

FIGURE 3-54

STEP 6 ▶

Select box 7, the one with the letters C, A, and B and the percent signs.

Excel highlights the selected pie chart format.

STEP 7 ▶

Choose the Next button on the ChartWizard – Step 3 of 5 dialog box. If a Microsoft Excel dialog box displays, choose the OK button. If necessary, change the settings in the ChartWizard – Step 4 of 5 dialog box to agree with those shown in Figure 3-55.

The ChartWizard – Step 4 of 5 dialog box displays showing a sample 3-D pie chart (Figure 3-55).

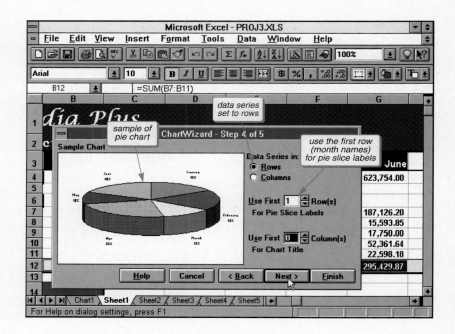

FIGURE 3-55

STEP 8 ▶

Choose the Next button in the ChartWizard – Step 4 of 5 dialog box.

The ChartWizard – Step 5 of 5 dialog box displays on the screen (Figure 3-56). The dialog box gives you the opportunity to add a legend and a chart title.

STEP 9 ▶

Type January to June Payroll Expenses **in the Chart Title box as shown in Figure 3-56.**

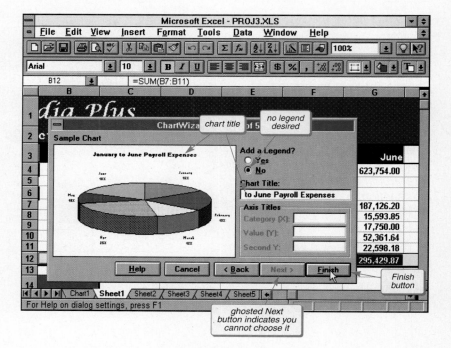

FIGURE 3-56

STEP 10 ▶

Choose the Finish button in the
ChartWizard – Step 5 of 5 dialog
box.

*Excel draws the 3-D pie chart and
displays it on a sheet titled Chart1
(Figure 3-57).*

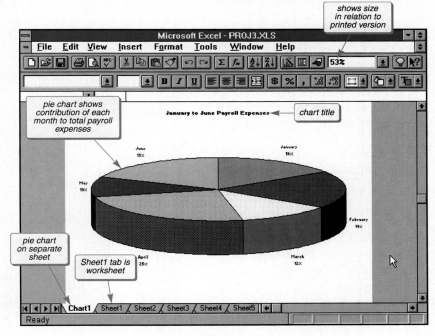

FIGURE 3-57

Each slice of the pie chart represents one of the six months, January through
June. The names of the months and the percent contribution to the total projected
payroll expense display outside the slices. The chart title, January to June Payroll
Expenses, displays immediately above the pie chart.

Excel determines the direction of the data series range (down a column or
across a row) on the basis of the selected range. Because the selection for the pie
chart is across the worksheet (ranges B3:G3 and B12:G12), Excel automatically sets
the data series to rows as shown in Figure 3-55.

Notice in the five ChartWizard dialog boxes (Figure 3-52 through Figure 3-56)
that you can return to the previous ChartWizard dialog box, return to the beginning of the ChartWizard, or create the chart with the options selected thus far
while any one of the five ChartWizard dialog boxes is on the screen.

Formatting the Chart Title and Chart Labels

In Project 2, the chart title was formatted by double-clicking it and entering
the format changes in the Format Chart Title dialog box. This project formats the
chart title and labels that identify the slices of the pie by selecting them and using
the Formatting toolbar.

TO FORMAT THE CHART TITLE AND LABELS ▼

STEP 1 ▶

Select the chart title by pointing to it and clicking the left mouse button.

Excel displays a box with black handles around the chart title.

STEP 2 ▶

Click the Font Size arrow on the Formatting toolbar and choose 20. Click the Font Color arrow on the Formatting toolbar

The Chart1 sheet displays as shown in Figure 3-58.

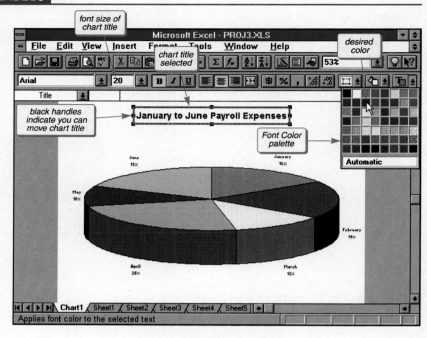

FIGURE 3-58

STEP 3 ▶

Choose blue (column 3, row 2) on the Font Color palette. Point to any one of the labels identifying the slices of the pie and click the left mouse button. Click the Font Size arrow on the Formatting toolbar and choose 12.

The chart title displays in blue, and all the labels increase slightly in size (Figure 3-59).

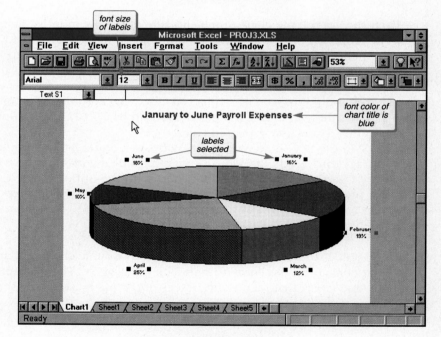

FIGURE 3-59

Notice the labels in Figure 3-59 have black handles. This means you can move and resize them. You can also select and format individual labels by pointing to a label after all the labels have been selected and clicking the left mouse button again.

Exploding the Pie Chart

The next step is to emphasize the slice representing the April payroll expenses by offsetting, or exploding, it from the rest of the pie. Perform the following steps to offset a slice of the pie chart.

TO EXPLODE THE PIE CHART ▼

STEP 1 ▶

Click the slice labeled April twice. Do not double-click.

Excel surrounds the April slice with black handles.

STEP 2 ▶

Drag the slice to the desired position, and release the left mouse button.

Excel redraws the pie chart with the April slice offset from the rest of the pie chart (Figure 3-60).

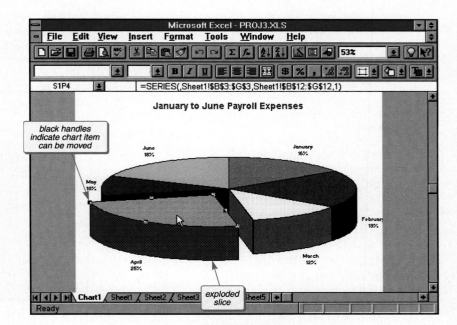

FIGURE 3-60

Although you can offset as many slices as you want, as you drag more slices away from the main portion of the pie chart, the slices become smaller. If you continue to offset slices, the pie chart becomes too small to have an impact on the reader.

Rotating the Pie Chart

In a 3-D chart, you can change the view to better display the section of the chart you are trying to emphasize. Excel allows you to control the rotation angle, elevation, perspective, height, and angle of the axes by using the **3-D View command** on the Format menu or shortcut menu.

To obtain a better view of the offset of the April slice, you can rotate the pie chart 80 degrees to the left. The **rotation angle** of a pie chart is defined by the line that divides the June and January slices (Figure 3-60). Excel initially draws a pie chart with one of the dividing lines pointing to 12:00 (or zero degrees). Complete the steps on the next page to rotate the angle of the pie chart.

TO ROTATE THE PIE CHART ▼

STEP 1 ▶

With the April slice selected, click the right mouse button.

The shortcut menu displays (Figure 3-61).

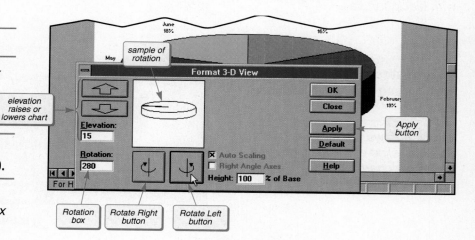

any chart item can be selected when you click right mouse button

3-D View command

shortcut menu

Clear
Insert Data Labels...
Insert Trendline...
Insert Error Bars...
Format Data Point...
Chart Type...
AutoFormat...
3-D View...
Format 3-D Pie Group...

FIGURE 3-61

STEP 2 ▶

Choose the 3-D View command.

The Format 3-D View dialog box displays.

STEP 3 ▶

Click the Rotate Left button (⟲) until the Rotation box displays 280.

Excel displays a sample of the rotated pie chart in the dialog box (Figure 3-62). Between clicks of the Rotate Left button, you can choose the Apply button to apply the current rotation to the pie chart.

sample of rotation

elevation raises or lowers chart

Format 3-D View

Elevation: 15

Rotation: 280

OK
Close
Apply
Default
Help

Apply button

Auto Scaling
Right Angle Axes
Height: 100 % of Base

Rotation box

Rotate Right button

Rotate Left button

FIGURE 3-62

STEP 4 ▶

Choose the OK button on the Format 3-D View dialog box. Click outside the chart area.

Excel displays the pie chart rotated to the left so the gap between the April slice and the main portion of the pie is more prominent (Figure 3-63).

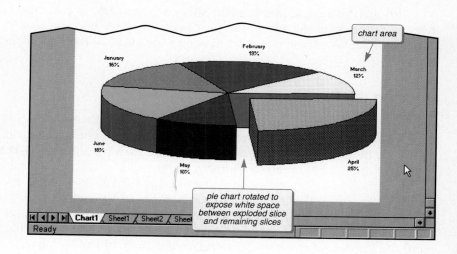

chart area

pie chart rotated to expose white space between exploded slice and remaining slices

FIGURE 3-63

Compare Figure 3-63 to Figure 3-60 on page E173. The offset of the April slice is more noticeable in Figure 3-63 because the pie chart has been rotated to the left to expose the white space between the main portion of the pie and the April slice.

Besides controlling the rotation angle, additional buttons and boxes in the Format 3-D View dialog box (Figure 3-62 on the previous page) allow you to control the elevation and height of the pie chart. When you change characteristics, Excel always redraws the pie chart in the small window in the Format 3-D View dialog box.

Changing the Colors of the Slices

The next step is to change the colors of the slices of the pie. The colors you see in Figure 3-63 are the default colors Excel uses when you first create a pie chart. The Project 3 chart requires the colors shown in Figure 3-65 on the next page. To change the colors of the slices, select them one at a time and use the Color button on the Formatting toolbar as shown in the following steps.

TO CHANGE THE COLORS OF THE SLICES ▼

STEP 1 ▶

Click the slice labeled April twice. Do not double-click.

Excel displays black handles around the April slice.

STEP 2 ▶

Click the Color button arrow on the Formatting toolbar.

The Color palette displays (Figure 3-64).

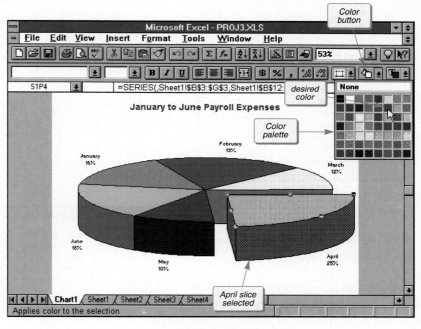

FIGURE 3-64

STEP 3 ▶

Choose teal (column 6, row 2) on the Color palette.

Excel changes the April slice to the color teal.

STEP 4 ▶

Repeat Step 1 through Step 3 and use the following colors on the Color palette for the months specified: January – yellow (column 6, row 1); February – red (column 3, row 1); March – tan (column 3, row 3); May – brown (column 4, row 2); and June – blue (column 3, row 2).

The pie chart displays as shown in Figure 3-65.

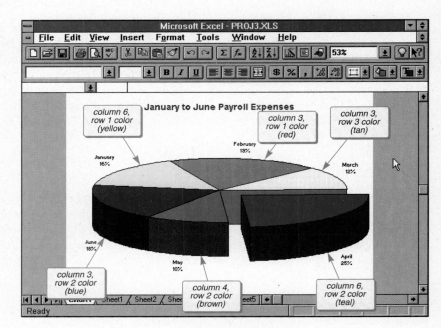

FIGURE 3-65

Adding a Text Box

Excel automatically adds some text to a chart, such as the labels that identify the slices. You can add even more text to clarify or emphasize a chart item. The next step is to add a **text box** with the text, Greatest Payroll Expenses.

TO ADD A TEXT BOX AND FORMAT ITS CONTENTS ▼

STEP 1 ▶

Click the Text Box button (▤) on the Standard toolbar.

The mouse pointer shape changes to a cross.

STEP 2 ▶

Move the mouse pointer approximately three-eighths of an inch above the S in the Sheet1 tab. Drag the mouse to the location shown in Figure 3-66.

A rectangle identifies the text box location on the chart sheet. When you release the left mouse button, the text box will disappear and an insertion point will appear.

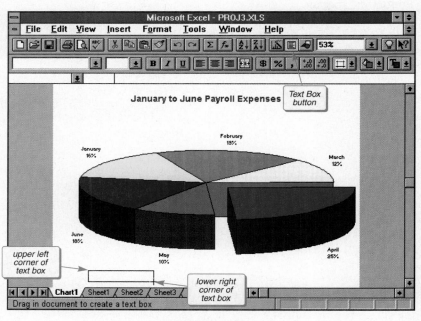

FIGURE 3-66

STEP 3 ►

Release the left mouse button and type Greatest Payroll Expense

The text displays below and to the left of the pie chart (Figure 3-67).

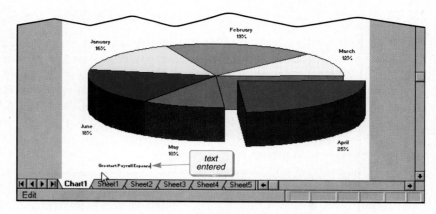

FIGURE 3-67

STEP 4 ►

Click the text, Greatest Payroll Expense and drag the text box to increase its width as shown in Figure 3-68. Make sure the text box is wide enough or the next step will not work properly.

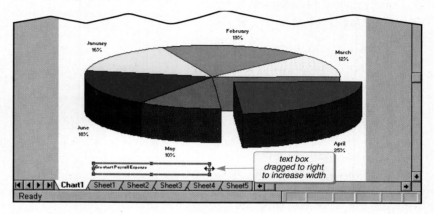

FIGURE 3-68

STEP 5 ►

With the text box selected, click the Font Size arrow on the Formatting toolbar and choose 20. Click the Bold button on the Formatting toolbar. Click the Font Color button arrow and choose the color red (column 3, row 1) on the Font Color palette.

The text in the text box displays as shown in Figure 3-69.

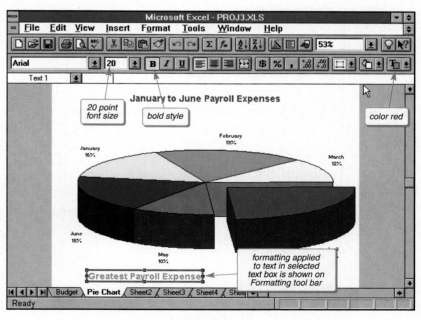

FIGURE 3-69

Adding and Formatting a Chart Arrow

You can add an arrow to the chart and point it at any chart item to emphasize it. To add the arrow, you click the **Arrow button** ( ) on the Drawing toolbar. Next, click the screen where you want the arrow to start. Then drag the arrow in the direction you want it to point. The following steps add and then format an arrow that begins on the right of the text added to the text box and extends toward the April slice.

TO ADD AND FORMAT A CHART ARROW ▼

STEP 1 ▶

Click the Drawing button on the Standard toolbar. If necessary, scroll down until the text box is on the screen.

Excel displays the Drawing toolbar docked at the bottom of the screen.

STEP 2 ▶

Click the Arrow button on the Drawing toolbar. Move the mouse pointer above and to the right of the last letter e in Expense. Drag the mouse pointer to a point immediately below the left edge of the April slice. Release the left mouse button.

An arrow displays between the text box and the April slice (Figure 3-70). The black handles indicate the arrow is selected.

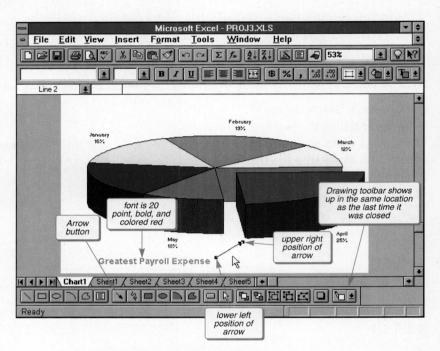

FIGURE 3-70

STEP 3 ▶

With the arrow selected and the mouse pointer pointing to it, click the right mouse button.

The shortcut menu displays (Figure 3-71).

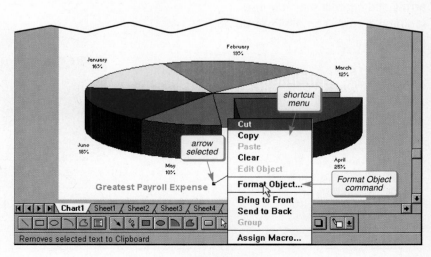

FIGURE 3-71

STEP 4 ▶

Choose the Format Object command. When the Format Object dialog box displays, click the Patterns tab, click the Color arrow, and select the color red (column 3, row 1 on the palette). Click the Weight arrow and select the heaviest weight line.

The Format Object dialog box displays with the selected settings (Figure 3-72).

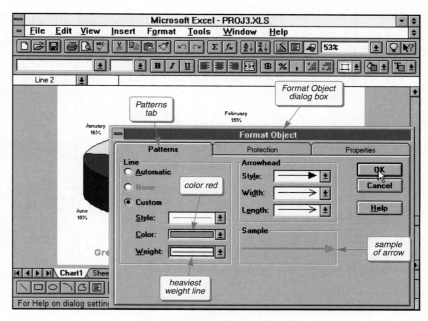

FIGURE 3-72

STEP 5 ▶

Choose the OK button in the Format Object dialog box. Click the Drawing button on the Standard toolbar to hide the Drawing toolbar. Press the ESC key to remove the selection from the arrow.

The formatted arrow displays as shown in Figure 3-73.

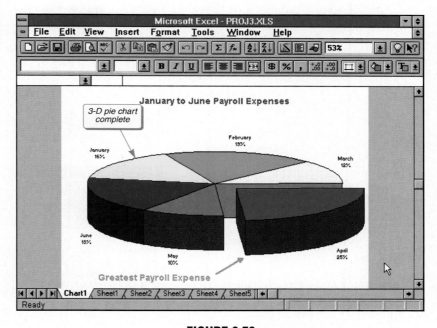

FIGURE 3-73

You can add as many arrows as you want to a chart. However, more than two arrows tend to clutter the chart. As you can see from the Format Object dialog box (Figure 3-72), you can modify the arrow to take on a variety of appearances.

The offset of the slice, the text, and the arrow pointing to the April slice clearly emphasize the month with the greatest projected payroll expenses in the pie chart.

Changing the Name of the Sheet Tabs and Rearranging the Order of the Sheets

The final step in creating the worksheet and pie chart in Project 3 is to change the names of the tabs at the bottom of the screen. The following steps show you how to rename the sheet tabs and reorder the sheets so the worksheet comes before the chart sheet.

TO RENAME THE SHEET TABS AND REARRANGE THE ORDER OF THE SHEETS ▼

STEP 1 ▶

Double-click the tab named Chart1 at the bottom of the screen. When the Rename Sheet dialog box displays, type `Pie Chart` (Figure 3-74).

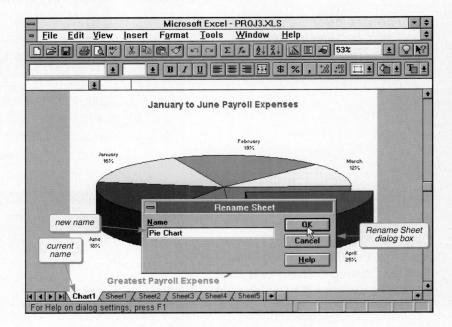

FIGURE 3-74

STEP 2 ▶

Choose the OK button in the Rename Sheet dialog box.

STEP 3 ▶

Repeat Step 1 and Step 2 for the Sheet1 tab. Type `Budget` for the tab name.

STEP 4 ▶

Drag the Budget tab to the left over the Pie Chart tab.

Excel rearranges the sequence of the sheets and displays the worksheet (Figure 3-75).

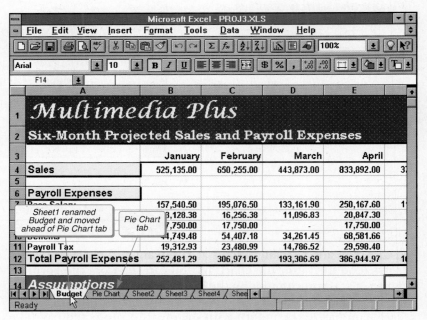

FIGURE 3-75

▶ CHECKING SPELLING, SAVING, PREVIEWING, AND PRINTING THE WORKBOOK

With the workbook complete, the next series of steps is to check spelling, save, preview, and print the workbook. The spell checker only checks the spelling of the selected sheets. Thus, before checking the spelling, hold down the SHIFT key and click the Pie Chart tab. Next, click the Spelling button on the Standard toolbar. After correcting any errors, save the workbook to disk by clicking the Save button on the Standard toolbar before attempting to print it.

Previewing and Printing the Workbook

With the worksheet and pie chart complete, the next step is to print the workbook. You may want to preview it first by clicking the Print Preview button on the Standard toolbar. Recall that Excel only previews selected sheets. Thus, if you want to preview both the worksheet and pie chart, hold down the SHIFT key and click the Pie Chart tab while the Budget sheet displays. Next, click the Print Preview button. After you are finished previewing, follow these steps to print the workbook and save it with the print settings.

TO PRINT THE WORKBOOK

Step 1: Ready the printer.

Step 2: Make sure the worksheet is on the screen. If both sheets are not selected, hold down the SHIFT key and click the Pie Chart tab.

Step 3: Point to the menu bar and click the right mouse button. Excel displays a shortcut menu.

Step 4: Choose the Page Setup command. When the Page Setup dialog box displays, select the Sheet tab and remove the X from the Gridlines check box by clicking it. Next, select the Page tab and select Landscape in the Orientation area. Choose the OK button in the Page Setup dialog box.

Step 5: Click the Print button on the Standard toolbar.

Step 6: Hold down the SHIFT key and click the Budget tab to deselect the Pie Chart tab.

Step 7: Click the Save button on the Standard toolbar to save the workbook with the print settings.

The worksheet and pie chart print as shown in Figure 3-76 on the next page.

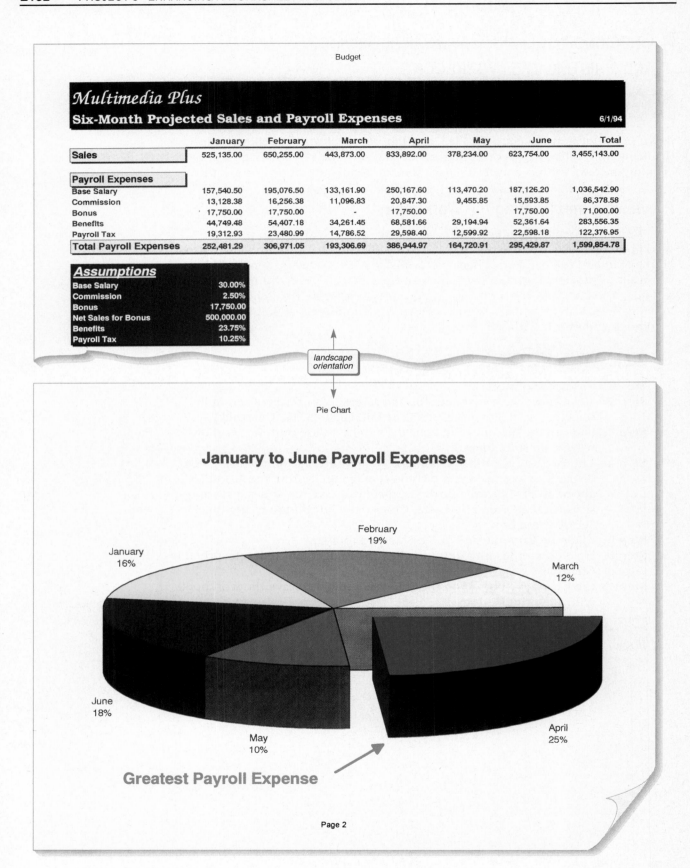

Budget

Multimedia Plus
Six-Month Projected Sales and Payroll Expenses
6/1/94

	January	February	March	April	May	June	Total
Sales	525,135.00	650,255.00	443,873.00	833,892.00	378,234.00	623,754.00	3,455,143.00
Payroll Expenses							
Base Salary	157,540.50	195,076.50	133,161.90	250,167.60	113,470.20	187,126.20	1,036,542.90
Commission	13,128.38	16,256.38	11,096.83	20,847.30	9,455.85	15,593.85	86,378.58
Bonus	17,750.00	17,750.00	-	17,750.00	-	17,750.00	71,000.00
Benefits	44,749.48	54,407.18	34,261.45	68,581.66	29,194.94	52,361.64	283,556.35
Payroll Tax	19,312.93	23,480.99	14,786.52	29,598.40	12,599.92	22,598.18	122,376.95
Total Payroll Expenses	252,481.29	306,971.05	193,306.69	386,944.97	164,720.91	295,429.87	1,599,854.78

Assumptions
Base Salary	30.00%
Commission	2.50%
Bonus	17,750.00
Net Sales for Bonus	500,000.00
Benefits	23.75%
Payroll Tax	10.25%

landscape orientation

Pie Chart

January to June Payroll Expenses

February
19%

January
16%

March
12%

June
18%

April
25%

May
10%

Greatest Payroll Expense

Page 2

FIGURE 3-76

▶ CHANGING THE VIEW OF THE WORKSHEET

ith Excel, you can easily change the view of the worksheet. For example, you can magnify or shrink the worksheet on the screen. You can also view different parts of the worksheet through **window panes**.

Shrinking and Magnifying the View of a Worksheet or Chart

To change the view of the worksheet, you can magnify (zoom in) or shrink (zoom out) the display of a worksheet or chart. When you magnify a worksheet, the characters on the screen become large and fewer columns and rows display. Alternatively, when you shrink a worksheet, more columns and rows display. Magnifying or shrinking a worksheet affects only the view; it does not change the window size or printout of the worksheet or chart. Perform the following steps to change the view.

TO SHRINK AND MAGNIFY THE DISPLAY OF A WORKSHEET OR CHART ▼

STEP 1 ▶

Click the Zoom Control box arrow on the Standard toolbar.

A drop-down list of percentages display (Figure 3-77).

FIGURE 3-77

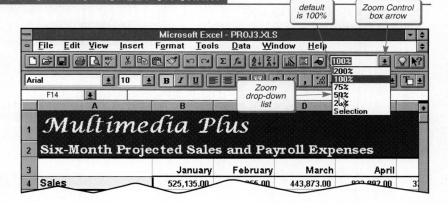

STEP 2 ▶

Choose 50% in the drop-down list.

Excel shrinks the display of the worksheet to a magnification of 50% of its normal display (Figure 3-78). With the worksheet zoomed to 50%, you can see more rows and columns than you did at 100% magnification.

STEP 3 ▶

Click the Zoom Control box arrow on the Standard toolbar and choose 100%.

Excel returns to a normal display.

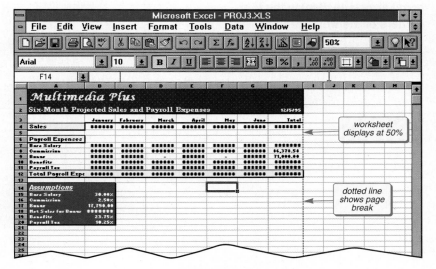

FIGURE 3-78

Notice in Figure 3-78 how you get a better view of the page breaks when you shrink the display of the worksheet. Depending on your printer driver, you may end up with different page breaks.

Splitting the Window into Panes

In Excel, you can split the window into two or four window panes so that you can view different parts of a large worksheet at the same time. To split the window into four panes, select the cell where you want the four panes to intersect. Next, choose the **Split command** from the Window menu. Use the following steps to split the window into four panes.

TO SPLIT A WINDOW INTO FOUR PANES ▼

STEP 1 ▶

Select cell D5, the intersection of the proposed four panes. Select the Window menu.

The Window menu displays as shown in Figure 3-79.

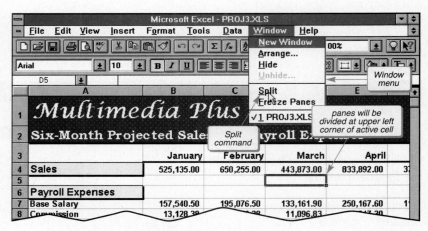

FIGURE 3-79

STEP 2 ▶

Choose the Split command. Use the scroll arrows to display the four corners of the worksheet.

Excel divides the window into four panes and the four corners of the work-sheet display (Figure 3-80).

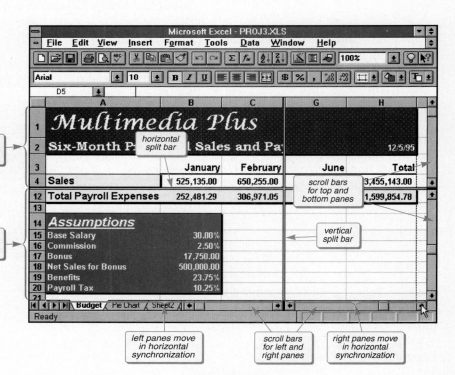

FIGURE 3-80

The four panes in Figure 3-80 are used to display the following: (1) the upper left pane displays the range A1:C4; (2) the upper right pane displays the range G1:H4; (3) the lower left pane displays the range A12:C20; and (4) the lower right pane displays the range G12:H20.

The vertical bar going up and down the middle of the window is called the **vertical split bar**. The horizontal bar going across the middle of the window is called the **horizontal split bar**. If you look closely at the scroll bars below the window and to the right of the window, you will see that the panes split by the horizontal split bar scroll together vertically. The panes split by the vertical split bar scroll together horizontally. To resize the panes, drag either split bar to the desired location in the window.

You can change the values of cells in any of the four panes. Any change you make in one pane also takes effect in the other panes.

If you want to split the window into only two panes instead of four, replace the previous two steps with the following: (1) position the mouse pointer on the **vertical split box** or the **horizontal split box** (Figure 3-81 on the next page); and (2) drag either split box to where you want to split the window.

You can also use the split bars when four panes are on the window to resize the panes. To remove one of the split bars from the window, drag the split box back to its original location or double-click the split bar. Follow these steps to remove both split bars.

TO REMOVE THE FOUR PANES FROM THE WINDOWS

Step 1: Position the mouse pointer at the intersection of the horizontal and vertical split bars.

Step 2: When the mouse pointer shape changes to a cross with four arrowheads (✛), double-click the left mouse button.

Excel removes the four panes from the window.

▶ CHANGING VALUES IN CELLS THAT ARE REFERENCED IN A FORMULA

Excel's automatic recalculation feature is a powerful tool that can be used to analyze worksheet data. Using Excel to scrutinize the impact of changing values in cells that are referenced by a formula in another cell is called **what-if analysis** or **sensitivity analysis**. Not only does Excel recalculate all formulas in a worksheet when new data is entered, it also redraws any associated charts.

In Project 3, the projected payroll expenses in the range A7:G11 are dependent on the **assumptions** in the range A15:B20. Thus, if you change any of the assumptions, Excel immediately recalculates the projected payroll expenses in rows 7 through 11 and the monthly total projected payroll expenses in row 12. The new values cause Excel to recalculate a new total projected payroll expense for the six-month period in cell H12. Because the monthly totals in row 12 change, Excel redraws the pie chart which is based on these numbers.

A what-if question for the worksheet in Project 3 might be, What if the first four assumptions in the range A15:B20 are changed as follows: Base Salary 30.00% to 27.00%; Commission 2.50% to 1.50%; Bonus $17,750.00 to $15,000.00; Net Sales for Bonus $500,000.00 to $600,000.00 — how would these changes affect the total projected payroll expenses in cell H12? To answer questions like this, you need to change only the first four values in the assumptions table. Excel immediately answers the question regarding the total projected payroll expenses in cell H12 by instantaneously recalculating these figures.

The following steps change the first four assumptions as indicated in the previous paragraph and determine the new total projected payroll expenses in cell H12. To ensure that the Assumptions table (range A14:B20) and the total projected payroll expenses in cell H12 show on the screen at the same time, the following steps also divide the window into two vertical panes.

TO ANALYZE DATA IN A WORKSHEET BY CHANGING VALUES

STEP 1 ▶

Use the vertical scroll bar to move the window so cell A4 is in the upper left corner of the screen.

STEP 2 ▶

Drag the vertical split box (**|**) from the lower right corner of the screen so the vertical split bar is positioned immediately to the right of column D and then release the left mouse button. Use the right scroll arrow in the right pane to display the totals in column H.

Excel divides the window into two vertical panes and shows the totals in column H in the pane on the right side of the window (Figure 3-81).

FIGURE 3-81

STEP 3 ▶

Enter 27% in cell B15, 1.50% in cell B16, 15,000 in cell B17, 600,000 in cell B18.

Excel immediately recalculates all the formulas in the worksheet, including the total projected payroll expenses in cell H12 (Figure 3-82).

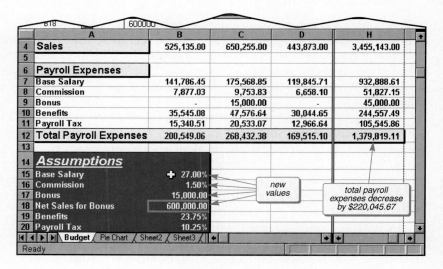

FIGURE 3-82

Each time you enter one of the new percent expenses, Excel recalculates the worksheet. This process usually takes less than one second, depending on how many calculations must be performed and the speed of your computer. Compare the total projected payroll expenses in Figures 3-82 and 3-81. By changing the values of the four assumptions (Figure 3-82), the total projected payroll expenses in cell H12, changes from $1,599,854.78 to $1,379,819.11. The change in the assumptions translates into a savings of $220,045.67 for the six-month period.

▶ GOAL SEEKING

If you know the result you want a formula to produce, you can use **goal seeking** to determine the value of a cell on which the formula depends. The following example re-opens PROJ3.XLS and uses the **Goal Seek command** on the Tools menu to determine the base salary percentage in cell B15 that yields a total projected payroll expense in cell H12 of $1,300,000.

TO GOAL SEEK ▼

STEP 1 ▶

Close PROJ3.XLS without saving changes by choosing the Close command on the File menu. Click the Open button on the Standard toolbar and reopen PROJ3.XLS. Drag the vertical split box to the right of column D. Select cell H12, the cell that contains the total projected payroll expense. Select the Tools menu.

The Tools menu displays (Figure 3-83).

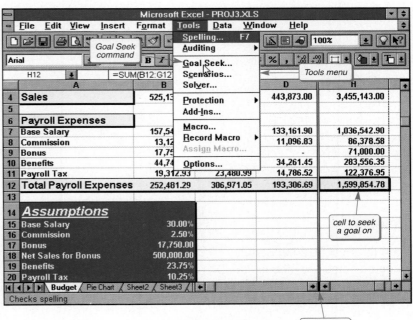

FIGURE 3-83

STEP 2 ▶

Choose the Goal Seek command on the Tools menu.

The Goal Seek dialog box displays. The Set cell box is automatically assigned the cell reference of the active cell in the worksheet (cell H12).

STEP 3 ▶

Type 1,300,000 in the To value box. Type B15 in the By changing cell box.

The Goal Seek dialog box displays as shown in Figure 3-84.

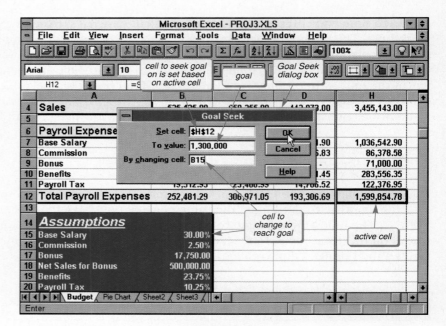

FIGURE 3-84

STEP 4 ▶

Choose the OK button on the Goal Seek dialog box.

Excel immediately changes cell H12 from 1,599,854.78 to the desired value 1,300,000.00. More importantly, Excel changes the base salary percentage in cell B15 to 23.52% (Figure 3-85).

STEP 5 ▶

When the Goal Seeking Status dialog box displays, choose the OK button.

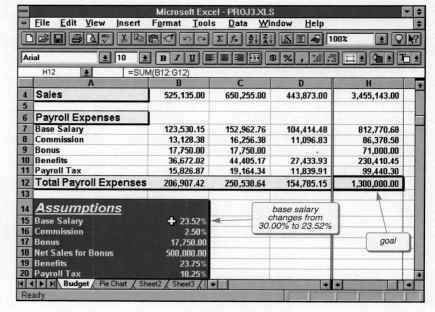

FIGURE 3-85

▲

Goal seeking allows you to change the value of only one cell referenced directly or indirectly in a formula in another cell. In this example, to change the total projected payroll expense in cell H12 to $1,300,000, the base salary percentage in cell B15 must decrease by 6.48% to 23.52%.

Notice that this goal seeking example does not require the cell to vary (cell B15) to be directly referenced in the formula or function. For example, the total projected payroll expense function in cell H12 is =SUM(B12:G12). There is no mention of the base salary percentage (cell B15) in the function. However, because the base salary percentage, on which the monthly sums in row 12 are based, is referenced in the formulas in rows 7 through 11, Excel is able to goal seek on the total projected payroll expense by varying the base salary percentage.

▶ PROJECT SUMMARY

Project 3 introduced you to working with worksheets that extend beyond the window. Using the fill handle, you learned how to create a series. The project presented steps and techniques showing you how to display hidden toolbars, how to freeze titles, and how to change the magnification of the worksheet. You displayed different parts of the worksheet through panes and improved the appearance of a chart. Finally, you used Excel to perform what-if analysis by means of goal seeking and by changing values in cells on which formulas depend.

▶ KEY TERMS AND INDEX

3-D View command *(E173)*
#REF! *(E147)*
absolute referencing *(E152)*
Arrow button *(E178)*
assumptions *(E136)*
AutoFill shortcut menu *(E140)*
Columns command *(E147)*
comparison operator *(E154)*
Copy button *(E143)*
Copy command *(E143)*
Cut command *(E145)*
date stamp *(E150)*
delete columns *(E147)*
Delete command *(E147)*
delete rows *(E147)*
docking a toolbar *(E162)*
drag and drop *(E145)*
drop shadow *(E162)*
Drawing button *(E178)*
Drawing toolbar *(E135, E161)*
exploded pie chart *(E167)*
Fill command *(E140)*

floating toolbar *(E162)*
Format Cells command *(E151)*
Format Object command *(E179)*
Format Painter button *(E140)*
format symbols *(E147)*
Freeze Panes command *(E148)*
freezing worksheet titles *(E148)*
General format *(E152)*
Goal Seek command *(E187)*
goal seeking *(E187)*
hiding a toolbar *(E166)*
horizontal split bar *(E185)*
horizontal split box *(E185)*
IF function *(E154)*
insert columns *(E147)*
Insert command *(E145)*
insert rows *(E145)*
Italic button *(E165)*
line weight *(E179)*
logical test *(E154)*
mixed cell reference *(E152)*
NOW function *(E150)*

Paste button *(E143)*
Paste command *(E143)*
pie chart *(E167)*
rotation angle *(E173)*
Rows command *(E145)*
sensitivity analysis *(E185)*
Split command *(E184)*
text box *(E176)*
Text Box button *(E176)*
toolbar dock *(E162)*
underline *(E166)*
Underline button *(E165)*
Undo Paste command *(E145)*
Unfreeze Panes command *(E157)*
vertical split bar *(E185)*
vertical split box *(E185)*
what-if analysis *(E185)*
window pane *(E183)*
Zoom Control box arrow *(E183)*

In Microsoft Excel, you can accomplish a task in a number of ways. The following table provides a quick reference to each task presented in this project with its available options. The commands listed in the Menu column can be executed using either the keyboard or mouse. Many of the commands in the Menu column are also available on the shortcut menu.

Task	Mouse	Menu	Keyboard Shortcuts
Add a Drop Shadow	Click Drop Shadow button on Drawing toolbar		
Copy a Selection onto the Clipboard	Click Copy button on Standard toolbar	From Edit menu, choose Copy	Press CTRL+C
Copy Cells	Drag selection to paste area while holding down CTRL key or use Copy and Paste buttons on Standard toolbar	From Edit menu, choose Copy; from Edit menu, choose Paste	Press CTRL+C and CTRL+V
Create a Series	Drag fill handle	From Edit menu, choose Fill	
Cut a Selection and Place It on the Clipboard	Click Cut button on Standard toolbar	From Edit menu, choose Cut	Press CTRL+X
Freeze Worksheet Titles		From Window menu, choose Freeze Panes	
Goal Seek		From Tools menu, choose Goal Seek	
Italicize	Click Italic button on Formatting toolbar	From Format menu, choose Cells	Press CTRL+I
Move Cells	Drag selection to its new location or use Cut and Paste buttons on Standard toolbar	From Edit menu, choose Cut; from Edit menu choose Paste	Press CTRL+X and CTRL+V
Paste a Selection from the Clipboard	Click Paste button on Standard toolbar	From Edit menu, choose Paste	Press CTRL+V
Remove Splits	Drag split bars or double-click split bars	From Window menu, choose Remove Split	
Show or Hide a Toolbar	Position mouse pointer in toolbar and click right mouse button	From View menu, choose Toolbars	
Split Window into Panes	Drag vertical split box or horizontal split box	From Window menu, choose Split	
Underline	Click Underline button on Formatting toolbar	From Format menu, choose Cells	Press CTRL+U
Unfreeze Worksheet Titles		From Window menu, choose Unfreeze Panes	
Zoom In or Zoom Out	Click Zoom Control arrow on Standard toolbar	From View menu, choose Zoom	

STUDENT ASSIGNMENT 1
True/False

Instructions: Circle T if the statement is true or F if the statement is false.

T F 1. If you enter 1899 in cell B3, 1900 in cell B4, select the range B3:B4, and then drag the fill handle down to cell B10, Excel assigns cell B10 the value 1900.

T F 2. To copy the text January in cell B3 to all the cells in the range B4:B10, hold down the ALT key while you drag the fill handle from cell B3 to cell B10.

T F 3. The Copy button on the Standard toolbar copies the selection onto the Clipboard.

T F 4. You can invoke the Paste command on the Edit menu by pressing the ENTER key.

T F 5. You can move a floating toolbar anywhere in the window.

T F 6. Excel has toolbar docks on each of the four sides of the window.

T F 7. You can dock more than one toolbar on a toolbar dock.

T F 8. You can dock any toolbar on any toolbar dock.

T F 9. You can freeze vertical titles (columns) but you cannot freeze horizontal titles (rows).

T F 10. The $ in a cell reference affects only the Move command on the Edit menu.

T F 11. If you save a workbook after changing the page setup characteristics, the next time you open the workbook the page characteristics will be the same as when you saved it.

T F 12. You can split a window into eight panes.

T F 13. You must enter a percentage value such as 5.3% as a decimal number (.053) in the formula bar.

T F 14. D23 is an absolute reference, and $D$23 is a relative reference.

T F 15. Although you can insert an entire row or entire column, you cannot insert a cell or range of cells within a row or column.

T F 16. Excel does not allow you to delete a row with a cell that is referenced elsewhere in the worksheet.

T F 17. When you copy cells, Excel adjusts the relative cell references in formulas copied to the paste area.

T F 18. Press the ESC key to remove the selection from a chart item.

T F 19. If you assign cell A4 the IF function =IF(A5 > A7, 1, 0) and cells A5 and A7 are equal to 7, then Excel displays the value 1 in cell A4.

T F 20. If you select a chart item and Excel surrounds it with black handles, then you can drag the chart item to any location in the window.

STUDENT ASSIGNMENT 2
Multiple Choice

Instructions: Circle the correct response.

1. Use function key _____ to change a relative reference in the formula bar to an absolute reference.
   a. F1
   b. F2
   c. F3
   d. F4

2. To use the drag and drop method for copying a range of cells, the mouse pointer must point to the border of the range and change to the _____ shape.
   a. cross
   b. block arrow
   c. block plus sign
   d. split double arrow

STUDENT ASSIGNMENT 2 (continued)

3. If you assign cell A5 the value 10, cell B6 the value 3, and cell B7 the function
=IF(A5 > 4 * B6, ''Valid'', ''Invalid'')
then _____ displays in cell B7.
   a. Valid
   b. Invalid
   c. #REF!
   d. none of the above
4. Which one of the following buttons in the ChartWizard dialog boxes instructs Excel to draw the chart using the options selected thus far?
   a. Next>
   b. Cancel
   c. <Back
   d. Finish
5. If you drag the fill handle to the right on cell A4, which contains Monday, then cell B4 will contain _____.
   a. Sunday
   b. Monday
   c. Tuesday
   d. #REF!
6. You can split the window into _____.
   a. two horizontal panes
   b. two vertical panes
   c. four panes
   d. none of the above
7. The horizontal and vertical split boxes are located _____.
   a. on the Standard toolbar
   b. on the Formatting toolbar
   c. next to the scroll arrows
   d. immediately to the left of the Select All button
8. To select nonadjacent cells, hold down the _____ key to make additional selections after you make the first selection.
   a. ALT
   b. SHIFT
   c. CTRL
   d. CAPS LOCK
9. You cannot dock a toolbar that contains a drop-down list box on the _____ of the window.
   a. bottom
   b. side
   c. top
   d. all of the above
10. When you insert rows in a worksheet, Excel _____ below the point of insertion to open up the worksheet.
    a. writes over the existing rows
    b. pushes up the rows
    c. reduces the height of the cells
    d. pushes down the rows

STUDENT ASSIGNMENT 3
Using the Standard and Formatting Toolbars

Instructions: The Standard and Formatting toolbars display above the formula bar in Figure SA3-3. Use Figure SA3-3 to answer the questions in this assignment.

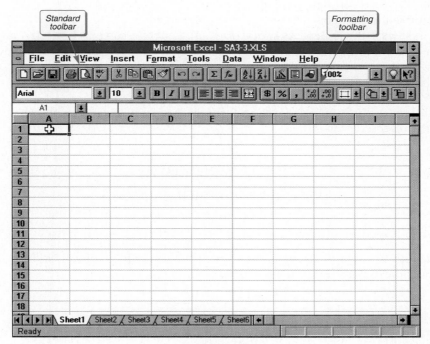

FIGURE SA3-3

1. Describe the function of the following buttons on the Standard toolbar.

    a. Undo button (⟲)   _____

    b. Format Painter button (◈)   _____

    c. AutoSum button (Σ)   _____

    d. ChartWizard button (▨)   _____

    e. Text Box button (▤)   _____

    f. Copy button (▤)   _____

2. Describe the function of the following buttons on the Formatting toolbar.

    a. Color button (▨▾)   _____

    b. Center Across Columns button (▨)_____

    c. Borders button (▦▾)   _____

    d. Bold button (**B**)   _____

    e. Comma Style button (,)   _____

    f. Increase Decimal button (▨)   _____

STUDENT ASSIGNMENT 4
Understanding the Insert and Delete Commands

Instructions: Fill in the correct answers

1. Assume you want to insert four rows between rows 5 and 6.
   a. Select rows _____ through _____
   b. From the shortcut menu, choose the _____ command.
2. You have data in rows 1 through 6. Assume you want to delete rows 2 thorough 4 and move rows up to replace them.
   a. Select rows _____ through _____
   b. From the shortcut menu, choose the _____ command.
   c. In which row would the data from row 6 be located? _____
3. Which command on the Edit menu results in formulas receiving the error message #REF! from cells referenced in the affected range? _____

STUDENT ASSIGNMENT 5
Understanding the IF Function

Instructions: Enter the correct answers.

1. Determine the truth value of the logical tests, given the following cell values: E1 = 500; F1 = 500; G1 = 2; H1 = 50; and I1 = 40. Enter true or false.

   a. $E1 < 400$ Truth value: _____

   b. $F1 = E1$ Truth value: _____

   c. $10 * H1 + I1 <> E1$ Truth value: _____

   d. $E1 + F1 >= 1000$ Truth value: _____

   e. $E1/H1 > G1 * 6$ Truth value: _____

   f. $5 * G1 + I1 = H1$ Truth value: _____

   g. $10 * I1 + 2 <= F1 + 2$ Truth value: _____

   h. $H1 - 10 < I1$ Truth value: _____

2. The active cell is cell F15. Write a function that assigns the value zero (0) or 1 to cell F15. Assign zero to cell F15 if the value in cell B3 is greater than the value in cell C12; otherwise assign 1 to cell F15.

   Function: _____

3. The active cell is cell F15. Write a function that assigns the value Credit OK or Credit Not OK to cell F15. Assign the label Credit OK if the value in cell A1 is not equal to the vlaue in cell B1; otherwise assign the label Credit Not OK.

   Function: _____

STUDENT ASSIGNMENT 6
Understanding Absolute, Mixed, and Relative Referencing

Instructions: Fill in the correct answers. Use Figure SA3-6 for problems 2 through 5.

FIGURE SA3-6

1. Write cell D15 as a relative reference, absolute reference, mixed reference with the row varying, and mixed reference with the column varying.

    Relative reference: _____   Mixed, row varying: _____

    Absolute reference: _____   Mixed, column varying: _____

2. Write the formula for cell B8 that multiplies cell B1 times the sum of cells B4, B5, and B6. Write the formula so that when it is copied to cells C8 and D8, cell B1 remains absolute. Verify your formula by checking it with the values found in cells B8, C8, and D8.

    Formula for cell B8: _____

3. Write the formula for cell E4 that multiplies cell A4 times the sum of cells B4, C4, and D4. Write the formula so that when it is copied to cells E5 and E6, cell A4 remains absolute. Verify your formula by checking it with the values found in cells E4, E5, and E6.

    Formula for cell E4: _____

4. Write the formula for cell B10 that multiplies cell B1 times the sum of cells B4, B5, and B6. Write the formula so that when it is copied to cells C10 and D10, Excel adjusts all the cell references according to the new location. Verify your formula by checking it with the values found in cells B10, C10, and D10.

    Formula for cell B10: _____

5. Write the formula for cell F4 that multiplies cell A4 times the sum of cells B4, C4, and D4. Write the formula so that when it is copied to cells F5 and F6, Excel adjusts all the cell addresses according to the new location. Verify your formula by checking it with the values found in cells F4, F5, and F6.

    Formula for cell F4: _____

COMPUTER LABORATORY EXERCISE 1
Using the Help Menu to Understand
IF Functions, Formulas, and What-if Analysis

Part 1 Instructions: Start Excel and perform the following tasks using a computer.

1. Choose the Search for Help on command from the Help menu.
2. Type `if functions` in the Search dialog box and choose the Show Topics button.
3. With the topic IF highlighted in the lower list, choose the Go To button.
4. Read the information displayed. Choose Print Topic from the Help window File menu to print the information.
5. To exit Help, double-click the Control-menu box in the Help window.

Part 2 Instructions: Start Excel and perform the following tasks using a computer.

1. Choose the Search for Help on command from the Help menu.
2. Type `formulas` in the Search dialog box.
3. In the upper list, select formulas, cell references in and then choose the Show Topics button.
4. In the lower list, choose the Go To button to display the Overview of Using References topic.
5. Read the information and then, under the See Also Help that appears at the bottom of the screen, click Changing a cell's reference type.
6. Read the information that appears in the How To window. Click the Print button in the How To window to print the information.
7. Click the Close button to close the How To window.
8. To exit Help, double-click the Control-menu box in the Help window.

Part 3 Instructions: Start Excel and perform the following tasks using a computer.

1. Choose the Search for Help on command from the Help menu.
2. Type `what-if` in the Search dialog box and then choose the Show Topics button.
3. In the lower list, choose the Go To button to display the Solving What-if Problems topic.
4. Click Seeking a specific solution to a formula using the Goal Seek command.
5. Read the information that appears in the How To window. Click the Print button in the How To window. Click the Close button in the How To window.
6. To exit Help, double-click the Control-menu box in the Help window.

COMPUTER LABORATORY EXERCISE 2
Using the Fill Handle and Mixed Cell Referencing

Instructions: Start Excel. Perform the tasks below Figure CLE3-2 to create the multiplication table shown.

	A	B	C	D	E	F	G	H	I	J	K	L	M	N	O	P
1	x	2	4	6	8	10	12	14	16	18	20	22	24	26	28	30
2	1	2	4	6	8	10	12	14	16	18	20	22	24	26	28	30
3	2	4	8	12	16	20	24	28	32	36	40	44	48	52	56	60
4	3	6	12	18	24	30	36	42	48	54	60	66	72	78	84	90
5	4	8	16	24	32	40	48	56	64	72	80	88	96	104	112	120
6	5	10	20	30	40	50	60	70	80	90	100	110	120	130	140	150
7	6	12	24	36	48	60	72	84	96	108	120	132	144	156	168	180
8	7	14	28	42	56	70	84	98	112	126	140	154	168	182	196	210
9	8	16	32	48	64	80	96	112	128	144	160	176	192	208	224	240
10	9	18	36	54	72	90	108	126	144	162	180	198	216	234	252	270
11	10	20	40	60	80	100	120	140	160	180	200	220	240	260	280	300
12	11	22	44	66	88	110	132	154	176	198	220	242	264	286	308	330
13	12	24	48	72	96	120	144	168	192	216	240	264	288	312	336	360
14	13	26	52	78	104	130	156	182	208	234	260	286	312	338	364	390
15	14	28	56	84	112	140	168	196	224	252	280	308	336	364	392	420
16	15	30	60	90	120	150	180	210	240	270	300	330	360	390	420	450
17	16	32	64	96	128	160	192	224	256	288	320	352	384	416	448	480
18	17	34	68	102	136	170	204	238	272	306	340	374	408	442	476	510

FIGURE CLE3-2

1. Change the width of all the columns in the worksheet to 4.57 characters.
2. Use the fill handle to create the series of numbers between column B and column P in row 1 (2, 4, 6, . . . , 30) and the series of numbers between rows 2 and 17 in column A (1, 2, 3,. . . ,17). Recall that the fill handle requires the first two entries to determine a numeric series.
3. Color the background of column A and row 1 purple (column 5, row 2 on the Color palette).
4. Add a bold outline around column A and then add a bold outline around row 1.
5. Enter the formula =$A2 * B$1 in cell B2. Copy the formula in cell B2 to the range B2:P18. Bold the range A1:P17.
6. Enter your name, course, computer laboratory exercise number (CLE3-2), date, and instructor name in column A in separate but adjacent cells beginning in cell A19. Save the workbook using the file-name CLE3-2.
7. Print the worksheet without gridlines.
8. Save the workbook again using the same filename
9. Press CTRL+` (single left quotation mark) to change the display to formulas. Print the formulas version in landscape orientation using the Fit To option on the Page tab in the Page Setup dialog box. Press CTRL+` (single left quotation mark) to change the display to values.

COMPUTER LABORATORY EXERCISE 3
Creating a Series

Instructions: Start Excel. Open CLE3-3 from the subdirectory Excel5 on the Student Diskette that accompanies this book. The worksheet shown in (Figure CLE3-3a) contains the initial values for eight different series.

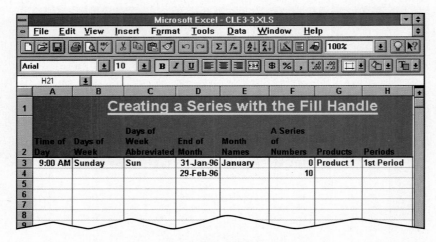

FIGURE CLE3-3a

Use the fill handle on one column at a time to propagate the eight different series through row 17 as shown in Figure CLE3-3b. For example, in column A, select cell A3 and drag the fill handle down to cell A17. Your final result should be 11:00 PM in cell A17. In column D, select the range D3:D4 and drag the fill handle down to cell D17. Save the workbook using the filename CLE3-3A. Print the worksheet on one page without cell gridlines.

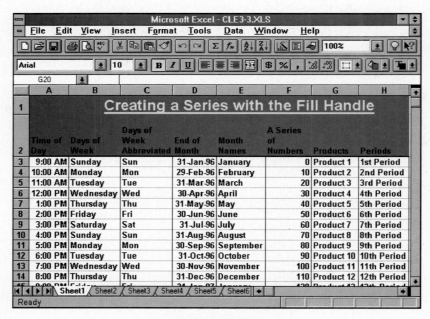

FIGURE CLE3-3b

COMPUTER LABORATORY ASSIGNMENT 1
Five-Year Projected Financial Statement

Purpose: To become familiar with entering IF functions, applying formulas that use absolute referencing, displaying the system date, charting, using panes, goal seeking, and what-if analysis.

Problem: You are a management trainee employed by Time Will Tell Inc. Each month for the first six months of your employment you work in a different department. This month you are working for the Information Systems (IS) department. Your IS supervisor observed from your resume that you learned Microsoft Excel in college and has requested that you build a Five-Year Projected Financial Statement based on figures available from 1995 (Figure CLA3-1A). Follow the instructions on the next page.

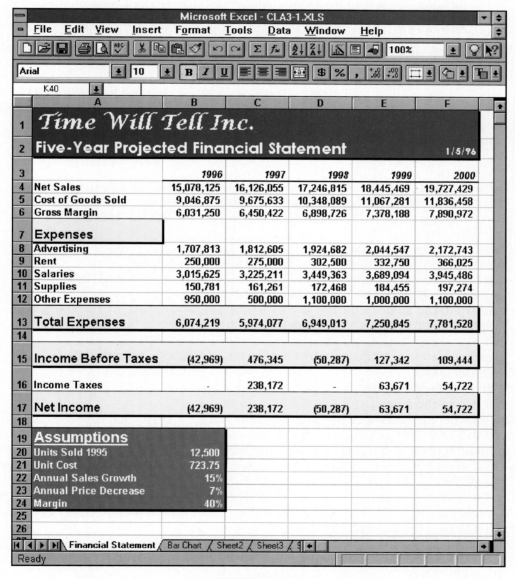

FIGURE CLA3-1a

(continued)

COMPUTER LABORATORY ASSIGNMENT 1(continued)

Part 1 Instructions: Perform the following tasks to create the worksheet shown in Figure CLA3-1a on the previous page.

1. Format the entire worksheet to bold, comma style with no decimal places by clicking the Select All button, the Bold button, the Comma Style button, and finally click the Decrease Decimal button on the Formatting toolbar twice. Enter the worksheet titles in cells A1 and A2. Enter the system date using the NOW function in cell F2. Format the date to the m/d/yy style.

2. Enter 1996 in cell B3, 1997 in cell C3, and generate the series 1996 through 2000 in the range B3:F3 using fill handle. Use the Cells command on the Format menu to assign the range B3:F3 the General format (Number tab, All category, General format code).

3. Enter the row titles in the range A4:A24. Change the font size in cells A7, A13, A15, and A17 to 12 point. Change the font size in cell A19 to 14 point and underline the characters in the cell.

4. Enter the following assumptions in the range B20:B24: Units Sold 1995: 12,500; Unit Cost: 723.75; Annual Sales Growth: 15%; Annual Price Decrease: 7%; Margin: 40%.
   Select the range B22:B24 and click the Percent Style button on the Formatting toolbar.

5. Change the following column widths: A = 23.43 and B through F = 11.00. Change the heights of rows 3, 7, 13, 15, 16, and 17 to 24.00 and row 19 to 18.00.

6. Complete the following entries:
   a. 1996 Sales (cell B4) = Units Sold 1995 * (Unit Cost/(1-Margin)) or =B20*(B21/(1-B24))
   b. 1997 Sales (cell C4) = 1996 Sales * (1+Annual Sales Growth)*(1-Annual Price Decrease) or =B4*(1+$B$22)*(1-$B$23)
   c. Copy cell C4 to the range D4:F4
   d. 1996 Cost of Goods Sold (cell B5) = 1996 Sales - (1996 Sales * Margin) or =B4*(1-$B$24)
   e. Copy cell B5 to the range C5:F5
   f. 1996 Gross Margin (cell B6) = 1995 Sales – 1995 Cost of Goods Sold or =B4-B5
   g. Copy cell B6 to the range C6:F6
   h. 1996 Advertising (cell B8) = $200,000+10%*1996 Sales or =200000+10%*B4
   i. Copy cell B8 to the range C8:F8
   j. 1996 Rent (cell B9) = $250,000
   k. 1997 Rent (cell C9) = 1996 Rent + 10%*1996 Rent or =B9*(1+10%)
   l. Copy cell C9 to the range D9:F9
   m. 1996 Salaries (cell B10) = 20% * 1996 Sales or =20%*B4
   n. Copy cell B10 to the range C10:F10
   o. 1996 Supplies (cell B11) = 1% * 1996 Sales or =1%*B4
   p. Copy cell B11 to the range C11:F11
   q. Other Expenses: 1996 = $950,000; 1997 = $500,000; 1998 = $1,100,000; 1999 = $1,000,000; and 2000 = $1,100,000
   r. 1996 Total Expenses (cell B13) = SUM(B8:B12)
   s. Copy cell B13 to the range C13:F13
   t. 1996 Income Before Taxes (cell B15 = 1996 Gross Margin – 1996 Total Expenses or =B6-B13
   u. Copy cell B15 to the range C15:F15
   v. 1996 Income Taxes (cell B16): If 1996 Income Before Taxes is less than zero, then 1996 Income Taxes equal zero; otherwise, 1996 Income Taxes equal 50% * 1996 Income Before Taxes or =IF(B15<0,0,50%*B15)
   w. Copy cell B16 to the range C16:F16
   x. 1996 Net Income (cell B17) = 1996 Income Before Taxes – 1996 Income Taxes or =B15-B16
   y. Copy cell B17 to the range C17:F17

7. Change the font in cell A1 to 20 point Lucida Calligraphy (or a similar font). Change the font in cell A2 to 16 point Century Gothic (or a similar font). Change the font in cell F2 to 10 point Century Gothic (or a similar font). Change the background and font colors and add drop shadows as shown in Figure CLA3-1a on the previous page.

8. Enter your name, course, computer laboratory assignment (CLA3-1), date, and instructor name in the range A27:A31. Save the workbook using the filename CLA3-1A.

9. Preview and print the worksheet without cell gridlines. Preview and print the formulas (CTRL+') in landscape orientation using the Fit to option button in the Page Setup dialog box. Press CTRL+` to display the values version of the worksheet.
10. Save the workbook again.

Part 2 Instructions: If you did not do Part 1, ask your instructor for a copy of CLA3-1. Draw a 3-D Column chart (Figure CLA3-1B) that compares the projected net incomes for years 1996 through 2000. Use the nonadjacent ranges B3:F3 and B17:F17. Add the chart title and format it as shown in Figure CLA3-1b. Rename and rearrange the tabs as shown in Figure CLA3-1b. Save the workbook using the filename CLA3-1B. Print both sheets.

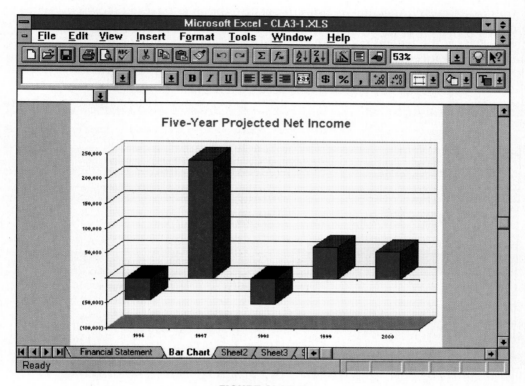

FIGURE CLA3-1b

Part 3 Instructions: If you did not do Parts 1 or 2, ask your instructor for a copy of CLA3-1. If the 3-D column chart is on the screen, click the Financial Statement tab to display the worksheet. Divide the window into two panes by dragging the horizontal split bar between rows 6 and 7. Use the scroll bars to display both the top and bottom of the worksheet. Using the numbers in the following table, analyze the effect of changing the annual sales growth (cell B22) and annual price decrease (cell B23) on the annual net incomes in row 17. Print both the worksheet and chart for each case.

CASE	ANNUAL SALES GROWTH	ANNUAL PRICE DECREASE	1997 RESULTING NET INCOME
1	5%	1%	$217,817
2	10%	-2%	$273,795
3	25%	10%	$275,830

Close CLA3-1B without saving it, and then re-open it. Use the Goal Seek command to determine a margin (cell B24) that would result in a net income of $500,000 for 1996 in cell B17. You should end up with a margin of 45%. Print only the worksheet after the goal seeking is complete. Do not save the workbook.

COMPUTER LABORATORY ASSIGNMENT 2
Modifying a Biweekly Payroll Worksheet

Purpose: To become familiar with entering IF functions with absolute referencing, freezing titles, zooming in and zooming out, and adding, changing, and deleting values and formats in a worksheet.

Note: Before you can begin this assignment, you must first complete Computer Laboratory Assignment 2 in Project 2 on page E134 or obtain the workbook CLA2-2 from your instructor.

Problem: Your supervisor in the Payroll department has asked you to modify the payroll workbook developed in Computer Laboratory Assignment 2 in Project 2 so that it appears as shown in Figure CLA3-2a. The major modifications include reformatting the worksheet, time-and-one-half for hours worked greater than 80, no federal tax if the federal tax is greater than the gross pay, and computation of the social security deduction. The worksheet (CLA2-2) created earlier in Project 2 is shown in Figure CLA2-2 on page E134.

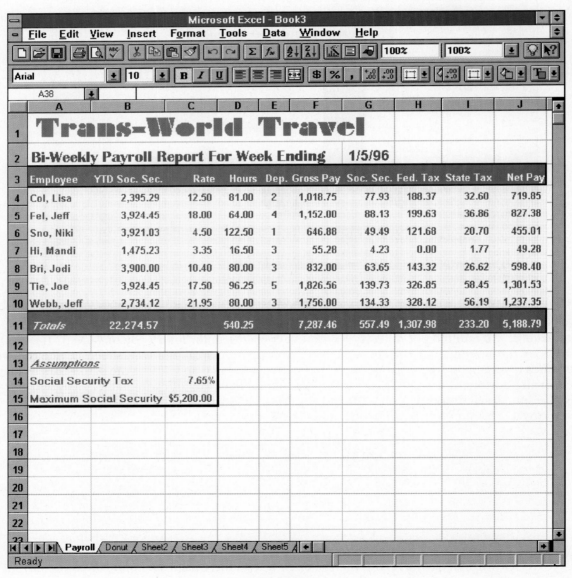

FIGURE CLA3-2a

Part 1 Instructions: Open the workbook CLA2-2 created in Project 2. Perform the following tasks:

1. Bold the entire worksheet. Delete rows 10 through 12. Insert a row above row 1. Enter the worksheet title, Trans-World Travel, in cell A1. Change the worksheet subtitle in row 2 to Bi-weekly Payroll Report for Week Ending. Assign the NOW function to cell G2 and format it to m/d/yy. Change the font in cell A1 to 24 point Braggadocio (or a similar font). Change the font in the range A2:G2 to 16 point Britannic Bold (or a similar font). Change the colors of the worksheet titles area so it appears as shown in Figure CLA3-2a.

2. Insert a new column between columns A and B. Title the new column YTD Soc. Sec.. Insert a new column between columns F and G. Title the new column Soc. Sec.. Format the column titles as shown in Figure CLA3-2a. Freeze the titles in column A and rows 1 through 3.

3. Increase the column widths and row heights as follows: A = 11.00; B = 13.00; C, F, G, I and J = 9.00; D = 7.00; E = 5.00; H = 8.00; row 2 = 24.00; row 3 = 21.00; rows 4 through 10 = 18.00; row 11 = 24.00; and rows 12 through 15 = 18.00.

4. Delete row 6 (Marci Di). Change Mandi Hi's number of dependents from 1 to 3.

5. Enter the following YTD social security values in row B.

NAME	YTD SOC. SEC.
Col, Lisa	$2,395.29
Fel, Jeff	3,924.45
Sno, Niki	3,921.03
Hi, Mandi	1,475.23
Bri, Jodi	3,900.00

6. Insert two new rows immediately above the Totals row. Add the following new employees:

EMPLOYEE	YTD SOC. SEC.	RATE	HOURS	DEPENDENTS
Tie, Joe	$3,924.45	$17.50	96.25	5
Webb, Jeff	2,734.12	21.95	80	3

7. Enter the Assumptions table in the range A13:C15 and format it as shown in Figure CLA3-2a. Place the titles in column A and the numbers in column C.

8. Change the background colors and font colors and add borders in the range A3:J11 as shown in Figure CLA3-2a.

9. Change the formulas to determine the gross pay in column F and the federal tax in column H.
   a. In cell F4, enter an IF function that applies the following logic:
      If Hours <= 80, then Gross Pay = Rate * Hours, otherwise Gross Pay = Rate * Hours + 0. 5 * Rate * (Hours - 80)
   b. Copy the IF function in cell F4 to the range F5:F10.
   c. In cell H4, enter the IF function that applies the following logic:
      If (Gross Pay - Dependents * 38. 46) > 0, then Federal Tax = 20% * (Gross Pay - Dependents * 38. 46), otherwise Federal Tax = 0
   d. Copy the IF function in cell H4 to the range H5:H10.

10. Copy the state tax and net pay formulas in the range I4:J4 to the range I10:H10.

11. An employee pays social security tax only if his or her YTD social security is less than the maximum social security in cell C15.
    a. Use the following logic to determine the social security tax for Lisa Col in cell G4:
       If Soc. Sec. Tax * Gross Pay + YTD Soc. Sec.> Maximum Soc. Sec., then Maximum Soc. Sec. - YTD Soc. Sec., else Soc. Sec. Tax * Gross Pay
    b. Copy the IF function to the range G5:G10.

(continued)

COMPUTER LABORATORY ASSIGNMENT 2 (continued)

    c. Make sure references to the values in the Assumptions table are absolute.

    d. Treat the social security tax as a deduction in determining the net pay.

    e. Determine any new totals as shown in row 11 of Figure CLA3-2a.

    f. Scroll over so the Net Pay column is adjacent to the row titles in column A.

12. Enter your name, course, computer laboratory assignment (CLA3-2), date, and instructor name in the range A18:A22. Save the workbook using the filename CLA3-2A.

13. Use the Zoom Control box on the Standard toolbar to change the view of the worksheet. One by one, select all the percents in the Zoom Control box. Change back to 100%.

14. Preview the worksheet in landscape orientation. Adjust column widths if number signs display in place of numbers. Print the worksheet without cell gridlines. Save the worksheet again.

15. Preview and print the formulas (CTRL+') in landscape orientation using the Fit to option button in the Page Setup dialog box. Close the worksheet without saving the latest changes.

Part 2 Instructions: If you did not do Part 1, ask your instructor for a copy of CLA3-2. Open the workbook CLA3-2A. Using the range A4:A10 (category names) and the range J4:J10 (data series), draw a donut chart (column 1, row 2 in the ChartWizard – Step 2 of 5 dialog box) with the labels inside each piece (Figure CLA3-2b). Add a chart title and format it appropriately. Add the text box with a drop shadow and the arrows as shown in Figure CLA3-2b. Format the text box and arrows appropriately. Rename and rearrange the tabs as shown in Figure CLA3-2b. Save the workbook using the filename CLA3-2B. Print both sheets.

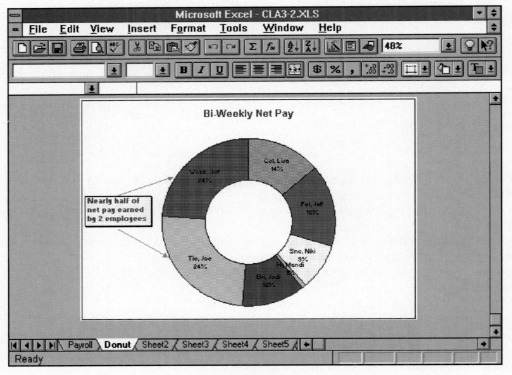

FIGURE CLA3-2b

Part 3 Instructions: If you did not do Parts 1 or 2, ask your instructor for a copy of CLA3-2. If the donut chart is on the screen, click the Payroll tab to display the worksheet. Using the numbers in the following table, analyze the effect of changing the Social Security Tax in cell C14 and the Maximum Social Security in cell C15. Print both the worksheet and chart for each case.

CASE	TAX	MAXIMUM SOCIAL SECURITY TAX	TOTAL SOCIAL SECURITY
1	8%	$5,000	$583.00
2	7.65%	5,200	557.49

COMPUTER LABORATORY ASSIGNMENT 3
Projected Quarterly Report

Purpose: To become familiar with creating a data series, using the Format Painter button, copying a range to a nonadjacent range, applying formulas that use absolute referencing, charting, goal seeking, and what-if analysis.

Problem: You are employed as a worksheet specialist by Plant A Tree Inc. The company utilizes assumptions, based on past business practice, to plan for the next quarter. You have been asked to create a worksheet similar to the one shown in Figure CLA3-3a. Follow the instructions on the next page.

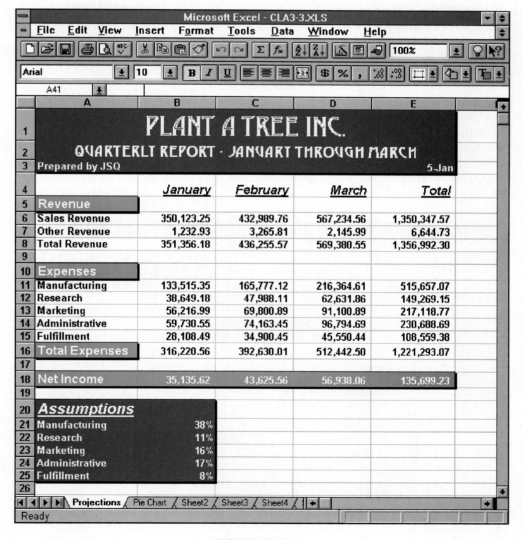

FIGURE CLA3-3a

(continued)

COMPUTER LABORATORY ASSIGNMENT 3 (continued)

Part 1 Instructions: Do the following to create the worksheet shown in Figure CLA3-3a.

1. Bold the entire worksheet. Enter the worksheet titles in cells A1, A2, and A3. Enter the NOW function in cell E3 and format it to d-mmm. Enter January in cell B4 and underline, italicize, and right align it. Use the fill handle to create the month series in row 4. Enter Total in cell E4 and use the Format Painter button on the Standard toolbar to format it the same as cell D4. Enter the row titles down through Assumptions in cell A20. Copy the row titles in the range A11:A15 to the range A21:A25.
2. Change the column widths as follows: A = 18.29; B through D = 13.71; and E = 14.86. Change the height of row 4 to 24.00.
3. Enter the sales revenue and other revenue from the table to the right in the range B6:D7.

	JANUARY	FEBRUARY	MARCH
Sales Revenue	$350,123.25	$432,989.76	$567,234.56
Other Revenue	1,232.93	3,265.81	2,145.99

4. Each of the expense categories in the range B11:D15 are determined by multiplying the total revenue for the month times the corresponding assumption in the Assumption table (range A20:B25). For example, the Manufacturing expense in cell B11 is equal to cell B21 times cell B8 or =B21*B8. Once the formulas are assigned to the range B11:B15, they can be copied to the range C11:D15. However, for the copy to work properly, you must make the first cell reference absolute. Thus, enter the following formulas in the designated cells:
    B11 = $B$21*B8; B12 = $B$22*B8; B13 = $B$23*B8; B14 = $B$24*B8; and B15 = $B$25*B8.
5. Use the SUM function to determine all the totals. The net income is equal to the total revenue for each month minus the total expenses for each month.
6. Enter your name, course, computer laboratory assignment (CLA3-3), date, and instructor name in the range A28:A32.
7. Save the workbook using the filename CLA3-3A.
8. Print the worksheet without cell gridlines. Preview and print the formulas (CTRL+') in landscape orientation using the Fit to option button in the Page Setup dialog box. Press CTRL+' to display the values version of the worksheet.
9. Save the workbook again.

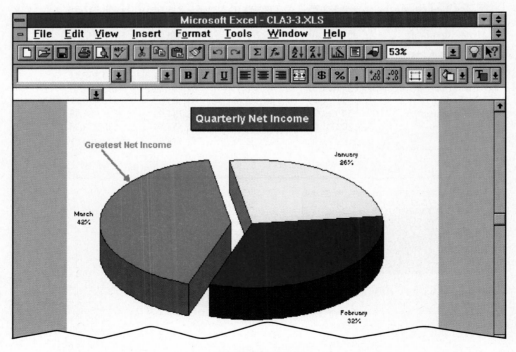

FIGURE CLA3-3b

Part 2 Instructions: If you did not do Part 1, ask your instructor for a copy of CLA3-3. Draw a 3-D pie chart (Figure CLA3-3b) that shows the monthly contribution to the quarterly net income. That is, chart the nonadjacent ranges B4:D4 (category names) and B18:D18 (data series).

Make the following changes to the pie chart:

1. Add the chart title and format it as shown in Figure CLA3-3b.
2. Explode the March slice.
3. Select a slice and use the 3-D View command on the shortcut menu to change the elevation to 30° and the rotation to 350°.
4. Change the color of the slices as shown in Figure CLA3-3b.
5. Add a text box with the phrase, Greatest Net Income, and an arrow pointing to the March slice. Format the text box and arrow as shown in Figure CLA3-3b.
6. Rename the tabs as follows: Chart1 to Pie Chart and Sheet1 to Projections. Rearrange the tabs so the Projections tab is to the left of the Pie Chart tab.
7. Save the workbook using the filename CLA3-3B.
8. Print both sheets.

Part 3 Instructions: If you did not do Parts 1 or 2, ask your instructor for a copy of CLA3-3. If the 3-D pie chart is on the screen, click the Projections tab to display the worksheet shown in Figure CLA3-3a. Using the numbers in the following table, analyze the effect of changing the assumptions in rows 21 through 25 on the quarterly net income in cell E18. Print both the worksheet and chart for each case.

	CASE 1	CASE 2	CASE 3
Manufacturing	35%	37%	40%
Research	10%	10%	15%
Marketing	14%	15%	17%
Administrative	16%	16%	20%
Fulfillment	5%	7%	5%

You should end up with the following quarterly net incomes in cell E18: Case 1 = $271,398.46; Case 2 = $203,548.85; and Case 3 = $40,709.77.

Close CLA3-3B without saving it and then re-open it. Use the Goal Seek command to determine the marketing percentage (cell B23) that would result in a quarterly net income of $200,000 in cell E18. (You should end up with a marketing percentage of 11%.) Print only the worksheet.

COMPUTER LABORATORY ASSIGNMENT 4
Stock Analysis Worksheet

Purpose: To become familiar with planning a worksheet.

Problem: You are rich and famous and own stock in many different companies. Your computer stock portfolio includes the companics listed in the following table on the next page. The number of shares you own in each company are in parentheses. Your investment analysts tell you that on average the computer industry will return 5% per year for the next ten years. Create a worksheet that organizes your computer stock portfolio and projects its annual worth for each of the next ten years. Make sure the 5% return is assigned to a cell so that you can modify this value as circumstances change.

(continued)

COMPUTER LABORATORY ASSIGNMENT 4 (continued)

HARDWARE	SOFTWARE	NETWORKING
Apple (5,000)	Autodesk (3,000)	3Com (2,500)
Compaq (11,500)	Borland (4,500)	Compaq (11,250)
DEC (6,550)	Lotus (11,250)	Novell (16,750)
IBM (22,500)	Microsoft (58,000)	
Intel (7,000)	Symantec (6,500)	

Instructions: Obtain the latest stock prices from the newspaper for your computer stocks. Using the figures in the table, compute the amount of your investment in each stock and list it under the current year. Next, use the 5% return per year to project the annual worth of these stocks for each of the next ten years. Group the companies in the worksheet by major segments (Hardware, Software, Networking). Show totals for each segment. Use goal seeking to modify the grand total by changing the appropriate cells. Use the techniques developed in this project to manipulate the large worksheet. Submit the following:

1. A description of the problem. Include the purpose of the worksheet, a statement outlining the results, the required data, and calculations.
2. A handwritten design of the worksheet.
3. A printed copy of the worksheet without cell gridlines.
4. A printed copy of the formulas in the worksheet.

▼

WORKING WITH TEMPLATES AND MULTIPLE WORKSHEETS IN A WORKBOOK

OBJECTIVES You will have mastered the material in this project when you can:

▸ Create and use a template
▸ Copy data between worksheets
▸ Utilize custom formats
▸ Create formulas that reference cells in different sheets in a workbook
▸ Change chart types
▸ Enhance embedded charts
▸ Summarize data using consolidation

▸ Add comments to cells
▸ Add a header or footer to a workbook
▸ Change the margins
▸ Drag a column in a chart to change the corresponding number in a worksheet
▸ Find text in the workbook
▸ Replace text in the workbook

▸ INTRODUCTION

There are business applications that require data from several worksheets to be summarized onto one worksheet. For example, many businesses maintain daily sales data on separate worksheets. At the end of the week, these businesses have seven worksheets of data, one for each day of the week, which is then summarized onto one worksheet for the entire week.

Excel's three-dimensional capabilities make it easy for you to complete this type of application. For example, the sales for each day would be maintained on a separate sheet in a workbook. The eighth sheet in the workbook would contain a summary of the seven daily sheets. You use the tabs at the bottom of the Excel window to move from sheet to sheet. Furthermore, Excel has the capability to reference cells found on different sheets, which allows you to easily summarize the daily sales data. You could even extend the application to summarize the weekly worksheets onto a monthly sheet and the monthly sheets onto a yearly sheet. The process of summarizing information found on multiple sheets is called **consolidation**.

Another important concept you will be introduced to in this project is the use of a template. A **template** is a special workbook you can use as a pattern to create new workbooks that are similar. A template usually consists of a **general format** (worksheet title, column and row titles, numeric format) and formulas that are common to all the worksheets. For example, with the daily sales application, the seven daily worksheets and the weekly worksheet would be identical, except for the numbers. For such an application, it is to your advantage to create a template, save it, and then copy it eight times to a workbook, once for each day of the week and once for the end-of-the-week summary.

Finally, this project introduces you to using the Find and Replace commands.

E209

▶ Project 4 — Beaviston Public Safety Division Budget Proposal

In June of each year, the controller for the town of Beaviston, Florida tenders to the town board a preliminary Public Safety Division budget for the next year. The Public Safety Division is made up of the Fire, Police, and Streets and Sanitation departments. Each of the three departments develops its own budget proposal for the upcoming year, which also includes the current year's budget and the variance between the two years. The individual department budget proposals are submitted to the controller and consolidated onto one budget proposal for the Public Safety Division. An example of the consolidation process is shown in Figure 4-1. Graphs that compare the next year's budget proposal to the current year's budget are included to illustrate the variances.

FIGURE 4-1

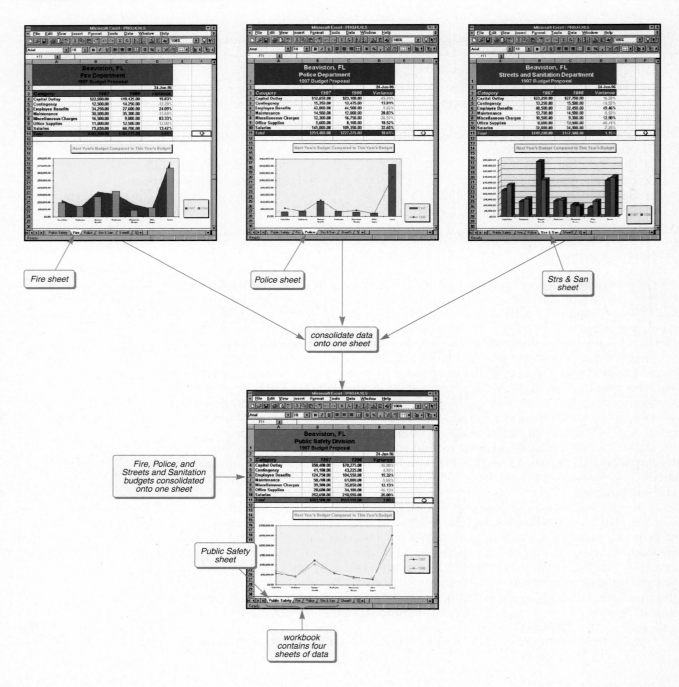

Because the three departments and division worksheets are similar, a template (Figure 4-2) is first created and then copied four times into the Public Safety Division Budget Proposal workbook. Thus, the objective of Project 4 is to create the template and use it to build the workbook made up of four sheets, one for each department and one for the division.

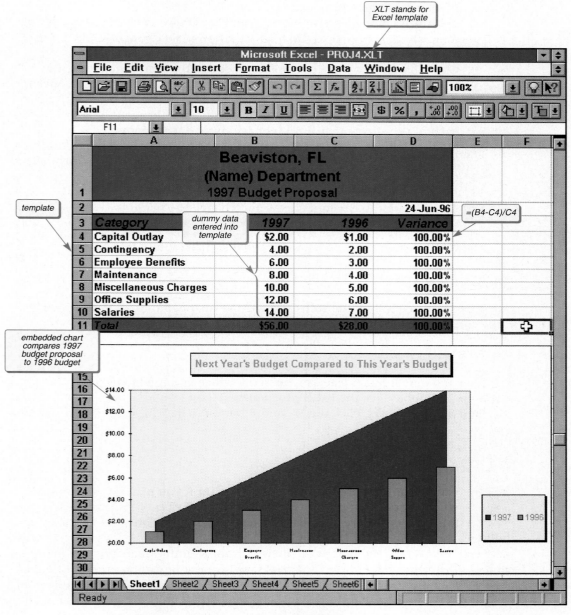

FIGURE 4-2

Template and Workbook Preparation Steps

The following list is an overview of how to build the template shown in Figure 4-2 and the workbook shown in Figure 4-1. If you are building the template and workbook on a personal computer, read these 14 steps without doing them.

1. Start the Excel program.
2. Apply the bold style to all the cells in the worksheet.

3. Increase the width of columns A through D, enter the worksheet titles, row titles, column titles, and system date.

4. Use the fill handle to enter dummy data for the 1996 budget and 1997 proposed budget. Next, determine department totals and enter the variance formulas in column D.

5. Save the workbook as a template using the filename PROJ4.XLT.

6. Format the template.

7. Create an embedded combination area and column chart as part of the template that compares the next year's proposed budget to the current year's budget. Format the chart.

8. Check spelling, save the template a second time, and then close it.

9. Open the template. Copy Sheet1 to Sheet2, Sheet3, and Sheet4. Save the workbook as PROJ4.XLS.

10. Modify the worksheet title, enter the data, and change the chart type on each of the sheets that represent the three departments.

11. Modify the worksheet title of the division sheet. Enter the SUM function and copy it to consolidate the data found on the three department sheets. Change the chart type.

12. Add workbook documentation to a cell on the division sheet.

13. Add a header to the four sheets and change the margins.

14. Save, preview, and print the workbook.

The following sections contain a detailed explanation of these steps.

Starting Excel

To start Excel, follow the steps you used at the beginning of Project 1. These steps are summarized below.

TO START EXCEL

Step 1: From Program Manager, open the Office group window.
Step 2: Double-click the Excel program-item icon.
Step 3: If necessary, click the Maximize button to maximize the Book1 window.

▶ CREATING THE TEMPLATE

L earning how to use templates is important if you plan to use a similar worksheet design in your workbooks. In the case of Project 4, there are four sheets (Figure 4-1) that are nearly identical. Thus, the first step in building the Public Safety Division Budget Proposal workbook is to create a template (Figure 4-2) that contains the labels, formulas, and formats that are found on each of the sheets. Once the template is saved to disk, it can be used as often as required to initiate a new workbook. Many worksheet users create a template for each application on which they work. The templates can be as simple as containing a special font you want to use in an application to more complex entries as is the case in the template for Project 4.

You create and modify a template using the same techniques you used in the worksheets in previous projects. The only difference between a worksheet and a template is in the way in which it is saved.

Bolding the Font and Changing Column Widths of the Template

The first step in this project is to change the font of the entire template to bold so all entries are emphasized and change the column widths as follows: A = 22.00 and B through D = 14.00.

TO BOLD THE FONT IN THE TEMPLATE AND CHANGE COLUMN WIDTHS

Step 1: Click the Select All button immediately above row heading 1 and to the left of column heading A.

Step 2: Click the Bold button on the Standard toolbar. Select cell A1.

Step 3: Move the mouse pointer to the border between column heading A and column heading B so the mouse pointer shape changes to a split double arrow. Drag the mouse pointer to the right until the width displayed in the reference area in the formula bar is equal to 22.00 and then release the left mouse button.

Step 4: Select columns B through D by pointing to column heading B and dragging though column heading D. Move the mouse pointer to the borderline between column headings D and E and drag the mouse to the right until the width displayed in the reference area is 14.00. Release the left mouse button.

Column A has a width of 22.00 and columns B through D have a width of 14.00.

Entering the Template Title and Row Titles

There are three lines of text in the template title in cell A1. To enter the three lines of text in one cell, press ALT+ENTER after each of the first two lines. After the third line, press the ENTER key or click the check box in the formula bar or press an arrow key as you have done in previous projects to complete a cell entry. You enter the row titles using the same steps as in earlier projects.

TO ENTER THE TEMPLATE TITLE AND ROW TITLES

Step 1: Select cell A1. Type `Beaviston, FL` and press ALT+ENTER. Type `(Name) Department` and press ALT+ENTER. Type `1997 Budget Proposal` and press the DOWN ARROW key twice.

Step 2: With cell A3 selected, type `Category` and press the DOWN ARROW key.

Step 3: Enter the remaining row titles in column A as shown in Figure 4-3 on the next page.

FIGURE 4-3

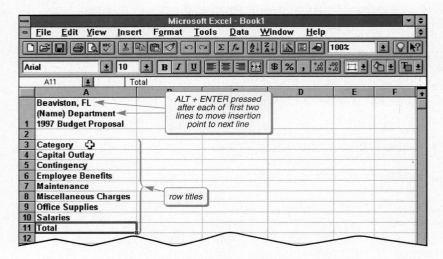

Pressing ALT+ENTER after each line in the template title in cell A1 causes the insertion point to move down one line in the cell. This procedure allows you to control the width of each line of text entered into a cell.

Excel will **wrap** text to the next line when a word will not fit on a line in a cell instead of overflowing it into the cell to the right. However, you have to first select the Wrap Text check box on the Alignment tab. To display the Alignment tab, choose the Format Cells command on the shortcut menu and click the Alignment tab.

Entering the Template Column Titles and System Date

The next step is to enter the column titles in row 3 and the system date in cell D2. If a cell entry contains only digits, such as 1997, then Excel considers it to be numeric. Because of the method this project presents to determine the sums in columns B and C and the chart range that will be selected later, enter the two numeric entries in row 3 as text. To enter a number as text, begin it with an apostrophe (') as shown in the following steps. The apostrophe (') is found on the key with the quotation marks (").

TO ENTER THE TEMPLATE COLUMN TITLES AND SYSTEM DATE ▼

STEP 1 ▶

Select cell B3. Type ′ 1997 and press the RIGHT ARROW key. Type ′ 1996 and press the RIGHT ARROW key. Type Variance and press the ENTER key.

STEP 2 ▶

Select the range B3:D3 and click the Align Right button on the Formatting toolbar.

STEP 3 ▶

Select cell D2. Type =now() and click the enter box or press the ENTER key.

The column titles and system date display as shown in Figure 4-4.

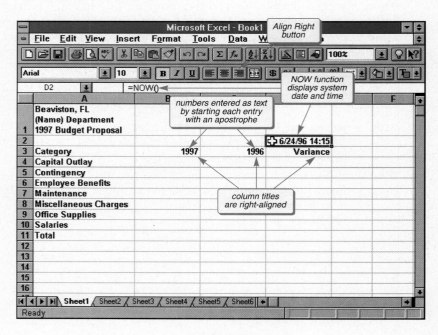

FIGURE 4-4

STEP 4 ▶

With the mouse pointer in cell D2, click the right mouse button and choose the Format Cells command. When the Format Cells dialog box displays, click the Number tab. Select Date in the Category box and d-mmm-yy in the Format Codes box. Choose the OK button.

The system date displays using the new format (Figure 4-5).

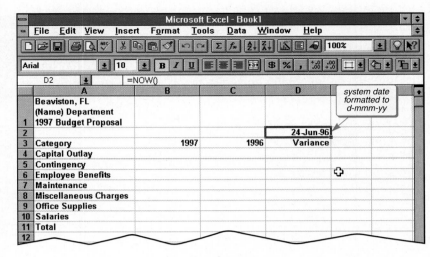

FIGURE 4-5

Entering Dummy Numbers and Summing Them in the Template

Dummy numbers are used in place of actual data in a template to verify the formulas. Usually, you select numbers that allow you to quickly check if the formulas are generating the proper results. In Project 4, the budget category dollar amounts are entered into the range B4:C10. The following steps use the fill handle to create a series of numbers in column B that begins with 2 and increments by 2 and a series of numbers in column C that begins with 1 and increments by 1. Recall from Project 3, to create a series, you must enter the first two numbers so Excel can determine the increment amount.

TO ENTER DUMMY NUMBERS AND SUM THEM IN THE TEMPLATE ▼

STEP 1 ▶

Enter 2 in cell B4, 4 in cell B5, 1 in cell C4, and 2 in cell C5. Select the range B4:C5 and drag the fill handle through cells B10 and C10.

Excel surrounds the range B4:C10 with a dark grey border (Figure 4-6).

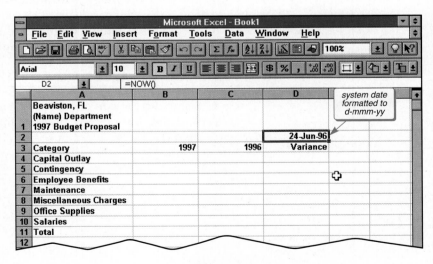

FIGURE 4-6

STEP 2 ►

Release the left mouse button.
Select the range B11:C11, and click
the AutoSum button on the Standard
toolbar.

*Excel assigns the sum of the val-
ues in the range B4:B10 to cell
B11 and the sum of the values in
the range C4:C10 to cell C11
(Figure 4-7).*

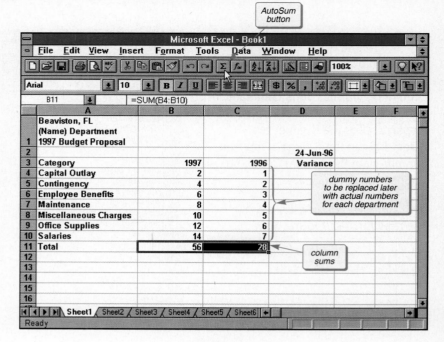

FIGURE 4-7

Notice, if 1997 in cell B3 and 1996 in cell C3 had been entered as numbers,
then Excel would have included them in the sums. Because they were entered
with an initial apostrophe, Excel considers them to be text, and therefore, does
not include them in the ranges to sum in cells B11 and C11.

Entering the Variance Formula in the Template

The variances in column D (see Figure 4-1 on page E210) are equal to the corresponding 1997 budget amount less the 1996 budget amount divided by the 1996
budget amount. For example, the formula to enter in cell D4 is =(B4-C4)/C4. This
formula displays a decimal result that indicates the percent increase or decrease in
the 1997 budget amount when compared to the 1996 budget amount. Once the
formula is entered into cell D4, it can be copied to the range D5:D11.

TO ENTER THE VARIANCE FORMULA IN THE TEMPLATE

Step 1: Select cell D4 and enter =(B4-C4)/C4
Step 2: With cell D4 selected, drag the fill handle down through cell D11, and
then release the left mouse button. Select cell F11.

*The formula is entered into cell D4 and copied to the range D5:D11 (Figure
4-8).*

Excel displays a 1 in each cell in the range D4:D11 because the numbers in column B are twice the corresponding numbers in column C. Thus, the 1s in column D represent 100% proposed budget increases between 1996 and 1997. Later, when the actual budget numbers replace the dummy numbers in columns B and C, these percent values will be different. Shortly, column D will be formatted so the numbers display as percents instead of whole numbers.

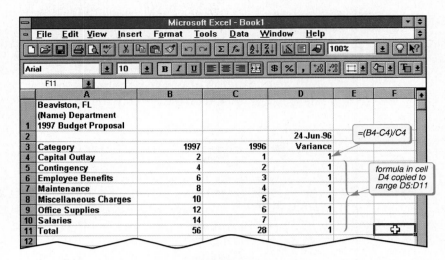

FIGURE 4-8

Saving the Template

Saving a template is accomplished in the same fashion as saving a workbook described in previous projects, except that you select Template in the Save File as Type box in the Save As dialog box. Excel saves the template with an extension of **.XLT**, which stands for Excel Template.

TO SAVE A TEMPLATE ▼

STEP 1 ▶

Click the Save button on the Standard toolbar. When the Save As dialog box displays, type `proj4` in the File Name box. Select drive A in the Drives drop-down list box.

STEP 2 ▶

Select Template from the Save File as Type drop-down list box.

The Save As dialog box displays as shown in Figure 4-9.

STEP 3 ▶

Choose the OK button. You may optionally enter summary information in the Summary Information dialog box. Choose the OK button.

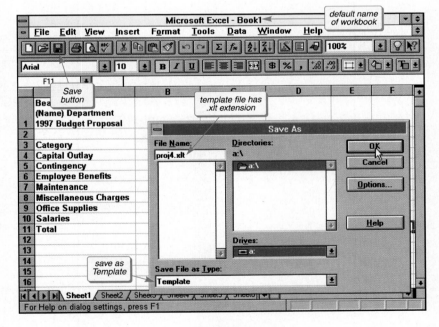

FIGURE 4-9

Excel saves the template proj4.xlt to the disk in drive A. The filename PROJ4.XLT displays in the title bar as shown in Figure 4-10.

The **Save File As Type box** allows you to save an Excel workbook in many different forms. For example, you can save a workbook (only the active sheet) as an ASCII file. A file stored in **ASCII file format** can be read by any software package. You can also save workbooks so other spreadsheet software such as Lotus 1-2-3 and Quattro Pro can read them.

▶ FORMATTING THE TEMPLATE

T he next step is to format the template so it displays as shown in Figure 4-10. Keep in mind that the formats selected will show up in each of the sheets for which the template is used. The following list summarizes the sequence of formatting to be applied.

1. Change the font size of the template title in cell A1. Center cell A1 across columns A through D.
2. Italicize and change the font size of the column titles in row 3. Italicize the row title Total in cell A11.
3. Assign the background color teal and a heavy border to the nonadjacent ranges A1:D1, A3:D3, and A11:D11.
4. Apply a Currency format to the nonadjacent ranges B4:C4 and B11:D11. Apply a Comma format to the range B5:C10.
5. Apply a Percent format to the range D4:D11.

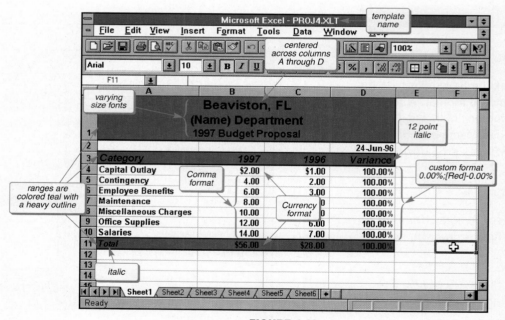

FIGURE 4-10

Applying Formats to the Template Title

To emphasize the template title in cell A1, the font size will be changed to the following: line 1 = 16 point; line 2 = 14 point; and line 3 = 12 point. Recall from page E85 in Project 2 that you can assign font sizes to individual characters or groups of characters in a cell. The following steps change the font size and center the template title across columns A through D. After the font size of the text in cell A1 is changed, but before it is centered, the text will wrap on several lines. As soon as cell A1 is centered across columns A through D, the text will wrap on three lines.

TO APPLY FORMATS TO THE TEMPLATE TITLES

Step 1: Double-click cell A1 to activate in-cell editing. Drag across the first line of text. Click the Font Size arrow on the Formatting toolbar and choose 16 point.

Step 2: With in-cell editing still active in cell A1, use the techniques described in Step 1 to change the font size of line 2 to 14 point and line 3 to 12 point. Click the check box in the formula bar or press the ENTER key.

Step 3: With cell A1 selected, drag through cell D1. Click the Center Across Columns button on the Formatting toolbar.

Step 4: Select the range A3:D3. Click the Font Size arrow on the Formatting toolbar and choose 12 point. Click the Italic button on the Formatting toolbar.

Step 5: Select cell A11 and click the Italic button on the Formatting toolbar.

The template displays as shown in Figure 4-11.

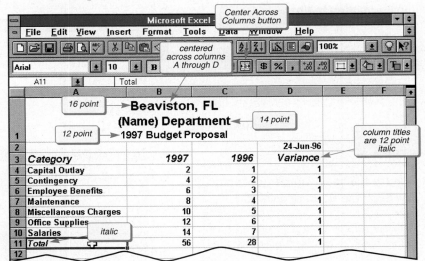

FIGURE 4-11

To help make the titles stand out even more, the background colors will be changed and a heavy outline will be drawn around these three areas.

TO CHANGE THE BACKGROUND COLOR AND ADD AN OUTLINE ▼

STEP 1 ▶

Hold down the CTRL key and drag through the ranges A1:D1, A3:D3, and A11:D11. Click the Color button arrow on the Formatting toolbar.

The Color palette displays (Figure 4-12).

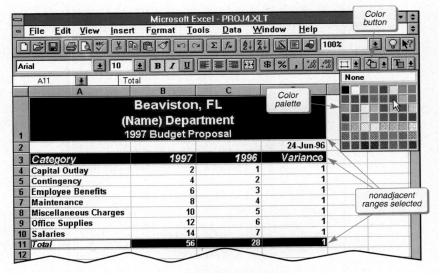

FIGURE 4-12

STEP 2 ▶

Choose teal (column 6, row 2) on the Color palette.

STEP 3 ▶

Click the Borders button arrow on the Formatting toolbar.

The Borders palette displays (Figure 4-13).

FIGURE 4-13

STEP 4 ▶

Choose the heavy border (column 4, row 3) on the Borders palette.

The template title, column titles, and total row display as shown in Figure 4-14.

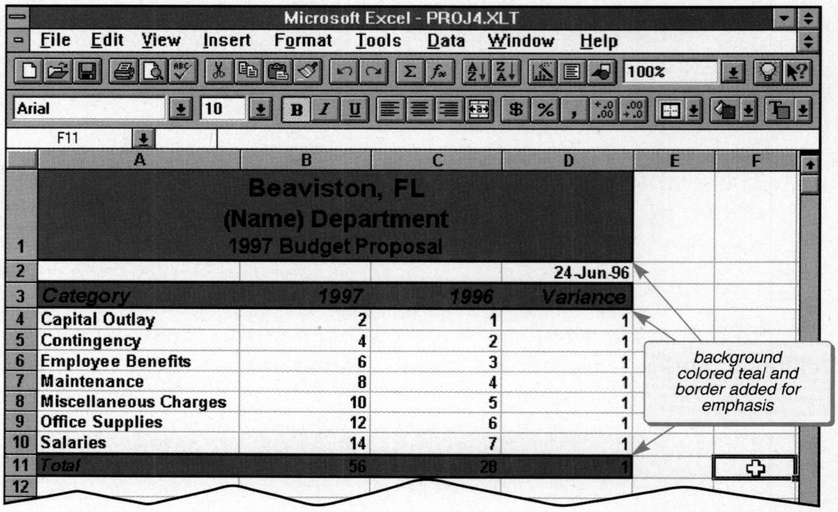

FIGURE 4-14

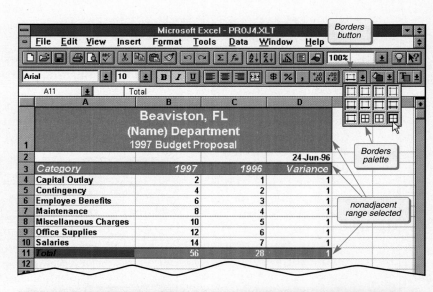

Applying Number Formats from the Format Cells Dialog Box

The first three projects used the buttons on the Formatting toolbar to apply format codes to the numbers in cells. These buttons offer limited formatting choices. Using the Format Cells dialog box, you can select from a larger number of format codes. A **format code** is a series of format symbols that define a format. For example, earlier in this project you formatted the system date in cell D2 using the format code d-mmm-yy.

The template in this project (see Figure 4-2 on page E211) calls for following the standard accounting convention for a table of numbers by adding dollar signs to the first row of numbers (row 3) and the totals row (row 11). To accomplish this task, you could select the range and click the Currency style button on the Formatting toolbar. However, the format code applied to the selected cells would result in applying a fixed dollar sign. A **fixed dollar sign** always displays in the same position in a cell regardless of the number of digits in the number. The alternative to a fixed dollar sign is a floating dollar sign. A **floating dollar sign** always displays immediately to the left of the first significant digit. Because this project uses a floating dollar sign, a format code must be selected in the Format Cells dialog box, instead of using the Currency Style button.

The following steps apply a format code to the ranges B4:C4 and B11:C11 using the Format Cells command on the shortcut menu. The steps then use the Comma Style button on the Formatting toolbar to format the range B5:C10.

TO APPLY A FORMAT CODE FROM THE FORMAT DIALOG BOX

STEP 1 ▶

Select the nonadjacent range B4:C4 and B11:C11 by holding down the CTRL key when you select the second range.

STEP 2 ▶

With the mouse pointer in one of the two selected areas, click the right mouse button.

Excel displays the shortcut menu (Figure 4-15).

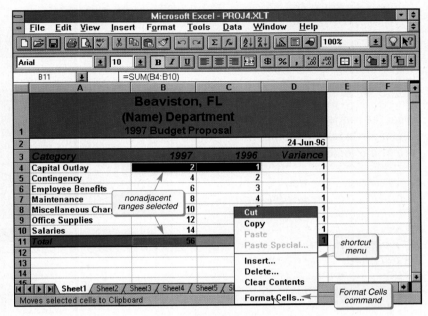

FIGURE 4-15

STEP 3 ▶

Choose the Format Cells command from the shortcut menu.

Excel displays the Format cells dialog box.

STEP 4 ▶

Click the Number tab. Select Currency in the Category box and the format code $#,##0.00_);($#,##0.00) in the Format Codes box.

The Format Cells dialog box displays as shown in Figure 4-16.

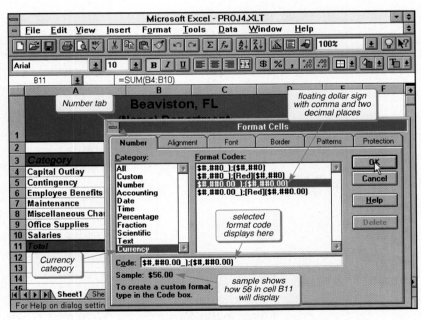

FIGURE 4-16

STEP 5 ▶

Choose the OK button in the Format Cells dialog box.

The selected ranges display as shown in Figure 4-17.

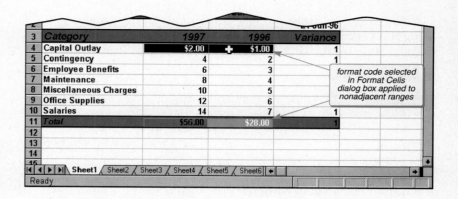

FIGURE 4-17

STEP 6 ▶

Select the range B5:C10 and click the Comma Style button on the Formatting toolbar.

Excel displays the numbers in the range B5:C10 using the Comma format (Figure 4-18). Later when larger numbers are entered into the worksheets that are based on the template, these numbers will include a comma.

FIGURE 4-18

Each format symbol within the format code $#,##0.00_);($#,##0.00) selected in Step 4 has special meaning. Table 4-1 summarizes the most frequently used format symbols and their meanings. For a complete listing of the format symbols, choose the Search for Help on command from the Help menu. Next, type `format codes` in the top box, and click the Show Topics button. When Number Format Codes displays in the lower box, choose the Go To button. Excel displays a table consisting of all the format symbols.

A format code can have up to four sections: positive numbers, negative numbers, zeros, and text as shown below. Each section is divided by a semicolon.

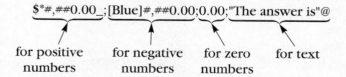

$*#,##0.00_;[Blue]#,##0.00;0.00;"The answer is"@

    for positive   for negative   for zero   for text
    numbers   numbers   numbers

For most applications, a format code will only have a positive section and, possibly, a negative section.

Creating a Customized Format Code

The next step is to format the variances in the range D4:D11. This project requires that positive numbers in this range display using the format code 0.00%. Negative numbers display in red using a format code of 0.00% with a leading minus sign. The required format code is 0.00%;[Red]-0.00%. As shown in

▶ **TABLE 4-1**

FORMAT SYMBOL	EXAMPLE OF SYMBOL	DESCRIPTION
General	General	Displays the number in General format, which means no dollar signs, no commas, no decimal point unless required, or no trailing zeros to the right of the decimal point.
#	###.##	Digit placeholder. If there are more digits to the right than there are number signs, Excel rounds the number. Extra digits to the left are displayed.
0 (zero)	#,##0.00	Same as number sign (#), except that if the number is less than one, Excel displays a zero in place of the one.
. (period)	#0.00	Ensures a decimal point will display in the number. Determines how many digits display to left and right of decimal point.
%	0.00%	Excel multiplies the value of the cell by 100 and displays a percent sign following the number.
, (comma)	#,##0.00	Displays the thousands separator.
$ or - or +	$#,##0.00;($#,##0.00)	Displays a floating dollar sign.
* (asterisk)	$* ##0.00	Displays a fixed sign ($, +, or -) to the left in cell followed by spaces until the first significant digit.
[color]	#.##;[Red]#.##	Displays the characters in the cell in the designated color. In the example, positive numbers display in the default color and negative numbers display in red.
_	#,##0.00_	Skips the width of the character that follows the underline.
()	#0.00;(#0.00)	Displays negative numbers surrounded by parentheses.

Figure 4-19, this format code is not available in the Percentage category in the Format Cells dialog box. Thus, it must be created by entering the format code in the Code box in the Format Cells dialog box. A format code that you create in the Code box is called a **custom format code**.

TO CREATE A CUSTOM FORMAT CODE ▼

FIGURE 4-19

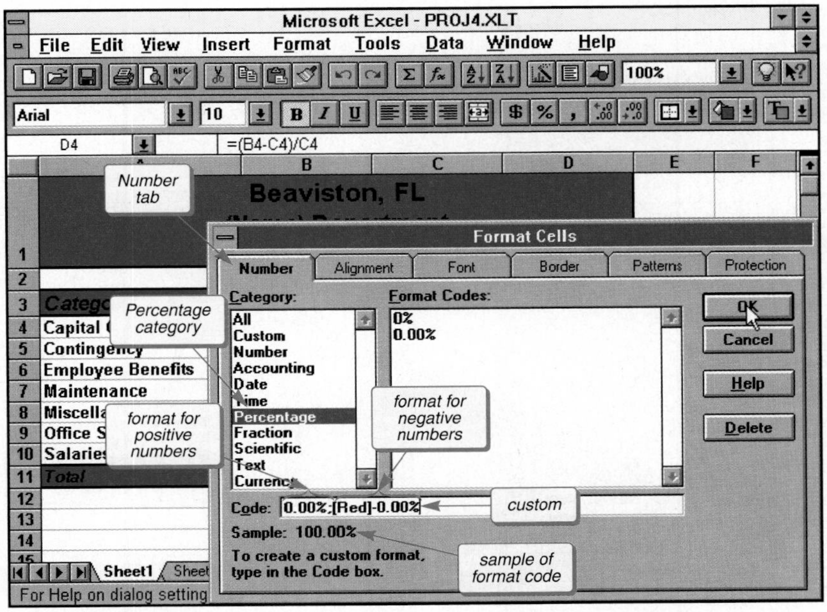

STEP 1 ▶

Select the range D4:D11. With the mouse pointer in the selected range, click the right mouse button. Choose the Format Cells command. When the Format Cells dialog box displays, select Percentage in the Category box to see if the required format code is available.

STEP 2 ▶

Because the format code is not available, click in the Code box and type 0.00%;[Red]-0.00%

The Format Cells dialog box displays as shown in Figure 4-19.
Make sure you type zeros and not the letter O in the code box.

STEP 3 ▶

Choose the OK button.

The percents in the range D4:D11 display as shown in Figure 4-20.

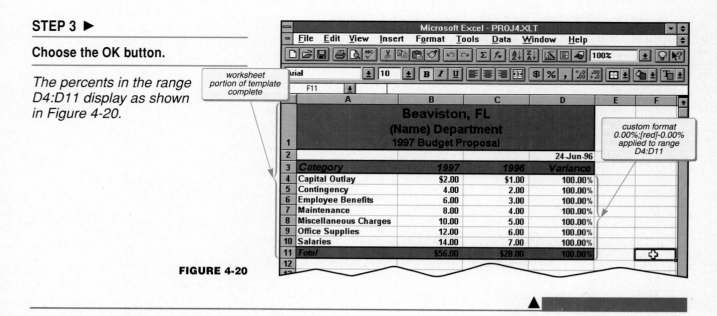

FIGURE 4-20

When you create a custom format code, Excel displays it in the Format Codes box to make it available for other cells in the workbook.

The worksheet portion of the template is complete. Save the template to disk as PROJ4.XLT before continuing with this project.

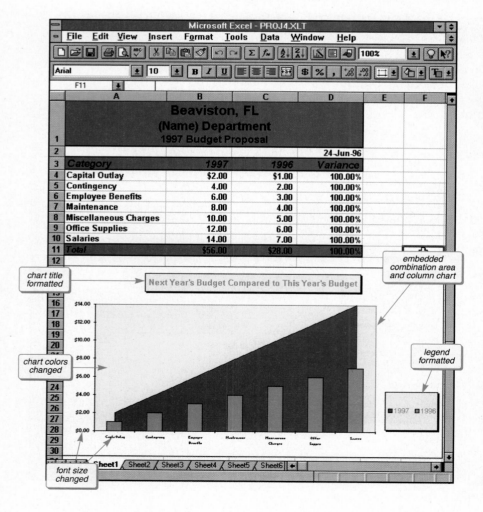

FIGURE 4-21

▶ ADDING A CHART TO THE TEMPLATE

The next step is to add an embedded combination area and column chart to the template in the range A13:F30 using the ChartWizard button on the Standard toolbar. The **combination area and column chart** allows you to compare two sets of numbers in one chart. In the proposed budget template, the chart compares next year's proposed budget (area) to the current year budget (column) as shown in Figure 4-21.

After creating the chart in this section, formats will be applied to the chart title, legends, and font along the axis. Techniques are then presented to resize and change the color of the chart.

Creating an Embedded Chart Using the ChartWizard Button

Recall from Project 1 that an embedded chart is one that resides on the same sheet as the numbers being charted. To create a combination area and column chart that compares next year's proposed budget to this year's budget, perform the following steps.

TO DRAW AN EMBEDDED COMBINATION AREA AND COLUMN CHART ▼

STEP 1 ▶

Select the range A3:C10. Click the ChartWizard button on the Standard toolbar and move the mouse pointer to the upper left corner of cell A13.

A marquis surrounds the range to chart, A3:C10. The mouse pointer shape changes to a cross hair with a chart symbol (Figure 4-22).

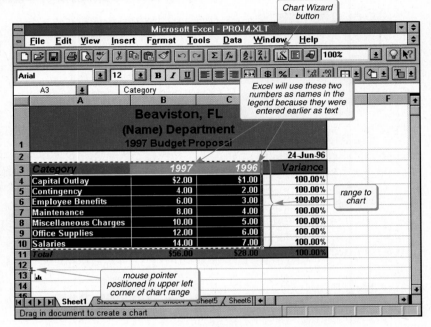

FIGURE 4-22

STEP 2 ▶

Hold down the ALT key and drag the mouse pointer to the lower right corner of the chart location (cell F30). Release the left mouse button and then release the ALT key.

The mouse pointer is positioned at the lower right corner of cell F30, and the chart area is surrounded by a solid line rectangle (Figure 4-23). Holding down the ALT key while you drag snaps the rectangle to the cell edge nearest the mouse pointer.

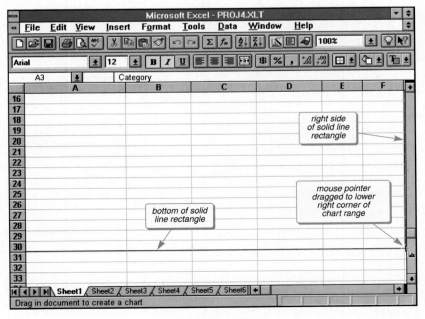

FIGURE 4-23

STEP 3 ▶

Release the left mouse button.

Excel responds by displaying the ChartWizard - Step 1 of 5 dialog box (Figure 4-24).The Range box contains the chart range. In this dialog box, you can change the range by typing a new one or dragging on a new range in the template.

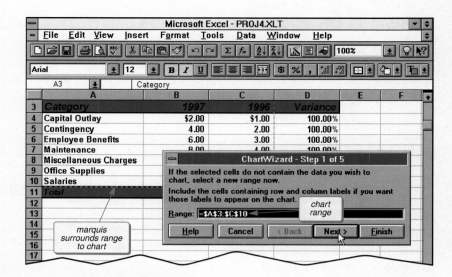

FIGURE 4-24

STEP 4 ▶

Choose the Next button in the ChartWizard – Step 1 of 5 dialog box.

The ChartWizard – Step 2 of 5 dialog box displays with fifteen charts from which to choose.

STEP 5 ▶

Select Combination (column 4, row 2).

Excel highlights the Combination chart type (Figure 4-25).

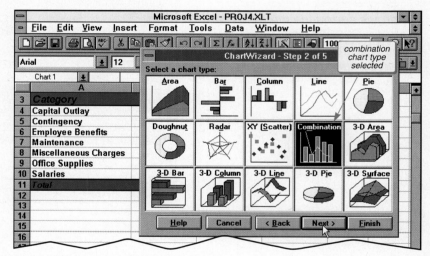

FIGURE 4-25

STEP 6 ▶

Choose the Next button in the ChartWizard – Step 2 of 5 dialog box.

The ChartWizard – Step 3 of 5 dialog box displays with six different built-in combination chart formats from which to choose.

STEP 7 ▶

Select box 4, the one with the area and column charts.

Excel highlights the selected combination chart format (Figure 4-26).

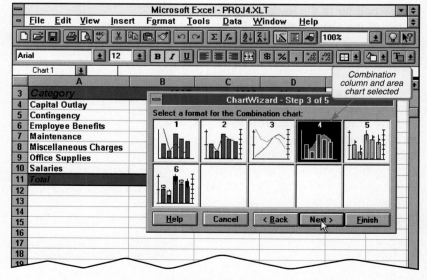

FIGURE 4-26

STEP 8 ▶

Choose the Next button in the ChartWizard – Step 3 of 5 dialog box.

The ChartWizard – Step 4 of 5 dialog box displays showing a sample of the combination chart (Figure 4-27).

FIGURE 4-27

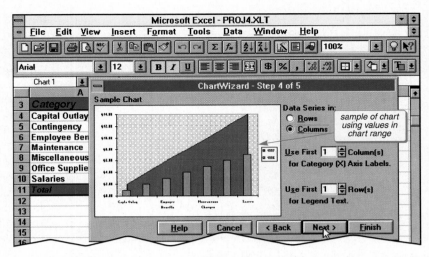

STEP 9 ▶

Choose the Next button in the ChartWizard – Step 4 of 5 dialog box.

The ChartWizard -– Step 5 of 5 dialog box displays. In this dialog box, you can add a chart title.

STEP 10 ▶

In the Chart Title box, type Next Year's Budget Compared to This Year's Budget **as shown in Figure 4-28.**

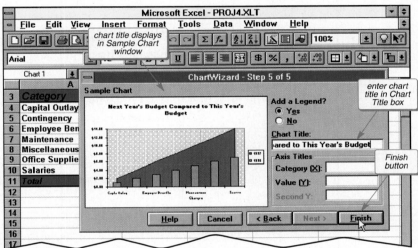

FIGURE 4-28

STEP 11 ▶

Choose the Finish button on the ChartWizard – Step 5 of 5 dialog box.

Excel draws the combination chart in the range A13:F30, selects it, and displays it (Figure 4-29). Notice that not all category names display along the horizontal axis. This problem will be resolved shortly.

FIGURE 4-29

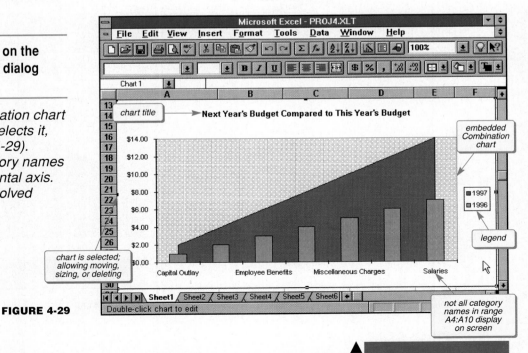

The embedded column chart in Figure 4-29 on the previous page compares the six budget categories proposed for next year (range B4:B10) to the six budget categories for this year (range C4:C10). The legend on the right side contains the two labels (1997 and 1996) in cells B3 and C3. Because the dummy numbers increase in a linear fashion in the worksheet portion of the template, the area and column charts also increase in a linear fashion from left to right.

Formatting the Chart Title

Before you can format a chart item in an embedded chart, the chart must be active. You activate a chart by double-clicking anywhere within the chart area. An active chart has a heavy gray border surrounding it. An **active chart** is different from a selected chart. A **selected chart** has a thin border with handles surrounding it. You *select* a chart to resize it or move it to another area on the sheet. You *activate* a chart to format it. Perform the following steps to activate the chart and format the chart title.

TO FORMAT THE CHART TITLE

Step 1: Double-click the embedded chart. Click the chart title. The embedded chart is surrounded by a heavy gray border. The chart title is surrounded by a heavy dark border.

Step 2: Click the Color button arrow and choose pale yellow (column 4, row 5) on the Color palette.

Step 3: Click the Font Color button arrow and choose red (column 3, row 1) on the Font Color palette.

Step 4: Click the Drawing button on the Standard toolbar. Dock the Drawing toolbar at the bottom of the window.

Step 5: Click the Drop Shadow button on the Drawing toolbar. Click outside the chart title.

The chart title displays as shown in Figure 4-30.

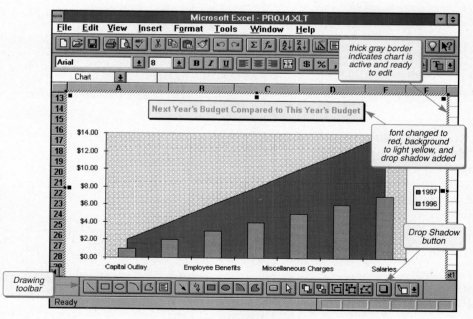

FIGURE 4-30

Resizing the Plot Area

The **plot area** is the rectangle (gray background in Figure 4-30) formed by the two axes in the chart area. The following steps show how to resize the plot area so the legend can be enlarged.

TO RESIZE THE PLOT AREA ▼

STEP 1 ▶

With the embedded chart active, click the gray colored background portion of the plot area. Point to the right center handle. Drag to the left approximately one inch.

The plot area is reduced in size (Figure 4-31).

STEP 2 ▶

Release the left mouse button.

The plot area is resized.

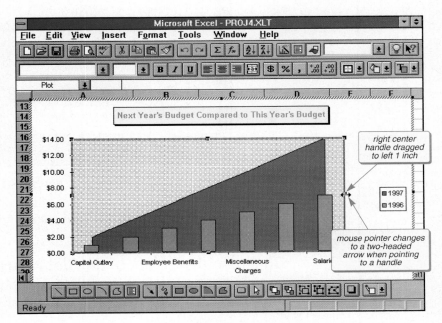

FIGURE 4-31

Formatting, Moving, and Resizing the Legend

The next step is to format, move, and resize the legend on the right side of the plot area. Perform the following steps.

TO FORMAT, MOVE, AND RESIZE THE LEGEND

Step 1: With the embedded chart active, select the legend by clicking on it. With the mouse pointer pointing to the center of the legend, drag it down to its new location (Figure 4-32 on the following page).

Step 2: Increase the size of the legend by dragging the handles so it is the same size as the legend in Figure 4-32.

Step 3: Click the Color button on the Formatting toolbar to change the background color to pale yellow.

Step 4: Click the Font Color button on the formatting toolbar to change the font color to red.

Step 5: Click the Drop Shadow button on the Drawing toolbar.

The legend displays as shown in Figure 4-32 on the following page.

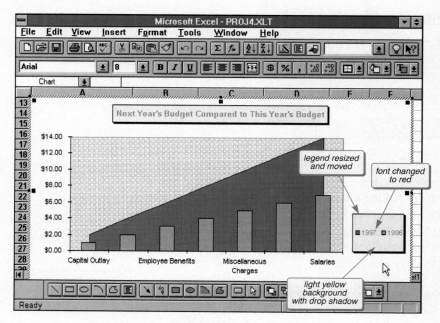

FIGURE 4-32

You can move the legend to any location in the chart area, including inside the plot area.

Changing the Colors of the Plot Area and Data Markers

The next step is to change the colors of the plot area and data markers. The **data markers** are the columns and purple area within the plot area.

TO CHANGE THE COLORS OF THE PLOT AREA AND DATA MARKERS

Step 1: With the chart area active, select the plot area by clicking it. Click the Color button on the Formatting toolbar to assign the color on the face of the Color button.

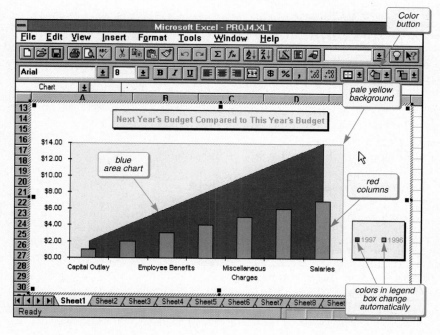

Step 2: Select all the columns by clicking one of them. Click the Color button arrow on the Formatting toolbar. Choose red (column 3, row 1) on the Color palette.

Step 3: Select the area chart by clicking it. Click the Color button arrow on the Formatting toolbar. Choose blue (column 1, row 4) on the Color palette.

The combination area and column chart appears as shown in Figure 4-33.

FIGURE 4-33

Notice that when you change the colors of the data markers, Excel also changes the colors of the identifiers within the legend.

Changing the Size of the Font on the Axes

The **category axis** (x-axis) is the horizontal line below the plot area in Figure 4-33. The **value axis** (y-axis) series is the vertical line to the left of the plot area. With the current size of the font (8 point) on the category axis, not all the labels display. Thus, the font size on the category axis must be reduced from 8 point to 4 point. To maintain a reasonable proportion between the labels on the axes, the font on the value axis will be changed to 6 point.

TO CHANGE THE SIZE OF THE FONT ON THE AXES

Step 1: Select the value axis (vertical axis) by pointing to it and clicking the left mouse button. Click in the Font Size box on the Formatting toolbar, type 6 and press the ENTER key.

Step 2: Select the category axis by pointing to it and clicking the left mouse button. Click in the Font Size box on the Formatting toolbar, type 4 and press the ENTER key.

The fonts along the axes display as shown in Figure 4-34.

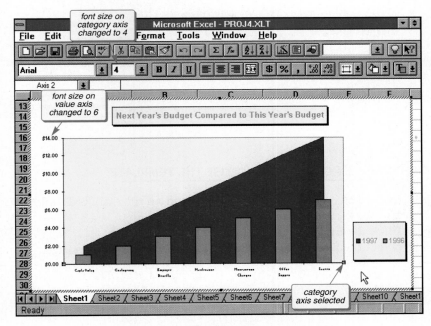

FIGURE 4-34

With the new font size (Figure 4-34), all seven category names display, instead of only four (Figure 4-33).

Checking Spelling, Saving, and Closing the Template

The template is complete (Figure 4-35). The next step is to check spelling, save the template, and then close it.

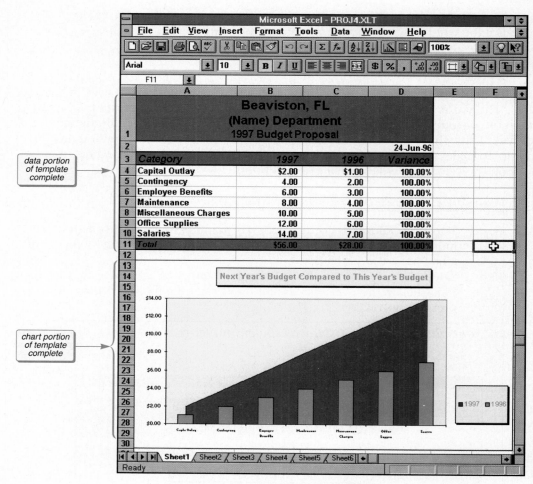

data portion
of template
complete

chart portion
of template
complete

FIGURE 4-35

TO CHECK SPELLING, SAVE, AND CLOSE THE TEMPLATE

Step 1: Select cell A1. Click the Spelling button on the Standard toolbar. Change any misspelled words.

Step 2: Click the Save button on the Standard toolbar.

Step 3: Select the File menu and choose the Close command.

The template is saved using the filename PROJ4.XLT. The template is removed from the Excel window.

▶ ALTERNATIVE USES OF TEMPLATES

Before continuing the use of templates to create the Public Safety Division Budget Proposal workbook, be aware that Excel provides additional uses of templates. You can specify font, formatting, column widths, or any other defaults by creating templates with the desired formats and saving them to the XLSTART subdirectory. The **XLSTART subdirectory** is called the **startup directory**. Templates stored in the XLSTART subdirectory are called **autotemplates**. After saving templates to this special subdirectory, you can select any one of them by choosing the **New command** from the File menu. If you store one of the templates in the XLSTART subdirectory using the filename BOOK.XLT, then Excel uses the formats you assigned to it every time you start Excel.

▶ CREATING A WORKBOOK FROM A TEMPLATE

With the template stored on disk, the second phase of this project involves using the template to create the Public Safety Division Budget Proposal workbook shown in Figure 4-1 on page E210. To create the new workbook, open the template. Next, use the Select All button to select the sheet the template is on and then copy it to the Clipboard. Click the Sheet2 tab and paste the Clipboard's contents. In similar fashion, paste the Clipboard's contents to sheet 3 and sheet 4. With the template copied to the four sheets, save the workbook using the filename PROJ4.XLS. The following steps create and save the Public Safety Division Budget Proposal workbook.

TO CREATE A WORKBOOK FROM A TEMPLATE ▼

STEP 1 ▶

Click the Open button on the Standard toolbar. When the Open dialog box displays, select drive A and select the template PROJ4.XLT. Choose the OK button in the Open dialog box. Excel opens the template PROJ4.XLT and changes the name in the title bar to Proj41.

Excel changes the name in the title bar to ensure that the workbook will not be mistakenly saved in place of the template PROJ4.XLT.

STEP 2 ▶

Click the Select All button and click the Copy button on the Standard toolbar.

The template is selected as shown in Figure 4-36. The template is also on the Clipboard.

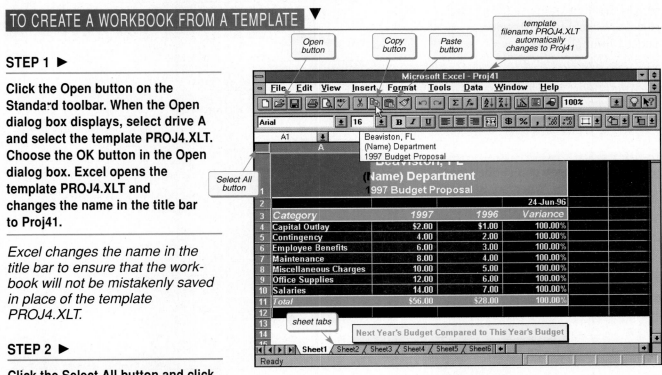

FIGURE 4-36

STEP 3 ▶

Click the Sheet2 tab. Click the Paste button on the Standard toolbar. Click the Sheet3 tab. Click the Paste button on the Standard toolbar. Click the Sheet4 tab. Click the Paste button on the Standard toolbar.

STEP 4 ▶

With Sheet4 tab active, hold down the SHIFT key and click the Sheet1 tab to select all four sheets. Click cell F11 so it is the active cell on all sheets. Hold down the SHIFT key and click the Sheet4 tab to deselect Sheet 1 through Sheet 3.

Excel removes the highlight from the four sheets and displays Sheet4 with cell F11 selected.

STEP 5

Select the File menu and choose the Save As command. When the Save As dialog box displays, type `PROJ4` in the File Name box. Select drive A. Choose the OK button.

Excel saves the Public Safety Division Budget Proposal workbook with four identical sheets to drive A using the filename PROJ4.XLS (Figure 4-37).

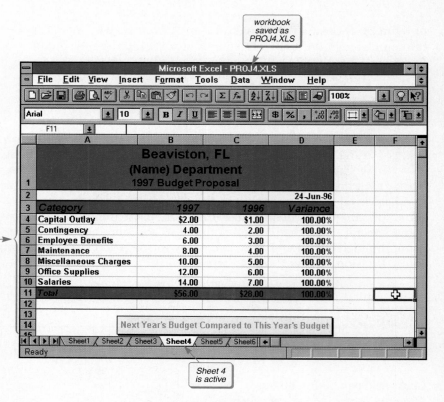

FIGURE 4-37

Modifying the Fire Sheet

   With the skeleton of the Public Safety Division Budget Proposal workbook created, the next step is to modify the individual sheets. The following steps change the title of the Fire sheet and enter the Fire Department's proposed budget numbers.

TO MODIFY THE FIRE SHEET

Step 1: Double-click the Sheet1 tab. When the Rename dialog box displays, type `Fire` in the Name box. Choose the OK button.
Step 2: Double-click cell A1, double-click (Name) in line 2, and type `Fire`
Step 3: Enter the data in Table 4-2 in the range B4:C10.
Step 4: Click the Save button on the Standard toolbar.

The Fire sheet displays as shown in Figure 4-38.

▸ **TABLE 4-2**

CELL	VALUE	CELL	VALUE
B4	22500	C4	19425
B5	12500	C5	14250
B6	34250	C6	27600
B7	30500	C7	35300
B8	16500	C8	9000
B9	11000	C9	12500
B10	75650	C10	66700

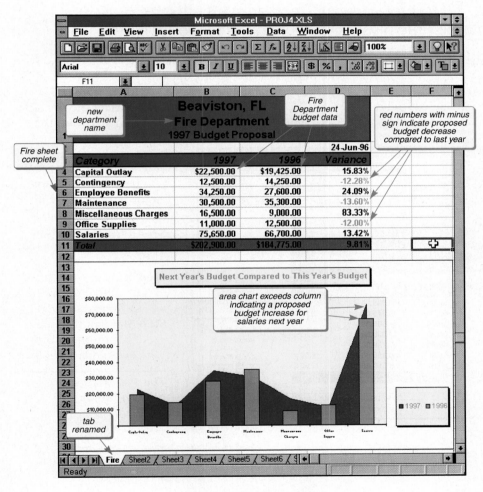

FIGURE 4-38

Notice as you enter the new data, Excel immediately updates the variances, displaying negative variances in red. In addition, Excel redraws the combination area and column chart found below the worksheet each time you enter a new value.

Modifying the Police Sheet

Three additional items that were not a problem with Fire sheet must be modified in the remaining three sheets as follows:

1. To differentiate between the four sheets in the workbook, the titles and total row are formatted with different colors. For example, the Police sheet uses white characters on a blue background.
2. Because of the way the sheets were created (copy and paste), the charts on the second, third, and fourth sheets all refer to the range A3:C10 on the Fire sheet. Thus, the charts will not be linked to the worksheet on the same sheet, unless the chart range is changed.
3. Each sheet has a different combination chart (see Figure 4-1 on page E210). Therefore, the chart type must be changed on the last three sheets.

The following steps modify the worksheet portion of the Police sheet.

TO MODIFY THE SPREADSHEET PORTION OF THE POLICE SHEET

Step 1: Double-click the Sheet2 tab. When the Rename dialog box displays, type `Police` in the Name box. Choose the OK button.

Step 2: Double-click cell A1 and replace (Name) in line 2 with `Police`

Step 3: Select the range A1:D1. Hold down the **CTRL** key and select the nonadjacent ranges A3:D3 and A11:D11. Click the Color button arrow on the Formatting toolbar. Choose blue (column 1, row 4) on the Color palette. Click the Font Color button arrow on the Formatting toolbar. Choose white (column 2, row 1) on the Font Color palette.

Step 4: Enter the data in Table 4-3 in the range B4:C10.

Step 5: Click the Save button on the Standard toolbar.

The Police sheet displays as shown in Figure 4-39.

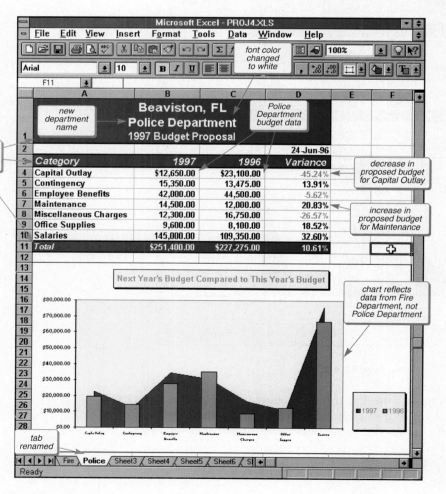

FIGURE 4-39

▶ **TABLE 4-3**

CELL	VALUE	CELL	VALUE
B4	12650	C4	23100
B5	15350	C5	13475
B6	42000	C6	44500
B7	14500	C7	12000
B8	12300	C8	16750
B9	9600	C9	8100
B10	145000	C10	109350

Notice in Figure 4-39, that although new data was entered into the Police sheet, its chart has not changed. In fact, the chart in Figure 4-39 is identical to the chart in Figure 4-38. This is because the Police sheet was created by copying the Fire sheet. The following steps change the chart range so it corresponds to the worksheet on the Police sheet.

TO CHANGE THE CHART RANGE ▼

STEP 1 ▶

Activate the chart on the Police sheet by double-clicking it.

A heavy gray border surrounds the chart. You may end up with the chart displaying in its own window. If this happens, click any cell in the worksheet and reduce the size of the chart so it fits in the window. Then double-click the chart again.

STEP 2 ▶

Click the ChartWizard button on the Standard toolbar.

Excel displays the ChartWizard – Step 1 of 2 dialog box which contains the Range box.

STEP 3 ▶

Drag over the sheet reference Fire! in the Range box.

The sheet reference is highlighted in the Range box (Figure 4-40).

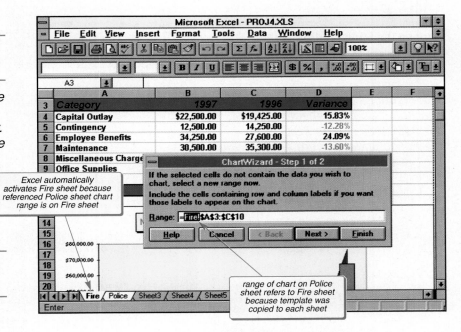

FIGURE 4-40

STEP 4 ▶

Press the DELETE key. Point to the Finish button in the ChartWizard – Step 1 of 2 dialog box.

The sheet reference Fire! disappears from the range box (Figure 4-41). When there is no sheet reference in the Range box, the range refers to the sheet the embedded chart is on.

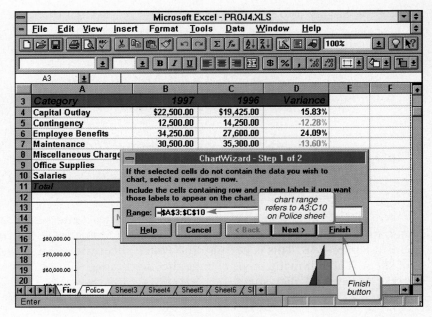

FIGURE 4-41

STEP 5 ▶

Choose the Finish button in the ChartWizard – Step 1 of 2 dialog box.

The combination area and column chart on the Police sheet reflect the data in the range A3:C10 of the Police sheet (Figure 4-42).

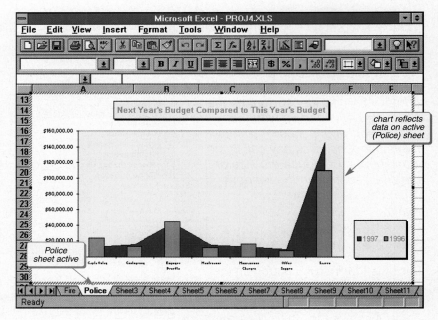

FIGURE 4-42

The next step is to change the chart type from a combination area and column chart to a combination line and column chart.

TO CHANGE THE CHART TYPE ▼

STEP 1 ►

If the embedded chart on the Police sheet is not active, double-click it.

A heavy gray border surrounds the chart.

STEP 2 ►

With the mouse within the chart area, click the right mouse button.

Excel displays a shortcut menu.

STEP 3 ►

Choose the AutoFormat command. When the AutoFormat dialog box displays, select the combination line and column chart (format number 1) in the Formats box.

The AutoFormat dialog box displays with the combination line and column chart selected (Figure 4-43).

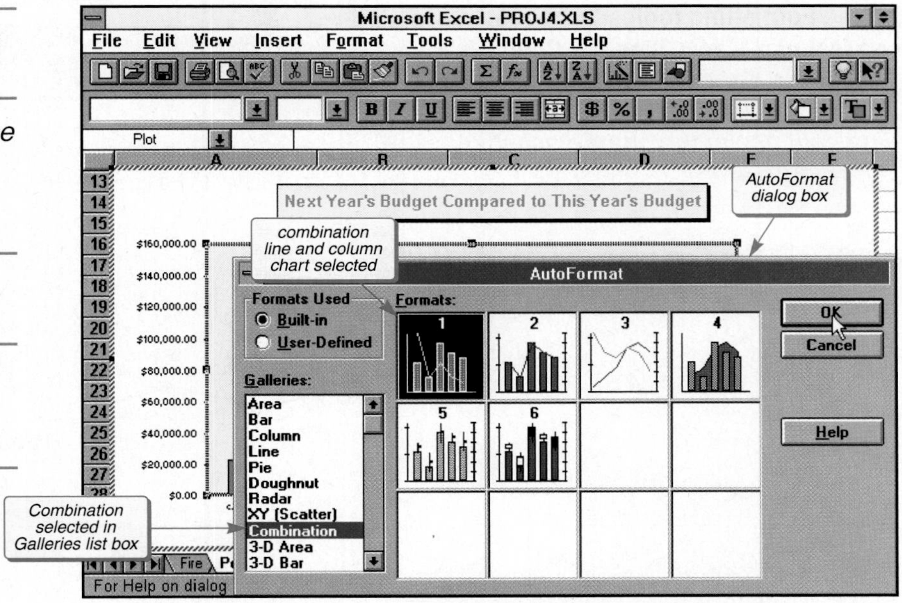

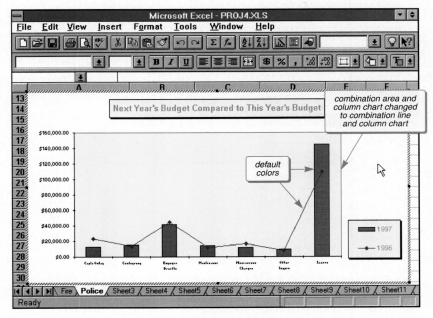

FIGURE 4-43

STEP 4 ►

Choose the OK button on the AutoFormat dialog box.

The combination area and column chart on the Police sheet is changed to a combination line and column chart (Figure 4-44).

FIGURE 4-44

STEP 5 ▶

Select the columns by clicking one of them. Click the Color button arrow on the Formatting toolbar. Choose red (column 1, row 2) on the Color palette.

The columns in the chart display in red (Figure 4-45).

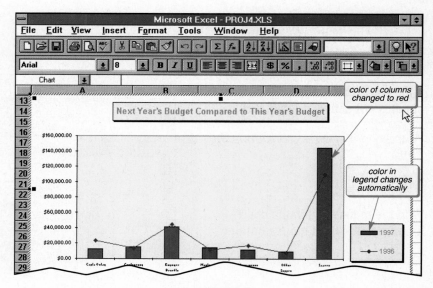

FIGURE 4-45

As indicated in the legend in Figure 4-45, the columns represent the 1997 proposed budget for the Police Department. The line represents the 1996 budget for the Police Department. You can see from the Salaries column in the chart that the Police Department is requesting a significant increase in its salary budget for 1997. The completed Police sheet displays as shown in Figure 4-46.

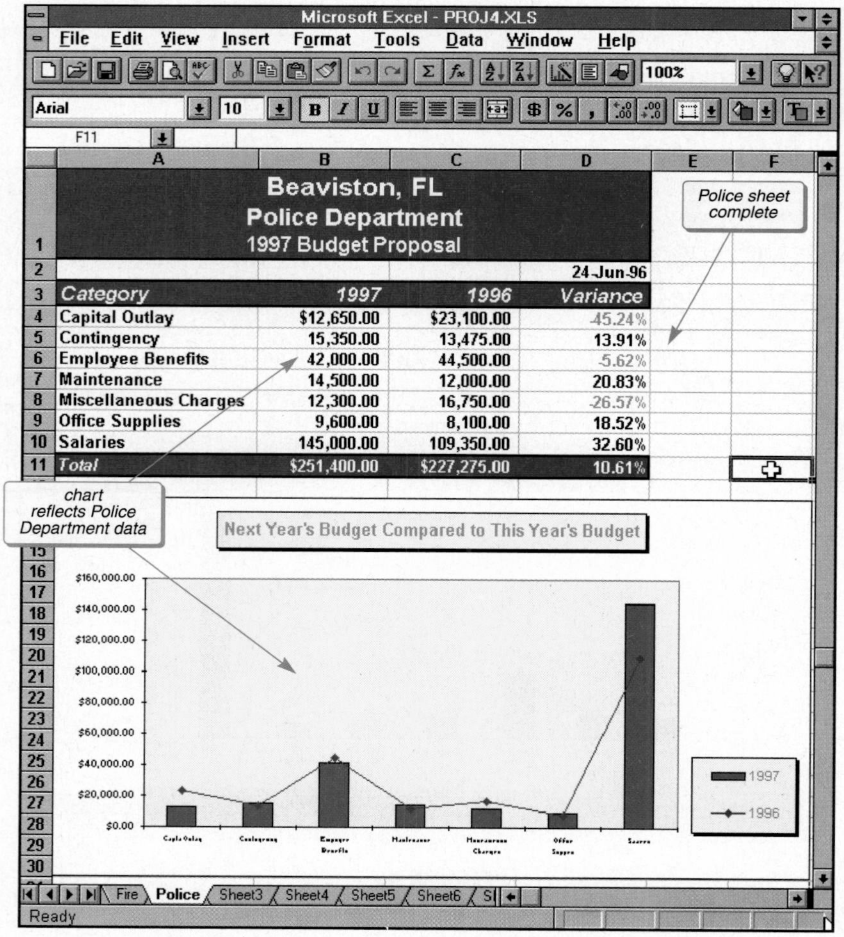

FIGURE 4-46

Modifying the Streets and Sanitation Sheet

As was done on the Police sheet, the data, color, chart range, and chart type must be changed on the Streets and Sanitation sheet. The following steps modify the worksheet portion of the Streets and Sanitation sheet.

TO MODIFY THE WORKSHEET PORTION OF THE STREETS AND SANITATION SHEET

Step 1: Double-click the Sheet3 tab. When the Rename dialog box displays, type Strs & San in the Name box. Choose the OK button.

Step 2: Double-click cell A1 and replace (Name) in line 2 with Streets and Sanitation

Step 3: Select the range A1:D1. Hold down the **CTRL** key and select the nonadjacent ranges A3:D3 and A11:D11. Click the Color button arrow on the Formatting toolbar. Choose green (column 2, row 2) on the Color palette. Click the Font Color button arrow on the Formatting toolbar. Choose white (column 2, row 1) on the Font Color palette.

Step 4: Enter the data in Table 4-4 on the next page in the range B4:B10.

Step 5: Click the Save button on the Standard toolbar.

The Streets and Sanitation sheet displays as shown in Figure 4-47.

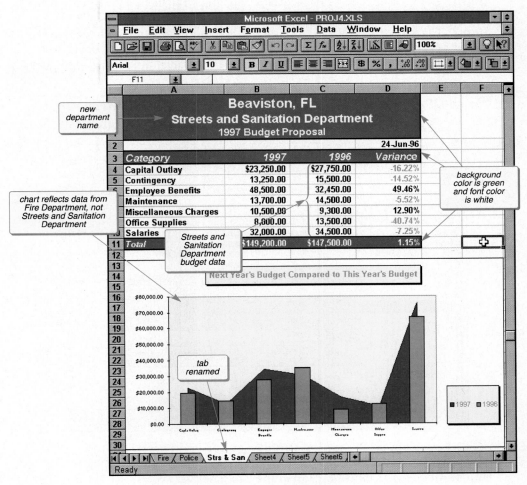

FIGURE 4-47

▸ **TABLE 4-4**

CELL	VALUE	CELL	VALUE
B4	23250	C4	27750
B5	13250	C5	15500
B6	48500	C6	32450
B7	13700	C7	14500
B8	10500	C8	9300
B9	8000	C9	13500
B10	32000	C10	34500

Here again, the new data is not reflected in the chart (Figure 4-47). The chart is identical to the one in Figure 4-38 because it was created by copying the Fire sheet. The following steps change the chart range.

TO CHANGE THE CHART RANGE

Step 1: Activate the chart on the Strs & San sheet by clicking it. A heavy gray border surrounds the chart.

Step 2: Click the ChartWizard tool on the Standard toolbar. Excel displays the ChartWizard – Step 1 of 2 dialog box which contains the Range box.

Step 3: Drag over the sheet reference Fire! in the Range box. Press the DELETE key.

The chart range refers to the Streets and Sanitation sheet (Figure 4-48).

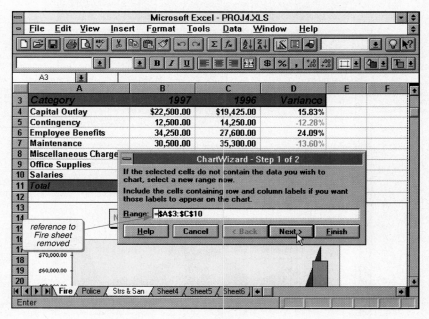

FIGURE 4-48

Step 4: Choose the Finish button in the ChartWizard – Step 1 of 2 dialog box.

The combination area and column chart reflect the data in the range A3:C10 of the Strs and San sheet (Figure 4-49).

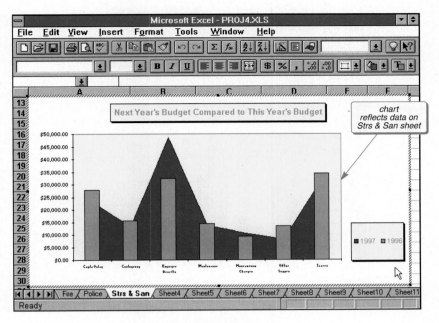

FIGURE 4-49

The next step is to change the Strs & San sheet's chart type from a combination area and column chart to a 3-D column chart.

TO CHANGE THE CHART TYPE ▼

STEP 1 ▶

With the chart area active and the mouse pointer within the chart area, click the right mouse button.

STEP 2 ▶

Choose the AutoFormat command. When the AutoFormat dialog box displays, select 3-D Column in the Galleries box. Select the column chart with gridlines (format number 4) in the Formats box.

The AutoFormat dialog box displays with the three-dimensional column chart selected (Figure 4-50).

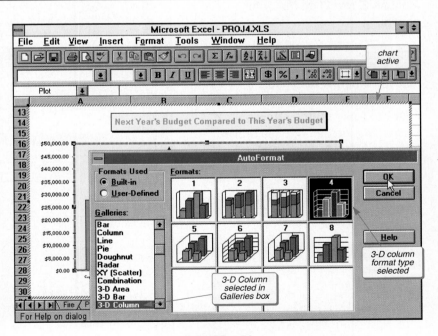

FIGURE 4-50

STEP 3 ▶

Choose the OK button in the AutoFormat dialog box.

The combination area and column chart on the Strs & San sheet is changed to a 3-D column chart (Figure 4-51).

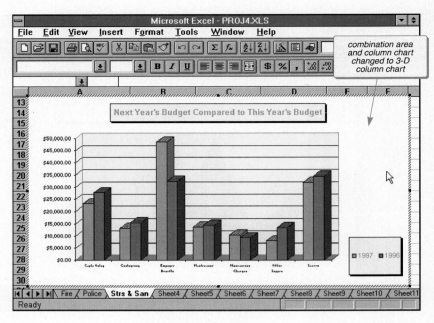

FIGURE 4-51

STEP 4 ▶

Select the blue columns (leftmost) by clicking one of them. Click the Color button arrow on the Formatting toolbar. Choose green (column 2, row 2) on the Color palette.

STEP 5 ▶

Select the purple columns (rightmost) by clicking one of them. Click the Color button arrow on the Formatting toolbar. Choose brown (column 4, row 2) on the Color palette.

The Streets and Sanitation sheet is complete as shown in Figure 4-52.

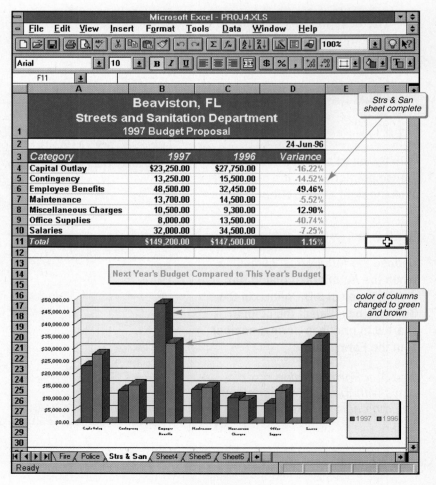

FIGURE 4-52

With the three department sheets complete, the next step is to modify the Public Safety Division sheet (Sheet4). However, before modifying Sheet4, it is important that you understand how to reference cells in other sheets in a workbook because this sheet contains the totals of the first three sheets.

▶ REFERENCING CELLS IN OTHER SHEETS IN A WORKBOOK

 o reference cells in other sheets in a workbook, you use the sheet name, also called the **sheet reference**. For example, you refer to cell B4 on the Fire sheet in the following fashion:

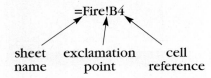

Thus, one way to add cell B4 on the first three sheets in this project and place the sum in cell B4 of the fourth sheet would be to select cell B4 on the fourth sheet and enter:

=Fire!B4+Police!B4+'Strs & San'!B4

Single quotation marks around the sheet name Strs & San are required because the name includes spaces. A much quicker way to find the sum of the **three-dimensional range** is to use the SUM function as follows:

=SUM('Fire:Strs & San'!B4)

The SUM argument ('Fire:Strs & San'!B4) instructs Excel to sum cell B4 on each of the three sheets (Fire, Police, and Strs & San). The colon (:) between the first sheet and the last sheet means to include these sheets and all sheets in between. A range that spans two or more sheets in a workbook, such as Fire!'Strs & San'!B4, is called a **3-D reference**.

A sheet reference, such as Fire!, is always absolute. Thus, unlike a relative cell reference, when you copy formulas, the sheet reference will remain constant.

Entering a Sheet Reference

You can enter a sheet reference by typing it or by clicking the sheet tab to activate it. When you click the sheet tab, Excel automatically adds the name followed by an exclamation point at the insertion point in the formula bar and activates the sheet. Next, click or drag through the cells you want to reference on the sheet.

If you are spanning sheets, click the first sheet, select the cell or range of cells, and then hold down the SHIFT key and click the last sheet. Excel will include the cell or range on the two sheets and all the sheets between. It will also add the colon between the first sheet and the last sheet referenced.

Modifying the Public Safety Sheet

The following paragraphs include steps that modify the Public Safety sheet so it summarizes the budget amounts for each category for the three departments and appears as shown in Figure 4-53.

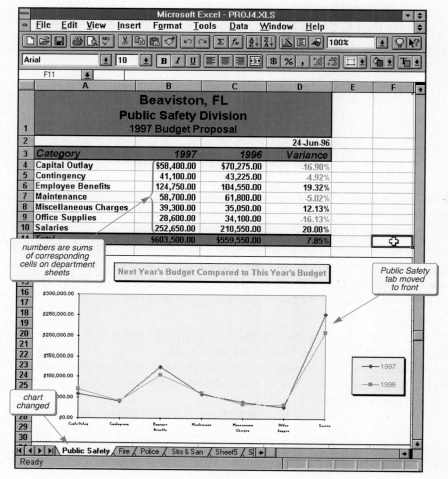

FIGURE 4-53

TO CHANGE THE BACKGROUND COLORS OF THE PUBLIC SAFETY SHEET

Step 1: Double-click the Sheet4 tab. When the Rename dialog box displays, type `Public Safety` in the Name box. Choose the OK button.

Step 2: Double-click cell A1 and replace (Name) `Department` in line 2 with `Public Safety Division`

Step 3: Select the range A1:D1. Hold down the CTRL key and select the nonadjacent ranges A3:D3 and A11:D11. Click the Color button arrow on the Formatting toolbar. Choose brown (column 4, row 2) on the Color palette.

The worksheet title, column titles, and total row display as shown in Figure 4-53.

Entering and Copying a 3-D Reference on the Public Safety Sheet

The next step in changing Sheet4 so it displays as shown in Figure 4-53 is to enter the SUM function in each of the cells in the range B4:C10. The SUM functions will determine the sums of the budget values for the three departments by category. Thus, cell B4 on the Public Safety sheet will be equal to the sum of the 1997 Capital Outlay amounts in cells Fire!B4, Police!B4, and Strs & San!B4.

TO ENTER AND COPY 3-D REFERENCES ON THE PUBLIC SAFETY SHEET ▼

STEP 1 ▶

With the Public Safety sheet active, select cell B4. Click the AutoSum button on the Standard toolbar.

The SUM function displays without a range (Figure 4-54).

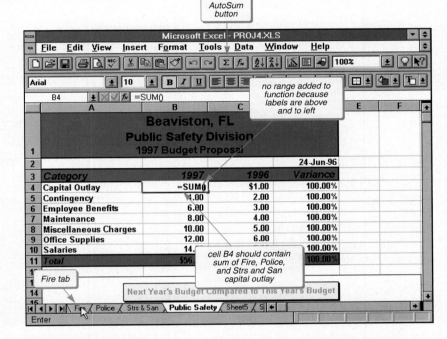

FIGURE 4-54

STEP 2 ▶

Click the Fire tab and select cell B4. Hold down the SHIFT key and click the Strs & San tab.

A marquis surrounds cell Fire!B4 (Figure 4-55). All four sheet tabs are highlighted. The Fire tab displays in bold because it is the active sheet. The SUM function displays in the formula bar.

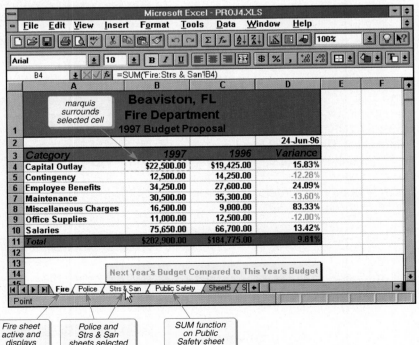

FIGURE 4-55

STEP 3 ▶

Click the enter box in the formula bar or press the ENTER key.

The Public Safety sheet becomes the active sheet. The sum of the cells Fire!B4, Police!B4, and Strs & San!B4 displays in cell B4 of the Public Safety sheet (Figure 4-56). The SUM function assigned to cell B4 displays in the formula bar.

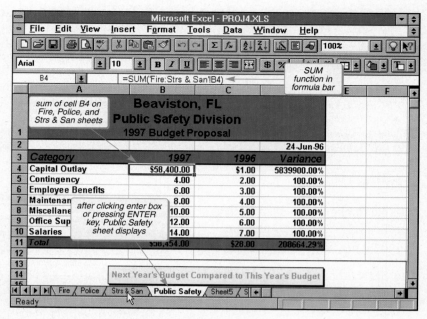

FIGURE 4-56

STEP 4 ▶

With cell B4 active, drag the fill handle through cell C4. Release the left mouse button.

Excel copies the formula in cell B4 to cell C4 (Figure 4-57). The cell reference in the SUM function in cell C4 references cell C4 on each of the three sheets.

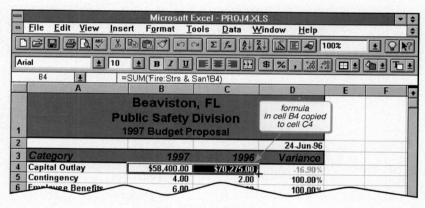

FIGURE 4-57

STEP 5 ▶

Select the range B4:C4 on the Public Safety sheet. Drag the fill handle down through cell C10.

Excel shades the border of the paste area (Figure 4-58).

FIGURE 4-58

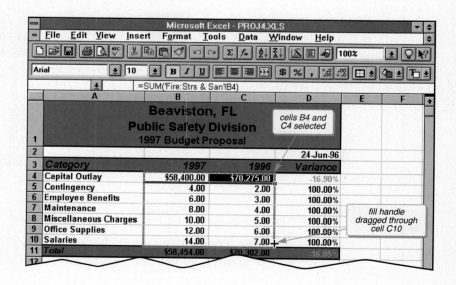

STEP 6 ►

Release the left mouse button.

Excel copies the formulas in cells B4 and C4 to the range B5:C10 (Figure 4-59).

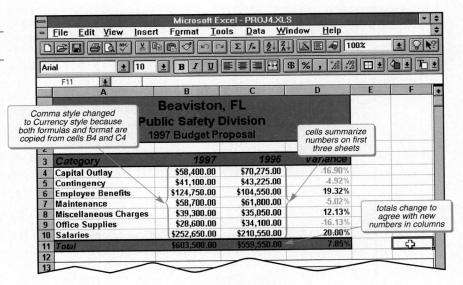

FIGURE 4-59

STEP 7 ►

Select the range B5:C10 and click the Comma Style button on the Formatting toolbar.

The worksheet portion of the Public Safety sheet is complete (Figure 4-60).

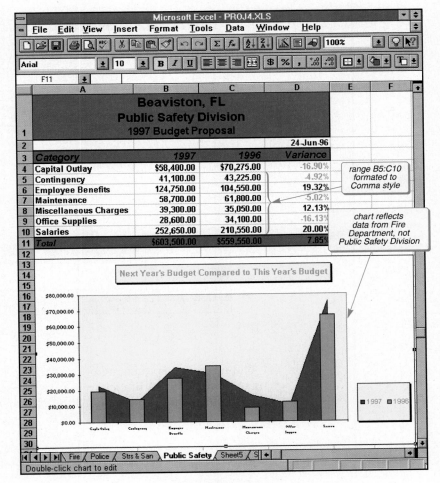

FIGURE 4-60

The reason for reformatting the range B5:C10 is because when you copy a cell, the format is also copied. Thus, the Currency style assigned to cell B4 earlier was copied to cell C4 and then to the range B5:C10.

A close look at Figure 4-60 on the previous page reveals that the embedded chart is using the range Fire!A3:C10 instead of Public Safety!A3:C10. Hence, the next step is to change the chart range.

TO CHANGE THE CHART RANGE

Step 1: Activate the chart on the Public Safety sheet by double-clicking it.

Step 2: Click the ChartWizard tool on the Standard toolbar. Excel displays the ChartWizard – Step 1 of 2 dialog box which contains the Range box.

Step 3: Drag over the sheet reference Fire! in the Range box. Press the **DELETE** key. Choose the Finish button in the ChartWizard – Step 1 of 2 dialog box.

The combination area and column chart reflects the data in the range A3:C10 of the Public Safety sheet (Figure 4-61).

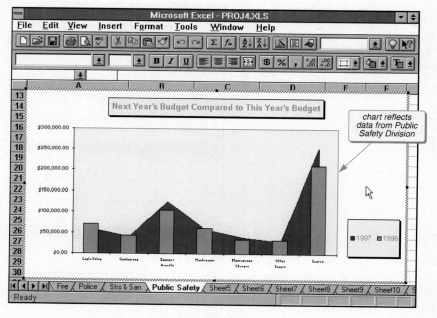

FIGURE 4-61

The next step is to change the chart type from a combination area and column chart to a line chart. A line chart is usually used to show a trend, but it can also be used to compare multiple series of numbers on the same chart.

TO CHANGE THE CHART TYPE ▼

STEP 1 ►

With the chart area active and the mouse pointer within the chart area, click the right mouse button.

STEP 2 ►

Choose the AutoFormat command. When the AutoFormat dialog box displays, select Line in the Galleries box. Select the line chart with data point markers (format number 1) in the Formats box.

The AutoFormat dialog box displays with the line chart with data point markers chart selected (Figure 4-62).

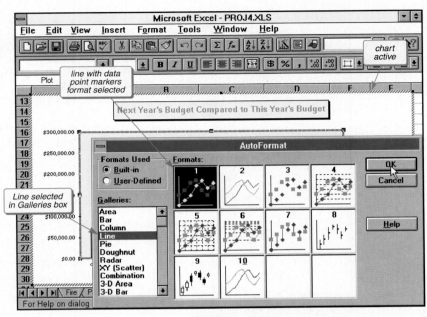

FIGURE 4-62

STEP 3 ►

Choose the OK button in the AutoFormat dialog box. Select cell F11 (or any other cell) to deactivate the chart area. Drag the Public Safety tab to the left of the Fire tab so it displays first in the workbook.

The combination area and column chart on the Public Safety sheet is changed to a line chart with data point markers (Figure 4-63). The Public Safety sheet is positioned first in the workbook.

STEP 4 ►

Click the Save button on the Standard toolbar to save the workbook.

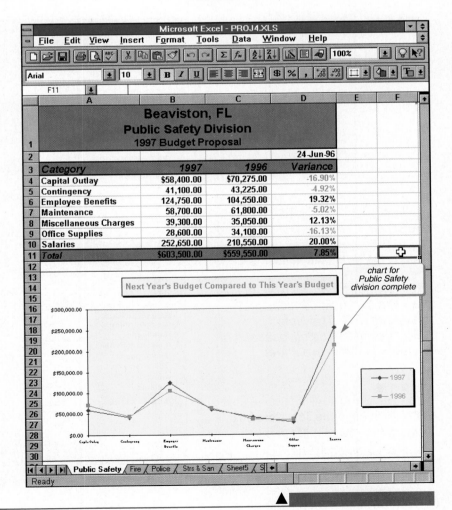

FIGURE 4-63

The workbook is complete. The next section introduces you to adding comments to a workbook.

▶ ADDING COMMENTS TO A WORKBOOK

Comments, or **notes**, in a workbook are used to describe the function of a cell, a range of cells, a sheet, or the entire workbook. Comments are used to identify workbooks and clarify entries that would otherwise be difficult to understand.

In Excel, you can assign comments to any cell in the workbook using the **Note command** on the Insert menu. Overall workbook comments should include the following:

1. Worksheet title
2. Author's name
3. Date created
4. Date last modified (use N/A if it has not been modified)
5. A short description of the purpose of the worksheet

The following steps add workbook comments to cell F1 on the Public Safety sheet.

TO ADD A NOTE TO A CELL ▼

STEP 1 ▶

Select cell F1 on the Public Safety sheet. Select the Insert menu.

The Insert menu displays (Figure 4-64).

FIGURE 4-64

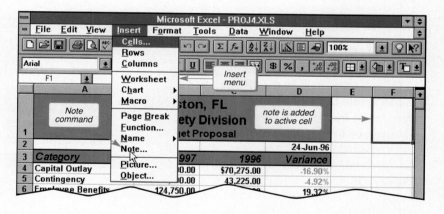

STEP 2 ▶

Choose the Note command.

Excel displays the Cell Note dialog box. The Cell box identifies the active cell (F1). The Notes in Sheet box lists the cell locations of all notes in the active sheet.

STEP 3 ▶

Enter the note in the Text Note box as shown in Figure 4-65. Press the ENTER key after each line.

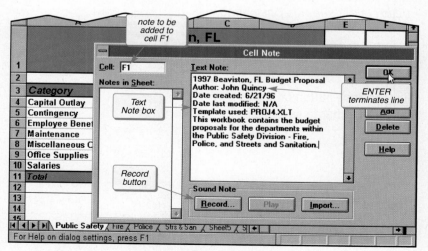

FIGURE 4-65

STEP 4 ►

Choose the OK button in the Cell Note dialog box.

*Excel adds a small red dot, called a **note indicator**, in the upper right corner of cell F1 to indicate a note has been added to it (Figure 4-66). If a red dot does not appear in the cell, choose the Options command from the Tools menu. Click the View tab and click Note Indicator.*

STEP 5 ►

Click the Save button on the Standard toolbar to save the workbook.

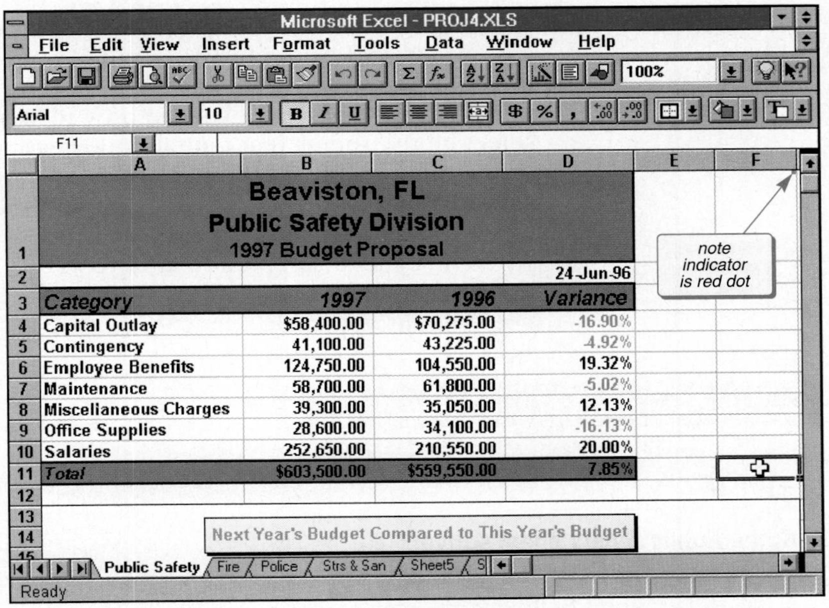

FIGURE 4-66

A red dot indicates that a cell has a note attached to it. To read the comment, or note, any time the sheet is active, select the cell with the note and choose the Note command from the Insert menu or press SHIFT+F2.

If you prefer not to display the note indicator (small red dot) in cell A1, choose the Options command from the Tools menu; and on the View tab, remove the x from the Note Indicator check box by clicking it. You can print notes attached to cells by selecting the **Notes check box** on the Sheet tab in the Page Setup dialog box.

Besides entering comments in the form of text, you can add an audio comment to a cell (up to two minutes) if you have a sound board, a microphone, and the appropriate software. To add the audio comment, select the **Record button** in the Cell Note dialog box (Figure 4-65). When a **sound note** (also called an **audio comment**) is added without a text note, the computer speaks the comment when you choose the Note command from the Insert menu or press SHIFT+F2.

► ADDING A HEADER AND FOOTER AND CHANGING THE MARGINS

A **header** prints at the top of a every page in a printout. A **footer** prints at the bottom of every page in a printout (see Figure 4-74 on page E258). By default, Excel prints the tab name as the header, .5 inch from the top, and the page number preceded by the word Page as a footer, .5 inch from the bottom. You can change the header and footer to print other types of information.

Sometimes you will want to change the margins to center a printout on the page or include additional columns and rows that would otherwise not fit. The **margins** in Excel are set to the following: top = 1 inch; bottom = 1 inch, left = .75 inch; and right = .75 inch.

Changing the header and footer, turning gridlines off, and changing the margins are all part of the function called **page setup**. You use the Page Setup command on the shortcut menu or File menu to carry out the page setup function. The following procedure shows you how to step through page setup. Be sure you select all the sheets that contain information before you change the header, footer, or margin, or some of the page setup characteristics will occur only on the selected sheet.

You should also be aware that Excel does not copy page setup characteristics when one sheet is copied to another. Thus, applying page setup characteristics to the template before copying it to the Public Safety Division Budget Proposal workbook would not work.

TO CHANGE THE HEADER AND FOOTER ▼

STEP 1 ►

With the Public Safety sheet active, hold down the SHIFT key and click the Strs & San tab. Point to the menu bar and click the right mouse button.

Excel displays a shortcut menu (Figure 4-67). The first four tabs at the bottom of the window are highlighted.

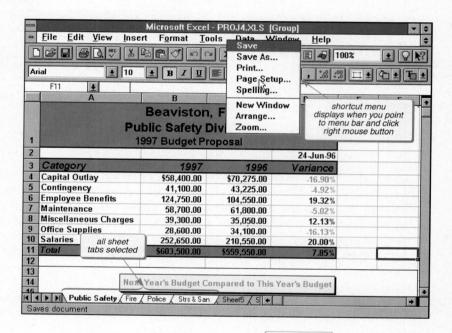

FIGURE 4-67

STEP 2 ►

Choose the Page Setup command.

The Page Setup dialog box displays.

STEP 3 ►

If necessary, click the Sheet tab in the Page Setup dialog box. In the Print box, click the Gridlines check box to remove the x. Point to the Header/Footer tab.

The Sheet tab on the Page Setup dialog box displays (Figure 4-68). The Gridlines check box is cleared.

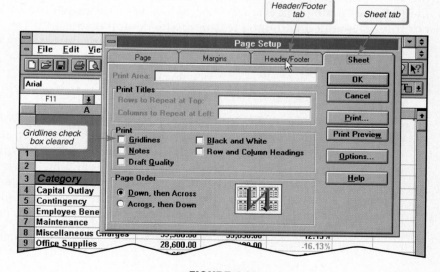

FIGURE 4-68

STEP 4 ▶

Click the Header/Footer tab.

Samples of the current header and footer display (Figure 4-69).

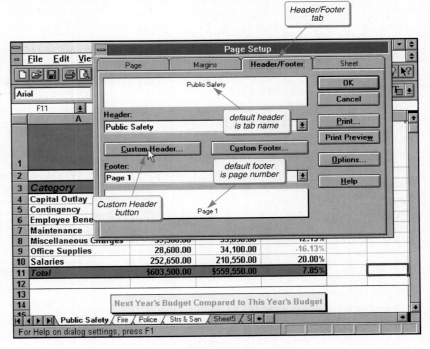

FIGURE 4-69

STEP 5 ▶

Choose the Custom Header button (Custom Header...).

The Header dialog box displays.

STEP 6 ▶

Click the Left Section box. Type John Quincy, Controller **and press the ENTER key to go to the next line. Type** Preliminary Budget Proposal **and click the Center Section. Click the Sheet Name button ( ) in the Header dialog box. Click the Right Section box. Type** Page **followed by a space and click the Page Number button ( ) in the Header dialog box. Type** of **followed by a space. Click the Total Pages button ( ).**

The Header dialog box displays with the new header as shown in Figure 4-70.

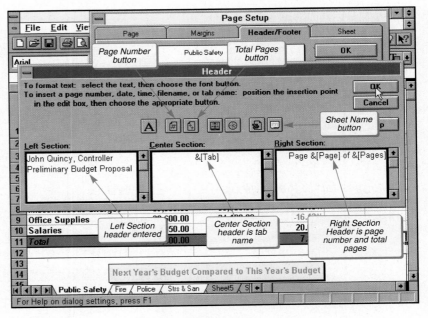

FIGURE 4-70

STEP 7 ▶

Choose the OK button in the Header
dialog box. Choose the Custom
Footer button (Custom Footer...)
(Figure 4-69). Drag across the footer
Page &[Page] and press the DELETE
key to remove it. Choose the OK
button in the Footer dialog box.

The Header/Footer tab in the Page
Setup dialog box displays as
shown in Figure 4-71.

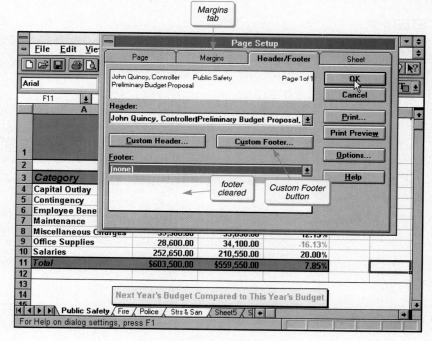

FIGURE 4-71

STEP 8 ▶

Click the Margins tab in the Page
Setup dialog box. Click the top box
and change the top margin to 1.5.
Click the Header box and change the
distance from the top of the page to
.75.

The Margins tab in the Page dia-
log box displays as shown in
Figure 4-72.

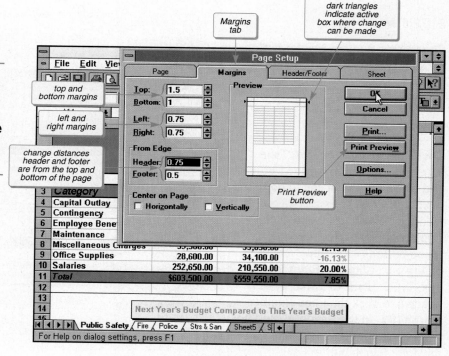

FIGURE 4-72

STEP 9 ▶

Choose the Print Preview button in the Page Setup dialog box to preview the workbook.

The Public Safety sheet displays as shown in Figure 4-73. Although difficult to read, the header displays at the top of the page. You can choose the Zoom button to get a better view of the page.

STEP 10 ▶

Choose the Close button when you are finished reviewing the preview. When control returns to the Page Setup dialog box, choose the OK button.

STEP 11 ▶

Click the Save button on the Standard toolbar to save the workbook with the new print settings.

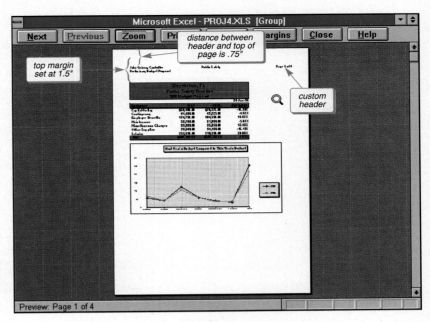

FIGURE 4-73

Notice when you click one of the buttons in the Header dialog box (Figure 4-70), Excel enters a code into the active section. A **code** such as &[Page] means insert the page number. Table 4-5 summarizes the buttons, their codes, and functions in the Header or Footer dialog box.

▶ **TABLE 4-5**

BUTTON	NAME	CODE	FUNCTION
Ⓐ	Font		Displays the Font dialog box
🔢	Page Number	&[Page]	Inserts a page number
🔢	Total Pages	&[Pages]	Insert the total number of pages
📅	Date	&[Date]	Inserts the system date
🕐	Time	&[Time]	Inserts the system time
📄	Filename	&[File]	Inserts the filename of the workbook
🗔	Sheet Name	&[Tab]	Inserts the tab name

Printing the Workbook

The following steps print the workbook.

TO PRINT THE WORKBOOK

Step 1: Ready the printer.
Step 2: If the four sheets in the workbook are not selected, click the Public Safety tab and then hold down the SHIFT key and click the Strs & San tab.
Step 3: Click the Print button on the Standard toolbar.

The workbook prints as shown in Figure 4-74.

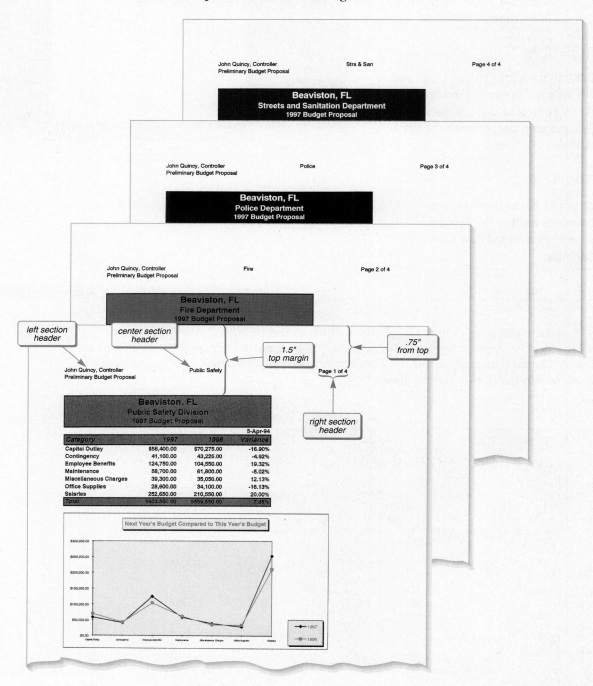

FIGURE 4-74

An alternative to using the SHIFT key and mouse to select the sheets in Step 2 is to point to one of the tabs and click the right mouse button. The **sheet tab shortcut menu** displays. Choose the **Select All Sheets** command. Other commands available on this shortcut menu include Insert, Delete, Rename, and Move or Copy. All these commands relate to manipulating sheets in a workbook. For example, you can use this menu to insert a new sheet, delete the active sheet, rename the active sheet, or move or copy the active sheet.

▶ CHANGING DATA IN THE WORKBOOK

If you change any data in the three department sheets, Excel immediately redraws the embedded chart. Because changing data also affects the Public Safety Division worksheet, its corresponding chart also changes. The following steps show how the chart for the Police Department changes when the 1997 proposed salary in cell B10 is changed from $145,000.00 to $90,000.00.

TO CHANGE DATA IN A WORKSHEET THAT AFFECTS THE EMBEDDED CHART

Step 1: Click the Police tab to select it. Select cell B10.

Step 2: Type 90000 and click the enter box in the formula bar or press the ENTER key.

Excel redraws the embedded chart (Figure 4-75).

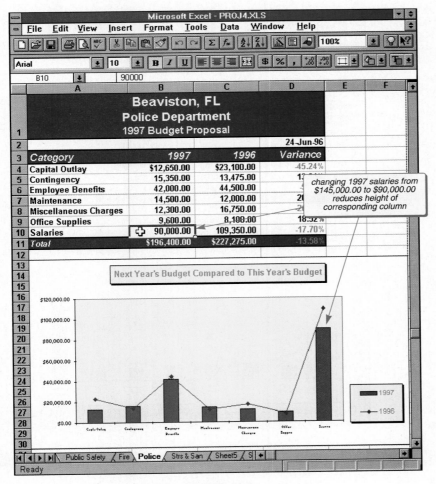

FIGURE 4-75

Compare the chart in Figure 4-75 to Figure 4-46 on page E240. You can see that the Salaries column is much shorter after changing the 1997 proposed salary from $145,000.00 to $90,000.00.

Changing Data in a Worksheet by Resizing a Column in the Chart

You can resize a column in the embedded chart, and Excel will change the corresponding data in the cell as shown in the following steps.

TO CHANGE DATA IN A WORKSHEET BY RESIZING A COLUMN IN A CHART ▼

STEP 1 ▶

Hold down the SHIFT key and click the Police tab, and then double-click within the embedded chart.

STEP 2 ▶

Select the Employee Benefits column. Point to the top center handle.

The column is surrounded by black handles which indicate the column can be resized (Figure 4-76).

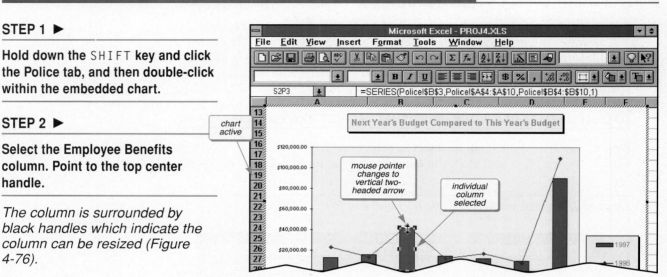

FIGURE 4-76

STEP 3 ▶

Drag the handle down to approximately $14,400. Notice the moving marker on the value axis as you drag down. Release the left mouse button. Select cell F11.

The Employee Benefits column in the embedded chart is shorter than it was before, and the value in the corresponding cell (B6) changes from $42,000.00 (Figure 4-75) to $14,400.00 (Figure 4-77).

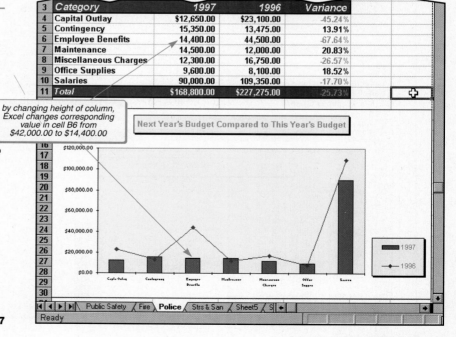

FIGURE 4-77

▶ FINDING AND REPLACING TEXT OR NUMBERS

T o find cells that contain specific characters, choose the **Find command** on the Edit menu. To find and replace characters in cells, choose the **Replace command** on the Edit menu.

Finding Text or Numbers

The following steps show you how to find the text *Misc* in *Miscellaneous Charges* (cell A8) in the workbook. If you select a range before invoking the Find command, Excel searches the range on the active sheet. If you select a cell, Excel searches all selected sheets. Excel searches row by row, beginning with row 1 of the active sheet. However, you can instruct Excel to search column by column selecting a check box in the Find dialog box.

TO FIND TEXT OR NUMBERS ▼

STEP 1 ▶

Click the Public Safety tab and then hold down the SHIFT key and click the Strs & San tab. Select the Edit menu and point to the Find command.

The Edit menu displays as shown in Figure 4-78.

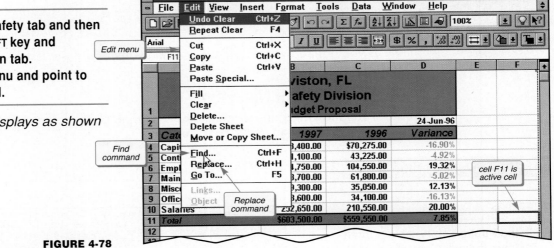

FIGURE 4-78

STEP 2 ▶

Choose the Find command. When the Find dialog box displays, type `Misc` in the Find What box. Choose the Find Next button (Find Next).

The Find dialog box displays as shown in Figure 4-79, and Excel activates the first cell containing the text Misc (cell A8).

STEP 3 ▶

Choose the Close button to close the Find dialog box or choose the Find Next button to find the next occurrence of Misc.

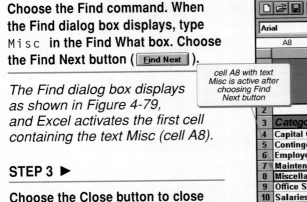

FIGURE 4-79

Using **wildcard characters** (*, or ?), you can find variations of the sequence of characters you type into the Find What box. The asterisk (*) represents any number of characters in that same position. The question mark (?) represents any character in that same position. For example, if you type *ies in the Find What dialog box, Excel will stop on any cell containing text that ends with ies. If you type S?1 in the Find What box, Excel will stop on any cell containing text that includes a sequence of characters with the letter S, followed by any character, followed by letter l. Table 4-6 summarizes the options found in the Find dialog box.

▶ **TABLE 4-6**

OPTION	FUNCTION
Find Next button	Finds next occurrence
Close button	Closes Find dialog box
Replace button	Displays the Replace dialog box where occurrence can be replaced
Search box	Instructs Excel to search across rows or down columns
Look in box notes	Instructs Excel to search in cell formulas, cell values, or cell notes
Match Case check box	Instructs Excel to be case sensitive
Find Entire Cells Only check box	Instructs Excel to find only exact and complete matches

If you hold down the SHIFT key when you choose the Find Next button, Excel finds the previous occurrence.

Replacing Text or Numbers

The following steps show you how to replace the first occurrence in the workbook of the word Salaries with Salary.

TO REPLACE TEXT OR NUMBERS ▼

STEP 1 ▶

Click the Public Safety tab and then hold down the SHIFT key and click the Strs & San tab. Select the Edit menu and point to the Replace command.

The Edit menu displays as shown earlier in Figure 4-78.

STEP 2 ▶

Choose the Replace command. When the Replace dialog box displays, type Salaries in the Find What box and type Salary in the Replace with box. Choose the Find Next button.

The Replace dialog box displays and Excel finds the first cell containing the word Salaries (cell A10) on the Public Safety sheet (Figure 4-80).

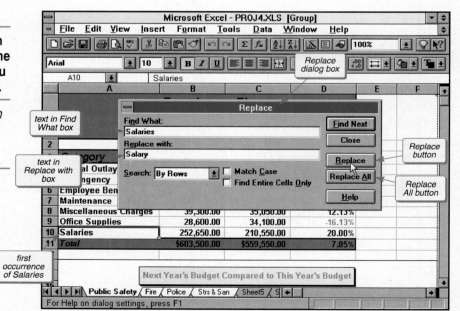

FIGURE 4-80

STEP 3 ▶

Choose the Replace button
(Replace).

Excel replaces the word Salaries with the word Salary in cell A10 (Figure 4-81) and finds the next occurrence of Salaries.

STEP 4 ▶

Choose the Close button to close the Replace dialog box without making the replacement and then click the Public Safety tab.

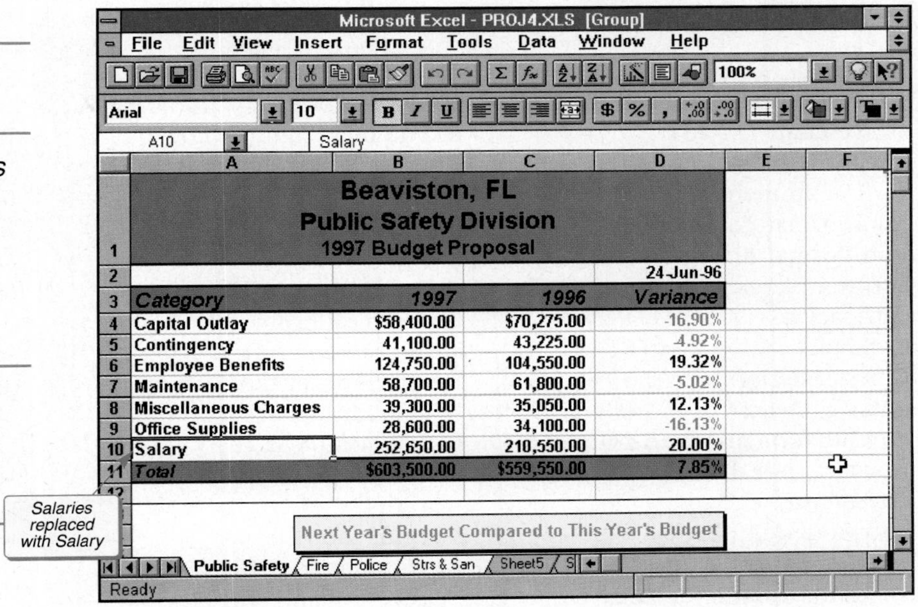

FIGURE 4-81

The **Replace All** button (Replace All) in the Replace dialog box (Figure 4-80) causes Excel to replace all occurrences of the text in the selected sheets. The remaining options in the Replace dialog box are the same as in the Find dialog box described in Table 4-6.

▶ PROJECT SUMMARY

Project 4 introduced you to creating and using a template, customizing formats, changing chart types, and enhancing embedded charts. Using the steps and techniques presented in the project, you learned how to reference cells in other sheets and add comments to a cell. To enhance a printout, you learned how to add a header and footer and change margins. Finally, you learned how to drag a column in a chart to change the corresponding number in the worksheet and how to find and replace text and numbers.

▶ KEY TERMS AND INDEX

QUICK REFERENCE

In Microsoft Excel, you can accomplish a task in a number of ways. The following table provides a quick reference to each task presented in this project with its available options. The commands listed in the Menu column can be executed using either the keyboard or mouse. Many of the commands in the Menu column are also available on the shortcut menu.

Task	Mouse	Menu	Keyboard Shortcuts
Add a Note		From Insert menu, choose Note	Press SHIFT+F2
Apply Custom Formats		From Format menu, choose Cells; click Number tab, then enter format code in Code box	
Change a Header/Footer		From File menu, choose Page Setup	
Change Margins		From File menu, choose Page Setup	
Copy a Sheet to Another Sheet	Click Select All button; click Copy button on Standard toolbar; click Sheet tab; click Paste button on Standard toolbar		Press CTRL+A to select sheet; press CTRL+C; click sheet tab; press CTRL+V

Task	Mouse	Menu	Keyboard Shortcuts
Display a Note		From Insert menu, choose Note	Press SHIFT+F2
Find Text		From Edit menu, choose Find	Press CTRL+F
Move to the Next or Previous Tab in a Workbook or Dialog Box			Press CTRL+PAGE DOWN (next sheet); press CTRL+PAGE UP (previous sheet)
Print a Note		From File menu, choose Page Setup	
Replace Text		From Edit menu, choose Replace	Press CTRL+H
Save a Template		From File menu, choose Save As; select Template in Save File As Type box	
Select a Grouping of Sheets	Click first sheet tab, hold down SHIFT key, then click last sheet tab	From sheet tab shortcut menu, choose Select All Sheets	
Select Nonadjacent Sheets	Click first sheet tab, hold down CTRL key, then click other sheet tabs		

S T U D E N T   A S S I G N M E N T S

STUDENT ASSIGNMENTS
STUDENT ASSIGNMENT 1 True/False

Instructions: Circle T if the statement is true or F if the statement is false.

T F   1. In Excel, formulas can reference cells found on different sheets of a workbook.

T F   2. Templates are not used to create new workbooks that are similar.

T F   3. Summarizing information that appears on multiple sheets of a workbook is referred to as consolidation.

T F   4. A template is saved with the same extension as a workbook.

T F   5. The purpose of dummy numbers is to fill in cells in a template.

T F   6. A fixed dollar sign will appear in the same position in a cell no matter how many digits there are in the number that follows it.

T F   7. Combination area and column charts show one set of numbers from a worksheet in two different formats on one chart.

T F   8. The value axis series is the horizontal line to the left of the plot area of a chart.

T F   9. A template may be copied to the clipboard and pasted to one or more sheets in a workbook.

T F 10. When a template is used to create a worksheet and embedded chart, the worksheet can be modified but the embedded chart cannot be modified.

T F 11. A three-dimensional range is indicated in Excel functions by sheet references that reference cells in other sheets of a workbook.

T F 12. Line charts are not used to show trends and are the same as area charts.

T F 13. A note indicator appears in the upper right corner of a cell to indicate a note has been attached to that particular cell.

(continued)

STUDENT ASSIGNMENT 1 (continued)

T F 14. If you have the appropriate hardware, an audio comment can be added to a cell.
T F 15. Workbook headers and footers appear only on the first page of a printout.
T F 16. Workbook margins including top, bottom, left, and right cannot be changed.
T F 17. The codes used in headers and footers will insert page numbers, system date, system time, the filename of the workbook, or the tab name.
T F 18. To display the shortcut menu with commands for manipulating sheets in a workbook, point to the title bar and click the right mouse button.
T F 19. You can resize a column in a chart to change data in its associated worksheet.
T F 20. A custom format code cannot be created in Excel.

STUDENT ASSIGNMENT 2
Multiple Choice

Instructions: Circle the correct response.

1. The Wrap Text check box is found on the _____ tab of the Format Cells dialog box.
   a. Number
   b. Alignment
   c. Fonts
   d. Protection
2. To enter numeric data as text, the number must begin with _____.
   a. a letter
   b. a quotation mark
   c. an apostrophe
   d. an exclamation point
3. Templates are saved with an extension of _____.
   a. .xlw
   b. .xls
   c. .tpt
   d. .xlt
4. Format codes are used to define formats for _____.
   a. numbers
   b. dates
   c. text
   d. all of the above
5. _____ around the chart indicates if a chart is active.
   a. A heavy gray border
   b. A turquoise border
   c. A thin border with handles
   d. A heavy border with handles
6. _____ around the chart indicates the chart is selected.
   a. A heavy gray border
   b. A turquoise border
   c. A thin border with handles
   d. A heavy border with handles
7. Comments are added to a workbook through the use of the _____ command on the Insert menu.
   a. Name
   b. Note
   c. Function
   d. Object

8. Excel automatically places a _____ at the bottom of each page in a printout.
   a. tab name
   b. filename
   c. page number
   d. date
9. The Excel function called page setup allows you to _____.
   a. copy pages of a workbook
   b. check the spelling of a workbook
   c. change the margins of a workbook
   d. select all the sheets of a workbook
10. Templates, called _____ are stored in the XLSTART subdirectory.
    a. autotemplates
    b. startup templates
    c. new templates
    d. format templates

STUDENT ASSIGNMENT 3
Understanding Dialog Boxes and Tabs

Instructions: Identify the command and tab that cause the dialog box and tab to display and allow you to make the indicated changes. Enter N/A in the Tab column if it does not apply.

CHANGE/TASK	COMMAND	TAB
1. Assign a note to a cell	_____	_____
2. Change the margins	_____	_____
3. Change the header	_____	_____
4. Remove gridlines	_____	_____
5. Change to a new chart type	_____	_____
6. Select all sheets	_____	_____
7. Rename a sheet	_____	_____
8. Insert a sheet	_____	_____
9. Find text	_____	_____
10. Replace text	_____	_____

STUDENT ASSIGNMENT 4
Understanding 3-D References

Instructions: The workbook in Figure SA4-4 is made up of five sheets labeled Dept1, Dept2, Dept3, Dept4, and Division. On the next page write the formula or function that accomplishes each of the specified tasks. Assume cell F2 is active on the Division sheet. Each of the five tasks is independent of the others.

FIGURE SA4-4

(continued)

STUDENT ASSIGNMENT 4 (continued)

1. Assign Division!F2 the sum of cell B10 on each of the department's sheets.

   Function: _____

2. Assign to cell Division!F2 the product of cell A1 on the Dept1 sheet and cell D5 on the Dept3 sheet.

   Formula: _____

3. Assign to cell Division!F2 cell H1 on the Division sheet times the quantity of cell R3 on the Dept2 sheet minus cell A6 on the Dept1 sheet.

   Formula: _____

4. Assign to cell Division!F2 the expression $(D \wedge 3 - 4 * F * H) / (4 - H)$ where the value of D is cell A8 on the Dept1 sheet, F is cell D3 on the Dept2 sheet, and H is cell B2 on the Dept3 sheet.

   Formula: _____

5. Assign to cell Division!F2 the value of cell B6 on the Dept3 sheet.

   Formula: _____

STUDENT ASSIGNMENT 5
Working with Customized Formats

Instructions:

Using Table 4-1 on page E223, determine the results that will display in the RESULTS IN and COLOR columns of Table SA4-5. Assume the column width of the cell that will display the value can hold 10 characters (including special characters). If the column width is not big enough, enter a series of 10 asterisks in the RESULTS IN column. Use the letter b to indicate positions containing blank characters.

PROBLEM	CELL CONTENTS	FORMAT APPLIED	RESULTS IN	COLOR
1	25	###.00	bbbbb25.00	N/A
2	-297.34	##0.00;[Red]-##0.00	bbb-297.34	Red
3	14.816	###.##		
4	-3841.92	#,##0.00;[Green]#,##0.00		
5	5281.42	$ #,##0.00		
6	214.76	$##,##0.00		
7	32	#,##0.00;[Red](#,##0.00)		
8	7	+##0.00		
9	0	#,###		
10	.14363	##.####		
11	99567.768	$##,##0.00		
12	.129	##0.00%		
13	.8	$#,##0.00		
14	412999351	$#,###,###		
15	7	+#,##0.00		

You may want to enter the numbers in cells (column width = 10.00) in a blank sheet and apply the formats to determine the answers. As examples, the first two problems in the table are complete. If the number displays in a color other than black, indicate the color in the color column, otherwise enter N/A.

STUDENT ASSIGNMENT 6
Understanding the Header and Footer Buttons

Instructions: Using the Header dialog box in Figure SA4-6, match the numbered bubbles to the codes labeled with letters.

LETTER	NUMBER
A	_____
B	_____
C	_____
D	_____
E	_____
F	_____

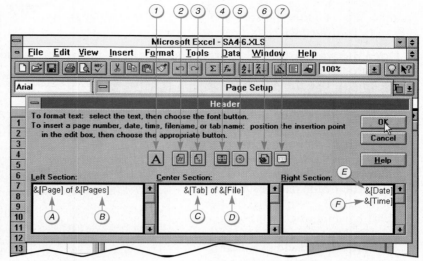

FIGURE SA4-6

COMPUTER LABORATORY EXERCISES

COMPUTER LABORATORY EXERCISE 1
Using the Help Menu to Understand 3-D References

Instructions: Start Excel and perform the following tasks using a computer.

1. Choose the Search for help on command from the Help menu. Type `format` in the top box of the Search dialog box. Choose the Show Topics button. With Number Format Codes selected in the lower box in the Search dialog box, choose the Go To button. When the information displays, read it, and then choose the Print Topic command from the File menu in the Help window. Double-click the Control-menu box in the Help window.
2. Choose the Search for help on command from the Help menu. Type `template` in the top box of the Search dialog box. Choose the Show Topics button. One at a time, select each topic in the lower box and choose the Go To button. Read and print each topic. When you are finished with the last one, double-click the Control-menu box in the Help window.
3. Choose the Search for help on command from the Help menu. Type `cell reference` in the top box of the Search dialog box. Select cell reference to other sheets in the upper list box. Choose the Show Topics button. Choose the Go To button. When the information displays, choose the Print button in the How To window. Close the Help menu.

COMPUTER LABORATORY EXERCISE 2
Enhancing a Chart

Instructions: Follow the steps below to modify the chart in the workbook CLE4-2.XLS so it displays as shown in Figure CLE4-2.

1. Open the workbook CLE4-2 from the subdirectory Excel5 on the Student Diskette.
2. Activate the chart by double-clicking it. Use the AutoFormat command on the shortcut menu to change the column chart to the 3-D area chart (Galleries box = 3-D Area and Formats box = 6). Change the color of the area chart to dark red (column 1, row 2) on the Color palette. Adjust the size and perspective of the chart by selecting it and dragging the handles.
3. Activate the Drawing toolbar to use the Drop Shadow and Arrow buttons. Format the chart title. Add and format the text box and arrow as shown in Figure CLE4-2.
4. Save the workbook using the filename CLE4-2A.
5. Add a header that includes your name and course number on two lines in the Left Section box, the computer laboratory exercise number (CLE4-2) in the Center Section box, and the system date and your instructor name on two lines in the Right Section box. Remove the footer.
6. Print the workbook without cell gridlines.
7. Save the workbook with the printsettings by clicking the Save button on the Standard toolbar.

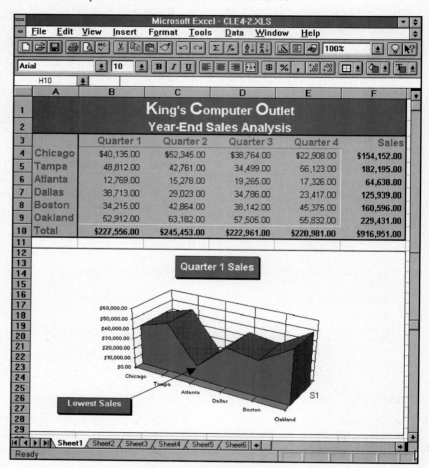

FIGURE CLE4-2

COMPUTER LABORATORY EXERCISE 3
Consolidating Data in a Workbook

Instructions: Perform the following steps to consolidate the four weekly payroll sheets into the monthly payroll sheet chart in the workbook CLE4-3.XLS. The Month Totals sheet should display as shown in the lower screen in Figure CLE4-3.

1. Open the workbook CLE4-3 from the subdirectory EXCEL5 on the Student Diskette.
2. One at a time, click the first four tabs and review the weekly totals. Click on the Month Totals tab to activate it.

3. Use the SUM function and 3-D references to sum the hours worked and gross pay for each employee to determine the monthly totals. See pages E247 through E249.

4. Save the workbook using the filename CLE4-3A.

5. Add a header that includes your name and course number on two lines in the Left Section box, the computer laboratory exercise number (CLE4-3) in the Center Section box, and the system date and your instructor name on two lines in the Right Section.

6. Print the workbook without cell gridlines.

7. Save the workbook with the print settings by clicking the Save button on the Standard toolbar.

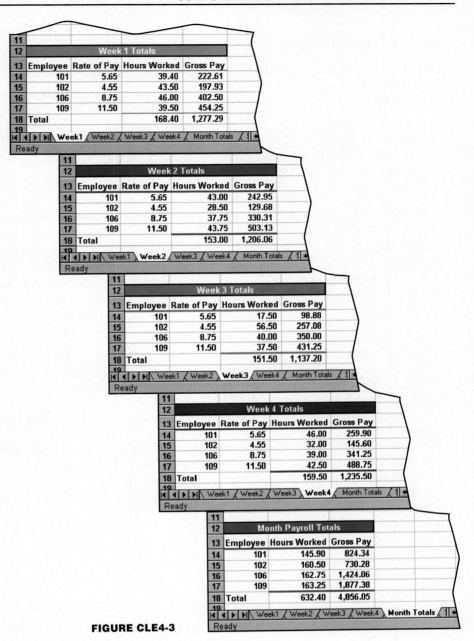

FIGURE CLE4-3

COMPUTER LABORATORY ASSIGNMENTS

COMPUTER LABORATORY ASSIGNMENT 1
Creating a Company Template

Purpose: To become familiar with creating, saving, and opening a template that changes Excel's defaults.

Problem: You are a summer intern in the Information Systems department at Southeast Airlines. Your specialty is designing worksheets. The company uses a product that allows people to share information across a computer network. Your supervisor has instructed you to create a company-specific template for employees to open when they use Excel (Figure CLA4-1a on the page).

(continued)

COMPUTER LABORATORY ASSIGNMENT 1 (continued)

Instructions: The template should include the following:

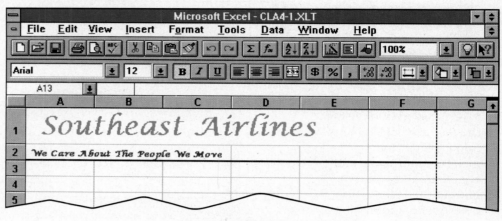

FIGURE CLA4-1a

1. Apply the comma format to all cells. Change the font of all cells to 12 point CG Times. Increase all column widths to 12. (**Hint**: Click the Select All button to make these changes).

2. Add a note to cell F1 identifying the template and its purpose (see page E252 for the type of information to include in the note). Include your name as the author.

3. Enter the titles in cells A1 and A2 as shown in Figure CLA4-1a. Change the font in cells A1 and A2 to Lucida Calligraphy (or something similar). In cell A1, change the font size and color to 26 point red. In cell A2, change the font size and color to 8 point blue. Draw a heavy bottom border across the range A2:F2.

4. Enter your name, course, computer laboratory assignment (CLA4-1), date, and instructor name in the range A8:A12.

5. Save the template using the filename CLA4-1. Remember, you must select Template in the Save File as Type box in the Save As dialog box when you save the template.

6. Print the template and note. To print the note, click the Note check box in the Sheet tab in the Page Setup dialog box. Your printout of page 2 should resemble Figure CLA4-1b. After the note prints, click the Note check box to toggle off printing the note.

7. Close the template. Open the template. Save the template as a regular workbook using the filename CLA4-1.

FIGURE CLA4-1b

> **Note:** Template for Southeast Airlines
> Author: John Quincy
> Date created: 6/24/96
> Date last modified: N/A
> This template changes the Excel defaults to those recommended by Southeast Airlines. To use this template, open it and then save it using a new filename.

COMPUTER LABORATORY ASSIGNMENT 2
Using a Template to Create a Multiple-Sheet Sales Analysis Workbook

Purpose: To become familiar with using a template to create a multiple-sheet workbook.

Problem: Unified Audio Center has outlets in Maui, Sanibel, and Bali. Each outlet sells products by telephone, by mail, by fax or to walk-in customers. The Information Systems department generates a year-end sales analysis workbook from a template. The workbook contains four sheets, one for each of the three outlets and one for the company. The Company Totals sheet displays as shown in Figure CLA4-2.

The template is stored in the subdirectory Excel5 on the Student Diskette. You have been assigned the task of creating the year-end sales analysis workbook from the template.

Instructions: Perform the following tasks:

1. Open the template CLA4-2.XLT from the subdirectory Excel5 on the Student Diskette. Click the Select All button and copy the template to the Clipboard. One at a time, paste the contents of the Clipboard to Sheet2, Sheet3, and Sheet4. Save the workbook using the filename CLA4-2.XLS.

2. Enter the data in Table CLA4-2 onto the three outlet sheets. Before entering the data on each sheet, rename the sheet tabs (Maui, Sanibel, Bali, and Company Totals). Change the title in cell A1 on each sheet. Change the chart range for the second and third sheets so it refers to the data on the same sheet the chart is on. Change the chart type and colors on these two sheets. Click the Save button on the Standard toolbar to save the workbook.

3. On the Company Totals sheet, use the SUM function, 3-D references, and the fill handle to total the corresponding cells on the three outlet sheets. Change the chart range and colors. The Company Totals sheet should resemble the one in Figure CLA4- 2. Save the workbook by clicking the Save button on the Stan-

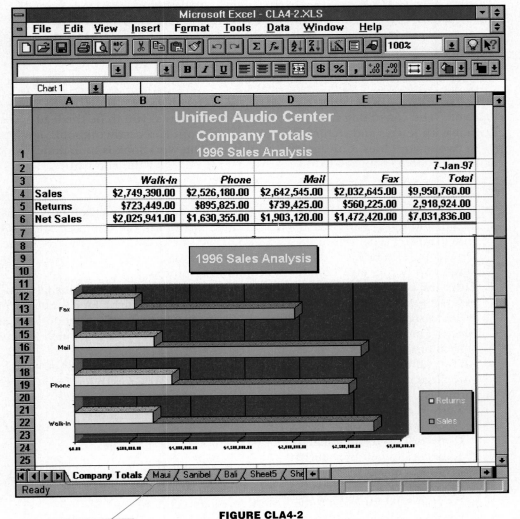

FIGURE CLA4-2

four sheets created from template CLA4-2.XLT

▶ **TABLE CLA4-2**

		MAUI	SANIBEL	BALI
Walk-In	Sales	$957,890	$879,150	$912,350
	Returns	325,450	123,675	274,324
Phone	Sales	792,800	754,730	978,650
	Returns	425,900	123,150	346,775
Mail	Sales	954,235	753,210	935,100
	Returns	123,000	211,675	404,750
Fax	Sales	786,400	592,345	653,900
	Returns	132,650	235,125	192,450

dard toolbar.

4. Select all four sheets. Change the header to include your name, course, computer laboratory exercise (CLA4-2.XLT), date, and instructor name. Change the footer to include the page number and total pages. Print the workbook without gridlines.

5. Save the workbook with the print settings.

COMPUTER LABORATORY ASSIGNMENT 3
Creating a Template and Consolidated Profit Forecast Sheet

Purpose: To become familiar with creating, saving, and opening a template and creating a multiple-sheet workbook.

Problem: The consulting firm you work for has assigned you to be the lead spreadsheet specialist on its account with Jewels and Denim Ltd. to create a Profit Forecast workbook. Jewels and Denim Ltd. has outlets in two major cities, Chicago and New York. The workbook is to include a worksheet and pie chart for each outlet and a summary worksheet with a pie chart for the company.

Instructions: Perform the following tasks:

1. Create the template in Figure CLA4-3. The column widths are as follows: A = 19.00; B through E = 12.00; and F = 13.00. Bold all cells. Change the font in the template title to Old Bookman (or something similar). The font in the first line of the title is 26 point. The font in the second line is 16 point. Draw a bottom border and italicize the column titles. Italicize the label Profit in cell A6 and draw a single top border and a double bottom border on row 6.

2. Enter the dummy data shown in Figure CLA4-3 into the Assumptions table in the range A8:E12. Format the text in the Assumptions section as shown in Figure CLA4-3. Enter all percents with a trailing percent sign (%). Format cell B9 to a Currency style with a floating dollar sign and two decimal places. Format the range B10:E12 to a Percentage style with two decimal places. Add the colors shown in Figure CLA4-3.

3. All the values that display in rows 4 through 6 are based on the assumptions in rows 8 through 12. A surcharge is added to the expenses whenever the Qtr Growth Rate is negative. Use the following formulas:
    a. Sales in cell B4: =B9
    b. Sales in cell C4: =B4 * (1 + C10)
    c. Copy cell C4 to the range D4:E4
    d. Expenses in cell B5: =IF(B10 < 0, B4 * (B11 + B12), B4 * B11)
    e. Profit in cell B6: =B4 - B5
    f. Copy the range B5:B6 to the range C5:E6
    g. Use the SUM function to determine totals in column F.

4. Create the 3-D pie chart that shows the contribution of each quarter to the total profit as shown in Figure CLA4-3. Use the chart ranges B3:E3 and B6:E6.

5. Save the template using the filename CLA4-3.XLT. Make sure the Save as File Type box is set to Template. Close the template.

6. Open the template. Copy the template to Sheet2., and Sheet3. Save the workbook using the filename CLA4-3.

7. Rename the tabs appropriately. Change the assumptions for Chicago to the following: Qtr1 Sales Amount = $598,000; Qtr2 Growth Rate = 3%; Qtr3 Growth Rate = -2.5%; Qtr4 Growth Rate = 1.5%; Qtr Expense Rate = 52%, 54.5%, 48.75%, and 54%; Surcharge = 2%, 1.75%, 3.5%, and 2.25%. Change the assumptions for New York to the following: Qtr1 Sales Amount = $675,000; Qtr2 Growth Rate = –3%; Qtr3 Growth Rate = 2%; Qtr4 Growth Rate = 4.75%; Qtr Expense Rate = 51%, 49.5%, 51%, and 57%; Surcharge = 1%, 2.25%, 1.75%, and 2%.

8. Delete the Assumptions table from the Summary sheet. Use 3-D references and the fill handle to determine totals on the Summary sheet. You should end up with the following totals in column F on the Summary sheet: Sales = $5,121,193.76; Expenses = $2,712,024.66; and Profit = $2,409,169.10.

9. Change the chart range so each pie chart refers to the data on the same sheet.

10. Save the workbook by clicking the Save button on the Standard toolbar.

11. Select all three sheets. Change the header to include your name, course, computer laboratory exercise (CLA4-3.XLT), date, and instructor name. Change the footer to include the page number and total pages. Print the workbook without gridlines.

12. Save the workbook by clicking the Save button on the Standard toolbar.

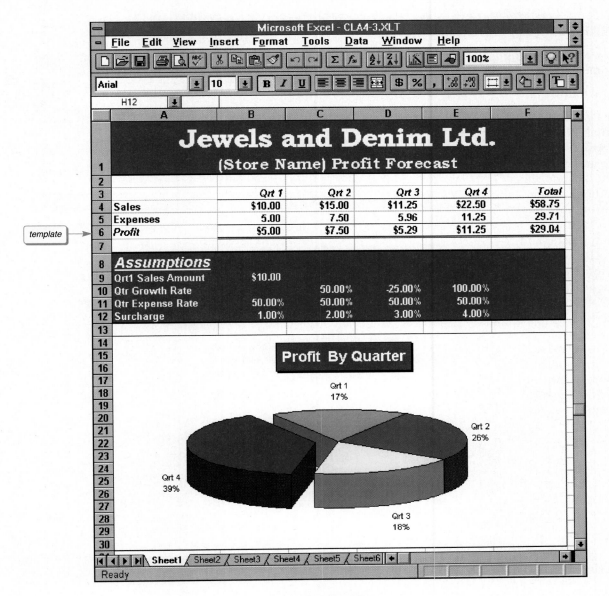

FIGURE CLA4-3

COMPUTER LABORATORY ASSIGNMENT 4
Creating a Template and Consolidated Balance Sheet

Purpose: To provide experience using Excel to create a template and consolidated balance sheet.

Problem: Some businesses are divided into smaller companies for the purpose of better organization. Tri-Quality International, by whom you are employed as an analyst is a parent to two companies — Modern Elek Avenue and Analog Haven. Create a template for the consolidated balance sheet workbook similar to the one in Figure CLA4-4 on the next page. Save the template using the filename CLA4-4. Close the template and then open it. Copy it to three sheets and then enter the data shown in Table CLA4-4 on the next page. Use 3-D references to consolidate the data on the first two sheets into one sheet that represents Tri-Quality International. Draw on a separate sheet in the workbook a 3-D pie chart that shows the consolidated contributions of each asset category to the total. Format the pie chart appropriately. Select all three sheets and enter your name, course, computer laboratory assignment number (CLA4-4), date, and instructor name as a header.

(continued)

COMPUTER LABORATORY ASSIGNMENT 4 (continued)

Save the workbook using the filename CLA4-4.

Submit the following:

1. A description of the problem. Include the purpose of the template and consolidated Balance Sheet workbook, a statement outlining the results, the required data, and calculations.

2. A printed copy of the template and workbook without gridlines.

3. A printed copy of the formulas in the summary sheet.

4. A short description explaining how to use the workbook.

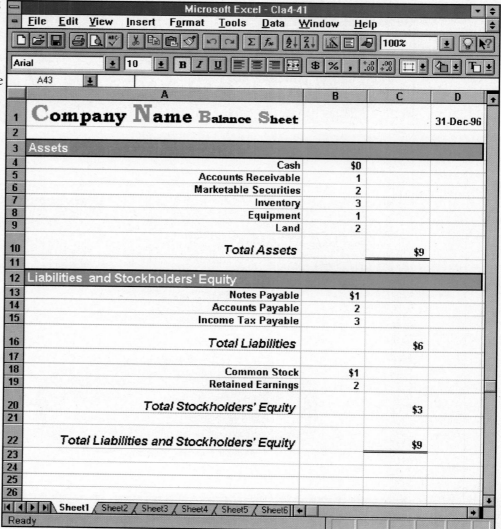

FIGURE CLA4-4

▸ **TABLE CLA4-4**

	MODERN ELK AVENUE	ANALOG HAVEN
Assets		
Cash	$211,000	$123,000
Accounts Receivable	72,500	63,500
Marketable Securities	179,150	213,500
Inventory	459,000	357,000
Equipment	213,000	114,000
Land	579,000	362,000
Liabilites and Stockholders' Equity		
Notes Payable	$62,500	$51,500
Accounts Payable	212,850	179,150
Income Tax Payable	73,000	49,500
Common Stock	585,200	625,100
Retained Earnings	780,100	327,750

MICROSOFT EXCEL 5 FOR WINDOWS

PROJECT FIVE

DATA TABLES, MACROS USING VISUAL BASIC, AND SCENARIO MANAGER

OBJECTIVES You will have mastered the material in this project when you can:

▸ Assign a name to a cell and refer to the cell in a formula by using the assigned name
▸ Determine the monthly payment of a loan using the financial function PMT
▸ State the purpose of the FV and PV functions
▸ Enter a series of percents using the fill handle
▸ Build a data table to analyze data in a worksheet

▸ Write a macro in Visual Basic to automate data entry into a worksheet
▸ Analyze worksheet data by changing values and goal seeking
▸ Use Excel's Scenario Manager to record and save different sets of what-if assumptions and the corresponding results of formulas
▸ Protect and unprotect cells

▸ INTRODUCTION

One of the more powerful aspects of Excel is its capability to analyze worksheet data or answer what-if questions. A what-if question regarding a loan might be, "What if the interest rate for a loan increases by 1% — how would the increase affect the monthly payment?" Or, "What if you know the result you want a formula in a worksheet to return, but you do not know the data required to attain that value?" Excel has the capability to quickly answer these types of questions and save you the time of performing trial-and-error analysis. In Project 3, you learned how to analyze data by using Excel's recalculation feature and goal seeking. This project revisits these two methods of analyzing data and describes two additional ones — data tables and Scenario Manager.

This project also introduces you to the use of macros and cell protection. You use a macro to reduce a series of actions to the click of a button or a keystroke. Cell protection ensures that you don't accidentally change values that are critical to the worksheet.

▶ PROJECT FIVE — WESAVU MONEY LOAN ANALYSIS WORKBOOK

Project 5 creates the WeSavU Money Loan Analysis workbook. The workbook is made up of three worksheets: (1) a worksheet that determines the monthly payment, total interest, and total cost for a loan; (2) a macro that instructs Excel to accept new loan data from the worksheet user; and (3) a worksheet that summarizes what-if questions. The latter is called a **Scenario Summary worksheet.**

The Loan Analysis worksheet (Figure 5-1) includes three distinct sections: (1) a loan analysis section in the range A1:B11; (2) a button titled New Loan in the range A13:A14 that, when clicked, executes the macro shown in Figure 5-2; and (3) a data table in the range D1:G16 that can be used to show the effect of different interest rates on the monthly payment, total interest, and total cost of the loan. The Scenario Summary worksheet will be shown and discussed later in this project.

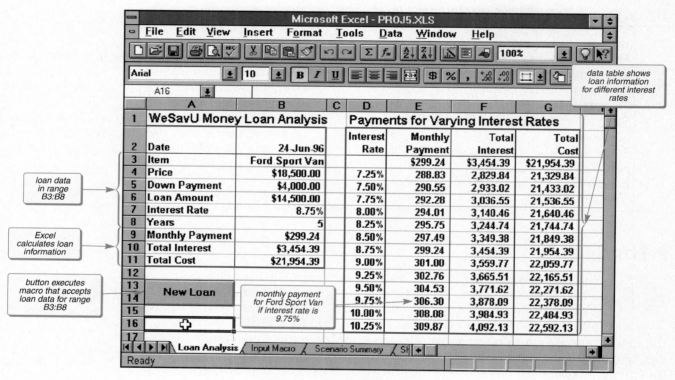

FIGURE 5-1

The loan analysis section on the left in Figure 5-1 answers the following question: What is the monthly payment (cell B9), total interest (cell B10), and total cost (cell B11) for a Ford Sport Van (cell B3) that costs $18,500.00 (cell B4), if the down payment is $4,000.00 (cell B5), the interest rate is 8.75% (cell B7), and the term of the loan is 5 years (cell B8)? As shown in Figure 5-1, the monthly payment is $299.24 (cell B9), the total interest is $3,454.39 (cell B10), and the total cost of the Ford Sport Van is $21,954.39 (cell B11). Excel determines the monthly payment in cell B9 using the PMT function. Formulas are used to calculate the total interest and total cost in cells B10 and B11. The loan analysis section of the worksheet can determine the answers to loan questions for the WeSavU Money Loan Company as fast as you can enter the new loan data in the range B3:B8.

The function of the button titled New Loan in the range A13:A14 (Figure 5-1) is to automate the entry of loan data. The button executes the macro in Figure 5-2 that simplifies the loan data entry into cells B3 through B8. Using a button that executes a macro to enter the loan data is especially helpful for users who know little about computers and worksheets.

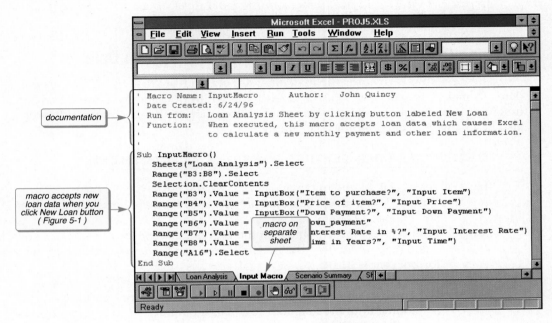

FIGURE 5-2

The third section of the worksheet in Figure 5-1 is the data table on the right side of the screen. Each time you enter new loan data into the worksheet, the data table recalculates new values for the monthly payment, total interest, and total cost for the different interest rates in column D. A **data table** is a powerful what-if tool because it can automate your data analyses and organize the answers returned by Excel. The data table in Figure 5-1 answers thirteen different what-if questions. The questions pertain to the effect the thirteen different interest rates in column D have on the monthly payment, total interest, and total cost. For example, what will be the monthly payment for the Ford Sport Van if the interest rate is 9.75%, instead of 8.75%? The answer, $306.30, is in cell E14.

The macro in Figure 5-2 is made up of a series of Visual Basic statements that are executed when you click the New Loan button (Figure 5-1). Visual Basic statements tell Excel to carry out an operation, such as select a range or clear the selection. Creating a macro is a form of **programming.** The programming language you use with Excel 5 is called **Visual Basic for Applications**, or **VBA**.

Changing the Font of the Entire Worksheet

After you start Excel, the first step in this project is to change the font of the entire worksheet to bold. By bolding the font, the characters in the worksheet stand out.

TO CHANGE THE FONT OF THE ENTIRE WORKSHEET

Step 1: Click the Select All button immediately above row heading 1 and to the left of column heading A (see Figure 5-3).
Step 2: Click the Bold button on the Formatting toolbar.

As you enter text and numbers onto the worksheet, they will display in Arial bold.

Entering the Worksheet Title, Row Titles, and System Date

The next step is to enter the loan analysis section title, row titles, and system date. To make the worksheet easier to read, the width of columns A and B and the height of rows 1 and 2 will be increased. The font size of the worksheet title will also be changed from 10 point to 12 point.

TO ENTER THE WORKSHEET TITLE, ROW TITLES, AND SYSTEM DATE

Step 1: Select cell A1 and enter `WeSavU Money Loan Analysis`
Step 2: With cell A1 active, click the Font Size arrow on the Formatting toolbar and choose 12.
Step 3: Position the mouse pointer on the border between row headings 1 and 2 and drag down until the height of row 1 in the reference area in the formula bar is 21.00.
Step 4: Select cell A2 and enter the row title `Date`
Step 5: Position the mouse pointer on the border between row headings 2 and 3 and drag until the height of row 2 in the reference area in the formula bar is 27.00.
Step 6: Enter the following row titles:

CELL	ENTRY	CELL	ENTRY	CELL	ENTRY
A3	Item	A6	Loan Amount	A9	Monthly Payment
A4	Price	A7	Interest Rate	A10	Total Interest
A5	Down Payment	A8	Years	A11	Total Cost

Step 7: Select columns A and B. Position the mouse pointer on the border between column headings B and C and drag until the width of column B in the reference area in the formula bar is 16.00.
Step 8: Select cell B2. Enter `=now()`
Step 9: With the mouse pointer in cell B2, click the right mouse button and choose the Format Cells command. When the Format Cells dialog box displays, click the Number tab if necessary, select Date in the Category box, and select d-mmm-yy in the Format Codes box. Choose the OK button.
Step 10: Click the Save button on the Standard toolbar. Save the workbook using the filename PROJ5.XLS.

The worksheet title, row titles, and system date display as shown in Figure 5-3.

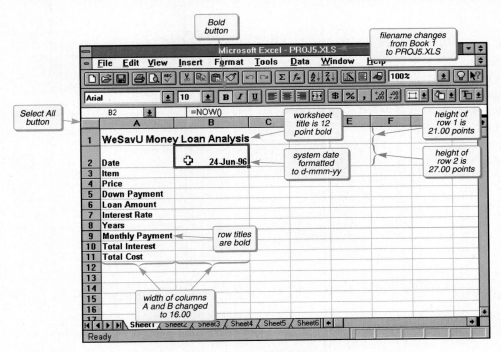

FIGURE 5-3

Outlining and Adding Borders to the Loan Analysis Section of the Worksheet

An **outline** is used to box-in an area of the worksheet so it stands out. In this case, the outline is used to separate the loan analysis section in the range A1:B11 from the data table in the range D1:G16. Light borders are also used within the outline to further subdivide the loan analysis text and numbers as shown in Figure 5-1 on page E278.

TO DRAW AN OUTLINE AND BORDERS ▼

STEP 1 ▶

Select the range A2:B11. With the mouse pointer in the selected range, click the right mouse button to display the shortcut menu.

The shortcut menu displays (Figure 5-4).

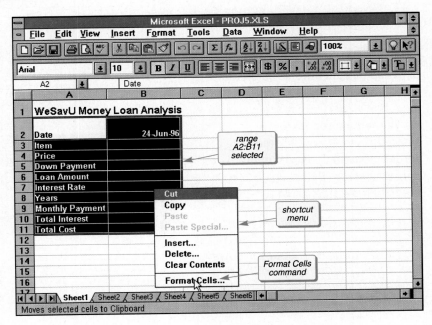

FIGURE 5-4

STEP 2 ►

Choose the Format Cells command. When the Format Cells dialog box displays, select the Border tab. Click the Color box arrow. Select red (column 1, row 2 on the palette). Select the regular border in the Style area (column 1, row 3). Click the Outline box in the Border area.

The **Border tab** in the Format Cells dialog box displays as shown in Figure 5-5.

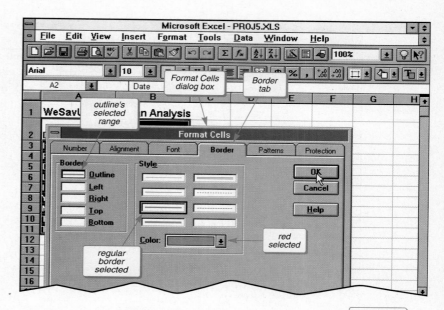

FIGURE 5-5

STEP 3 ►

Choose the OK button in the Format Cells dialog box. Select the range A2:B2. Click the arrow on the Borders button on the Formatting toolbar.

The loan analysis section of the worksheet displays along with the Border palette as shown in Figure 5-6.

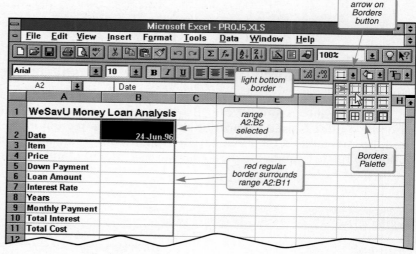

FIGURE 5-6

STEP 4 ►

Click the bottom border (column 2, row 1) on the Borders palette. Select the range A2:A11. Click the arrow on the Borders button on the Formatting toolbar. Click the right border (column 4, row 1) on the Borders palette. Select cell B13 to deselect the range A2:A11.

The loan analysis section is outlined in red. It has a border dividing row 2 from the rest of the rows and a right border dividing the two columns (Figure 5-7).

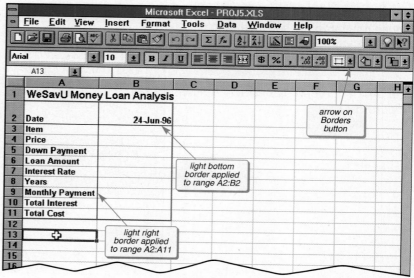

FIGURE 5-7

Entering the Loan Data

According to the worksheet in Figure 5-1 on page E278, the item to be purchased, the price of the item, the down payment, the interest rate, and the number of years until the loan is paid back are entered into cells B3 through B5 and cells B7 and B8. These five values make up the loan data.

TO ENTER THE LOAN DATA

Step 1: Select cell B3. Enter Ford Sport Van and click the Align Right button on the Formatting toolbar. Select cell B4 and enter 18500. Select cell B5 and enter 4000.

Step 2: Skip cell B6 and select cell B7. Enter 8.75%. Select cell B8 and enter 5.

The loan data displays in the worksheet as shown in Figure 5-8. The interest rate is formatted to the 0.00% Percent style because the percent sign (%) was typed as part of the entry in cell B7.

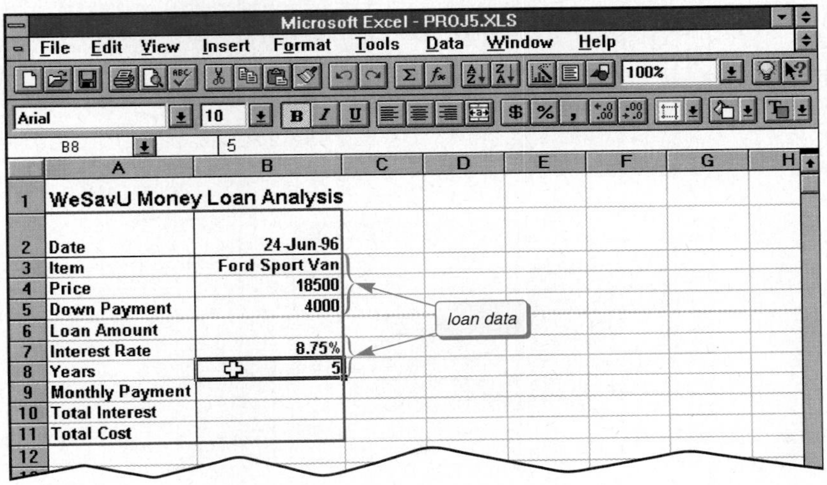

FIGURE 5-8

The four remaining entries in the loan analysis section of the worksheet, loan amount (cell B6), monthly payment (cell B9), total interest (cell B10), and total cost (cell B11), require formulas that reference cells B4, B5, B7, and B8. The formulas will be entered referencing names assigned to cells instead of cell references because names are easier to remember than cell references.

▶ CREATING NAMES BASED ON ROW TITLES

Naming a cell that you plan to reference in a formula helps make the formula easier to read and remember. For example, the loan amount in cell B6 is equal to the price in cell B4 less the down payment in cell B5. Therefore, according to what you learned in the earlier projects, you can write the loan amount formula in cell B6 as =B4 - B5. However, by assigning the corresponding row titles in column A as the names of cells B4 and B5 you can write the loan amount formula as =Price – Down_Payment which is clearer and easier to remember than =B4 - B5.

To name cells, you first select the range encompassing the row titles that include the names and the cells to be named (range A4:B11). Next, you use the **Name command** on the Insert menu, then choose the **Create command** on the cascading menu. In the **Create Names dialog box**, you select Top Row, Left Column, Bottom Row, or Right Row depending on where the names are located in relation to the cells to be named. In this case, the names are the row titles in column A. Therefore, you select Left Columns. On the basis of the range you select prior to invoking the command, Excel will make a selection of its own, which you can change in the Create Names dialog box.

In the following steps, each row title in the range A4:A11 is assigned to the adjacent cell in column B. Because the data in cell B2 and the item in cell B3 will not be referenced in formulas, there is no need to include them in the range.

TO CREATE NAMES ▼

STEP 1 ▶

Select the range A4:B11. Select the Insert menu and choose the Name command.

The range A4:B11 is selected and Excel displays the Name command cascading menu (Figure 5-9).

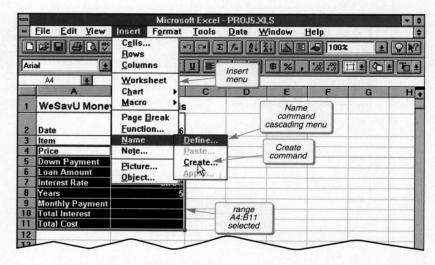

FIGURE 5-9

STEP 2 ▶

Choose the Create command from the cascading menu.

Excel displays the Create names dialog box (Figure 5-10). Excel automatically selects the Left Column box because the general direction of the range in Step 1 is downward.

STEP 3 ▶

Choose the OK button in the Create Names dialog box.

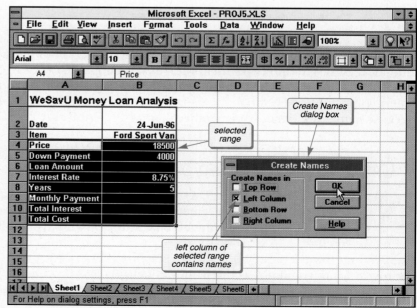

FIGURE 5-10

After Step 3, you can use the names in the range A4:A11 in formulas to reference the adjacent cells in the range B4:B11. Excel is not case-sensitive with respect to names of cells. Hence, you can enter the names of cells in formulas in uppercase or lowercase. Some names, such as Down Payment in cell A5, include a space because they are made up of two words. To use a name in a formula that is made up of two or more words, replace any space with the underscore character (_). For example, Down Payment is written as down_payment when you want to reference the adjacent cell B5. Consider these three additional details regarding the assignment of names to cells:

1. A name can be a minimum of one character or a maximum of 255 characters.

2. If you want to assign a name that is not a text item in an adjacent cell, use the Define command on the cascading menu shown in Figure 5-9 or select the cell or range and type the name in the reference area in the formula bar.

3. The worksheet names display in alphabetical order in the Name box when you click the Name box arrow (Figure 5-11).

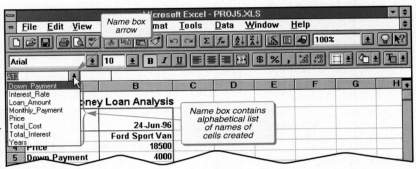

FIGURE 5-11

Using the Name Box and Point Mode to Enter a Formula

The next step is to enter in cell B6 the formula =Price – Down_Payment. You can enter the formula as you have in the previous projects by using the keyboard and the Point mode. However, the Name box offers an alternative to the Point mode that allows you to point to the names of cells, instead of to the cells themselves. The following steps show how to use the Point mode and the Name box to enter the formula =Price – Down_Payment in cell B6.

TO ENTER THE LOAN AMOUNT FORMULA USING THE NAME BOX ▼

STEP 1 ▶

Select cell B6. Type = and click the Name box arrow in the formula bar.

The Name box displays with Loan_Amount selected because the cell it names (cell B6) is the active one (Figure 5-12).

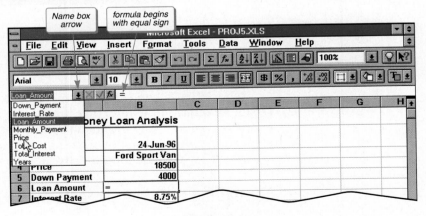

FIGURE 5-12

STEP 2 ▶

Click the name Price in the Name drop-down list box. Press the SPACEBAR, type a minus sign (-), and press the SPACEBAR.

The first term in the formula displays in the formula bar and in cell B6 (Figure 5-13). Pressing the SPACEBAR inserts spaces before and after the minus sign for readability.

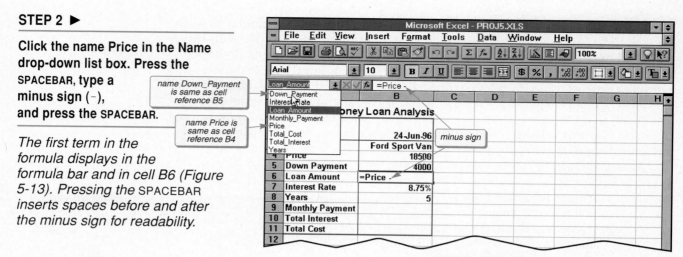

FIGURE 5-13

STEP 3 ▶

Click the Name box arrow in the formula bar. Click the name Down_Payment in the Name drop-down list box. Click the enter box or press the ENTER key.

Excel assigns the formula =Price – Down_Payment to cell B6 and displays the result of the formula (14500) in cell B6 (Figure 5-14).

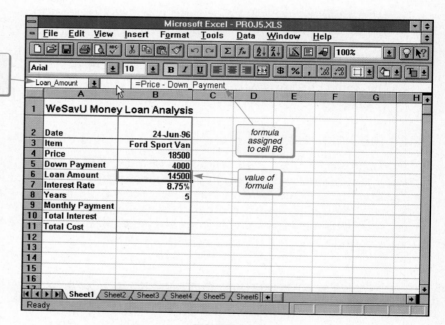

FIGURE 5-14

Notice that when cell B6 is selected, Excel displays the name of the cell (Loan_Amount) in the reference area in the formula bar instead of the cell reference B6. Besides using the Name box to assign names in formulas, you can click a name in the Name drop-down list box to select the cell it names. For example, to select cell B9, click on Monthly_Payment in the Name drop-down list box.

Formatting to Currency Style with a Floating Dollar Sign

After entering the loan amount formula, the next step is to format the nonadjacent ranges B4:B6 and B9:B11 to the Currency style with a floating dollar sign.

TO FORMAT TO CURRENCY STYLE WITH A FLOATING DOLLAR SIGN ▼

STEP 1 ▶

Select the range B4:B6. Hold down the CTRL key and select the range B9:B11. With the mouse pointer in one of the selected ranges, click the right mouse button to display the shortcut menu. Choose the Format Cells command. When the Format Cells dialog box displays, click the Number tab. Select Currency in the Category box and $#,##0.00_);[Red]($#,##0.00) in the Format Codes box.

The Format Cells dialog box displays as shown in Figure 5-15.

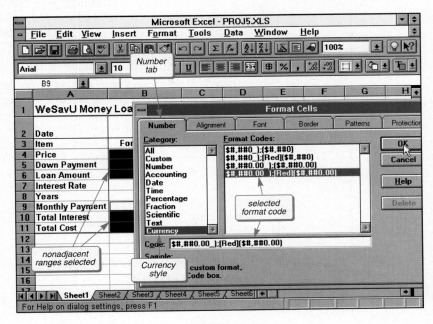

FIGURE 5-15

STEP 2 ▶

Choose the OK button in the Format Cells dialog box.

The price, down payment, and loan amount in the range B4:B6 have been formatted to Currency style and display as shown in Figure 5-16. Later when numbers display in the range B9:B11, they will display using the Currency style.

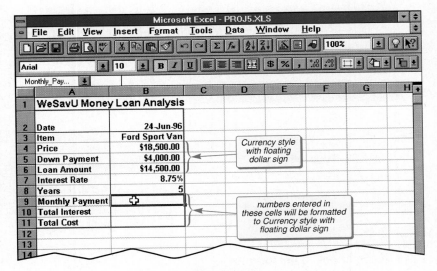

FIGURE 5-16

An alternative to formatting the numbers to the Currency style as described in the previous steps is to enter the numbers in the desired format. For example, the number 18500 could have been entered earlier as $18,500.00 and the Currency style with a floating dollar sign would have been automatically assigned to the cell. The same can be said for the remaining dollar amounts entered earlier. A third alternative is to enter the dollar amount in cell B4 and then use the Format Painter button on the Standard toolbar to format the remaining cells containing dollar amounts.

▶ **DETERMINING THE MONTHLY PAYMENT**

U sing Excel's PMT function, you can determine the monthly payment (cell B9) on the basis of the loan amount (cell B6), the interest rate (cell B7), and the term of the loan (cell B8). The general form of the **PMT function** is

=PMT(rate, payments, loan amount)

where rate is the interest rate per payment period, payments is the number of payments, and loan amount is the amount of the loan. Rate, payments, and loan amount are called **arguments.**

In the worksheet shown in Figure 5-16 on the previous page, cell B7 is equal to the annual interest rate. However, loan institutions calculate the interest, which is their profit, on a monthly basis. Thus, the first value in the PMT function is Interest_Rate / 12 (cell B7 divided by 12) instead of Interest_Rate (cell B7). The number of payments (or periods) is equal to 12 * Years (12 times cell B8) because there are twelve months, or twelve payments, per year.

Excel considers the value returned by the PMT function to be a debit and therefore, returns a negative number as the monthly payment. To display the monthly payment as a positive number precede the loan amount with a negative sign. Thus, the loan amount is equal to -Loan_Amount. The PMT function for cell B9 becomes the following:

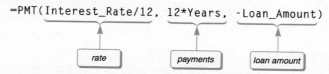

The following steps use the PMT function to determine the monthly payment in cell B7.

TO ENTER THE PMT FUNCTION ▼

STEP 1 ▶

Select cell B9. Type
=pmt(interest_rate / 12, 12 * years, -loan_amount)

STEP 2 ▶

Click the enter box in the formula bar or press the ENTER key.

Excel displays the monthly payment of $299.24 in cell B9 (Figure 5-17) for a loan amount of $14,500.00 (cell B6) with an annual interest rate of 8.75% (cell B7) for five years (cell B8). Notice that with cell B9 selected, the PMT function displays in the formula bar.

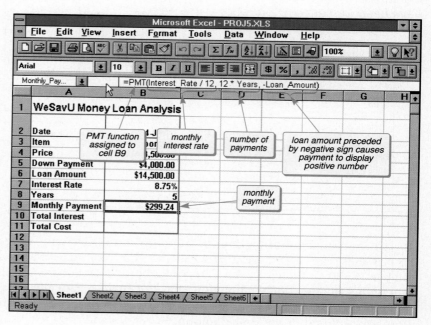

FIGURE 5-17

An alternative way to enter the PMT function is by using the Function Wizard button on the Standard toolbar. In addition, using the Point mode along with the Name box arrow in the formula bar, you can select the cells representing the rate, payment, and loan amount.

Besides the PMT function, Excel has fifty-two additional **financial functions** to help you solve the most complex financial problems. These functions save you from entering long, complicated formulas to obtain the results you require. Table 5-1 summarizes three of the most often used financial functions.

▸ **TABLE 5-1**

FUNCTION	DESCRIPTION
FV(rate, periods, payment)	Returns the future value of an investment based on periodic, constant payments and constant interest rate.
PMT(rate, periods, loan amount)	Returns the periodic payment of a loan.
PV(rate, periods, payment)	Returns the present value of an investment made up of a series of payments.

To view a complete list of Excel's financial functions, select the Help menu and choose the Search for Help on command. When the Search dialog box displays, type `financial functions` in the top box. Choose the Show Topic button. Select Financial Functions in the lower box and choose the Go To button. Excel responds by displaying a list of all the financial functions. An alternative to using the Help menu to learn about the financial functions is to click the Function Wizard button on the Standard toolbar as described in the following steps.

**TO OBTAIN INFORMATION ON FINANCIAL
FUNCTIONS USING THE FUNCTION WIZARD BUTTON**

Step 1: Select any empty cell in the worksheet. Click the Function Wizard button on the Standard toolbar.

Step 2: Select Financial in the Function Category box when the Function Wizard – Step 1 of 2 dialog box displays.

Step 3: One by one, select the functions in the Function Name box and read the description below the Function Category box.

Step 4: When you are finished, choose the Cancel button in the Function Wizard – Step 1 of 2 dialog box.

▶ DETERMINING THE TOTAL INTEREST AND TOTAL COST

The next step is to determine the total interest (the loan institution's profit) and the borrower's total cost of the item being purchased. The total interest (cell B10) is equal to:

12 * Years * Monthly_Payment – Loan_Amount

The total cost of the item to be purchased (cell B11) is equal to:

12 * Years * Monthly_Payment + Down_Payment

To enter the total interest and total cost formulas, perform the steps on the following page.

TO DETERMINE THE TOTAL INTEREST,
TOTAL COST, AND SAVE THE WORKBOOK

Step 1: Select cell B10. Enter the formula:

`=12 * years * monthly_payment - loan_amount`

Step 2: Select cell B11. Enter the formula:

`=12 * years * monthly_payment + down_payment`

Step 3: Click the Save button on the Standard toolbar to save the workbook using the filename PROJ5.XLS.

Excel displays the total interest, $3,454.39, in cell B10 and the total cost of the Ford Sport Van to be purchased, $21,954.39, in cell B11 (Figure 5-18).

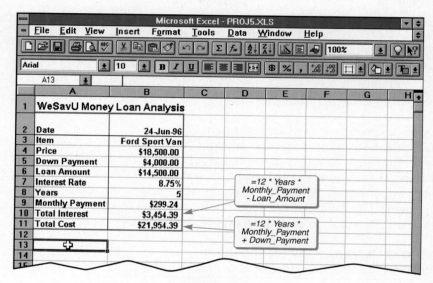

FIGURE 5-18

With the loan analysis section of the worksheet complete, you can determine the monthly payment, total interest, and total cost for any reasonable loan data. After entering the data table in the next section, alternative loan data will be entered to illustrate Excel's recalculation feature.

▶ USING A DATA TABLE TO ANALYZE WORKSHEET DATA

The next step is to build the data table section of the worksheet in the range D1:G16 (right side of Figure 5-19). A **data table** is a range of cells that shows the answers to formulas in which different values have been substituted.

You have already seen that if a value is changed in a cell referenced elsewhere in a formula in the worksheet, Excel immediately recalculates and stores the new value in the cell assigned the formula. What if you want to compare the results of the formula for several different values? It would be unwieldy to write down or remember all the answers to the what-if questions. This is where a data table becomes useful because it will organize the answers in the worksheet for you automatically.

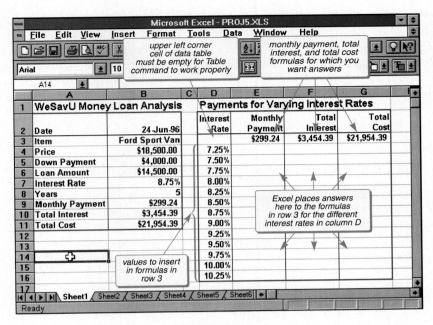

FIGURE 5-19

Data tables are built in an unused area of the worksheet. You may vary one or two values and display the results of the specified formulas in table form. The right side of Figure 5-19 illustrates the makeup of a one-input data table. With a **one-input data table**, you vary one cell reference (in this project, cell B7, the interest rate) and Excel fills the table with the results of one or more formulas. In this project, they are the monthly payment, total interest, and total cost.

The interest rates that will be used to analyze the loan formulas in this project range from 7.25% to 10.25% in increments of 0.25%. The data table (Figure 5-20) illustrates the impact of varying the interest rate on three formulas: the monthly payment (cell B9), total interest paid (cell B10), and the total cost of the item to be purchased (cell B11).

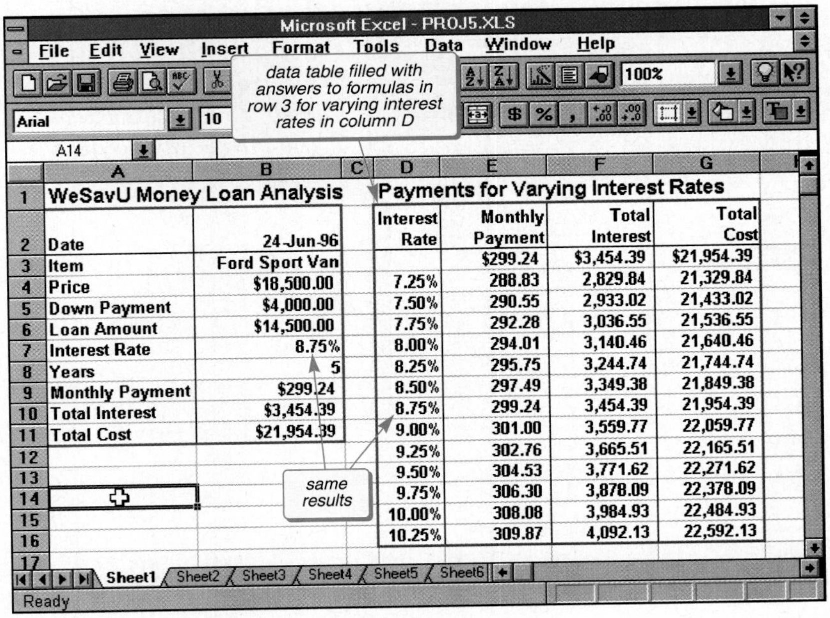

FIGURE 5-20

The steps that follow are used to construct the data table in Figure 5-20: (1) adjust the widths of columns C through G; (2) enter the data table title and column titles in the range D1:G2; (3) use the data fill handle to enter the varying interest rates in column D; (4) enter the formulas in the range E3:G3 for which the data table is to determine answers; (5) use the **Table command** on the **Data menu** to define the range D3:G16 as a data table and identify the interest rate in cell B7 as the **input cell**, the cell to vary; and (6) outline the data table to highlight it. The techniques to accomplish these tasks are presented on the following pages.

Changing Column Widths and Entering Titles

First, the columns are set to specific widths so the data table will fit in the same window with the loan analysis section. Keep in mind you may have to adjust the widths of columns after the numbers and text are assigned to the cells because large numbers that won't fit in a cell cause Excel to display number signs (#) in the cell. When you design a worksheet, you make the best possible estimate of column widths and then change them later as required.

**TO CHANGE COLUMN WIDTHS AND ENTER THE
DATA TABLE TITLE AND COLUMN TITLES**

Step 1: Use the mouse to change the widths of columns C through G as follows: C = 3.00; D = 6. 71; and E, F, and G = 11. 29.

Step 2: Select cell D1 and enter Payments for Varying Interest Rates

Step 3: Click the Font Size arrow on the Formatting toolbar and choose 12.

Step 4: Enter the following in the range D2:G2:

CELL	ENTRY
D2	Interest ALT+ENTER Rate
E2	Monthly ALT+ENTER Payment
F2	Total ALT+ENTER Interest
G2	Total ALT+ENTER Cost

Step 5: Select the range D2:G2. Click the Align Right button on the Formatting toolbar.

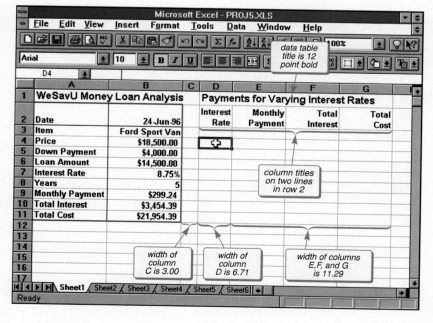

The data table title and column headings display as shown in Figure 5-21. Pressing ALT + ENTER *in Step 4 instructs Excel to continue the entry on the next line of the cell.*

FIGURE 5-21

Creating a Percent Series Using the Fill Handle

After changing the column widths and entering the titles, the next step is to create the percent series in column D using the fill handle.

TO CREATE A PERCENT SERIES USING THE FILL HANDLE ▼

STEP 1 ▶

Enter 7.25% in cell D4 and 7.50% in cell D5.

STEP 2 ▶

Select the range D4:D5 and point to the fill handle. Drag the fill handle down through cell D16.

Excel shades the border of the paste area (Figure 5-22).

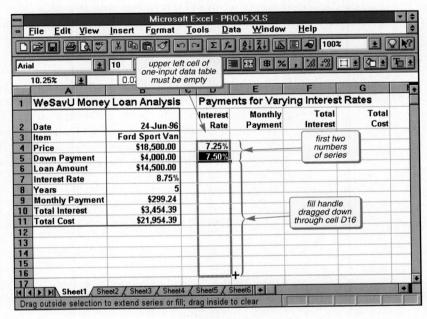

FIGURE 5-22

STEP 3 ▶

Release the mouse button. Select cell E3.

Excel generates the series of numbers, 7.25% to 10.25% in increments of 0.25%, in the range D4:D16 (Figure 5-23).

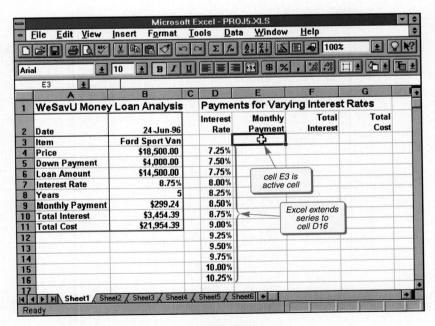

FIGURE 5-23

The percents in column D are the values Excel uses to compute the formulas entered at the top of the data table in row 3. Notice that the series beginning with 7.25% in column D was not started in cell D3 because the cell immediately above the series and to the left of the formulas in the data table (Figure 5-22 on the previous page) must be empty for a one-input data table.

Entering the Formulas in the Data Table

The next step in creating the data table is to enter the three formulas in row 3 in cells E3, F3, and G3. The three formulas are the same as the monthly payment formula in cell B9, the total interest formula in cell B10, and the total cost formula in cell B11.

Excel provides three ways to enter these formulas in the data table: (1) retype the formulas in cells E3, F3, and G3; (2) copy cells B9, B10, and B11 to cells E3, F3, and G3, respectively; or (3) enter the formulas =Monthly_Payment in cell E3, =Total_Interest in cell F3, and enter =Total_Cost in cell G3. Recall that earlier in this project cells B9 through B11 were assigned names.

Using the names preceded by an equal sign to define the formulas in the data table has two advantages: (1) it is more efficient; and (2) if you change any of the formulas in the range B9:B11, the formulas at the top of the data table are automatically updated.

TO ENTER AND FORMAT THE FORMULAS IN THE DATA TABLE

Step 1: With cell E3 selected, enter =Monthly_Payment
Step 2: Select cell F3. Type =Total_Interest
Step 3: Select cell G3. Type =Total_Cost
Step 4: Select the range E3:G3. Click the Currency Style button on the Formatting toolbar.

The results of the formulas display in the range E3:G3 (Figure 5-24).

Here again, the formulas could have been entered using the Point mode and the Name box arrow in the formula bar.

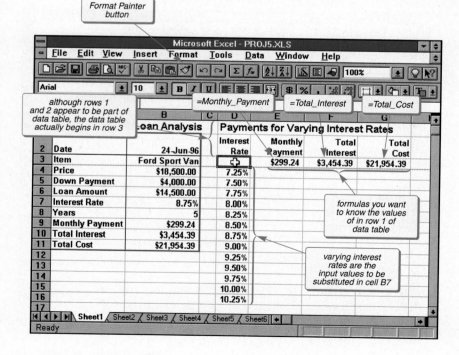

FIGURE 5-24

Defining the Data Table

After creating the interest rates in column D and assigning the formulas in row 3, the next step is to define the range D3:G16 as a data table.

TO DEFINE A RANGE AS A DATA TABLE ▼

STEP 1 ▶

Select the range D3:G16. Select the Data menu.

*Excel displays the Data menu (Figure 5-25). Notice in the worksheet that the range D3:G16 does not include the data table title in row 1 and column headings in row 2. The column headings are **NOT** part of the data table even though they identify the columns in the table.*

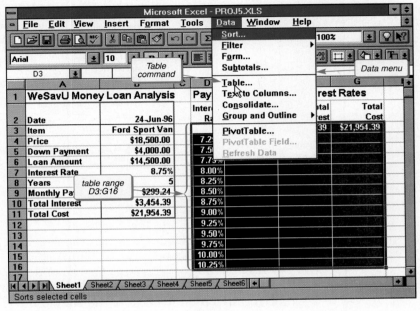

FIGURE 5-25

STEP 2 ▶

Choose the Table command from the Data menu. When the Table dialog box displays, select the Column Input Cell box in the Table dialog box. Click cell B7 or type $B$7, the input cell.

*A marquis surrounds the selected input cell B7 and Excel assigns cell B7 to the Column Input Cell box in the **Table dialog box** (Figure 5-26).*

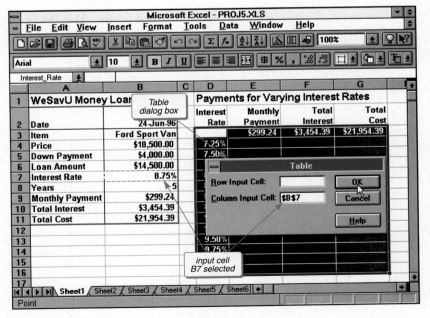

FIGURE 5-26

STEP 3 ▶

Choose the OK button in the Table dialog box.

Excel immediately fills the data table by calculating the three formulas at the top of the data table for each interest rate in column D (Figure 5-27).

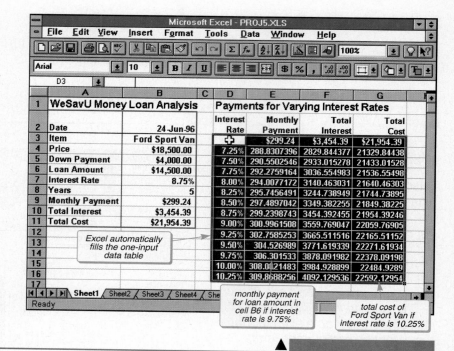

FIGURE 5-27

Notice in Figure 5-27 that the data table displays the monthly payment, total interest, and total cost for the interest rates in column D. For example, if the interest rate is 9.75% (cell D14) instead of 8.75% (cell B7), the monthly payment is $306.30 (cell E14) instead of $299.24 (cell B9). If the interest rate is 10.25% (cell D16) then the total cost of the Ford Sport Van is approximately $22,592.13 (cell G16) instead of $21,954.39 (cell B11). Thus, a 1.5% increase in the interest rate results in a $637.74 increase in the total cost of the Ford Sport Van.

TO OUTLINE AND FORMAT THE DATA TABLE AND SAVE THE WORKBOOK

Step 1: Select the range E4:G16. Click the Comma Style button on the Formatting toolbar.

Step 2: Select the range D2:G16. With the mouse pointer in the selected range, click the right mouse button.

Step 3: When the shortcut menu displays, choose the Format Cells command. When the Format Cells dialog box displays, click the Border tab.

Step 4: Click the Color box arrow on the Border tab. Select red (column 1, row 2 on the palette). Select Outline in the Border box. Select the regular border in the Style box (column 1, row 3). Choose the OK button in the Format Cells dialog box.

Step 5: Select the range D2:G2. Click the arrow on the Borders button on the Formatting toolbar. Choose the light bottom border (column 2, row 1) on the Borders palette.

Step 6: Select the range D2:F16. Click the Borders button arrow on the Formatting toolbar. Choose the light right border (column 4, row 1) on the Borders palette.

Step 7: Double-click the Sheet1 tab. When the Rename dialog box displays, type `Loan Analysis` and choose the OK button.

Step 8: Click the Save button on the Standard toolbar to save the workbook using the filename PROJ5.XLS.

The worksheet displays as shown in Figure 5-28.

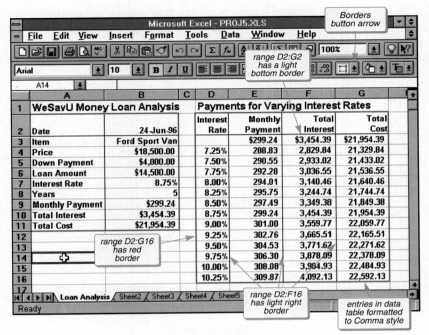

FIGURE 5-28

The following list details important points you should know about data tables:

1. The input cell must be a cell reference in the formula(s) you are analyzing.
2. You can have as many active data tables in a worksheet as you want.
3. You delete a data table as you would any other item on a worksheet. That is, select the data table and press the DELETE key.
4. For a data table with one varying value, the cell in the upper left corner of the table (cell D3 in Figure 5-28) must be empty.
5. To add additional formulas to a one-input data table, enter them in adjacent cells in the same row as the current formulas and define the entire range as a data table by using the Table command on the Data menu.
6. A one-input data table can vary only one value, but can analyze as many formulas as you want.

ENTERING NEW LOAN DATA

With the loan analysis and data table sections of the worksheet complete, you can use them to generate new loan information. For example, assume you want to purchase a $178,500.00 house. You have $36,500.00 for a down payment and want the loan for 15 years. The loan company is currently charging 8.75% interest for a 15-year loan. The following steps show how to enter the new loan data.

TO ENTER NEW LOAN DATA

Step 1: Select cell B3. Enter the item to be purchased, House
Step 2: Select cell B4. Enter the price of the house, 178500
Step 3: Select cell B5. Enter the down payment, 36500
Step 4: Leave the interest rate at 8.75% in cell B7.
Step 5: Select cell B8. Enter the number of years, 15

Excel automatically recalculates the loan information in cells B6, B9, B10, B11, and the data table (Figure 5-29 on the following page). Do not save the workbook with the changes.

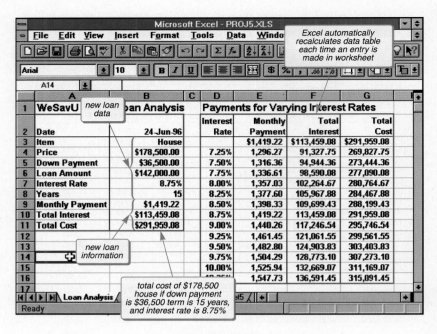

FIGURE 5-29

You can use the worksheet to calculate the loan information for any reasonable loan data. As you can see from Figure 5-29, the monthly payment for the house is $1,419.22. The total interest (loan institution's profit) is $113,459.08. The total cost of the house is $291,959.08.

▶ CREATING A MACRO TO AUTOMATE LOAN DATA ENTRY

A **macro** is made up of a series of Visual Basic statements that tell Excel how to complete a task. A macro like the one shown in Figure 5-30 is used to automate routine workbook tasks such as entering new data into a worksheet. Macros are almost a necessity for worksheets that are built to be used by people who know little or nothing about computers and worksheets.

For example, in the previous section new loan data was entered to calculate new loan information. However, the user who enters the data must know what cells to select and how much loan data is required to obtain the desired results. To facilitate entering the loan data, a worksheet and macro can be set up so the user simply clicks a button to execute the macro. The instructions that make up the macro (Figure 5-30) then guide the user through entering the required loan data in the range B3:B8.

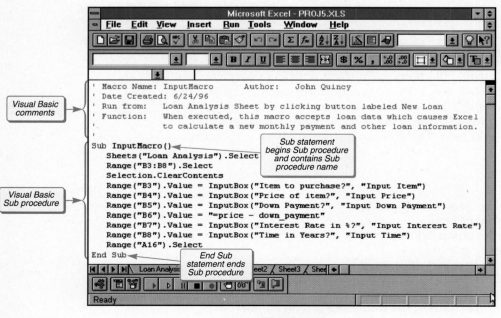

FIGURE 5-30

Visual Basic Statements

Visual Basic for Applications is a powerful programming language available with Excel that you can use to carry out most of the workbook activity described thus far in this book. Visual Basic statements (or **Visual Basic code**) are entered on a **module sheet**. **Visual Basic statements** are instructions to Excel. In the case of Project 5, all the statements are entered into a single **Sub procedure**. A Sub procedure begins with a **Sub statement** and ends with an **End Sub statement** (Figure 5-30).

The Sub statement includes the name of the Sub procedure. This Sub procedure name is important because it is used later to run the macro. In Project 5, the Sub procedure name used is InputMacro, but it could be any name with fewer than 40 characters.

Remark statements begin with the word **Rem** or an apostrophe ('). In Figure 5-30, there are six remark lines prior to the Sub statement. These remarks contain overall Sub procedure documentation, and therefore, are optionally placed above the Sub statement. Rem statements have no effect on the execution of a macro.

This project is concerned with using the seven Visual Basic statements and one Visual Basic function listed in Table 5-2. InputBox is a **function**, instead of a statement because it returns a value to the Sub procedure.

▸ **TABLE 5-2**

VISUAL BASIC STATMENTS*	DESCRIPTION
Rem or '	Initiates a comment for human consumption
Sub name ()	Begins a Sub procedure
Sheets("sheet name").Select	Selects the worksheet to affect
Range("range").Select	Selects a range
Selection.ClearContents	Clears the selected range
Range("cell").Value	Assigns the value following the equal sign to the cell
Inputbox("Message", "Title of Dialog Box)	Displays *Message* in a dialog box with the title *Title of Dialog Box*
End Sub	Ends the Sub procedure

Planning a Macro

When you execute a macro, Excel steps through the Visual Basic statements one at a time beginning at the top of the Sub procedure. Excel bypasses any statements that begin with Remark, Rem, or an apostrophe ('). Thus, when you plan a macro you should remember that the order in which you place the statements in the Sub procedure determines the sequence of execution.

Once you know what you want the macro to do, write it out on paper. Before entering the macro into the computer, desk-check it. Put yourself in the position of Excel and step through the instructions and see how it affects the worksheet. Testing a macro before entering it is an important part of the development process and is called **desk-checking.**

You should add comments before each Sub procedure because they help you remember the purpose of the macro at a later date.

Inserting a Module Sheet

You write a macro on a module sheet, which is a blank sheet with no cells. You insert a module sheet by choosing the Macro command on the Insert menu. The following steps show how to insert a module sheet.

TO INSERT A MODULE SHEET ▼

STEP 1 ▶

With the Loan Analysis worksheet on the screen choose the Macro command from the Insert menu.

Excel displays a cascading menu (Figure 5-31).

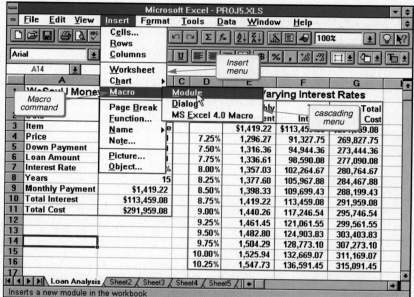

FIGURE 5-31

STEP 2 ▶

Choose the Module command from the cascading menu.

*Excel inserts a module sheet with the name Module1 on its tab (Figure 5-32). The insertion point is in column 1 of the first line. The **Visual Basic toolbar** displays. If the Visual Basic toolbar does not display, point to any toolbar, click the right mouse button, and choose Visual Basic from the shortcut menu. If necessary, drag the Visual Basic toolbar below the tabs.*

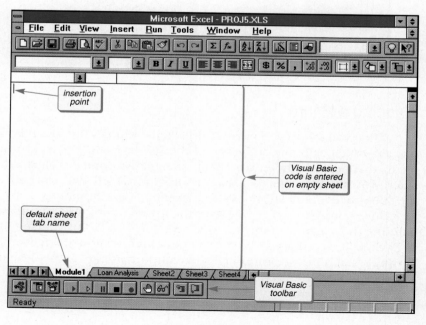

FIGURE 5-32

Entering the Macro on the Module Sheet

You enter a macro by typing the lines of Visual Basic code (statements) the same way you would if you were using word processing software. The macro editor is a full-screen editor. Thus, you can move the insertion point to previous lines to make corrections. At the end of a line, press the ENTER key or use the DOWN ARROW key to move to the next line. If you make a mistake in a statement and notice it, use the arrow keys and the DELETE or BACKSPACE key to correct it.

Each time you type a line and move the insertion point to the next line, Excel checks the syntax of the statement. If you overlook an error, such as a missing parenthesis, Excel displays the line in red and also displays a dialog box to alert you that the previous statement is in error. When you are finished entering the macro, move to another sheet by clicking a sheet tab.

TO ENTER A MACRO ON A MODULE SHEET ▼

STEP 1 ▶

Type the six Rem statements as shown in Figure 5-33.

Excel automatically displays the remark lines in green after you press the ENTER key or DOWN ARROW key.

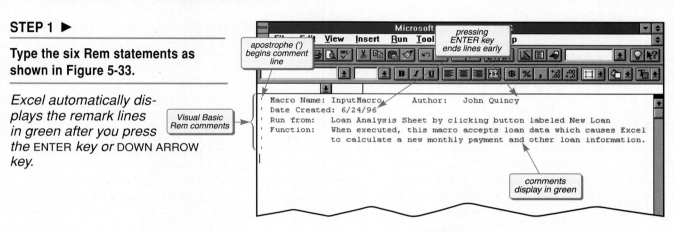

FIGURE 5-33

STEP 2 ▶

Type the Sub procedure as shown in Figure 5-34. Indent all lines between the Sub statement and End Sub statement for clarity. Double-click the Module1 tab. When the Rename Sheet dialog box displays, type `Input Macro` **and choose the OK button.**

STEP 3 ▶

Drag the Input Macro tab and position it between the Loan Analysis tab and Sheet2 tab.

The module sheet displays as shown in Figure 5-34.

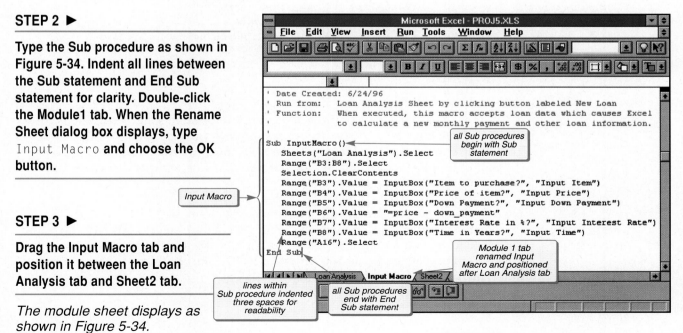

FIGURE 5-34

More About Macros and Visual Basic Statements

When the module sheet is active, Excel displays a Visual Basic toolbar docked at the bottom of the screen. Figure 5-35 describes the function of each button. Once you begin writing macros on your own, you will find these buttons to be handy, especially for testing macros.

For more information on the Visual Basic toolbar, choose the Search for Help on command from the Help menu. When the Search dialog box displays, type Visual Basic toolbar in the top box. Choose the Show Topic button. Select Visual Basic Toolbar in the bottom box and choose the Go To button. Close the Help window when you are finished.

There is a much more to Visual Basic for Applications than is presented here. Your central focus, however, is to understand the basic makeup of a Visual Basic statement. For example, each statement within the Sub procedure includes a period. On the left side of the period you tell Excel the object on the worksheet you want to affect. An **object** can be a cell, a range, a chart, a button, the worksheet, or the workbook. On the right side of the period, you tell Excel what you want to do to the object. The right side of the period is called the **property**. For example,

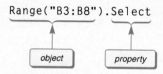

Thus, when the macro executes, the statement identifies the range B3:B8 (object) and selects it (property), as if you used the mouse to drag across the range B3:B8 in the worksheet to select it. In several of the statements in Figure 5-34, there are equal signs. An equal sign instructs Excel to make an assignment to a cell. For example,

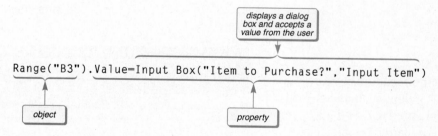

When executed as part of the macro, this Range.Value statement assigns to cell B3 the value entered by the user in response to the dialog box.

Because the second and third statement in the Sub procedure clear the range B3:B8, the formula in cell B6 has to be reentered. When executed, the seventh statement in the Sub procedure:

```
Range("B6").Value = "=price - down_payment"
```
reenters in cell B6 the formula =price - down_payment.

The next to the last statement in the Sub procedure selects cell A16, the same as if you clicked cell A16 in the worksheet. Finally, the last statement in the Sub procedure, End Sub, ends the Sub procedure and control returns to the worksheet from which the Sub procedure was executed.

For additional information on Visual Basic statements, select the Help menu and choose the Contents command. Choose Programming with Visual Basic by clicking it. You can also choose the Examples and Demos command on the Help menu, and then choose Using Visual Basic.

Using a macro is a two-step process. First, you enter the macro on a module sheet as was done earlier in this project. Next, you execute it. There are several ways to execute a macro. For example, you can click the **Run Macro button** on the Visual Basic toolbar (Figure 5-35). Another way is to create a button on the worksheet or on a toolbar, assign the macro to it, and then click the button. This project details the steps to assign a macro to a button on the worksheet.

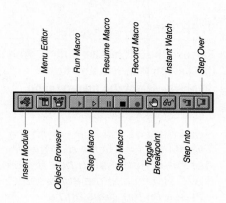

FIGURE 5-35

► ADDING A BUTTON TO THE WORKSHEET TO EXECUTE A MACRO

T o create a button, you use the **Create Button button** on the Drawing toolbar. You size and locate a button in the same way you did a chart in the earlier projects. You then assign the macro to it by using the name in the Sub statement (InputMacro). Finally, you change the name on the button by editing it. The following steps show how to create a button and assign to it the macro InputMacro. Recall, that InputMacro was the name placed earlier in the Sub statement.

TO ADD A BUTTON TO THE WORKSHEET AND ASSIGN A MACRO TO IT ▼

STEP 1 ►

Click the Loan Analysis tab to activate the worksheet. Click the Drawing button on the Standard toolbar. Dock the Drawing toolbar at the bottom of the screen.

STEP 2 ►

Click the Create Button button on the Drawing toolbar. Drag the mouse pointer from the top left corner of cell A13 to the lower right corner of cell A14.

Excel draws a light border around the button area (Figure 5-36).

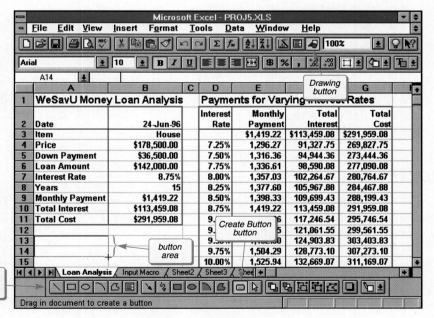

FIGURE 5-36

STEP 3 ▶

Release the left mouse button. When the Assign Macro dialog box displays, select the macro name InputMacro.

*Excel displays the button with the title Button 1 and also displays the **Assign Macro dialog box** (Figure 5-37). Notice that the button has handles on the sides and a shaded border. The handles and shaded border indicate you can resize and relocate the button on the worksheet after the Assign Macro dialog box is closed.*

STEP 4 ▶

Choose the OK button in the Assign Macro dialog box. Click the Drawing button on the Standard toolbar to close the Drawing toolbar. Drag across the button title, Button 1, and type the new button title `New Loan`

STEP 5 ▶

Select cell A16 to lock in the new button title.

The button with the title New Loan displays in the range A13:A14 on the worksheet (Figure 5-38).

STEP 6 ▶

Click the Save button on the Standard toolbar to save the workbook using the filename PROJ5.XLS.

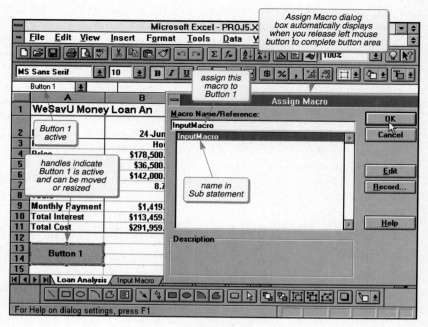

FIGURE 5-37

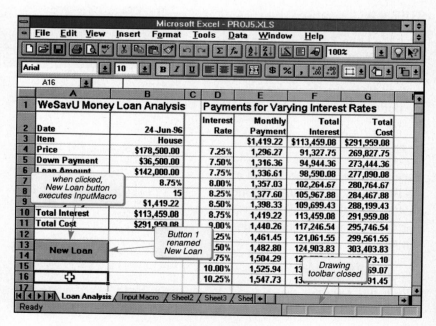

FIGURE 5-38

If you want to resize, relocate, or change the name of the button any time after Step 6, hold down the CTRL key and click the button. Once the button is surrounded by the shaded border and handles, you can modify it. You can also choose the **Assign Macro command** from the Tools menu or shortcut menu to assign a different macro to the button. When you finish editing the button, select any cell to deselect it.

▶ EXECUTING THE MACRO

Follow the steps below to enter the loan data: Item — 25' Cabin Cruiser; Price — $32,550.00; Down Payment — $8,250.00; Interest Rate — 10.25%; Years — 7. You should be aware that when the macro executes, the second and third statements clear the range. Thus, any formula in the worksheet that includes the operation of division may result in the display of the diagnostic message **#DIV/0!** in the cell.

TO EXECUTE THE MACRO AND ENTER NEW LOAN DATA ▼

STEP 1 ▶

Click the New Loan button. When Excel displays the Input Item dialog box with the prompt message, Item to purchase?, type 25' Cabin Cruiser (Figure 5-39).

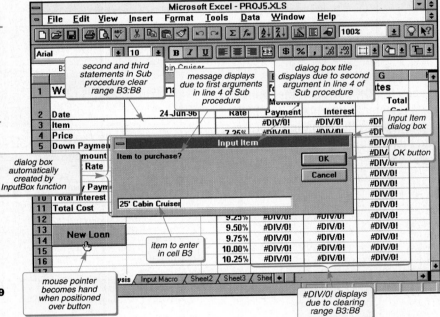

FIGURE 5-39

STEP 2 ▶

Choose the OK button in the Input Item dialog box or press the ENTER key. When Excel displays the Input Price dialog box with the prompt message, Price of item?, type 32550 (Figure 5-40).

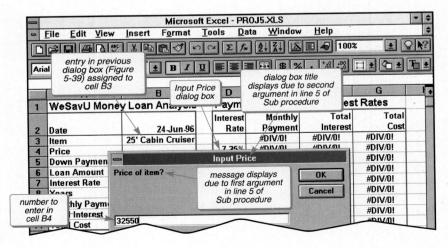

FIGURE 5-40

STEP 3 ▶

Choose the OK button in the Input Price dialog box. When Excel displays the Input Down Payment dialog box with the prompt message, Down Payment?, type 8250 (Figure 5-41).

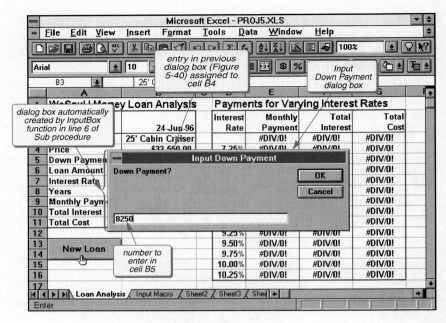

FIGURE 5-41

STEP 4 ▶

Choose the OK button in the Input Down Payment dialog box. When Excel displays the Input Interest Rate dialog box with the prompt message, Interest Rate in %?, type 10.25% (Figure 5-42).

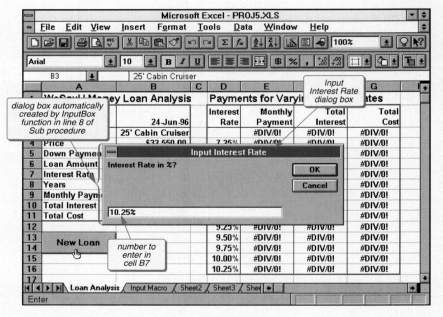

FIGURE 5-42

STEP 5 ▶

Choose the OK button in the Input Interest Rate dialog box. When Excel displays the Input Time dialog box with the prompt message, Time in Years?, type 7 (Figure 5-43).

STEP 6 ▶

Choose the OK button in the Input Time dialog box.

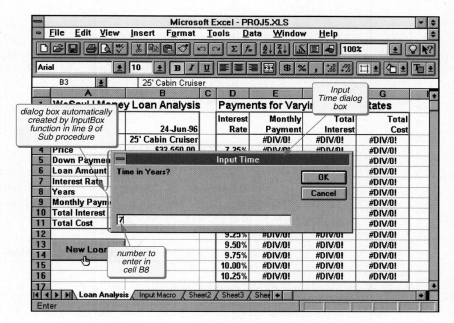

FIGURE 5-43

Excel recalculates the loan information for the new loan data, and cell A16 is the active cell (Figure 5-44). Figure 5-44 shows that the monthly payment is $406.55 (cell B9), the total interest is $9,850.59 (cell B10), and the total cost is $42,400.59 (cell B11) for the 25' Cabin Cruiser. In addition, Excel automatically recalculates new results in the data table (range D3:G16) for the new loan data.

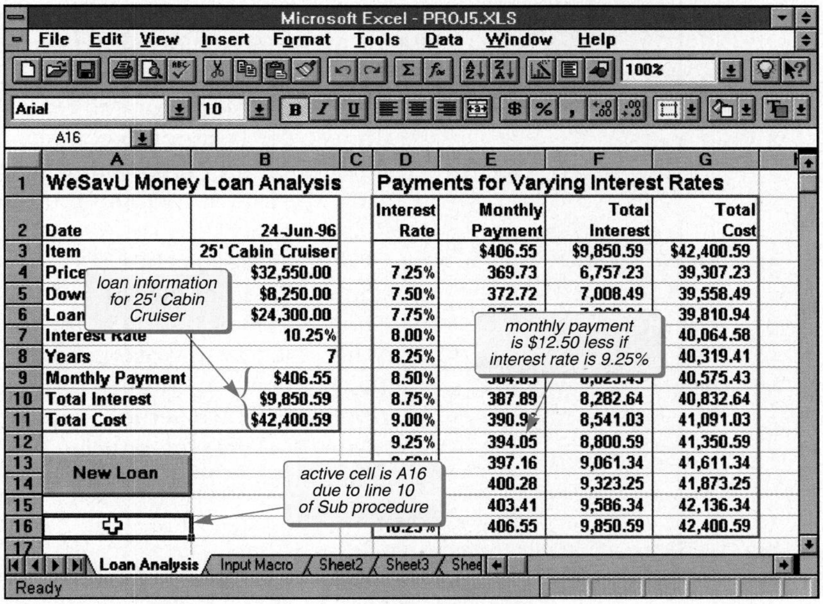

FIGURE 5-44

▶ RECORDING A MACRO

Excel has a **Macro Recorder** that creates a macro automatically from the actions you perform and commands you choose. The Macro Recorder can be turned on, during which time it records your activities, and then turned off to terminate the recording. What you do during the time it is turned on can be **played back** (executed) as often as you want. Thus, the Macro Recorder is like a tape recorder in that it records everything you do to a workbook over a period of time. Once the macro is recorded, you can do one of the following to play it back.

1. Assign the macro to a button on the worksheet as was done earlier in this project and click the button.
2. Assign the macro to a custom button on a toolbar and click the button.
3. Choose the **Macro command** on the Tools menu.
4. Click the **Run Macro button** (▶) on the Visual Basic toolbar.
5. Add a command to the Tools menu that plays back the macro and then choose the command.
6. Assign the macro to a graphic, such as a chart, so when you click it, the macro plays back.

The following series of steps shows you how to record a macro to print the Loan Analysis worksheet in landscape orientation and then return the orientation to portrait. To guard against macro catastrophes, the workbook is saved before invoking the Macro Recorder.

TO RECORD A MACRO TO PRINT THE LOAN ANALYSIS WORKSHEET IN LANDSCAPE

Step 1: Click the Save button on the Standard toolbar to save the workbook using the filename PROJ5.XLS.

Step 2: From the Tools menu, choose Record Macro, and then choose Record New Macro from the cascading menu.

Step 3: When the Record New Macro dialog box displays, type the macro name `PrintLandscape` in the Macro Name box.

Step 4: Choose the OK button in the Record New Macro dialog box. Excel displays the **Stop Macro button** in its own toolbar and displays the message "Recording" on the status bar at the bottom of the screen. The Macro Recorder is on. Whatever actions you do are recorded.

Step 5: Complete the following actions:
    a. Point to the menu bar and click the right mouse button.
    b. Choose the Page Setup command.
    c. When the Page Setup dialog box displays, click the Page tab.
    d. Click the Landscape option button.
    e. Click the Sheet tab.
    f. Click the Gridlines box.
    g. Choose the Print button.
    h. Choose the OK button in the Print dialog box.
    i. When the Printing dialog box disappears, point to the menu bar and click the right mouse button.
    j. Choose the Page Setup command
    k. When the Page Setup dialog box displays, click the Page tab, click the Portrait option button, and then choose the OK button.

Step 6: Click the Stop Macro button.

Notice that you are able to step through the actions and see the results as the macro is recorded. If you recorded the wrong actions, select the Tools menu, and choose the Macro command. When the **Macro dialog box** displays, select the name of the macro (PrintLandscape) and choose the Delete button and then start recording again.

Playing Back a Recorded Macro

The following steps show you how to play back the recorded macro Print-Landscape by choosing the Macro command on the Tools menu.

TO PLAY BACK A RECORDED MACRO

Step 1: From the Tools menu, choose the Macro command.
Step 2: When the Macro dialog box displays, select the macro name PrintLand-scape in the Macro Name/Reference box.
Step 3: Choose the Run button (▶) in the Macro dialog box.
Step 4: Click the Save button to save the workbook using the filename PROJ5.XLS.

The Excel window blinks as the macro is executed. The report prints as shown in Figure 5-45.

WeSavU Money Loan Analysis

Date	24-Jun-96
Item	25' Cabin Cruiser
Price	$32,550.00
Down Payment	$8,250.00
Loan Amount	$24,300.00
Interest Rate	10.25%
Years	7
Monthly Payment	$406.55
Total Interest	$9,850.59
Total Cost	$42,400.59

Payments for Varying Interest Rates

Interest Rate	Monthly Payment	Total Interest	Total Cost
	$406.55	$9,850.59	$42,400.59
7.25%	369.73	6,757.23	39,307.23
7.50%	372.72	7,008.49	39,558.49
7.75%	375.73	7,260.94	39,810.94
8.00%	378.75	7,514.58	40,064.58
8.25%	381.78	7,769.41	40,319.41
8.50%	384.83	8,025.43	40,575.43
8.75%	387.89	8,282.64	40,832.64
9.00%	390.96	8,541.03	41,091.03
9.25%	394.05	8,800.59	41,350.59
9.50%	397.16	9,061.34	41,611.34
9.75%	400.28	9,323.25	41,873.25
10.00%	403.41	9,586.34	42,136.34
10.25%	406.55	9,850.59	42,400.59

FIGURE 5-45

You can view the macro that the Macro Recorder created by clicking the right tab scrolling button, and when the Module1 tab appears, click it. As you can see from the Module 1 sheet, the PrintLandscape macro is 70 Visual Basic statements long. Also notice when the Module1 sheet is active, the Visual Basic toolbar appears at the bottom of the screen. Click the Loan Analysis tab if it is not active.

For more information on using the Macro Recorder, choose the Search for Help on command from the Help menu. Type macro recorder in the top box and choose the Show Topics button. Select Overview of Writing and Editing a Macro in the lower box and choose the Go To button.

▶ GOAL SEEKING TO DETERMINE THE DOWN PAYMENT FOR A SPECIFIC MONTHLY PAYMENT

I f you know the result you want a formula to produce, you can use **goal seeking** to determine the value of a cell on which the formula depends. The example on the following page uses the Goal Seek command to determine the down payment so the monthly payment for the 25' Cabin Cruiser will be exactly $300.00.

TO DETERMINE THE DOWN PAYMENT FOR A SPECIFIC MONTHLY PAYMENT ▼

STEP 1 ►

Select cell B9, the cell with the monthly payment amount. From the Tools menu, choose the Goal Seek command. When the Goal Seek dialog box displays, enter 300 in the To value box. Select the By changing cell box. In the worksheet, use the mouse pointer to select cell B5.

The Goal Seek dialog box displays as shown in Figure 5-46. Notice in the dialog box that the first entry indicates the cell you want to seek a goal on (cell B9), the second box indicates the specific value you are seeking ($300.00), and the third box indicates the cell to vary (cell B5).

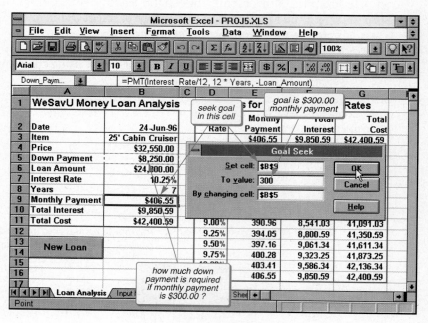

FIGURE 5-46

STEP 2 ►

Choose the OK button in the Goal Seek dialog box.

Excel displays the Goal Seek Status dialog box indicating it has found an answer. Excel also changes the monthly payment in cell B9 to the goal ($300.00) and changes the down payment in cell B5 to $14,618.83 (Figure 5-47).

STEP 3 ►

Choose the OK button in the Goal Seek Status dialog box.

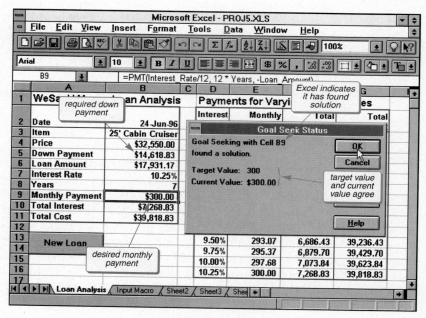

FIGURE 5-47

Thus, according to Figure 5-47, if the 25' Cabin Cruiser costs $32,550.00, the interest rate is 10.25%, the term is 7 years, and you want to pay exactly $300.00 a month, then you must pay a down payment of $14,618.83.

Notice in this goal seeking example, it is not required that the cell to vary be directly referenced in the formula or function. For example, the monthly payment formula in cell B9 is =PMT(interest_rate / 12, 12 * years, loan_amount). There is no mention of the down payment in the PMT function. However, because the loan amount, which is referenced in the PMT function, is based on the down payment, Excel is able to goal seek on the monthly payment by varying the down payment.

You can reset the worksheet to the values displayed prior to goal seeking by choosing the Cancel button while the Goal Seek Status dialog box is on the screen. If the dialog box is no longer on the screen, you can reset the worksheet by clicking the Undo button on the Standard toolbar or selecting the Edit menu and choosing the Undo Goal Seek command. The Undo Goal Seek command is only available until a new entry is made into the worksheet.

▶ USING SCENARIO MANAGER TO ANALYZE DATA

An alternative to using a data table to analyze worksheet data is to use Excel's Scenario Manager. The **Scenario Manager** allows you to record and save different sets of what-if assumptions (data values) called **scenarios**. For example, earlier in this project (Figure 5-29 on page E298), a monthly payment of $1,419.22 was determined for the following loan data: Item — House; Price —$178,500.00; Down Payment — $36,500.00; Interest Rate — 8.75%; and Years —15. One scenario for the house loan might be, "What is the monthly payment, total interest, and total cost if the interest rate is the same (8. 75%) but the number of years changes from 15 to 30?" Another scenario might be: "What is the monthly payment, total interest, and total cost if the interest rate is increased by 1% to 9.75% and the number of years remains at 15?" Each set of values represents a what-if assumption. The primary uses of Scenario Manager are to:

1. Create different scenarios with multiple sets of changing cells.
2. Build a summary worksheet that contains the different scenarios.
3. View the results of each scenario on your worksheet.

The following sections show how to use the Scenario Manager for each of the procedures just listed. Once you create the scenarios, you can instruct Excel to build the summary worksheet. The summary worksheet the Scenario Manager generates is actually an outlined worksheet (Figure 5-48) you can print and manipulate like any other worksheet. An **outlined worksheet** is one that contains symbols (buttons) above and to the left that allow you to collapse and expand rows and columns.

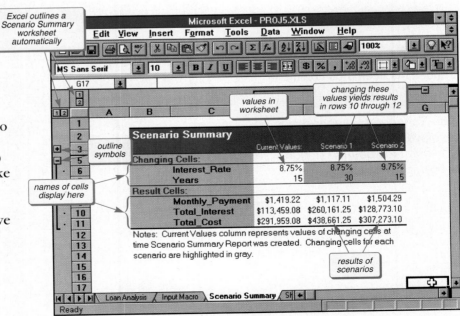

FIGURE 5-48

Before illustrating the Scenario Manager, click the New Loan button and enter the loan data for the house as shown in Figure 5-29 on page E298.

The following steps create the two scenarios and the Scenario Summary worksheet shown in Figure 5-48 on the previous page by using the **Scenarios command** on the Tools menu. The worksheet illustrates the monthly payment, total interest, and total cost for two scenarios and for the current values in the Loan Analysis worksheet. The current interest rate equals 8.75% and the current years equal 15 (Figure 5-29). The first scenario sets the interest rate to 8.75% and the number of years to 30. The second scenario sets the interest rate to 9.75% and the number of years to 15.

TO CREATE SCENARIOS AND A SCENARIO SUMMARY WORKSHEET ▼

STEP 1 ▶

With the loan data for the house in Figure 5-29 entered, select the Tools menu (Figure 5-49).

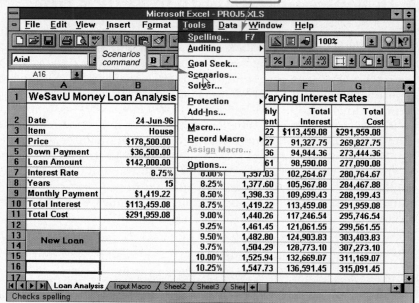

FIGURE 5-49

STEP 2 ▶

Choose the Scenarios command from the Tools menu.

The Scenario Manager dialog box displays informing you there are no scenarios defined (Figure 5-50).

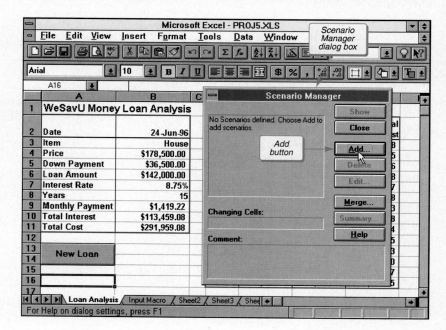

FIGURE 5-50

STEP 3 ▶

Choose the Add button to add a scenario. When the Add Scenario dialog box displays, type `Scenario 1` in the Scenario Name box, click in the Changing Cells box, and drag over the range B7:B8 in the worksheet.

Excel displays a marquis around the cells in the worksheet to change (interest rate in cell B7 and years in cell B8) and assigns the range B7:B8 to the Changing Cells box in the Add Scenario dialog box (Figure 5-51).

FIGURE 5-51

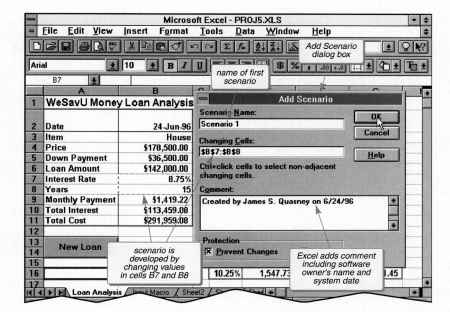

STEP 4 ▶

Choose the OK button in the Add Scenario dialog box. When the Scenario Values dialog box displays, select the Years box and type `30`

*The **Scenario Values dialog box** displays as shown in Figure 5-52.*

FIGURE 5-52

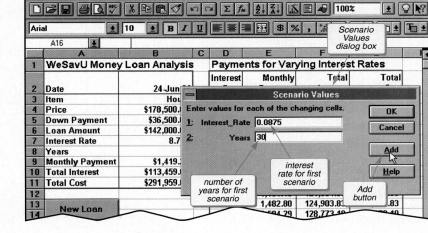

STEP 5 ▶

Choose the Add button in the Scenario Values dialog box to add the second scenario. When the Add Scenario dialog box displays, type `Scenario 2` in the Scenario Name box.

The Add Scenario dialog box displays as shown in Figure 5-53. Notice that Excel automatically assigns the range $B$7:$B$8 to the Changing Cells box because this range is used in the prior scenario.

FIGURE 5-53

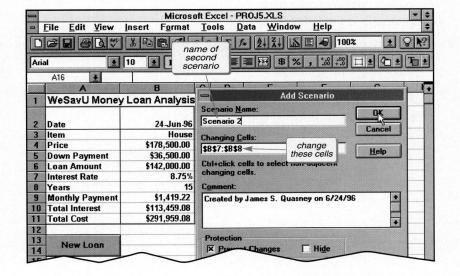

STEP 6 ▶

Choose the OK button in the Add Scenario dialog box. When the Scenario Values dialog box displays, enter 9.75% in the Interest_Rate box and 15 in the Years box.

The Scenario Values dialog box displays as shown in Figure 5-54.

FIGURE 5-54

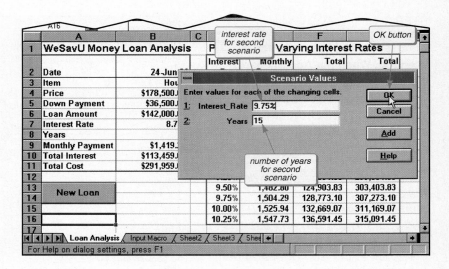

STEP 7 ▶

Because this is the last scenario to create, choose the OK button in the Scenario Values dialog box.

The Scenario Manager dialog box displays with the two named scenarios (Figure 5-55).

FIGURE 5-55

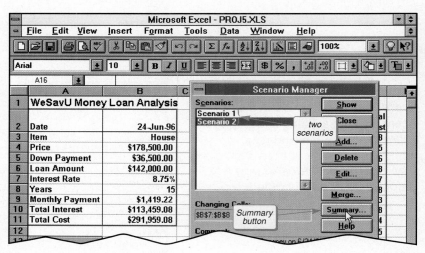

STEP 8 ▶

Choose the Summary button (Summary...) in the Scenario Manager dialog box. When the Scenario Summary dialog box displays, click in the Result Cells box and drag over the range B9:B11 to indicate the cells you want results for.

*The **Scenario Summary dialog box** displays as shown in Figure 5-56.*

FIGURE 5-56

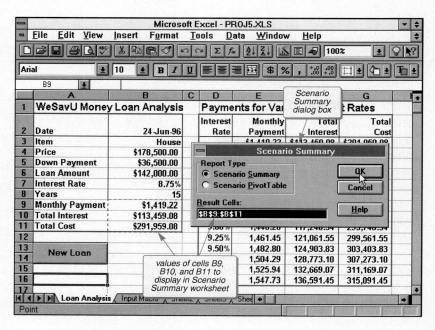

STEP 9 ▶

Choose the OK button in the Scenario Summary dialog box. Drag the Scenario Summary tab to the immediate right of the Input Macro tab.

The Scenario Summary worksheet displays as shown in Figure 5-57.

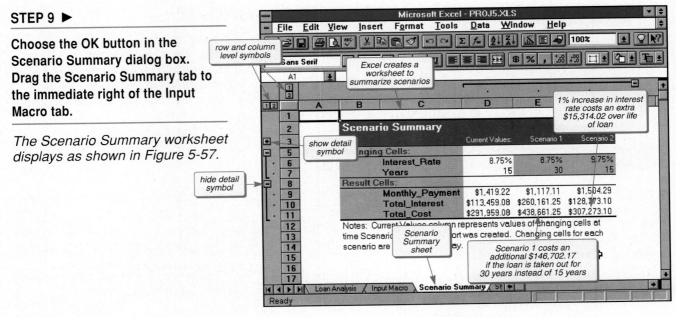

FIGURE 5-57

The Scenario Summary worksheet in Figure 5-57 shows the results of the current values (column D) in the Loan Analysis worksheet and two scenarios in columns E and F. Compare the Scenario 1 column to the Current Values column. In the Scenario 1 column, the interest rate is the same as in the Current Values column, but the length of time is 30 years instead of 15 years. Because the loan is for twice the length of time, the monthly payment decreases by $302.11 per month, but the total cost of the loan increases by $146,702.17 to $438,661.25. In the Scenario 2 column, the number of years is the same as the Current Values column, but the interest rate is 1% greater. The 1% change increases the monthly payment by $85.07 per month and the total cost of the house to $307,273.10 or $15,314.02 more than the loan data in the Current Values column.

Working with an Outlined Worksheet

Excel automatically outlines the Scenario Summary worksheet. The **outline symbols** display above the worksheet and to the left (Figure 5-57). You click the outline symbols to expand or collapse the worksheet. For example, if you click the **show detail symbol** (⊞) Excel displays additional rows or columns that are summarized on the displayed row or column. If you click a **hide detail symbol** (⊟), Excel hides any detail rows that extend through the length of the corresponding **row level bar** (⌐). or **column level bar** (⌐▪) You can also expand or collapse a worksheet by clicking the **row level symbol** (½) or **column level symbol** (⊡12) above and to the left of row title 1. An outline is especially useful when working with large worksheets. To remove an outline, choose the **Group and Outline command** on the Data menu, then choose the **Clear Outline command** from the cascading menu.

Applying Scenarios Directly to the Worksheet

When you work with scenarios, it is not necessary to create the Scenario Summary worksheet shown in Figure 5-57. You can create the scenarios following the first seven steps of the previous example and then use the Show button in the Scenario Manager dialog box to apply the scenarios directly to the worksheet for which they were created. The following steps show how to apply the two scenarios created earlier directly to the worksheet.

TO APPLY SCENARIOS DIRECTLY TO THE WORKSHEET ▼

STEP 1 ▶

Click the Loan Analysis tab. Select the Tools menu and choose the Scenarios command.

The Scenario Manager dialog box displays (Figure 5-58).

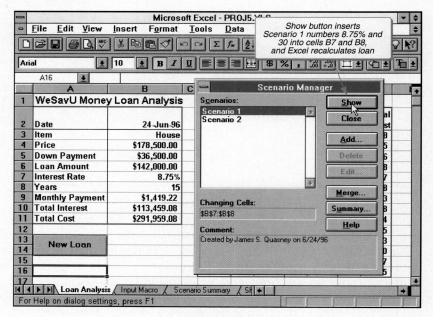

FIGURE 5-58

STEP 2 ▶

With Scenario 1 selected in the Scenarios box, choose the Show button (Show).

Excel inserts the numbers from Scenario 1 into the worksheet and recalculates all formulas (Figure 5-59). Notice that the entries in the range B7:B11 have changed so they agree with the results in column E of the Scenario Summary Report worksheet shown in Figure 5-57 on the previous page.

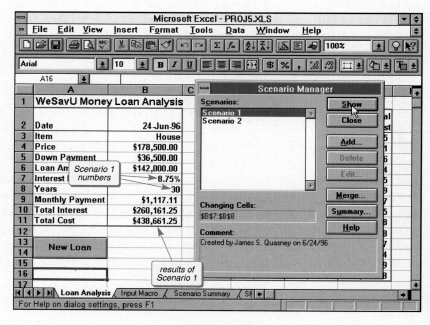

FIGURE 5-59

STEP 3 ▶

Select Scenario 2 in the Scenarios box in the Scenario Manager dialog box. Choose the Show button.

Excel inserts the numbers from Scenario 2 into the worksheet and recalculates all formulas (Figure 5-60). Here again, the results in the worksheet agree exactly with column F of the Scenario Summary worksheet shown in Figure 5-57 on page E315.

STEP 4 ▶

Choose the Close button in the Scenario Manager dialog box. Click the Save button on the Standard toolbar.

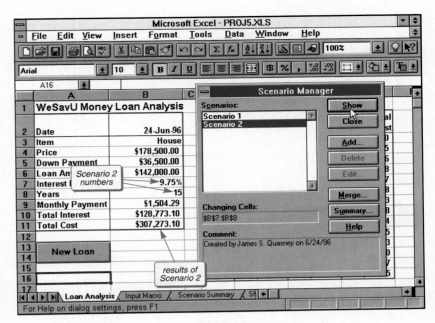

FIGURE 5-60

You can undo the scenario results by clicking the Undo button on the Standard toolbar or choosing the Undo Show command on the Edit menu. If you want, you can then choose the Redo Show command on the Edit menu to change the worksheet back to the results of the scenario.

Scenario Manager is an important what-if tool for organizing your assumptions. Using Scenario Manager, you can define different scenarios with up to 32 changing cells per scenario. Once you have entered the scenarios, you can show them one by one as illustrated in the previous example or you can create the Scenario Summary worksheet.

Before moving on to the next section, change the value in cell B7 to 8.75% and the value in cell B8 to 15. The worksheet should generate the results shown in Figure 5-58.

▶ PROTECTING THE WORKSHEET

When you build a worksheet that will be used by people who know little or nothing about computers and worksheets, it is important to protect the cells in the worksheet that you don't want changed, such as cells that contain text and formulas. In the Loan Analysis worksheet (see Figure 5-61 on the next page), there are only five cells that the user should be allowed to change: the item in cell B3; the price in cell B4; the down payment in cell B5; the interest rate in cell B7; and the years in cell B8. Also, because of the way the macro assigned to the New Loan button works, cell B6 should be unprotected. The remaining cells in the worksheet should be protected so that they cannot be changed by the user.

When you create a new worksheet, all the cells are unprotected. **Unprotected cells**, or **unlocked cells**, are cells with values you can change at any time while **protected cells**, or **locked cells**, are cells that you cannot change. If a cell is protected and the user attempts to change its value, Excel displays a dialog box with a message indicating the cells are protected.

You should protect cells only after the worksheet has been fully tested and displays the correct results. Protecting a worksheet is a two-step process:

1. Select the cells you want to leave unprotected and change their cell protection settings to unprotected.
2. Protect the entire worksheet.

At first glance, these steps may appear to be backwards. However, once you protect the entire worksheet, you cannot change anything including the protection of individual cells. Thus, you first deal with the cells you want to leave unprotected and then protect the entire worksheet.

The following steps show how to protect the Loan Analysis worksheet.

TO PROTECT A WORKSHEET ▼

STEP 1 ▶

Select the range B3:B8, the range to unprotect. With the mouse pointer in the selected range, click the right mouse button.

Excel displays the shortcut menu (Figure 5-61).

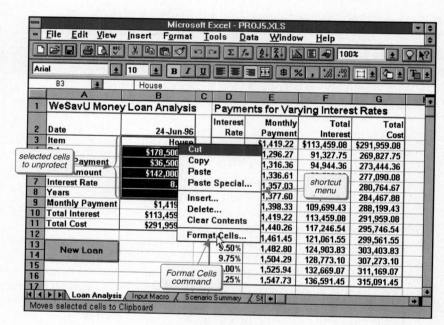

FIGURE 5-61

STEP 2 ▶

Choose the Format Cells command. When the Format Cells dialog box displays, click the Protection tab. Click the Locked check box.

*The **Protection tab** in the Format Cells dialog box displays with the x removed from the **Locked check box** (Figure 5-62).*

STEP 3 ▶

Choose the OK button in the Format Cells dialog box.

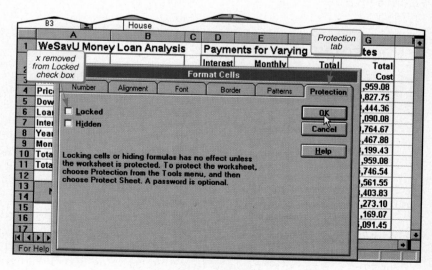

FIGURE 5-62

STEP 4 ▶

Select the Tools menu. Choose the Protection command.

Excel displays the Tools menu and cascading menu (Figure 5-63).

all cells are unprotected until protect sheet command is chosen

all cells have locked attribute except for range B3:B8

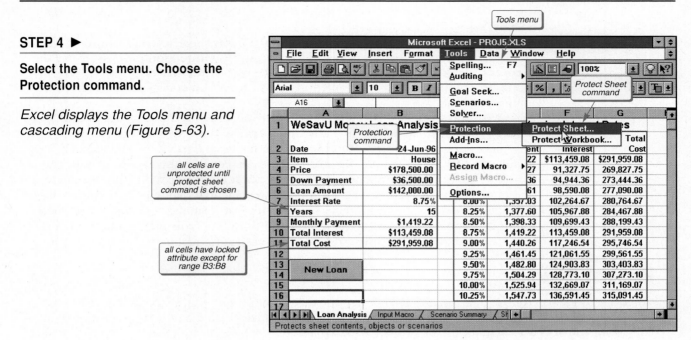

FIGURE 5-63

STEP 5 ▶

Choose the Protect Sheet command from the cascading menu.

*Excel displays the **Protect Sheet dialog box** (Figure 5-64).*

STEP 6 ▶

Choose the OK button in the Protect Sheet dialog box. Click the Save button on the Standard toolbar to save the protected workbook.

All the cells in the worksheet are protected, except for the range B3:B8. The range B3:B8 includes the cells in which you enter new loan data.

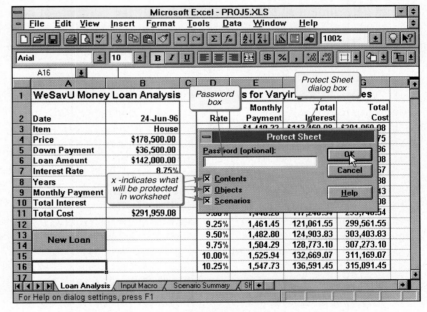

FIGURE 5-64

Notice in the Protect Sheet dialog box in Figure 5-64 that you can add a password. You add a **password** when you want to keep others from changing the worksheet from protected to unprotected. You can also click any of the three check boxes (Contents, Objects, and Scenarios) shown in Figure 5-64 to unprotect them. Contents refers to the entries in the worksheet. Objects are charts and buttons. Scenarios refer to those scenarios associated with the worksheet being protected.

The protection only pertains to the active worksheet. If you want to protect additional sheets, select them before you begin the protection process or use the **Protect Workbook command** on the cascading menu that displays (Figure 5-63 on the previous page) when you choose the Protection command from the Tools menu.

With the worksheet protected, you can still execute the macro InputMacro by clicking the New Loan button at any time because the cells referenced (B3:B8) by the macro are unprotected. However, if you try to change any protected cell, Excel displays a dialog box with a diagnostic message. For example, try to change the row title Item in cell A3. When you type the first character with cell A3 selected, Excel responds by displaying a diagnostic message in a dialog box. If you want to change any cells in the worksheet such as titles or formulas, unprotect the document by choosing the Protection command from the Tools menu, and then choose the **Unprotect Sheet command** from the cascading menu.

▶ PROJECT SUMMARY

In Project 5, you learned how to apply the PMT function to determine the monthly payment of a loan. The project presented steps and techniques showing you how to analyze data by creating a data table and working with the Scenario Manager. This project also explained how macros are used to automate worksheet tasks. You learned how to build a macro that accepts loan data. Once the macro was built, you used the Create Button button to assign the macro to a button in the worksheet. Using the button, you executed the macro. You also learned how to record a macro and play it back. Finally, you learned how to protect a document so a user can change only the contents of cells that you left unprotected.

▶ KEY TERMS AND INDEX

In Microsoft Excel, you can accomplish a task in a number of ways. The following table provides a quick reference to each task presented in this project with its available options. The commands listed in the Menu column can be executed using either the keyboard or mouse. Many of the commands in the Menu column are also available on the shortcut menu.

Task	Mouse	Menu	Keyboard Shortcuts
Borders	Click Borders button arrow on Formatting toolbar	From Format menu, choose Cells	Press CTRL+1
Create a Button	Click Create Button button on Drawing toolbar		
Create a Data Table		From Data menu, choose Table	
Create a Macro	Click Insert Module button on Visual Basic toolbar		
Create a Scenario Summary Worksheet		From Tools menu, choose Scenarios	
Display the Visual Basic toolbar	Point to any toolbar and click right mouse button, then choose Visual Basic	From Insert menu, choose Macro, then choose Module	
Edit a Button	CTRL+click button to edit		
Name Cells	Click in reference area in formula bar and type name	From Insert menu, choose Name, then choose Create	Press CTRL+SHIFT+F3
Outline a Range	Click Borders button arrow on Formatting toolbar	From Format menu, choose Cells	Press CTRL+SHIFT+&
Protect a Worksheet		From Tools menu, choose Protection, then choose Protect Sheet	
Record a Macro	Click Record Macro button on Visual Basic toolbar	From Tools menu, choose Record Macro, then choose Record New Macro	
Run (or Execute or Play Back) a Macro	Click Run Macro button on Visual Basic toolbar	From Tools menu, choose Macro	
Select a Named Range	Click name in name box in formula bar	From Edit menu, choose Go To	Press F5
Stop Recording a Macro	Click Stop Macro button on Visual Basic toolbar		
Unprotect a Worksheet		From Tools menu, choose Protection, then choose Unprotect Sheet	
Unprotect Cells		From Format menu, choose Cells	

STUDENT ASSIGNMENT 1
True/False

Instructions: Circle T if the statement is true or F if the statement is false.

T   F   1. A Visual Basic statement in a macro tells Excel to carry out an activity such as select a cell or clear a selection.

T   F   2. You can click a name in the Name box to append the name to a formula you are creating.

T   F   3. To efficiently assign a label (such as a row title) in the worksheet to an adjacent cell, select the Insert command, choose the Name command, and then choose the Define command.

T   F   4. If cell B4 is named Balance and cell B5 is named Payment, then the formula =B4 - B5 can be written as =Balance - Payment.

T   F   5. A data table is a cell that answers what-if questions.

T   F   6. The cell you vary in a one-input data table is called the input cell.

T   F   7. Use the Open command from the File menu to create a module sheet.

T   F   8. A macro is made up of a series of Visual Basic statements.

T   F   9. The Visual Basic statement, Selection.ClearContents, is used to clear the selected cell or range of cells.

T   F   10. You end a Sub procedure with the End Sub statement.

T   F   11. In a Visual Basic Sub procedure, to specify a range in the active worksheet, use the object Range("range").

T   F   12. A module sheet has cells similar to a worksheet.

T   F   13. Desk-checking refers to checking the Windows desktop.

T   F   14. The Create Button button is on the Standard toolbar.

T   F   15. To edit a button on the worksheet, hold down the CTRL key and click the button to edit.

T   F   16. When executed, the macro function InputBox causes a dialog box to display.

T   F   17. The Scenario Manager can be used to organize answers to what-if questions in a worksheet.

T   F   18. When you open a new workbook it is unprotected.

T   F   19. Select the cells to unprotect after you protect the entire worksheet.

T   F   20. If you attempt to change the value of a protected cell, Excel immediately returns control to Windows.

STUDENT ASSIGNMENT 2
Multiple Choice

Instructions: Circle the correct response.

1. A worksheet that summarizes what-if questions is called a _____.
   a. scenario
   b. outlined worksheet
   c. Report worksheet
   d. Scenario Summary worksheet

2. To name a cell, use the _____ command on the Insert menu.
   a. Name
   b. Paste Function
   c. Apply Names
   d. Paste Name

3. When the name of a cell is made up of two or more words, replace the spaces between the words with _____ when you use the name in a formula.
   a. minus signs (-)
   b. number signs (#)
   c. circumflexes (^)
   d. underscores (_)

4. Use the _____ function to determine a monthly payment on a loan.
   a. FV
   b. PMT
   c. PV
   d. NOW

5. If payments are to be made on a monthly basis and the length of the loan is given in years, then _____ for the periods argument in the PMT function.
   a. multiply years by 12
   b. divide years by 12
   c. enter years
   d. multiply years by 365

6. Data tables are usually created _____.
   a. in an unused area of the worksheet
   b. on a toolbar
   c. in a cell
   d. on a chart sheet

7. In a one-input data table, the input cell _____.
   a. must be referenced directly or indirectly in the formula(s) at the top of the data table
   b. is the upper left corner cell of the worksheet
   c. is a range of cells
   d. must be defined on the module sheet

8. In a macro, use the _____ property to assign a value to a cell.
   a. Assign
   b. Clear
   c. Select
   d. Value

9. For a one-input data table to work properly, _____.
   a. the upper left cell must be empty
   b. the input cell must be on another worksheet
   c. the input cell must be blank
   d. the input cell must be defined as the upper left cell in the data table

10. After creating a module sheet, return to the worksheet by _____.
   a. selecting the Window menu
   b. clicking the worksheet tab
   c. choosing the Open command on the File menu
   d. entering the End Sub statement

STUDENT ASSIGNMENT 3
Understanding Functions, Data Analysis, and Worksheet Protection

Instructions: Fill in the correct answers.

1. Write a function to determine the monthly payment (PMT function) on a loan of $75,000.00, over a period of 20 years, at an annual interest rate of 8.4%. Make sure the function returns the monthly payment as a positive number.

   Function: _____

2. Write a function to determine the future value (FV function) of a $100.00 a month investment for 10 years if the interest rate is fixed at 6% and compounded monthly.

   Function: _____

(continued)

STUDENT ASSIGNMENT 3 (continued)

3. Write a function to determine the present value (PV function) or how much it would cost, for an annuity that pays $500.00 a month for 20 years and pays 8% compounded monthly. Display the cost of the annuity as a positive number by placing a minus sign before the monthly payment.

    Function: _____

4. Explain the purpose of a data table.

    _____

    _____

    _____

5. Describe what Scenario Manager is used for.

    _____

    _____

    _____

6. Explain the difference between a protected cell and an unprotected cell. How do you change the contents of a cell that is protected?

    _____

    _____

    _____

STUDENT ASSIGNMENT 4
Understanding Excel Menus and Commands

Instructions: Identify the menu and initial command (command on cascading menu not required) that displays the dialog box that allows you to make the indicated change.

	MENU	COMMAND
1. Name cells	_____	_____
2. Create a data table	_____	_____
3. Create a macro sheet	_____	_____
4. Record a macro	_____	_____
5. Change the macro assigned to a button	_____	_____
6. Protect a worksheet	_____	_____
7. Unprotect cells	_____	_____
8. Draw a color outline	_____	_____
9. Seek a goal for a cell assigned a formula	_____	_____
10. Create a Scenario Summary worksheet	_____	_____

STUDENT ASSIGNMENT 5
Understanding Macro Functions

Instructions: Assume a module sheet is open. In the space provided, write the Visual Basic statement that completes the specified task.

1. Select the range A1:D23 on the worksheet: _____

2. Clear the selected range: _____

3. Assign the formula =B6 - B7 to cell A10 in the worksheet: _____

4. Accept a value from the user and assign it to cell G25 in the worksheet: _____

   _____

5. End the Sub procedure: _____

STUDENT ASSIGNMENT 6
Understanding Worksheet Entries

Instructions: Indicate how you would make the suggested corrections.

Part 1:   In the worksheet in Figure SA5-6a the monthly payment, total interest, total cost, and data table results display in red within parentheses. The red color and parentheses indicate negative numbers. What would you do to display the results as positive numbers? (**Hint:** Review the formula in the formula bar.)

Change the formula in cell: _____ to _____

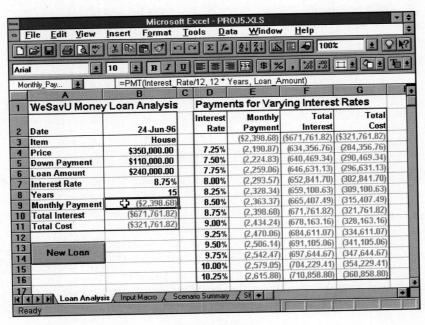

FIGURE SA5-6a

(continued)

STUDENT ASSIGNMENT 6 (continued)

Part 2:   In the worksheet in Figure SA5-6b, some or all of the loan data in the range B3:B8 was entered incorrectly. The loan data should be as follows: Item — House; Price — $178,500.00; Down Payment — $36,500.00; Interest Rate — 10.75%; and Years — 15. Explain the error and method of correction.

Error: _____

Method of correction: _____

	Microsoft Excel - PROJ5.XLS	
File	**Edit** **View** **Insert** **Format** **Tools** **Data** **Window** **Help**	

	A	B	C	D	E	F	G
1	WeSavU Money Loan Analysis			Payments for Varying Interest Rates			
2	Date	24-Jun-96		Interest Rate	Monthly Payment	Total Interest	Total Cost
3	Item	House			$127,208.33	###########	###########
4	Price	$178,500.00		7.25%	1,296.27	91,327.75	269,827.75
5	Down Payment	$36,500.00		7.50%	1,316.36	94,944.36	273,444.36
6	Loan Amount	$142,000.00		7.75%	1,336.61	98,590.08	277,090.08
7	Interest Rate	1075.00%		8.00%	1,357.03	102,264.67	280,764.67
8	Years	15		8.25%	1,377.60	105,967.88	284,467.88
9	Monthly Payment	$127,208.33		8.50%	1,398.33	109,699.43	288,199.43
10	Total Interest	$22,755,500.00		8.75%	1,419.22	113,459.08	291,959.08
11	Total Cost	$22,934,000.00		9.00%	1,440.26	117,246.54	295,746.54
12				9.25%	1,461.45	121,061.55	299,561.55
13	New Loan			9.50%	1,482.80	124,903.83	303,403.83
14				9.75%	1,504.29	128,773.10	307,273.10
15				10.00%	1,525.94	132,669.07	311,169.07
16				10.25%	1,547.73	136,591.45	315,091.45
17							

Loan Analysis / Input Macro / Scenario Summary / Sh

Ready

FIGURE SA5-6b

COMPUTER LABORATORY EXERCISES

COMPUTER LABORATORY EXERCISE 1
Using the Help Menu to Learn About Data Tables and Macros

Instructions: Start Excel and perform the following tasks.

1. Choose the Contents command from the Help menu. Choose Using Microsoft Excel. Choose Solving Problems by Analyzing Data. Choose Solving What-If Problems. One at a time, choose the eight items in the list, read them, and print them. Close the Help window.
2. Select the Help menu and choose the Examples and Demos command. When the Examples and Demos window displays, choose Performing What-If Analysis. When you finish with the first tutorial, choose Using Visual Basic.
3. Select the Help menu and choose the Search for Help on command. In the top box, type `Visual Basic` and choose the Show Topic button. One at a time, read and print the help information on each of the following topics:
   a. Overview of Writing and Editing a Macro
   b. Recording code into an existing macro
   c. Writing a macro

COMPUTER LABORATORY EXERCISE 2
Creating a One-Input Data Table

Instructions: Start Excel. Open the worksheet CLE5-2 from the subdirectory Excel5 on the Student Diskette that accompanies this book. As shown in Figure CLE5-2a, the worksheet computes the proposed annual salary (cell B4) from the proposed percent salary increase (cell B2) and the current annual salary (cell B3).

Perform the following tasks to create the one-input data table shown in Figure CLE5-2b.

1. Select the range A4:B4. Choose the Name command from the Insert menu, then choose the Create command to assign the name in cell A4 to cell B4.
2. Enter and format the data table title and column titles in the range A6:B7 as shown in Figure CLE5-2b. Use the fill handle to create the series of numbers in the range A9:A14.
3. Assign cell B8 the formula =proposed_salary.
4. Create a data table in the range A8:B14. Use cell B2 as the column input cell.
5. Draw borders around the data table as shown in Figure CLE5-2b.
6. Save the worksheet using the filename CLE5-2A. Print the worksheet without cell gridlines.
7. Use the goal seeking capabilities of Excel to determine the proposed percent increase in cell B2 if the proposed salary in cell B4 is set to $25,500,000. Your final result should be 0.59% in cell B2. Print the worksheet.

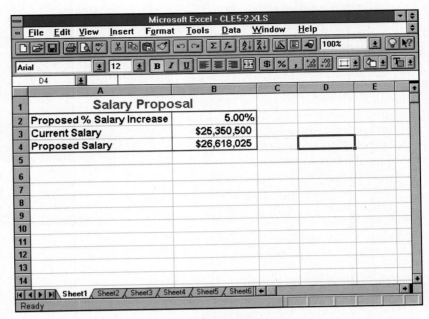

FIGURE CLE5-2a

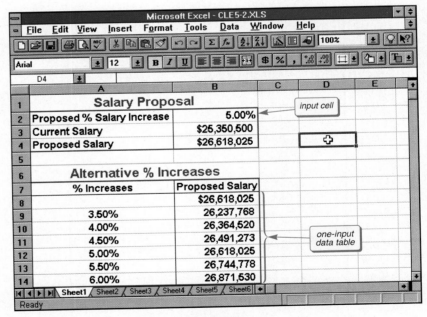

FIGURE CLE5-2b

COMPUTER LABORATORY EXERCISE 3
Assigning a Command Macro to a Button

Instructions: Start Excel and perform the following tasks.

1. Open the worksheet CLE5-3 from the subdirectory Excel5 on the Student Diskette that accompanies this book.

2. Click the Input Macro tab and print the macro. Click the Inventory Listing tab. Click the Drawing button on the Standard toolbar to display the Drawing toolbar. Add the button shown in Figure CLE5-3a. Assign the macro titled Input-Macro (Figure CLE5-3b) to the button. Change the title of the button to Acceptable Total Parts.

3. Unprotect cell D9 and then protect the worksheet.

4. Click the Acceptable Total Parts button and enter 100000. The words in the Excessive Parts column (column F) change based on the value entered. Print the worksheet without cell gridlines. Use the button to enter 79000. Print the worksheet without gridlines.

5. Save the worksheet as CLE5-3A.

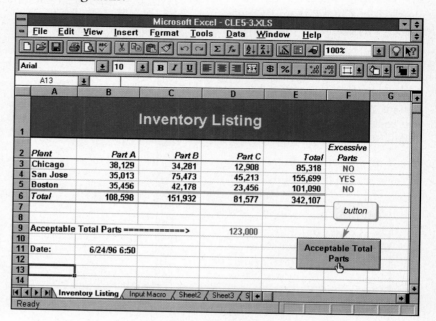

FIGURE CLE5-3a

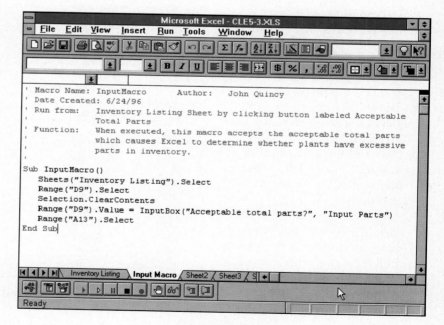

FIGURE CLE5-3b

COMPUTER LABORATORY ASSIGNMENT 1
Determining the Monthly Mortgage Payment

Purpose: To become familiar with using the PMT function, names, one-input data tables, macros, and buttons.

Problem: You are a part-time consultant for the Crown Loan Company. You have been asked to build a worksheet (Figure CLA5-1a) that determines the monthly mortgage payment and includes a one-input data table that shows the monthly payment, total interest, and total cost of a mortgage for varying years. The worksheet will be used by loan officers who know little about computers and worksheets. Thus, create a macro (Figure CLA5-1b on the following page) that will guide the user through entering the mortgage data. Assign the macro to a button on the worksheet.

FIGURE CLA5-1a

Instructions: Perform the following tasks:

1. Bold the entire worksheet.
2. Enter the Mortgage Payment section of the worksheet. Assign cell B2 the NOW function so it displays the system date and time. It is not necessary that you display the exact date shown in Figure CLA5-1a. Create names for the range B3:B6 using the Name command on the Insert menu. Assign cell B6 the following formula using the Point mode and the name box in the formula bar:
   =PMT(Interest_Rate / 12, 12 * Years, -Principal)
3. Enter the following mortgage data: Principal = $100,000; Interest Rate = 9.50%; Years = 30. Format the range B3:B6 as shown in Figure CLA5-1a.

(continued)

COMPUTER LABORATORY ASSIGNMENT 1 (continued)

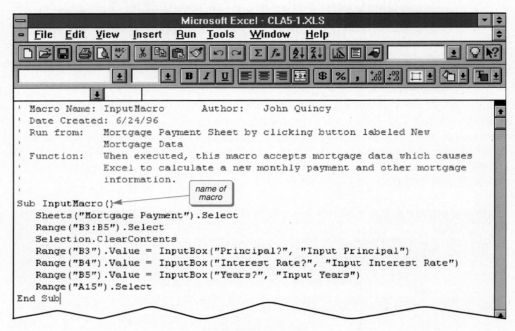

FIGURE CLA 5-1b

4. Enter the Payments for Varying Years section of the worksheet. Assign cell E3 the formula, =Monthly_Payment, cell G3 the formula, =12 * Years * Monthly_Payment, and cell F3 the formula, =G3 - Principal. Use the fill handle to create the series in the range D4:D15. Create a data table in the range D3:G15 using the Table command on the Data menu. Use cell B5 as the input cell.

5. Color the worksheet and add drop shadows as shown in Figure CLA5-1a.

6. Add your name, course, computer laboratory assignment number (CLA5-1), date, and instructor name in column A beginning in cell A14. Save the worksheet using the filename CLA5-1. Print the worksheet without cell gridlines. Rename the tab for the worksheet Mortgage Payment.

7. Use the Macro command on the Insert menu to create the macro in Figure CLA5-1b. Rename the tab for the macro Input Mortgage Data.

8. Click the Mortgage Payment tab. Display the Drawing toolbar. Create the button shown below the Mortgage Payment section in Figure CLA5-1a on the previous page. Assign the macro InputMacro to the button. Hide the Drawing toolbar. Unprotect the range B3:B5. Protect the worksheet. Click the Save button on the Standard toolbar to save the worksheet.

9. Use the button to determine the mortgage payment for the following mortgage data and print the worksheet for each data set: (a) Principal — $63,500, Interest Rate — 7.75%, and Years —15; (b) Principal — $343,250, Interest Rate — 8.25%, and Years — 30. The Mortgage Payment for (a) is $597.71 and for (b) $2,578.72.

COMPUTER LABORATORY ASSIGNMENT 2
Determining the Future Value of an Investment

Purpose: To become familiar with using the FV function, names, two-input data tables, macros, and buttons.

Problem: The insurance company you work for is in need of a Future Value worksheet that its agents can use with a portable computer when they visit clients. A future value computation tells the user what a constant monthly payment is worth after a period of time if the insurance company pays a fixed interest rate.

An agent survey indicates they want a worksheet similar to the one in Figure CLA5-2a that includes not only a future value computation, but also a **two-input data table** that determines future values for varying interest rates and monthly payments. The survey indicates that the agents know little about computers and worksheets. Thus, you must create a macro (Figure CLA5-2b on the following page) that will guide the agent through entering the future value data. Assign the macro to a button.

Instructions: Perform the following tasks:

1. Bold the entire worksheet.
2. Enter the Future Value Computations section of the worksheet. Assign cell B2 the NOW function so it displays the system date. Format the system date so it appears as shown in Figure CLA5-2a. Enter the data in cells B3, B4, and B5 as shown in Figure CLA5-2a. Create names for the range B3:B6. Assign cell B6 the following formula:
   =FV(Interest_Rate / 12, 12 * Years, -Monthly_Payment)
   Assign cell B7 the following formula:
   =12 * Years * Monthly_Payment

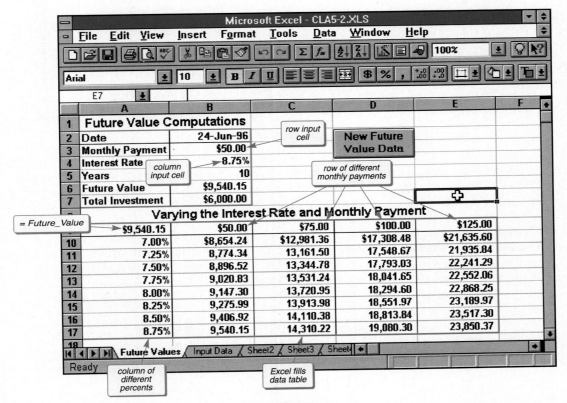

FIGURE CLA5-2a

3. Enter the Varying the Interest Rate and Monthly Payment data table. Assign cell A9 the formula, =Future_Value. Assign cells B9, C9, D9, and E9 the following monthly payments, $50.00, $75.00, $100.00, and $125.00, respectively. Use the fill handle to create the series in the range A10:A17. Create a data table in the range A9:E17 using the Table command from the Data menu. Use cell B3 as the row input cell and cell B4 as the column input cell. Rename the Sheet1 tab Future Values.
4. Add your name, course, computer laboratory assignment number (CLA5-2), date, and instructor name in column A beginning in cell A19. Save the workbook using the filename CLA5-2. Print the worksheet without cell gridlines with the future value data shown in Figure CLA5-2a.
5. Use the Macro command from the Insert menu to create the macro in Figure CLA5-2b on the following page. Rename the tab Input Data. Print the macro.

(continued)

COMPUTER LABORATORY ASSIGNMENT 2 (continued)

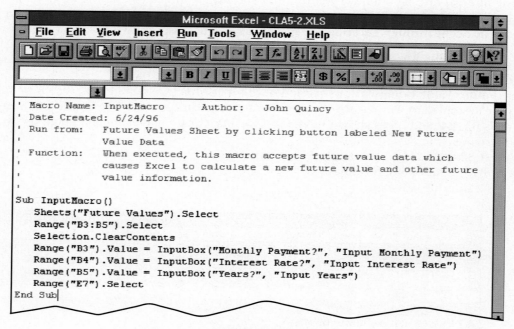

```
'  Macro Name: InputMacro      Author:   John Quincy
'  Date Created: 6/24/96
'  Run from:     Future Values Sheet by clicking button labeled New Future
'                Value Data
'  Function:     When executed, this macro accepts future value data which
'                causes Excel to calculate a new future value and other future
'                value information.
'
Sub InputMacro()
    Sheets("Future Values").Select
    Range("B3:B5").Select
    Selection.ClearContents
    Range("B3").Value = InputBox("Monthly Payment?", "Input Monthly Payment")
    Range("B4").Value = InputBox("Interest Rate?", "Input Interest Rate")
    Range("B5").Value = InputBox("Years?", "Input Years")
    Range("E7").Select
End Sub
```

FIGURE CLA5-2b

6. Click the Future Values tab. Display the Drawing toolbar. Create the button shown in column D in Figure CLA5-2a. Assign the macro InputMacro to the button. Hide the Drawing toolbar. Unprotect the range B3:B5. Protect the worksheet. Click the Save button on the Standard toolbar to save the workbook.

7. Use the New Future Value Data button (Figure CLA5-2a) to determine the future value for the following data and print the worksheet for each data set: (a) Monthly Payment — $100.00, Interest Rate — 7.25%, and Years — 30; (b) Monthly Payment — $300.00, Interest Rate — 9.25%, and Years —10. The Future Value for (a) is $128,189.33 and for (b) is $58,881.96.

COMPUTER LABORATORY ASSIGNMENT 3
Building an Amortization Table and Analyzing Data

Purpose: To become familiar with the PMT and PV functions. To understand how to develop an amortization table and use goal seeking and the Scenario Manager to analyze data.

Problem: Each student in your Office Automation course is assigned a *live project* with a local company. You have been assigned to the Crown Loan Company to generate the loan information worksheet in Figure CLA5-3a and the Scenario Summary worksheet in Figure CLA5-3b. The president also wants you to demonstrate the goal seeking capabilities of Excel.

Instructions: Perform the following tasks to create the two worksheets:

1. Enter the worksheet title in cell A1. Enter the text in the ranges A2:A4 and D2:D4. Enter 13500 in cell B2, 2300 in cell B3, 7.75% in cell E2, and 5 in cell E3 (Figure CLA5-3a). Create names for the cells in the range B2:B4 and E2:E4 by using the names in the adjacent cells. In cell B4, enter the formula:
=Price - Down_Pymt. In cell E4, enter the PMT function:
=PMT(Rate / 12, 12 * Years, -Loan_Amount)

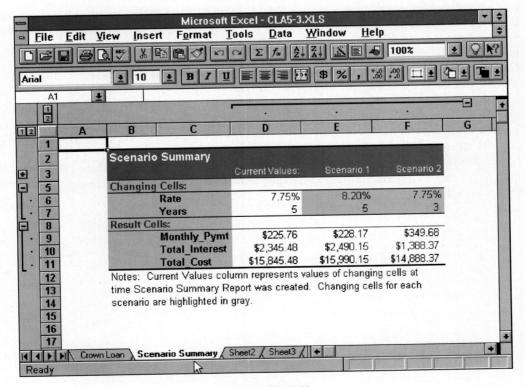

FIGURE CLA5-3a

FIGURE CLA5-3b

COMPUTER LABORATORY ASSIGNMENT 3 (continued)

2. Enter the column titles for the amortization schedule in the range A5:E13. Use the fill handle to generate the years in the range A6:A10.

3. Assign the formulas and functions to the cells indicated in the table below:

CELL	FORMULA OR FUNCTION
B6	=Loan_Amount
C6	=IF(A6 <= Years, PV(Rate / 12, 12 * (Years - A6), -Monthly_Pymt), 0)
D6	=B6 - C6
E6	=IF(B6 > 0, 12 * Montly_Pymt - D6, 0)
B7	=C6
D11	=SUM(D6:D10)
E11	=SUM(E6:E10)
E12	=Down_Pymt
E13	=D11 + E11 + E12

4. Copy cell B7 to the range B8:B10. Copy the range C6:E6 to the range C7:E10. Draw the borders shown in Figure CLA5-3a. Rename the tab Crown Loan.

5. Save the workbook using the file name CLA5-3. Print the worksheet without cell gridlines with the loan data and loan information in Figure CLA5-3a.

6. Unprotect the ranges B2:B4 and E2:E3. Protect the worksheet. Save the worksheet.

7. Use Excel's goal seeking capabilities to determine the down payment required for the loan data in Figure CLA5-3a if the monthly payment is set to $200.00. The down payment that results for a monthly payment of $200.00 is $3,577. 87. Print the worksheet. Change the down payment in cell B3 back to $2,300.00.

8. Unprotect the worksheet. Name cell E11 Total_Interest by choosing the Name command from the Insert menu, and then choosing the Define command from the cascading menu. Use the same command to assign the name Total_Cost to cell E13. These names will show up in the Scenario Summary worksheet in the next step. Protect the worksheet.

9. Use Scenario Manager to create a Scenario Summary worksheet (Figure CLA5-3b) for the following scenarios: (1) Interest Rate — 8.2% and Years — 5 and (2) Interest rate — 7.75% and Years — 3. After the Scenario Summary worksheet displays, move the Scenario Summary tab to the immediate right of the Crown Loan tab. Print the Scenario Manager worksheet. Activate the Crown Loan worksheet and save the workbook.

COMPUTER LABORATORY ASSIGNMENT 4
Planning a Mortgage Payment Worksheet

Purpose: To become familiar with planning a worksheet.

Problem: You are a consultant working for Fair Loan Company. You have been assigned to create a worksheet similar to the one in Figure CLA5-3a and a Scenario Summary worksheet similar to the one in Figure CLA5-3b. In the worksheet you are to create, the amortization table should be extended to 30 years. See Computer Laboratory Assignment 3 for the formulas to use.

Create a macro to accept the loan data. Assign the macro to a button in the worksheet. Create a Scenario Summary worksheet that shows the monthly mortgage payment, total interest, and total cost for a 30-year loan with three different interest rates. Add a one-input data table to the worksheet that analyzes the monthly mortgage payment, total interest, and total cost for varying interest rates between 5.00% and 10.00% in increments of .25%.

Record a macro that saves and prints the workbook by clicking one button on the worksheet.

Instructions: Design and create the Mortgage Payment worksheet. Develop your own test data. Enter your name, course, computer laboratory assignment number (CLA5-4), date, and instructor name in column A in separate but adjacent cells. Save the workbook using the filename CLA5-4. Submit the following:

1. A description of the problem. Include the purpose of the worksheet, a statement outlining the results, the required data, and calculations.
2. A handwritten design of the worksheet.
3. A printed copy of the worksheet, macro, and Scenario Summary worksheet.
4. A printed copy of the formulas in the worksheet.
5. A short description explaining how to use the worksheet.

MICROSOFT EXCEL 5 FOR WINDOWS

P R O J E C T   S I X

SORTING AND FILTERING A WORKSHEET DATABASE

OBJECTIVES You will have mastered the material in this project when you can:

▸ Create a database
▸ Use a data form to display records, add records, delete records, and change field values in a database
▸ Sort a database on one field or multiple fields
▸ Display automatic subtotals
▸ Use a data form to find records that meet comparison criteria

▸ Filter data to display records in a database that meet comparison criteria
▸ Use the advanced filtering features to display records in a database that meet comparison criteria
▸ Apply database functions to generate information about the database
▸ Analyze a database using a pivot table

▶ INTRODUCTION

In this project, you will learn about the database capabilities of Excel. A **worksheet database**, also called a **database** or **list**, is an organized collection of data. For example, telephone books, grade books, and lists of company employees are databases. In these cases, the data related to a person is called a **record**, and the data items that make up a record are called **fields**. In a list of company employees, some of the fields would be name, hire date, and age.

A worksheet's row and column structure can easily be used to organize and store a database (Figure 6-1). Each row of a worksheet can be used to store a record and each column can store a field. In addition, a row of column titles at the top of the worksheet is used as **field names** to identify each field.

Once you create a database in Excel, you can do the following:

1. Add and delete records.
2. Change the values of fields in records.
3. Sort the records so they appear in a different order.
4. Determine subtotals for numeric fields.
5. Display records that meet comparison criteria.
6. Analyze data using database functions.
7. Summarize information about the database using a pivot table.

This project illustrates all seven of these database capabilities.

▶ PROJECT SIX — N-VIRO PERSONNEL DATABASE

N-Viro is an environmental consulting firm with 15 employees. The personnel data maintained by N-Viro is shown in Figure 6-1. The field names, columns, types of data, and column widths are described in Table 6-1. Because the N-Viro Personnel Database is visible on the screen, it is important that it be readable. Therefore, some of the column widths in Table 6-1 are determined from the field names and not the maximum length of the data.

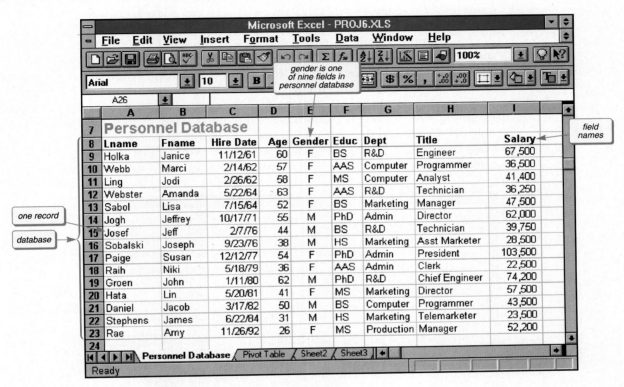

FIGURE 6-1

▶ **TABLE 6-1**

COLUMN TITLES (FIELD NAMES)	COLUMN	TYPE OF DATA	COLUMN WIDTH
Lname	A	Text	10.00
Fname	B	Text	8.00
Hire Date	C	Date	9.00
Age	D	Numeric	5.00
Gender	E	Text	7.00
Educ	F	Text	5.00
Dept	G	Text	9.00
Title	H	Text	13.00
Salary	I	Numeric	9.00

As you will see when creating a database, the column titles (field names) play an important role in the commands you issue to manipulate the data in the database. These column titles must be text and can contain a maximum of 255 characters. However, it's best to keep them short, as shown in row 8 of Figure 6-1 on the previous page.

One difference between the N-Viro Personnel Database in Figure 6-1 and the worksheets discussed in previous projects is the location of the data on the worksheet. In all of the previous worksheets, you began the entries in row 1. When you enter a database onto a worksheet, you usually leave several rows empty above it for adding entries that are used to analyze the data.

Once the N-Viro personnel database is entered onto the worksheet, it will be sorted and manipulated to illustrate how you can quickly generate information. One way to generate database information is to create a pivot table. A **pivot table** gives you the capability to summarize data in the database and then rotate the table's row and column titles to give you different views of the summarized data. Figure 6-2 illustrates two views of the same pivot table. In this pivot table, the salary of the employees is summarized by department and gender. Compare the top worksheet in Figure 6-2 to the bottom one. Notice how the row and column titles have been interchanged to give you different views of the same data.

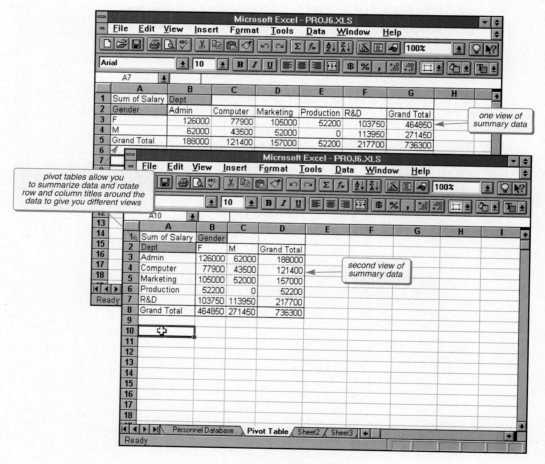

FIGURE 6-2

Project Steps

The following list is an overview of this project. If you are building this project on a personal computer, read these 13 steps without doing them.

1. Start the Excel program.
2. Enter and format the database title and column titles.
3. Assign the column titles in row 8 and the row immediately below it the name Database. Save the workbook.
4. Enter the employee records into the database using a data form.
5. Display employee records using a data form.
6. Sort the employee records in the database.
7. Determine salary subtotals.
8. Use a data form to display employee records that meet a comparison criteria in the database one at a time.
9. Filter the database using the AutoFilter command.
10. Filter the database using the Advanced Filter command.
11. Extract employee records from the database that meet comparison criteria.
12. Apply database functions to the database to generate information.
13. Create and manipulate a pivot table.

The following pages contain a detailed explanation of these steps.

Starting Excel and Setting Up the Database

Start Excel in the same manner described in the previous projects. Once a blank worksheet displays, follow these steps to change the column widths to those specified in Table 6-1; change the height of row 7 to 18 points; and enter and format the database title and column titles. Although Excel does not require the database title in cell A7, it is a good practice to include one on the worksheet to show where the database begins.

TO SET UP THE DATABASE

Step 1: Use the mouse to change the column widths as follows: A = 10.00, B = 8.00, C = 9.00, D = 5.00, E = 7.00, F = 5.00, G = 9.00, H = 13.00, and I = 9.00.

Step 2: Select cell A7 and enter Personnel Database

Step 3: Click the Font Size button on the Formatting toolbar and choose 14. Position the mouse pointer on the border between row heading 7 and row heading 8. When the mouse pointer changes to a split double arrow, drag down until 18.00 displays in the reference area.

Step 4: Enter the column titles in row 8 as shown in Figure 6-1 on page E337. Hold down the CTRL key and select the range A8:I8. Click the Bold button on the Formatting toolbar. Click the Font color button on the Formatting toolbar and choose red (column 1, row 2).

Step 5: With the mouse pointer in the selected range (A8:I8), click the right mouse button. Choose the Format Cells command. Click the Border tab. Click the Color box arrow in the Style area and choose dark red (column 1, row 2). Click the regular border in the Style area (column 1, row 2). Click the Bottom box in the Border area. Choose the OK button.

Step 6: Click column heading E to select the column. Click the Center button on the Formatting toolbar so all entries in column E will be centered. Click column title I to select the column. Click the Comma Style button on the Formatting toolbar. Click the Decrease Decimal button on the Formatting toolbar twice so all entries in column I will display using the Comma style with zero decimal places. Select cell A10.

The worksheet displays as shown in Figure 6-3.

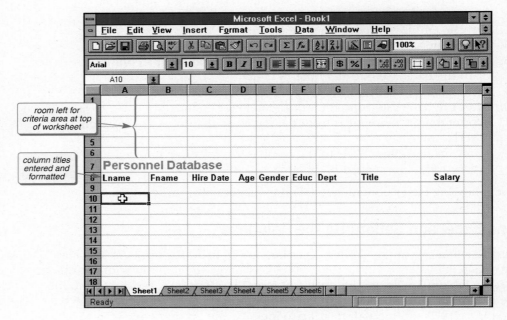

FIGURE 6-3

▶ CREATING A DATABASE

Although Excel can usually identify a **database range** on a worksheet without any qualifications, it is best to give it the name Database. Using the name Database eliminates any confusion when commands are entered to manipulate the database. Thus, to create the N-Viro Personnel Database shown in Figure 6-1, you define the name Database to be the range A8:I9 by selecting the range and typing Database in the reference area in the formula bar. The range assigned to the name Database encompasses the column titles (row 8) and one blank row (row 9) below the column titles. The blank row is for expansion of the database. As records are added using a data form, Excel automatically expands the range of the name Database to encompass the last record. The following steps also rename the Sheet1 tab as Personnel Database and save the workbook using the filename PROJ6.XLS.

TO NAME THE DATABASE AND SAVE THE WORKBOOK ▼

STEP 1 ►

Select the range A8:I9. Click in the reference area in the formula bar and type Database

STEP 2 ►

Press the ENTER key.

The worksheet displays as shown in Figure 6-4.

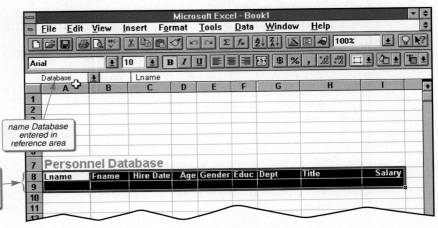

FIGURE 6-4

STEP 3 ►

Select cell A9. Double-click the Sheet1 tab at the bottom of the screen. When the Rename Sheet dialog box displays, type Personnel Database **and choose the OK button.**

STEP 4 ►

Select any cell in the worksheet. Click the Save button on the Standard toolbar. When the Save As dialog box displays, type proj6 in the File name box. Select drive A in the Drives box, and then choose the OK button. If the Summary Info dialog box displays, enter any appropriate information and then choose the OK button.

The worksheet displays as shown in Figure 6-5.

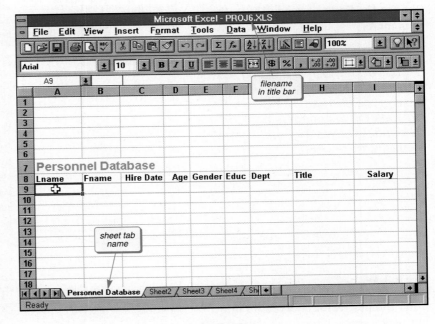

FIGURE 6-5

Entering Records into the Database Using a Data Form

After defining the name Database to be two rows long, a data form is used to enter the personnel records. **A data form** is a dialog box in which Excel includes the field names in the database and corresponding boxes in which you enter the field values. The following steps add the employee records to the N-Viro Personnel Database as shown in Figure 6-1 on page E337.

TO ENTER RECORDS INTO A DATABASE USING A DATA FORM ▼

STEP 1 ▶

Select the Data menu and point to the Form command (Figure 6-6).

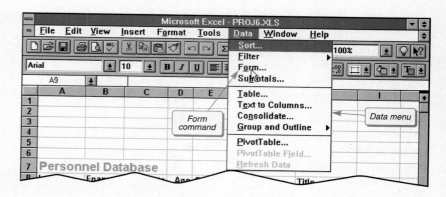

FIGURE 6-6

STEP 2 ▶

Choose the Form command from the Data menu.

Excel displays the data form (Figure 6-7), which is a dialog box, with the tab title Personnel Database in the title bar. The data form includes the field names and corresponding boxes for entering the field values.

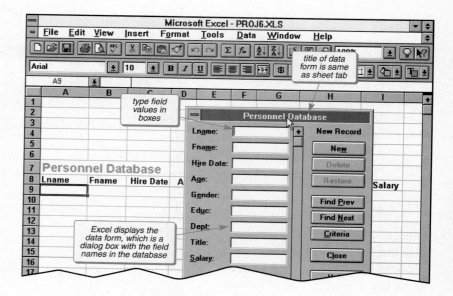

FIGURE 6-7

STEP 3 ▶

Enter the first personnel record into the data form as shown in Figure 6-8. Use the mouse or the TAB key to move the insertion point down to the next box and the SHIFT+TAB keys to move the insertion point to the previous box in the data form.

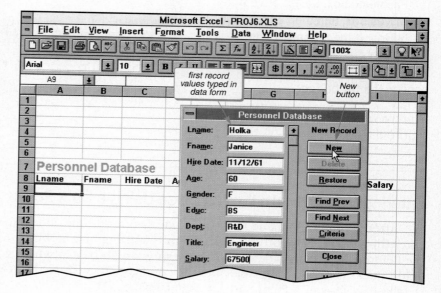

FIGURE 6-8

STEP 4 ▶

Choose the New button (New) in the data form or press the ENTER key. Type the second personnel record into the data form as shown in Figure 6-9.

Excel adds the first personnel record to row 9 in the database range on the worksheet, and the second record displays in the data form (Figure 6-9).

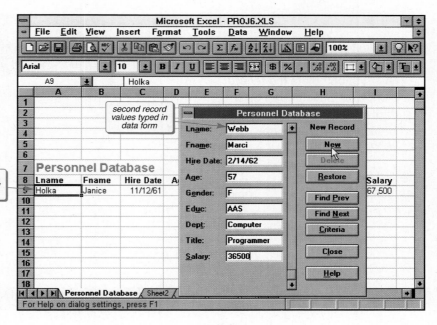

FIGURE 6-9

STEP 5 ▶

Choose the New button in the data form or press the ENTER key to enter the second personnel record. Enter the next twelve personnel records in rows 11 through 22 of Figure 6-1 on page E337 using the data form. Type the last personnel record in row 23 of Figure 6-1.

Excel enters the records into the database range as shown in Figure 6-10. The last record displays in the data form.

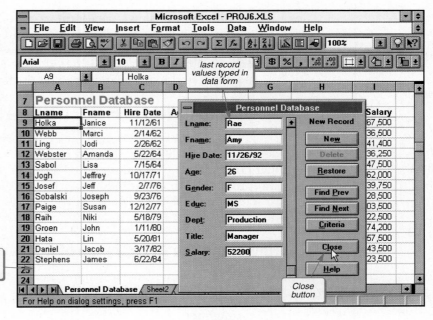

FIGURE 6-10

STEP 6 ▶

With the last record typed in the data form, choose the Close button (Close) to complete the record entry. Click the Save button on the Standard toolbar to save the workbook using the filename PROJ6.XLS.

The N-Viro Personnel Database displays as shown in Figure 6-11.

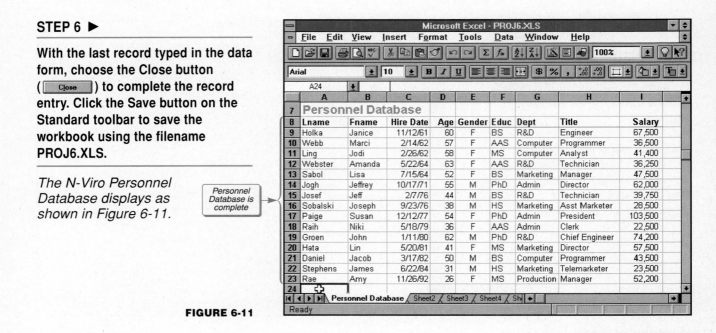

Personnel Database is complete

FIGURE 6-11

In addition to using a data form to build a database, you can enter the records in the same fashion as you entered data onto previous worksheets and then define the name Database to be all the columns and rows (A8:I23). This project presents the data form because it is considered to be a more accurate and reliable method of data entry, and it automatically extends the range of the name Database.

Moving from Field to Field on a Data Form

To move from field to field on a data form, you can use the TAB key as described earlier in Step 3 or you can hold down the ALT key and press the key that corresponds to the underlined letter in the name of the field to which you want to move. An underlined letter in a field name is called an **access key**. Thus, to select the field titled Fname in Figure 6-11 you can hold down the ALT key and press the M key (ALT+M) because m is the access key for the field name Fname.

Reviewing the Appearance of the N-Viro Personnel Database

Refering to the data shown in Figure 6-11, notice the following:

1. In column C, the dates are right-justified because Excel treats dates as numbers.
2. Excel formats the dates in the data form (Figure 6-12) to the m/d/yyyy style when you enter them in the form mm/dd/yy.
3. The Gender codes in column E are centered because Step 6 on page E340 applied the center format to column E, which means all entries in column E will be centered.
4. The salary entries in column I display using the Comma style with no decimal places because Step 6 on page E340 applied this format to column I.

Guidelines to Follow When Creating a Database

Listed in Table 6-2 are some guidelines to use when creating a database in Excel.

▶ **TABLE 6-2**

Database Size and Location on Worksheet
1. Do not enter more than one database per worksheet.
2. Maintain at least one blank row between a database and other worksheet entries.
3. Do not store other worksheet entries in the same rows as your database.
4. Define the name Database to be the database range.
5. A database can have a maximum of 256 fields and 16,384 records on a worksheet.

Column Titles (Field Names)
1. Place column titles in the first row of the database.
2. Do not use blank rows or rows with dashes to separate the column titles from the data.
3. Apply a different format to the column titles and data. For example, bold the column titles and display the data below the column titles using a regular style. Varying the format between the column titles and data is necessary only if you do not assign the name Database to the database range.
4. Column titles (field names) can be up to 255 characters in length.

Contents of Database
1. Each column should have similar data. For example, employee gender should be in the same column for all employees.
2. Do not use spaces in data to improve readability.
3. format the data to improve readability, but do not vary the format in a column.

▶ USING A DATA FORM TO VIEW RECORDS AND CHANGE DATA

A t any time while the worksheet is active, you can use the Form command on the Data menu to display records, add new records, delete records, and change the data in records. When a data form is initially opened, Excel displays the first record in the database. To display the sixth record as shown in Figure 6-12, you choose the Find Next button (**Find Next**) until the sixth record displays. Each time you choose the Find Next button, Excel advances to the next record in the database. If necessary, you can use the Find Prev button (**Find Prev**) to back up to a previous record. You can also use the UP ARROW key and DOWN ARROW key or the vertical scroll bar to the left of the buttons to move among records.

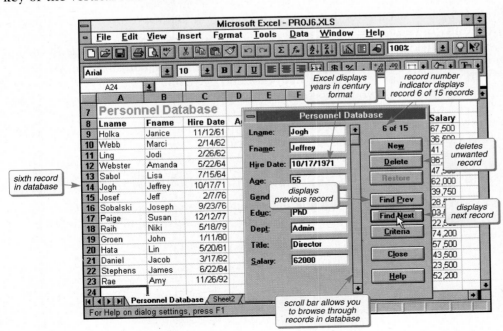

FIGURE 6-12

To change data in a record, you first display it in a data form. Next, you select the fields to change, one at a time. Finally, you use the DOWN ARROW key or the ENTER key to confirm the field changes. If you change field values in a data form and then select the Find Next button to move to the next record, the field changes will not be made.

To add a new record, you choose the New button. A data form always adds the new record to the bottom of the database. To delete a record, you first display it in a data form and then choose the Delete button (Delete). Excel automatically moves all records below the deleted record up one row.

Printing a Database

Printing the database is accomplished using the same procedures you followed in earlier projects. If there is data on the worksheet that is not part of the database you want to print, then follow these steps to print only the database.

TO PRINT A DATABASE

Step 1: Point to the menu bar and click the right mouse button.
Step 2: Choose the Page Setup command from the shortcut menu. Click the Sheet tab. Turn off gridlines. Type `Database` in the Print Area box.
Step 3: Choose the OK button.
Step 4: Ready the printer and click the Print button on the Standard toolbar.

Later, if you want to print the entire worksheet, remove the name Database from the Print Area box on the Sheet tab in the Page Setup dialog box.

▶ SORTING A DATABASE

The data in a database is easier to work with and more meaningful if the records are arranged in sequence on the basis of one or more fields. Arranging records in sequence is called **sorting**. Data is in **ascending sequence** if it is in order from lowest to highest, earliest to most recent, or in alphabetical order. For example, the records were entered into the N-Viro Personnel Database beginning with the earliest hire date to the most recent hire date. Thus, the database in Figure 6-12 on the previous page is sorted in ascending sequence by hire date. Data that is in sequence from highest to lowest in value is in **descending sequence**.

Sort by clicking the **Sort Ascending button** (⬛) or **Sort Descending button** (⬛) on the Standard toolbar or by choosing the **Sort command** on the Data menu. If you're sorting on a single field (column), use one of the Sort buttons on the Standard toolbar. If you're sorting on multiple fields, use the Sort command on the Data menu. Make sure you select a cell in the field to sort on before you click the button. The field you select to sort the records on is called the **sort key**. The first sort example reorders the records by last name.

Sorting the Database by Last Name in Ascending Sequence

To sort the records by last name in ascending sequence, select a cell in column A and click the Sort Ascending button on the Standard toolbar as shown in the following steps.

TO SORT A DATABASE BY LAST NAME IN ASCENDING SEQUENCE ▼

STEP 1 ▶

Select cell A9 and point to the Sort Ascending button on the Standard toolbar (Figure 6-13).

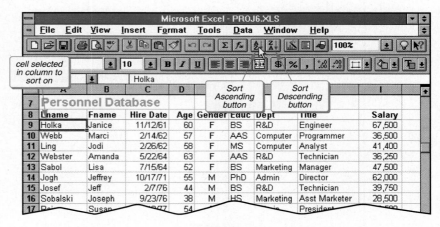

FIGURE 6-13

STEP 2 ▶

Click the Sort Ascending button.

Excel sorts the database by last name in ascending sequence (Figure 6-14).

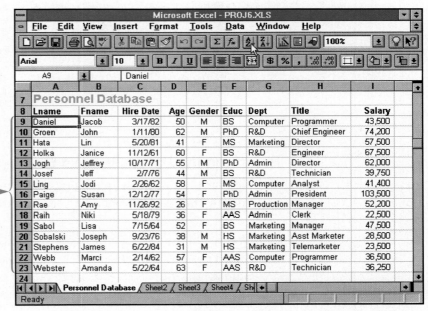

FIGURE 6-14

Sorting the Database by Last Name in Descending Sequence

To sort the records by last name in descending sequence, select a cell in column A and click the Sort Descending button on the Standard toolbar as shown in the steps on the next page.

TO SORT A DATABASE BY LAST NAME IN DESCENDING SEQUENCE

Step 1: Select cell A9.

Step 2: Click the Sort Descending button on the Standard toolbar.

Excel sorts the database by last name in descending sequence (Figure 6-15).

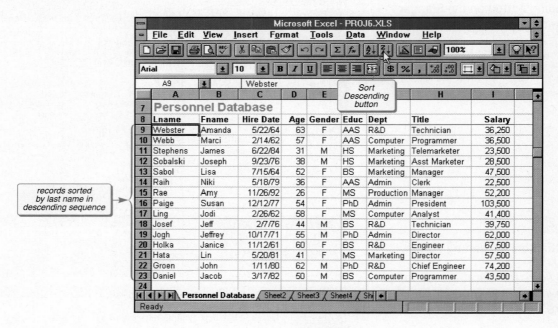

records sorted by last name in descending sequence

FIGURE 6-15

Returning the Database to Its Original Order

Follow these steps to change the sequence of the records back to their original order by hire date in ascending sequence.

TO RETURN THE DATABASE TO ITS ORIGINAL ORDER

Step 1: Select cell C9.

Step 2: Click the Sort Ascending button on the Standard toolbar.

Excel reorders the records in their original sequence by hire date (Figure 6-16).

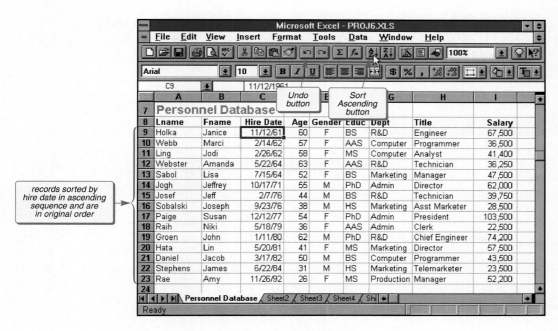

FIGURE 6-16

Undoing a Sort

If you are not satisfied with the results of a sort, you can undo it by immediately using one of the following proecedures:

1. Click the **Undo button** on the Standard toolbar.
2. Choose the **Undo Sort command** from the Edit menu.

These two procedures will only work if you have not entered any commands since the sort operation. For example, after sorting by last name in descending sequence, if you click the Undo button on the Standard toolbar, Excel displays the records in their most recent order — by last name in ascending sequence. If you click the Undo button a second time, Excel displays the records by last name in descending sequence. Thus, the Undo button does not allow you to revert back to an original order once multiple sorts have taken place. For this reason, it is a good idea to enter records into a database in sequence on one of the fields so you can display the database in its original order when necessary. Some Excel users use the fill handle to create a series in an additional field in the database that is used only to reorder the records into their original sequence.

Sorting the Database on Multiple Fields

Excel allows you to sort a maximum of three fields at a time. The sort example that follows uses the Sort command on the Data menu to sort the N-Viro Personnel Database by salary (column I) within education (column F) within gender (column E). In this case, gender is the **major sort key** (Sort By field), education is the **intermediate sort key** (First Then By field), and salary is the **minor sort key** (Second Then By field). The first two keys will be sorted in ascending sequence. The salary field will be sorted in descending sequence.

The phrase *sort by salary within education within gender* means that the records are arranged in sequence by gender code. Within gender, the records are arranged in sequence by education code. Within education, the records are arranged in sequence by salary.

TO SORT A DATABASE ON MULTIPLE COLUMNS ▼

STEP 1 ▶

With a cell in the database selected, select the Data menu.

The Data menu displays (Figure 6-17).

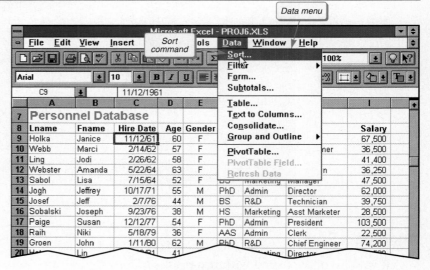

FIGURE 6-17

STEP 2 ▶

Choose the Sort command. When the Sort dialog box displays, click the Sort By arrow.

The Sort By drop-down list shows the field names in the database (Figure 6-18).

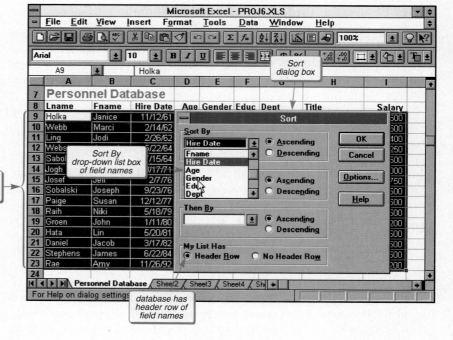

FIGURE 6-18

STEP 3 ▶

Select Gender in the Sort By drop-down list. Click the first Then By box arrow and select Educ. Click the second Then By arrow and then select Salary. Click the Descending option button in the second Then By area.

The Sort dialog box displays as shown in Figure 6-19.

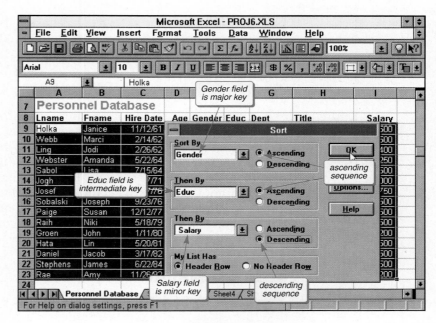

FIGURE 6-19

STEP 4 ▶

Choose the OK button in the Sort dialog box.

Excel sorts the personnel database by salary within education within gender as shown in Figure 6-20.

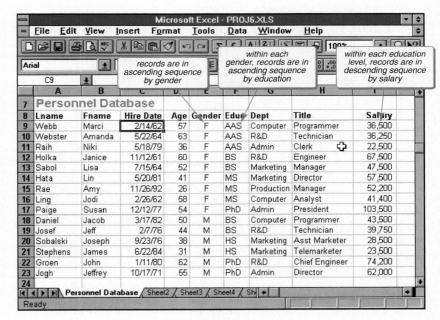

FIGURE 6-20

In Figure 6-20, the records are in ascending sequence by the gender codes (F or M) in column E. Within each gender code, the records are in ascending sequence by the education codes (AAS, BS, HS, MS, PhD) in column F. Finally, within the education codes, the salaries are in descending sequence in column I. Remember, if you make a mistake in a sort operation, you can reorder the records into their original sequence by immediately clicking the Undo button on the Standard toolbar.

Because Excel sorts the database using the current order of the records, the previous example could have been completed by sorting on one field at a time, beginning with the least important one.

Sorting with More than Three Fields

Excel allows you to sort on more than three fields by sorting two or more times. The most recent sort takes precedence. Hence, if you plan to sort on four fields, you sort on the three least important keys first and then sort on the major key. If you want to sort on fields, Lname within Title within Dept within Gender, you first sort on Lname (Second Then By column) within Title (first Then By column) within Dept (Sort By column). After the first sort operation is complete, you finally sort on the Gender field by selecting one of the Gender field cells and clicking the Sort Ascending button on the Standard toolbar.

▶ DISPLAYING AUTOMATIC SUBTOTALS IN A DATABASE

Displaying **automatic subtotals** is a powerful tool for summarizing data in a database. Excel only requires that you sort the database on the field for which you want subtotals to be based and then use the **Subtotals command** on the Data menu. The field you sort on, prior to choosing the Subtotals command, is called the **control field**. When the control field changes, Excel displays a subtotal for the numeric fields you select in the Subtotal dialog box. For example, if you sort on the Dept field and request subtotals on the Salary field, then Excel displays a salary subtotal every time the Dept field changes, and a salary grand total for the entire database.

In the Subtotal dialog box, you select the subtotal function you want to use. The most often used subtotal functions are listed in Table 6-3.

▸ **TABLE 6-3**

SUBTOTAL FUNCTIONS	DESCRIPTION
Sum	Sums a column
Count	Counts the number of entries in a column
Average	Determines the average of numbers in a column
Max	Determines the maximum value in a column
Min	Determines the minimum value in a column

Besides displaying subtotals, Excel also creates an outline for the database. The following example shows you how to display salary subtotals by department. Because the insertion of subtotals increases the number of rows, the Zoom Control box on the Standard toolbar is used to display the entire database.

TO DISPLAY SALARY SUBTOTALS BY DEPARTMENT ▼

STEP 1 ►

Select cell G9. Click the Sort Ascending button on the Standard toolbar.

The N-Viro Personnel Database displays by department in ascending sequence as shown in Figure 6-21.

FIGURE 6-21

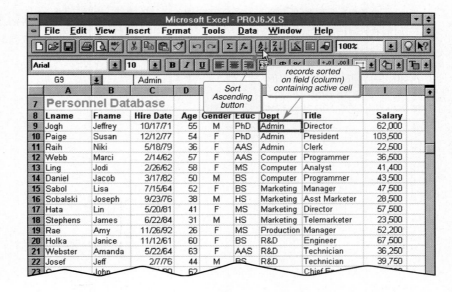

STEP 2 ►

Select the Data menu.

The Data menu displays (Figure 6-22).

FIGURE 6-22

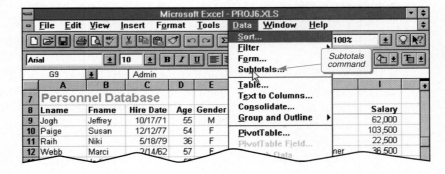

STEP 3 ►

Choose the Subtotals command. When the Subtotals dialog box displays, click the At Each Change in box arrow and select Dept. Select Salary in the Add Subtotal to box.

The Subtotal dialog box displays as shown in Figure 6-23. The At Each Change in box contains the Dept field. The Use Function box contains Sum by default. In the Add Subtotal to box, the Salary field is selected.

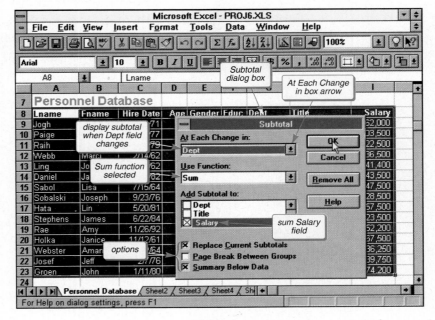

FIGURE 6-23

STEP 4 ▶

Choose the OK button.

Excel inserts new rows in the N-Viro Personnel Database. Each new row contains salary subtotals for each department (Figure 6-24). The database is also outlined and extends beyond the window.

Excel displays database with outline

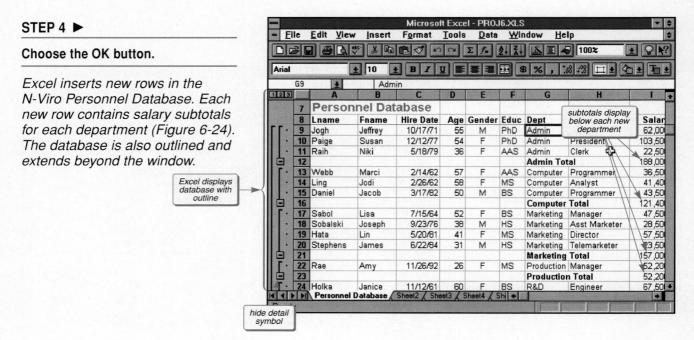

hide detail symbol

FIGURE 6-24

Notice in Figure 6-24 that Excel has added subtotal rows in the middle of the database. Names for each subtotal row are derived from the department names. Thus, in row 12, the text *Admin Total* precedes the actual total salary of $188,000 for the Administration department.

Zooming Out on a Worksheet and Hiding and Showing Detail Data in a Subtotaled Database

The following steps show how to use the Zoom Control box on the Standard toolbar to reduce the size of the display so all records show. The steps also illustrate how to use the outline features of Excel to display only the total rows.

TO ZOOM OUT ON A WORKSHEET AND HIDE AND SHOW DETAIL IN A SUBTOTALED DATABASE ▼

STEP 1 ►

Click the Zoom Control box arrow on the Standard toolbar. Choose 75%.

Excel displays the worksheet in reduced form so all the rows and columns in the database, including the subtotals and grand total, display (Figure 6-25).

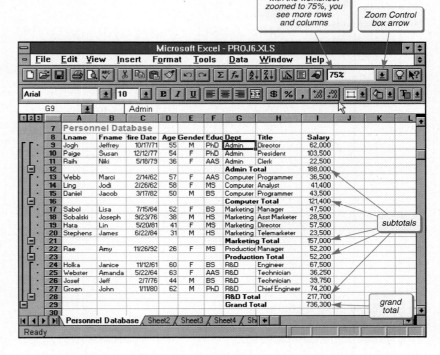

FIGURE 6-25

STEP 2 ►

Click the row level 2 symbol in the group next to the Select All button to hide all detail rows.

Excel displays only the subtotal and grand total rows (Figure 6-26).

STEP 3 ►

Click the row level 3 symbol next to the Select All button to display hidden detail rows. Click the Zoom Control box and choose 100%.

Excel displays the worksheet in normal size (Figure 6-24).

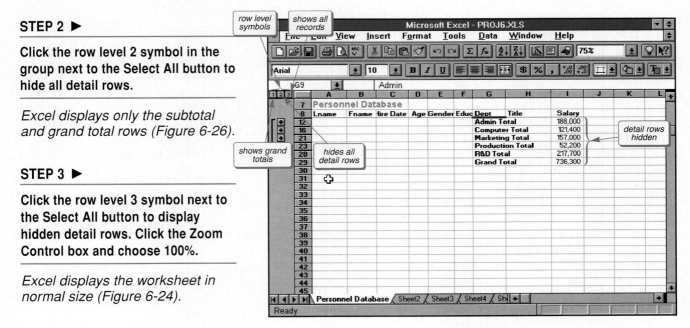

FIGURE 6-26

By utilizing the outlining features of Excel, you can quickly hide and show detail data. You should be aware that when you hide data, you can chart the resulting rows and columns as if they are adjacent to one another. Thus, in Figure 6-26 you can chart the salary subtotals as an adjacent range even though they are not in adjacent rows when the worksheet displays in normal form.

Removing Subtotals from the Database

Excel provides two ways to remove subtotals and the accompanying outline from a database. First, you can click the Undo button on the Standard toolbar or use the Undo Subtotals command on the Edit menu if you have not entered any commands since creating the subtotals. Second, you can choose the Remove All button in the Subtotal dialog box. The following steps show how to use the Remove All button.

TO REMOVE SUBTOTALS FROM A DATABASE ▼

STEP 1 ▶

Select the Data menu and choose the Subtotals command.

Excel selects the database and displays the Subtotal dialog box (Figure 6-27).

STEP 2 ▶

Choose the Remove All button (Remove All).

Excel removes all total rows and the outline from the database so it displays as shown earlier in Figure 6-21 on page E353.

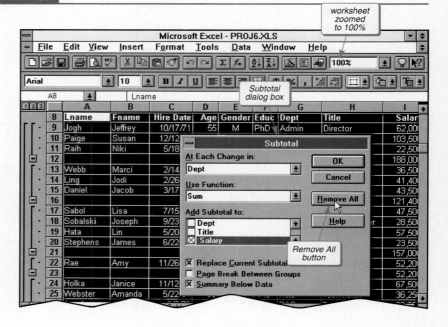

FIGURE 6-27

From the previous sections, you can see how easy it is to add and remove subtotals from a database. This allows you to quickly generate the type of information that database users require to help them make decisions about products or company direction.

Before moving on to the next section, follow these steps to sort the N-Viro Personnel Database into its original order by hire date in ascending sequence.

TO SORT THE DATABASE BY HIRE DATE

Step 1: Select cell C9.
Step 2: Click the Sort Ascending button on the Standard toolbar.

The records in the N-Viro Personnel Database are sorted by hire date in ascending sequence (Figure 6-16 on page E349).

▶ FINDING RECORDS USING A DATA FORM

To find records in the database that pass a test made up of comparison criteria, you can use the Find Prev and Find Next buttons together with the Criteria button (⬜ Criteria ⬜) in the data form. **Comparison criteria** are one or more conditions that include the field names and entries in the corresponding boxes in a data form. For example, you can instruct Excel to find and display only those records that pass the test:

Hire Date < 1/1/80 **AND** Gender = F **AND** Age < 40

For a record to display in the data form, it has to pass **All** three parts of the test. Finding records that pass a test is useful for maintaining the database. When a record that passes the test displays in the data form, you can change the field values or delete it from the database.

You use the same relational operators (=, <, >, >=, ≥ <=, ≤ and <>) to form the comparison criteria in a data form that you used to formulate conditions in IF functions in Project 3. The following steps illustrate how to use a data form to find records that pass the following test:

Age ≥ 40 **AND** Gender = M **AND** Education <> AAS **AND** Salary > $40,000.

TO FIND RECORDS USING A DATA FORM ▼

STEP 1 ▶

From the Data menu, choose the Form command.

The first record in the N-Viro Personnel Database displays in the data form (Figure 6-28).

STEP 2 ▶

Choose the Criteria button in the data form.

Excel displays the data form with blank boxes.

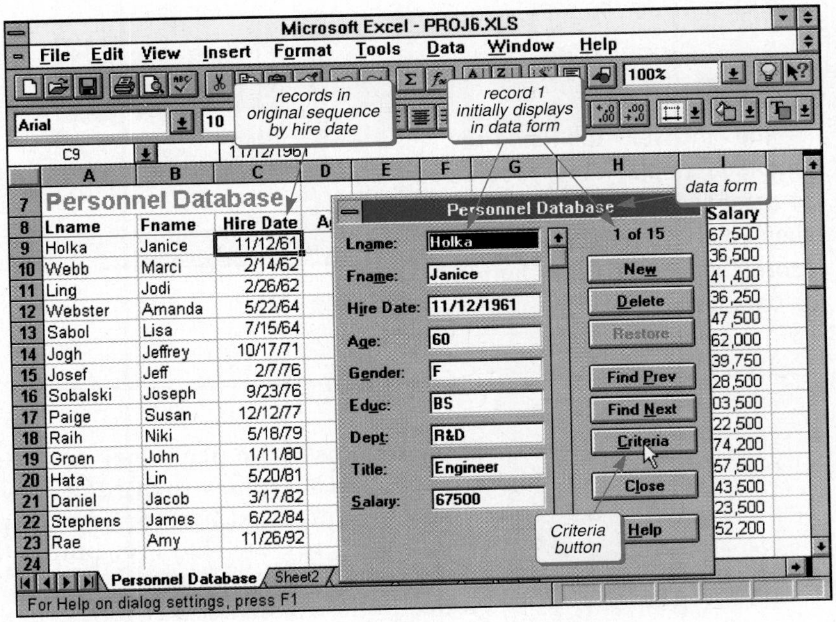

FIGURE 6-28

STEP 3 ▶

Type >=40 **in the Age box,** =M **in the Gender box,** <>AAS **in the Educ box, and** >40000 **in the Salary box.**

The data form displays with the comparison criteria as shown in Figure 6-29. The comparison criteria are 40 years or older, any degree other than AAS and earning a salary greater than $40,000.

FIGURE 6-29

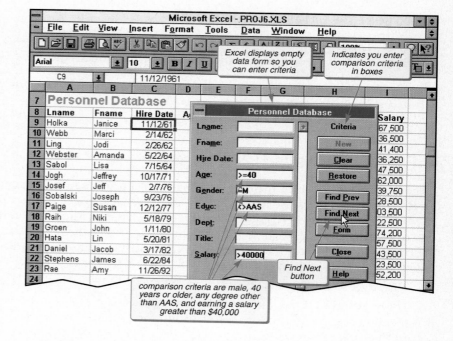

STEP 4 ▶

Choose the Find Next button in the data form.

Excel immediately displays the first record in the database (record 6) that passes the test (Figure 6-30). Mr. Jeffrey Jogh is a 55 year old male with a PhD who earns $62,000. The first 5 records in the database failed the test.

STEP 5 ▶

Use the Find Next and Find Prev buttons to display other records in the database that pass the test. When you have finished displaying records, select the Close button in the data form.

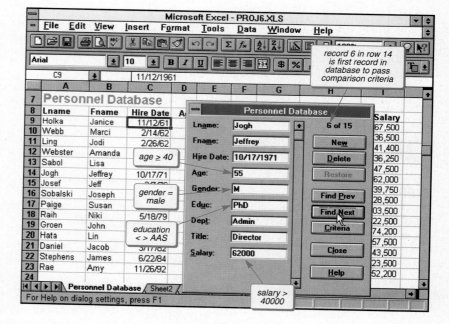

FIGURE 6-30

Three records in the personnel database pass the test: record 6 (Mr. Jeffrey Jogh), record 11 (Mr. John Groen), and record 13 (Mr. Jacob Daniel). Each time you choose the Find Next button, Excel displays the next record that passes the test. You can also use the Find Prev button to display the previous record that passed the test.

Notice in the comparison criteria established in Figure 6-29, no blank characters appear between the relational operators and the values. Leading or trailing blank characters have a significant impact on text comparisons. For example, there is a big difference between =M and = M.

Excel is not **case-sensitive**. That is, Excel considers uppercase and lowercase characters in a criteria comparison to be the same. For example, =m is the same as =M.

Using Wildcard Characters in Comparison Criteria

For text fields, you can use **wildcard characters** to find records that share certain characters in a field. Excel has two wildcard characters, the question mark (?) and the asterisk (*). The **question mark** (?) represents any single character in the same position as the question mark. For example, if the comparison criteria for Lname (last name) is =We?b, then any last name passes the test that has the following: We as the first two characters, any third character, and the letter b as the fourth character. Webb (record 2 in row 10) passes the test.

Use the **asterisk** (*) in a comparison criteria to represent any number of characters in the same position as the asterisk. Jo*, *e, Web*r, are examples of valid text with the asterisk wildcard character. Jo* means all text that begins with the letters Jo. Jogh (record 6 in row 14) and Josef (record 7, row 15) pass the test. The second example, *e, means all text that ends with the letter e. Paige (record 9 in row 17) and Rae (record 15 in row 23) pass the test. The third example, Web*r, means all text that begins with the letters Web and ends with the letter r. Only Webster (record 4 in row 12) passes the test.

If the comparison criteria calls for searching for a question mark (?) or asterisk (*), then precede either one with a tilde (~). For example, to search for the text What?, enter What~? in the comparison criteria.

Using Computed Criteria

A **computed criteria** involves using a formula in a comparison criteria. For example, the computed criterion formula =Age > Salary / 1000 in the Age field on a data form finds all records whose Age field is less than the corresponding Salary field divided by 1000.

▶ FILTERING A DATABASE USING AUTOFILTER

An alternative to using a data form to find records that pass a test is to use AutoFilter. Whereas the data form displays one record at a time, **Auto Filter** enables you to display all the records that meet a criteria as a subset of the database. AutoFilter hides records that do not pass the test, thus displaying only those that pass the test.

You apply AutoFilter to a database by choosing the Filter command on the Data menu, and then choosing AutoFilter from the cascading menu. Excel responds by adding drop-down arrows directly on the field names at the top of the database in row 8. Clicking an arrow displays a list of the unique items in the field (column). If you select an item from the list, Excel immediately hides records that do not contain the item. The item you select from the drop-down list is called the **filter criterion**. If you select an item from a second field, Excel displays a subset of the first subset.

The following steps show how to use AutoFilter to display those records in the N-Viro Personnel Database that pass the following test:

Gender =M **AND** Educ =PhD

TO APPLY AUTOFILTER TO A DATABASE ▼

STEP 1 ▶

Select any cell in the database.
Select the Data menu and choose
the Filter command.

*Excel displays a cascading menu
(Figure 6-31).*

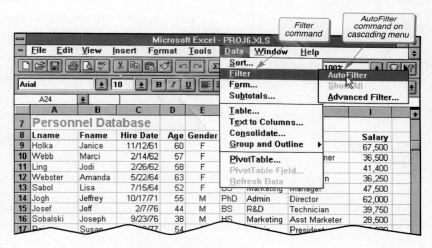

FIGURE 6-31

STEP 2 ▶

Choose the AutoFilter command.

*Drop-down arrows appear on each
field name in row 8 (Figure 6-32).*

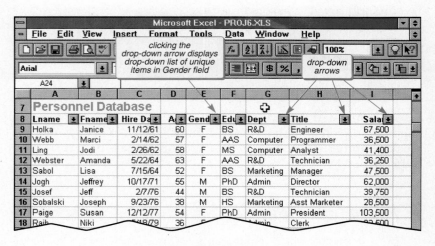

FIGURE 6-32

STEP 3 ▶

Click the Gender drop-down arrow.

*A list of the entries F and M in the
Gender field displays (Figure
6-33). (All), (Custom...), (Blanks),
and (NonBlanks) are found in
every AutoFilter drop-down list.
When you first choose the AutoFilter command, the filter criterion for
each field in the database is set to
All. Thus, all records display.*

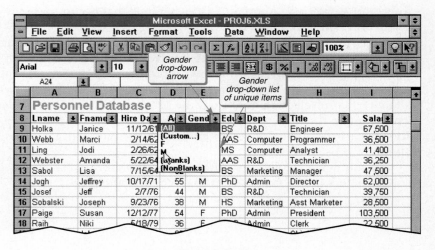

FIGURE 6-33

STEP 4 ►

Select M from the Gender drop-down list. Click the Educ arrow.

Excel hides all records representing females. Thus, only records representing males display (Figure 6-34). The Educ drop-down list of entries displays.

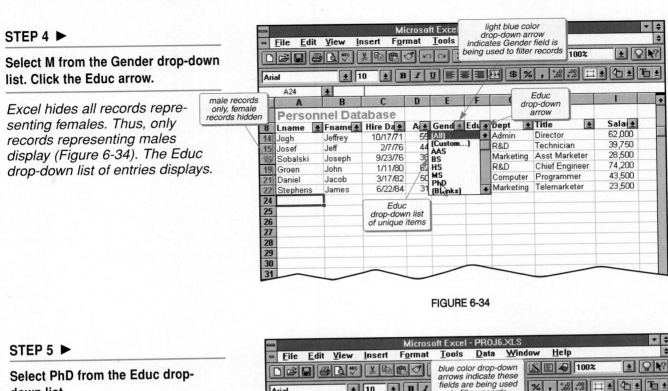

FIGURE 6-34

STEP 5 ►

Select PhD from the Educ drop-down list.

*Excel hides all records representing males that do not have a PhD. Only two records pass the filter criterion Gender = M **AND** Educ = PhD (Figure 6-35).*

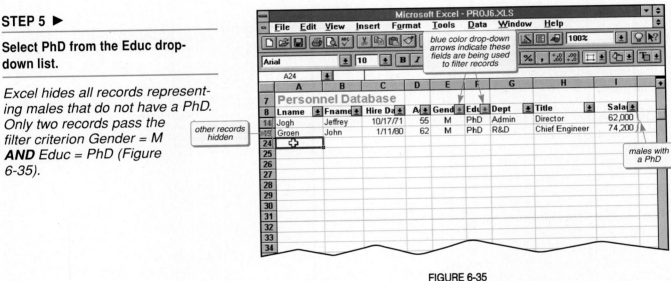

FIGURE 6-35

It is important to note that Excel adds the second filter criterion to the first. Thus, there are two tests that each record must pass to display as part of the final subset of the database. Listed below are some important points regarding AutoFilter.

1. When AutoFilter is active, Excel displays in blue the row headings and drop-down arrows used to establish the filter.
2. If you have multiple lists (other columns of data) on the worksheet, select a cell within the database prior to choosing the AutoFilter command.
3. If a single cell is selected before applying AutoFilter, Excel assigns arrows to all field names in the database. If you select certain field names, Excel assigns arrows to only the selected field names.

4. To find the rows with blank cells in a field, select Blanks from the drop-down list for that field. To find rows with nonblank cells in a field, select the NonBlanks option from the drop-down list for that field.

5. To remove a filter criterion for a single field, select the All option from the drop-down list for that field.

6. Automatic subtotals should be added to a filtered database only after applying AutoFilter, because Excel does not recalculate after selecting the filter criterion.

Removing AutoFilter

To display all records and remove the drop-down arrows, choose the Filter command from the Data menu, then choose the AutoFilter command. To display all records and keep the drop-down arrows on the field names, choose the **Show All command** on the Filter cascading menu. The following steps illustrate how to display all records and remove the drop-down arrows.

TO REMOVE AUTOFILTER ▼

STEP 1 ▶

Select a cell in the database. Select the Data menu and choose the Filter command.

The Data menu and cascading menu display as shown in Figure 6-36.

STEP 2 ▶

Choose the AutoFilter command.

All the records in the N-Viro Personnel Database display as shown in Figure 6-31 on page E360. The AutoFilter command is like a toggle switch. Choose it once and the drop-down arrows are added to the field names. Choose it again, and the drop-down arrows are removed and any hidden records display.

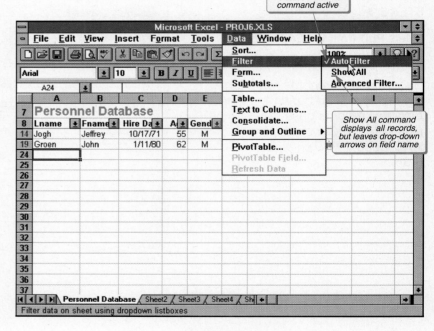

FIGURE 6-36

Entering Custom Criteria with AutoFilter

One of the options available in all the drop-down lists is (Custom...). The **(Custom...)** option allows you to enter custom criteria, such as multiple options in a drop-down list and ranges of numbers. The following steps show how to display records in the N-Viro Personnel Database that represent employees whose ages are in the range 40 to 50 inclusive ($40 \leq Age \leq 50$).

TO ENTER CUSTOM CRITERIA ▼

STEP 1 ►

Select the Data menu and choose the Filter command, then choose the AutoFilter command. Click the Age drop-down arrow.

The Age drop-down list displays (Figure 6-37).

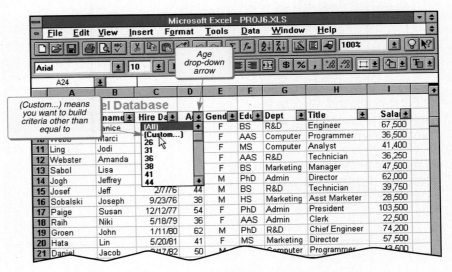

FIGURE 6-37

STEP 2 ►

Select the (Custom...) option. When the Custom AutoFilter dialog box displays, select the >= comparison operator in the top left box. Type 40 in the top right box. Select the <= comparison operator in the bottom left box. Type 50 in the bottom right box.

The Custom AutoFilter dialog box displays as shown in Figure 6-38.

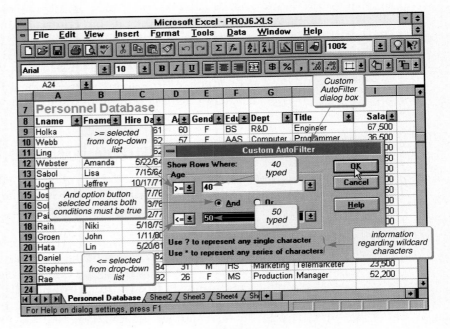

FIGURE 6-38

STEP 3 ►

Choose the OK button in the Custom AutoFilter dialog box.

The records in the N-Viro Personnel Database that represent employees whose ages are between 40 and 50 inclusive display (Figure 6-39). Records that represent employees whose age are not between 40 and 50 inclusive are hidden.

STEP 4 ►

Select the Data menu and choose the Filter command. Choose the AutoFilter command from the cascading menu.

All records in the N-Viro Personnal Database display as shown in Figure 6-31 on page E360.

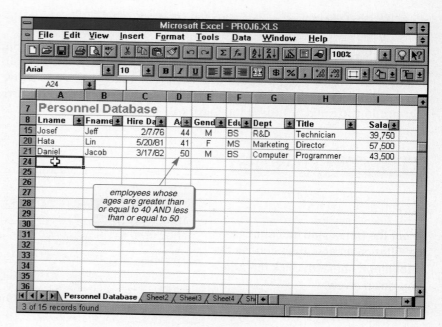

FIGURE 6-39

Notice in the Custom AutoFilter dialog box in Figure 6-38 on the previous page that you can select the And or Or operator to indicate whether both parts of the criteria must be true (And) or only one of the two must be true (Or). Use the And, operator when the custom criteria is continuous over a range of values, such as Age between 40 **AND** 50 inclusive ($40 \leq Age \leq 50$). Use the Or operator when the custom criteria is not continuous, such as Age less than or equal to 40 **OR** greater than or equal to 50 ($40 \geq Age \geq 50$).

As with data forms, you can use wildcard characters to build the custom criteria as described at the bottom of the Custom AutoFilter dialog box in Figure 6-38.

► CREATING A CRITERIA RANGE ON THE WORKSHEET

I nstead of using a data form or AutoFilter to establish criteria, you can set up a **criteria range** on the worksheet and use it to manipulate records that pass the comparison criteria. To set up a criteria range, you copy the database field names to another area of the worksheet, preferably above the database in case, it is expanded downward or to the right in the future. Next, you enter the comparison criteria in the row immediately below the field names in the criteria range. Then you name the criteria range Criteria. After naming the criteria range, use the **Advanced Filter command** on the Filter cascading menu. The following steps show how to set up criteria in the range A2:I3 to find records that pass the test: Gender =M **AND** Age >40 **AND** Salary >50000.

TO SET UP A CRITERIA RANGE ON THE WORKSHEET ▼

STEP 1 ►

Select the database title and field names in the range A7:I8. Click the Copy button on the Standard toolbar. Select cell A1. Press the ENTER key to copy the contents on the Clipboard to the paste area A1:I2. Change the title in cell A1 from Personnel Database to `Criteria Area`. Enter `>40` in cell D3. Enter `M` in cell E3. Enter `>50000` in cell I3.

The worksheet in Figure 6-40 displays.

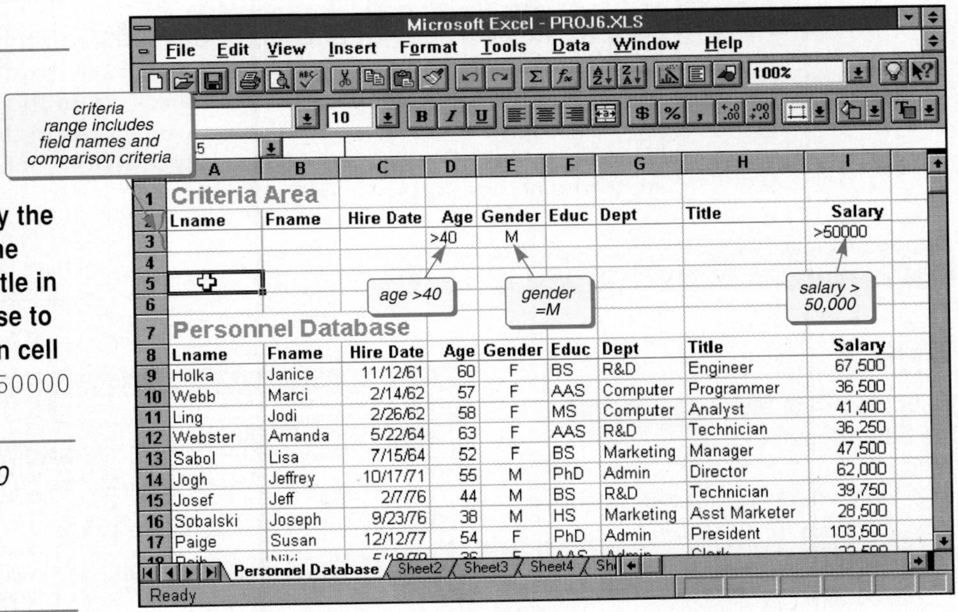

STEP 2 ►

Select the range A2:I3. In the reference area in the formula bar, type `Criteria` and press the ENTER key.

The name Criteria is defined to be the range A2:I3. The Advanced AutoFilter command will automatically recognize the range named Criteria as the criteria range.

FIGURE 6-40

Remember these important points about setting up a criteria range:

1. Do not begin a test for equality involving text (Gender =M) with an equal sign because Excel will assume the text (M) is a range name rather than text.
2. If you include a blank row in the criteria range (for example, rows 2 and 3 and the blank row 4), all records will pass the test.
3. To ensure the field names in the criteria range are spelled exactly the same as in the database, use the Copy command to copy the database field names to the criteria range as illustrated in the previous steps.
4. The criteria range is independent of the criteria set up in a data form.
5. You can print the criteria range by entering the name Criteria in the Print Area box on the Sheet tab in the Page Setup dialog box as discussed earlier for printing a database range (see page E346).

▶ DISPLAYING RECORDS THAT MEET A CRITERIA USING THE ADVANCED FILTER COMMAND

he Advanced Filter command is similar to the AutoFilter command, except that it does not add drop-down arrows to the field names. Instead, it uses the comparison criteria set up on the worksheet in a criteria range (A2:I3). Follow these steps to display the records in the database that pass the test (Gender = M **AND** Age > 40 **AND** Salary > 50000) defined in the previous set of steps and shown in Figure 6-40.

TO DISPLAY RECORDS USING THE ADVANCED FILTER ▼

STEP 1 ▶

Select the Data menu and choose the Filter command.

The Data menu and a cascading menu display (Figure 6-41).

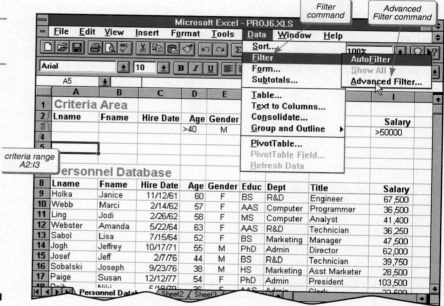

FIGURE 6-41

STEP 2 ▶

Choose the Advanced Filter command.

The Advanced Filter dialog box displays (Figure 6-42). In the Action area, the Filter the List, in-place option button is selected automatically. Excel selects the database (range A8:I23) in the List Range box, because it is assigned the name Database. Excel also selects the criteria range (A2:I3) in the Criteria Range box, because it is assigned the name Criteria.

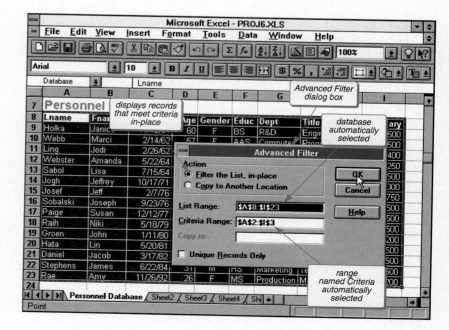

FIGURE 6-42

STEP 3 ▶

Choose the OK button.

Excel hides all records that do not meet the comparison criteria, leaving only two records on the worksheet (Figure 6-43). Jeffrey Jogh (row 14) and John Groen (row 19) are the only two in the personnel database that are older than 40, male, and earn a salary greater than $50,000.

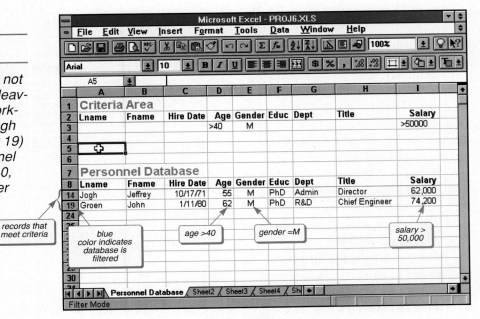

FIGURE 6-43

Notice the Advanced Filter command displays a subset of the database in the same fashion as the AutoFilter command. The primary difference between the two is that the Advanced Filter command allows you to create more complex comparison criteria, because the criteria range can be as many rows long as necessary, allowing for many sets of comparison criteria.

To display all records in the N-Viro Personnel Database, select the Data menu and choose the Filter command, then choose the Show All command.

▶ EXTRACTING RECORDS

I f you select the Copy to Another Location in the Action area of the Advanced Filter dialog box (Figure 6-42), Excel copies the records that pass the test to another part of the worksheet, rather than displaying a subset of the database. The location where the records are copied to is called the **extract range.** The way the extract range is set up is similar to the way the criteria range was set up earlier. Once the records that pass the test in the criteria range are **extracted** (copied), you can manipulate and print them as a group.

Creating the Extract Range

To create an extract range, copy the field names of the database to an area on the worksheet, preferably well below the database range. Next, name the range containing the field names Extract by using the reference area. Finally, use the Advanced Filter command to extract the records. The following steps show how to set up an extract range below the N-Viro Personnel Database.

TO CREATE AN EXTRACT RANGE ON THE WORKSHEET ▼

STEP 1 ▶

Select the database title and field names in the range A7:I8. Click the Copy button on the Standard toolbar. Select cell A27. Press the ENTER key to copy the contents on the Clipboard to the paste area A27:I28. Change the title in cell A27 from Personnel Database to Extract Area. Select the range A28:I28. Type the name Extract in the reference area in the formula bar and press the ENTER key. Select any cell on the worksheet. Select the Data menu and choose the Filter command.

The worksheet displays as shown in Figure 6-44. Notice that the name Extract is only assigned the field names in row 28. Excel will automatically copy the records to the rows below the range named Extract.

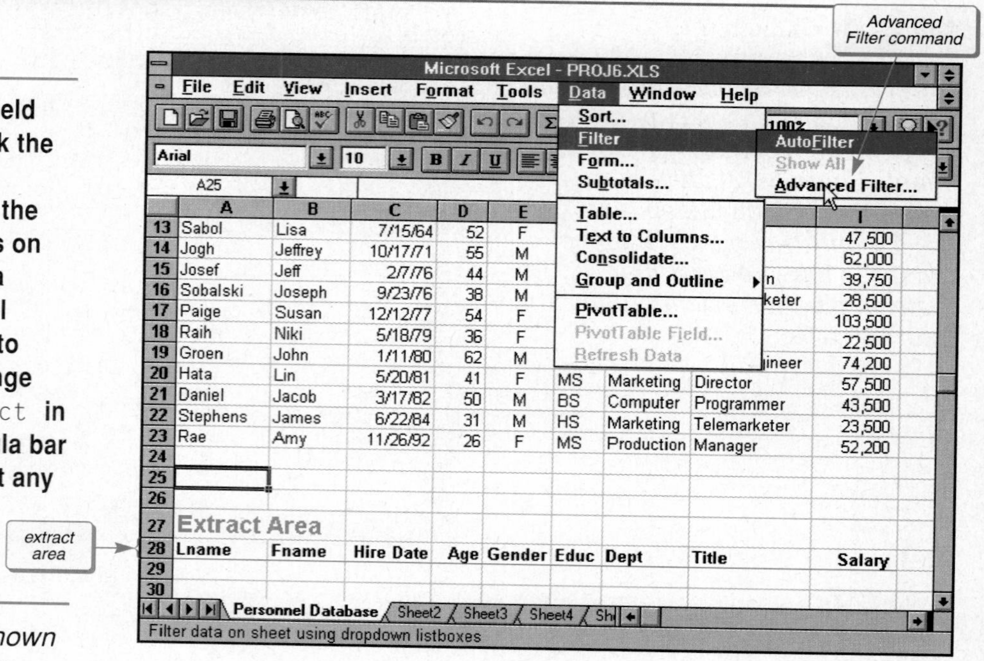

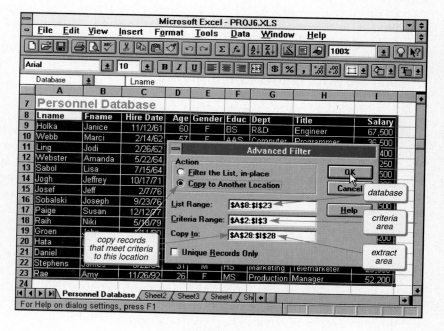

FIGURE 6-44

STEP 2 ▶

Choose the Advanced Filter command from the cascading menu. When the Advanced Filter dialog box displays, select the Copy to Another Location option button in the Action area.

Excel automatically assigns the range A8:I23 to the List Range box because the range A8:I23 is named Database (Figure 6-45). It also assigns the range named Criteria (A2:I3) to the Criteria Range box and the range named Extract (A28:I28) to the Copy to box.

FIGURE 6-45

STEP 3 ▶

Choose the OK button.

Excel copies the records from the N-Viro Personnel Database that pass the test described in the criteria range (see Figure 6-43) to the extract range (Figure 6-46).

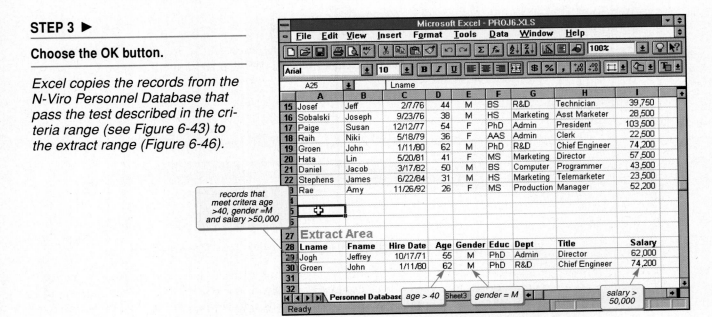

FIGURE 6-46

When you set up the extract range, you do not have to copy all the field names in the database to the proposed extract range. Instead of using the copy command, you can copy only those field names you want and they can be in any order. You can also type the field names, but it is not recommended.

When you choose the Advanced Filter command and select the Copy to Another Location option button, Excel clears all the cells below the field names in the extract range. Hence, if you change the comparison criteria in the criteria range and choose the Advanced Filter command a second time, Excel clears the original extracted records before it copies the records that pass the new test.

In the previous example, the extract range was defined as a single row containing the field names (range A28:I28). When you define the extract range as one row long (the field names), any number of records can be extracted from the database because Excel will use all the rows below row 28 to the bottom of the worksheet. The alternative is to define an extract range with a fixed number of rows. However, if you define a fixed-size extract range, and if more records are extracted than there are rows available, Excel displays a dialog box with a diagnostic message indicating the extract range is full.

▶ MORE ABOUT COMPARISON CRITERIA

T he way you set up the comparison criteria in the criteria range determines the records that will pass the test when you use the Filter command. Different comparison criteria are described on the next page.

A Blank Row in the Criteria Range

If the criteria range contains a blank row, then all the records in the database pass the test. For example, the blank row in the criteria range in Figure 6-47 causes all records to pass the test.

FIGURE 6-47

Using Multiple Comparison Criteria with the Same Field

If the criteria range contains two or more entries under the same field name, then records that pass either comparison criterion pass the test. For example, the criteria range in Figure 6-48 causes all records that represent employees who have an AAS degree **OR** a BS degree to pass the test.

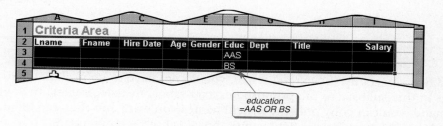

FIGURE 6-48

If an **AND** applies to the same field name (Age >50 **AND** Age <55), then you must duplicate the field name (Age) in the criteria range. That is, add the field name Age to the right of Salary in column I, delete the name Criteria by using the Name command on the Insert menu, and then define the name Criteria in the reference area to be equal to the new range that includes the second Age field.

Comparison Criteria in Different Rows and Under Different Fields

When the comparison criteria under different field names are in the same row, then records pass the test only if they pass all the comparison criteria. If the comparison criteria for the field names are in different rows, then the records must pass only one of the tests. For example, in the criteria range in Figure 6-49, all records that represent employees who are greater than 60 years old **OR** earn more than $70,000 pass the test.

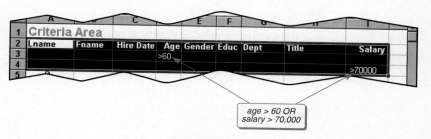

FIGURE 6-49

▶ USING DATABASE FUNCTIONS

Excel has twelve database functions that you can use to evaluate numeric data in a database. One of the functions is called the **DAVERAGE function**. As the name implies, you use the DAVERAGE function to find the average of numbers in a database field that pass a test. This function serves as an alternative to finding an average using the Subtotals command on the Data menu. The general form of the DAVERAGE function is

=DAVERAGE(database, "field name", criteria range)

where database is the name of the database, field name is the name of the field in the database, and criteria range is the comparison criteria or test to pass.

In the following steps, the DAVERAGE function is used to find the average age of the female employees and the average age of the male employees in the N-Viro Personnel Database.

TO USE THE DAVERAGE DATABASE FUNCTION

Step 1: Enter the field name Gender twice, once in cell K1 and again in cell L1. Enter the code for females F in cell K2. Enter the code for males M in cell L2.

Step 2: Enter Average Female Age in cell M1. Enter Average Male Age in cell M2.

Step 3: Enter the database function =daverage(database, "Age", K1:K2) in cell O1.

Step 4: Enter the database function =daverage(database, "Age", L1:L2) in cell O2.

Step 5: Select the range O1:O2. Click the Decrease Decimal button on the formatting toolbar until only one decimal place appears.

Excel computes and displays the average age of the females in the database (49.7) in cell O1 and the average age of the males in the database (46.7) in cell O2 (Figure 6-50).

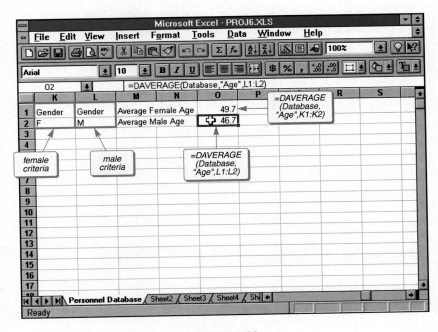

FIGURE 6-50

Notice in Figure 6-50 on the previous page the first value (Database) in the function references the database defined earlier in this project (range A8:I23). The second value ("Age") identifies the field on which to compute the average. Excel requires that you surround the field name with quotation marks unless the field has been assigned a name through the reference area in the formula bar. The third value (K1:K2 for the female average) defines the criteria range.

Other database functions that are similar to the functions described in previous projects include the DCOUNT, DMAX, DMIN, and DSUM functions. For a complete list of the database functions, click the Function Wizard button on the Standard toolbar. When the FunctionWizard – Step 1 of 2 dialog box displays, select Database in the Function Category list box. The database functions display in the Function Name list box.

▶ CREATING A PIVOT TABLE TO ANALYZE DATA

A pivot table gives you the capability of summarizing data in the database and then rotating the table's row and column titles to give you different views of the summarized data. You usually create a pivot table on another page in the same workbook as the database you are analyzing, although you can create it on the same sheet as the worksheet.

The **PivotTable command** on the Data menu starts the PivotTable Wizard, which guides you through creating a pivot table. The **PivotTable Wizard** does not modify the database in any way. It uses the data in the database to generate information.

The pivot table to be created in this project is shown in Figure 6-51. The table summarizes salary information by gender and department for the N-Viro Personnel Database built earlier in this project.

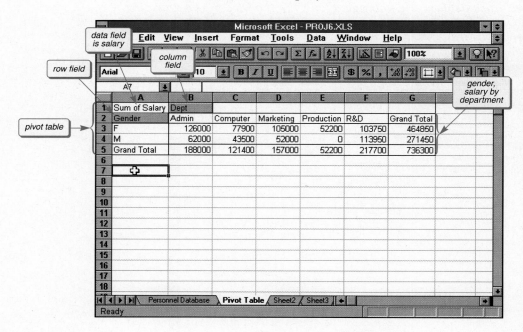

FIGURE 6-51

To create the pivot table in Figure 6-51, you need only select three fields from the database when requested by the PivotTable Wizard:

1. row field
2. column field
3. data field

In Figure 6-51, the row field is Gender — female (F) and male (M). The column field is the Dept — Admin, Computer, Marketing, Production, and R&D. The data field is Salary. Grand total salaries automatically display for the row and column fields in row 5 and in column G. For example, from the table in Figure 6-51, you can see in the Computer department, the female employees are paid a total salary of $77,900, while the male employees are paid a total salary of $43,500. Column G shows that all females in the company are paid $464,850 and all males are paid $271,450. The total company salary, $736,300, displays in cell G5.

The data analysis power of pivot tables is found in its ability to allow you to view the data by interchanging or pairing up the row and column fields by dragging the buttons located over cells A2 and B1 in Figure 6-51. The process of rotating the field values around the data field will be discussed later in this project.

To create the pivot table shown in Figure 6-51, perform the following steps.

TO CREATE A PIVOT TABLE ▼

STEP 1 ▶

Press CTRL+HOME, and then select cell A24 so the database displays on the screen. Select the Data menu and point to the PivotTable command.

The database displays on the screen, and then the Data menu displays. The mouse pointer points to the PivotTable command (Figure 6-52).

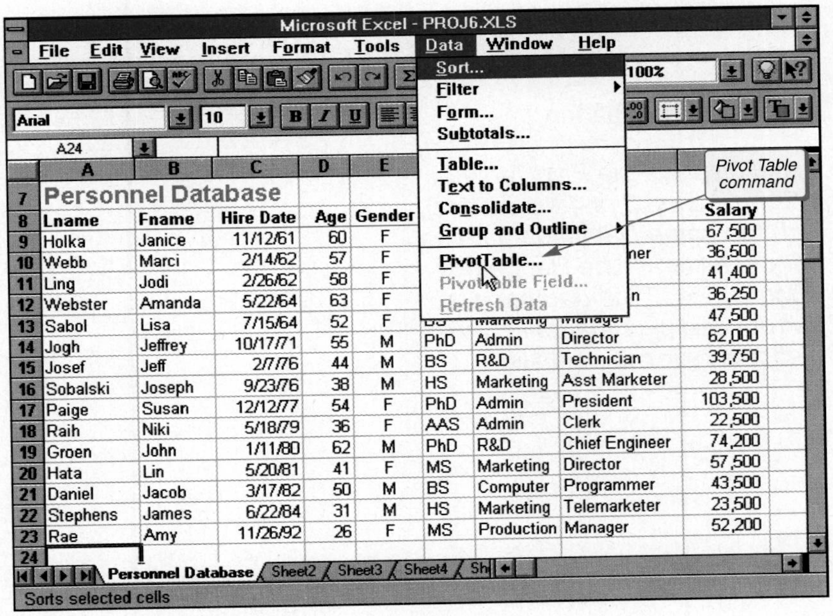

FIGURE 6-52

STEP 2 ▶

Choose the PivotTable command.

The PivotTable Wizard – Step 1 of 4 dialog box displays (Figure 6-53). The Microsoft Excel List or Database option button is selected automatically, because the default option is to use the database on the worksheet.

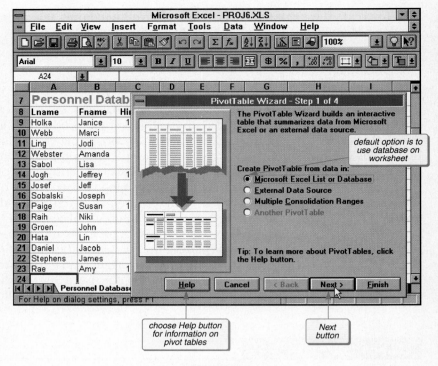

FIGURE 6-53

STEP 3 ▶

Choose the Next button.

Excel displays the PivotTable Wizard – Step 2 of 4 dialog box with the name Database automatically selected in the Range box (Figure 6-54). The database is surrounded by a marquis, which disappears in the next step.

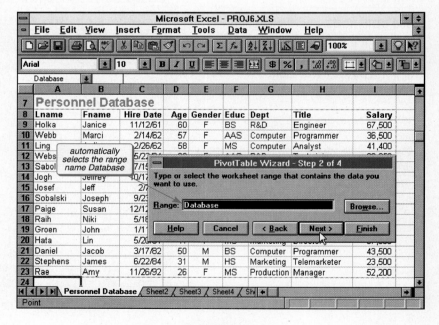

FIGURE 6-54

STEP 4 ▶

Choose the Next button.

Excel displays the PivotTable Wizard – Step 3 of 4 dialog box (Figure 6-55). At the top of the dialog box are instructions and definitions that help you create the pivot table. On the right side of the dialog box are buttons, one for each field in the N-Viro Personnel Database. You drag these buttons to locations (ROW, COLUMN, and DATA) in the middle of the dialog box.

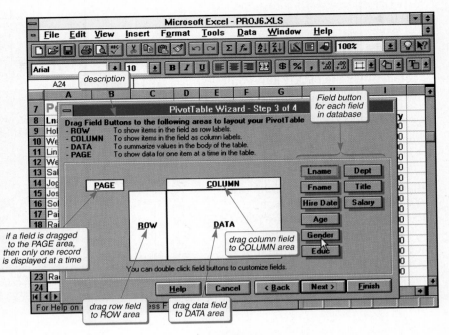

FIGURE 6-55

STEP 5 ▶

Drag the Gender button (Gender) to the ROW area. Drag the Dept button (Dept) to the COLUMN area. Drag the Salary button (Salary) to the DATA area.

The PivotTable Wizard – Step 3 of 4 dialog box displays as shown in Figure 6-56.

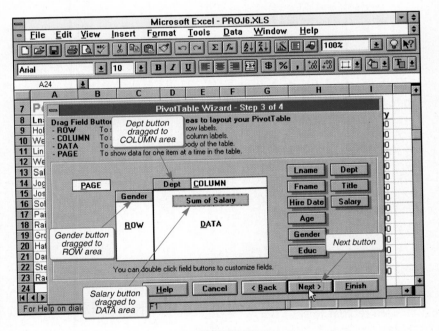

FIGURE 6-56

STEP 6 ▶

Choose the Next button. With the PivotTable Starting Cell box selected, press the DELETE key. Point to the Finish button.

The PivotTable Wizard – Step 4 of 4 dialog box displays (Figure 6-57). At the top right corner of the dialog box, Excel's starting location for the pivot table is blank and the pivot table name is Pivot-Table1. When you leave the Pivot Table Starting Cell box blank, Excel automatically creates the pivot table on a new sheet. The mouse pointer points to the Finish button.

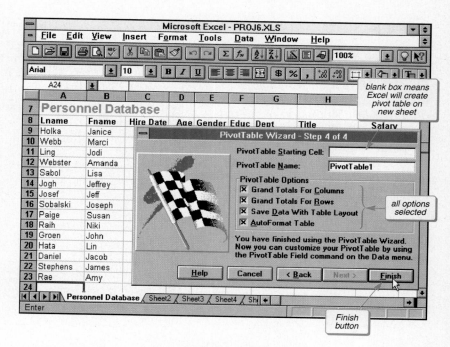

FIGURE 6-57

STEP 7 ▶

Choose the Finish button. Double-click the Sheet17 tab and rename it Pivot Table. Drag the Pivot Table tab to the immediate right of the Personnel Database tab.

Excel creates and displays the pivot table on a new sheet as shown in Figure 6-58. The pivot table summarizes the salaries by gender and department.

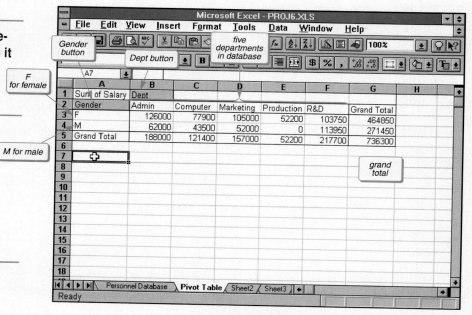

FIGURE 6-58

STEP 8 ▶

Click the Save button on the Standard toolbar to save the workbook using the filename PROJ6.XLS.

Once the pivot table is created you can treat it like any other worksheet. Thus, you can print or chart a pivot table. If you update the data in the N-Viro Personnel Database, choose the **Refresh Data command** from the Data menu or shortcut menu to update the corresponding pivot table.

Changing the View of a Pivot Table

You can rotate the row and column fields around the data field by dragging the buttons on the pivot table from one side of the salary data to another. For example, if you drag the Dept button on top of the Gender button, you change the view of the pivot table to the one in Figure 6-59a. As you will note, if you interchange the Dept and Gender buttons by dragging them to their new locations, you get the view shown in Figure 6-59b.

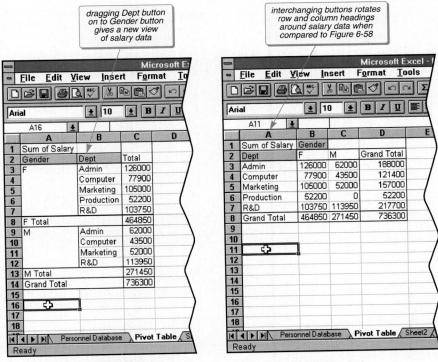

FIGURE 6-59a   **FIGURE 6-59b**

Query and Pivot Toolbar

When you first create a pivot table, Excel may display the Query and Pivot toolbar shown in Figure 6-60. The buttons allow you to quickly modify the appearance of the pivot table. You can also use the buttons to reenter the PivotTable Wizard and refresh the data after updating the database.

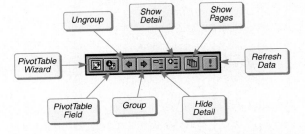

FIGURE 6-60

▶ PROJECT SUMMARY

In Project 6, you learned how to create, sort, and query a database. Creating a database involves naming a range in the worksheet Database. After naming the range, you can then add, change, and delete records in the database through a data form. Sorting a database is presented in steps using the Sort Ascending and Sort Descending buttons on the Standard toolbar or by using the Sort command on the Data menu. Once a database is sorted, you can use the Subtotals command on the Data menu to generate subtotals that display within the database range. Filtering a database involves displaying a subset of the database or copying (extracting) records that pass a test. Finally, you learned to use database functions and the pivot tables to analyze data in the database.

▶ KEY TERMS AND INDEX

QUICK REFERENCE

In Microsoft Excel, you can accomplish a task in a number of ways. The following table provides a quick reference to each task presented in this project with its available options. The commands listed in the Menu column can be executed using either the keyboard or mouse. Many of the commands in the Menu column are also available on the shortcut menu.

Task	Mouse	Menu	Keyboard Shortcuts
AutoFilter	Click AutoFilter button (custom)	From Data menu, choose Filter, then choose AutoFilter	
Advanced Filter		From Data menu, choose Filter, then choose Advanced Filter	
Data Form		From Data menu, choose Form	
Pivot Table	Click PivotTable Wizard on Query and Pivot toolbar	From Data menu, choose Pivot Table	
Refresh Data in Pivot Table	Click Refresh Data button on Query and Pivot toobar	From Data menu, choose Refresh Data	
Remove Subtotals		From Data menu, choose Subtotals, then choose Remove All button	
Sort	Click Sort Ascending button or Sort Descending button on Standard toolbar	From Data menu, choose Sort	
Subtotals		From Data menu, choose Subtotals	

STUDENT ASSIGNMENT 1
True/False

Instructions: Circle T if the statement is true or F if the statement is false.

T F 1. The series of numbers 1, 2, 3, 4, 5, 6 is in descending sequence.

T F 2. The column titles in a database are used as field names.

T F 3. When you name a database using the reference area in the formula bar, select only the row that contains the field names.

T F 4. A data form is not a dialog box.

T F 5. To add a new record to the database using a data form, select the New button.

T F 6. Excel treats dates as text.

T F 7. Excel allows you to sort on up to four fields at one time.

T F 8. A criteria range consisting of field names and empty cells below the field names will cause Excel to process all the records in the database.

T F 9. The wildcard character asterisk (*) can only be used at the end of text that is part of the comparison criteria.

T F 10. When you use the Subtotals command and apply the SUM function, Excel also displays grand totals.

T F 11. In the phrase sort "age within seniority within trade," age is the major key.

T F 12. To find records that pass a test using a data form, you first must set up a criteria range in the worksheet.

T F 13. To undo a sort operation, click the Undo button on the Standard toolbar before issuing any other commands.

T F 14. Excel is not case-sensitive when evaluating comparison criteria.

T F 15. Use the Refresh Data command on the Data menu to clear a worksheet.

T F 16. The DAVERAGE function is used to find the average of numbers in a database field that pass a test.

T F 17. A pivot table is used to summarize data and display different views of the data.

T F 18. Blank characters are significant in text-type comparison criteria.

T F 19. The criteria range in a worksheet is independent of the criteria set up in a data form.

T F 20. Each time you add a record using a data form to a range named Database, Excel expands the range of Database by one row.

STUDENT ASSIGNMENT 2
Multiple Choice

Instructions: Circle the correct response.

1. Which one of the following commands adds drop-down arrows to the field names at the top of the database?
   a. Subtotals
   b. AutoFilter
   c. Form
   d. Pivot Table

(continued)

E379

STUDENT ASSIGNMENT 2 (continued)

2. Which one of the following characters when used in comparison criteria represents any character in the same position?
   a. tilde (~)
   b. number sign (#)
   c. asterisk (*)
   d. question mark (?)

3. To copy all records that pass a test defined in a criteria range, use the _____ command on the Filter cascading menu.
   a. Filter
   b. Advanced Filter
   c. Subtotals
   d. Show All

4. When a data form is first opened, Excel displays the _____ record in the database.
   a. first
   b. last
   c. blank
   d. second

5. If you make a mistake and sort a database on the wrong field, immediately select the _____ command from the Edit menu.
   a. Clear
   b. Replace
   c. Undo Sort
   d. Repeat Sort

6. To select a field in a database to sort on when the Sort dialog box displays, enter the _____ in the Sort By box.
   a. cell reference of the field (column) in the first record
   b. cell reference of the field (column) in the last record
   c. cell reference of any cell in the field (column)
   d. all of the above will work

7. With a data form active and criteria defined, use the _____ button to display the former record in the database that passes the test.
   a. Find Next
   b. Find Prev
   c. New
   d. Close

8. A database field name referenced in a database function must be surrounded by _____.
   a. quotation marks (")
   b. apostrophes (')
   c. brackets ({ })
   d. colons (:)

9. The Pivot Table command on the Data menu is used to create a _____.
   a. chart
   b. database
   c. summary table
   d. scenario

10. To set up a criteria range that will cause the Filter command to process all records, include a(n) _____ in the criteria range.
    a. blank cell under the first field name
    b. asterisk under all field names
    c. ="" under all field names
    d. blank row

STUDENT ASSIGNMENT 3
Understanding Sorting

Instructions: In the spaces below Figure SA6-3, write the sort order of the records in the Personnel Database in Figure SA6-3. Use the term *within* to describe the sort order. For example, minor field *within* intermediate field *within* major field. Also indicate the sequence (ascending or descending) of each field.

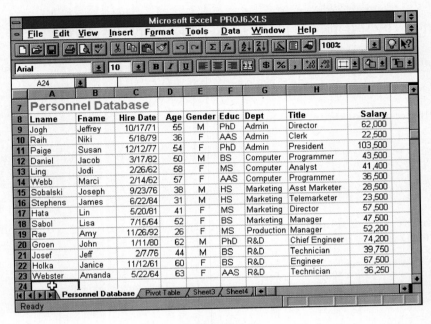

FIGURE SA6-3

Order: _____ within _____ within _____

Field(s) in ascending sequence: _____ _____   Field(s) in descending sequence: _____

STUDENT ASSIGNMENT 4
Understanding Dialog Boxes and Commands

Instructions: Identify the menu and command that carry out the operation or cause the dialog box to display and allow you to make the indicated changes. Make an entry in the Cascading Menu column only if it applies.

	MENU	COMMAND	CASCADING MENU
1. Sort a database	_____	_____	_____
2. Undo a sort operation	_____	_____	_____
3. Add subtotals to a database	_____	_____	_____
4. Add drop-down arrows to the field names in a database	_____	_____	_____
5. Name a Database range	_____	_____	_____
6. Filter a database using a criteria range	_____	_____	_____
7. Create a pivot table	_____	_____	_____
8. Display a data form	_____	_____	_____

STUDENT ASSIGNMENT 5
Understanding Comparison Criteria

Instructions: Assume that the tables that accompany each of the following problems make up the criteria range. Fill in the comparison criteria to select records from the database in Figure 6-1 on page E337 according to these problems. To help you better understand what is required for this assignment, the answer is given for the first problem.

1. Select records that represent male employees who are less than 30 years old.

Lname	Fname	Hire Date	Age	Gender	Educ	Dept	Title	Salary
			<30	M				

2. Select records that represent employees whose title is Manager or Director.

Lname	Fname	Hire Date	Age	Gender	Educ	Dept	Title	Salary

3. Select records that represent employees whose last names begin with "Jo", education is BS, and are assigned to the R&D department.

Lname	Fname	Hire Date	Age	Gender	Educ	Dept	Title	Salary

4. Select records that represent employees who are at least 30 years old and were hired before 1/1/90.

Lname	Fname	Hire Date	Age	Gender	Educ	Dept	Title	Salary

5. Select records that represent male employees or employees who are at least 50 years old.

Lname	Fname	Hire Date	Age	Gender	Educ	Dept	Title	Salary

6. Select records that represent female engineer employees who are at least 40 years old and whose last names begin with the letter H.

Lname	Fname	Hire Date	Age	Gender	Educ	Dept	Title	Salary

STUDENT ASSIGNMENT 6
Understanding Filtering a Database

Instructions: Using Figure SA6-6, answer the following questions:

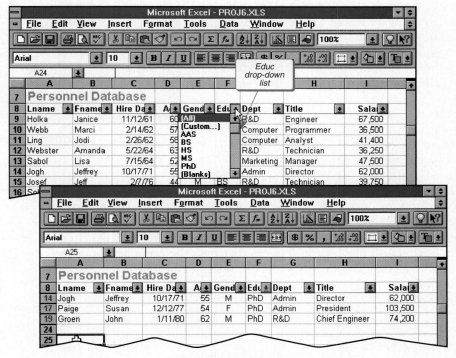

FIGURE SA6-6

1. Which menu name and command names display the drop-down arrows on the field names in row 8 of the top screen in Figure SA6-6? _____

2. How do you display the Educ drop-down list? _____

3. Which option in the Educ drop-down list would you select to generate the display in the bottom screen in Figure SA6-6? _____

C O M P U T E R   L A B O R A T O R Y   E X E R C I S E S

COMPUTER LABORATORY EXERCISE 1
Using a Data Form to Maintain a Database

Instructions: Start Excel. Open the workbook CLE6-1 from the subdirectory Excel5 on the Student Diskette that accompanies this book. The first sheet in the workbook is shown in Figure CLE6-1 on the next page. It contains a database of union employees.

(continued)

COMPUTER LABORATORY EXERCISE 1 (continued)

Perform the following tasks:

1. Choose the Form command on the Data menu. Select the Find Next button and display each record.
2. The three types of maintenance performed on databases are: (a) change the values of fields, (b) add records, and (c) delete records. Use a data form to complete the type of maintenance specified in the first column of the table below to the records identified by employee name in the Union Database shown in Figure CLE6-1.
3. Add your name as the last record in the database. If necessary, increase the width of column A so your name fits. Enter an age of 35 and a department number of 3. Use your course number for the Trade field. Use your division number for the Years of Seniority field.
4. Save the workbook using the filename CLE6-1A.
5. Print the database with gridlines off. Click the Save File button on the Standard toolbar to save the workbook.
6. With a data form active, choose the Criteria button. Enter the following criteria: Age <32, Dept = 3. Select the Form button and display the records that pass the comparison criteria by using the Find Next and Find Prev buttons. How many records pass the comparison criteria? When you are finished, choose the Close button.
7. Close the workbook.

5	Union Database					
6	Employee	Gender	Age	Dept	Trade	Years of Seniority
7	Jordon, David	M	48	1	Operator	7
8	Peat, Jeffrey	M	27	1	Machinist	5
9	Hill, Judith	F	36	2	Operator	12
10	Abram, Paul	M	30	2	Machinist	8
11	Jenings, Carl	M	35	1	Oiler	15
12	Lyndowe, Jodi	F	32	3	Oiler	13
13	Jean, Marcell	F	23	1	Operator	4
14	Lerner, Nicole	F	20	3	Machinist	1
15	Pylerski, Alex	M	45	2	Operator	23
16	Delford, James	M	25	3	Oiler	3

Union / Sheet2 / Sheet3 / Sheet4 / Sheet5 / Sheet6
Ready

FIGURE CLE6-1

TYPE OF MAINTENANCE	EMPLOYEE	GENDER	AGE	DEPT	TRADE	YEARS OF SENIORITY
Change	Peat, Jeffrey		32	3		
Change	Delford, James				Machinist	7
Delete	Lerner, Nicole					
Delete	Abram, Paul					
Add	Daniels, Jacob	M	48	1	Oiler	0
Add	Beet, Sharon	F	22	2	Operator	0

COMPUTER LABORATORY EXERCISE 2
Sorting a Database and Determining Subtotals

Part 1 Instructions: Start Excel. Open the workbook CLE6-2 (Figure CLE6-2a) from the subdirectory Excel5 on the Student Diskette that accompanies this book. Sort the database according to the six sort problems below. Print the database for each sort problem without gridlines. Save the workbook with each sort solution using the file name CLE6-2x, where x is the sort problem number. For each sort problem, open the original workbook CLE6-2.

1. Sort the database into descending sequence by division.

2. Sort the database by district within division. Both sort keys are to be in ascending sequence.

3. Sort the database by department within district within division. All three sort keys are to be in ascending sequence.

4. Sort the database into descending sequence by sales.

5. Sort the database by department within district within division. All three sort keys are to be in descending sequence.

6. Sort the database by salesperson within department within district within division. All four sort keys are to be in ascending sequence.

FIGURE CLE6-2a

Part 1 Instructions: One at a time, close all the workbooks created in Part 1 by using the Close command on the File menu. Next, open the workbook CLE6-2 (Figure CLE6-2a) from the subdirectory Excel5 on the Student Diskette. Sort the database by department within district within division. Select ascending sequence for all three sort keys. Use the Subtotals command to generate subtotals by division. Type 90% in the Zoom Control box on the Standard toolbar so the worksheet appears as shown in Figure CLE6-2b. Print the database with the subtotals. Use the Subtotals command to remove the subtotals. Choose 100% from the Zoom box drop-down list box on the Standard toolbar. Close the workbook.

FIGURE CLE6-2b

COMPUTER LABORATORY EXERCISE 3
Filtering a Database

Instructions: Start Excel and perform the following tasks:

1. Open the workbook CLE6-3 from the subdirectory Excel 5 on the Student Diskette that accompanies this book. The workbook displays with the drop-down arrows as shown in Figure CLE6-3. Step through each filter exercise in the table below and print the results for each with gridlines off.

To complete a filter exercise, select the appropriate drop-down arrow and option. Use the (Custom...) option in filter exercises 2, 3, 4, 5, 7, and 9. After you print the filtered list solution for each, choose the Show All command on the Filter cascading menu before you begin another filter exercise. When you are finished with the last filter exercise, remove the drop-down arrows by choosing the AutoFilter command on the Filter cascading menu. You should end up with the following number of records: 1 = 3; 2 = 3; 3 = 2; 4 = 1; 5 = 4; 6 = 2; 7 = 7; 8 = 2; 9 = 1; and 10 = 10.

FILTER	EMPLOYEE	GENDER	AGE	DEPT5	TRADE	SENIORITY
1		M		1		
2	Begins with letter J					
3			>32 and <40			
4		F			Operator	>10
5						>5 and <15
6				3	Oiler	
7				1 or 3		
8		M		2		
9		M	<30	3		

	Employee	Gender	Age	Dep	Trade	Years of Senior
7	Jordon, David	M	48	1	Operator	7
8	Peat, Jeffrey	M	27	1	Machinist	5
9	Hill, Judith	F	36	2	Operator	12
10	Abram, Paul	M	30	2	Machinist	8
11	Jenings, Carl	M	35	1	Oiler	15
12	Lyndowe, Jodi	F	32	3	Oiler	13
13	Jean, Marcell	F	23	1	Operator	4
14	Lerner, Nicole	F	20	3	Machinist	1
15	Pylerski, Alex	M	45	2	Operator	23
16	Delford, James	M	25	3	Oiler	3

FIGURE CLE6-3

COMPUTER LABORATORY ASSIGNMENTS

COMPUTER LABORATORY ASSIGNMENT 1
Building and Sorting a Database of Prospective Programmers

Purpose: To become familiar with building a database using a data form and sorting a database.

Problem: You are an applications software specialist for Computer People, Inc. You have been assigned the task of building the Prospective Programmer Database shown in Figure CLA6-1. Create the database beginning in row 6 of the worksheet. Use the information in the table (opposite).

Prospective Programmer Database

	Name	Gender	Age	Years	QBasic	COBOL	C	VBA	Excel	Access
8	Bulva, Jim	M	32	5	Y	N	N	Y	Y	N
9	Chab, Sarah	F	23	2	N	Y	N	N	Y	Y
10	Rose, Claudia	F	26	4	Y	Y	N	Y	N	Y
11	Zingo, Arnie	M	24	2	Y	N	N	Y	N	Y
12	Milan, Tony	M	38	15	Y	Y	Y	N	Y	N
13	Biagi, John	M	29	7	N	Y	N	Y	N	Y
14	Holka, John	M	20	1	N	Y	Y	N	Y	Y
15	Lock, Nikole	F	42	12	Y	N	Y	N	N	Y
16	Daniel, Jacob	M	34	19	Y	Y	N	N	N	Y
17	Kay, Julie	F	49	16	N	N	N	N	Y	Y

FIGURE CLA6-1

▶ **TABLE CLA6-1**

COLUMN HEADINGS (FIELD NAMES)	COLUMN	TYPE OF DATA	COLUMN WIDTH
Name	A	Text	13
Gender	B	Text	8
Age	C	Numeric	5
Years	D	Numeric	7
Qbasic	E	Text	8
COBOL	F	Text	8
C	G	Text	5
VBA	H	Text	6
Excel	I	Text	7
Access	J	Text	9

Instructions: Perform the following tasks:

1. Bold the entire worksheet. Change the column widths as described in the preceding table. Enter the database title and column titles (field names) as shown in Figure CLA6-1. Use the reference area in the formula bar to define the name Database as the range A7:J8. Use the Form command on the Data menu to display a data form to enter the ten records.

2. Enter your name, course, computer laboratory exercise (CLA6-1), date, and instructor name in the range A30:A34. Print the worksheet without gridlines. Save the workbook using the filename CLA6-1.

3. Sort the records in the database into ascending sequence by name. Print the sorted version.

4. Sort the records in the database by age within gender. Select ascending sequence for the gender code and ascending sequence for the age. Print the sorted version.

COMPUTER LABORATORY ASSIGNMENT 2
Filtering the Prospective Programmer Database

Purpose: To become familiar with finding records that pass a test using a data form, and to filter a database using the AutoFilter and Advanced Filter commands.

Problem: Complete the filtering operations on the Prospective Programmer Database described in Parts 1, 2, and 3 of this assignment. If you were not required to build the database in Computer Laboratory Assignment 1, ask your instructor for a copy of CLA6-1.

Part 1 Instructions: Open the workbook CLA6-1 (Figure CLA6-1). Save the workbook using the filename CLA6-2. Use the Criteria button on a data form to enter the comparison criteria for the following tasks. Use the Find Next button on the data form to find the records that pass the comparison criteria. Write down and submit the names of the prospective programmers who pass the comparison criteria for tasks a through d.

a. Find all records that represent prospective programmers who are male and can program in COBOL.

b. Find all records that represent prospective programmers who can program in QBasic and VBA and use Excel.

c. Find all records that represent prospective female programmers who are at least 29 years old and can use Access.

d. Find all records that represent prospective programmers who know Excel and Access.

(continued)

COMPUTER LABORATORY ASSIGNMENT 2 (continued)

e. All prospective programmers who did not know Access were sent to a seminar on the software package. Use the Find Next button to locate the records of these programmers and change the Access field entry on the data form from the letter N to the letter Y. Make sure you press the ENTER key or press the DOWN ARROW key after changing the letter. Save the database using the filename CLA6-2A. Print the worksheet without gridlines. Close CLA6-2A.

Part 2 Instructions: Open the workbook CLA6-2. Use the AutoFilter command on the Filter cascading menu and redo Part 1 a, b, c, and d. Use the Show All command on the Filter cascading menu before starting problems b, c, and d. Print the worksheet without gridlines for each problem. Change the laboratory assignment number in the range A30:A34 to CLA6-22x, where x is the problem letter. Choose the Auto Filter command on the Filter cascading menu to remove the drop-down arrows. Close CLA6-2 without saving it.

Part 3 Instructions: Open the workbook CLA6-2. Add a criteria range by copying the database title and field names (range A7:J8) to range A1:J2. Change cell A1 to Criteria Area. Use the reference area in the formula bar to name the criteria range (A1:J2) Criteria. Add an extract range by copying the database title and field names (range A7:J8) to range A21:J22. Change cell A21 to Extract Area. Use the reference area in the formula bar to name the extract range (A1:J2) Extract. Your worksheet should look similar to the screen in Figure CLA6-2a.

FIGURE CLA6-2a

Use the Advanced Filter command on the Filter cascading menu to extract records that pass the tests in tasks a through e below. Change the laboratory assignment number in the range A30:A34 to CLA6-23x, where x is the problem letter. Print the entire worksheet without gridlines after each extraction.

a. Extract the records that represent prospective programmers who are female (Figure CLA6-2b).

b. Extract the records that represent prospective programmers who can program in QBasic and cannot program in VBA.

c. Extract the records that represent prospective male programmers who are at least 30 years old and can use Excel.

d. Extract the records that represent prospective programmers who know VBA and Access.

e. Extract the records that represent prospective programmers who do not know how to use any programming language. Save the workbook using the filename CLA6-2B.

FIGURE CLA6-2b

COMPUTER LABORATORY ASSIGNMENT 3
Finding Subtotals and Creating a Pivot Table for an Order Entry Database

Purpose: To become familiar with building a database using a data form, displaying subtotals, zooming, and creating a pivot table.

Problem: You are employed as a spreadsheet specialist in the order entry department of JM Sports, Inc. You have been given the following assignments:

1. Develop an order entry database that keeps track of the outstanding orders (Figure CLA6-3a on the next page).
2. Display subtotals of the number ordered and amount (Figure CLA6-3b on the next page).
3. Create a pivot table for summarizing the amount (Figure CLA6-3c on the next page).

Part 1 Instructions: Perform the following tasks to create the database shown in the range A6:G17 in Figure CLA6-3a.

1. Change the font of the worksheet to bold. Change the column widths to the following: A = 9, B = 11, C = 8, D = 16, E = 12, F = 11, and G = 12. Enter and format the database title and field names in the range A5:G6. Center entries in column B. Align the field names as shown in row 6 in Figure CLA6-3a.
2. Enter the first record without using a data form. Enter the formula =E7 * F7 in cell G7. Define the name Database as the range A6:G7. Use a data form to enter the remaining order records.
3. Enter your name, course, computer laboratory assignment (CLA6-3a), date, and instructor name in the range A20:A24.
4. Save the workbook using the filename CLA6-3. Use the Page Setup command on the File menu or shortcut menu to change the left and right margins to 0.5 inch and turn off gridlines. Print the worksheet. Click the Save button on the Standard toolbar to save the workbook.

(continued)

COMPUTER LABORATORY ASSIGNMENT 3 (continued)

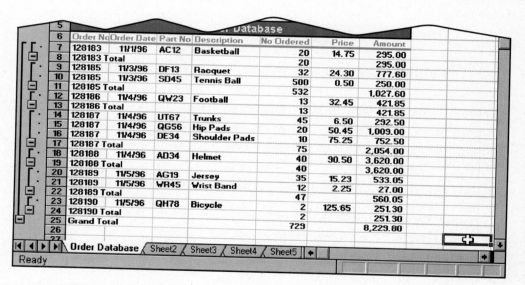

FIGURE CLA6-3a

	A	B	C	D	E	F	G
4							
5				Order Database			
6	Order No	Order Date	Part No	Description	No Ordered	Price	Amount
7	128183	11/1/96	AC12	Basketball	20	14.75	295.00
8	128185	11/3/96	DF13	Racquet	32	24.30	777.60
9	128185	11/3/96	SD45	Tennis Ball	500	0.50	250.00
10	128186	11/4/96	QW23	Football	13	32.45	421.85
11	128187	11/4/96	UT67	Trunks	45	6.50	292.50
12	128187	11/4/96	QG56	Hip Pads	20	50.45	1,009.00
13	128187	11/4/96	DE34	Shoulder Pads	10	75.25	752.50
14	128188	11/4/96	AD34	Helmet	40	90.50	3,620.00
15	128189	11/5/96	AG19	Jersey	35	15.23	533.05
16	128189	11/5/96	WR45	Wrist Band	12	2.25	27.00
17	128190	11/5/96	QH78	Bicycle	2	125.65	251.30
18							

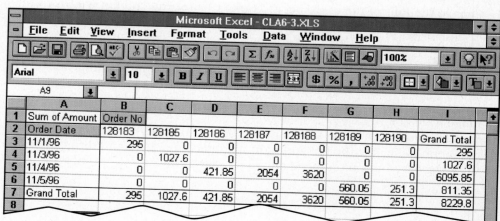

FIGURE CLA6-3b

	A	B	C	D	E	F	G	H	I
1	Sum of Amount	Order No							
2	Order Date	128183	128185	128186	128187	128188	128189	128190	Grand Total
3	11/1/96	295	0	0	0	0	0	0	295
4	11/3/96	0	1027.6	0	0	0	0	0	1027.6
5	11/4/96	0	0	421.85	2054	3620	0	0	6095.85
6	11/5/96	0	0	0	0	0	560.05	251.3	811.35
7	Grand Total	295	1027.6	421.85	2054	3620	560.05	251.3	8229.8
8									

FIGURE CLA6-3c

Part 2 Instructions: Perform the following tasks to develop the subtotals shown in Figure CLA6-3b.

1. Select a cell within the range of Database. Choose the Subtotals command on the Data menu and determine totals for the No Ordered and Amount fields by the Order No field.
2. Change the magnification of the worksheet to 75% (Figure CLA6-3b).
3. Print the worksheet.
4. Hide detail records so only total rows display. Print the worksheet.
5. Change the magnification back to 100%. Use the Subtotals command on the Data menu to remove subtotals.

Part 3 Instructions: Using the Order Database, create the pivot table shown in Figure CLA6-3c on a separate worksheet. The table summarizes dollar amount information by order number and order date.
Use the Pivot Table command to create the pivot table. Print the pivot table without gridlines. Drag the Order No and Order Date buttons around on the pivot table to obtain different views of the information. Save the workbook using the filename CLA6-3A.

COMPUTER LABORATORY ASSIGNMENT 4
Creating a Video Cassette Database

Purpose: To become familiar with planning, creating, and manipulating a database.

Problem: Obtain a list of at least fifteen movies from a nearby video store or library with the following information: movie title, year made, movie type (comedy, science fiction, suspense, drama, religious), director, producer, number of academy awards, and cost of the video. Create a video cassette database. Sort the database in alphabetical order by movie title. Create subtotals of the cost of videos by type. Using different combinations of comparison criteria, filter the database. For example, display movies that were produced prior to 1990 and have a movie type equal to comedy. Also, create a pivot table that summarizes the cost by type and director.

Enter your name, course, computer laboratory assignment number (CLA6-4), date, and instructor name well below the database in column A in separate but adjacent cells. Save the workbook using the filename CLA6-4.

Instructions: Submit the following:
1. A description of the problem. Include the purpose of the database, a statement outlining the required data, and calculations.
2. A handwritten design of the database.
3. A printed copy of the worksheet without gridlines.
4. A short description explaining how to use the worksheet.

MICROSOFT EXCEL 5 FOR WINDOWS

▼

OBJECT LINKING AND EMBEDDING (OLE)

You will have mastered the material in this project when you can:

- Start two applications
- Explain source document, destination document, and object
- Select a range to copy in the source document
- Copy the selected range in the source document to the Clipboard
- Switch from the source document application to the destination document application
- Paste the object on the Clipboard in the destination document

- Embed the object on the Clipboard in the destination document
- Link the object on the Clipboard to the destination document
- Tile two application windows on the screen to view both at the same time
- Drag and drop an object between tiled applications
- Embed an existing file or create and embed an object without leaving an application

---

▶ INTRODUCTION

One of the powerful features of Windows applications is that you can incorporate parts of documents or entire documents called **objects** from one application in another application. For example, you can copy a worksheet in Excel to a document in Word. In this case, the worksheet in Excel is called the **source document** (copied from) and the document in Word is called the **destination document** (pasted to or linked to). Copying objects between applications can be accomplished in three ways:

1. Copy and paste
2. Copy and embed
3. Copy and link

All of the Microsoft Office applications (Word 6, Excel 5, Access 2, and PowerPoint 4) allow you to use these three methods to copy objects between the applications.

E392

The method you select depends on what you plan to do after the task is complete. The first method, *copy and paste*, involves using the Copy and Paste buttons. The latter two methods, *copy and embed* and *copy and link*, are referred to as **Object Linking and Embedding**, or **OLE**. Each of these three methods is presented in this project. The following paragraphs describe the differences among the three methods.

Method 1 – Copy and Paste   When an object is copied from the source document and pasted in the destination document (standard **copy and paste**), it becomes part of the destination document. The object may be edited, but the editing features are, for the most part, limited to those available in the destination document. Thus, if you copy and paste an Excel worksheet into a Word document, the worksheet displays as a Word table and you use Word to edit the table. If you change values that are totaled, the totals will not be adjusted. This method is further weakened because you cannot directly copy and paste an embedded chart into a Word document. In addition, if you change the table contents in the Word document, the changes are *not* reflected in the worksheet when you display it later in Excel, because no link back to the worksheet is established. Of the three methods described, the *copy and paste* is by far the weakest. On the positive side, the *copy and paste* method is quick and easy.

Method 2 – Copy and Embed   When the same object is copied and embedded in a destination document, it becomes part of the document itself as with the *copy and paste* method. However, more importantly, the editing features made available are those of the source document's application. Thus, if you **copy and embed** an Excel worksheet in a Word document, it displays much like a worksheet in the Word document. When you double-click the worksheet to edit it, the menu bar and toolbars at the top of the Word screen change to the Excel menu bar and toolbars. Hence, when you copy and embed, you edit the worksheet in Word, but with Excel editing capabilities. Here again, if you change the worksheet in the Word document using Excel editing capabilities, the changes are **not** reflected in the worksheet when you display it later in Excel. You can also embed a worksheet with an embedded chart. In addition, the chart in the Word document will change when you change the data on which it depends.

You would choose *copy and embed* over *copy and paste* when you want to use the source application's editing capabilities or, as in this project, you want to copy an embedded chart. You would choose *copy and embed* over *copy and link* (method 3) when the object is fairly stable, or you don't need to have the most current version of the object in your document, or the object is small. Another reason to choose the *copy and embed* method would be when you plan to use the destination document and you do not have a copy of the source document.

Remember, when you copy and embed, the object is saved along with the destination document, thus taking up additional disk storage.

Method 3 – Copy and Link   When the same object is copied and linked to a destination document, the system returns to the source application when you edit the object because only a **link**, or reference, is established. Thus, if you **copy and link** an Excel worksheet to a Word document, it displays similarly to a worksheet in the Word document, but it does not take up space in the document (i.e., the worksheet is not saved with the Word document).

When you click the worksheet to edit, the system switches you to the source application (Excel). Hence, when you copy and link, you edit the object in the source application. For example, if you link an Excel worksheet to a Word document and you double-click the object while Word is active, Windows will start Excel and open the linked worksheet. Any changes you make to the worksheet will show up in the Word document.

Use *copy and link* over the first two methods when an object is likely to change and you want to make sure the object always reflects the changes in the source document or if the object is large, such as a video clip or sound clip. Thus, if you link a worksheet to a memorandum, and update the worksheet weekly, any time you open the memorandum the latest update of the worksheet will display.

Another useful feature is tiling. With the use of tiling, it is possible to start two or more applications, open documents in each of the applications, and place all of the open application's windows on the screen. When some Windows applications are tiled, such as the latest versions of Word, Excel, Access, and PowerPoint, you can copy and embed by using drag and drop between tiled applications.

▶ PROJECT SEVEN — KING'S COMPUTER OUTLET WEEKLY SALES MEMORANDUM

Each week, the vice president of sales for King's Computer Outlet sends out a memorandum to the regional sales managers showing the previous week's daily sales for all regions. She currently uses only Word to produce the memorandum that includes a table of the daily sales. The wording in the memorandum remains constant week to week. The table of daily sales changes each week.

She recently heard of the OLE capabilities of Microsoft's applications packages and would like to use them so she can create the basic memorandum (upper left screen in Figure 7-1) using Word and maintain the daily sales in a worksheet (upper right screen in Figure 7-1) using Excel. She would like to insert the worksheet from Excel into the Word document (bottom screen Figure 7-1). She plans to experiment with OLE and has decided to test each of the three methods described in the previous section: *copy and paste*; *copy and embed*; and *copy and link*.

▶ COPYING AND PASTING AN OBJECT BETWEEN APPLICATIONS

The first method being used to incorporate the worksheet in the document is a familiar one. It involves a copy and paste. You start Word and open the memorandum shown in the upper left screen in Figure 7-1. Next, you switch to Program Manager, start Excel, and open the worksheet shown in the upper right screen of Figure 7-1. While in Excel, you copy to the Clipboard the portion of the worksheet (called the object) you want to paste in the Word document. In this first example, the range A3:G10 is copied. Finally, you switch to Word and paste the object on the Clipboard into the memorandum. The chart below the data in the upper right screen in Figure 7-1 (range A12:G25) is not included because the *copy and paste* method cannot be used to copy an embedded chart.

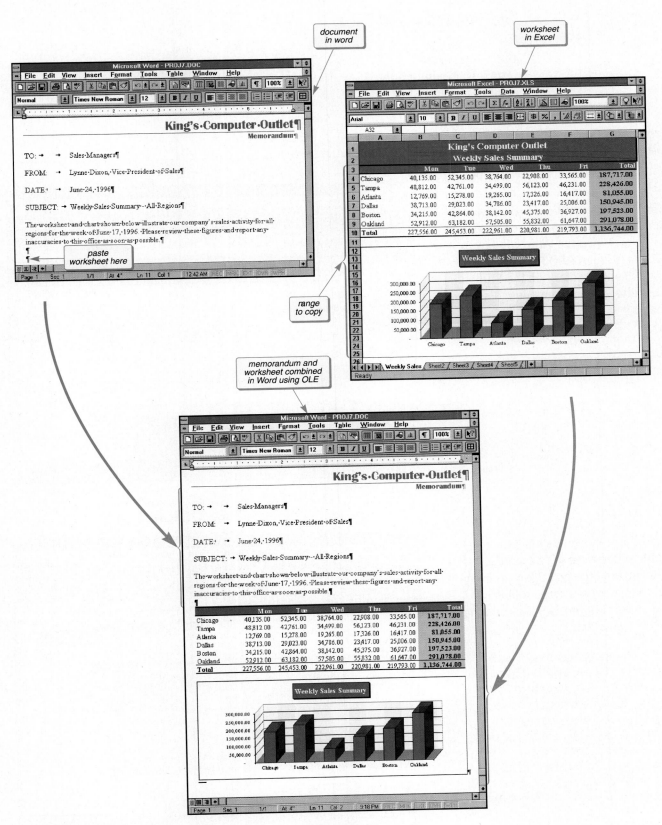

FIGURE 7-1

Starting Word and Excel

To start Word, the Windows Program Manager must display on the screen and the Microsoft Office group window must be open. Once Word is started and the appropriate document is opened, switch to Windows Program Manager, start Excel, and open the appropriate worksheet as shown in the following steps.

TO START WORD AND EXCEL ▼

STEP 1 ▶

Double-click the Word program-item icon in the Microsoft Office group window. When the Word window displays, open PROJ7.DOC from the Excel5 subdirectory on the Student Diskette that accompanies this book.

The memorandum shown in Figure 7-2 displays.

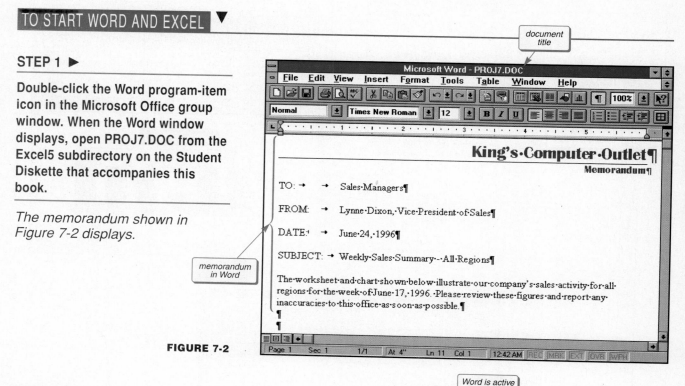

FIGURE 7-2

STEP 2 ▶

Hold down the ALT key. While holding down the ALT key, press the TAB key until the box titled Program Manager appears in the middle of the screen (Figure 7-3). Release the TAB key and then the ALT key.

Windows switches to Program Manager. When you press ALT+TAB the first time with Word active, Windows displays the box representing the most recent active application. Because these steps started with Program Manager and then started Word, the first time you press ALT+TAB, the Program Manager box displays.

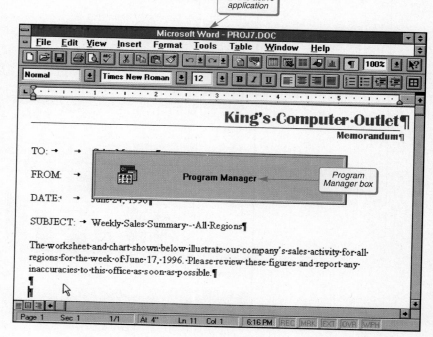

FIGURE 7-3

STEP 3 ▶

Double-click the Excel program-item icon in the Microsoft Office group window. When the Excel window displays, open PROJ7.XLS from the Excel5 subdirectory on the Student Diskette.

The worksheet shown in Figure 7-4 displays. There are two applications open at this time, Word and Excel. Excel is the active application.

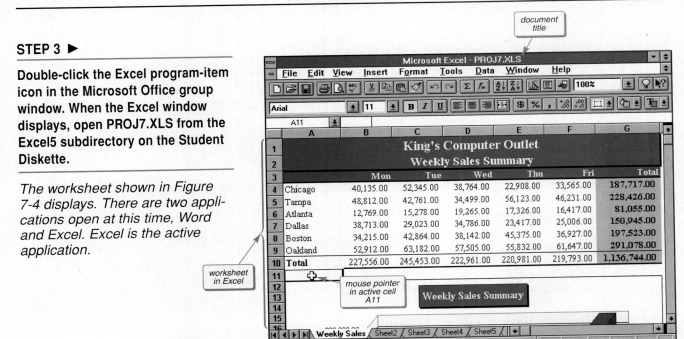

FIGURE 7-4

With the memorandum opened in Word and the worksheet opened in Excel, the next step is to complete the *copy and paste* operation.

Copying the Object in the Source Document and Pasting It in the Destination Document

The steps on the next two pages show how to copy the range A3:G10 to the Clipboard, switch to Word, and paste the object on the Clipboard below the last paragraph in the memorandum.

TO COPY AN OBJECT IN EXCEL AND PASTE IT IN WORD ▼

STEP 1 ▶

With Excel active and
PROJ7.XLS on the screen,
select the range A3:G10 (Figure 7-5).

STEP 2 ▶

Click the Copy button on the
Standard toolbar.

*A marquis surrounds the range
A3:G10 indicating it has been
copied to the Clipboard.*

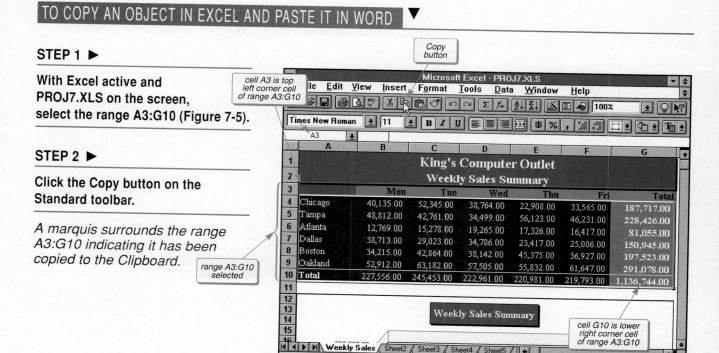

FIGURE 7-5

STEP 3 ▶

Hold down the ALT key and press the
TAB key until the box shown in the
middle of the screen contains the
title Microsoft Word – PROJ7.DOC.
Release the TAB key and then the ALT
key. Press CTRL+END.

*The document PROJ7.DOC dis-
plays with the insertion point at the
bottom of the document as shown
in Figure 7-6.*

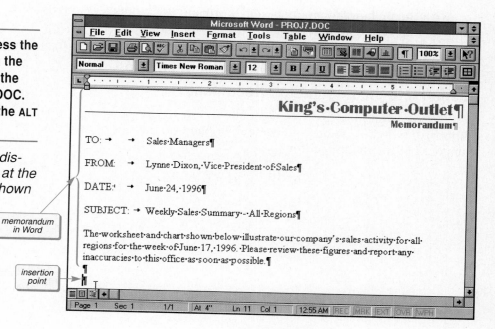

FIGURE 7-6

STEP 4 ▶

Click the Paste button.

The object on the Clipboard (range A3:G10 from PROJ7.XLS) is copied into the Word document as a table beginning at the insertion point (Figure 7-7).

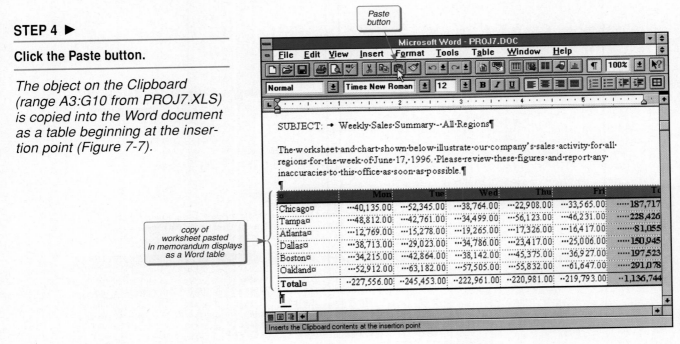

copy of worksheet pasted in memorandum displays as a Word table

FIGURE 7-7

The copy and paste operation is complete. The memorandum contains an object that was originally created in Excel. Although this method of inserting a portion of an Excel worksheet into a Word document is relatively simple, it lacks the required editing capabilities. For example, if any of the numbers change, you would probably make the adjustments to the worksheet in Excel and complete the copy and paste again. You could change the numbers in the table in Word, but then there would be inconsistency between the table in the Word document and the Excel worksheet.

Saving, Printing, and Closing the Memorandum

The following steps save, print, and close the memorandum.

TO SAVE, PRINT, AND CLOSE THE MEMORANDUM

Step 1: With Word active, use the Save As command on the File menu to save the memorandum to drive A using the filename PROJ7A.DOC.

Step 2: Click the Print button on the Standard toolbar. The memorandum prints as shown in Figure 7-8 on the next page.

Step 3: Choose the Close command from the File menu.

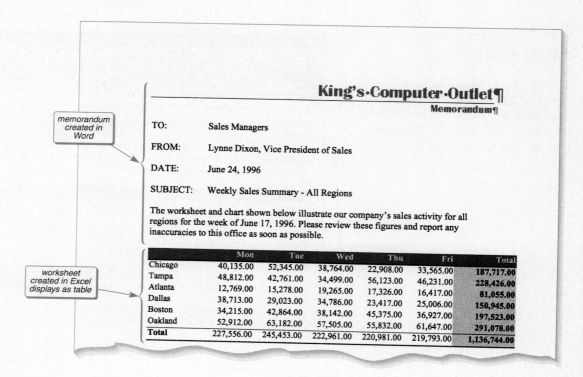

memorandum created in Word

worksheet created in Excel displays as table

King's·Computer·Outlet¶

Memorandum¶

TO: Sales Managers

FROM: Lynne Dixon, Vice President of Sales

DATE: June 24, 1996

SUBJECT: Weekly Sales Summary - All Regions

The worksheet and chart shown below illustrate our company's sales activity for all regions for the week of June 17, 1996. Please review these figures and report any inaccuracies to this office as soon as possible.

	Mon	Tue	Wed	Thu	Fri	Total
Chicago	40,135.00	52,345.00	38,764.00	22,908.00	33,565.00	187,717.00
Tampa	48,812.00	42,761.00	34,499.00	56,123.00	46,231.00	228,426.00
Atlanta	12,769.00	15,278.00	19,265.00	17,326.00	16,417.00	81,055.00
Dallas	38,713.00	29,023.00	34,786.00	23,417.00	25,006.00	150,945.00
Boston	34,215.00	42,864.00	38,142.00	45,375.00	36,927.00	197,523.00
Oakland	52,912.00	63,182.00	57,505.00	55,832.00	61,647.00	291,078.00
Total	227,556.00	245,453.00	222,961.00	220,981.00	219,793.00	1,136,744.00

FIGURE 7-8

Copying and pasting an object between applications using the Copy and Paste buttons is a quick and easy way for the vice president of sales for King's Computer Outlet to add the worksheet information to the memorandum. However, with this method, it was not possible to copy the chart in the worksheet to the memorandum. Also, if the table in the memorandum is modified, the table will no longer agree with the worksheet unless it too is modified.

▶ COPYING AND EMBEDDING AN OBJECT BETWEEN APPLICATIONS

The *copy and embed* method involves using the Copy button and the Paste Special command on the Edit menu. As with the *copy and paste* method, you start both applications and open the document and worksheet. With Excel active, you copy the portion of the worksheet (range A3:G25) you want to the Clipboard. Once the object is on the Clipboard, you return to Word and use the **Paste Special command** to paste the object on the Clipboard into the memorandum.

Using the Paste Special Command to Embed an Object

Follow these steps to open the Word document, copy the worksheet to the Clipboard, and embed the worksheet in the Word document.

TO COPY AND EMBED AN OBJECT BETWEEN APPLICATIONS ▼

STEP 1 ▶

With Word active, open PROJ7.DOC from the Excel5 subdirectory on the Student Diskette.

The memorandum shown in Figure 7-9 displays.

STEP 2 ▶

Hold down the ALT key. While holding down the ALT key, press the TAB key until the box titled **Microsoft Excel – PROJ7.XLS** appears in the middle of the screen (Figure 7-3 on page E396). Release the TAB key and then the ALT key. If Excel is not active, start Excel from Program Manager and open PROJ7.XLS from the Excel5 subdirectory on the Student Diskette.

Excel is active and the worksheet PROJ7.XLS displays.

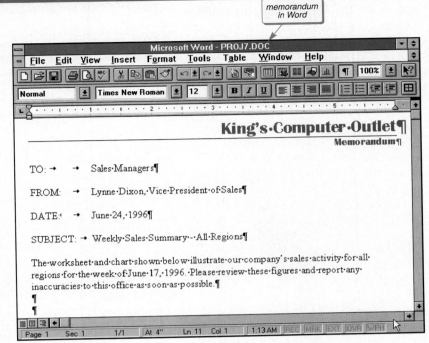

FIGURE 7-9

STEP 3 ▶

Select the range A3:G25 and click the Copy button on the Standard toolbar.

A marquis surrounds the range A3:G25 (Figure 7-10) indicating that a copy of it is on the Clipboard.

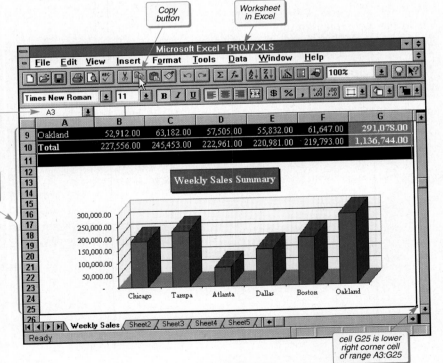

FIGURE 7-10

STEP 4 ▶

Hold down the ALT key and press the TAB key until the box shown in the middle of the screen contains the title Microsoft Word – PROJ7.DOC. Release the TAB key and then the ALT key. Press CTRL+END. Select the Edit menu.

Word is active and the Edit menu displays as shown in Figure 7-11.

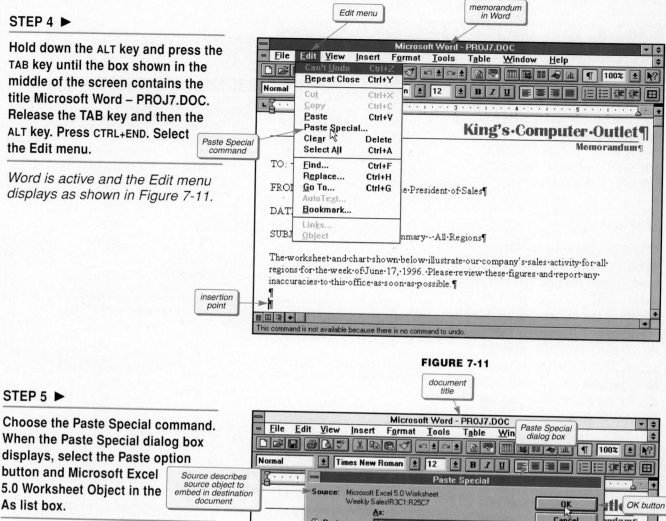

FIGURE 7-11

STEP 5 ▶

Choose the Paste Special command. When the Paste Special dialog box displays, select the Paste option button and Microsoft Excel 5.0 Worksheet Object in the As list box.

*The **Paste Special dialog box** displays as shown in Figure 7-12.*

FIGURE 7-12

STEP 6 ▶

Choose the OK button.

The object (range A3:G25 of the worksheet) on the Clipboard is pasted into the Word document (Figure 7-13).

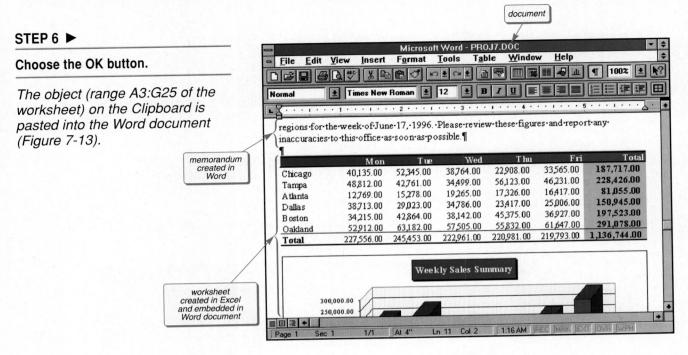

FIGURE 7-13

If you paste the object and the results are not what you expect, click the Undo button on the Standard toolbar or choose the Undo command from the Edit menu. If you have entered other commands between the time you embed the document and your decision to remove the object, click the embedded object to select it and press the DELETE key.

Saving and Printing the Memorandum

The following steps save and print the memorandum with the embedded worksheet.

TO SAVE AND PRINT THE MEMORANDUM

Step 1: With Word active, use the Save As command on the File menu to save the memorandum with the embedded worksheet to drive A using the filename PROJ7B.DOC.

Step 2: Click the Print button on the Standard toolbar.

The memorandum prints as shown in Figure 7-14 on the next page.

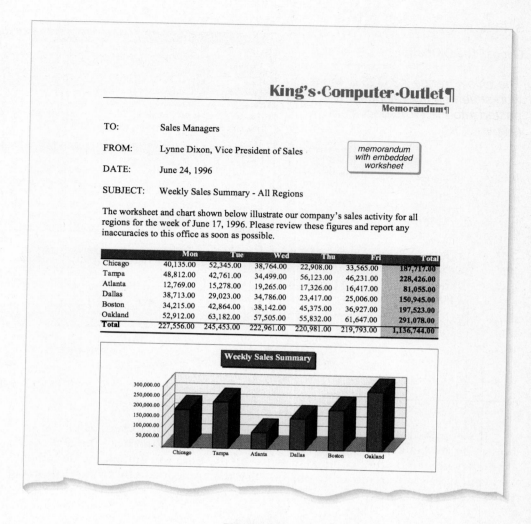

FIGURE 7-14

As you can see from Figure 7-14, the worksheet is added to the bottom of the memorandum as required (see Figure 7-1 on page E395). The next section shows how to edit the worksheet portion of the document. Because the worksheet is embedded in the Word document, the size of the file PROJ7B.DOC on disk is larger than the original memorandum (PROJ7.DOC).

Editing the Embedded Object

To change information in the worksheet portion of the memorandum, you do not have to make the changes in Excel, delete the worksheet from the memorandum, and then copy and embed again. All you have to do is double-click the worksheet while in Word.

When you double-click the embedded worksheet, the Word toolbars immediately change to Excel toolbars. The status bar changes. Except for the File and Window menus, the menu bar also changes. Thus, you use the editing capabilities of Excel while Word is the active application. This is called **in-place activation**. The following steps show how to change the contents of cell B8 from $34,215.00 to $14,217.00 and the contents of cell C9 from $63,182.00 to $3,182.00 while Word is the active application. As the changes are made, the chart is redrawn to represent the new sales amounts.

TO EDIT THE EMBEDDED WORKSHEET ▼

STEP 1 ▶

With Word active, point to the embedded worksheet and double-click.

Excel surrounds the worksheet in the memorandum with a heavy blue border as shown in Figure 7-15. The Excel menu bar, toolbars, formula bar, and status bar display on the screen, even though the title bar shows that Word is active. An Excel window has been opened within Word and the Excel source document displays in the Excel window. Notice the column and row headings and the vertical scroll bar within the Excel window. The mouse pointer changes from an I-beam to a block plus sign.

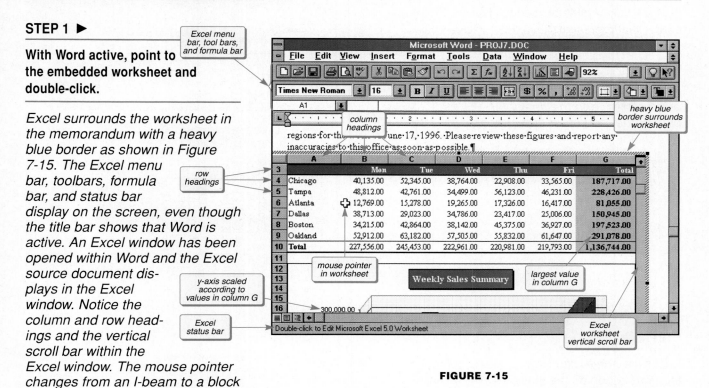

FIGURE 7-15

STEP 2 ▶

Use the Excel scroll bar to scroll down so row 8 displays at the top of the window. Select cell B8 and enter `14217`. Select cell C9 and enter `3182`.

The new numbers display in cells B8 and C9 and the chart is redrawn to represent the new amounts.(Figure 7-16). The new total amounts cause the y-axis in the chart to be rescaled. The largest amount at the top of the y-axis on the chart was 300,000.00. It is now 250,000.00.

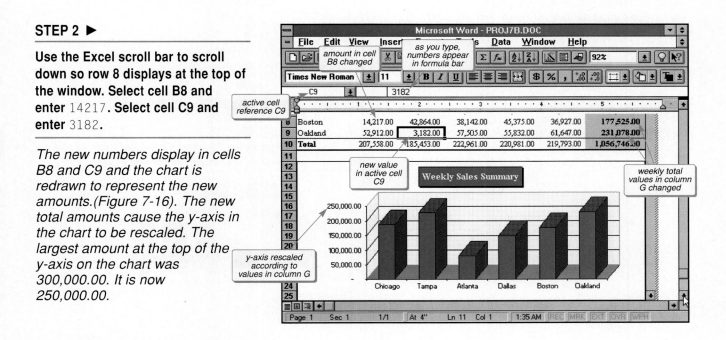

FIGURE 7-16

STEP 3 ▶

Double-click outside the heavy blue border that represents the Excel window.

The Word menu bar, tool-bars, ruler, and status bar are restored, and the heavy blue border no longer sur-rounds the Excel embedded object. The mouse pointer changes from a block plus sign to an I-beam (Figure 7-17).

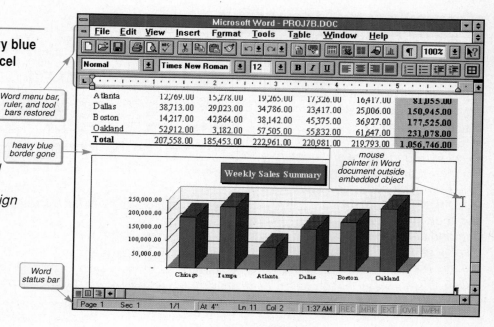

FIGURE 7-17

STEP 4 ▶

Ready the printer and click the Print button on the Standard toolbar.

The memorandum prints with the new values and redrawn chart (Figure 7-18).

STEP 5 ▶

Choose the Close command from the File menu to close PROJ7.DOC. Do not save the changes.

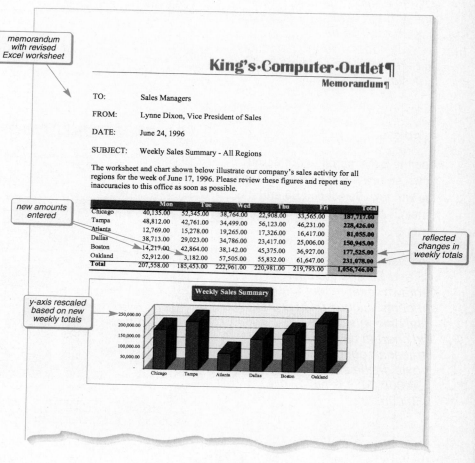

FIGURE 7-18

As shown in Figure 7-15 on page E405, when an object is embedded in a document, you can open one application from within another by double-clicking the object. You can then use the editing capabilities of the source application. However, the embedded worksheet has no connection to the original worksheet from which it was copied. Thus, the changes made to the worksheet while Word was active will not show up in the worksheet PROJ7.XLS, if you open it later in Excel.

▶ COPYING AND LINKING AN OBJECT BETWEEN APPLICATIONS

Unlike the previous two methods, when you link an object, you are not making a copy of it in the destination document. You create a link to the source document that contains the object. Thus, when you initiate an edit of a linked object by double-clicking on it in the destination document, the system activates the **source application**. In the case of the memorandum and worksheet in this project, when you link the worksheet to the memorandum and double-click the worksheet, the system activates Excel and opens the appropriate worksheet. The following steps show how to copy and link the worksheet to the memorandum.

TO COPY AND LINK AN OBJECT BETWEEN APPLICATIONS ▼

STEP 1 ▶

With Word active, open PROJ7.DOC from the Excel5 subdirectory on the Student Diskette. Hold down the ALT key. As you hold down the ALT key, press the TAB key until the box titled **Microsoft Excel – PROJ7.XLS** appears in the middle of the screen (Figure 7-3 on page E396). Release the TAB key and then the ALT key. If Excel is not active, start Excel from Program Manager and open PROJ7.XLS from the Excel subdirectory on the Student Diskette.

Excel is active and the worksheet PROJ7.XLS displays. You can link objects only from saved documents. Thus, it is important that PROJ7.XLS exists on disk.

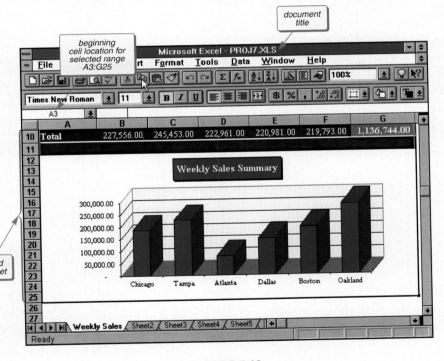

FIGURE 7-19

STEP 2 ▶

Select the range A3:G25 and click the Copy button on the Standard toolbar.

The range A3:G25 (Figure 7-19) is copied on to the Clipboard.

STEP 3 ▶

Hold down the ALT key and press the TAB key until the box shown in the middle of the screen contains the title Microsoft Word – PROJ7.DOC. Release the TAB key and then the ALT key. Press CTRL+END. Choose the Paste Special command from the Edit menu. Select the Paste Link option button. Select Microsoft Excel 5.0 Worksheet Object in the As list box.

The Paste Special dialog box displays as shown in Figure 7-20.

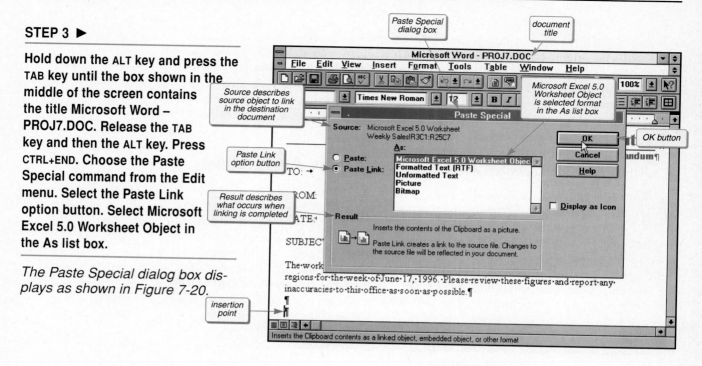

FIGURE 7-20

STEP 4 ▶

Choose the OK button

The object (range A3:G25 of the worksheet) on the Clipboard is paste linked to the Word document (Figure 7-21).

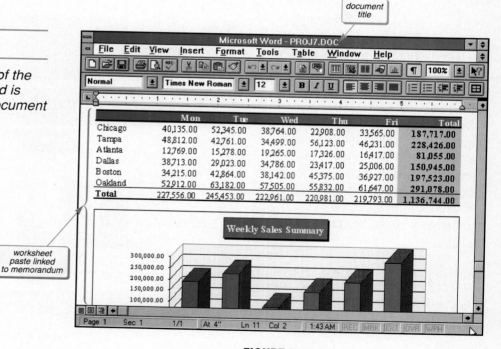

	Mon	Tue	Wed	Thu	Fri	Total
Chicago	40,135.00	52,345.00	38,764.00	22,908.00	33,565.00	187,717.00
Tampa	48,812.00	42,761.00	34,499.00	56,123.00	46,231.00	228,426.00
Atlanta	12,769.00	15,278.00	19,265.00	17,326.00	16,417.00	81,055.00
Dallas	38,713.00	29,023.00	34,786.00	23,417.00	25,006.00	150,945.00
Boston	34,215.00	42,864.00	38,142.00	45,375.00	36,927.00	197,523.00
Oakland	52,912.00	63,182.00	57,505.00	55,832.00	61,647.00	291,078.00
Total	227,556.00	245,453.00	222,961.00	220,981.00	219,793.00	1,136,744.00

FIGURE 7-21

It appears the result in Figure 7-21 is the same as the result achieved by copying and embedding shown earlier in Figure 7-13 on page E403. However, there is a big difference. In Figure 7-13, the object is embedded, or made part of the Word document. In Figure 7-20, the object is linked and, therefore, is not part of the Word document. The difference becomes apparent when you edit the two documents. Before editing the linked worksheet, the following section saves and prints the Word document and then exits both Word and Excel.

Saving and Printing the Memorandum and Exiting Word and Excel

Use the following steps to save and print the memorandum and exit both Word and Excel so you can see how Windows treats a linked object when the source application is closed.

TO SAVE, PRINT, AND EXIT WORD AND EXCEL

Step 1: With Word active, use the Save As command on the File menu to save the memorandum to drive A using the filename PROJ7C.

Step 2: Click the Print button on the Standard toolbar.

Step 3: Double-click the Control-menu box to exit Word.

Step 4: Press ALT+TAB to activate Excel, if it does not display on the screen when you exit Word. Double-click the Control-menu box to close Excel. Do not save changes.

The memorandum prints as shown in Figure 7-14 on page E404. When the memorandum is saved to disk, the link (reference) to the worksheet is saved with it. Because it is only a link, the size of the memorandum file is not as large as when the worksheet was embedded in the document earlier.

Starting Word and Opening a Document with a Linked Object

The following steps open the memorandum with the linked worksheet.

TO START WORD AND OPEN A DOCUMENT WITH A LINKED OBJECT

Step 1: With Program Manager active and the Microsoft Office group window open, double-click the Word program-item icon.

Step 2: Click the Open button on the Standard toolbar and open PROJ7C.DOC from drive A.

The memorandum with the linked worksheet displays as shown earlier in Figure 7-21. Word takes considerably longer to open the document because of the link to the worksheet. Once the memorandum is open, Word is active but Excel remains closed.

Editing the Linked Worksheet

When you double-click the worksheet in the Word document, Windows automatically starts Excel, makes it the active application, and opens the original worksheet PROJ7.XLS. The following steps change the contents of cell B8 from $34,215.00 to $14,217.00 and the contents of cell C9 from $63,182.00 to $3,182.00. As the changes are made, the chart is redrawn to represent the new sales amounts. When you return to Word using the ALT+TAB keys, the worksheet represents the most recent changes.

TO EDIT THE LINKED WORKSHEET ▼

STEP 1 ►

With Word active, point to the linked worksheet and double-click.

Windows starts Excel and displays the worksheet PROJ7.XLS in a minimized window.

STEP 2 ►

Click the Maximize button in the PROJ7.XLS window and then scroll down so the worksheet appears as shown in Figure 7-22.

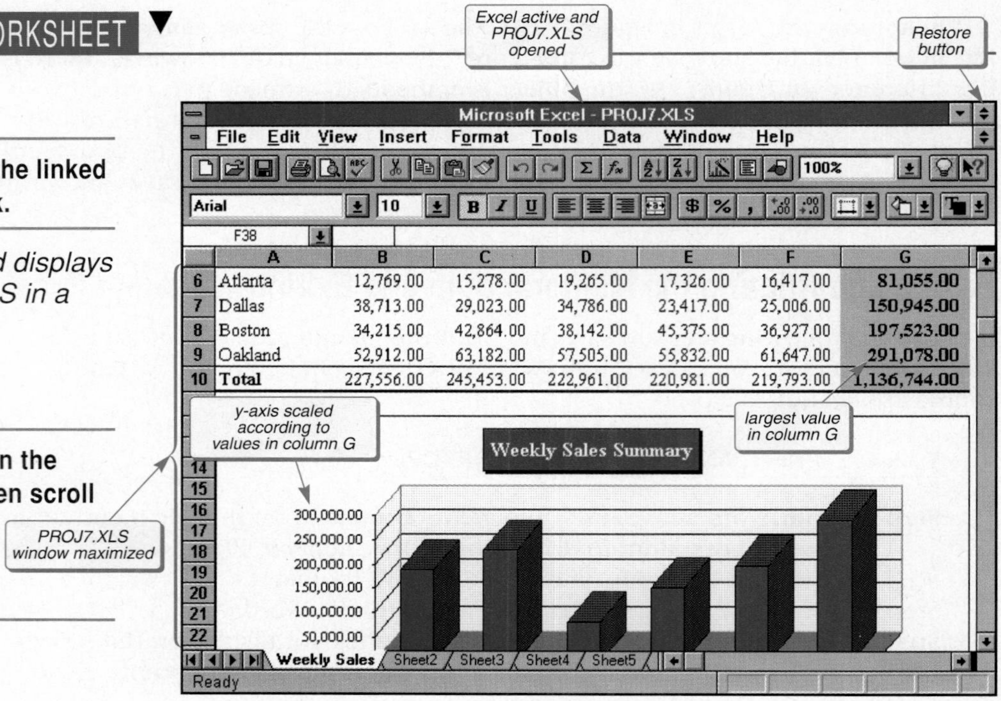

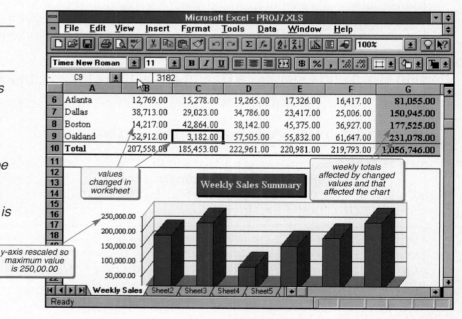

FIGURE 7-22

STEP 3 ►

Select cell B8 and enter 14217. Select cell C9 and enter 3182.

The new numbers display in cells B8 and C9 and the chart is redrawn to represent the new amounts in column G (Figure 7-23). The new total amounts cause the y-axis in the chart to be rescaled. The largest amount at the top of the y-axis on the chart was 300,000.00 (Figure 7-22). It is now 250,000.00.

FIGURE 7-23

STEP 4 ▶

Hold down the ALT key and press the TAB key until the box shown in the middle of the screen contains the title Microsoft Word – PROJ7C.DOC. Release the TAB key and then the ALT key.

Windows switches to Word. The memorandum displays with the worksheet updated (Figure 7-24).

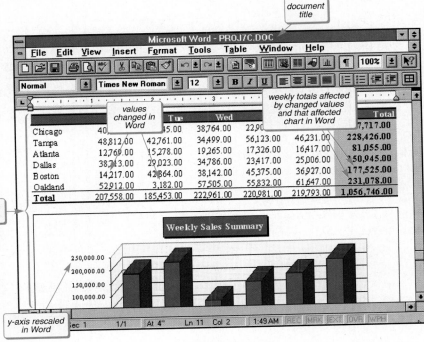

FIGURE 7-24

Displaying and Modifying the Links

To check the links to a document you can choose the **Links command** on the Edit menu. If the command is ghosted, no links exist. You can link as many objects as you want to a document provided you have enough main memory. The following steps show how to check the links.

TO DISPLAY AND EDIT THE LINKS ▼

STEP 1 ▶

Press CTRL+HOME to move the insertion point to the top of the document. Select the Edit menu (Figure 7-25).

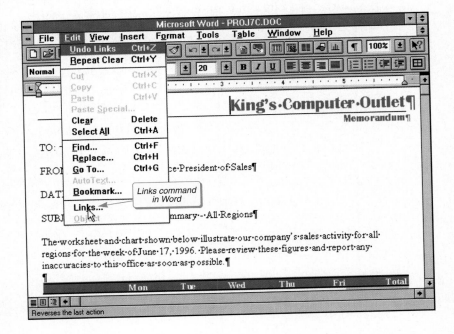

FIGURE 7-25

STEP 2 ►

Choose the Links command.

The **Links dialog box** displays
(Figure 7-26). The Source File
list box displays the links. In
this case, there is a link to
PROJ7.XLS on drive A to
PROJ7.DOC. The sheet name and
range display in row-column form .
That is, R3 stands for row 3.
The three dots following R3
mean to the end of the
worksheet (R25).

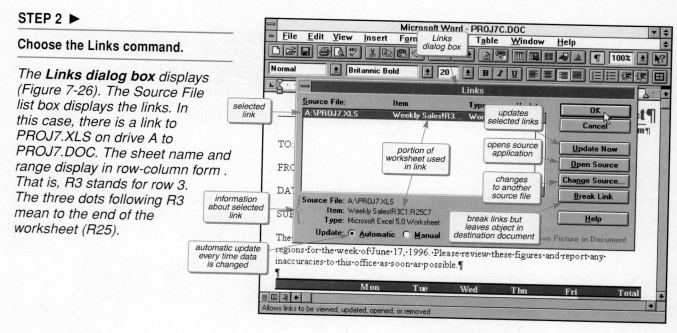

FIGURE 7-26

Both internal links and external links display in the Links dialog box. **Internal links** refer to links within Word itself. **External links** refer to other applications such as Excel. While the Links dialog box is on the screen, you can change links to other files or remove links. For more information, choose the Help button in the Links dialog box.

Saving and Printing the Memorandum and Exiting Word and Excel

The following steps save and print the memorandum. Then, both Word and Excel are closed. Excel is closed *without* saving changes. Thus, when the memorandum is opened later, the updates to the linked object will not appear.

TO SAVE, PRINT, AND EXIT WORD AND EXCEL

Step 1: With Word active, use the Save As command on the File menu to save the memorandum to drive A using the filename PROJ7D.DOC.

Step 2: Click the Print button on the Standard toolbar.

The memorandum prints as shown in Figure 7-18 on page E406.

Step 3: Double-click Word's Control-menu box to exit Word.

Excel becomes the active document and PROJ7.XLS displays.

Step 4: Double-click Excel's Control-menu box to exit Excel.

The Microsoft Excel dialog box shown in Figure 7-27 displays.

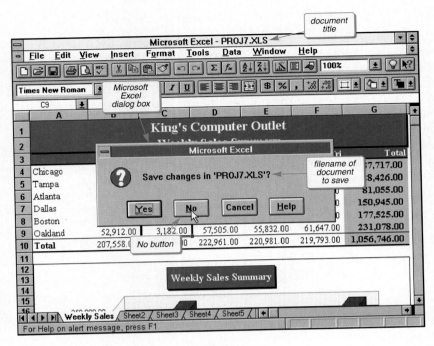

FIGURE 7-27

Step 5: Choose the No button.

The worksheet PROJ7.XLS is closed and the changes made earlier in Step 3 on page E410 (Figure 7-23) are lost.

Step 6: With Program Manager on the screen, double-click the Word program-item icon in the Microsoft Office group window. Open PROJ7C.DOC from drive A.

The memorandum with the linked worksheet displays (Figure 7-28). The changes made earlier do not show up because the Excel worksheet was not saved in Step 5.

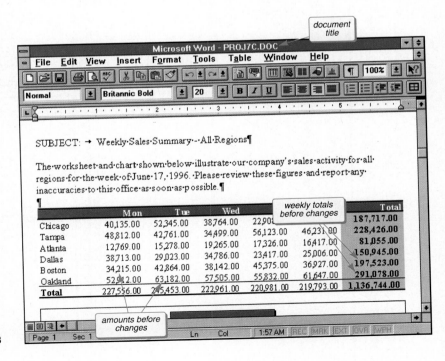

FIGURE 7-28

Step 7: Double-click the Word Control-menu box to exit Word.

Consider this important point in the last set of steps. Even though the memorandum was saved after the worksheet was updated, the updates did not show up in Figure 7-28 on the previous page because the worksheet was not saved when Excel was closed in Step 5. This example further solidifies the fact that the linked worksheet is independent of the memorandum. Thus, the worksheet must be saved for the updates to show when the memorandum is opened later. This was not true when the *copy and embed* method was used earlier.

You can see that if the vice president of sales plans to maintain the worksheet in Excel and send out the memorandum once a week, then the *copy and link* is the better choice over the *copy and paste* and *copy and embed*.

▶ TILING APPLICATIONS AND USING DRAG AND DROP TO COPY AND EMBED

Earlier in this project, the *copy and embed* method was presented using the Copy button and Paste Special command. An alternative procedure to copy and embed is to tile the applications and then drag and drop the object from the source document to the destination document. To use this procedure with the memorandum and worksheet, you first start Excel, open PROJ7.XLS, then start Word, and open PROJ7.DOC. With Word on the screen, you switch to Excel and tile. **Tiling** is the process of arranging the open windows in smaller sizes to fit next to each other on the desktop. Each application will display in its own window in the same fashion group windows display in Program Manager. You can then use the drag and drop procedure to copy and embed.

The following steps start the applications and open the memorandum and worksheet.

TO START EXCEL AND WORD AND MINIMIZE PROGRAM MANAGER

Step 1: With Program Manager on the screen, double-click the Excel program-item icon in the Microsoft Office group window. If necessary, click the Maximize button in the Excel title bar. Open PROJ7.XLS.

Step 2: Hold down the ALT key and press the TAB key until the box shown in the middle of the screen contains the title Program Manager. Release the TAB key and then the ALT key.

Step 3: Double-click the Word program-item icon to start Word. If necessary, click the Maximize button in the Word window. Open PROJ7.DOC.

Step 4: Hold down the ALT key and press the TAB key until the box shown in the middle of the screen contains the title Program Manager. Release the TAB key and then the ALT key. Click the Program Manager Minimize button.

Both Word and Excel are running and the memorandum and worksheet are open. Word is the active application. Program Manager is minimized.

The next step is to tile so both Word and Excel are visible on the desktop.

TO TILE APPLICATIONS ▼

STEP 1 ▶

With Word active, click the Control-menu box.

The Control menu displays as shown in Figure 7-29.

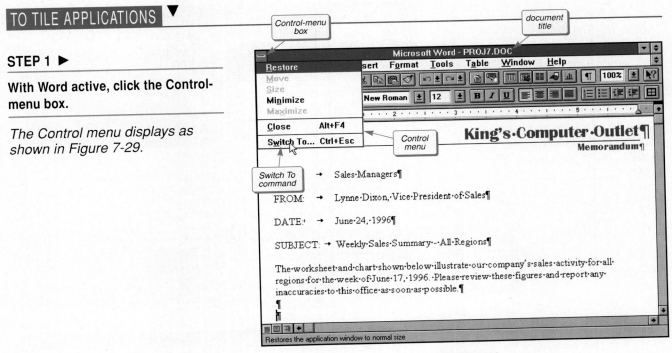

FIGURE 7-29

STEP 2 ▶

Choose the Switch To command.

Windows displays the Task List window (Figure 7-30).

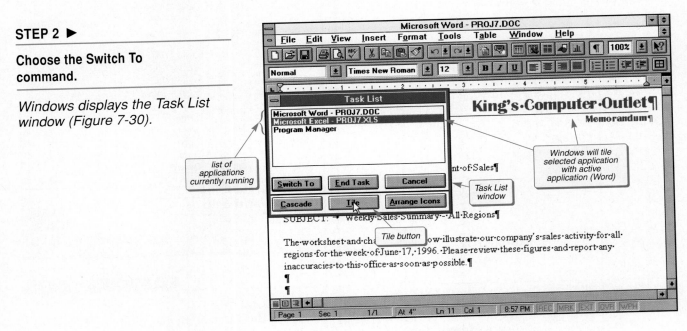

FIGURE 7-30

STEP 3 ▶

Choose the Tile button ([___Tile___]).
Point to the bottom border of the
Word window so the mouse pointer
becomes a double-headed arrow
(⇳) **(Figure 7-31).**

*Windows displays two windows
with Word in the left window and
Excel in the right window (Figure
7-31).*

FIGURE 7-31

STEP 4 ▶

**Drag the border to the bottom of the
desktop. Do the same with the Excel
window.**

*The Word and Excel windows dis-
play side by side as shown in
Figure 7-32. Because the Excel
window was the last one resized, it
is the active application. Recall
that the active application
has a darker title bar.*

FIGURE 7-32

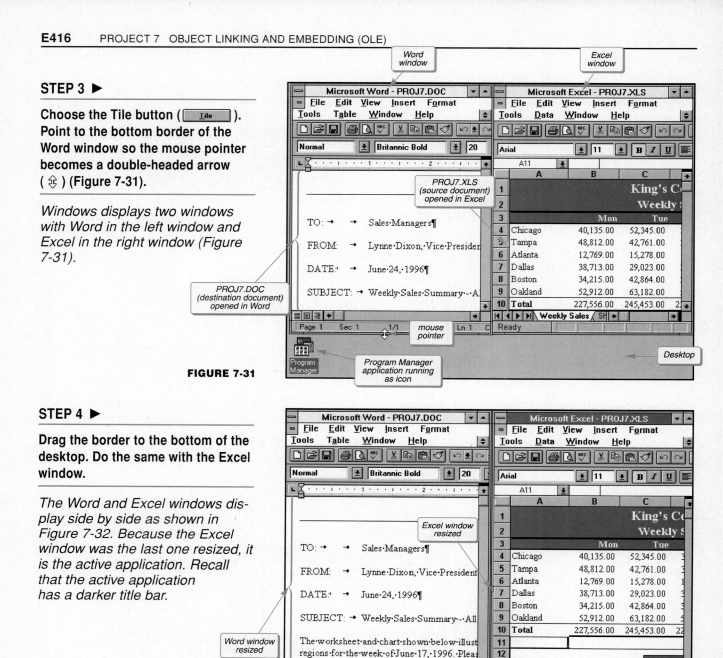

Besides tiling applications, you can use the Control menu (Figure 7-30) to
switch to another application (similar to pressing ALT+TAB), close an application, or
cascade applications. When you **cascade**, the applications windows overlap so
each title bar is visible. When the applications are cascaded, you can bring any
application window to the top of the desktop by clicking the application's title bar.

Using the Drag and Drop Procedure Between
Tiled Applications to Copy and Embed

The following steps show how to copy and embed between the two tiled
applications using the drag and drop procedure. With drag and drop, you select

the worksheet range, point to the border of the range, hold down the CTRL key, drag over to the memorandum, release the left mouse button and then the CTRL key.

TO DRAG AND DROP BETWEEN TILED APPLICATIONS

STEP 1 ►

Click in the Word window and scroll down so the last paragraph mark displays. Click in the Excel window and select the range A3:G25. Point to the border of the range so the mouse pointer changes to a block arrow.

The selected range and mouse pointer display as shown in Figure 7-33.

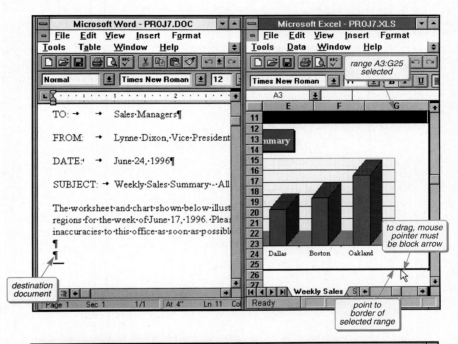

FIGURE 7-33

STEP 2 ►

With the mouse pointer displaying as a block arrow, hold down the CTRL key so the mouse pointer changes to a block arrow with a small plus sign ( ). While holding down the CTRL key, drag the mouse to the last paragraph mark in the Word window. Release the left mouse button and then release the CTRL key.

The range A3:G25 from the work-sheet is embedded into the memo-randum (Figure 7-34).

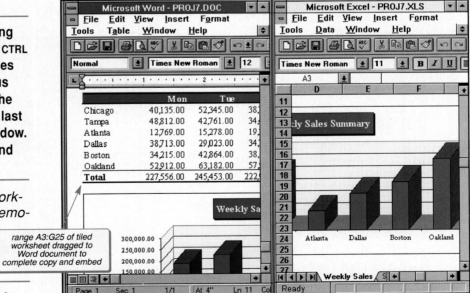

FIGURE 7-34

STEP 3 ►

Click the Excel Maximize button to maximize the Excel window. Press ALT+TAB to activate Word. Click the Maximize button to maximize the Word window. Double-click the Control-menu box in the Word title bar to exit Word. Do not save the changes. When the Excel window displays, close Excel without saving changes to the workbook.

Consider the following important points when using the drag and drop technique between tiled applications.

1. You must select the range to copy and point to the border.
2. The mouse pointer must be a block arrow before you hold down the CTRL key.
3. You must first release the left mouse button before you release the CTRL key or Windows will move instead of copy.

▶ EMBEDDING OBJECTS USING THE OBJECT COMMAND

The prior OLE examples used the Clipboard to transfer the information between applications. An alternative method is to use the **Object command** on the Insert menu. The primary differences between using the Object command and the Clipboard are the following:

1. The Object command allows you to embed without ever leaving the destination document.
2. With the Object command, you can embed an existing file or create a new object from one of the applications on your system (Figure 7-35). You cannot, however, embed part of a document as was done when the range A3:G25 was embedded using the Paste option in the Paste Special dialog box.

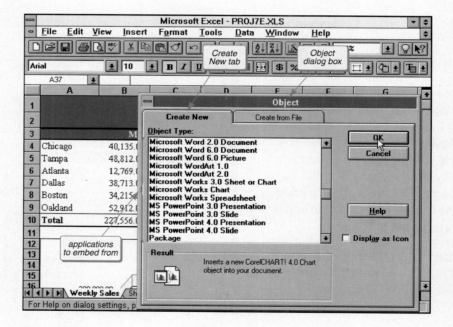

FIGURE 7-35

In some applications, such as Word and PowerPoint, you can use the Insert Microsoft Excel worksheet button (⊞) on the Standard toolbar to embed an empty workbook. Once the empty workbook is embedded in the Word or PowerPoint document, you can utilize Excel's capabilities to create the workbook without ever leaving the application.

▶ PROJECT SUMMARY

Project 7 introduced you to the three methods for copying objects between a source document and a destination document: (1) *copy and paste*; (2) *copy and embed*; and (3) *copy and link*. The *copy and paste* method is quick and easy, but limited. *The copy and embed* method makes the object part of the destination document and allows you to use the editing capabilities of the source application. The *copy and link* method establishes a link in the destination document to the object in the source document, instead of making it part of the destination document. When you edit a linked object, Windows activates the source application and opens the document that the object is part of. You learned how to copy and embed by using the drag and drop procedure between tiled applications. Finally, you learned that you can use the Object command on the Insert menu to embed objects from other applications without leaving the destination application.

▶ KEY TERMS AND INDEX

cascade *(E416)*
Control menu *(E415)*
copy and embed *(E393)*
copy and link *(E393)*
copy and paste *(E393)*
destination document *(E392)*
external links *(E412)*
in-place activation *(E404)*
internal links *(E412)*

link *(E393)*
Links command *(E411)*
Links dialog box *(E412)*
Object command *(E418)*
Object Linking and Embedding *(E393)*
objects *(E392)*
OLE *(E393)*
Paste Link option button *(E408)*

Paste option button *(E402)*
Paste Special command *(E400)*
Paste Special dialog box *(E402)*
source application *(E407)*
source document *(E392)*
Switch To command *(E415)*
Task List window *(E415)*
tiling *(E414)*

QUICK REFERENCE

In Microsoft Excel, you can accomplish a task in a number of ways. The following table provides a quick reference to each task presented in this project with its available options. The commands listed in the Menu column can be executed using either the keyboard or mouse. Many of the commands in the Menu column are also available on the shortcut menu.

Task	Mouse	Menu	Keyboard Shortcuts
Copy and Embed Between Applications	Select object in source document; click Copy button; switch to destination document; from Edit menu, choose Paste Special, then select Paste option	Select object in source document; from Edit menu choose Copy; switch to destination document; from Edit menu, choose Paste Special, then select Paste option	Select object in source document; press CTRL+C; switch to destination document; from Edit menu, choose Paste Special, then select Paste option
Copy and Link Between Applications	Select object in source document; click Copy button; switch to destination document; from Edit menu, choose Paste Special, then select Paste Link option	Select object in source document; from Edit menu choose Copy; switch to destination document; from Edit menu, choose Paste Special, then select Paste Link option	Select object in source document; press CTRL+C; switch to destination document; from Edit menu, choose Paste Special, then select Paste Link option

(continued)

QUICK REFERENCE (continued)

Task	Mouse	Menu	Keyboard Shortcuts
Copy and Paste Between Applications	Select object in source document; click Copy button; switch to destination document; click Paste button	Select object in source document; from Edit menu choose Copy; switch to destination document; from Edit menu, choose Paste	Select object in source document; press CTRL+C; switch to destination document; press CTRL+V
Edit Embedded or Linked Object Without Leaving an Application	Double-click on object in Word or PowerPoint, click Excel button on Standard toolbar	From Insert menu, choose Object	
Edit Links		From Edit menu, choose Links	
Tile or Cascade	Click Control-menu box; choose Switch To		Press CTRL+ESC

S T U D E N T   A S S I G N M E N T S

STUDENT ASSIGNMENT 1
True/False

Instructions: Circle T if the statement is true or F if the statement is false.

T F 1. An object can be an entire worksheet.

T F 2. The source document is the one that contains the object to copy.

T F 3. Use the Paste button on the Standard toolbar to embed an object.

T F 4. When you copy and link, the object is saved along with the destination document.

T F 5. OLE stands for Object Linking and Embedding.

T F 6. When you use the copy and paste method, a range of cells is pasted into a Word document as a table.

T F 7. When you edit an embedded object, Windows automatically updates the source document on disk.

T F 8. Click an embedded object to edit it.

T F 9. Use the Link command in the source document to check links.

T F 10. Use the copy and embed method when an object is fairly stable.

T F 11. Embed large objects, link small objects.

T F 12. Use the copy and link method when an object is likely to change.

T F 13. Double-click the Control-menu box of the active application to tile.

T F 14. The copy and link method establishes a reference, or link, to the source document in the destination document .

T F 15. Drag and drop between applications means that the object is cut from one document and pasted (embedded) into another.

T F 16. The Undo button cannot undo a paste.

T F 17. You can link only one document to another.
T F 18. The Links command allows you to update a link.
T F 19. If the Links command on the Edit menu is ghosted, then there is no link to the active document.
T F 20. Windows cannot display two or more applications on the screen at one time.

STUDENT ASSIGNMENT 2
Multiple Choice

Instructions: Circle the correct response.

1. To exchange data with other applications so you can use the editing capabilities of the source application and save the object as part of the destination document, use the _____ method.
   a. copy and paste
   b. copy and embed
   c. copy and link
   d. either b or c
2. To paste an object from a worksheet into a Word document as a Word table, use the _____ method.
   a. copy and paste
   b. copy and embed
   c. copy and link
   d. either a or c
3. To paste an object so only a reference to the object is assigned to the destination document, use the _____ method.
   a. copy and paste
   b. copy and embed
   c. copy and link
   d. none of the above
4. To paste so when you edit the object, the toolbars in the destination document change to the source application, use the _____ method.
   a. copy and paste
   b. copy and embed
   c. copy and link
   d. undo and repeat
5. When you copy and link and the object is edited, Windows will _____.
   a. save the source document when you return to the destination document
   b. not save the source document unless you instruct it to do so
   c. save the source document when you save the destination document
   d. not save the source document even if you instruct it to do so
6. When you edit an embedded object in a destination document, Windows will _____.
   a. save the source document when you click outside the object
   b. not save the source document
   c. save the source document when you save the destination document
   d. none of the above
7. Which one of the menus on the menu bar do not refer to the embedded object when you double-click it to edit?
   a. File
   b. Edit
   c. Format
   d. Help

(continued)

STUDENT ASSIGNMENT 2 (continued)

8. The keyboard shortcut for displaying the Task List window is _____.
   a. CTRL+C
   b. CTRL+ESC
   c. CTRL+V
   d. CTRL+ENTER

9. To display the Task List window, choose the Switch To command on the _____ menu.
   a. Tools
   b. Edit
   c. Control
   d. File

10. To display applications behind one another on the desktop with the title bar of each application showing, use the _____ button in the Task List dialog box.
    a. Cascade
    b. Tile
    c. Switch To
    d. Arrange Icons

STUDENT ASSIGNMENT 3
Understanding Button Functions

Instructions: Fill in the descriptions in the space provided.

1. Describe the function of the following buttons in the Task List window

   a. Switch To (Switch To) _____

   b. End Task (End Task) _____

   c. Cancel (Cancel) _____

   d. Cascade (Cascade) _____

   e. Tile (Tile) _____

   f. Arrange Icons (Arrange Icons) _____

2. Describe the function of the following buttons in the Links dialog box.

   a. Update Now (Update Now) _____

   b. Open Source (Open Source) _____

   c. Change Source (Change Source...) _____

   d. Break Link (Break Link) _____

STUDENT ASSIGNMENT 4
Matching

Instructions: Match the method in column 2 with the statement in column 1

When you want to

_____ 1. Edit the object using the source application
even when the source document is not available.

_____ 2. Include an object that is maintained separately
from the destination document.

_____ 3. Include a very large object.

_____ 4. Change a worksheet to a table in Word.

_____ 5. Include an object that changes often and
you want the latest copy in the destination
document when it is opened.

Use this method

a. copy and paste
b. copy and embed
c. copy and link

STUDENT ASSIGNMENT 5
Short Answer

Instructions: Answer the following questions.

1. How do you activate an embedded object to edit?

_____

2. Which menu contains the Switch to command for tiling?

_____

3. Which command do you use to change links in a destination document?

_____

4. How do you remove a link?

_____

5. How do you display only one application on the desktop when applications are tiled?

_____

6. Using keyboard shortcuts, how do you return to the destination document after editing a linked
object in the source application?

_____

7. How do you remove an embedded object?

_____

STUDENT ASSIGNMENT 6
Understanding OLE

Instructions: Summarize the differences between the three methods of moving an object from one application to another: copy and paste, copy and embed, and copy and link.

_____

_____

_____

_____

_____

_____

C O M P U T E R   L A B O R A T O R Y   E X E R C I S E S

COMPUTER LABORATORY EXERCISE 1
Using the Help Menu to Understand OLE, Drag and Drop, and Tiling

Part 1 Instructions: Start Excel and perform the following tasks using a computer.

1. Choose the Search for Help on command from the Help menu.
2. Type ole in the Search dialog box.
3. Use the Scroll box to find and select OLE, embedding in other applications.
4. Choose the Show Topics button.
5. With the topic Embedding a Microsoft Excel object in another application highlighted in the lower list, choose the Go To button.
6. Read the information that displays. Choose the Print button in the How To window.
7. Close the How To window.
8. Choose the Search button and scroll to OLE, linking source worksheets to dependents.
9. Select this topic and choose the Show Topics button.
10. With the topic Linking a Microsoft Excel document to a document from another application highlighted in the lower list, choose the Go To button.
11. Read the information that displays. Choose the Print button in the How To window.
12. Choose the Close button in the How To window.
13. To exit Help, double-click the Control-menu box in the Help window.

Part 2 Instructions: Start Excel and perform the following tasks using a computer:

1. Choose the Index command from the Help menu.
2. Click the O button.
3. Find Object command (Insert menu) in the list that displays and click Create From File tab.
4. Read the information that displays. Choose the Print Topic command on the File menu.
5. To exit Help, double-click the Control menu box in the Help window.

Part 3 Instructions: Start Excel and perform the following tasks using a computer:

1. Choose the Search for Help on command on the Help menu.
2. Type dragging, between applications in the Search dialog box.
3. Choose the Show Topics button.
4. With Dragging data between applications highlighted in the lower box, choose the Go To button.
5. Read the information that displays. Choose the Print Topic command from the File menu.
6. Choose the Close button in the How To window.
7. Choose the Search button.
8. Type tiling. With tiling windows, Arrange command highlighted in the upper box, choose the Show Topics button.
9. With the topic Arrange and Arrange Icons Commands (Window Menu) highlighted in the lower box, choose the Go To button.
10. Read the information that displays. Choose the Print Topic command from the File menu.
11. To exit Help, double-click the Control-menu box in the Help window.

COMPUTER LABORATORY EXERCISE 2
Object Linking and Embedding

The manager of the accounting department at the firm where you work has directed you to solve an applications problem. She would like to keep all of the branch managers up to date regarding the monthly office expenses incurred at each of the branch locations. She currently does this by using Word to generate a new memorandum each month to summarize the information she has in a worksheet in Excel. As her assistant, you have been instructed to find a way to reuse the same memorandum each month and somehow incorporate the worksheet information directly in the memorandum.

Part 1 Instructions: Start Word and open the memorandum CLE7-2.DOC from the Excel5 subdirectory on the Student Diskette that accompanies this book. Use the ALT and TAB keys to return to Program Manager and start Excel. In Excel open the worksheet CLE7-2.XLS in the Excel5 subdirectory on the Student Diskette.

Perform the tasks that follow to copy and paste the worksheet in the memorandum (Figure CLE7-2a).

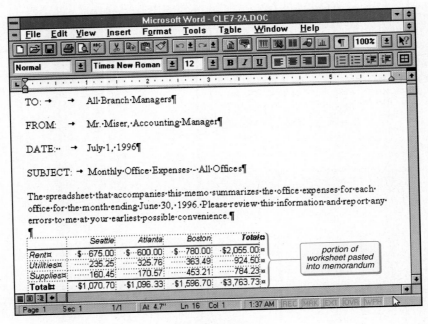

FIGURE CLE7-2a

(continued)

COMPUTER LABORATORY EXERCISE 2 (continued)

1. With Excel active and the CLE7-2 workbook opened, select the range A2:E6 and click the Copy button on the Standard toolbar.
2. Use the ALT and TAB keys to return to Word.
3. Press CTRL+END to place the insertion point at the bottom of the memorandum.
4. Click the Paste button.
5. Save the document using the filename CLE7-2A.DOC.
6. Print the document.
7. Close Word and Excel. Do not save changes to the workbook.

Part 2 Instructions: Start Word and open the memorandum CLE7-2.DOC from the Excel5 subdirectory on the Student Diskette. Use the ALT and TAB keys to return to Program Manager and start Excel. Open the workbook CLE7-2.XLS from the Excel5 subdirectory on the Student Diskette.

Perform the tasks that follow to copy and embed the worksheet into the memorandum (Figure CLE7-2b).

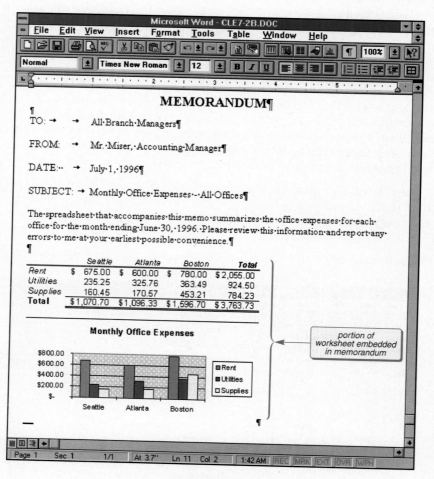

FIGURE CLE7-2b

1. With Excel active and the CLE7-2 workbook opened, select the range A2:F17 and click the Copy button on the Standard toolbar.
2. Use the ALT and TAB keys to return to Word.
3. Press CTRL+END to place the insertion point at the bottom of the memorandum.
4. Choose the Paste Special command on the Edit menu and embed the object (range A2:F17 of the worksheet) on the Clipboard.
5. Save the document using the filename CLE7-2B.DOC.
6. Print the document.
7. Close Word and Excel. Do not save changes to the workbook.

Part 3 Instructions: Start Word and open the memorandum CLE7-2.DOC from the Excel5 subdirectory on the Student Diskette. Use the ALT and TAB keys to return to Program Manager and start Excel. In Excel open the worksheet CLE7-2.XLS from the Excel5 subdirectory on the Student Diskette.

Perform the tasks that follow to copy and link the worksheet (range A2:F17) to the memorandum. The memorandum should appear as shown in Figure CLE7-2b.

1. With Excel active and the CLE7-2 workbook opened, select the range A2:E17 and click the Copy button on the Standard toolbar.
2. Use the ALT and TAB keys to return to Word.
3. Press CTRL+END to place the insertion point at the bottom of the memorandum.
4. Choose the Paste Special command on the Edit menu and link the object (object (range A2:F17 of the worksheet) on the Clipboard to the memorandum.
5. Save the document to the Excel5 subdirectory on the Student Diskette using the filename CLE7-2C.DOC.
6. Print the document.
7. Close both Word and Excel. Do not save changes to the workbook.

COMPUTER LABORATORY EXERCISE 3
Object Linking and Embedding Clip Art

Part 1 Instructions: Start Excel and open the workbook CLE7-3.XLS from the Excel5 subdirectory on the Student Diskette. Use the ALT and TAB keys to return to Program manager and start Word.

Perform the tasks that follow to copy and embed the clip art, shown in Figure CLE7-3a into the worksheet CLE7-3.XLS.

1. With Word active, choose the Picture command on the Insert menu and open the Windows file, blusedan.wmf (Figure CLE7-3a).
2. Select the picture in Word and click the Copy button on the Standard toolbar.
3. Use the ALT and TAB keys to return to Excel.
4. Click a cell below the data in the worksheet.
5. Choose the Paste Special command on the Edit menu and embed the car below the data in the worksheet.
6. Select the car and resize it so it has the same width as the data in the worksheet (Figure CLE7-3b).
7. Save the workbook using the filename CLE7-3A.XLS.
8. Print the worksheet without gridlines. Click the Save button on the Standard toolbar.
9. Close Excel. Close Word. Do not save changes to the document in Word.

FIGURE CLE7-3a

(continued)

COMPUTER LABORATORY EXERCISE 3 (continued)

Part 2 Instructions: Start Excel and open the workbook CLE7-3.XLS from the Excel5 subdirectory on the Student Diskette. Use the ALT and TAB keys to return to Program manager and start Word.

Perform the tasks that follow to copy and link the picture shown in Figure CLE7-3c to CLE7-3.XLS as an icon.

1. With Word active, choose the Picture command on the Insert menu and open the Windows clip art, motorcrs.wmf

2. Select the picture and click the Copy button on the Standard toolbar.

3. Use the ALT and TAB keys to return to Excel.

4. Click cell G1 on the worksheet.

5. Choose the Paste Special command on the Edit menu and link the flags to the worksheet as an icon. Move and resize the icon as it appears as shown in Figure CLE7-3d.

6. Select the icon and double-click to view it in Word. Use ALT+TAB to return to Excel.

7. Save the workbook using the filename CLE7-3B.XLS.

8. Print the worksheet without gridlines. Click the Save button on the Standard toolbar and close Excel.

9. Save the Word document using the filename CLE7-3B.DOC. and close Word.

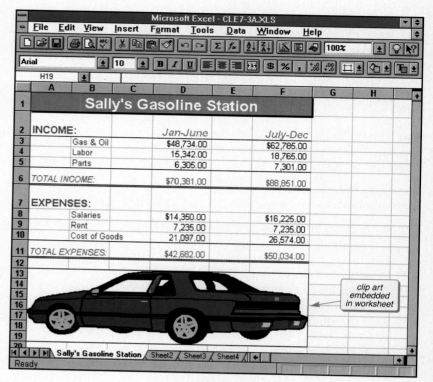

FIGURE CLE7-3b

FIGURE CLE7-3c

FIGURE CLE7-3d

COMPUTER LABORATORY ASSIGNMENT 1
Editing a Table Pasted in a Word Document from an Excel Workbook

Purpose: To edit a table in Word that was pasted from an Excel worksheet.

Instructions: Start Word and open the document CLE7-2A.DOC. If you did not complete Part 1 of Computer Laboratory Exercise 2 on page E425, ask your instructor for a copy of CLE7-2A.DOC (Figure CLE7-2a on page E425). Add $100.00 to the rent for each city. Adjust the totals so they are correct. Save the document using the filename CLA7-1.DOC. Print the document. Close Word.

COMPUTER LABORATORY ASSIGNMENT 2
Editing a Worksheet Embedded in a Word Document

Purpose: To edit a worksheet embedded in a Word document.

Instructions: Start Word and open the document CLE7-2B.DOC. If you did not complete Part 2 of Computer Laboratory Exercise 2 on page E426, ask your instructor for a copy of CLE7-2B.DOC. Double-click the embedded worksheet (Figure CLE7-2b on page E426). Add $100.00 to the rent for each city. Save the document using the filename CLA7-2.DOC. Print the document. Close Word.

COMPUTER LABORATORY ASSIGNMENT 3
Editing a Worksheet Linked to a Word Document

Purpose: To edit a worksheet linked to a Word document.

Instructions: Start Word and open the document CLE7-2C.DOC from the Excel5 subdirectory on the Student Diskette. If you did not complete Part 3 of Computer Laboratory Exercise 2 on page E427, ask your instructor for a copy of CLE7-2C.DOC. Use the Links command on the Edit menu to make sure that CLE7-2.XLS is linked to CLE7-2C.DOC. Also check to be sure that CLE7-2.XLS is in the indicated directory on your Student Diskette. Double-click the linked worksheet (Figure CLE7-2b on page E426). Add $100.00 to the rent for each city. Save the document using the filename CLA7-3.DOC. Print the document. Close Word. Save the workbook using the filename CLA7-3.XLS. Activate Word and choose the Links command on the Edit menu. Verify that the linked workbook has changed to CLA7-3.XLS.

COMPUTER LABORATORY ASSIGNMENT 4
Embedding and Linking a Consolidated Balance Sheet

Purpose: To provide experience using OLE to embed a consolidated worksheet in a memorandum and link a consolidated worksheet to a memorandum.

Problem: One of your responsibilities as the manager of accounting for Tri-Quality International, is to inform the board of directors about the company's financial status. You have a workbook you created in Computer Laboratory Assignment 4 in Project 4 on page E275 that includes the company's balance sheet. If you did not complete Computer Laboratory Assignment 4 in Project 4, see your instructor for a copy of the workbook CLA4-4.XLS.

Instructions: Write a memorandum to the board of directors that includes the consolidated balance sheet from the workbook CLA4-4 (see page E275). Create two versions of the memorandum, one in which the balance sheet is embedded and the other in which the balance sheet is linked. Edit the balance sheet in both memorandums. Submit printed copies of the memorandums.

INDEX